Handbook of
Behavioral and Emotional Problems in Girls

Issues in Clinical Child Psychology

Series Editors: **Michael C. Roberts,** *University of Kansas—Lawrence, Kansas*
Lizette Peterson, *University of Missouri—Columbia, Missouri*

CHILDREN AND DISASTERS
Edited by Conway F. Saylor

HANDBOOK OF ADOLESCENT HEALTH RISH BEHAVIOR
Edited by Ralph J. DiClemente, William B. Hensen, and Lynn E. Ponton

HANDBOOK OF BEHAVIORAL AND EMOTIONAL PROBLEMS IN GIRLS
Edited by Debora J. Bell, Sharon L. Foster, and Eric J. Mash

HANDBOOK OF CHILD ABUSE RESEARCH AND TREATMENT
Edited by T. Steuart Watson and Frank M. Gresham

HANDBOOK OF CHILDREN'S COPING: Linking Theory and Intervention
Edited by Sharlene A. Wolchik and Irwin N. Sandler

HANDBOOK OF DEPRESSION IN CHILDREN AND ADOLESCENTS
Edited by William M. Reynolds and Hugh F. Johnson

HANDBOOK OF MENTAL HEALTH SERVICES FOR CHILDREN, ADOLESCENTS,
AND FAMILIES
Edited by Ric G. Steele and Michael C. Roberts

HANDBOOK OF PSYCHOTHERAPIES WITH CHILDREN AND FAMILIES
Edited by Sandra W. Russ and Thomas H. Ollendick

HANDBOOK OF RESEARCH IN PEDIATRIC AND CLINICAL CHILD PSYCHOLOGY
Edited by Dennis Drotar

HANDBOOK OF SCHOOL MENTAL HEALTH: Advancing Practice and Research
Edited by Mark D. Weist, Steven W. Evans, and Nancy A. Lever

INTERNATIONAL HANDBOOK OF PHOBIC AND ANXIETY DISORDERS IN
CHILDREN AND ADOLESCENTS
Edited by Thomas H. Ollendick, Neville J. King, and William Yule

MENTAL HEALTH INTERVENTIONS WITH PRESCHOOL CHILDREN
Edited by Robert D. Lyman and Toni L. Hembree-Kigin

SCHOOL CONSULTATION: Conceptual and Empirical Bases of Practice
William P. Erchul and Brian K. Martens

SUCCESSFUL PREVENTION PROGRAMS FOR CHILDREN AND ADOLESCENTS
Joseph A. Durlak

A continuation Order Plan is available for this series. A continuation order will bring delivery of each new volume immediately upon publication. Volumes are billed only upon actual shipment. For further information please contact the publisher.

Handbook of
Behavioral and Emotional Problems in Girls

Edited by

Debora J. Bell

University of Missouri-Columbia
Columbia, MO

Sharon L. Foster

Alliant International University
San Diego, CA

Eric J. Mash

University of Calgary
AB, Canada

Kluwer Academic / Plenum Publishers
New York, Boston, Dordrecht, London, Moscow

Library of Congress Cataloging-in-Publication Data

Handbook of behavioral and emotional problems in girls / edited by Debora J. Bell, Sharon
  L. Foster, Eric J. Mash.
    p.   cm.—(Issues in clinical child psychology)
  Includes bibliographical references and index.
  ISBN 0-306-48673-3
  1. Behavior disorders in children.   2. Emotional problems of children.   3. Behavior
  disorders in teenagers.   4. Emotional problems of teenagers.   5. Girls—Mental health.
  6. Teenage girls—Mental health.   7. Problem children—Mental health.   I. Bell,
  Debora J.   II. Foster, Sharon L.   III. Mash, Eric J.   IV. Series.

  RJ506.B44H247 2005
  618.92′89′0082—dc22

                                                                        2004054839

ISBN 0-306-48673-3

© 2005 by Kluwer Academic/Plenum Publishers, New York
233 Spring Street, New York, New York 10013

http://www.kluweronline.com

10 9 8 7 6 5 4 3 2 1

A C.I.P. record for this book is available from the Library of Congress

Permissions for books published in Europe: permissions@wkap.nl
Permissions for books published in the United States of America: permissions@wkap.com

Printed in the United States of America

To the memory of Lizette Peterson, Ph.D. (1951–2002), Byler Endowed Chair and Curators Professor, University of Missouri-Columbia. Dr. Peterson was the quintessential clinical scientist, dedicated to improving children's lives through her research, clinical work, and mentoring of young scholars. Dr. Peterson planted the seeds for this book and her vision and spirit live on in its pages.

Contributors

Anne Marie Albano Columbia University, New York, NY 10032-2626

Judy A. Andrews Oregon Research Institute, Eugene, OR 97403

Sandra T. Azar The Pennsylvania State University, University Park, PA 16804-3000

Karen Bearman Miller St. Mary's Child Development Center, West Palm Beach, FL

Debora J. Bell University of Missouri-Columbia, Columbia, MO 65211

Dara R. Blachman University of California, Berkeley, CA 94720-1650

Christy M. Buchanan Wake Forest University, Winston-Salem, NC 27109-7778

Ana Mari Cauce University of Washington, Seattle, WA 98195

Claire V. Crooks Center for Research on Violence against Women and Children, The University of Western Ontario, London, Ontario, Canada N6A 5B8

Sunita Duggal National Institute of Mental Health, Bethesda, MD 20892-2606

Elisabeth M. Dykens John F. Kennedy Center & Peabody College, Vanderbilt University, Nashville, TN 37235

Sharon L. Foster Alliant International University, San Diego, CA 94720-1650

Stephen P. Hinshaw University of California, Berkeley, CA 94720-1650

Robert M. Hodapp John F. Kennedy Center & Peabody College, Vanderbilt University, Nashville, TN 37235

Dan R. Hoyt University of Nebraska, Lincoln, NE 68588-0324

Kathleen Koeing Yale University Child Study Center, New Haven, CT 06520

Amy Krain New York University School of Medicine, New York, NY 10016

Dawn A. Kurtz University of Southern California, Los Angeles, CA 90089-0411

Annette M. La Greca University of Miami, Coral Gables, FL 33124

Eric J. Mash University of Calgary, Calgary, Albert, T2N 1

Jennie G. Noll University of Southern California, Los Angeles, CA 90089-0411

Matthew Paradise University of North Carolina, Greensboro, NC 27402

Eleanor Race National Institute of Mental Health, Bethesda, MD 20892-2606

Katreena L. Scott Ontario Institute for Studies in Education, The University of Toronto, Toronto, Ontario M5S 1V6

Linda Smolak Kenyon College, Gambier, OH 43022-0000

Angela Stewart Les B. Whitbeck, Matthew Paradise, & Dan R. Hoyt

Penelope K. Trickett University of Southern California, Los Angeles, CA 90089-0411

Katherine D. Tsatsanis Massachusetts General Hospital, Harvard Medical School

Les B. Whitbeck University of Nebraska, Lincoln, NE 68588-0324

David A. Wolfe Center for Addiction and Mental Health, The University of Toronto, Toronto, Ontario M5T 1R8

Arlene Young Simon Fraser University, Burnaby, British Columbia, Canada, V5A 1S6

Carolyn Zahn-Waxler National Institute of Mental Health, Bethesda, MD 20892-2606

Ken J. Zucker Center for Addiction and Mental Health-Clarke Division, Toronto, Ontario M5T 1R8

Contents

I

Introduction

1

Understanding Behavioral and Emotional Problems in Girls

DEBORA J. BELL, SHARON L. FOSTER, and ERIC J. MASH

"What are little girls made of? Sugar and spice and everything nice; that's what little girls are made of . . . "(Mother Goose nursery rhyme)

"There are no good girls gone wrong, just bad girls found out"
Mae West, American Actress (1892–1980)

Historically, girls have evoked images of sweetness and light, purity and beauty. In this fairytale land of youth, girls are angels and princesses, characterized by positive adjustment and certainly not by behavioral or emotional problems. However, as Mae West observed, in reality female children and adolescents are much more complex, with both positive and negative aspects to their development and adjustment. Unfortunately, the complexity has been understudied in the developmental psychopathology literature. Compared to the amount of research attention given to boys' development and adjustment, girls have been relatively neglected. This lack of attention has obvious negative implications for our ability to understand girls' development and our efforts to promote optimal development and to remediate problematic development.

Recent research on disorders of childhood and adolescence such as conduct disorders (Moffitt, Caspi, Rutter, & Silva, 2001), attention deficit hyperactivity disorder (ADHD; Hinshaw, 2002), anxiety disorders

DEBORA J. BELL • University of Missouri-Columbia, Columbia, Missouri, 65211.
SHARON L. FOSTER • Alliant International University, San Diego, California, 92131. **ERIC J. MASH** • University of Calgary, Calgary, Alberta, T2N 1N4.

(Lewinsohn, Gotlib, Lewinsohn, Seeley, & Allen, 1997), mood disorders (Rudolph, Hammen, & Daley, in press), and other disorders (Mash & Barkley, 2003; Mash & Wolfe, 2005) indicates that the epidemiology, expression, developmental pathways, and causes of these problems in girls may differ from those for boys. Increasingly, the field of developmental psychopathology is recognizing the special aspects of female development, behavior and adjustment needed to understand psychopathology in girls (Crick & Zahn-Waxler, 2003). To date, however, an integrative conceptual framework for understanding different forms of psychopathology in girls is lacking. Much important knowledge about girls' behavior problems is relatively new, and has not been presented in a single source. The aim of this volume is to compile the best and most current knowledge and research findings regarding behavioral and emotional problems in girls through childhood and adolescence, organized within a developmental and contextual framework. We believe that the time is ripe for a volume like this and that it will be an invaluable resource to students, mental health researchers, and practitioners as they conceptualize and address behavioral and emotional problems in girls.

OVERVIEW OF THIS BOOK

This book includes chapters written by some of the leading scholars in developmental psychopathology, many of whom have focused specifically on girls in their own research. The chapters cover a broad range of disorders, problems, and life experiences that affect girls' adjustment, including disruptive behavior disorders, emotional problems, developmental and learning disorders, health-related problems such as eating disorders and illness, and negative life experiences such as abuse, violence, and homelessness. Some of the topics, such as mood and anxiety disorders, eating disorders, and sexual abuse, have traditionally been considered "girl problems" and are obvious choices for a book on girls' adjustment. However, disruptive behavior disorders, typically considered more problematic for boys, "aren't just for boys anymore." The chapters on ADHD, conduct problems, and substance use and abuse focus on how girls act out throughout childhood and adolescence. Beyond simply focusing on problems that are most prevalent for girls, or only on differences in problem behaviors between boys and girls, the chapters in this book focus on how girls express and experience diverse forms of problematic behavior and adjustment, as well as theory and evidence regarding etiology, developmental course, correlates, and outcomes of problem behaviors among girls in particular.

A notable strength of the chapters in this volume is their use of a developmental psychopathology framework (Pennington, 2002). Information about girls' problematic adjustment is grounded in an understanding of girls' typical development, and in the context of biological, psychosocial, environmental, and cultural issues. This perspective has decided advantages over simply examining sex differences in behavioral and emotional adjustment. Literature in developmental psychology clearly shows that boys' and girls' development differs. As a result, problems in development (e.g., particular areas of risk or resilience, or ways in which stress or dysfunction is likely to be expressed) are also likely to differ. Additionally, regardless of sex differences, the mechanisms by which boys and girls develop adjustment problems may differ, due to differences in biological and psychological development, as well as to the gendered culture(s) in which children develop. The chapters also focus on implications of our current knowledge for the future of the field of developmental psychopathology in general and for girls in particular. Issues of how we define and diagnose disorder or maladjustment are considered; for some problems (e.g, conduct disorders; Zoccolillo, Tremblay, & Vitaro, 1996) different diagnostic criteria or cutoffs for girls and boys may be warranted. Future research needs are presented, with recommendations for both content and methodology. Chapter authors also address clinical implications, and discuss how assessment, treatment, and prevention efforts may need to be tailored to issues particularly relevant to girls.

Prior to embarking on our presentation of specific problems that girls can experience, we consider some of the issues involved in understanding the state of the literature on girls' behavioral and emotional problems, discuss important aspects of a developmental psychopathology framework, and present a brief foundational overview of girls' development as it is relevant to these problems. We also preview some of the wealth of information covered in subsequent chapters, focusing on common themes in girls' behavioral and emotional problems that emerge across problem areas, as well as the implications of these commonalities for assessment, diagnosis, treatment, and prevention that seem to emerge from the literature. At the same time, what we know about girls' adjustment problems is outstripped by what we do not know, and the literature throughout this book prompts many questions and directions for future research. We highlight several of these issues, examining both the content of needed research as well as the methods that are most promising for advancing the field.

As we move through our discussion of girls' development and psychopathology, we should offer a note about our use of several terms. First, we use the term *girls* to refer broadly to female youth throughout childhood and adolescence. Where adolescence or post-pubertal status is particularly important to the point under consideration, we specify this by referring to adolescent girls or young women. Second, the focus of our book is on behavioral and emotional problems that girls may *exhibit* or *encounter*. Some of the problems that girls exhibit constitute disorders as outlined by diagnostic classification systems such as the Diagnostic and Statistical Manual for Mental Disorders (e.g., *DSM-IV*; American Psychiatric Association, 2000). Other problems that girls experience represent stressors or negative life experiences that may affect their adjustment. The term *psychopathology* is most properly limited to disorder, but we sometimes use it to refer more broadly to both disorder and stressor-related adjustment problems. We do not mean to pathologize girls who experience negative life events (adjustment problems in the context of extreme stressors such as abuse may be considered quite normal), but simply to emphasize the behavioral or emotional aspects of girls' functioning that may interfere with their development, health, and happiness. We also use the term "psychopathology" as a shorthand term for a developmental psychopathology approach to understanding girls' functioning.

Finally, the terms sex and gender are used frequently throughout the book as we discuss our understanding of girls' behavioral and emotional problems in the context of, or in comparison to, what we know about boys. Although the terms are often used somewhat interchangeably, we attempt to use *sex* to refer to the phenotypic classification (presumed to be a marker for biological status) of girl versus boy based on observable physical characteristics. The term *gender* encompasses sex or gender roles and other aspects of culturally influenced sex-related identity. Although gender and gender identity are related to a child's sex, they are not synonymous with it. In our view, much research that compares boys and girls examines sex differences; whether these differences signify differences in biological status or culturally influenced gender are typically not studied explicitly or separately. In fact, Rutter, Caspi, and Moffitt (2003) suggest that attempts to distinguish between sex and gender differences via terminology may create a false dichotomy, by implying that social and biological influences operate separately from one another. Thus, we use the term "sex" to refer simply to the subject classification variable without any assumption about biological versus social influence, but use "gender" when we want to highlight particular socialization factors.

GIRLS' PSYCHOPATHOLOGY: WHY DON'T WE KNOW MORE?

A question even more basic than why we do not know more about girls' behavioral and emotional problems is why we need to know more. As mentioned above, until recently, the preponderance of literature on the development of behavior problems has largely ignored issues of sex and gender. One major exception has been in studies of developmental epidemiology, where findings have pointed to large sex differences in incidence and prevalence of some behavior problems at some ages. Contrary to the "sugar and spice" notion, girls are not always the fairer, or better-adjusted, sex. For example, depression and eating disorders are far more prevalent among teenage girls than boys, with depression affecting as many as 35% of girls by the time they reach adulthood and subthreshold eating disorders affecting as many as 10% of girls, rates that range from 2 to 10 times the rates for boys (Smolak, this volume; Zahn-Waxler, Race, and Duggal, this volume). Physical aggression and ADHD are more prevalent among boys across age groups, but both problems occur in girls, although frequently with different symptom expression than in boys (Foster, this volume; Hinshaw & Blachman, this volume). Thus, the number of girls experiencing adjustment problems is not insignificant, although it is frequently different from the number of boys experiencing similar problems. Further, this number could be even higher, since current criteria for diagnosing commonly occurring disorders such as conduct problems and ADHD may underestimate the prevalence of these problems in girls.

Studies showing differences in rates of behavior problems for boys and girls have had several consequences, some positive and some negative. One positive consequence is that when a disorder is common in one sex, researchers are intrigued and devote effort to understanding that disorder and factors related to its etiology and maintenance in that sex. One downside to this interest, however, has been that studies of that disorder may focus on the sex in which the disorder is most common, to the relative exclusion of the sex in which the disorder is less common. For example, the literature on ADHD is much more heavily populated with studies of boys than girls, and so we have less knowledge about this disorder in girls. Similarly, our knowledge about boys with depression or eating disorders is also quite limited. Unfortunately, however, it is not uncommon to see theories developed and findings related to etiology framed as though they applied equally to boys and girls. Many key theories of aggression and delinquency, for example, are based on all-male samples. The literature on eating disorders, on the other hand, is dominated by all-female samples. Other literatures (e.g., mental retardation; Hodapp & Dykens, this volume) often do not consider sex or gender as relevant variables, so the extent to which their theories and findings apply to boys or girls specifically is unknown.

Given epidemiological evidence that girls and boys differ in the types and rates of adjustment problems, why have sex and gender received so little attention as relevant issues in children's behavioral and emotional problems? There are several probable reasons for the neglect of sex and gender issues. One is practical—some disorders are relatively rare in females (or males), making it difficult to recruit sufficient participants to study the problem. For example, very few males display eating disorders while relatively few females meet current criteria for ADHD. Other disorders such as autism and Asperger's Syndrome are rare in both boys and girls and investigators are loathe to compromise statistical power by looking at sex differences or by studying only girls.

A second reason for the absence of a focus on gender is the implicit assumption that behavioral and emotional problems and their causes are universal and that findings with boys can be readily generalized to girls. In the last few decades, traditional developmental psychology has seen a move away from this "universal truth" approach to behavior and development (Rutter & Sroufe, 2000). Similarly, research on gender development, studies showing that boys and girls differ in presentation of many behavior problems, and biological and multicultural approaches to psychopathology and intervention have all challenged these "universal causes and patterns" assumptions in the study of boys' and girls' development. Explicit discussion of different pathways of development for different subgroups of children has opened the door to examining girls and boys separately.

Clearly, sex and gender, like ethnicity, are important sources of variability in children's behavior. However, like ethnicity, they are only marker variables. Knowing that boys and girls differ in rates of certain types of problem behaviors tells us nothing about the mechanisms that might produce these differences (Rutter et al., 2003). Thus, it is not enough to show that boys and girls differ. This is only the beginning of the story. Far more interesting questions pertain to how socialization experiences, biologically based variables, and environmental or cultural contexts and demands interact over time to produce different patterns of adjustment for boys and girls. Equally interesting questions focus just on girls, independent of how they compare to boys. For example, looking at girls with problematic adjustment in relation to typically developing girls is important in its own right, and not only informs our understanding of how developmental trajectories can be altered or interrupted, but also offers sensible templates upon which to base diagnostic decisions and treatment or prevention goals. Helping girls with problems become more similar to better-adjusted girls seems a much more profitable goal than helping these girls become more like boys. Fortunately, some investigators are beginning to examine these more interesting questions, as illustrated throughout this volume.

A DEVELOPMENTAL PSYCHOPATHOLOGY FRAMEWORK FOR UNDERSTANDING GIRLS' ADJUSTMENT PROBLEMS

Some of the same limitations just described in the study of the roles of sex and gender in youth development are exactly the sorts of issues that led to the emergence of the field of developmental psychopathology. It became increasingly clear that developmental theories that attempted to provide universal explanations of development across domains, individuals, and the lifespan were inadequate, as were theories of psychopathology that seemed to expect that single, disorder-specific causes could be identified for each form of psychopathology (Kazdin & Kagan, 1994; Rutter & Sroufe, 2000). These theories failed to appreciate crucial aspects of dimensionality; continuities and discontinuities in functioning; the notions of equifinality (different causes for the same outcome) and multifinality (the same cause leading to different outcomes); and the complex interplay of biological, genetic, and other individual difference characteristics with environmental and cultural processes in influencing development and adjustment (Cicchetti & Rogosch, 1996; Rutter & Sroufe, 2000).

Developmental psychopathology, defined concisely by Rutter and Sroufe as "the study of the origins and course of individual patterns of behavioral maladaptation" (Rutter & Sroufe, 2000, p. 265; Sroufe & Rutter, 1984, p. 18), encompasses these issues that complicate and contextualize our understanding of development and disorder. Several issues central to a developmental psychopathology approach are also of particular relevance to our conceptualization of girls' behavioral and emotional adjustment. For example, development is considered a dynamic process in which a person (who brings genetic and biological characteristics, learning histories, and cognitive and affective processing to any interaction) influences and is influenced by her environment. Two issues are key here. First, the child's development and adjustment are in constant flux, a work in progress. Second, the child's development is multiply determined, with functioning at any particular point in time resulting from this interaction of personal and environmental factors. Beyond the sheer number of influencing factors, it is important to note that both genetic and environmental influences are thought to operate in a probabilistic rather than deterministic fashion (Rutter & Sroufe, 2000). Thus, a comprehensive understanding of girls' adjustment must incorporate the range of person and environment characteristics that may be operating, and must acknowledge the iterative nature of functioning (e.g., see Hankin & Abramson, 2001, for an example of a theory of depression that posits a causal chain for girls that includes genetic, cognitive, and interpersonal influences).

A developmental psychopathology perspective to girls' adjustment emphasizes the importance of understanding not only *what* personal (genetic and otherwise) and physical or sociocultural environmental influences are operating to produce specific outcomes for girls, but *how* these causal processes are operating over time (e.g., pathways) and in concert with each other. For example, it is informative to know what combination of influences may serve as risk factors for girls' development of depression or eating disorders, or as protective factors for girls' low rates of early-onset conduct problems. It is unlikely that these factors are simply the mirror images of factors that place boys at higher risk for conduct problems and lower risk for mood and eating problems. Even if the factors per se are the same, however, they may interact differently or play out differently over time for girls. The types of child-rearing environments that predict resilience to adversity may also differ for boys and girls. For example, Werner (1995) in the longitudinal children of Kauai study, found that resilience in girls was related to a household that combined risk taking and independence with support from a female caregiver. In contrast, resilience in boys was related to a household with a male role model that was characterized by structure, rules, and some encouragement of emotional expressiveness. Thus, research on one sex will not necessarily inform us well about the other sex. Furthermore, it is important to ground this information in the context of developmental tasks and processes that are normative for girls in their particular cultural context as they mature into adulthood, a topic we discuss in more detail in the next section.

Continuities and discontinuities of development are also relevant to a developmental psychopathology approach to understanding girls' adjustment. Overall, evidence suggests that girls' psychopathology is more discontinuous throughout childhood and adolescence than boys' (Keenan & Shaw, 1997). For example, girls' display of behavior and temperament problems in early childhood declines substantially during pre-adolescent childhood, but then increases again, particularly in areas of mood problems (Nolen-Hoeksema & Girgus, 1994) but also to some extent in externalizing problems (Moffitt et al., 2001).

Thus, a developmental psychopathology perspective offers a normal development foundation and an understanding of development that incorporates multiple personal and environmental characteristics that influence one another in complex probabilistic, mutual, and ongoing ways, and allows for both continuities and discontinuities in development. This perspective has the richness and complexity to advance our understanding of the expression, course, and process of girls' behavioral and emotional problems as they relate to girls' and women's development more generally, as well as how they relate to what we know about boys' adjustment.

GIRLS' DEVELOPMENT

At the core of the developmental psychopathology approach is an appreciation of typical development. Perhaps one of the most important truths about development is that it is a process (versus an outcome) that affects all living organisms in some similar ways—organisms begin life and grow, usually in size and almost certainly in complexity. For male and female children, the common features of development are numerous. Embryos begin as relatively undifferentiated cellular structures that multiply and differentiate to form the brain, organs, and limbs; infants are born with largely rudimentary abilities in physical, cognitive, and social functioning that throughout childhood and adolescence become language, motor coordination, thought, emotion, and social interaction. Both boys and girls negotiate the developmental tasks of self-regulation (of motor behavior, cognitive activity, emotion), communication (through language and action), and social interaction (e.g., with caregivers, peers). Throughout childhood, as skills become more complex and advanced, so too do independence and autonomy, the child's ability to be an active agent in his or her survival and interaction with the environment. Indeed, we could say that the major developmental task of childhood is to grow into independent adulthood, with the cognitive, affective, physical, and social skills to function smoothly in the world. From an evolutionary psychology perspective, we could also add that a further, and perhaps penultimate, task is to produce and rear the next generation of children in order to perpetuate the species (Geary, 1998).

Given the commonalities in developmental tasks, outcomes, and processes for male and female humans, it is not surprising that child development has focused largely on children as a group rather than on boys and girls separately. However, important differences also exist. Working backward and considering first the tasks of procreation and child rearing, males and females across species have different biological and behavioral roles in this process. Biologically speaking, females in most species have primary responsibility for pregnancy and childbirth. Obviously, this requires certain biological characteristics and processes. From a psychological perspective, specific physiological, cognitive, affective, and behavioral characteristics would also have adaptive value—for example, the oxytocin that aids in childbirth and lactation also enhances emotional and behavioral attachment to new offspring (Frank & Young, 2000). In most cultures, women have primary responsibility for raising children, especially during early years. For this role, characteristics such as nurturance and relationship focus are beneficial to caring for children who are relatively dependent and immature. The fact that females are typically in this early caregiving role also suggests that adjustment problems in girls (who become adult women) may be an especially important risk factor for psychopathology in the next generation, as research on the effects of maternal depression on their offspring would indicate (Goodman & Gotlib, 2002).

Given differences in the biological capabilities and normative roles of adult men and women, it makes sense that boys' and girls' development would diverge in specific abilities that provide the foundations for these functions. In addition to biologically based differences, cultures influence human behavior in ways that may go well beyond childrearing. For example, cultures differ in the roles that men and women tend to adopt in providing financial and material resources for the family (e.g., careers), in social relationships (e.g., friendships, dating), and in recreational or leisure activities. Although the extent to which these roles are influenced by biological or social factors has been the subject of much debate (Maccoby, 1998), it is generally agreed that their development begins in childhood. Thus, it is important to appreciate the distinct ways in which girls develop across biological, cognitive, emotional, and social domains, with attention to how environmental influences such as socialization from family, school, and the broader culture may influence and interact with development in ways relevant to psychopathology.

At the same time, it is important to realize that there are large individual differences within each gender. Thus, although socialization and biological development may differ generally for boys and girls as a group, individual girls can vary widely on rates of development and exposure to gender-related socialization processes, as can boys. One key task of developmental psychopathologists is to explain this within-gender variation, particularly as it relates to the development and maintenance of maladaptive behavior.

Biological Development

Biologically, girls begin with a developmental advantage over boys. In utero and throughout infancy, girls have higher survival rates, better immune function, and faster biological development, with evidence suggesting that lack of prenatal exposure to testosterone accounts for this relative advantage (Keenan & Shaw, 1997; Geary, 1998, 2002). Faster development has been implicated as a protective factor against mild genetic anomalies and learning disabilities in girls. In general, girls show fewer early-onset disorders associated with neurodevelopmental impairment than boys. Some evidence also suggests that young girls show better physiologic response to stress (Keenan & Shaw, 1997). Thus, young girls seem biologically better prepared to master the developmental tasks of infancy and toddlerhood, and to approach school-age, when they are approximately 1 year ahead of boys in physical maturity (Eme, 1992).

Interestingly, biological and hormonal factors have been implicated in girls' early expression of sex-typed behaviors. For example, hormonal factors have been proposed to account for girls' interest in infants (Maccoby, 1998) and greater orientation toward people, a tendency that appears as early as 1 day of age (Geary, 2002). Toy and play preferences have also been shown to vary with prenatal exposure to hormones, with androgen exposure in girls being related to a preference for boy playmates and sex-typed boy toys (Ruble & Martin, 1998).

Biological differences play an important role in discussions of boys' and girls' development at all ages, although some developmental periods such as puberty may figure more prominently (Hayward, 2003). In adolescence, hormonal changes associated with puberty in girls emerge and seem to function as risk rather than protective factors. Girls' increases in negative and depressed mood during puberty may be related to increases in estrogen (Angold, Worthman, & Costello, 2003; Kessler, 2000; Parry, 2000), although the evidence for this is inconsistent and the increases in depression may also reflect environmental and socialization stressors experienced by adolescent girls (Rudolph, 2002). Early puberty seems to place girls at particular risk for adjustment problems, although again, whether this reflects biological or environmental factors is uncertain (Ruble & Martin, 1998). Differences between boys' and girls' physical abilities, particularly strength-based abilities, also increase during puberty (Geary, 2002), and may contribute to adjustment difficulties for girls who are accustomed to and value physical or athletic parity with their male peers. In sum, biological factors may confer some facilitative or protective effects on girls' early development, while conferring risk during the adolescent years.

Cognitive and Language Development

Evidence for differences between boys' and girls' cognitive development is mixed, but where present, seems to be most strongly related to advanced language development for girls (Keenan & Shaw, 1997; Maccoby, 1998). Among young children, girls have larger vocabularies than boys and show relative advances in using language to label and describe objects, events, and personal experience and preferences. They tend to initiate verbal interchanges more frequently and show greater responsiveness to the verbalizations of others. Interestingly, these sex differences remain even after controlling for the potential effects of parent attention and teaching on language use (Geary, 2002; Keenan & Shaw, 1997).

Although there is little evidence of sex differences in overall cognitive functioning or IQ, girls and boys do seem to differ on the ways in which they attend to and process information (Geary, 1998, 2002). For example, when engaged in exploratory play, boys and girls remember similar amounts, but different types, of spatial information; boys remember routes whereas girls remember landmarks. Even in infancy, boys are more likely to attend to physical aspects of their environments (e.g., lights, sounds) whereas girls tend to attend to the consequences of environmental objects or events (e.g., attending to others' responses).

Sex differences in cognitive abilities have been proposed to explain the male preponderance of certain disorders such as autism. For example, Baron-Cohen (2002) has hypothesized that individuals with autism fall at the extreme high end of a continuum of cognitive abilities associated with "systemizing" (drive to construct systems that helps to understand the inanimate world), and at the extreme low end of abilities associated with "empathizing" (identifying emotions and thoughts that help to understand the social world). Although both abilities are present in both sexes, males are presumed to show relatively more systemizing and females more empathizing. Frequent interests and behaviors that occur among individuals with autism and Asperger's Syndrome (e.g., attention to detail, collecting, interest in mathematics, mechanical knowledge, scientific and technical information) are presumed to reflect an extreme on the systemizing dimension of the male brain, and a relative absence of empathizing (e.g., mindreading, empathy, eye contact, communication) (Baron-Cohen, Richler, Bisarya, Gurunathan, & Wheelwright, 2003; Baron-Cohen & Wheelwright, 2004).

Throughout the school-age years, including adolescence, girls' achievement in selected academic and cognitive domains frequently declines relative to boys'. Girls express less interest, confidence, and sometimes ability in areas such as math and science. However, this may be more a function of socialization factors than cognitive abilities per se; parents and teachers are frequently less encouraging of girls' achievement in math and science, and attribute successes to hard work rather than ability (Jacobs & Eccles, 1992; Jussim & Eccles, 1992). Similarly, the finding that parents are three times more likely to explain science to boys than girls, even at a young age, suggests that socialization processes may be contributing to a gender gap in scientific literacy even prior to any formal science instruction in grade school (Crowley, Callanan, Tenenbaum, & Allen, 2001).

Social-Emotional Development

Girls show some distinct patterns of social-emotional development that seem particularly relevant for understanding their behavioral and emotional adjustment. For example, from very early ages, social interaction and play preferences differ for boys and girls. Whereas boys' play is characterized by attention to objects (e.g., tools, inanimate mechanical objects, constructing), action (e.g., rough-and-tumble play, action hero play), and personal achievement and power, girls are more likely to engage in play with relationship and family themes and when using objects in play, to incorporate them into relationship-oriented fantasy (Geary, 2002; Maccoby, 2002; Nicolopoulou, 1997). For example, Geary (2002) describes young African girls using everyday inanimate objects as "dolls" or "babies" when no dolls were available. By preschool and middle childhood, children are much more likely to play with same-sex than opposite-sex peers, likely because of shared interests and play styles (Maccoby, 1998). Parents and adults tend to encourage sex-typed play in young children, in their toy offerings and play styles, although they frequently give girls greater leeway in cross-sex activities. Interestingly, however, there is little evidence that parents have any substantial influence on children's play activity or partner preferences. However, some evidence suggests that children display more interest in novel toys labeled as "for their sex" and imitate same-sex models who are distinctively sex-appropriate (Maccoby, 1998; Powlishta, Sen, Serbin, Poulin-DuBois, & Eichstedt, 2001).

Girls' relational focus continues throughout childhood and adolescence (Maccoby, 2002; Crick & Zahn-Waxler, 2003). Girls think and talk more about their relationships, particularly the emotional aspects, than boys do. Their play is more likely than boys' to be characterized by cooperation and harmony, and themes of relationships and family. When girls have interpersonal conflicts, they are more likely to behave in relationally aggressive ways (aggression intended to harm someone's relationship) than in overtly aggressive ways (Underwood, 2003). Girls' emotional development also has a relational focus. For example, from young childhood, girls show advances, relative to boys, in their ability to regulate and express their own emotions, as well as their understanding of and responses to emotions of others (Keenan & Shaw, 1997; Maccoby, 1998). Girls are more likely to talk about emotions, although this might reflect language abilities more than emotional development. They demonstrate social perspective-taking and emotion-regulation abilities, by inhibiting negative emotions in the presence of others if these negative emotions might distress the other person, and by showing distress or guilt if another person is wronged. They also show empathy and concern for others, and display prosocial (e.g., helping) responses appropriate to the situation.

As girls mature, they retain this relative emphasis on inhibiting expression of negative affect and demonstrating positive, prosocial emotions, particularly in the presence of others (Maccoby, 1998, 2002; Crick & Zahn-Waxler, 2003). Some researchers (e.g., Brown & Gilligan, 1992; Tolman & Brown, 2001) argue that especially by adolescence, girls become very concerned about reading other people for signs of approval and disapproval and may "act" how they think others want them to rather than displaying their true feelings and opinions. Brown and Gilligan (1992) refer to this "loss of voice," or an adolescent girl's decision to give up herself for the sake of the relationship, as a risk factor for problems with self-esteem, identity development, and emotional problems. Additional evidence suggests that this more cooperative, polite, and other-focused interaction style may disadvantage girls and young women in mixed-sex groups (Maccoby, 2002). For example, although these women are frequently liked, they may be seen as less competent and be given less authority or fewer opportunities to participate or advance professionally.

IMPLICATIONS OF GIRLS' DEVELOPMENT FOR BEHAVIORAL AND EMOTIONAL PROBLEMS

Our brief review of girls' development suggests many reasons why girls might be protected from some developing some problems but at increased risk for developing others. For example, the combination of good language development and relational focus should increase young girls' chances of developing good interpersonal relationships with family and friends. By being able to express themselves, girls should be more able to get their needs met and they may be interesting conversation partners (especially for older children or adults who are used to interacting verbally). By virtue of their ability to predict others' emotions and to regulate their own emotion expression, young girls may develop social skills that lead them to be desirable interaction partners. Thus, early interpersonal relationships may be mutually satisfying for girls, and may increase the chances of girls' future interpersonal success. At the same time, the downside of this combination of emotion regulation and relational focus is Gilligan's "loss of voice," which may be particularly harmful for adolescent girls as they approach developmental tasks of autonomy and are faced with a conflict between expressing independence and being perfect, nice, agreeable, and dependent (Hey, 1997; Tolman & Brown, 2001). This conflict can be further complicated by an interaction with socioeconomic status, whereby girls from low-income families may need to work, thus heightening the conflict between dependence and autonomy. Alternatively, it can be lessened in cultures (e.g., African American) that support more independent thought in young women (Tolman & Brown, 2001). In addition, if the hypothesis that girls' peer groups are characterized by generally high rates of verbal skill and friendship connections is true, the lack of these skills may be particularly problematic for girls who fail to meet normative expectations.

Thus, girls' risk and resilience is best understood in the context of the tasks of normal development and the typical developmental progression and issues for girls, as well as in the context of the girls' unique socialization experiences. Subsequent chapters of this book offer a great deal of information about girls' risk for a variety of disorders and negative life experiences. For some of these issues, such as depression, eating disorders, and sexual abuse, girls' risk is relatively high, either in general or relative to boys, and the knowledge base is accordingly large. In other words, "girl" problems have been studied in girls. Other disorders, such as developmental disorders (learning disabilities, mental retardation, pervasive developmental disorders, ADHD) and gender identity disorders are relatively uncommon for girls and the literature is smaller. Finally, several issues are simply *different* for girls than for boys (e.g., aggression, dating violence, substance use and abuse, coping with stressors such as chronic illness, homelessness, and physical abuse and neglect); in these cases, girls may show distinctive patterns of symptom expression, course, or outcomes. Despite major differences in the amount and focus on girls across problem areas, several themes are apparent. We present these briefly.

First, consistent with a developmental psychopathology framework, girls' problems in adjustment are often consistent with what we know about their typical development. Girls' coping with negative life experiences is a clear example of this. For example, girls may show resilience or better adjustment than boys in areas of relative developmental strength (e.g., language use, emotion expression and regulation, relationship support), and have problems in areas of developmental vulnerability (e.g., putting others' needs ahead of their own, confidence, autonomy). For example, Miller and LaGreca (this volume) summarize data showing that girls coping with chronic illness tend to do better than boys in areas such as emotional expression, support-seeking, and behavioral conduct. When they do have problems, they are likely to be in confidence or self-esteem. Similarly, homeless girls (Cauce, Stewart, Whitbeck, Paradise, & Hoyt, this volume) are at particular risk for depression and sexual victimization, and although their rates of conduct problems exceed those of housed girls, they are still less likely than (homeless) boys to display overtly aggressive behavior.

A second theme is that puberty is a specific time of challenge for girls across disorders and problem areas (Hayward, 2003). Both internalizing (Albano & Krain, this volume; Smolak, this volume; Zahn-Waxler, Race, & Duggal, this volume) and externalizing (Andrews, this volume; Foster, this volume) problems increase for girls during puberty. Zahn-Waxler et al. review several theories regarding increases in depression in adolescent girls. These emphasize influences such as gender intensification (whereby expectations that adolescent girls behave in ways that are dependent, helpless, passive, and self-sacrificing, are strengthened; Hill & Lynch, 1983), hormones (Cyranowski, Frank, Young, & Shear, 2000), cognitive vulnerability (Hankin & Abramson, 2001), and interpersonal stress (Rudolph et al., in press) that may become particularly relevant in adolescence. Similarly, Smolak presents theories of eating disorders that highlight maladaptive eating as a way to regain the loss of voice and loss of control that accompanies adolescence for many females (Smolak & Munsterteiger, 2002), or a response to objectification of women's bodies that becomes more salient at puberty (Fredrickson & Roberts, 1997). Foster's description of potential mechanisms of risk for adolescent girls' conduct problems includes a similar combination of personal (e.g., distorted cognitions) and environmental (e.g., exposure to delinquent peers, especially males) that may be especially likely to occur in adolescence.

A third theme in our chapters is that of the gender paradox of severity and comorbidity. This notion derives from the polygenetic multiple threshold model, a theory that attempts to explain gender differences in prevalence of behavior problems (see Eme, 1992, for review). This model specifically examines problems that are more prevalent among boys than girls (e.g., ADHD, autism) and advances the hypothesis that girls—who are less prone than boys to develop the problem—are nonetheless more likely to be severely afflicted once the problem occurs (Eme, 1992). Investigators have interpreted "more severe affliction" as either (a) more severe forms or symptoms associated with the disorder or problem per se, or (b) more frequent comorbid occurrence of behavior problems above and beyond the problem under investigation. In fact, support for this theoretical framework is quite mixed, whether one examines severity of disorder per se or whether one looks at comorbid problems (Eme, 1992; Foster, this volume;

Hinshaw & Blachman, this volume; Koenig & Tsatsanas, this volume). At the same time, this theoretical framework has prompted researchers to examine gender-specific patterns of behavior problems and symptoms and comorbid problems for boys and girls. In addition, this and other theories focus on possible mechanisms for understanding gender differences. The mechanisms that could explain gender differences include (Eme, 1992; Moffitt et al., 2001; Smolak, this volume; Young, this volume; Zahn-Waxler et al., this volume): (a) boys and girls may be exposed to different environmental and genetic risk and protective factors, (b) boys and girls may be exposed to different levels of the same risk and protective factors, (c) boys and girls may show different biological susceptibility to risk, (d) boys and girls may have different mechanisms of gene expression (such that genetic influences may be amplified or diminished among girls, relative to boys), (e) boys and girls may require different thresholds of risk for serious problems to develop, perhaps due to sex differences in their biological or genetic makeup; (f) boys and girls encounter different environmental or cultural challenges that differentially prompt the emergence of particular problems.

Despite the emphasis on comparing males and females that is evident in some writing related to gender and disorder, the chapters in this volume illustrate, without exception, the importance of understanding each of girls' difficulties in the context of environmental and socialization factors that are particularly important for girls. Several of these factors, such as societal encouragement of girls' prosocial and sometimes overly agreeable or compliant behavior; the importance of, but dissatisfaction with, body image for adolescent girls; and the role of autonomy-dependency conflicts in girls' adjustment, have already been discussed. Socialization of girls to value compliance, beauty, and an other-focus may also play a role in girls' victimization (e.g., in girls taking blame for abuse and coping passively; Azar, this volume; Wolfe, Scott, & Crooks, this volume). Similarly, Andrews (this volume) suggests that body image concerns may be implicated in girls' smoking as a way to maintain weight loss. Socialization (along with a potential genetic predisposition to value relationships) may also make the consequences of some disorders especially troublesome for girls. For example, girls with developmental disorders that impair social skills (e.g., ADHD, learning disorders, pervasive developmental disorders) may experience particular frustration or depression because of their inability to function successfully in a developmental domain that has special significance for females.

Societal and cultural factors are also implicated in the definition of disorder for girls. For example, cultural norms providing more leeway for sex-atypical behavior in girls have been proposed to account for lower rates of diagnosis of gender identity disorder in girls (Zucker, this volume). Such norms have also been suggested as influencing the types of behaviors that are considered symptoms of ADHD and conduct disorder, such that girls' rates of these disorders are substantially lower than boys' (Hinshaw & Blachman, this volume; Foster, this volume).

CURRENT ISSUES AND FUTURE DIRECTIONS

Theory

As indicated in this chapter and throughout the book, many theories of the development of behavior disorders have not explicitly considered whether the symptoms they describe and the pathways they propose are equally applicable for boys and girls. We cannot assume that theories developed for boys will apply equally well to girls. In some instances they may, but it is also likely that specific theories will be needed to account for the presentations and developmental pathways of at least some problems in girls. As discussed below, current assessment of many disorders relies on diagnostic and assessment systems that emphasize the symptom profile of the sex for which the disorder is most common. Thus, the symptom lists for ADHD and conduct disorder include behaviors most typically expressed by males, whereas the symptom list for depression and eating disorders include behaviors as most typically expressed by females. Similarly, theories of development of these disorders are frequently developed based on what we know about the problem in the sex in which it is most common. Even when symptoms are similar for boys and girls, the factors leading to the behavior or the function and impact of such behavior on the environment may differ.

One way to test theoretical mechanisms involved in the development of behavior problems is to study girls as an important population in their own right. Indeed, it could be argued that the study of gender differences may undermine understanding of gender-specific pathways to specific behavior problems by leading to too much focus on differences between the genders at the expense of understanding mechanisms at work within each gender. Furthermore, a focus on girls might force greater attention to variables and circumstances particularly salient in girls' development—variables that might not receive attention if mixed-gender samples were included.

Research

In addition to studies that focus specifically on girls, research on the development of emotional and behavioral problems in girls would benefit from increased attention to several methodological issues. First, it is important to focus on variables, theoretical frameworks, and situations that are particularly relevant to girls. For example, given the importance of relational issues in girls' typical development, the impact of social relations and support are likely to be important in the development, maintenance, and consequences of many disorders. Similarly, our understanding of girls' relative "strength" in emotion regulation suggests both that disorders of under- and over-regulation are of interest, and that any measurement of emotion in girls is likely influenced by their ability to regulate emotional expression. Second, researchers who study both boys and girls should move beyond gender differences to illuminate mechanisms involved in creating these differences (Rutter et al., 2003). Often researchers explain gender differences by speculating about differences in how boys and girls were socialized, but fail to measure these socialization variables to test whether in fact they mediate or explain observed gender differences. Third, when researchers study gender as a factor that may moderate the relationships between risk or protective factors and behavior problems, it is imperative that their sample size be sufficient to detect significant interactions between gender and the risk or protective variables of interest (Crick & Zahn-Waxler, in press). This is a particularly important issue because statistical power to detect interaction effects is often markedly lower than power to detect the main effects (Aiken & West, 1991).

Another important factor for future research is the need to consider differences between clinical and community samples. Girls who come to the attention of mental health professionals may differ from unreferred girls with similar levels of behavior problems in the community in important ways. Due to referral practices and other family and community dynamics or norms, girls with particular types of problems will be referred for treatment. For example, girls with gender-atypical behavior problems such as aggression or hyperactivity may be referred for treatment at lower levels of distress than girls with more gender-typical issues such as depression, simply because it stands out more to parents or teachers.

It is also important to consider comorbidity issues, particularly with clinical samples. For example, many of the correlates of aggression, antisocial behavior, and substance use in girls are quite similar (Andrews, this volume; Foster, this volume). The same is true of anxiety and depression among girls (Albano & Krain, this volume; Zahn-Waxler, this volume). This is not surprising given the high comorbidity between each of these pairs of difficulties. Thus, studies of one disorder are likely to include girls with both problems. It is likely that some risk factors are specific to particular difficulties while others operate more generally to put girls at risk for various types of problems. It will be difficult to tease these apart, however, unless researchers assess a variety of behavior problems in their female samples and explicitly address comorbidity issues in girls' development.

Finally, it is important for researchers to examine the interaction of sex with other factors such as time (i.e., development) or intelligence. For example, sex seems to interact with development in the prevalence and expression of conduct problems, with the male advantage for conduct problems in childhood narrowing in adolescence and increasing again in young adulthood and beyond (Foster, this volume). Similarly, gender differences among children with autism are larger in the normal range of intellectual functioning than at lower levels of intelligence (Baron-Cohen, 2002; Koenig & Tsatsanis, this volume). These interactions suggest different developmental pathways and different sets of putative causal factors.

Assessment and Diagnosis

The framework espoused here raises several issues relevant to the assessment and diagnosis of girls' problems. A key issue in diagnosis lies in the relevance and sensitivity of diagnostic criteria for assessing girls.

This issue is particularly salient with any disorder for which prevalence rates are much higher in one gender than another (e.g., ADHD, CD, depression, eating disorders). As mentioned earlier, when this occurs and when criteria are based in part on research findings, the criteria are more likely to reflect the characteristic "problem profile" of the dominant gender. Thus, it is likely that criteria for female-dominated problems will be particularly relevant for girls, whereas criteria used to diagnose male-dominated problems may miss important features of girls' problems. Diagnostic criteria need to be scrutinized for inclusion of typical problem behaviors for both genders, recognizing that problem behaviors that describe a disorder may take different forms depending on whether the child is a boy or a girl (Crick & Zahn-Waxler, 2003). Assessment approaches used for diagnosis must reflect gender-related differences in behaviors or symptoms used to establish diagnoses so that symptom lists are sufficiently inclusive to capture behaviors that capture the diagnostic criteria but may differ in form for females and males.

Considering the development of problems specifically in girls mandates a focus on assessing problems in the context of normal developmental processes and tasks, both gender-specific and gender-nonspecific. Many developmental tasks are similar for boys and girls; both must learn to communicate and play cooperatively with others, master academic skills, and—in teenage years—formulate an identity and emancipate from the family of origin. But the nuances of these common developmental tasks can differ for boys and girls. For example, girls interact in smaller groups of friends than boys, placing a presumed premium on conversation skills for girls and game-playing skills for boys. As a consequence, contexts in which problems occur may vary somewhat as well. Similar issues with regard to diagnostic issues have been raised with regard to age and culture, where it is important to define abnormal development in the context of adaptive development for the age or cultural group in question. Thus, comprehensive assessment of girls' adjustment should include assessment in girl-relevant (as well as age-relevant and culture-relevant) contexts.

Finally, assessment tools that rely on normative data would be wise to publish gender-specific norms, so that girls can be compared to girls and boys to boys. This is not to imply that different cutoffs for disorder should automatically be applied if the genders differ in overall levels of a particular problem behavior. Not only does this risk "overpathologizing" the gender with the lower cutoff (Crick & Zahn-Waxler, 2003), but gender differences in rates of serious problems most likely occur for legitimate reasons having to do with differential exposure to risk factors, as described by many authors in this volume. Different cutoffs or thresholds for diagnosis should be established with great caution and only after considerable evidence of differential sensitivity and specificity of cutoff scores in predicting important outcomes for boys versus girls.

Prevention and Treatment

Treatment and prevention efforts should be built on an understanding of the factors that propel some girls toward serious problems and that maintain those problems once they have been established. Yet treatment and prevention approaches for most behavior problems in childhood and adolescence, like most assessment instruments, have virtually ignored gender-related issues. A first and obviously necessary step in creating gender-sensitive treatment approaches will be to examine whether the best available evidence-based interventions are equally effective for boys and girls, and to examine factors that contribute to treatment outcome for each gender separately.

It is likely that somewhat different treatment and prevention approaches will be required to maximize treatment effectiveness for girls and boys. We say this because if different factors are involved in the development of disorder among males and females, different approaches would be necessary to address those factors that are causally implicated in girls' behavior problems. Chapters in this volume in fact suggest that—although many factors that contribute to problems are similar for boys and girls— some clearly differ or matter more for girls than for boys. Even if the same risk factors are involved in the development of male and female disorders, it seems that gender-sensitive treatment approaches may maximize effectiveness of treatment. For example, consider social skills training, commonly used with children diagnosed with ADHD and antisocial behavior problems. Boys' and girls' peer groups differ in their composition and customary activities. Training that situates skill building in the types of activities girls are likely to encounter presumably should enhance generalization to girls' common encounters in their natural environment.

In addition, treatment is often initiated by, and relies on involvement of, adults (parents, teachers) in the girls' environment. Adults may voice different concerns about the same behaviors for boys versus girls. For example, in our experience parents of acting out teenage girls are typically more concerned about the girls' time away from home and friends of the opposite sex than are parents of acting out boys, principally based on concerns about possible pregnancy and its ramifications for girls. Thus, the presenting problem may be driven in part by whether the child is male or female. In addition, the ways in which clinicians involve parents and teachers may differ for boys versus girls. As mentioned earlier, parents and teachers tend to socialize and interact with boys and girls differently. Considering the socialization practices that are more normative for girls than for boys (and vice versa) may help clinicians develop parent and teacher interventions that fit within their customary ways of behaving and are thus more acceptable to them.

Prevention efforts, too, could benefit from increased attention to gender-related issues of the sort just discussed. The specific targets of prevention will likely differ for girls and boys, as the rates of disorder or problem area, the severity of diagnosed cases, and the specific symptoms or problem behaviors within diagnoses differ across sex. For example, depression, as a more common issue for adolescent girls than boys, is an obvious area for prevention efforts. Prevention of conduct problems, a lower-rate disorder among girls, may also be a fruitful prevention target if one broadens more traditional views of conduct problems to include relational aggression and dating violence. However, the qualities that may protect against the development of one disorder may exacerbate the like-lihood of another. Socialization practices that encourage girls to inhibit their expression of anger and hostility, for example, may protect girls from developing problems with over-aggression, but provide a breeding ground for depression (Crick & Zahn-Waxler, in press). Thus, the multiple (and sometimes conflicting) consequences of addressing particular prevention targets should be considered. Similarly, as mentioned earlier, girls grow up to be women who, in most societies, have primary (or at least large) responsibility for child-rearing. Thus, the consequences of prevention and treatment extend into the next generation as the behavioral and emotional adjustment of mothers impacts the socialization and development of their children.

The process of effective prevention efforts are also likely to differ for girls and boys. The most effective prevention efforts may indeed be those that are sensitive to girls' normative development (e.g., their typical areas of biological, cognitive, psychological, and interpersonal strength and vulner-ability), interaction styles and contexts, and socialization experiences. As is the case with treatment, designing prevention programs that account for girls' relative strengths in areas such as language and emotion regulation, and their relational focus, may increase the likelihood that girls resonate to, participate in, and benefit from these programs. Finally, prevention efforts should be nested within a broad view of how girls in different cultures are socialized at various ages, and how this socialization can go awry. Charac-teristics that are protective at one age may become risk factors later (e.g., their social relationship focus may protect them against conduct problems but heighten risk for depression in adolescence).

CONCLUSIONS

An ever-increasing group of researchers is attending to the behavioral and emotional adjustment of female youth. For several problem areas, mostly those that are relatively rare in girls, our understanding of girls' experiences is fairly rudimentary—we have information on prevalence for girls, but symptom descriptions and issues of etiology, outcome, and co-morbid conditions are essentially based on what we know about the disor-ders in boys or in mixed-sex samples that are too small for males and females to be considered separately. For problem areas that are more prevalent for girls, we have a much deeper understanding of how girls experience and express difficulty, what factors increase risk or provide protection, and what we can expect regarding the broader picture of co-morbidity and prognosis. Like the initial developments in child psychology and psychopathology, which were embedded in an understanding of adult development and disorder, our initial efforts to understand girls' behavioral and emotional adjustment have developed largely in the context of what we know of boys' adjustment. However, we see promising advances in the de-velopment of theories that are sensitive to or specific to girls, taking into ac-count the unique aspects of girls' biological, cognitive, and social-emotional development and contexts. We also see advances in research that assesses girls' behavioral and emotional problems in the context of female development and adjustment. The chapters in this volume present the state of the field in diverse areas of child adjustment problems. They are exciting in what they communicate about current knowledge of girls' behavioral and emotional problems, and in their vision for future study. However, our longer-term aspiration for the field is the development of empirically supported theories that embed our understanding of girls into a larger understanding of youth (including both boys and girls), and human behavior (across the lifespan). These theories would encompass our understanding of girls as they are similar to and different from each other, from boys, from adult women and men, within the context of age and culture, and would represent the ideal in developmental psychopathology. Much research is moving in this direction, but the field is ripe for further advances. Hopefully, this book will inspire some of these.

REFERENCES

Albano, A. M., & Krain, A. (2005). Anxiety disorders in girls. In D. J. Bell, S. L. Foster, & E. J. Mash (Eds.), *Handbook of behavioral and emotional problems in girls* (pp. 79–115). New York: Kluwer Academic/Plenum Publishers.

Aiken, L. S., & West, S. G. (1991). *Multiple regression: Testing and interpreting interactions.* Thousand Oaks, CA: Sage.

American Psychiatric Association (2000). *Diagnostic and statistical manual of mental disorders* (4th ed., text rev.). Washington, DC: Author.

Andrews, J. A. (2005). Substance abuse in girls. In D. J. Bell, S. L. Foster, & E. J. Mash (Eds.), *Handbook of behavioral and emotional problems in girls* (pp. 181–209). New York: Kluwer Academic/Plenum Publishers.

Angold, A., Worthman, C., & Costello, E. J. (2003). Puberty and depression. In C. Hayward (Ed.), *Gender differences at puberty* (pp. 137–164). New York: Cambridge University Press.

Azar, S. T. (2005). Physical abuse and neglect in girls and women. In D. J. Bell, S. L. Foster, & E. J. Mash (Eds.), *Handbook of behavioral and emotional problems in girls* (pp. 321–326). New York: Kluwer Academic/Plenum Publishers.

Baron-Cohen, S. (2002). The extreme male brain theory of autism. *Trends in Cognitive Sciences, 6,* 248–254.

Baron-Cohen, S., Richler, J., Bisarya, D., Gurunathan, N., & Wheelwright, S. (2003). The systemizing quotient: An investigation of adults with Asperger syndrome or high-functioning autism, and normal sex differences. *Philosophical Transactions of the Royal Society: Biological Sciences, 358,* 361–374.

Baron-Cohen, S., & Wheelwright, S. (2004). The empathy quotient: An investigation of adults with Asperger Syndrome or high functioning autism, and normal sex differences. *Journal of Autism and Developmental Disorders, 34,* 163–175.

Brown, L., & Gilligan, C. (1992). *Meeting at the crossroads.* Cambridge MA: Harvard University Press.

Cauce, A. M., Stewart, A., Whitbeck, L. B., Paradise, M., & Hoyt, D. R. (2005). Girls on their own: Homelessness in female adolescents. In D. J. Bell, S. L. Foster, & E. J. Mash (Eds.), *Handbook of behavioral and emotional problems in girls* (pp. 439–522). New York: Kluwer Academic/Plenum Publishers.

Cicchetti, D., & Rogosch, F. Q. (2002). A developmental psychopathology perspective on adolescence. *Journal of Consulting and Clinical Psychology, 70,* 6–20.

Crick, N. R., & Zahn-Waxler, C. (2003). The development of psychopathology in males and females: Current progress and future challenges. *Development and Psychopathology, 15,* 719–742.

Crowley, K., Callanan, M. A., Tenenbaum, H. R., & Allan, E. (2001). Parents explain more often to boys than to girls during shared scientific thinking. *Psychological Science, 12,* 258–261.

Cyranowski, J. M., Frank, E., Young, E., & Shear, M. K. (2000). Adolescent onset of the gender difference in lifetime rates of major depression. *Archives of General Psychiatry, 57,* 21–27.

Eme, R. F. (1992). Selective female affliction in the developmental disorders of childhood: A literature review. *Journal of Clinical Child Psychology, 21,* 354–364.

Foster, S. L. (2005). Aggression and antisocial behavior in girls. In D.J. Bell, S. L. Foster, & E. J. Mash (Eds.), *Handbook of behavioral and emotional problems in girls* (pp. 149–180). New York: Kluwer Academic/Plenum Publishers.

Frank, E., & Young, E. (2000). Pubertal changes and adolescent challenges: Why do rates of depression rise precipitously for girls between ages 10 and 15 years? In E. Frank (Ed.), *Gender and its effects on psychopathology* (pp. 85–102). Washington, DC: American Psychiatric Press.

Fredrickson, B., & Roberts, T. (1997). Objectification theory: Toward understanding women's lived experiences and mental health risks. *Psychology of Women Quarterly, 21,* 173–206.

Geary, D. C. (1998). *Male, female: The evolution of human sex differences.* Washington, DC: American Psychological Association.

Geary, D. C. (2002). Sexual selection and human life history. *Advances in Child Development and Behavior, 30,* 41–100.

Goodman, S. H., & Gotlib, I. H. (Eds.). (2002). *Children of depressed parents: Mechanisms of risk and implications for treatment.* Washington, DC: American Psychological Association.

Hankin, B. L., & Abramson, L.Y. (2001). Development of gender differences in depression: An elaborated cognitive vulnerability-transactional stress theory. *Psychological Bulletin, 127,* 773–796.

Hayward, C. (Ed.) (2003). *Gender differences at puberty.* New York: Cambridge University Press.

Hey, V. (1997). *The company she keeps: An ethnography of girls' friendships.* London: University of London Press.

Hill, J. P., & Lynch, M. E. (1983). The intensification of gender-related role expectations during early adolescence. In J. Brooks-Gunn and A. Petersen (Eds.), *Girls at puberty: Biological and psychosocial perspectives* (pp. 201–228). New York: Plenum Press.

Hinshaw, S. P. (2002). Process, mechanism and explanation related to externalizing behavior in developmental psychopathology. *Journal of Abnormal Child Psychology, 30,* 431–446.

Hinshaw, S. P., & Blachman, D. R., (2005). Attention-deficit/hyperactivity disorder in girls. In D.J. Bell, S.L. Foster, & E. J. Mash (Eds.), *Handbook of behavioral and emotional problems in girls* (pp. 117–147). New York: Kluwer Academic/Plenum Publishers.

Hodapp, R. M., & Dykens, E. M. (2005). Problems of girls and young women with mental retardation (intellectual disabilities). In D. J. Bell, S. L. Foster, & E. J. Mash (Eds.), *Handbook of behavioral and emotional problems in girls* (pp. 239–262). New York: Kluwer Academic/Plenum Publishers.

Jacobs, J. E., & Eccles, J. S. (1992). The impact of mothers' gender-role stereotype beliefs on mothers' and children's ability perceptions. *Journal of Personality and Social Psychology, 63,* 932–944.

Jussim, L., & Eccles, J. S. (1992). Teacher expectations II: Construction and reflection of student achievement. *Journal of Personality and Social Psychology, 63,* 947–961.

Kazdin, A. E., & Kagan, J. (1994). Models of dysfunction in developmental psychopathology. *Clinical Psychology: Science and Practice, 1,* 35–52.

Keenan, K., & Shaw, D. (1997). Developmental and social influences on young girls' early problem behavior. *Psychological Bulletin, 12,* 95–113.

Kessler, R. C. (2000). Gender differences in major depression: Epidemiological findings. In E. Frank (Ed.), *Gender and its effects on psychopathology* (pp. 61–84). Washington, DC: American Psychiatric Press.

Koenig, K., & Tsatsanas, K. D. (2005). Pervasive developmental disorders in girls. In D. J. Bell, S. L. Foster, & E. J. Mash (Eds.), *Handbook of behavioral and emotional problems in girls* (pp. 211–237). New York: Kluwer Academic/Plenum Publishers.

Lewinsohn, P. M., Gotlib, I. H., Lewinsohn, M., Seeley, J. R., & Allen, N. B. (1997). Gender differences in anxiety disorders and anxiety symptoms in adolescents. *Journal of Abnormal Psychology, 107*, 109–117.

Maccoby, E. E. (1998). *The two sexes: Growing up apart, coming together*. Cambridge, MA: Harvard University Press.

Maccoby, E. E. (2002). Gender and social exchange: A developmental perspective. In W. G. Graziano & B. Laursen (Eds.), *Social exchange in development* (pp. 87–106). San Francisco: Jossey-Bass.

Mash, E. J., & Barkley, R. A. (Eds.). (2003). *Child psychopathology* (2nd ed.). New York: Guilford.

Mash, E. J., & Wolfe, D. A. (2005). *Abnormal child psychology* (3rd ed.). Belmont, CA: Wadsworth.

Miller, K. B., & La Greca A. M. (2005). Adjustment to chronic illness in girls. In D. J. Bell, S. L. Foster, & E. J. Mash (Eds.), *Handbook of behavioral and emotional problems in girls* (pp. 489–522). New York: Kluwer Academic/Plenum Publishers.

Moffitt, T. E., Caspi, A., Rutter, M., & Silva, P. A. (2001). *Sex differences in antisocial behavior*. New York: Cambridge University Press.

Nicolopoulou, A. (1997). Worldmaking and identity formation in children's narrative playacting. In B. Cox & C. Lightfoot (Eds.), *Sociogenic perspectives in internalization* (pp. 257–287). Hillsdale, NJ: Lawrence Erlbaum.

Nolen-Hoeksema, S., & Girgus, J. (1994). The emergence of gender differences in depression during adolescence. *Psychological Bulletin, 115*, 424–443.

Parry, B. L. (2000). Hormonal basis of mood disorders in women. In E. Frank (Ed.), *Gender and its effects on psychopathology* (pp. 3–22). Washington, DC: American Psychiatric Press.

Pennington, B. F. (2002). *The development of psychopathology*. New York: Guilford.

Powlishta, K. K., Sen, M. G., Serbin, L. A., Poulin-DuBois, D., & Eichstedt, J. A. (2001). From infancy through middle childhood: The role of cognitive and social factors in becoming gendered. In R. K. Unger (Ed.), *Handbook of the psychology of women and gender* (pp. 116–132). New York: Wiley.

Ruble, D. N., & Martin, C. L. (1998). Gender development. In W. Damon & N. Eisenberg (Eds.), *Handbook of child psychology, Vol 3: Social, emotional, and personality development* (pp. 933–1016). New York: Wiley.

Rudolph, K. D. (2002). Gender differences in emotional responses to interpersonal stress during adolescence. *Journal of Adolescent Health, 30S*, 3–13.

Rudolph, K. D., Hammen, C., & Daley, S. E. (in press). Adolescent mood disorders. In D. A. Wolfe & E. J. Mash (Eds.), *Behavioral and emotional disorders in adolescents: Nature, assessment and treatment*. New York: Guilford.

Rutter, M., Caspi, A., & Moffitt, T. E. (2003). Using sex differences in psychopathology to study causal mechanisms: Unifying issues and research strategies. *Journal of Child Psychology and Psychiatry, 44*, 1092–1115.

Rutter, M., & Sroufe, L. A. (2000). Developmental psychopathology: Concepts and challenges. *Development and Psychopathology, 12*, 265–296.

Smolak, L. (2005). Eating disorders in girls. In D.J. Bell, S. L. Foster, & E. J. Mash (Eds.), *Handbook of behavioral and emotional problems in girls* (pp. 463–480). New York: Kluwer Academic/Plenum Publishers.

Smolak, L., & Munsterteiger, B. (2002). The relationship of gender and voice to depression and eating disorders. *Psychology of Women Quarterly, 26*, 234–241.

Sroufe, L. A., & Rutter, M. (1984). The domain of developmental psychopathology. *Child Development, 55*(1), 17–29.

Tolman, D. L., & Brown, L. M. (2001). Adolescent girls' voices: Resonating resistance in body and soul. In R. K. Unger (Ed.), *Handbook of the psychology of women and gender* (pp. 133–155). New York: Wiley.

Underwood, M. K. (2003). *Social aggression among girls*. New York: Guilford.

Werner, E. E. (1995). Resilience in development. *Current Directions in Psychological Science, 4*, 81–85.

Wolfe, D. A., Scott, K., & Crooks, C. (2005). Abuse and violence in adolescent girls' dating relationships. In D. J. Bell, S. L. Foster, & E. J. Mash (Eds.), *Handbook of behavioral and emotional problems in girls* (pp. 381–414). New York: Kluwer Academic/Plenum Publishers.

Young, A. R. (2005). Learning disorders in girls. In D. J. Bell, S. L. Foster, & E. J. Mash (Eds.), *Handbook of behavioral and emotional problems in girls* (pp. 263–283). New York: Kluwer Academic/Plenum Publishers.

Zahn-Waxler, C., Race, E., and Duggal, S. (2005). Mood symptoms and disorders in girls. In D. J. Bell, S. L. Foster, & E. J. Mash (Eds.), *Handbook of behavioral and emotional problems in girls* (pp. 25–77). New York: Kluwer Academic/Plenum Publishers.

Zoccolillo, M., Tremblay, R., & Vitaro, F. (1996). *DSM-III-R* and *DSM-III* criteria for conduct disorder in preadolescent girls: Specific but insensitive. *Journal of the American Academy of Child and Adolescent Psychiatry, 35*, 461–470.

Zucker, K. J. (2005). Gender identity disorder in girls. In D. J. Bell, S. L. Foster, & E. J. Mash (Eds.), *Handbook of behavioral and emotional problems in girls* (pp. 285–319). New York: Kluwer Academic/Plenum Publishers.

II

Emotional Disorders

2

Mood Disorders and Symptoms in Girls

CAROLYN ZAHN-WAXLER, ELEANOR RACE, and SUNITA DUGGAL

Women are two to three times more likely to experience unipolar depressive disorders as seen in both community-based and clinically referred samples (Kessler, McGonagle, Swartz, Blazer, & Nelson, 1993; Nolen-Hoeksema, 1990; Weissman & Klerman, 1978; Weissman, Leaf, Bruce, & Florio, 1988). This is true whether depression is diagnosed as a (mood) disorder or measured along a continuum of symptom severity. Knowledge of factors that alter the course of depression can help improve both prevention and treatment efforts. Early intervention is important given the negative developmental trajectory for depression in childhood and adolescence (Harrington, Fudge, Rutter, Pickles, & Hill, 1990).

In this chapter we examine the antecedents, correlates, and consequences of girls' depression during childhood and in adolescence. Both diagnostic and dimensional assessments of depression are considered in an effort to understand the processes by which girls become progressively and disproportionately more afflicted than males over time. Most of the relevant research has been conducted with adolescents, since this is when the differential rates of depression begin to approximate those of men and women. However, a developmental psychopathology perspective dictates the need to examine infancy, early and middle childhood. Processes that come into play earlier in development could create vulnerability to girls' later high rates depression as well as early signs of depressive symptoms that go unnoticed at the time.

Most theories of depression have been developed to explain the origins for all individuals affected, not just females. Some theories, however, do

CAROLYN ZAHN-WAXLER, ELEANOR RACE, and SUNITA DUGGAL • National Institute of Mental Health, Bethesda, MD, 20892-2606.

focus specifically on risk factors common or unique to females. Both approaches are necessary to understand more fully why girls are more likely than boys to succumb to incapacitating feelings of sadness. This raises several questions. Are triggers similar or different for girls and boys? Do girls react similarly or differently than boys to the same triggers? And what causes some girls but not others to develop depression? The focus then is on both main effects (i.e., similar causes of depression in females and males) and interactions (factors that uniquely or better predict depression in females).

DEFINITIONS AND DIAGNOSIS OF DEPRESSION

While there are several theories of depression, operational definitions are mainly atheoretical. Definitions focus on combinations of symptoms that result in psychiatric diagnoses or symptom severity scores. Major depressive disorder as defined in the Diagnostic and Statistical Manual of Mental Disorders (American Psychiatric Association, 1994) is characterized by at least one major depressive episode involving a cluster of five or more symptoms that must include either a depressed mood (or irritable mood in children and adolescents), or a loss of interest or pleasure in almost all activities most of the day. Other symptoms include disturbances in appetite or weight, sleep (insomnia or hypersomnia), and motor activity (psychomotor agitation or retardation); fatigue or low energy; feelings of worthlessness or excessive guilt; diminished ability to think, concentrate, or make decisions; and recurrent thoughts of death or suicidal ideation or a suicidal plan or attempt. Symptoms must be present most of the time, persist for a least 2 weeks and cause significant impairment. Sometimes psychotic features are present. Dysthymic disorder is a chronic, less severe form with fewer symptoms, but that persist for at least 1 year in children and adolescents. Here we review research on nonpsychotic unipolar depressive disorders and symptoms. We do not consider manic or hypomanic symptoms that are part of bipolar and cyclothymic disorders and are quite rare in children and adolescents.

ASSESSMENT AND EXPRESSION OF DEPRESSION
IN FEMALES

Questions have been raised about the extent to which higher rates of depression in female than males represent actual population differences versus assessment differences, potential biases, or problems with validity of diagnostic criteria. Researchers have examined the *DSM* criteria used to make diagnoses as well as self-report measures such as the Beck Depression Inventory (Beck, Steer, & Garbin, 1988) and the Children's Depression

Inventory (Sitarerios & Kovacs, 1999) to address these questions. Most of the research has been conducted with adults. Mental health specialists, particularly male clinicians, are more likely to overdiagnose depression in women (Loring and Powell, 1988; Potts, Burnam, & Wells, 1991). However, in a literature review on clinician bias Lopez (1989) concluded that findings were mixed.

Some have suggested that the diagnostic criteria for depression may contribute to its greater prevalence in females. Findings here have also been inconclusive. Angst and Dobler-Mikola (1984) found that women reported more symptoms than men, with the median at five symptoms for women and three for men. Because women had better recall of symptoms over time, they more often reported a history of depression of the past 1 year. Angst and Dobler-Mikola inferred that current diagnostic criteria capture depression better in women than men. Young, Fogg, Scheftner, Keller, and Fawcett (1990) found that women only report more symptoms at higher levels of depression, such that differences in symptom reports were due to differences in depression, not to diagnostic criteria. For the Beck Depression Inventory, except for body image disturbance, there was no gender-related item bias (Byrne, Baron, & Campbell, 1993). Adolescent males and females interpret items on the BDI in the same way, indicated by the same factor structure, although females endorse more items (Santor, Ramsay, & Zuroff, 1994).

In general, measures of depression are quite sensitive to symptom expression in females. Girls' self-reports correlate with observer and clinician ratings of depression, while boys' do not, or do so to a lesser extent (Berard, Boermeester, Hartman, & Rust, 1997; Jolly, Wiesner, Wherry, Jolly, et al., 1994). However, Kornstein and McEnany (2000) note that because women tend to have more atypical symptoms of depression (e.g., weight gain, hypersomnia, somatization, and extreme rejection sensitivity) and more comorbid anxiety symptoms, self-report measures that do not include such symptoms may not be as accurate for women. In a recent review, Piccinelli and Wilkinson (2000) concluded that while artifact may contribute slightly to more depression in females, the substantial sex differences in depression are genuine.

Females do display a different constellation of depressive symptoms than males, particularly more anxiety, more somatic symptoms, greater sleep disturbance, weight gain, increased appetite, psychomotor retardation, and body image disturbance (Campbell, Byrne, & Baron, 1992; Canals, Blade, Carbajo, & Domenech-Llaberia, 2001; Donnelly and Wilson, 1994; Frank, Carpenter, & Kupfer, 1987; Kornstein, Schatzberg, Thase, Yonkers, et al., 2000; Kornstein, Schatzberg, Yonkers, Thase, et al., 1995; Smucker, Craighead, Craighead, & Green, 1986; Young, Scheftner, Fawcett, & Klerman 1990). Increased appetite and weight gain seem to be the most distinct symptoms in women and adolescent girls. Higher rates of crying, sadness, and negative self-concept have been noted for school-age and adolescent girls (Campbell, et al., 1992; Canals, et al., 2001; Donnelly and Wilson, 1994; Smucker, et al., 1986).

COMORBIDITY AND ASSOCIATED FEATURES
OF DEPRESSION

In both prepubertal children and adolescents, major depressive episodes and dysthymic disorder frequently occur in conjunction with other disorders, most commonly with anxiety disorders (see reviews by Angold, Costello, & Erkanli, 1999; Brady & Kendall, 1992). Comorbidity rates for depressive and anxiety disorders can range as high as 70%, with rates from 20% through 50% most likely to be reported. If subclinical anxiety is also considered, rates of cooccurrence with depression are even higher. Depression is also comorbid with disruptive behavior disorders, attention deficit disorders, and in adolescence with substance-related disorders and eating disorders (Nottlemann & Jensen, 1995). Because anxiety disorders and eating disorders are more prevalent in girls (and disorders that involve externalizing problems more prevalent in boys), different constellations of gender-based comorbidities can be expected. Comorbidity of depressive and anxiety disorders is much more common in girls than boys (Lewinsohn, Rohde, & Seeley, 1995); moreover, depression that is comorbid with more than one anxiety disorder is virtually exclusive to females (Lewinsohn, Zinbarg, Seeley, Lewinson, & Sack, 1997). Female gender and presence of a coexisting anxiety disorder are also related to severity of initial depression (McCauley, Myers, Mitchell, Calderon, et al., 1993).

Persons experiencing a major depressive episode frequently present with tearfulness, irritability, brooding, obsessive rumination, anxiety, phobias, excessive worry about physical health, and complaints of pain. Often there are problems in relationships and effective functioning in other settings (e.g., school, work). The core symptoms of major depression are the same for children and adolescents, although the prominence of symptoms may change with age (American Psychiatric Association, 1994). In childhood, when girls do not exceed boys in rates of depression, somatic complaints, irritability, and social withdrawal are particularly common. Psychomotor retardation and hypersomnia are more common in adolescence when girls exceed boys in depression rates. Associated features for dysthymic disorder are similar to those for major depression. The most common symptoms are feelings of inadequacy, loss of interest, social withdrawal, guilt or brooding, irritability or anger, decreased activity and productivity.

Culture can influence the experience and communication of depression. Depression in some cultures may be experienced largely in somatic terms, rather than as sadness or guilt. Complaints of "nerves" or headaches (in Latino and Mediterranean cultures), of weakness, fatigue or "imbalance" (in Asian cultures), of problems of the "heart" (in Middle Eastern cultures) are examples of different ways depression is expressed. Given that females experience more depression than males across cultures, one can assume these different forms of expression also occur most commonly in females.

EPIDEMIOLOGY OF DEPRESSION

Depression is rare in preschoolers with estimates ranging from .4% and .9% (Kashani & Carlson, 1987; Kashani, Holcomb, & Orvaschel, 1986), and uncommon in school-aged children with estimates from 1.8% to 6.3% (Anderson, Williams, McGee, & Silva, 1987; Poznanski & Mokros, 1994). The prevalence of depression increases dramatically after puberty, particularly in girls. The lifetime prevalence of major depression in adolescent females is between 20.8% and 31.6% (Kessler et al.,1993; Lewinsohn, Hops, Roberts, Seeley et al., 1993; Lewinsohn, Rohde, & Seeley, 1998), while the estimated prevalence of subclinical depression in adolescent girls is as high as 59% (Roberts, Andrews, Lewinson, & Hops, 1990). The 1-year first incidence of major depression for girls is 7.14% (Lewinsohn et al., 1993). Lewinsohn et al. (1998) estimate that 35% of girls will have had at least one episode of major depression by the age of 19 years.

The rates of depression in childhood are comparable for boys and girls (with boys showing slightly higher rates), but while the rates dramatically increase around puberty for girls, they remain the same for boys or increase to a lesser extent (Anderson, Williams, McGee, & Silva, 1987; Angold & Rutter, 1992). Studies based both on diagnostic interviews and standardized self-reports indicate that this change in prevalence rates begins around the ages of 13–15 years (Angold, Costello, & Worthman, 1998; Ge, Lorenz, Conger, Elder et al., 1994; Petersen, Sargiani, & Kennedy, 1991; Wichstrom, 1999). There is a 4–23% increase in diagnosed depression in adolescents between the ages of 15 to 18 years (Hankin, Abramson, Moffitt, Silva, & McGee (1998). After puberty, the lifetime prevalence of depression in females is two times that of adolescent males, and 1-year first incidence of depression is 1.6% greater for females than males (Lewinsohn et al., 1993). Sex differences in depression are found consistently across cultures within the United States and the world, controlling for income, education, and occupation (McGrath, Keita, Strickland, & Russo, 1990; Weissman, Bland, Canino, Faravelli et al., 1996).

GENERAL THEORIES OF DEPRESSION

The earliest systematic theories originated from psychoanalytic and psychodynamic approaches, which emphasized the role of early adverse family experiences. This was followed by behavioral and cognitive theories that focused initially on environmental stress and traumas, and then on the cognitions individuals develop about themselves that can contribute to depression. In recent decades biological and genetic explanations have become prominent. Here we highlight major themes of these approaches and consider their relevance to the high rates of depression in females that emerge in adolescence. We also describe approaches that emphasize interactions of biological, and environmental processes thought to produce depression, especially in girls. In subsequent sections we present the empirical research pertinent to these different approaches. Finally, we consider the implications for treatment and future research.

Psychoanalytic, Psychodynamic, and Relational Theories

Early psychoanalytic theory emphasized unresolved childhood experiences that result in adult depression, in particular the loss of a real or imagined love object. One common theme is that repeated disappointments and parental failures to meet the child's psychological needs may give rise to depression. Unconscious reactions to perceptions of aversive early childhood circumstances were thought to result over time in harsh superego development as extreme guilt, self-blame, and unrealistically high standards became internalized. Adult depression, but not childhood depression, was believed to result from these internalized processes. Children were deemed incapable of the ego- and cognitive-developmental processes required to experience sustained, internalized sadness, guilt, and misery that underlie depression. While this belief has been refuted (see review by Zahn-Waxler & Kochanska, 1990), its entrenchment in the literature for so many years severely hampered research on early childhood depression.

Psychoanalytic and psychodynamic views of family relations influenced later research on parenting practices and family processes associated with child and adolescent depression. Based on an attachment perspective, a family environment characterized both by close relationships and the fostering of autonomy was thought to promote healthy psychological development and low risk for depression. To the extent that autonomy promotion and secure relationships are threatened or lessened for girls, these environmental factors could contribute to greater depression. Examples of socialization experiences studied in relation to depression include parental rejection, criticality, hostility, lack of warmth, and family conflict (e.g., Ge, Best, Conger, & Simons, 1996; McCauley, Pavidis, & Kendall, 2001; Sheeber, Hops, Alpert, Davis et al., 1997). Girls may be particularly affected, either because they are more often exposed to these events or because they experience the same negative family events more keenly than boys.

Behavioral and Cognitive Learning Theories

Behavioral theories of depression focus on learning and environmental contingencies. Overmier and Seligman (1967) demonstrated how depressive symptoms could be learned. Dogs initially exposed to uncontrollable shock became impaired in subsequent efforts to escape from or control shock. The paradigm was applied to other species (Maier & Seligman, 1976; Mineka & Henderson, 1985), culminating in the "learned helplessness" model of depression where the organism learns to give up on challenging, aversive, stressful situations. This model when applied to humans was expanded to include cognitive distortions characterized by certain negative attributional styles in adults (Abramson, Seligman, & Teasdale, 1978).

A crosscutting theme of several cognitive-behavioral theories is that repeated, uncontrollable aversive environmental experiences result in cognitive distortions (e.g., negative schemas, biased attributions, negative self-
concept; Beck, 1967). These distortions can create risk for or become part
of the depressive experience. People with negative attributional styles believe negative events result from their own actions and characteristics.
Problems are viewed as stable and unchangeable and the person as personally flawed. Conversely, positive events are seen as externally caused
and outside of one's own control (McCauley et al., 2001).

Several studies have examined associations between cognitive style
and depression in children and established the relevance of adult models
to children (e.g. Seligman, Peterson, Kaslow, Tanenbaum et al., 1984). To
the extent that girls are raised in environments that foster the development
of helplessness and distorted negative self-views, their risk for depression
will be heightened. Recent extensions of cognitive models emphasize maladaptive, self-defeating coping styles based on cognitive distortions likely
to be more common in girls than boys.

Biological and Genetic Models

A number of models hypothesize genetic and biologically based factors
as major contributors to depressive symptoms and disorders. Inheritance
of depression is examined in behavioral and molecular genetics research.
Studies of twins, adopted children, and intergenerational transmission indicate that depression runs in families and genetics plays a significant
role. However, efforts to identify genetic markers based on analysis of DNA
structure have not yet yielded reliable, replicable findings. Research on
the psychophysiology of depression has focused on overactivation, un-
deractivation, and other abnormalities of particular biological systems.
This has included hormones associated with the hypothalamic-pituitary-
adrenal (HPA) axis system, both those involved in pubertal development
and reproduction (e.g., testosterone and estrogen) and those involved in
the stress-response system (e.g., cortisol). We focus here mainly on research with adults to provide a framework for later discussion of biological
research on depression in children and adolescents, and its relevance to
gender.

With respect of overactivation of the stress-response system, many
depressed adult patients have elevated basal cortisol, show a flattening
of the circadian rhythm, and fail to suppress cortisol production in response to the dexamethazone suppression test (DST) (Akil, Haskett, Young,
Grunhaus et al., 1993). High reactivity to stress has also been examined
in relation to the autonomic nervous system function (ANS). High resting
heart rates and low electrodermal activity and reactivity often are found for
adult depressed patients (Lahmeyer & Bellur, 1987; Thorell, Kjellman, &
D'Elia, 1987).

Other biological processes associated with depression include brain
chemistry and circuitry. Several neurotransmitters have been linked
to the pathophysiology of mood disorders, for example, serotonergic,

noradrenergic, and GABAergic systems. Information about brain regions and circuitry comes from accumulated research based on brain lesions, neuroimaging, and electroencephalographic (EEG) activity. The left frontal brain region is associated with approach and positive emotions; the right frontal lobe is involved in internalizing patterns of withdrawal and negative emotions that include sadness and depressed mood. Studies of mood have implicated both frontal and parietal regions of both left and right hemispheres (Davidson, 1994; Heller, 1990). Individuals with depressed moods show frontal lobe asymmetry, reflected mainly in low activation of the left hemisphere, or high activation of the right hemisphere, relative to controls. Depression also has been associated with reduced activity in the right parietal region. Relations between frontal and parietal lobe activity remain to be studied, as do interconnections of cortical and limbic systems involved in the regulation of moods, including depression. Neurochemical transmission between limbic and cortical structures that affect arousal and activation of various brain structures may be a crucial link in the cortical or subcortical interaction (Heller, 1990). A decade ago, Heller (1993) proposed ways in which these processes might differ for females and males to produce more depression in females, but there has been no systematic research on this topic since then.

A Biobehavioral Model of the Development of Depression

Ultimately, depression will be best understood in terms of how biological and environmental processes interact to produce the prolonged negative moods, cognitions, and behavior patterns that define depression. From this point of view, youth depression would be attributed to a combination of environmental stressors and biological vulnerability, that is, a diathesis stress model is used to explain the emergence of clinical depression. An integrative model by Post and colleagues (Post et al., 1996) places affective illness in the context of an evolving developmental neurobiological framework and a series of molecular neurobiological adaptations. Environmental experiences are postulated to affect the expression of depression, including psychosocial stressors and the neurobiology of episode recurrence. In this view, social support may inhibit illness progression by decreasing the perception and neurobiological impact of stressors. Later we consider an application of this model to explain how girls may become particularly likely to develop entrenched, internalized distress that culminates over time in depression.

THEORIES OF DEPRESSION IN GIRLS

One of the first serious attempts to understand depression in adolescent girls can be found in the gender-intensification hypothesis (Hill & Lynch, 1983). In this view, cultural reinforcement of the feminine ideal or stereotype promotes behaviors that are dependent, relationship-driven, emotional, helpless, passive, and self-sacrificing. These behaviors are hypothesized to create risk for depression. Before puberty, gender roles are more fluid and girls are not expected to adhere to them. At puberty, however, expectations change and girls subscribe more to these roles. Others have suggested that any attempt to understand depression in adolescent girls must take into account their strong interpersonal orientation that affects the feminine self-concept (Stattin & Magnusson, 1990) and mood states. Several recent theories have been proposed to explain high rates of depression in adolescent females (Cyranowski, Frank, Young, & Shear, 2000; Hankin & Abramson, 2001; Nolen-Hoeksema & Girgus (1994).

Nolen-Hoeksema and Girgus (1994) present three hypotheses: (1) the causes of depression are the same for girls and boys, but become more prevalent for girls in adolescence, (2) there are different causes for depression in girls and boys, and the causes for girls become more prevalent in early adolescence, and (3) girls are more likely than boys to carry risk factors for depression even before early adolescence, but the risk factors only lead to depression in the face of challenges that increase in early adolescence. They looked at risk factors in personality, biology, and social challenges to find support for the proposed models. Model 3 provided the best fit with existing data, suggesting that vulnerability factors more common to girls than boys may be present in childhood but do not lead to obvious depression until adolescence when girls are faced with multiple biological and social challenges. Childhood risk factors more common for girls were low instrumentality, dominance, and aggression (Nolen-Hoeksema & Girgus, 1994).

Cyranowski et al. (2000) propose that female gender socialization and increased levels of hormones such as oxytocin (which is associated with reproduction and caregiving) at puberty can intensify the need for affiliation in girls. This, in turn, can contribute to a difficult adolescent transition and a depressogenic diathesis. Gender intensification would result from such vulnerabilities as insecure attachments to parents, an anxious or inhibited temperament, and low instrumental coping skills. These factors are thought to interact with stressful life events, particularly those in the interpersonal domain, to cause depression.

Hankin and Abramson (2001) advance a cognitive vulnerability-stress model in which preexisting vulnerabilities (resulting from genetics, personality, and environmental adversity) contribute to cognitive vulnerabilities and the likelihood of experiencing negative events. The elaborated causal chain posits that negative events contribute to initial levels of general negative affect, which include anxious and depressive affect. Following these immediate emotional reactions, individuals seek causal attributions and those with cognitive vulnerabilities select attributions that ultimately lead to depression. This, in turn leads to more negative events, which creates a cycle of repetition of depressive experiences. This model helps explain the greater depression in girls, because girls report more general negative affect (neuroticism), experience more negative events such as sexual abuse, and more show more cognitive vulnerability in the form of rumination and negative inferential style (Hankin & Abramson, 2001).

While no current framework can provide a full etiological account of depression in females, these models represent important efforts to integrate biological and social factors that interact to increase girls' risk for depression. In our overview of theories of depression, we moved from nurture to nature to interactive, transactional models. This reflects the history of theory development. In our subsequent review of empirical research on the etiology of depression we begin with work that focuses on endogenous factors (biology, genetics). We then consider factors that focus on environmental factors (socialization, life stressors and events, culture). Finally, we review work on personality and social-cognitive factors that influence how people understand and interpret their feelings and events in their lives. This organizational framework underscores the need for an interactive, developmental theory in which innate, biological vulnerabilities are more likely to result in depression when the child (a) is exposed to particular socialization practices and life experiences and (b) develops particular social-cognitive views of herself and the world. Such a diathesis-stress model is increasing favored as a means to understand the etiology of depression. Throughout, it is important to bear in mind that none of the etiologic factors reflect "pure" biological, environmental, or cognitive influences.

ETIOLOGY OF DEPRESSION: GENETIC AND BIOLOGICAL FACTORS

Genetic Factors

Estimates of heritability of major depression range from 31–42% (Kendler & Prescott, 1999; Sullivan, Neale, & Kendler, 2000) to as high as 70% (Kendler, Neale, Kessler, Heath et al., 1993a). Depressive symptoms also show heritability (Kendler, Walters, Truett, Heath et al., 1994). Although heritability estimates for depressive disorders are the same for men and women, Kendler, Gardner, Neale, and Prescott (2001) found that women have 30% more heritability of depression if depression is defined according to *DSM-III-R* criteria where impairment is considered. In this study, three diagnostic criteria of increasing narrowness were used: *DSM-III-R*, *DSM-III-R* plus impairment, and Washington University. Heritability of sex differences was not evident for the two more narrow definitions.

Genetics are also involved in the etiology of depression through their effect on sensitivity to environmental events. Silberg Rutter, Neale, and Eaves (2001) found that genetics had a larger effect on the development of depression in adolescent girls who had experienced a negative event in the previous year than on those who did not. Similarly, Kendler and his colleagues (Kendler, 1998; Kendler, Kessler, Walters, MacLean et al., 1995) found that individuals at greater genetic risk were twice as likely to develop major depression in response to a severe stressor than people at lower genetic risk. In addition, genetic risk was found to alter sensitivity to the environment specifically for women (Kendler, Kessler et al., 1995).

Genes also exert some control over exposure to environments that increase the likelihood of developing depression (Kendler, 1998). Serious stressors can occur regardless of genetic risk, but a number of events are more likely to occur to adults at high genetic risk for depression. Examples include assault, difficulties in marriage, divorces and breakups, job loss, serious illness, and financial difficulties (Kendler, 1998; Kendler & Karkowski-Shuman, 1997). Similarly, as girls reach puberty, their negative life events are more genetically mediated (Silberg et al., 1999), with 30% of the variance in stability of depression due to genetic factors. Nonshared environmental factors within and outside the family, including differential treatment of children by parents (Plomin, 1994) also have an impact on depression. The interaction of genetic and environmental factors is implicated in the development of more severe forms of depression (Rende, Plomin, Reiss, & Hetherington, 1993).

Biological Processes

Hormones and Pubertal Development

The robust nature of the marked increase in rates of depression in girls in adolescence has raised the question of the role of biological processes associated with puberty. This has been studied in terms of hormones that increase during puberty, timing of puberty, physical bodily changes, and interactions of body change and weight gain.

Angold and colleagues (Angold, Costello, & Worthman, 1998; Angold, Costello, Erklani, & Worthman, 1999) have examined the influence of hormones and body development on depression. Angold et al. (1998) found that pubertal development (measured by Tanner stages), but not age, accounted for increased rates of depression. Boys showed higher rates of depression than girls before reaching Tanner stage III (the midpoint of puberty when body changes become apparent but before menarche). Girls showed much higher rates of depression than boys at and after Tanner stage III (Angold et al., 1998). Angold et al. (1999) then measured hormones associated with pubertal development and reproduction, namely testosterone, estrogen and estradiol, luteinizing hormone, and follicle-stimulating hormone. Testosterone and estrodial were more strongly related to depression than Tanner stages. A link between hormones (specifically estradiol) and later depressive affect has been shown even after the course of a year (Paikoff, Brooks-Gunn, & Warren, 1991). It would be valuable in future research on hormones and depression to study these processes in middle childhood, and also to examine the role of oxytocin for reasons previously noted (Cyranowski et al., 2000; Frank and Young, 2000).

Early puberty in girls (but not boys) is associated with more depression. Young girls may have not yet acquired coping skills to deal with the pressures and stresses of early physical maturation. While Angold et al. (1998) and others did not find an effect of pubertal timing on depression, several others have found such associations. Girls who reach puberty earlier are more likely to have or to develop depressive symptoms than those who reach puberty on time (e.g., Brooks-Gunn & Warren, 1989; Ge, Conger, & Elder, 1996; Graber, Lewinson, Seeley, & Brooks-Gunn, 1997; Hayward, Killen, Wilson, Hammer et al., 1997; Paikoff et al., 1991; Stice, Presnell, & Bearman, 2001). Stice et al. (2001) also show that high body mass, body dissatisfaction, and dieting partially mediate the link between early puberty and depression.

Early puberty results from a complex mix of biological, social, and contextual factors. Genes, as well as environmental influence like nutrition, exercise, and weight play a role. Depression in mothers may induce early puberty in daughters (Ellis & Garber, 2000), as well as the presence of unrelated adult male father figures. The latter finding reported by others as well (e.g., Moffitt, Caspi, Belsky, & Silva, 1992). Animal studies suggest that chemicals known as pheromones produced by unrelated adult males accelerate female pubertal development. A similar process may occur for girls, indicating the need for research on how alterations of the social or parenting environment could alter hormonal changes in girls.

The Stress-Response System in Children and Adolescents

While high cortisol levels and a flattening of the circadian rhythm have been identified in depressed adults, the patterns are less clear in depressed children and adolescents (Birmaher et al., 1996; Klimes-Dougan, Hastings, Granger, Usher et al., 2001), though some similar patterns have been noted (see Klimes-Dougan et al., 2001; Ryan & Dahl, 1993). A longitudinal study of adolescents (Goodyer, Tamplin, & Altham, 2000) has shown that high early morning cortisol levels predict later major depression for both females and males, in an additive model that also included initial depressive symptoms, personal disappointments, and recent losses. Because depression is infrequent in childhood it is useful to cast a wider net for early biological markers by focusing more broadly on closely related internalizing symptoms of anxiety, fearfulness, and shyness or inhibition. Not only are anxiety and depressed mood highly correlated throughout development, but also there is now evidence (reviewed in a later section) that anxiety is a developmental precursor of child and adolescent depression. High basal cortisol (particularly early morning) and stress responses have been noted in behaviorally inhibited, shy children (Kagan, Resnick, & Snidman, 1988; Schmidt, Fox, Rubin, Sternberg et al., 1997). Internalizing symptoms and related temperamental characteristics also are more likely than externalizing symptoms to be related to high cortisol levels.

Links between HPA axis functioning and psychopathology can differ for males and females. In adolescents who were normal, depressed, or depressed with comorbid externalizing problems (Klimes-Dougan et al., 2001), females with depressive symptoms, in contrast to other groups, did not show the typical diurnal pattern of high early morning cortisol levels and a decrease in production across the course of the day. These girls also showed a more gradual decline in cortisol following discussion of a conflict. In a longitudinal study of younger children (Smider, Essex, Kalin, Buss et al., 2002), girls showed higher cortisol levels than boys at the age of 4.5 years. High cortisol predicted more depression and anxiety a year and a half later for girls only. Girls' greater physiological reactivity may reflect early proneness to later depressive symptoms.

Other Physiological Correlates of Internalizing Symptoms

Behavioral inhibition, which can be a precursor to depression, has been associated with a sympathetically more reactive cardiovascular system in young children (Kagan & Snidman, 1999). Girls typically have higher heart rates than boys. Greater autonomic reactivity is a physiological index of anxiety and may be an early risk factor for later depression. In one study of 4–5-year-old children with and without early emotional and behavioral problems, girls showed slightly higher heart rates during mood inductions. Moreover, girls with problems that included anxiety and depression showed very high levels of skin conductance (palmer sweat), another physiological index of anxiety (Zahn-Waxler, Cole, Welsh, & Fox, 1995).

Neural Correlates

While research with children and adolescents is limited, some studies indicate patterns of brain activity in children at risk like those of depressed adults. Infants and young children of depressed mothers show reduced left frontal EEG activity (e.g., see Dawson, Frey, Self, Panagiotides et al., 1999). Systematic sex differences have not been reported, but the issue merits further study. Sex differences can be seen in regional patterns of brain activity in adults with a history of childhood-onset depression (Miller, Fox, Cohen, Forbes et al., 2002). EEG asymmetry scores (indicating higher right and lower left frontal brain activity) are linked to vulnerability to negative mood states and depression. Here, women with a history of childhood depression had higher right midfrontal alpha suppression, and men with childhood depression had higher left midfrontal alpha suppression, relative to participants without childhood depression.

ETIOLOGY OF DEPRESSION: ENVIRONMENTAL FACTORS

The Role of the Family Environment

Substantial evidence suggests that family processes and dynamics play a role in the etiology of depression in children and adolescents of both sexes. To date, sex differences in the relationship between family processes and depression have been less studied, though some evidence indicates that different experiences and treatment may place girls at greater risk.

Parental Depression

Parental depression (most often studied in mothers) creates substantial risk in offspring for developing depression (Beardslee, Versage, & Gladston, 1998; Davies & Windle, 1997; Downey & Coyne, 1990; Garber, Keiley, & Martin, 2002; Graham & Easterbrooks, 2000; Hammen, Burge, Burney, & Adrian, 1990; Hops, 1996; Shiner & Marmorstein, 1998; Strober, 2001). Offspring are at greater risk for depression, if both parents are depressed (Birmaher, Ryan, Williamson, Brent et al., 1996; McCauley et al., 2001). The lifetime risk of depression for children with a depressed parent has been estimated at 45% (Hammen et al., 1990). Because depression has a substantial heritable component and does run in families, it is commonly assumed that children of depressed parents are at increased risk for depression because of genetic similarity. However, the experiences of these children can differ markedly as well.

Compared with nondepressed controls, depressed parents are, on average, less reciprocal, attuned, and engaged in interactions with their children as early as infancy. In addition to the sadness that marks depression, depressed parents may also express a greater range and less control of other negative emotions such as anxiety, guilt, irritability, and hostility. Children exposed to a depressed parent's despair and lack of pleasure in daily activities can come to experience these emotions through processes of contagion and imitation. Depressed parents often model helpless, passive styles of coping. They also tend to use discipline and control methods that are either ineffectual or too harsh and coercive, and that also involve guilt induction (see reviews by Beardslee et al., 1998; Cummings et al., 2001; Downey & Coyne, 1990; Gelfand & Teti, 1990; Goodman & Gotlib, 1999; Zahn-Waxler, 2000). Cummings, DeArth-Pendley, Schudlich, and Smith (2001) suggest that families in which a parent is depressed are more dysfunctional in communicating with one another, have more trouble resolving problems within the family, and model a style of coping with one's emotions that portrays negative emotions as overwhelming, painful, and difficult to handle. Thus, in a variety of ways, children's experiences with a depressed parent could contribute to their own depression.

Increasing evidence suggests that girls are more susceptible to the influences of maternal depression than are boys (Boyle & Pickles, 1997; Conger, Conger, Elder, Lorenz et al., 1993; Cummings et al., 2001; Hops, 1996). As adolescent girls mature, the effects of maternal depression on their development of depression become stronger. Several longitudinal studies have shown long-term effects of maternal depression on later development of depression in daughters but not sons (Davies & Windle, 1997; Duggal, Carlson, Sroufe, & Egeland, 2001; Fergusson, Horwood, & Lynsky (1995). In one study, adolescent daughters, but not sons, who provided comfort and suppressed their own aggression showed an increase in depressive symptoms over time (Davis, Sheeber, Hops, & Tildesley, 2000). Klimes-Dougan and Bolger (1998) found that adolescent females were more likely than males to provide active support to their depressed mothers. These girls also expressed more sadness, worry, and withdrawal, as well as heightened feelings of responsibility for the mother's depression. Daughters may be more susceptible to their mothers' unhappiness and depression because they spend more time with them and have stronger emotional ties to their mothers (Gurian, 1987). Modeling of depressive behavior by mothers may be particularly salient to girls and linked to sex roles for women and girls.

Parental Discord and Divorce

Parental conflict and divorce have also been implicated in children's symptoms of depression. Depression of a parent can itself lead to marital conflict and vice versa, and frequently they cooccur (Beardslee et al., 1998; Conger et al., 1993; Cummings et al., 2001; Davies & Windle, 1997; Downey & Coyne, 1990; Strober, 2001). Marital discord and divorce lead both to internalizing problems (depression, anxiety), for which females generally are at higher risk and externalizing problems (aggression, antisocial behavior), for which females generally are at lower risk than males. Adolescents who view their families as poorly adjusted show more depression and lower self-esteem than adolescents more satisfied with their families (Ohannessian, Lerner, Lerner, & von Eye, 1994).

Parental divorce can influence the development of depression in adolescents through increased family conflicts, financial difficulties, unavailability of parents, and changes in the family (Aseltine, 1996). Divorce is associated with less parental warmth and involvement, which can also contribute to depression in adolescents (Aseltine, 1996). When exposed to family conflict and discord, adolescent girls are at greater risk than boys for developing depression and related problems (Aseltine, 1996; Crawford, Cohen, Midlarsky, & Brook, 2001; Dadds, Atkinson, Turner, Blum et al., 1999; Formoso, Gonzales, & Aiken, 2000; Garnefski, 2000; Vuchenich, Emery, & Cassidy, 1988). Girls show higher levels of interpersonal caring orientation and involvement in the problems of others (particularly mothers) than boys, and these qualities contribute to girls' higher rates of depressed mood (Gore, Aseltine, & Colton, 1993). These interactions were interpreted as suggesting that in family stress situations that negatively influence the mental health of both boys and girls, having a strong caring orientation or involvement in family problems is particularly harmful to girls.

Parent-Child Relationships

Children who spend more time with their families and have better relationships with their parents show less depression than those who do not (Field, Diego, & Sanders, 2002). Those who have less intimate relationships with their parents and less physical affection also show more depression and lower self-esteem than those who are closer to their parents (Field et al., 2001). Less support from one's family, and particularly one's mother, is related to more depression and difficulty among adolescents (Aseltine, Gore, & Colten, 1994; Barrerra & Garrison-Jones, 1992; Ge et al., 1994; McFarlane, Bellissimo, & Norman, 1995).

The impact of familial support and relationships with parents can be particularly great for girls. In a 4-year longitudinal study of stressful life events and depressive symptoms in adolescence (Ge et al., 1994), girls (but not boys) living with less supportive mothers were more vulnerable to negative life changes. Changes in depressive symptoms were related to changes in stressful life events only for girls. In another study, conflict with the mother that was associated with submissive coping was related to concurrent depression and predicted increases in these symptoms 1 year later for adolescent daughters but not sons (Powers & Welsh, 1999).

Still other research indicates that a close relationship with one's parents can serve as a protective factor against developing depression for girls (Leadbeater, Kuperminc, Blatt, & Hertzog, 1999). Girls who view their parents as very caring are relatively unlikely to develop depression, though girls whose fathers were overprotective showed more depressive symptoms (Avison & McAlpine, 1992). Parental overprotection may create a diminished sense of mastery and independence that, in turn, may lead to depression. Consistent with this idea, Allen, Hauser, Eickholt, Bell et al. (1994) found that problems in gaining autonomy from parents (mainly from mothers) was linked to depression. The difficulties girls face balancing their need for family support and intimacy with their need for increased autonomy in adolescence may play a role in the development of their higher rates of depression (McGrath, Keita, Strickland, & Russo, 1990).

Child Maltreatment

Physical and sexual abuse have been linked to depression in children and adolescence. While sexual abuse is by no means restricted to parents or parental or authority figures in the family, much of it does occur in this context. About 6.8–19% of girls and 3–7.3% of boys are exposed to some form of childhood sexual abuse (Cutler & Nolen-Hoeksema, 1991). Experiencing abuse places youths, girls more so than boys, at increased risk for the development of depression (Cutler & Nolen-Hoeksema, 1991; Fergusson, Horwood, & Lynsky, 1996; Kendler, Bulik, Silberg Hettema et al., 2000; Weiss, Longhurst, & Mazure, 1999; Whiffen & Clark, 1997). Girls are more likely to know the abuser than boys, which may reduce self-esteem and create interpersonal difficulties, both of which are related to depression. The relationship between childhood abuse and later depression is accounted for, only in part, by other concurrent risk factors (e.g., parental psychopathology and family dysfunction), according to genetically informed research designs. This provides a basis for inferring a causal relation between childhood sexual abuse and psychopathology (Fergusson et al., 1996; Kendler et al., 2000).

Women may experience more severe forms of abuse (Cutler & Nolen-Hoeksema, 1991), which has been linked to a greater risk of developing a disorder (Fergusson et al., 1996). Moreover, women may engage in more self-blame following abuse than men, which could lead to more depressive symptoms. Although these generalizations are based on research with adult women, it is reasonable to assume that girls and female adolescents would experience guilt and shame as well, and be equally affected (if not more so). Weiss and colleagues (1999) propose a biobehavioral model, suggesting that early stress in the form of abuse can alter the function and regulation of the HPA axis and create vulnerability to depression. To the extent that the HPA axis is more responsive to stress in females than males, this would heighten risk for depression.

Environmental Stress and Support at Adolescence

Stressful Life Events

Once girls reach early adolescence, their worlds change dramatically. Physical maturation alters the ways in which others react to them. There are school changes, that is, from elementary to middle school, or from middle school to high school, and the peer environment undergoes major transformations. Dating, friendships, and academic and extracurricular performance related to entry to college assume greater importance, and adolescents are expected to act with more maturity. This environment creates unique stressors and challenges with which many adolescents are not yet prepared to cope, contributing to the etiology of depression, particularly for girls (Avison & McAlpine, 1992; Ge et al., 1994; Goodyer, 2001; Goodyer, Kolvin, & Gatzanis, 1987; McCauley et al., 2001; Silberg et al., 1999).

Life stress and negative life events increase for girls after the age of 13 (Brooks-Gunn, 1992; Ge et al., 1994) and contribute to the rise in their rates of depression (Avison & McAlpine, 1992; Brooks-Gunn, 1991; Cyranowski et al., 2000; Ge et al., 1994). Examples include school problems (Silberg et al., 1999), romantic problems (Kendler & Gardner, 2001; Silberg, Pickles, Rutter, Hewitt et al., 1999), school transition (McCauley et al., 2001), increased pressure to perform (McCauley et al., 2001), personal disappointments (Goodyer, 2001), personal loss or loss of a relationship (Goodyer, 2001; Lewinsohn et al., 1998), interpersonal events (Rudolph, Hammen, Burge, Lindberg et al., 2000; Williamson, Birmaher, Anderson, & Al-Shabbout et al., 1998), and friendship difficulties (Goodyer, Wright, & Altham, 1990).

Some researchers report that girls are not more exposed than boys to stressful life events, and similarly, they are not more vulnerable to the effects of these events (Avison & McAlpine, 1992; Gore, Aseltine, & Colton, 1992; Kendler et al., 2001). Others indicate that girls do report more negative events, or that they may experience the same events as more negative than boys (Goodyer et al., 2001; Gore et al., 1992). Girls tend to show different patterns in the relationship between life events and depression than boys, particularly after puberty (Ge et al., 1994; Silberg et al., 1999). Females are more likely than males to experience or be affected by the stresses of others, which also would create vulnerability to depression.

The timing of major life events is also crucial in understanding the role of the environment in the etiology of depression. Girls going through multiple life changes simultaneously (i.e., puberty, changing schools, family disruptions, etc.) are more at higher risk than those dealing with one at a time. This is particularly true for girls who experience puberty at the same time they move to different, larger, more challenging schools (Simmons, Burgeson, & Carlton-Ford, 1987). Pubertal timing more often corresponds with school change for girls than boys; this could contribute to their increase in rates of depression at this time (Petersen et al., 1991). Cyranowski et al. (2000) hypothesize that the increase in interpersonal stressors related to friendship roles and dating during adolescence, interacts with girls' increased need for affiliation, making girls more vulnerable to the depression following a negative interpersonal event.

Distinctions have been made between "dependent" life events and "independent" life events. Dependent events are those in which the person contributes to the event through her own actions (e.g., interpersonal problems, breaking up with someone, failing a test). Independent events are not influenced by the person experiencing the event (e.g., death of a relative, a natural disaster). Both types of events can contribute to the etiology of depression (Kendler et al., 1999; Williamson et al., 1995). Dependent interpersonal events, in particular, are closely tied with depression for adolescent girls (Rudolph et al., 2000). In a longitudinal study of adolescents (Ge et al. 1994), changes in uncontrollable events were associated with increases in girls' but not boys' depressive symptoms. Moreover, changes in depressive symptoms were related to change in stressful events only for girls.

Stress and negative life events are related to the onset of depression, but their impact differs depending on whether the episode is the first onset of depression or a recurrent episode. Kendler and colleagues (Kendler, Thornton, & Gardner, 2000; Kendler, Thornton, & Prescott, 2001) report that stressful events contribute strongly to the first onset of depression, but their influence diminishes with each subsequent episode. They suggest that once someone is primed for depression, she no longer requires a major environmental stressor to provoke recurrence.

Social Support

At adolescence, girls begin to rely less heavily on their parents for support and guidance and instead turn to their peers. Girls tend to care more about their relationships with peers than do boys (Simmons & Blyth, 1987). Girls are generally more satisfied with their peer relationships than are boys (Colarossi & Eccles, 2000) and experience more intimate and higher-quality relationships (Field et al., 2002). Positive peer relationships and social support can directly help to reduce the risk of depression (Field et al., 2002; Sabatelli & Anderson, 1991). They may also work indirectly by increasing self-esteem and self-efficacy as well (McFarlane et al., 1995; Simmons & Blyth, 1987). However, if girls rely too heavily on peer support, they may be at greater risk for depression (Barrera & Garrison-Jones,

1992). Moreover, the literature does not uniformly suggest that girls have better social relationships than boys. Benenson and Christakos (2003) found that girls' closest friendships were more fragile and vulnerable to termination than those of boys, which could also create risk for depression.

Adolescents with friends who engage in more delinquent or deviant behavior are at a greater risk of developing depression than those with peers who do not. Thus, the type of peer support will determine the degree of risk or protection that friendship affords for developing depression (Brendgan, Vitaro, & Bukowski, 2000). Having fewer friends, feeling unpopular, or being rejected by peers also places girls at risk (Field et al., 2001; Bell-Dolan, Foster, & Christopher, 1995; Boivin, Poulin, & Vitaro, 1994; Hecht, Inderbitzin, & Bukowski, 1998). Girls neglected by their peers are somewhat less at risk than rejected girls (Bell-Dolan et al., 1995; Hecht et al., 1998), possibly because they may have other peer groups. In addition, active bullying or victimization can have deleterious effects on girls, contributing to the development of depression (Crick & Grotpeter, 1996; Hecht et al., 1998; Neary & Joseph, 1994).

The Role of Socioeconomic Status and Culture

Socioeconomic Status (SES)

Socioeconomic status and the environment it creates for adolescents can influence the development of depression. Girls from lower-income backgrounds are at greater risk than those from families with average or above-average incomes (Graham & Easterbrooks, 2000; Roberts, Roberts, & Chen, 1997). The same is true for girls who have a lower perceived standard of living or whose parents have less education (Gore et al., 1992). However, being in a high socioeconomic class is not necessarily a protective factor for girls, as they are still at greater risk for depression than boys. SES may be a risk factor because economically disadvantaged children develop a lower sense of mastery over their surroundings due to (a) experiencing more negative life events and (b) being poorly equipped to deal with such events. Also, Conger et al. (1993) found that economic difficulties can lead to parental stress and depression along with disrupted parenting practices, which in turn affect girls' depression.

Women typically have lower social standing than men in most cultures. Women are expected to help support a family financially as well as to carry the majority of the parenting responsibilities, which result in greater chronic stress and strain (Nolen-Hoeksema, Larson, & Grayson, 1999). Female children and adolescents are able to see their mothers and female role models coping with the difficulties adult women face. As girls reach puberty and begin to feel the pressures of more intense gender socialization, they may see the hardships their mothers face as what they should expect for themselves. This could cause girls to feel hopeless about their futures and make them less invested in academics or other goals they may have had earlier.

Culture

Around the world, the lifetime rates of depression vary significantly. Taiwan has the lowest reported rates at 1.5% and Beirut has the highest at 19% (Weissman, Bland, Canino, Faravelli et al., 1996). It is not clear why rates vary so much, though Beirut's history of war and turmoil may explain some of the greater prevalence in that country. However, though the rates themselves differ, women consistently have higher rates of depression than men across all cultures (Kleinman & Cohen, 1997; Weissman et al., 1996). Ratios of women to men vary across cultures with a 1.6 to 1 ratio in Beirut and Taiwan to a 3.1 to 1 ratio in West Germany (Weissman et al., 1996). In Chile, women have rates of depression five times that of men, and in China, women have rates nine times greater than men (Kleinman & Cohen, 1977). The fact that females are at greater risk than males across cultures implicates genetic or biological factors in the etiology of depression. The fact that ratios vary across countries and cultures also implicates the role of culture and environment. Developmental cross-cultural studies would help to determine the ways in which biology, culture, and socialization interact to produce the sex differences in rates and ratios of depression. They would also be informative of when in development, the cultural differences in female-to-male rates of depression begin to emerge.

The United States is known for being a "melting pot," with many cultures coexisting and contributing to the overarching American culture. These different cultures and ethnic groups may also have different rates of depression, with corresponding implications for how these symptoms and problems develop. Roberts et al. (1997) compared adolescents among different ethnic groups within the United States and found that one group, namely, Mexican Americans, had higher rates of depression than other groups. While the Latinos only had elevated depression rates when they were poor, other studies (Mirowsky & Ross, 1984; Ross, Mirowsky, & Cockerham, 1983) have found that culture plays a role, beyond the effects of poverty. In these studies, Mexican Americans had a more fatalistic outlook and belief in external (locus of) control than Anglo-Americans, and these views were related to higher rates of depression. A fatalistic outlook was most strongly related to depression in Mexican American women.

Within Asian ethnic groups in America, adolescents who maintained a closer connection to their ethnic culture and were less integrated to mainstream culture had higher rates of depression than those more oriented toward American culture (Nguyen, Messe, & Stollak, 1999; Wong, 2001). Thus Asian ethnic groups living in the United States may be less vulnerable to depression, to the extent that they assimilate into mainstream culture. The same is not true for African Americans. African American adolescents, who distanced themselves from their communities and ethnic backgrounds in order to succeed in academics, were at higher risk for depression (Arroyo & Zigler, 1995).

One aspect of African-American culture that may protect girls from depression is its conception of the ideal female. White American culture is oriented toward an emphasis on appearance, beauty, and a thin body in females. This emphasis is related to the development of depression in puberty, when girls develop bodies that do not match the thin ideal (Allgood-Merten, Lewinson, & Hops, 1990; Stice & Bearman, 2001; Wichstrom, 1999)). African-American culture emphasizes personality traits, grooming, and a heavier body type and deemphasizes competition to be beautiful relative to White culture (Parker, Nichter, Nichter, Vucovic et al., 1995). While early puberty is linked to depression in Caucasian girls, this was not found for African-American and Hispanic girls (Haywood, Gotlib, Schraedley, Litt et al., 1999).

ETIOLOGY OF DEPRESSION: COPING STYLES, COGNITIONS, SOCIAL TRAITS AND STEREOTYPES

Certain traits or characteristics more often seen in females than males may make them more prone to depression. Both biological processes and socialization experiences may shape these qualities. But regardless of origins, they reflect important individual differences in core aspects of how some people cope with negative events, interpret these events, and more generally view themselves that increase risk for depression.

Coping Styles

While some people cope actively by addressing problems with actions, others cope more passively, thinking or talking about a problem without taking any direct action to fix it. This more passive style, referred to as rumination, is directly related to the development of depression (Harrington & Blankenship, 2002; Nolen-Hoeksema, 1987, 1991; Nolen-Hoeksema & Girgus, 1994). Rumination tends to increase and prolong negative mood. This, along with a diminished sense of mastery and control over negative events, can make individuals more prone to future negative events and negative affect (Nolen-Hoeksema et al., 1999). Some have found that low sense of mastery is related to depression specifically in girls (Avison & McAlpine, 1992).

Overwhelmingly, the literature has shown that girls and women, more so than men and boys, ruminate (Hankin & Abramson, 1999; Nolen-Hoeksema, 1987, 1991; Nolen-Hoeksema and Girgus, 1994; Nolen-Hoeksema et al., 1999). This difference not only accounts for some of the gender difference seen in rates of depression, but also mediates the relationship between gender and depression (Nolen-Hoeksema et al. 1999). Possible explanations include the socialization of girls to be interpersonally dependent rather than instrumental and independent, to emphasize emotion rather than action, and to express impulses in an inward-directed fashion (Cyranowski et al., 2000; Gjerde & Block, 1996; Hankin & Abramson, 2001). Indeed, girls do show more awareness of their emotional and inner states and more frequently engage in self-reflection (Avison & McAlpine, 1992). Corumination, which involves excessive discussion of personal problems typically within the context of close dyadic relationships, is much more common in girls than boys. While corumination can be part of high-quality friendships, it also predicts depression and hence is a risk factor (Rose, 2002).

Cognitive Styles, Guilt, and Self-Esteem

Cognitive distortions (e.g., negative schemas, biased attributions, negative self-concept) often involve an overgeneralized sense of responsibility for negative events, in which one feels helpless, inadequate, and blameworthy. Such depressogenic cognitive styles are linked to greater risk for depression in children and adolescents as well as adults. In a longitudinal study of adolescents (Garber et al., 2002) attributional styles that became more negative over time were associated with initial higher levels of mother-reported depression in youth and increases over time in youth-reported depressive symptoms.

These negative attributional styles are not only present in currently depressed individuals, but also in individuals vulnerable to developing depression (e.g., Lewinsohn et al., 1998; McCauley et al., 2001). Hankin and Abramson (1999) concluded that cognitive vulnerability often does not mediate the gender differences in depression. However, in a later review Hankin and Abramson (2001) conclude that girls are more cognitively vulnerable, and when coupled with a tendency to experience more negative events, girls will be at greater risk. While guilt is not explicitly a part of negative attributional style, its presence can be inferred. The emotion of guilt (blameworthy, at fault) is strongly linked to depression and is more common in females than males (Zahn-Waxler, Cole, & Barrett, 1991). Similarly, negative views of the self may contribute to the development of depression in girls (Allgood-Merten et al., 1990; Avison & McAlpine, 1992; Block & Gjerde, 1990; Gjerde & Block, 1996; Lewinsohn et al., 1998). Self-esteem is lower in females than males (Harter, 1993) and it decreases in females during adolescence (Block & Robins, 1993) just as their depression rates begin to soar.

Social Traits

Interpersonal orientation is a trait more common in females than males and reflects the premium they place on interpersonal relationships. Because girls are more invested in these relationships than boys (Leadbeater et al., 1999; Simmons & Blyth, 1987), they may be at greater risk for becoming depressed when relationships are disrupted or changed, as often happens at adolescence (Cyranowski et al., 2000; Leadbeater et al., 1999). Heightened interpersonal focus and dependence on others are inversely related to traits of independence, agency, and instrumentality, which can protect against depression (Allgood-Merten et al., 1990; Nolen-Hoeksema & Girgus, 1994). Girls show fewer of these instrumental traits than do boys. This interpersonal vulnerability may lead to feelings of helplessness, fear of abandonment, and a need for intimacy and nurturance (Leadbeater et al., 1999).

Sex Roles, Sex Stereotypes, and Self-Definition

Traditional feminine socialization can encourage girls to sacrifice their own needs in order to care for others, and to suppress their own thoughts and preferences in relationships. Traditional feminine sex role traits in the extreme are not conducive to healthy psychological development. Instruments that measure feminine traits typically use adjectives that reflect (a) a caring orientation (e.g. "compassionate," "understanding," "sympathetic," "sensitive to others' needs," "eager to sooth hurt feelings," and (b) an immature, submissive, deferential style ("child-like," "yielding," "soft-spoken," "shy," "gullible," "flatterable") (Bem, 1978).

Girls characterized by the feminine ideal or stereotype are more often engaged in behaviors that are dependent, relationship-driven, emotional, helpless, passive, and self-sacrificing (Aube et al., 2000; Hart & Thompson, 1996; Hill & Lynch, 1983; Wichstrom, 1999). Each of these behaviors or coping styles is associated with risk for depression. In contrast, traits associated masculine sex role, which mainly reflect competence and achievement (e.g. "assertive," "athletic," "a leader," self-reliant," "forceful," "strong personality") protect against depression. Aube et al. (2000) found that girls who felt overly responsible for the welfare of others, and who experienced difficulties being assertive, had higher levels of depression than boys, and this difference was more marked in older than younger adolescents.

As girls mature, many place more emphasis on conforming to the sex roles set out by their cultures (Allgood-Merten et al., 1990; Aube et al., 2000; Hart & Thompson, 1996; Huselid & Cooper, 1994; Wichstrom, 1999). One important aspect of conformity concerns lack of self-expression and self-assertion. Harter and colleagues found that the "loss of voice" and low self-worth in adolescence, more common to females than males and implicated in depression, is restricted to a subset of girls who endorse a feminine orientation (Harter, Walters, Whitesell, & Kastilic, 1998). Loss of voice refers to the display of false self-behavior, including suppression of opinions. Jack (1991) proposed that some girls and women adopt schemas regarding appropriate gender role behavior in close relationships that contribute to their vulnerability to depression. The schema of "self-silencing" refers to inhibition of self-expression to avoid interpersonal conflict, putting others' needs first, and presenting oneself as compliant in spite of inner resentment. Overcompliance is a risk factor for depression whether or not inner resentment is present. However, such resentment may signal a form of depression where anger is present but so are efforts to stifle it. Feminine sex role, per se, does not create depression. Some aspects of traditional female sex roles such as sympathy and compassion are adaptive and valued qualities. Links to depression would depend upon the extent to which feminine sex role impairs functioning, as well as the extent to which other risk factors are present.

A DEVELOPMENTAL PSYCHOPATHOLOGY PERSPECTIVE

Childhood Precursors of Adolescent Depression

Most of the work reviewed to this point has focused on explanations for the appearance of sex differences in depression at adolescence (see Zahn-Waxler, 2000), with limited attention to childhood precursors or early signs and symptoms. Early developmental research on psychopathology had emphasized disruptive problems less common to girls than boys, such as anti-social behaviors, attention deficits and hyperactivity. These problems often begin quite early in children's lives and show substantial continuity across time. Not only are girls much less likely than boys to engage in disruptive, antisocial ways during childhood, when they do aggress they are more likely also to be depressed and anxious. This "gender paradox of comorbidities" (Loeber & Keenan, 1994) indicates that even "poorly behaved" girls experience greater internal pressures, constraints, and distress than boys with similar problems. Moreover, in the absence (as well as the presence) of externalizing problems, comorbid anxiety and depression are more common in girls than boys. Different comorbidity patterns in childhood may provide early clues not only about sex differences in depression but also about why some girls are at higher risk than others.

Research on sex differences in childhood provides a means to examine how extreme expressions of normative differences may create greater risk for depression in girls than boys. Developmental hypotheses have been advanced that focus on early risk factors for later (higher rates of) depression in girls than boys (Block & Gjerde, 1990; Block, Gjerde, & Block, 1991; Gurian, 1987; Keenan, 2003; McCauley, Pavlidis, & Kendall, 2001; Nolen-Hoeksema & Girgus, 1994; Zahn-Waxler, 2000; Zahn-Waxler, Cole, & Barrett, 1991). We will consider child characteristics as well as socialization experiences prior to adolescence, within a developmental psychopathology framework. We examine how depression might emerge in childhood and show continuity over time, though not necessarily as phenotypic depressive emotions and behaviors.

A Developmental Psychopathology Framework

Developmental psychopathology has been defined as "the study of the origins and course of individual patterns of behavioral maladaptation" (Sroufe & Rutter, 1984, 18). Because clinical problems generally do not arise *de novo,* but rather emerge over time from prodromal or subclinical symptoms, a developmental perspective allows for the study of the evolution of disorder (Cicchetti & Toth, 1995; Post et al., 1996). Endogenous and exogenous risk factors interact to determine developmental outcomes. Under optimal conditions, children become increasingly well regulated and organized in their functioning over time in most aspects of their lives, including social, emotional, cognitive, and physical domains. They move from adequate and adaptive functioning within the family into a world that also includes other authority figures (e.g., their teachers), peers, and playmates.

They learn to care for others, to socialize, to negotiate, to resolve conflicts, to regulate their emotions, and to protect, defend, and assert themselves. They develop adequate-to-highly effective repertoires for dealing with life's challenges.

The repertoires children develop for dealing with the worlds they inhabit differ, to some degree, for girls and boys. The most robust differences observed include greater aggression in boys (Coie & Dodge, 1998) and more prosocial, caring behaviors in girls (Eisenberg & Fabes, 1998). These serve as prototypes for masculine and feminine behaviors, respectively. While myth, dogma, and societal stereotyping may contribute to these differences, empirical data overwhelmingly confirm the existence of these differences and from an early age. Child behaviors that reflect feminine qualities, when combined with particular socialization practices may set an even earlier course toward depression. Although the gender intensification hypothesis was developed to explain the higher rates of depression that emerge in girls in adolescence, it also is relevant to processes that may be set in motion earlier in childhood (Zahn-Waxler, 1993). While extreme feminine sex role is not the only factor expected to place girls at risk, it is important to consider it from a developmental perspective because of the later established links observed between stereotypically feminine behaviors and depression.

The Etiologic Role of Anxiety in Depression

Unlike disruptive behavior problems, depression does not show a great deal of stability from childhood to adolescence. It may be a discontinuous phenomenon, reflecting the fact that depression is relatively rare in childhood. Or, continuity may be present but take a less direct form. In one study, inhibited 3-year-olds were unassertive and depressed at 21 years (Caspi, 2000). Anxiety, which does show stability over time (e.g., Ialongo, Edelsohn, Werthamer-Larrson, Crockett et al., 1995), is part of a developmental continuity process relevant to the etiology of depression in females. In one longitudinal study girls (but not boys) with inhibited temperament as toddlers were likely to be impaired in adolescence with generalized social anxiety (Schwartz, Snidman, & Kagan, 1999). Already by 6 years of age, girls are twice as likely as boys to have experienced an anxiety disorder (Lewinsohn, Gotlib, Lewinsohn, Seeley et al., 1998). And normatively, young girls worry more than boys (Silverman, LaGreca, & Wasserstein, 1995).

Several longitudinal studies now suggest that anxiety is often an integral feature of depression, that it precedes depression developmentally, and hence may be a prodromal sign of depression. Anxiety disorders in childhood and adolescence often precede and predict later depressive disorders. Initial evidence was based on retrospective accounts of lifetime histories obtained from diagnostic interviews. For example, in one study of children with comorbid anxiety and depression, two-thirds became anxious before they became depressed (Kovacs, Gatsonis, Paulauskas, & Richards, 1989). Several prospective, longitudinal studies have found that anxiety temporally precedes depression in children, adolescents, and even young adults (e.g., Breslau, Schultz, & Peterson, 1995; Cole, Peeke, Martin, Truglio, & Seroczynski, 1998; Lewinsohn, Gotlib, & Seeley, 1995). Also, prepubertal-onset anxiety disorder precedes later recurrent major depressive disorder across several generations of families at high risk for depression (Warner, Weissman, Mufson, & Wickramaratne, 1999).

An expanded rumination model can help to explain developmental links between early anxiety and later depression. While research on rumination and depression has focused on ruminative responses *to* depression beginning in adolescence, the process of rumination is likely to be present *before* depression develops. Rumination involves worry, perseveration, and even obsession (at times) about one's inner state. Anxiety and worry have childhood origins, hence rumination is likely to begin early as well. Rumination can feed upon itself to magnify problems, overwhelm the child, and eventually create depression. The process of rumination can maintain or exacerbate depression by augmenting accessibility and recall of negative events (Bower, 1981).

Biological processes also are implicated in the evolution of anxiety into depression. Because anxiety involves dysregulation of limbic, vegetative, and autonomic systems, the heightened, sustained arousal can eventually tax these systems in ways that cause the organism to shut down and withdraw from environmental stimulation, in short to become depressed. Not all forms of depression are preceded by anxiety, and anxiety does not always lead to depression. But the pathway from anxiety to depression occurs with sufficient regularity to postulate that anxiety plays an etiologic role. Because females are more likely than males not only to develop mood disorders and symptoms, but also to have comorbid anxiety, we would expect that girls would also more often experience a developmental pathway from anxiety to depression than boys.

Early Predisposing Child Characteristics

Early Channeling of Distress

Depressive mood does not manifest itself in a uniform fashion, and its form of expression may be gender-linked. Gjerde (1995) reported that dysphoric adolescent males often expressed their unhappiness directly and without hesitation, by acting on the world in an aggressive, hostile manner. This is consistent with a psychodynamic theory where aggression reflects masked depression. Dysphoric symptoms in female adolescents, in contrast, were characterized by introspection, absence of open hostility, and a mostly hidden preoccupation with self. This fits the psychodynamic view of depression as aggression turned inward. Moreover, the differences in how these adolescent girls and boys experience and express dysthymia could be seen earlier in development. As early as at 7 years of age, boys who later showed dysthymia were aggressive, self-aggrandizing, and undercontrolled, whereas dysthymic girls were intropunitive, oversocialized, and overcontrolled, anxious and introspective (Block, Gjerde, & Block, 1991).

Young girls who later became depressed also had close relationships. Similar subclinical patterns may be seen even earlier in development. In one study of young children, negative affectivity (composite of anger, anxiety, sadness) predicted internalizing problems in girls and externalizing problems in boys (Rothbart, Ahadi, & Hershey, 1994). Fear and sadness were related to prosocial traits (more common in girls), while irritability and anger were related to antisocial traits (more common in boys).

Sex Role Stereotypes

As early as preschool, children have clear stereotypes about the different ways in which females and males behave. This has been found consistently with regard to the different toys, games, and activities engaged in by the two sexes, as well as in children's perceptions of adult roles and professions. Children also hold sex-stereotypic views of the emotions associated with internalizing and externalizing problems, with anger seen as a male trait and sadness as a female trait (Karbon, Fabes, Carlo, & Martin, 1992). Moreover, these children believed that males lack the capacity to experience sadness, hence viewing the emotion at the center of the depressive experience as unique to females.

Normative Sex Differences in Emotions and Behaviors

Early constitutional advantages for girls may make them more amenable to socialization, more likely to adhere to social norms and responsibilities, and less likely to engage in disruptive behaviors. Young girls, on average, show greater language skills, more rapid physical maturation, and better regulation than boys (see review by Keenan & Shaw, 1997). As early as the second year of life, girls show higher levels of empathy and prosocial behavior (Zahn-Waxler, Robinson, & Emde, 1992). Young girls also are more developmentally advanced in other social-emotional domains. Two-year-old girls show greater affective discomfort and remorse following transgression than boys (Cummings, Hollenbeck, Iannotti, Radke-Yarrow, & Zahn-Waxler, 1986; Kochanska, De Vet, Goldman, Murray, & Putnam, 1994) and their anger is more likely to be linked to feelings of guilt and shame (Zahn-Waxler & Robinson, 1995). Preschool girls are better at affective perspective-taking than boys, showing greater understanding of others' problems (Denham, McKinley, Couchard, & Holt, 1990).

Young girls are more able than boys, to control negative emotion under conditions of disappointment (Cole, 1986; Saarni, 1994). This may reflect their heightened awareness of others' affective states and sensitivity to the impact of their anger and distress on others. This greater social awareness develops early and is seen at all ages (see review by Brody, 1985). Preschool girls show greater frustration tolerance, impulse control, and self-regulation than boys. At the same time, they express more sadness and fear in emotionally challenging situations, suggesting greater internalized distress (Zahn-Waxler, Schmitz, Fulker, Robinson, & Emde, 1996). Girls are more likely than boys to report expressing sadness and pain

(Zeman & Garber, 1996), and to use more emotional than aggressive strategies (Zeman & Shipman, 1998). In contrast, boys are more likely to dissemble sadness (Zeman & Shipman, 1997). Girls' greater emotionality and openness to the expression of sadness could, under some circumstances, make it difficult to modulate this emotion.

Girls spend more time indoors, interact in smaller groups, have one or two best friends, and engage in more turn-taking than boys. Girls also engage in less public play in large groups and use less body contact (Maccoby, 1991). Boys tend to issue direct commands and establish dominance physically, whereas girls attempt to influence each other with compliments, requests for advice, or imitation. These differences affect the interactions of girls with boys. Preschool girls have difficulty influencing boys, although boys do not have difficulty influencing girls (Serbin, Sprafkin, Elman, & Doyle, 1984). Thus, the sphere of influence for girls is more confined from early on in life, and they have less impact than boys in group settings. This may lead to feelings of helplessness and anxiety about how to function in the larger world. Young girls use affiliation to cope with interpersonal conflict more than boys, (Zahn-Waxler et al., 1994), which is a less direct, assertive way to deal with problems. This also may limit the development of other important instrumental skills.

Except for their lessened ability to influence others, young girls show developmental advantage. This has led to the creation of a myth—the "benign childhood myth for girls," and another paradox—the "developmental paradox of female resilience and depression." It is difficult to understand why girls, who appear resilient and relatively impervious to childhood mental disorders, later show so many internalizing disorders. The paradox may reflect the possibility that resilience can mask problems present early in development where the depressive experience takes a different or subtler form. Many of the qualities identified earlier in young girls as linked to later depression (e.g., highly socialized, emotionally regulated, and intelligent) (Block & Gjerde, 1990; Gjerde & Block, 1996) would be more likely to be seen by adults as adaptive rather than problematic. Intelligence in girls may predict later depression as girls may be less encouraged than boys to make full use of their cognitive abilities.

Dienstbier (1984) has proposed that different temperaments might lead to different emotion-attributional styles and levels of guilt. Proneness to emotional tension should result in intense discomfort and distress following transgression. When distress is internal, the child is more likely to experience the links between tension and transgression, and come to experience anticipatory anxiety. Temperamentally anxious children may develop "affective maps" or "somatic markers" of their experiences where threat or stress-related information becomes particularly salient (Derryberry & Reed, 1994; Damasio, Tranel, & Damasio, 1991). This physiological reactivity may facilitate the early, rapid development of mechanisms related to conscience, such as guilt and restraint from wrongdoing.

Guilt and anxiety are more common in girls than boys in childhood, and anxiety is associated with autonomic arousal (e.g., heart rate elevation and electrodermal activity). Therefore, girls may more readily develop somatic markers that facilitate internalization of norms and standards of conduct, but that also create more sustained inner distress as they begin to dwell on problems. Because females are more emotionally responsive to the problems of *others* than males, they are likely to become more aroused and stressed by a wide range of interpersonal contexts. Ruminative scripts may begin to develop that lead to more entrenched, generalized anxiety and depression that is serious in nature. The higher rates of rumination in adolescent and adult females than males may begin at much earlier ages.

Socialization Risk Factors for Girls

Several of the socialization experiences discussed earlier were linked to depression in both boys and girls. They do not appear to be directed more often toward girls (e.g., harsh, punitive parenting) and do not uniquely predict depression in girls. Additional research based mainly on normative, often middle-class samples, is relevant to the socialization of female depression, by virtue of examining different treatment of girls and boys. Girls are more often socialized in ways that interfere with self-actualization, that is, to be dependent, compliant, and unassertive (Kavanagh & Hops, 1994). From a young age, girls are perceived as being more fragile and dependent and are therefore more protected and socialized to be dependent on interpersonal relationships (Gurian, 1987; Hill & Lynch, 1983). This socialization does not prepare girls to handle conflict in interpersonal relationships or to develop a sense of mastery over their environment. Rather, it would be expected to lead to the feelings of helplessness that can culminate in depression.

Preschool girls asked to explain why they succeed or fail on performance tasks express more self-derogation while boys give more self-enhancing explanations (Burgner & Hewstone, 1993). This may reflect different parental socialization practices around achievement issues. In a study by Alessandri and Lewis (1993), 3-year-old girls achieved as much as boys, but received more negative evaluations, and less praise and attention from their middle-class parents than boys for similar accomplishments. Shyness and dependency are treated more positively in females than males, which may help to confirm their anxiety and uncertainty (Simpson & Stevenson-Hinde, 1985).

Mothers more often show disapproval when their infant daughters display anger (i.e., by frowning), but support the expression of anger in male infants (i.e., with looks of empathic concern) (Malatesta & Haviland, 1982). Mothers more often accept anger and retaliation as an appropriate response to another's anger in their 2–3-year-old sons, but encourage their daughters to resolve anger by reestablishing the damaged relationship (Fivush, 1989, 1991). Mothers of 2-year-olds require their girls more than boys, to relinquish toys to guests (Ross, Tesla, Kenyon, & Lollis, 1990). This may contribute to daughters feeling less entitled, and less likely when there is a struggle, to try to keep things that they want. Parents of 3-year-olds are more likely to override and negate the verbal assertions of their daughters than those of their sons (Kerig, Cowan, & Cowan, 1993).

Mothers of 2-year-olds more often reason with their daughters than sons, pointing out the harmful consequences for others of their aggression (Smetana, 1989). Mothers appear to show greater authenticity in their expressions of anger toward preschool daughters than sons (Cole, Teti, & Zahn-Waxler, in press).

This body of work suggests that normatively girls are oversocialized and boys are undersocialized regarding appropriate social behaviors. Moreover, they provide a framework for understanding why girls are more likely than boys to mask their anger, disappointment, and frustration.

Parents often have higher expectations for mature interpersonal behavior in girls, are less tolerant of their anger and misbehavior, and more likely to override or negate assertive behaviors in girls than boys. Many of the socialization practices directed more often toward girls contain messages that reflect pressures to be prosocial, suppress anger, and curtail antisocial behavior. Suppression of anger, assertion, and other forms of self-expression may heighten internalized distress. Over time this may result in the indecision, self-criticism, self-blame, and low self-esteem that become part of the phenomenology of the depressive experience.

In addition, parents socialize their sons' and daughters' expression and experience of emotion differently, which may contribute to higher rates of depression in girls. Parents discuss more emotions, particularly sadness with daughters, but avoid discussing or showing anger (Brody & Hall, 1993; Fivush, 1989, 1991). Brody and Hall (1993) also suggest that girls are expected to have more internalizing negative emotions (such as sadness and fear) and less anger than boys. This socialization by family and peers begins at an early age, reinforcing internalizing emotions in girls and but failing to equip girls with adaptive ways to deal with their anger.

Social-Cognitive Filters and Triggers for Depression

The abrupt appearance of depressive symptoms in adolescents and adults, without clear environmental precipitants, is sometimes taken as evidence for the primacy of biological processes that become operative at this time. However, this depression may be based, in part, on earlier stress and trauma. Post and colleagues (Post et al., 1996; Meyersburg & Post, 1979) proposed a crucial role of stressful or traumatic life events in precipitating initial depressive episodes in genetically predisposed persons. Initial episodes lead to future episodes that occur in closer proximity over time and eventually without environmental triggers. This model was derived from work on the "kindling" of seizure disorders in which seizures may become more spontaneously generated over the years.

Based on the work of Post and colleagues, Goodwin and Jamison (1990) thus have argued that depression appearing "out of the blue" in young adults may have origins in early traumatic environmental events that helped to create subsequent biological vulnerability. Repeated exposure to aversive psychological stimulation may sensitize individuals so that later in development relatively brief exposures to (similar) environmental stress and trauma, or even thoughts and images that serve as reminders, may induce depression. So far we have discussed early socialization experiences that could create risk as well as early biological vulnerability (e.g., anxious arousal). However, we have not yet described characteristics of some children (often girls) that, given these contexts and conditions, would make them likely to develop internalized "reminders" (i.e., thoughts and images that trigger depressive thoughts) even in the absence to traumatic experiences.

We propose that girls are more likely than boys to experience and interpret their environments in ways that create depressive cognitions. Because of their strong interpersonal orientation, girls are often in close physical proximity to caregivers. This can influence how the family climate is represented in conscious and unconscious memory, the scripts girls develop about early family life, and the accessibility of these memories. The literature on emotion language provides clues about how negative emotions and cognitions become fused as young girls are drawn into a communication process that is depressogenic in nature (see review by Zahn-Waxler, 2000). Parents (particularly mothers), as noted, talk more about internalizing emotions (sadness, fear), providing greater detail and elaboration, with daughters than sons. Distressed and depressed parents talk more about these negative emotions than well mothers (Zahn-Waxler, 2000). Thus young girls in these families will most often be privy to these communications, providing more frequent occasions for girls to internalize negative scripts that provide ready access to emotionally based material.

Greater access to negative affect-based memories about family life or other social relationships (e.g., with teachers, friends, and classmates) that are unhappy and conflictual may reflect a nascent form of ruminative coping and negative cognitions that may contribute to later depression. Since this process is likely to occur more often with young daughters than sons, girls may come to dwell more on negative events where they have little or no control. Through a complex set of processes, socialization is thought to prime these memories and affective, physiological arousal to stamp them into memory. There are many ways in which early negative emotions, behaviors, and cognitions combine and lead to later depression, particularly for girls. We consider here one prototypic model, that is, how being the young girl of a depressed parent can create a depresssogenic style whereby she comes to feel guilty, blameworthy, and generally responsible for bad things that happen. Other conditions (e.g., early sexual abuse) would be expected to have a similar effect.

During the preschool years children can readily become overinvolved in parental conflict and distress. For example, they try to get fighting parents to make up or to cheer up a depressed mother (Cummings, Zahn-Waxler, & Radke-Yarrow, 1981; Radke-Yarrow, Zahn-Waxler, Richardson, Susman, & Martinez, 1994). Not only do they become highly emotionally involved and try to help, but they also develop *scripts* of overinvolvement in other's distress that include themes of empathy and guilt (Zahn-Waxler, Kochanska, Krupnick, & McKnew, 1990). These patterns are more common in girls than boys. Preschool children of depressed mothers are particularly likely to try to help them (Radke-Yarrow et al., 1994). Thus girls of depressed mothers are the most likely to become overinvolved in another's distress. At the same time, young girls, but not boys, of depressed mothers also may show unassertive, submissive ways of coping with their own conflict (Hay, Zahn-Waxler, Cummings, & Iannotti, 1992).

These patterns of participation in parental conflict and distress suggest one possible model for intergenerational transmission of features of depression. In attributional theories, adult depression is characterized by overwhelming feelings of both helplessness and responsibility. The fact that young children with an emotionally distressed caregiver fundamentally cannot help the parent would be expected to lead to feelings of helplessness and failure. The belief, however, that they can create change would be intermittently reinforced by their occasional successful efforts. These children also become part of a large climate of despair by their close proximity to parental distress, with contagion of mood a likely outcome. Thus, young children, more often girls, could experience depression-like symptoms of helplessness and responsibility early and repeatedly due to empathic overinvolvement. These girls could come to feel that life requires more from them than they can give, leading to defeatism and encroaching on the development of autonomy and self-esteem.

Earlier we described a number of studies in which depression and caregiving in older girls were linked to having a depressed mother. Although family stress negatively impacts the mental health of both girls and boys, having a strong, caring orientation or involvement in family processes in the context of parental psychopathology and discord is seen as particularly harmful to girls (Gore et al., 1993). The research with young children suggests that these harmful processes for girls can be set into play well before adolescence, indeed in the early formative years. To the extent that other early potential risk factors known to distinguish girls and boys are also present, the deleterious effects will be exacerbated (Essex, Klein, Cho, & Kraemer, 2003).

INTERVENTION AND TREATMENT OF DEPRESSION IN GIRLS

Treatment of Depression

Cognitive-behavioral and interpersonal therapy has been used with success in treating depressed adolescents (Kovacs & Sherill, 2001), consistent with studies of adults (Brems, 1995; Clarke, Rohde, Lewinson, Hops et al., 1999; Kovacs, Rush, Beck, & Hollon, 1981; Lewinsohn & Gotlib, review, 1995; Mazure, Keita, & Blehar, 2002; Weissman et al., 1981). Cognitive-behavioral therapies focus on active change in thought patterns and behaviors, to interfere with ruminative tendencies that maintain depressive states. Interpersonal therapy focuses on resolution of relationship difficulties. Depressed adolescents have benefited from group therapy, as well as a CBT course known as Adolescent Coping With Depression (Clarke & Lewinsohn, 1989). It focuses on attending to one's mood, increasing social skills and activities, and reducing negative or ir-rational cognitions (Clarke et al., 1999). Interpersonal Psychotherapy for Depressed Adolescents (IPTA; Musfon, Weissman, Moreau, & Garfinkel, 1999; Mufson, Moreau, & Weissman, 1996) has been shown to be effective for depressed adolescents in randomized, controlled studies. Youths with subclinical symptoms also benefited from cognitive restructuring and role-playing designed to increase social skills. Treatments that include family members and are based on interactional, interpersonal models can also be effective, for example, Family Therapy for Depressed Adolescents (FTDA; Diamond & Siqueland, 1995) and Interpersonal Family Therapy (Schwartz, Kaslow, Racusin, & Carton, 1998).

Particular issues that require attention when females are treated for depression include body image, gender roles, and possible abuse or victimization (Davis and Padesky, 1989; McGrath et al., 1990). Treatment of depressed adolescent girls requires further consideration of their developmental stage. It is important to help girls negotiate increasing independence in the adolescent years after having been socialized to be dependent on and derive identity from their families. More generally, the therapist must take into account the many contexts of the adolescent and the demands made on her in each environment (McGrath et al., 1990).

Women respond differently than men to psychopharmacological treatment of depression. Higher percentages of body fat, lower amounts of gastric acid, and a longer time to empty the stomach all contribute to differences in drug effects, such as a greater experience of side effects and a longer-lasting effect of the drug (Kornstein & McEnany, 2000). In addition, women respond most favorably to SSRIs than to tricyclics (Kornstein, 2001; Korenstein & McEnany, 2000). These issues remain to be addressed regarding the treatment of adolescent girls.

Prevention of Depression

A number of prevention programs for children and adolescents have been developed. A group cognitive-based program, a school-based program, and a family-based program have all been successful in reducing future incidence of depressive disorder in adolescents (see reviews by Asarnow, Jaycox, & Thompson, 2001; Beardslee & Gladstone, 2001). The cognitive program, Coping With Stress, is based on cognitive distortion theories of depression (Clarke et al., 1995). Adolescents with high subclinical depressive symptomatology are targeted in this program. The school-based prevention program also targets children with high scores on self-report measures of depression or parental conflict (Jaycox, Reivich, Gillham, & Seligman, 1994). It includes both a cognitive training module and a social problem-solving module that focuses on modifying explanatory styles. Finally, the family-based intervention targets children at risk for depression as a result of having a parent with affective disorder (Beardslee & Gladstone, 2001). It is administered by a clinician to individual families or in group lecture to parents to help them deal with marital and family problems that may affect their children. While both interventions were effective, participants in the clinician-based intervention experienced more favorable outcomes.

Other interventions have shown more limited success, for example, those aimed at improving behavioral skills (Stark, Reynolds, & Kaslow, 1987; Clarke, Hawkins, Murphy, & Sheeber, 1993) or at teaching coping skills (Petersen, Leffert, Graham, Alwin et al., 1997). Interventions that promote direct, clear, assertive communication merit further attention. Given that girls' problems in this area begin early, often in the family setting, opportunities to develop and practice these skills with parents could be particularly useful. To date, there are no comprehensive programs specifically designed for girls, despite the facts that they (a) are more likely to develop depression than boys and (b) have certain characteristics and vulnerability factors that would suggest the appropriateness of specialized treatments. Longitudinal research now shows that the developmental phenomenology of major depression differs in boys and girls, including the timing and types of patterns of comorbid disorders (Kovacs, Obrosky, Scott, & Sherrill, 2003). Such information may help to identify optimal timing of efforts to reduce depressive symptoms and treat comorbid disorders, and help select developmentally appropriate target symptoms in girls.

There is now a considerable body of research that is relevant to the development of depressive symptomatology in girls. This research could be used to provide updated information to the public, parents, and children and to further inform the development of comprehensive prevention programs. Optimally, prevention would be proactive and designed from a developmental perspective. From infancy onward, girls are learning to organize and manage their emotional experiences and they are receiving messages from others about who they are and how they fit into the world. Long before girls become active agents of change in their own lives, they are profoundly affected by attitudes, beliefs, and behavior of their parents.

Positive parenting, an important component of treatment of depression in offspring, holds even more potential as a component of prevention programs. The question is when and how to get parents involved in prevention programs. Some prevention programs have targeted parents with affective disorder. Examples of other possible target groups include parents with (a) subclinical depressive symptoms, (b) other psychopathology or troubled relationships, (c) considerable life stress, (d) lack of sufficient knowledge of child development and effective parenting and (e) genetic risk for depression. Emphasis would be placed both on training of parenting skills and helping parents to identify vulnerability factors in their girls that may require extra knowledge and initiative in the parenting process.

The transition from childhood into adolescence and adulthood is thought to be particularly difficult for females because of the conflict between remaining dependent on authority figures, particularly mothers, and striving for autonomy and independence. Females often construe separation as an act of aggression (Gilligan, 1982), where strivings toward selfhood run the risk of severing relational ties. Interventions, like normal development, should lead to integration of relational and self-definitional issues in order to progress toward more mature expressions in both developmental domains (Leadbeater, Blatt, & Quinlan, 1995).

Interventions would be expected to be most effective if they focus both on helping the girl develop a secure sense of personal competence (e.g., in academics, work, sports, artistic activities), in the context of supportive, reliable and stable relationships. Thus, girls should be encouraged to develop their individual identities, to pursue their own interests, and to take steps toward independence with adequate safety provisions prior to puberty. Parents may need assistance as well in dealing with their changing roles with respect to their daughters.

It is important for parents to be aware of the significance of pubertal changes. Physical changes that accompany puberty for girls include culturally devalued ones such as an increase in body fat. Because body dissatisfaction is implicated in the development of depression in female girls (Allgood-Merten, Lewinsohn, & Hops, 1990), efforts to minimize it are important. While festive rituals in many world cultures mark puberty, developed societies have tended to foster negative attitudes (Brooks-Gunn & Reiter, 1990). Parents could be taught to encourage private family rituals to celebrate the onset of menarche and put physical changes in a positive light.

Suppression of anger by girls can also contribute to feelings of helplessness, powerlessness, and passivity, which can then lead to depression. Many parents, mothers in particular, have had the experience of being punished as children for expressing their anger. They may find it difficult to understand that their daughters can become socially responsible and caring persons while still being allowed to express anger, having themselves learned in childhood that these were incompatible processes. Parents can be more effective in helping their daughters to label and accept their emotions if they fully understand the adaptive value of anger and the situations in life in which anger is appropriate and useful. Parents need to learn that curtailment and criticism of angry feelings in daughters may lead to sadness and self-blame in situations of conflict and distress. It is important that girls not be treated differently than their brothers in this regard, given societal predilections to tolerate anger in boys. Parents' modeling of effective management of anger as well as sadness and anxiety also will be beneficial.

As children enter school, teachers become another important source of influence. Teachers could be sensitized to pay attention to the needs of girls even though they may not be expressed as loudly or disruptively as the needs of boys. For example, every time a teacher attends to a child who is acting out in some way, the teacher could take a moment to talk to, or recognize in some other way, a child who is not misbehaving or garnering attention in some other noisy manner. Quiet children, more often girls, can be encouraged to speak in ways that allay their anxiety and do not threaten them. More generally, both teachers and parents need to become more sensitive to subtle signs of internalized distress in young girls, and not to simply view being nice, compliant, and quiet as "the way girls are." The "loss of voice" by some girls in adolescence probably has much earlier origins and could be targeted for intervention in childhood in order that girls begin to feel listened to and heard at this time.

In addition to the socializing role of parents and teachers, the influence of peers becomes more prominent over time, particularly by adolescence with the acceleration of gender-differential socialization. The substance of prescribed gender roles is conveyed with great redundancy in most cultures. Despite some progress in Western culture regarding respect for confidence and independence personified by female athletes, the thin, conventionally attractive, not overly assertive "feminine" woman is still the cultural ideal. Girls are exposed to cultural messages long before puberty, but as they enter puberty, they may begin to compare their developing bodies and personalities unfavorably to those of models and actresses who seemingly fit the mold. It is important to help girls learn to think critically about cultural messages. Some of this training could occur in the context of groups that provide peer education and support.

CONCLUSIONS

An etiological theory that integrates social or environmental, cognitive or personality, and biological factors leading to sex differences in depression has not yet been established (Piccinelli & Wilkenson, 2000). We are at the beginning stages in understanding the etiology of depression in girls and planning efficacious treatments and early interventions. Because problems may be underrecognized in young girls, we will need to increase the sensitivity of our observing lens—to be sure that qualities of being well behaved, polite, socially sensitive and responsible, emotionally attuned, and slow to express anger, frustration, and disappointment, do not serve as cover for unseen hurts and fears. This is a special challenge because girls' greater proclivities with language, emotional expressivity, and ability to take others' perspectives can often interfere with the process of delving more deeply into the quality of their own lives. Some of these girls, under certain conditions of risk, will start to treat others' needs more seriously than their own and to minimize their own goals and ambitions. Eventually this can corrode self-esteem and even create confusion about who they really are. Anxiety may both underlie and result from these confusions, and the weight of this anxiety may develop over time into depression, as these young girls do not learn coping skills that reflect self-assertion.

We argue, then, that early constitutional and environmental risk factors act cumulatively over time to help create the precipitous increase in depressive symptoms in vulnerable girls as they transition into a period of development that should be preparing them for adulthood. Many of the vulnerability factors observed in adolescence may be present much earlier. This is not to say that some depression may not really appear "out of the blue" or that early vulnerabilities inevitably produce depression. Misfiring of neurons and alterations of brain chemistry may affect neurotransmitters in ways that inexplicably plunge individuals into darkness and despair, even when environmental adversity has been minimal. But often, early signs of depression may be apparent to the astute observer (if we better knew what to look for) or to the affected individual (if she were sensitized to the incipient cues), and alterations of the environment at this time might prevent the later expression of depressive symptoms. In addition to the need for better observations, it will also be necessary to establish better analytic and research techniques, to utilize large sample sizes, and to conduct longitudinal research that covers a wide age span of childhood to adolescence. Only then will it be possible to understand early less apparent sex differences that contribute to the growth of depression in the early growth of depression. In a recent longitudinal study (Cole, Tram, Martin, Hoffman et al., 2002), for example, cross-domain latent growth curve analysis revealed that sex differences in symptom *growth* in childhood preceded the emergence of mean *level* sex differences that are seen in adolescence.

It is a vast and inevitably probabilistic undertaking to identify long-term and short-term precipitants (i.e., distal and proximal causes) of depression. In addition to the existing recommendations, we emphasize the need for further qualitative and quantitative distinctions between of levels and types of depression. Throughout this chapter we have assumed that generalizations from nonclinical female samples apply to clinically depressed girls and vice versa. Evidence supports this generalization, which also fits with the fact that subclinical depression often evolves into a clinical disorder over time. However, further research is needed to support or refute these assumptions. Moreover, some of the early signs of depression may not be directly reflected in current diagnostic criteria or symptom definitions. They will require expanded consideration of the nature of depression in young children, girls in particular.

Most research is based on existing diagnostic criteria and more broadly on the psychiatric and psychological instruments used to assess symptoms and disorders. While these have been an essential part of the initial research process, their use can create forced, unnatural similarities between different levels and kinds of depression. At this point we should look more closely into the phenomenology of depressive experiences. Research on personality traits, emotion regulation patterns, and styles of social interaction of females and males, can begin to provide fundamental information about similarities and differences in ways females and males experience depression.

Given that mood disorders at their core reflect problems of emotion regulation it is surprising that there has been so little research devoted to understanding the development of the emotions that underlie depression and to use this as a way to further parse the phenomenology of depression. When does sadness becomes a mood state rather than an emotional response to particular situations? Enduring a sad mood is central to the definition of depression but other emotions are arguably as important in the etiology of depressive symptoms and disorders. From a developmental perspective, early affective biases or mood states that may precede or be a part of the depressive experience are likely also to involve worry and anxiety; guilt, shame, lack of pleasure (anhedonia); suppression *or* unmodulated expression of anger and hostility; and empathic overarousal where the self, becomes fused or submerged in the problems of others. Moral emotions such as guilt were first implicated in adult depression by Freud who emphasized childhood precursors of the disorder, seen in a harsh superego or conscience and internalization of criticism and blame. Different configurations of emotional profiles may provide ways to differentiate sub-types of depression, both as they develop and once they are established.

We have identified a number of biological, social, and cognitive factors, initially thought to be implicated mainly in the adolescent depression. Many of these vulnerability and risk factors are also present, or in formative stages, prior to the emergence of sex differences in depression in adolescence. It is not always clear when a particular vulnerability is a predictor of depression and when it is itself a manifestation of depression. We propose that sex differences in depression are present earlier but are not identified as such, given the requirement for functional impairment and the ease with which symptoms remain hidden. If a girl is doing well in school and getting along with others, including family, teachers, and friends, depression is not considered as a possibility. However, many depressed individuals at all ages are able to function in society, yet still suffer from serious sadness and lack of pleasure in their lives. This possibility seems no less true for young children, particularly girls.

No one risk factor is likely to create depression. Depression is a consequence of cumulative risk factors that culminate in serious mood disturbances over time and the processes by which this occurs is transactional in nature. Sometimes the constellations of risk factors will be similar in terms of their role in predicting depression, reflecting a similar etiology for boys and girls. Sometimes similar constellations for boys and girls will be differentially predictive of later depressive symptoms. And sometimes the initial configurations will differ, as will patterns of prediction over time. All of these possibilities need to be taken into account in order to fully understand rates, severity levels, and qualitative features of depression in females.

This is part of the larger issue of the kinds of conceptual models that will ultimately be needed to understand the origins, progression, and amelioration of (different types of) depression. For example, both sex-neutral and sex-specific depression models have been advanced. For sex-neutral models, one (more parsimonious) model based on depression theory is specified, and the gender difference in depression can be derived from specific factors in the general model. Sex-specific models require separate models for girls and boys. They are necessary when gender interacts with etiologic risk factors in predicting depression as we saw earlier, for example, when maternal depression predicted later depression in girls but not boys, or when stress reactivity predicted depression in girls but not boys. Such interactions can be notoriously difficult to detect given the statistical approaches available (McClelland & Judd, 1993). Hence their presence in the real world often will be underestimated and sometimes remain unidentified. These issues must be addressed if we are to further our understanding of factors particular to depression in females.

The links between early puberty and depression in females but not males and their more frequent experiencing of certain vegetative symptoms, speak to the likely role of biological factors in the nature of their psychological problems. These connections signal something unique about female reproductive and hormonal systems, in conjunction with the ways that evolution, culture, and society have prepared them for roles of child-bearing and child rearing, which creates heightened risk for depression. While there are many other aspects of being a female that contribute to their depression, this is one clearly defined sex difference that would suggest the utility of a (female) sex-specific model for some hypotheses about the etiology of depression.

Although the focus of this chapter has been on depression in girls, we need to remember that our understanding of their depression is enhanced by comparative research with boys. For many years, girls were mainly excluded from research on antisocial behavior and development because their aggression and violence was not nearly so frequent and serious at that of boys. However, this ignored the fact that a substantial number of girls engage in these behaviors and it prevented us from learning more about other ways in which they bring harm to others. Moreover, it kept us from learning about factors that contribute uniquely to aggression in either sex, and hence it hampered more generally, progress in research on the etiology of antisocial behavior. The most useful conceptual models of depression in children and adolescents will be those that do not repeat the errors of the past. It is essential to study both girls and boys in order to identify their common and unique risk factors for depression.

It will be important in this process to avoid stereotyping "female" and "male" depression in ways that correspond exclusively to sex-role stereotypes. If we do this we will miss many aspects of depression in females that do not fit neatly into the etiologic domains discussed. As one important example, depression is often accompanied by anger, irritability, and hostility. Depressed individuals can be critical and judgmental of others, unable or unwilling to accept responsibility for their actions, and ready to blame others for their misfortunes. This was illustrated in the descriptions of the child-rearing practices of some depressed parents. These hostile, judgmental patterns would appear to be a far cry from the "nice girl" syndrome we have emphasized, again illustrating the need to explore further different subtypes of depression. Analysis of different comorbidity patterns would be expected to play an important role in this process. In addition to the Axis I comorbid disorders already considered, including the developmental significance of anxiety as a precursor to depression, mood disorders are often comorbid with Axis II personality disorders in adults. Personality disorders variously reflect impulsivity, self-absorption, self-serving and antisocial behaviors, disregard for others, problems regulating anger, failures to internalize responsibility, and to take others' perspectives. They include borderline personality disorder, narcissistic personality disorder, histrionic personality disorder, and antisocial personality disorder.

Sex differences "favoring" females are most prevalent for borderline personality disorder, with 75% of diagnosed cases being women. The essential feature of borderline personality disorder is a pervasive pattern of instability of interpersonal relationships, self-image and affects, marked impulsivity, and self-destructive behavior. Frequently, they express inappropriate, intense anger, or have difficulty controlling their anger. They may display extreme sarcasm, enduring bitterness, or verbal outbursts. These expressions of anger are often followed by shame and guilt or feelings of being evil. This disorder is said to begin in early adulthood, but this is probably more of a reflection of that fact that the requisite research has not been conducted.

Because personality traits are, by definition, longstanding in nature, marked personality disturbances would be unlikely to occur out of the blue. However, there has been no research on the developmental origins of borderline personality disorder. This, again, is in marked contrast to research on the developmental origins of antisocial personality disorder, which is much more commonly diagnosed in men. Depression seen in borderline women, as well as in women with other personality disorders will be experienced very differently by them, their family and friends, than depression in females that is unaccompanied by a personality disorder. Understanding the development of personality traits in girls, and how they may intersect with depressive experiences will give rise to an expanded knowledge base regarding the origins of depression.

Transactional models are essential for understanding depression in girls. Depression is made up of cognitions, emotions, behaviors, and dysregulated physiological and neural states. These factors will need to be studied in concert if we are to develop more comprehensive theories and treatment paradigms. Researchers have identified many relevant variables and offered several bio-behavioral models, but have comprehensively tested relatively few of these models, particularly from a developmental perspective. Because the nature and "nurture" of depression are intricately interconnected and synergistically interactive over time, careful longitudinal assessment of etiologic processes and analysis of their predictive role in the appearance of depressive symptoms and syndromes are essential. Only in this way will it become possible to fully understand the etiology and expression of depression in females.

REFERENCES

Abramson, L. Y., Alloy, L. B., Hogan, M. E., Whitehouse, W. G., Donovan, P., Rose, D. T., et al. (2002). Cognitive vulnerability to depression: Theory and evidence. In R. L. Leahy & E. T. Dowd (Eds.), *Clinical advances in cognitive psychotherapy: Theory and application* (pp. 75–92). New York: Springer.

Abramson, L. Y., Seligman, M. E. P., & Teasdale, J. D. (1978). Learned helplessness in humans: Critique and reformulation. *Journal of Abnormal Psychology, 87*, 49–74.

Akil, H., Haskett, R. F., Young, E. A., Grunhaus, L., Kotun, J., Weinberg, V., et al. (1993). Multiple HPA profiles in endogenous depression: Effects of age and sex on cortisol and beta-endorphin. *Biological Psychiatry, 33*, 73–81.

Alessandri, S. M., & Lewis, M. (1993). Parental evaluation and its relation to shame and pride in young children. *Sex Roles, 29,* 335–343.

Allen, J. P., Hauser, S. T., Eickholt, C., Bell, K. L., & O'Connor, T. G. (1994). Autonomy and relatedness in family interactions as predictors of expressions of negative adolescent affect. *Journal of Research on Adolescence, 4,* 535–552.

Allgood-Merten, B., Lewinsohn, P. M., & Hops, H. (1990). Sex differences and adolescent depression. *Journal of Abnormal Psychology, 99,* 55–63.

American Psychiatric Association (1994). *Diagnostic and statistical manual of mental disorders* (4th ed.). Washington, DC: Author.

Anderson, J. C., Williams, S. M., McGee, R., & Silva, P. A. (1987). DSM-III disorders in preadolescent children: Prevalence in a large sample from the general population. *Archives of General Psychiatry, 44,* 69–76.

Angold, A., Costello, E. J., & Erkanli, A. (1999). Comorbidity. *Journal of Child Psychology and Psychiatry, 40,* 57–87.

Angold, A., Costello, E. J., Erkanli, A., & Worthman, C. (1999). Pubertal changes in hormone levels and depression in girls. *Psychological Medicine, 29,* 1043–1053.

Angold, A., Costello, E. J., & Worthman, C. M. (1998). Puberty and depression: The roles of age, pubertal status and pubertal timing. *Psychological Medicine, 28,* 51–61.

Angold, A., & Rutter, M. (1992). Effects of age and pubertal status on depression in a large clinical sample. *Development and Psychopathology, 4,* 5–28.

Angst, J., & Dobler-Mikola. A. (1984). Do the diagnostic criteria determine the sex ratio in depression? *Journal of Affective Disorders, 7,* 189–198.

Arroyo, C. G., & Zigler, E. (1995). Racial identity, academic achievement, and the psychological well-being of economically disadvantaged adolescents. *Journal of Personality and Social Psychology, 69,* 903–914.

Asarnow, J. R., Jaycox, L. H., & Thompson, M. C. (2001). Depression in youth: Psychosocial interventions. *Journal of Clinical Child Psychology, 30,* 33–47.

Aseltine, R. H. (1996). Pathways linking parental divorce with adolescent depression. *Journal of Health and Social Behavior, 37,* 133–148.

Aseltine, R. H., Gore, S., & Colten, M. E. (1994). Depression and the social developmental context of adolescence. *Journal of Personality and Social Psychology, 67,* 252–263.

Aube, J., Fichman, L., Saltaris, C., & Koestner, R. (2000). Gender differences in adolescent depressive symptomatology: Towards an integrated social-developmental model. *Journal of Social and Clinical Psychology, 19,* 297–313.

Avison, W. R., & McAlpine, D. D. (1992). Gender differences in symptoms of depression among adolescents. *Journal of Health and Social Behavior, 33,* 77–96.

Barrera, M., & Garrison-Jones, C. (1992). Family and peer social support as specific correlates of adolescent depressive symptoms. *Journal of Abnormal Child Psychology, 20,* 1–16.

Beardslee, W. R., & Gladstone, T. R. G. (2001). Prevention of childhood depression: Recent findings and future prospects. *Biological Psychiatry, 49,* 1101–1110.

Beardslee, W. R., Versage, E., & Gladstone, T. (1998). Children of affectively ill parents: A review of the past ten years. *Journal of the American Academy of Child and Adolescent Psychiatry, 37,* 1134–1141.

Beck, A. T. (1967). Depression: Clinical, experimental and theoretical aspects. New York: Hoeber.

Beck, A. T., Steer, R. A., & Garbin, M. G. (1988). Psychometric properties of the Beck Depression Inventory: Twenty-five years of evaluation. *Clinical Psychology Review, 8,* 77–100.

Bell-Dolan, D. J., Foster, S. L., & Christopher, J. S. (1995). Girls' peer relations and internalizing problems: Are socially neglected, rejected, and withdrawn girls at risk? *Journal of Clinical Child Psychology, 24,* 463–473.

Bem, S. L. (1978). *Bem sex role inventory manual.* Palo Alto, CA: Mind Garden.

Benenson, J. F., & Christakos, A. (2003). The greater fragility of females' versus males' closest same-sex friendships. *Child Development, 74,* 1123–1129.

Berard, R. M. F., Boermeester, F., Hartman, N., & Rust. A. L. (1997). The use of depression rating scales in an adolescent psychiatric population: Sex and age differences. *International Journal of Adolescent Medicine and Health, 9,* 313–320.

Birmaher, B., Ryan, N. D., Williamson, D. E., Brent, D. A., Kaufman, J., Dahl, R. E., et al. (1996). Childhood and adolescent depression: A review of the past 10 years. Part I. *Journal of the American Academy of Child and Adolescent Psychiatry, 35,* 1427–1439.

Block, J., & Gjerde, P. F. (1990). Depressive symptoms in late adolescence: A longitudinal perspective on personality antecedents. In J. E. Rolf, A. S. Masten, D. Cicchetti, K. H. Nuchterlein, & S. Weintraub (Eds.), *Risk and protective factors in the development of psychopathology* (pp. 334–360). New York: Cambridge University Press.

Block, J. H., Gjerde, P. F., & Block, J. H. (1991). Personality antecedents of depressive tendencies in 18-year-olds: A prospective study. *Journal of Personality and Social Psychology, 60,* 726–738.

Block, J., & Robins, R. W. (1993). A longitudinal study of consistency and change in self-esteem from early adolescence to early adulthood. *Child Development, 64,* 901–923.

Boivin, M., Poulin, F., & Vitaro, F. (1994). Depressed mood and peer rejection in childhood. *Development and Psychopathology, 6,* 483–498.

Bower, G. (1981). Mood and memory. *American Psychologist, 36,* 129–148.

Boyle, M. H., & Pickles, A. (1997). Maternal depressive symptoms and ratings of emotional disorder symptoms in children and adolescents. *Journal of Child Psychology and Psychiatry, 38,* 981–992.

Brady, E. U., & Kendall, P. C. (1992). Comorbidity of anxiety and depression in children and adolescents. *Psychological Bulletin, 3,* 244–255.

Brems, C. (1995). Women and depression: A comprehensive analysis. In E. E. Beckham & W. R. Leber (Eds.), *Handbook of Depression* (2nd ed., pp. 539–566). New York: Guilford.

Brendgen, M., Vitaro, F., & Bukowski, W. M. (2000). Deviant friends and early adolescents' emotional and behavioral adjustment. *Journal of Research on Adolescence, 10,* 173–189.

Bresleau, N., Schultz, L., & Peterson, E. (1995). Sex differences in depression: A role for preexisting anxiety. *Psychiatry Research, 58,* 1–12.

Brody, L. R. (1985). Gender differences in emotional development: A review of theories and research. *Journal of Personality, 53,* 102–149.

Brody, L. R., & Hall, J. A. (1993). Gender and emotion. In M. Lewis & J. M. Haviland (Eds.), *Handbook of emotions* (pp. 447–460). New York: Guilford.

Brooks-Gunn, J. (1991). How stressful is the transition to adolescence for girls? In M. E. Colton & S. Gore (Eds.), *Adolescent stress: Causes and consequences. Social institutions and social change* (pp.131–149). Hawthorne, NY: Aldine de Gruyter.

Brooks-Gunn, J. (1992). Growing up female: Stressful events and the transition to adolescence. In T. M. Field, P. M. McCabe, & N. Schneiderman (Eds.), *Stress and coping in infancy and childhood* (pp.119–145). Hillsdale, NJ: Erlbaum.

Brooks-Gunn, J., & Reiter, E. O. (1990). The role of pubertal processes. In S. S. Feldman & G. R. Elliot (Eds.), *At the threshold: The developing adolescent* (pp.16–56). Massachusetts: Harvard University Press.

Brooks-Gunn, J., & Warren, M. P. (1989). Biological and social contributions to negative affect in young adolescent girls. *Child Development, 60,* 40–55.

Burgner, D., & Hewstone, M. (1993). Young children's causal attributions for success and failure: "Self-enhancing" boys and "self-derogating" girls. *British Journal of Developmental Psychology, 11,* 125–129.

Byrne, B. M., Baron, P., & Campbell, T. L. (1993). Measuring adolescent depression: Factorial validity and invariance of the Beck Depression Inventory across gender. *Journal of Research on Adolescence, 3,* 127–143.

Campbell, T.L., Byrne, B.M., & Baron, P. (1992). Gender differences in the expression of depressive symptoms in early adolescents. *Journal of Early Adolescence, 12,* 326–338.

Canals, J., Blade, J., Carbajo, G., & Domenech-Laberia, E. (2001). The Beck Depression Inventory: Psychometric characteristics and usefulness in nonclinical adolescents. *European Journal of Psychological Assessment, 17,* 63–68.

Caspi, A. (2000). The child is the father of the man: Personalities continuities from childhood to adulthood. *Journal of Personality and Social Psychology, 78,* 158–172.

Cicchetti, D., & Toth, S. L. (1998). The development of depression in children and adolescents. *American Psychologist, 53,* 221–241.

Clarke, G. N., Hawkins, W., Murphy, M., & Sheeber, L. (1993). School-based primary prevention of depressive symptomatology in adolescents: Findings from two studies. *Journal of Adolescent Research, 8,* 183–204.

Clarke, G. N., Hawkins, W., Murphy, M., Sheeber, L. B., Lewinsohn, P. M., & Seeley, J. R. (1995). Targeted prevention of unipolar depressive disorder in an at-risk sample of high school adolescents. *Journal of the American Academy of Child and Adolescent Psychiatry, 34,* 312–321.

Clarke, G. N., & Lewinsohn, P. M. (1989). The Coping With Depression Course: A group psychoeducational intervention for unipolar depression. *Behaviour Change, 6,* 54–69.

Clarke, G. N., Rohde, P., Lewinsohn, P. M., Hops, H., & Seeley, J. R. (1999). Cognitive-behavioral treatment of adolescent depression. *Journal of the American Academy of Child and Adolescent Psychiatry, 38,* 272–279.

Coie, J. D., & Dodge, K. A. (1998). The development of aggression and antisocial behavior. In W. Damon (Series Ed.) & N. Eisenberg (Vol. Ed.), *Handbook of child psychology, Vol. 3: Social, emotional and personality development* (5th ed., pp. 779–861). New York: Wiley.

Colarossi, L. G., & Eccles, J. S. (2000). A prospective study of adolescents' peer support: Gender differences and the influence of parental relationships. *Journal of Youth and Adolescence, 29,* 661–678.

Cole, D. A., Peeke, L. G., Martin, J. M., Truglio, R., & Seroczynski, A. D. (1998). A longitudinal look at the relation between depression and anxiety in children and adolescents. *Journal of Consulting and Clinical Psychology, 66,* 451–460.

Cole, D. A., Tram, J. M., Martin, J. M., Hoffman, K. B., Ruiz, M. D., Jacquez, F. M., et al. (2002). Individual differences in the emergence of depressive symptoms in children and adolescents: A longitudinal investigation of parent and child reports. *Journal of Abnormal Psychology, 111,* 156–165.

Cole, P. M. (1986). Children's spontaneous control of facial expression. *Child Development, 57,* 1309–1321.

Cole, P. M., Teti, L. O., & Zahn-Waxler, C. (in press). Mutual emotion regulation and the stability of conduct problems between preschool and early school age. *Development and Psychopathology.*

Conger, R. D., Conger, K. J., Elder, G. H., Lorenz, F. O., Simons, R. L., & Whitbeck, L. B. (1993). Family economic stress and adjustment of early adolescent girls. *Developmental Psychology, 29,* 206–219.

Crawford, T. N., Cohen, P., Midlarsky, E., & Brook, J. S. (2001). Internalizing symptoms in adolescents: Gender differences in vulnerability to parental distress and discord. *Journal of Research on Adolescence, 11,* 95–118.

Crick, N., & Grotpeter, J. K. (1996). Children's treatment by peers: Victims of relational and overt aggression. *Development and Psychopathology, 8,* 367–380.

Cummings, E. M., DeArth-Pendley, G., Schudlich, T. D. R., & Smith, D. A. (2001). Parental depression and family functioning: Toward a process-oriented model of children's adjustment. In S. R. H. Beach (Ed.), *Marital and family processes in depression: A scientific foundation for clinical practice* (pp. 89–110). Washington, DC: American Psychological Association.

Cummings, E. M., Zahn-Waxler, C., & Radke-Yarrow. M. (1981). Young children's responses to expressions of anger and affection by others in the family. *Child Development, 52,* 1274–1282.

Cutler, S. E., & Nolen-Hoeksema, S. (1991). Accounting for sex differences in depression through female victimization: Childhood sexual abuse. *Sex Roles, 24,* 425–438.

Cyranowski, J. M., Frank, E., Young, E., & Shear, M. K. (2000). Adolescent onset of the gender difference in lifetime rates of major depression. *Archives of General Psychiatry, 57,* 21–27.

Dadds, M. R., Atkinson, E., Turner, C., Blums, G. J., & Lendich, B. (1999). Family conflict and child adjustment: Evidence for a cognitive-contextual model of intergenerational transmission. *Journal of Family Psychology, 13,* 194–208.

Damasio, A. R., Tranel, D., & Damasio, H. (1991). Somatic markers and the guidance of behavior: Theory and preliminary testing. In H. S. Levin, H. M. Eisenberg & A. L. Benton (Eds.), *Frontal lobe function and dysfunction* (pp. 217–229). New York: Oxford University Press.

Davidson, R. J. (1994). Asymmetric brain function, affective style, and psychopathology: The role of early experience and plasticity. *Development and Psychopathology, 6,* 741–758.

Davies, P. T., & Windle, M. (1997). Gender-specific pathways between maternal depressive symptoms, family discord, and adolescent adjustment. *Developmental Psychology, 33,* 657–668.

Davis, D., & Padesky, C. (1989). Enhancing cognitive therapy with women. In A. Freeman, & K. M. Simon, L. E. Beutler, & H. Arkowitz (Eds.), *Comprehensive handbook of cognitive therapy* (pp. 535–557). New York: Plenum Press.

Davis, B., Sheeber, L., Hops, H., & Tildesley, E. (2000). Adolescent responses to depressive parental behaviors in problem-solving interactions: Implications for depressive symptoms. *Journal of Abnormal Child Psychology, 5,* 451–465.

Dawson, G., Frey, K., Panagiotides, H., Yamada, E., Hessl, D., & Osterling, J. (1999). Infants of depressed mothers exhibit atypical frontal electrical brain activity during interactions with mother and a familiar, nondepressed adult. *Child Development, 70,* 1058–1066.

Denham, S. A., McKinley, M., Couchard, E. A., & Holt, R. (1990). Emotional and behavioral predictors of preschool peer ratings. *Child Development, 61,* 1145–1152.

Derryberry, D., & Reed, M. A. (1994). Temperament and the self-organization of personality. *Development and Psychopathology, 6,* 653–676.

Diamond, G., & Siqueland, L. (1995). Family therapy for the treatment of depressed adolescents. *Psychotherapy: Theory, Research, Practice, Training, 32,* 77–90.

Dienstbier, R. A. (1984). The role of emotion in moral socialization. In C. Izard, J. Kagan, & R. Zajonc (Eds.), *Emotions, cognition and behavior.* New York: Cambridge University Press.

Donnelly, M., & Wilson, R. (1994). The dimensions of depression in early adolescence. *Personality and Individual Differences, 17,* 425–430.

Downey, G., & Coyne, J. C. (1990). Children of depressed parents: An integrative review. *Psychological Bulletin, 108,* 50–76.

Duggal, S., Carlson, E. A., Sroufe, L. A., & Egeland, B. (2001). Depressive symptomatology in childhood and adolescence. *Development and Psychopathology, 13,* 141–162.

Eisenberg, N., & Fabes, R. A. (1998). Prosocial development. In William Damon (Series Ed.) & N. Eisenberg (Vol. Ed.), *Handbook of child psychology, Vol. 3, Social, emotional, and personality development.* (pp. 701–778), New York: Wiley.

Ellis, B. J., & Garber, J. (2000). Psychosocial antecedents of variations in girls' pubertal timing: Maternal depression, stepfather presence, and marital and family stress. *Child Development, 71,* 485–501.

Essex, M. J., Klein, M. H., Cho, E., & Kraemer, H. C. (2003). Exposure to maternal depression and marital conflict: Gender differences in children's later mental health problems. *Journal of the American Academy of Child and Adolescent Psychiatry, 42,* 728–737.

Fergusson, D. M., Horwood, L. J., & Lynsky, M. T. (1995). Maternal depressive symptoms and depressive symptoms in adolescents. *Journal of Child Psychology and Psychiatry and Allied Disciplines, 36,* 1161–1178.

Fergusson, D. M., Horwood. L. J., & Lynskey, M. T. (1996). Childhood sexual abuse and psychiatric disorder in young adulthood: II. Psychiatric outcomes of childhood sexual abuse. *Journal of the American Academy of Child and Adolescent Psychiatry, 35,* 1365–1374.

Field, T., Diego, M., & Sanders, C. (2001). Adolescent depression and risk factors. *Adolescence, 36,* 491–498.

Field, T., Diego, M., & Sanders, C. (2002). Adolescents' parent and peer relationships. *Adolescence, 37,* 121–130.

Fivush, R. (1989). Exploring sex differences in the emotional content of mother-child conversations about the past. *Sex Roles, 20,* 675–691.

Fivush, R. (1991). Gender and emotion in mother-child conversations about the past. *Journal of Narrative and Life History, 1,* 325–341.

Formoso, D., Gonzales, N. A., & Aiken, L. S. (2000). Family conflict and children's internalizing and externalizing behavior: Protective factors. *American Journal of Community Psychology, 28,* 175–199.

Frank, E., Carpenter, L. L., & Kupfer, D. J. (1987). Sex differences in recurrent depression: Are there any that are significant? *American Journal of Psychiatry, 145,* 41–45.

Frank, E., & Young, E. (2000). Pubertal changes and adolescent challenges: Why do rates of depression rise precipitously for girls between ages 10 and 15 years? In E. Frank (Ed.), *Gender and its effects on psychopathology* (pp. 85–102). Washington, DC: American Psychiatric Press.

Garber, J., Keiley, M., & Martin, N. C. (2002). Developmental trajectories of adolescents' depressive symptoms: Predictors of change. *Journal of Consulting and Clinical Psychology, 70,* 79–95.

Garnefski, N. (2000). Age differences in depressive symptoms, antisocial behavior, and negative perceptions of family, school, and peers among adolescents. *Journal of the American Academy of Child and Adolescent Psychiatry, 39,* 1175–1181.

Ge, X., Best, K., Conger, R. D., & Simons, R. L. (1996). Parenting behaviors and the occurrence and co-occurrence of adolescent depressive symptoms and conduct problems. *Developmental Psychology, 32,* 717–731.

Ge, X., Conger, R. D., & Elder, G. H. (1996). Coming of age too early: Pubertal influences on girls' vulnerability to psychological distress. *Child Development, 67,* 3386–3400.

Ge, X., Lorenz, F. O., Conger, R. D., Elder, G. H., & Simons, R. L. (1994). Trajectories of stressful life events and depressive symptoms during adolescence. *Developmental Psychology, 30,* 467–483.

Gelfand, D. M., & Teti, D. M. (1990). The effects of maternal depression on children. *Clinical Psychology Review, 10,* 329–353.

Gilligan, C. (1982). *In a different voice: Psychological theory and women's development.* Cambridge, MA: Harvard University Press.

Gjerde, P. F. (1995). Alternative pathways to chronic depressive symptoms in young adults: Gender differences in developmental trajectories. *Child Development, 66,* 1277–1300.

Gjerde, P. F., & Block, J. (1996). A developmental perspective on depressive symptoms in adolescence: Gender differences in autocentric-allocentric modes of impulse regulation. In D. Cicchetti & S. Toth (Eds.), *Adolescence: Opportunities and challenges* (Vol. 7, pp. 167–196). Rochester, NY: University of Rochester Press.

Goodman, S. H., & Gotlib, I. H. (1999). Risk for psychopathology in the children of depressed mothers: A developmental model for understanding mechanisms of transition. *Psychological Review, 106,* 458–490.

Goodwin, F. F., & Jamison, K. (1990). *Manic-depressive illness.* New York: Oxford University Press.

Goodyer, I. M. (2001). Life events: Their nature and effects. In I. M. Goodyer (Ed.), *The depressed child and adolescent* (2nd ed., pp. 204–232). New York: Cambridge University Press.

Goodyer, I., Kolvin, I., & Gatzanis, S. (1987). The impact of recent undesirable life events on psychiatric disorders in childhood and adolescence. *British Journal of Psychiatry, 151,* 179–184.

Goodyer, I. M., Tamplin, H.J., & Altham, P. M. E. (2000). Recent life events, cortisol, dehydroepiandrosterone and the onset of major depression in high-risk adolescents. *British Journal of Psychiatry, 177,* 499–504.

Goodyer, I., Wright, C., & Altham, P. (1990). The friendships and recent life events of anxious and depressed school children. *British Journal of Psychiatry, 156,* 689–698.

Gore, S., Aseltine, R. H., & Colton, M. E. (1992). Social structure, life stress, and depressive symptoms in a high school-aged population. *Journal of Health and Social Behavior, 33,* 97–113.

Gore, S., Aseltine, R. H., & Colten, M. E. (1993). Gender, social-relational involvement, and depression. *Journal of Research on Adolescence, 3,* 101–125.

Graber, J. A., Lewinsohn, P. M, Seeley, J. R., & Brooks-Gunn, J. (1997). Is psychopathology associated with the timing of pubertal development? *Journal of the American Academy of Child and Adolescent Psychiatry, 36,* 1768–1776.

Graham, C. A., & Easterbrooks, M. A. (2000). School-aged children's vulnerability to depressive symptomatology: The role of attachment security, maternal depressive symptomatology, and economic risk. *Development and Psychopathology, 12,* 201–213.

Gurian, A. (1987). Depression in young girls: Early sorrows and depressive disorders. In R. Formanek, & A. Gurian, (Ed.), *Women and depression: A lifespan perspective. Springer Series: Focus on women* (Vol. 11, pp. 57–83). New York: Springer.

Hammen, C., Burge, D., Burney, E., & Adrian, C. (1990). Longitudinal study of diagnoses in children of women with unipolar and bipolar affective disorder. *Archives of General Psychiatry, 47,* 1112–1117.

Hankin, B., & Abramson, L.Y. (1999). Development of gender differences in depression: Description and possible explanations. *Annals of Medicine, 31,* 372–379.

Hankin, B. L., & Abramson, L. Y. (2001). Development of gender differences in depression: An elaborated cognitive vulnerability-transactional stress theory. *Psychological Bulletin, 127,* 773–796.

Hankin, B. L., Abramson, L. Y., Moffitt, T. E., Silva, P. A., & McGee, R. (1998). Development of depression from preadolescence to young adulthood: Emerging gender differences in a 10-year longitudinal study. *Journal of Abnormal Psychology, 107,* 128–140.

Harrington, J. A., & Blankenship, V. (2002). Ruminative thoughts and their relation to depression and anxiety. *Journal of Applied Social Psychology, 32,* 465–485.

Harrington, R., Fudge, H., Rutter, M., Pickles, A., & Hill, J. (1990). Adult outcomes of childhood and adolescent depression: Psychiatric status. *Archives of General psychiatry, 47,* 465–473.

Hart, B. I., & Thompson, J. M. (1996). Gender role characteristics and depressive symptomatology among adolescents. *Journal of Early Adolescence, 16,* 407–426.

Harter, S. (1993). Vision of self: Beyond the me in the mirror. In R. Dienstbier (Ed.), *Nebraska Symposium on Motivation:* Vol. 40. *Developmental Perspectives on Motivation* (pp. 99–144). Lincoln: University of Nebraska Press.

Harter, S., Waters, P. L., Whitesell. N. R., & Kastilic, D. (1998). Level of voice among high-school females and males: Relational context, support, and gender orientation. *Developmental Psychology, 34,* 892–901.

Hay, D. H., Zahn-Waxler, C., Cummings, E. M., & Iannotti, R. J. (1992). Young children's views about conflict with peers: A comparison of the daughters and sons of depressed and well women. *Journal of Child Psychology and Psychiatry, 33,* 669–683.

Hayward, C., Gotlib, I. H., Schraedley, P. K., & Litt, I. F. (1999). Ethnic differences in the association between pubertal status and symptoms of depression in adolescent girls. *Journal of Adolescent Health, 25,* 143–149.

Hayward, C., Killen, J. D., Wilson, D. M., Hammer, L. D., Litt, I. F., Kraemer, H. C., et al. (1997). Psychiatric risk associated with early puberty in adolescent girls. *Journal of the American Academy of Child and Adolescent Psychiatry, 36,* 255–262.

Hecht, D. B., Inderbitzen, H. M., & Bukowski, A. L. (1998). The relationship between peer status and depressive symptoms in children and adolescents. *Journal of Abnormal Child Psychology, 26,* 153–160.

Heller, W. (1990). The neuropsychology of emotion. Developmental patterns and implications for psychopathology. In N. L. Stein, B. Leventhal, & T. Trabasso (Eds.), *Biological and psychological approaches to emotion* (pp. 167–211). Hillsdale, NJ: Erlbaum.

Heller, W. (1993). Gender differences in depression: Perspectives from neuropsychology. *Journal of Affective Disorders, 29,* 129–143.

Hill, J. P., & Lynch, M. E. (1983). The intensification of gender-related role expectations during early adolescence. In J. Brooks-Gunn & A. Petersen (Eds.), *Girls at puberty: Biological and psychosocial perspectives* (pp. 201–228). New York: Plenum Press.

Hops, H. (1996). Intergenerational transmission of depressive symptoms: Gender and developmental considerations. In C. Mundt & M. J. Goldstein (Eds.), *Interpersonal factors in the origin and course of affective disorders* (pp. 113–129). London, England: Gaskell/Royal College of Psychiatrists.

Huselid, R. F., & Cooper, M. L. (1994). Gender roles as mediators of sex differences in expressions of pathology. *Journal of Abnormal Psychology, 103,* 595–603.

Ialongo, N., Edelsohn, G., Werthamer-Larrson, Crockett, L., et al. (1995). The significance of self reported anxious symptoms in first grade children: Prediction to anxious symptoms and adaptive functioning in first grade. *Journal of Child Psychology & Psychiatry & Allied Disciplines, 36,* 427–37.

Jack, D. C. (1991). *Silencing the self: Women and depression.* Cambridge, MA: Harvard University Press.

Jaycox, L. H., Reivich, K., Gillham, J., & Seligman, M. E. P. (1994). Prevention of depressive symptoms in children. *Behavior Research and Therapy, 32,* 801–816.

Jolly, J. B., Wiesner, D. C., Wherry, J. N., Jolly, J. M., & Dykman, R. A. (1994). Gender and the comparison of self and observer ratings of anxiety and depression in adolescents. *Journal of the American Academy of Child and Adolescent Psychiatry, 33,* 1284–1288.

Kagan, J., Resnick, J. S., & Snidman, N. (1988). Biological bases of childhood shyness. *Science, 240,* 167–171.

Kagan, J., & Snidman, N. (1999). Early childhood predictors of adult anxiety disorders. *Biological Psychiatry, 46,* 1536–1541.

Karbon, M., Fabes, R. A., Carlo, G., & Martin, C. L. (1992). Preschoolers' beliefs about sex and age differences in emotionality. *Sex Roles, 27,* 377–390.

Kashani, J. H., & Carlson, G. A. (1987). Seriously depressed preschoolers. *American Journal of Psychiatry, 144,* 348–350.

Kashani, J. H., Holcomb, W. R., & Orvaschel, H. (1986). Depression and depressive symptoms in preschool children from the general population. *American Journal of Psychiatry, 143,* 1138–1143.

Kavanagh, K., & Hops, H. (1994). Good girls? Bad boys? Gender and development as contexts for diagnosis. In T. H. Ollendick & R. J. Prinz (Eds.), *Advances in Clinical Child Psychology,* (Vol. 16, pp. 45–79). New York: Plenum.

Keenan, K. (2000). Emotion dysregulation as a risk factor for child psychopathology. *Clinical Psychology—Science and Practice, 7,* 418–434.

Keenan, K., & Shaw, D. (1997). Developmental and social influences on young girls' early problem behavior. *Psychological Bulletin, 121,* 95–113.

Kendler, K. S. (1998). Major depression and the environment: A psychiatric genetic perspective. *Pharmacopsychiatry, 31,* 5–9.

Kendler, K. S., Bulik, C. M., Silberg, J., Hettema, J. M., Myers, J., & Prescott, C. A. (2000). Childhood sexual abuse and adult psychiatric and substance use disorders in women: An epidemiological and cotwin control analysis. *Archives of General Psychiatry, 57,* 953–959.

Kendler, K. S., & Gardner, C. O. (2001). Monozygotic twins discordant for major depression: A preliminary exploration of the role of environmental experiences in the aetiology and course of illness. *Psychological Medicine, 31,* 411–423.

Kendler, K. S., Gardner, C. O., Neale, M. C., & Prescott, C. A. (2001). Genetic risk factors for major depression in men and women: Similar or different heritabilities and same or partly distinct genes? *Psychological Medicine, 31,* 605–616.

Kendler, K. S., & Karkowski-Shuman, L. (1997). Stressful life events and genetic liability to major depression: Genetic control of exposure to the environment? *Psychological Medicine, 27,* 539–547.

Kendler, K. S., Karkowski, L. M., & Prescott, C. A. (1999). Causal relationship between stressful life events and the onset of major depression. *American Journal of Psychiatry, 156,* 837–841.

Kendler, K. S., Kessler, R. C., Walters, E. E., MacLean, C., Neale, M. C., Heath, A. C., et al. (1995). Stressful life events, genetic liability, and onset of an episode of major depression. *American Journal of Psychiatry, 152,* 833–842.

Kendler, K. S., Neale, M. C., Kessler, R. C., Heath, A. C., & Eaves, L. J. (1993). The lifetime history of major depressive disorder in women: Reliability of diagnosis and heritability. *Archives of General Psychiatry, 50,* 863–870.

Kendler, K. S., & Prescott, C. A. (1999). A population-based twin study of lifetime major depression in men and women. *Archives of General Psychiatry, 56,* 39–44.

Kendler, K. S., Thornton, L. M., & Gardner, C. O. (2000). Stressful life events and previous episodes in the etiology of major depression in women: An evaluation of the "kindling" hypothesis. *American Journal of Psychiatry, 157,* 1243–1251.

Kendler, K. S., Thornton, L. M., & Prescott, C. A. (2001). Gender differences in the rates of exposure to stressful life events and sensitivity to their depressogenic effects. *American Journal of Psychiatry, 158,* 587–593.

Kendler, K. S., Walters, E. E., Truett, K. R., Heath, A. C., Neale, M. C., Martin, N. G., et al. (1994). Sources of individual differences in depressive symptoms: Analysis of two samples of twins and their families. *American Journal of Psychiatry, 151,* 1605–1614.

Kerig, P. K., Cowan, P. A., & Cowan, C. P. (1993). Marital quality and gender differences in parent-child interaction. *Developmental Psychology, 29,* 931–939.

Kessler, R. C., McGonagle, K. A., Swartz, M., Blazer, D. G., & Nelson, C. B. (1993). Sex and depression in the National Comorbidity Survey I: Lifetime prevalence, chronicity and recurrence. *Journal of Affective Disorders, 29*, 85–96.

Kleinman, A., & Cohen, A. (1997). Psychiatry's global challenge. *Scientific American*, 86–89.

Klimes-Dougan, B., & Bolger (1998). Coping with maternal depressed affect and depression: Adolescent children of depressed and well mothers. *Journal of Youth and Adolescence, 27*, 1–15.

Klimes-Dougan, B., Hastings, P. D., Granger, D. A., Usher, B. A., & Zahn-Waxler, C. (2001). Adrenocortical activity in at-risk and normally developing adolescents: Individual differences in salivary cortisol basal levels, diurnal variation, and responses to social challenges. *Development and Psychopathology, 13*, 695–719.

Kochanska, G., DeVet, K., Goldman, M., Murray, K., & Putnam, S. P. (1994). Maternal reports of conscience development and temperament in young children. *Child Development, 65*, 852–868.

Kornstein, S. G. (2001). The evaluation and management of depression in women across the life span. *Journal of Clinical Psychiatry, 62*, 11–17.

Kornstein, S. G., & McEnany, G. (2000). Enhancing pharmacologic effects in the treatment of depression in women. *Journal of Clinical Psychiatry, 61*, 18–27.

Kornstein, S. G., Schatzberg, A. F., Thase, M. E., Yonkers, K. A., McCullough, J. P., Keitner, G. I., et al. (2000). Gender differences in chronic major and double depression. *Journal of Affective Disorders, 60*, 1–11.

Kornstein, S. G., Schatzberg, A. F., Yonkers, K. A., Thase, M. E., Keitner, G. I., Ryan, C. E., et al. (1995). Gender differences in presentation of chronic major depression. *Psychopharmacology Bulletin, 31*, 711–718.

Kovacs, M., Gatsonis, C., Paulauskas, S. L. & Richards, C. (1989). Depressive disorders in childhood: IV. A longitudinal study of comorbidity with and risk for anxiety disorders. *Archives of General Psychiatry, 46*, 776–782.

Kovacs. M., Obrosky, D. S., Scott, D. & Sherrill, J. (2003). Developmental changes in the phenomenology of depression in girls compared to boys from childhood onward. *Journal of Affective Disorders, 74*, 33–48.

Kovacs, M., Rush, A. J., Beck, A. T., & Hollon, S. D. (1981). Depressed outpatients treated with cognitive therapy or pharmacotherapy. *Archives of General Psychiatry, 38*, 33–39.

Kovacs, M., & Sherrill, J. T. (2001). The psychotherapeutic management of major depressive and dysthymic disorders in childhood and adolescence: Issues and prospects. In I. M. Goodyer (Ed.), *The depressed child and adolescent* (2nd ed., pp. 325–352). Cambridge, MA: Cambridge University Press.

Lahmeyer, H. W., & Bellur, S. N. (1987). Cardiac regulation and depression. *Journal of Psychiatric Research, 21*, 1–6.

Leadbeater, B. J., Blatt, S. J., & Quinlan, D. M. (1995). Gender-linked vulnerabilities to depressive symptoms, stress, and problem behaviors in adolescents. *Journal of Research in Adolescence, 51*, 1–29.

Leadbeater, B. J., Kuperminc, G. P., Blatt, S. J., & Hertzog, C. (1999). A multivariate model of gender differences in adolescents' internalizing and externalizing problems. *Developmental Psychology*, 1268–1282.

Lewinsohn, P. M., & Gotlib, I. H. (1995). Behavioral theory and treatment of depression. In E. E. Beckham & W. R. Leber (Eds.), *Handbook of Depression* (2nd Ed., pp. 539–566). New York: Guilford.

Lewinsohn, P. M., Gotlib, I. H., Lewinsohn, M., Seeley, J. R., & Allan, N. B. (1998). Gender differences in anxiety disorders and anxiety symptoms in adolescents. *Journal of Abnormal Psychology, 107*, 109–117.

Lewinsohn, P. M., Gotlib, I. H., & Seeley, J. R. (1995). Adolescent psychopathology: IV. Specificity of psychosocial risk factors for depression and substance abuse in older adolescents. *Journal of the American Academy of Child and Adolescent Psychiatry, 34*, 1221–1229.

Lewinsohn, P. M., Hops, H., Roberts, R. E., Seeley, J. R., & Andrews, J. A. (1993). Adolescent psychopathology: I. Prevalence and incidence of depression and other DSM-III-R disorders in high school students. *Journal of Abnormal Psychology, 102*, 133–144.

Lewinsohn, P. M., Rohde, P., & Seeley, J. R. (1995). Adolescent psychopathology: III. The clinical consequences of comorbidity. *Journal of the American Academy of Child and Adolescent Psychiatry, 34,* 510–519.

Lewinsohn, P. M., Rohde, P., & Seeley, J. R. (1998). Major depressive disorder in older adolescents: Prevalence, risk factors, and clinical implications. *Clinical Psychology Review, 18,* 765–794.

Lewinsohn, P. M., Zinbarg, R., Seeley, J. R., Lewinsohn, M., & Sack, W. H. (1997). Lifetime comorbidity among anxiety disorders and between anxiety disorders and other mental disorders in adolescents. *Journal of Anxiety Disorders, 11,* 377–394.

Loeber, R., & Keenan, K. (1994). The interaction between conduct disorder and its comorbid conditions: Effects of age and gender. *Clinical Psychology Review, 14,* 497–523.

Lopez, S. R. (1989). Patient variable biases in clinical judgment: Conceptual overview and methodological considerations. *Psychological Bulletin, 106,* 184–203.

Loring, M., & Powell, B. (1988). Gender, race, and DSM-III: A study of the objectivity of psychiatric diagnostic behavior. *Journal of Health and Social Behavior, 29,* 1–22.

Maccoby, E. E. (1990). Gender and relationships: A developmental account. *American Psychologist, 45,* 513–520.

Maier, S., & Seligman, M. E. P. (1976). Learned helplessness: Theory and evidence. *Journal of Experimental Psychology: General, 105,* 3–46.

Malatesta, C. Z., & Haviland, J. (1982). Learning display rules: The socialization of emotion expression in infancy. *Child Development, 53,* 991–1003.

Mazure, C. M., Keita, G. P., & Blehar, M. C. (2002). *Summit on women and depression: Proceedings and recommendations.* Washington, DC: American Psychological Association.

McCauley, E., Myers, K., Mitchell, J., Calderon, R., Schloredt, K., & Treder, R., (1993). Depression in young people: Initial presentation and clinical course. *Journal of the American Academy of Child and Adolescent Psychiatry, 32,* 714–722.

McCauley, E., Pavlidis, K., & Kendall, K. (2001). Developmental precursors of depression: The child and the social environment. In I. M. Goodyer (Ed.), *The depressed child and adolescent* (2nd ed., pp. 46–78). New York: Cambridge University Press.

McClelland, G. H., & Judd, C. M. (1993). Statistical difficulties of detecting interactions and moderator effects. *Psychological Bulletin, 114,* 376–390.

McFarlane, A. H., Bellissimo, A., & Norman, G. R. (1995). The role of family and peers in social self-efficacy: Links to depression in adolescence. *American Journal of Orthopsychiatry, 65,* 402–410.

McGrath, E., Keita, G. P., Strickland, B. R., & Russo, N. F. (1990). *Women and depression: Risk factors and treatment issues.* Washington, DC: American Psychological Association.

Meyersberg, H. A., & Post, R. M. (1979). A holistic developmental view of neural and psychological processes. *British Journal of Psychiatry, 135,* 139–155.

Miller, A., Fox, N. A., Cohn, J. F., Forbes, E. E., Sherrill, J. T., & Kovacs, M. (2002). Regional patterns of brain activity in adults with a history of childhood-onset depression: Gender differences and clinical variability. *American Journal of Psychiatry, 159,* 934–940.

Mineka, S., & Henderson, R. (1985). Controllability and predictability in acquired motivation. *Annual Review of Psychology, 36,* 495–529.

Mirowsky, J., & Ross, C.E. (1984). Mexican culture and its emotional contradictions. *Journal of Health and Social Behavior, 25,* 2–13.

Moffitt, T. E., Caspi, A., Belsky, J., & Silva, P. A. (1992). Childhood experience and the onset of menarche: A test of a sociobiological model. *Child Development, 63,* 47–58.

Mufson, L., Moreau, D., & Weissman, M. M. (1996). Focus on relationships: Interpersonal therapy for depressed adolescents. In Hibbs, E. D. & Jensen, P. S. (Eds.), *Psychosocial treatments for child and adolescent disorders: Empirically based strategies for clinical practice.* (pp. 137–155). Washington, DC: American Psychological Association.

Mufson, L., Weissman, M. M., Moreau, D., & Garfinkel, P. (1999). Efficacy of interpersonal psychotherapy for depressed adolescents. *Archives of General Psychiatry, 56,* 573–579.

Neary, A., & Joseph, S. (1994). Peer victimization and its relationship to self-concept and depression among schoolgirls. *Personality and Individual Differences, 16,* 183–186.

Nguyen, H. H., Messe, L. A., & Stollak, G. E. (1999). Toward a more complex understanding of acculturation and adjustment: Cultural involvements and psychosocial functioning in Vietnamese youth. *Journal of Cross-Cultural Psychology, 30,* 5–31.

Nolen-Hoeksema, S. (1987). Sex differences in unipolar depression: Evidence and theory. *Psychological Bulletin, 101,* 259–282.

Nolen-Hoeksema, S. (1990). *Sex differences in depression.* Stanford, CA: Stanford University Press.

Nolen-Hoeksema, S. (1991). Responses to depression and their effects on the duration of depressive episodes. *Journal of Abnormal Psychology, 100,* 569–582.

Nolen-Hoeksema, S., & Girgus, J. S. (1994). The emergence of gender differences in depression during adolescence. *Psychological Bulletin, 115,* 424–443.

Nolen-Hoeksema, S., Larson, J., & Grayson, C. (1999). Explaining the gender difference in depressive symptoms. *Journal of Personality and Social Psychology, 77,* 1061–1072.

Nottlemann, E. D., & Jensen, P. S. (1995). Comorbidity of disorders in children and adolescents: Developmental perspectives. *Advances in Clinical Child Psychology, 17,* 424–443.

Ohannessian, C. M., Lerner, R. M., Lerner, J. V., & von Eye, A. (1994). A longitudinal study of perceived family adjustment and emotional adjustment in early adolescence. *Journal of Early Adolescence, 14,* 371–390.

Overmier, J. B., & Seligman, M. E. P. (1967) Effects of inescapable shock upon subsequent escape and avoidance responding. *Journal of Comparative and Physiological Psychology, 63,* 28–33.

Paikoff, R. L., Brooks-Gunn, J., & Warren, M. P. (1991). Effects of girls' hormonal status on depressive and aggressive symptoms over the course of one year. *Journal of Youth and Adolescence, 20,* 191–215.

Parker, S., Nichter, M., Nichter, M., Vuckovic, N., Sims, C., & Ritenbaugh, C. (1995). Body image and weight concerns among African American and White adolescent females: Differences that make a difference. *Human Organization, 54,* 103–114.

Petersen, A. C., Leffert, N., Graham, B., Alwin, J., & Ding S. (1997). Promoting mental health during the transition into adolescence. In J. Schulenberg & J. L. Maggs (Eds.), *Health Risks and developmental transitions during adolescence* (pp.471–497). New York: Cambridge University Press.

Petersen, A. C., Sarigiani, P. A., & Kennedy, R. E. (1991). Adolescent depression: Why more girls? *Journal of Youth and Adolescence, 20,* 247–271.

Piccinelli, M., & Wilkinson, G. (2000). Gender differences in depression: Critical review. *British Journal of Psychiatry, 177,* 486–492.

Plomin, R. (1994). Genetic research and the identification of environmental illnesses. *Journal of Child Psychology and Psychiatry and Allied Disciplines, 35,* 817–834.

Post, R. M., Weiss, S. R. B., Leverich, G. S., George, M. S., Frye, M., & Ketter, T. A. (1996). Developmental psychobiology of cyclic affective illness: Implications for early therapeutic intervention. *Development and Psychopathology, 8,* 273–305.

Potts, M. K., Burnam, M. A., & Wells, K. B. (1991). Gender differences in depression detection: A comparison of clinician diagnosis and standardized assessment. *Psychological Assessment, 3,* 609–615.

Powers, S. I., & Welsh, D. P. (1999). Mother-daughter interactions and adolescent girls' depression. In M. Cox & J. Brooks-Gunn (Eds.), *Conflict and closeness: The formation, functioning, and stability of families* (pp. 243–281). Mahwah, NJ: Erlbaum.

Poznanski, E. O., & Mokros, H. B. (1994). Phenomenology and epidemiology of mood disorders in children and adolescents. In W. M. Reynolds & H. F. Johnston (Eds.), *Handbook of depression in children and adolescents: Issues in clinical child psychology* (pp. 19–39). New York: Plenum.

Radke-Yarrow, M., Zahn-Waxler, C., Richardson, D. T., Susman, A., & Martinez, P. (1994). Caring behavior in children of clinically depressed and well mothers. *Child Development, 65,* 1405–1414.

Rende, R. D., Plomin, R., Reiss, D., & Hetherington, E. M. (1993). Genetic and environmental influences on depressive symptomatology in adolescence: Individual differences and extreme scores. *Journal of Consulting and Clinical Psychology, 34,* 1387–1398.

Roberts, R. E., Roberts, C. R., & Chen, Y. R. (1997). Ethnocultural differences in prevalence of adolescent depression. *American Journal of Community Psychology, 25,* 95–110.

Roberts, R. W., Andrews, J. A., Lewinsohn, P. M., & Hops, H. (1990). Assessment of depression in adolescents using the Center for Epidemiologic Studies Depression Scale. *Psychological Assessment, 2*, 122–128.

Rose, A. J. (2002). Co-rumination in the friendships of girls and boys. *Child Development, 73*, 1830–1843.

Ross, C. E., Mirowsky, J., & Cockerham, W. C. (1983). Social class, Mexican culture, and fatalism: Their effects on psychological distress. *American Journal of Community Psychology, 11*, 383–399.

Ross, H., Telsa, C., Kenyon, B., & Lollis, S. (1990). Maternal intervention in toddler peer conflict: The socialization of principles of justice. *Developmental Psychology, 26*, 994–1003.

Rothbart, M. K., Ahadi, S. A., & Hershey, K. L. (1994). Temperament and social behavior in childhood. *Merrill-Palmer Quarterly, 40*, 21–39.

Rudolph, K. D., Hammen, C., Burge, D., Lindberg, N., Herzberg, D., & Daley, S. E. (2000). Toward an interpersonal life-stress model of depression: The developmental context of stress generation. *Development and Psychopathology, 12*, 215–234.

Ryan, N. D., & Dahl, R. E. (1993). The biology of depression in children and adolescents. In J. J. Mann & D. H. Kupfer (Eds.) *Biology of depressive disorders, Part B: Subtypes of depression and comorbid disorders. The depressive illness series* (Vol. 4, pp. 37–58). New York: Plenum.

Saarni, C. (1984). An observational study of children's attempts to monitor their expressive behavior. *Child Development, 55*, 1504–1513.

Sabatelli, R. M., & Anderson, S. A. (1991). Family system dynamics, peer relationships, and adolescents' psychological adjustment. *Family Relations, 40*, 363–369.

Santor, D., Ramsay, J. O., & Zuroff, D. C. (1994). Nonparametric item analyses of the Beck Depression Inventory: Evaluating gender item bias and response option weights. *Psychological Assessment, 6*, 255–270.

Schmidt, L. A., Fox, N. A., Rubin, K. H., Sternberg, E., Gold, P. W., Smith, C. C., et al. (1997). Behavioral and neuroendocrine responses in shy children. *Developmental Psychobiology, 30*, 127–140.

Schwartz, C. E., Snidman, N., & Kagan, J. (1999). Adolescent social anxiety as an outcome of inhibited temperament in childhood. *Journal of the American Academy of Child and Adolescent Psychiatry, 38*, 1008–1015.

Schwartz, J. A., Kaslow, N. J., Racusin, G. R., & Carton, E. R. (1998). Interpersonal family therapy for childhood depression. In Van Hasselt, V. B. & Hersen, M. (Eds.), *Handbook of psychological treatment protocols for children and adolescents.* Mahwah, NJ: Erlbaum.

Seligman, M. E. P., Peterson, C., Kaslow, N., Tanenbaum, R. L., Alloy, L. B., & Abramson, L. Y. (1984). Attributional style and depressive symptoms among children. *Journal of Abnormal Psychology, 93*, 235–238.

Serbin, L. A., Sprafkin, C., Elman, M., & Doyle, A. (1984). The early development of sex differentiated patterns of social influence. *Canadian Journal of Social Science, 14*, 350–363.

Shiner, R. L., & Marmorstein, N. R. (1998). Family environments of adolescents with lifetime depression. *Journal of the American Academy of Child and Adolescent Psychiatry, 37*, 1152–1160.

Silberg, J., Pickles, A., Rutter, M., Hewitt, J., Simonoff, E., Maes, H., et al. (1999). The influence of genetic factors and life stress on depression among adolescent girls. *Archives of General Psychiatry, 56*, 225–232.

Silberg, J., Rutter, M., Neale, M., & Eaves, L. (2001). Genetic moderation of environmental risk for depression and anxiety in adolescent girls. *British Journal of Psychiatry, 179*, 116–121.

Silverman, W. K., La Greca, A. M., & Wasserstein, S. (1995). What do children worry about? Worries and their relation to anxiety. *Child Development, 66*, 671–686.

Simmons, R. G., & Blyth, D. A. (1987). Moving into adolescence: The impact of pubertal change and school context. New York: Aldine de Gruyter.

Simmons, R. G., Burgeson, R., & Carlton-Ford, S. (1987). The impact of cumulative change in early adolescence. *Child Development, 58*, 1220–1234.

Simpson, A. E., & Stevenson-Hinde, J. (1985). Temperamental characteristics of three-to-four-year-old boys and girls and child-family interactions. *Journal of Child Psychology and Psychiatry, 26,* 43–53.

Sitarenios, G., & Kovacs, M. (1999). Use of the Children's Depression Inventory. In M. E. Maruish (Ed.), *The use of psychological testing for treatment planning and outcomes assessment* (2nd ed., pp. 267–298). Mahwah, NJ: Erlbaum.

Smetana, J. G. (1989). Toddlers' social interactions in the context of moral and conventional transgressions in the home. *Developmental Psychology, 25,* 499–509.

Smider, N. A., Essex, M. J., Kalin, N. H., Buss, K. A., Klein, M. H., Davidson, R. J., et al. (2002). Salivary cortisol as a predictor of socioemotional adjustment during kindergarten: A prospective study. *Child Development, 73,* 75–92.

Smucker, M. R., Craighead, W. E., Craighead, L. W., & Green, B. J. (1986). Normative and reliability data for the Children's Depression Inventory. *Journal of Abnormal Child Psychology, 14,* 25–39.

Sroufe, L. A., & Rutter, M. (1984). The domain of developmental psychopathology. *Child Development, 55,* 17–29.

Stark, K. D., Reynolds, W. M., & Kaslow, N. J. (1987). A comparison of the relative efficacy of self-control therapy and a behavioral problem-solving therapy for depression in children. *Journal of Abnormal Child Psychology, 15,* 91–113.

Stattin, H., & Magnusson, D. (1990). *Pubertal maturation in female development.* Hillsdale, NJ: Erlbaum.

Stice, E., & Bearman, S. K. (2001). Body-image and eating disturbances prospectively predict increases in depressive symptoms in adolescent girls: A growth curve analysis. *Developmental Psychology, 37,* 597–607.

Stice, E., Presnell, K., & Bearman, S. K. (2001). Relation of early menarche to depression, eating disorders, substance abuse, and comorbid psychopathology among adolescent girls. *Developmental Psychology, 37,* 608–619.

Strober, M. (2001). Family-genetic aspects of juvenile affective disorders. In I. M. Goodyer (Ed.). *The depressed child and adolescent* (2nd ed., pp. 179–203). Cambridge, MA: Cambridge University Press.

Sullivan, P. F., Neale, M. C., & Kendler, K. S. (2000). Genetic epidemiology of major depression: Review and meta-analysis. *American Journal of Psychiatry, 157,* 1552–1562.

Thorell, L. H., Kjellman, B. F., & D'Elia, G. (1987). Electrodermal activity in antidepressant medicated and unmedicated depressive patients and in healthy matched subjects. *Acta Psychiatrica Scandinavica, 76,* 684–692.

Vuchinich, S., Emery, R., & Cassidy, J. (1988). Family members as third parties in dyadic family conflict: Strategies, alliances and outcomes. *Child Development, 59,* 1293–1302.

Warner, V., Weissman, M. M., Mufson, L., & Wickramaratne, P. J. (1999). Grandparents, parents and grandchildren at high risk for depression: A three-generation study. *Journal of the American Academy of Child and Adolescent Psychiatry, 38,* 289–296.

Weiss, E. L., Longhurst, J. G., & Mazure, C. M. (1999). Childhood sexual abuse as a risk factor for depression in women: Psychosocial and neurobiological correlates. *American Journal of Psychiatry, 156,* 816–828.

Weissman, M. M., Bland, R. C., Canino, G. J., Faravelli, C., Greenwald, S., et al. (1996). Cross-national epidemiology of Major Depression and Bipolar Disorder. *Journal of the American Medical Association, 276,* 293–299.

Weissman, M. M., & Klerman, G. L. (1978). Epidemiology of mental disorders. *Archives of General Psychiatry, 35,* 705–712.

Weissman, M. M., Klerman, G. L., Prusoff, B. A., Sholomskas, D., & Padian, N. (1981). Depressed outpatients: Results one year after treatment with drugs and/or interpersonal psychotherapy. *Archives of General Psychiatry, 38,* 51–55.

Weissman, M. M., Leaf, P. J., Bruce, M. L., & Florio, L. (1988). The epidemiology of dysthymia in five communities: Rates, risks, comorbidity, and treatment. *American Journal of Psychiatry, 145,* 815–819.

Whiffen, V. E., & Clark, S. E. (1997). Does victimization account for sex differences in depressive symptoms? *British Journal of Clinical Psychology, 36,* 185–193.

Wichstrom, L. (1999). The emergence of gender differences in depressed mood during adolescence: The role of intensified gender socialization. *Developmental Psychology, 35,* 232–245.

Williamson, D. E., Birmaher, B., Anderson, B. P., Al-Shabbout, M., & Ryan, N. D. (1995). Stressful life events in depressed adolescents: The role of dependent events during the depressive episode. *Journal of the American Academy of Child and Adolescent Psychiatry, 3,* 591–598.

Williamson, D. E., Birmaher, B., Frank, E., Anderson, B. P., Matty, M. K., & Kupfer, D. J. (1998). Nature of life events and difficulties in depressed adolescents. *Journal of the American Academy of Child and Adolescent Psychiatry, 37,* 1049–1057.

Wong, S. (2001). Depression level in inner-city Asian American adolescents: The contributions of cultural orientation and interpersonal relationships. *Journal of Human Behavior in the Social Environment, 3,* 49–64.

Young, M. A., Fogg, L. F., Scheftner, W. A., Keller, M. B., & Fawcett, J. A. (1990). Sex differences in the lifetime prevalence of depression: Does varying the diagnostic criteria reduce the female/male ratio? *Journal of Affective Disorders, 18,* 187–192.

Young, M. A., Scheftner, W. A., Fawcett, J., & Klerman, G. L. (1990). Gender differences in the clinical features of unipolar major depressive disorder. *The Journal of Nervous and Mental Disease, 178,* 200–203.

Zahn-Waxler, C. (1993). Warriors and worriers: Gender and psychopathology. *Development and Psychopathology, 5,* 79–89.

Zahn-Waxler, C. (2000). The development of empathy, guilt, and the internalization of distress: Implications for gender differences in internalizing and externalizing problems. In R. Davidson (Ed.), *Anxiety, depression, and emotion* (pp. 222–265). New York: Oxford University Press.

Zahn-Waxler, C., Cole, P. M., & Barrett, K.C. (1991). Guilt and empathy: Sex differences and implications for the development of depression. In J. Garber & K. A. Dodge (Eds.), *Emotional regulation and dysregulation* (pp. 243–272). Cambridge, England: Cambridge University Press.

Zahn-Waxler, C., Cole, P. M., Richardson, D. T., Friedman, R. J., Michel, M. K., & Belouad, F. (1994). Social problem-solving in disruptive preschool children: reactions to hypothetical situations of conflict and distress. *Merrill-Palmer Quarterly, 40,* 98–119.

Zahn-Waxler, C., Cole, P. M., Welsh, J. D., & Fox, N. A. (1995). Psycho-physiological correlates of empathy and prosocial behaviors in preschool children with behavior problems. *Development and Psychopathology, 7,* 27–48.

Zahn-Waxler, C., & Kochanska, G. (1990). The development of guilt. In R. Thompson (Ed.), *Nebraska Symposium on Motivation, 1988: Socioemotional development* (Vol. 36, pp. 183–258). Lincoln: University of Nebraska Press.

Zahn-Waxler. C., Kochanska, G., Krupnick, J., & McKnew, D. (1990). The development of guilt in children of depressed and well mothers. *Developmental Psychology, 26,* 51–59.

Zahn-Waxler, C., & Robinson, J. (1995). Empathy and guilt: early origins of feelings of responsibility. In K. Fisher & J. Tangney (Eds.), *Self-conscious emotions: Shame, guilt, embarrassment, and pride* (pp. 143–173). New York: Guilford.

Zahn-Waxler, C., Robinson, J., & Emde, R. N. (1992). The development of empathy in twins. *Developmental Psychology, 28,* 1038–1047.

Zahn-Waxler, C., Robinson, J., Schmitz, S., Emde, R. N., & Fulker, D. (1996). Behavior problems in five-year-old MZ and DZ twins: Genetic and environmental influences, patterns of regulation and control. *Development and Psychopathology, 8,* 103–122.

Zeman, J., & Garber J. (1996). Display rules for anger, sadness and pain: It depends on who is watching. *Child Development, 67,* 957–973.

Zeman, J., & Shipman, K. (1997). Social-contextual influences on expectancies for managing anger and sadness: The transition from middle childhood to adolescence. *Developmental Psychology, 33,* 917–924.

Zeman, J., & Shipman, K. (1998). Influence of social context on children's affect regulation: A functionalist perspective. *Journal of Nonverbal Behavior, 22,* 11–165.

3

Anxiety and Anxiety Disorders in Girls

ANNE MARIE ALBANO and AMY KRAIN

Throughout the course of the 20th century the role of women in society has evidenced dramatic changes that continue through the present day. During this time period, American women were finally granted valuable civil rights and the power to make decisions for themselves. Many women rose into positions of authority and control in nearly every field, from business and industry, to education, government and law, medicine, science, and beyond. The range of lifestyle choices also became more open for women, a clear and distinct change from eras past. Indeed, girls need look no further than the popular media to find female role models representing the range of lifestyle and career choices before them, from Maya Angelou to Sally Ride, Madonna to Ruth Bader Ginsburg, Hillary Clinton to Mia Hamm. It is unclear, however, whether these welcome and hard-fought choices have also ushered in a range of stressors and risks to girls' physical and emotional health that were unknown to our foremothers during their early years of development. In this chapter we explore a well-documented but poorly understood phenomenon, that girls and women evidence higher rates of many fears and anxiety disorders than their male peers.

BRIEF HISTORICAL CONTEXT OF ANXIETY DISORDERS IN FEMALES

There are perhaps two infamous women well known for their anxiety reactions. The first, Lady Macbeth, was fictional but immortalized by William Shakespeare in his classic play, *Macbeth.* Haunted by the knowledge of her role in the death of King Duncan, Lady Macbeth's anxiety was

ANNE MARIE ALBANO • Columbia University, New York, NY, 10032-2626. AMY KRAIN • New York University School of Medicine, New York, NY, 10016.

expressed through compulsive handwashing, a symbolic attempt to rid herself of her anxiety and guilt. Interestingly, Shakespeare created Lady Macbeth well before the science of epidemiology was founded, so his portrayal of her suffering was based on his own observations of human nature and embellished with the use of literary devices. The second woman who is best remembered for her anxiety states was Bertha Pappenheim, a young woman who lived into the early 1900s. Bertha Pappenheim may well be responsible for Freud's conceptualization of unconscious conflict as the primary cause of human anxiety and emotional suffering. Better known as Anna O., Ms. Pappenheim was a patient of Freud and Josef Breuer, and suffered with a range of physiological and psychological symptoms including paralysis, tics, speech anomalies, and "nervous" coughs. The study of Anna O. was significant to Freud's theory and model of hysteria, which established certain symptomatology associated with pathological anxiety states as decidedly "feminine." These are two "classic" examples of how women typically are portrayed in literature and the media, and how being female is widely associated throughout Western culture with being more anxious, guilt-ridden, obsessed, and fragile, than men.

Historically, research on gender variations in anxiety disorders has been circumscribed to epidemiological studies evaluating differences between males and females for prevalence rates of fears and various anxiety disorders. Studies of children's fears consistently find that girls self-report or are reported by others to have a greater number of fears and greater fearfulness than boys (Gullone & King, 1993; Ollendick, Yang, Don, Xia, & Lin, 1995). Epidemiological studies have demonstrated that anxiety disorders are more common in girls than in boys, and that these differences become more pronounced during adolescence. For example, Lewinsohn and his colleagues (Lewinsohn, Gotlib, Lewinsohn, Seeley, & Allen, 1998) examined gender differences in a study of 1,079 adolescents who never met criteria for any disorder, 95 who had recovered from an anxiety disorder, and 47 who had a current anxiety disorder. The results demonstrated that females were more likely than males to be diagnosed as a current case or recovered case. Further, the rate at which girls develop anxiety disorders was shown to be faster than that of boys. By age six, twice as many girls had developed an anxiety disorder than boys. Also, female adolescents, both current and recovered cases, obtained significantly higher anxiety symptom scores than males. Girls also had more difficulty than boys with certain psychological factors associated with the development of anxiety. Girls reported more major life events, higher self-consciousness, lower self-esteem, more physical illness or symptoms, poorer self-rated physical health, and less exercise. Conversely, girls also reported higher self-rated social competence, greater emotional reliance, more social support from friends, and less obesity than boys. However, controlling for these factors did not change the gender differences in anxiety disorder diagnoses. Complicating these results is the problem of understanding the sequencing of the anxiety and associated psychological factors. The Lewinsohn study relied on the retrospective recall of the adolescents. Whether these psychological variables existed prior to the development of the anxiety, or were the by-product of the anxiety disorder, remain unknown and the subject for further, prospective study.

Sex differences in the prevalence of anxiety disorders continue through adolescence and adulthood (Roza, Hofstra, van der Ende, & Verhulst, 2003). The National Comorbidity Survey (NCS) examined the prevalence of psychiatric disorders in a community sample of 8,098 women and men between the ages of 15 and 65 years (Kessler et al., 1995). Consistently, more women than men were found to suffer from an anxiety disorder at some point in their lives. Social phobia was associated with a lifetime occurrence rate of 15% of women and 11% of men. Similarly, 6.6% of women and 3.6% of men reported generalized anxiety disorder (GAD), with the prevalence increasing with age to 10.3% in women over 45 years of age as compared to 3.6% for men over 45 years of age. These higher prevalence rates of anxiety in women as compared to men are also found for most other anxiety disorders including panic disorder, phobias, posttraumatic stress disorder (PTSD) (Bourdon et al., 1988; Breslau, Davis, Andreski, & Peterson 1991), and to a lesser degree, obsessive-compulsive disorder (OCD) (Pigott, 1999). Thus, starting with subclinical fears in childhood and continuing with the anxiety disorders through adolescence and into adulthood, girls and women show higher prevalence rates for the occurrence of these conditions. Despite consistent evidence of sex differences in rates of anxiety, the nature of these disparities is not well understood. In addition, whether this gender difference results in significant psychosocial and related impairments in functioning is also not well studied. We explore these sex differences and their implications throughout the remainder of this chapter.

DESCRIPTION OF ANXIETY DISORDERS IN GIRLS

Anxiety disorders are among the most common conditions affecting children and adolescents (Albano, Chorpita, & Barlow, 2003; Morris & March, 2004). Eleven of 15 epidemiological reports estimate the prevalence of anxiety disorders in youth to be greater than 10% (Pine, 1994), with surveys conducted in the United States demonstrating prevalence rates to range from 12% to 20% (Achenbach et al. 1995; Gurley, Cohen, Pine, & Brook, 1996; Shaffer et al. 1996). An individual anxiety disorder may occur alone, but more often anxiety disorders are associated with high overlap in symptomatology and are often comorbid with each other and with other internalizing disorders such as depression (e.g., Brady & Kendall, 1992). In addition to their high prevalence, childhood anxiety disorders are also associated with significant impairment in school performance, family relationships, and social functioning (Ialongo, Edelsohn, Werthamer-Larsson, Crockett, & Kellam, 1994, 1995). Children with anxiety disorders are considered as impaired as children with disruptive behavior disorders on many measures including teachers' global perceptions of competence (Benjamin, Costello, & Warren, 1990). Moreover, anxiety in childhood and adolescence is associated with impairment extending into adulthood and predicts adult anxiety disorders, major depression, suicide attempts, and psychiatric hospitalization (Achenbach et al. 1995; Ferdinand & Verhulst 1995; Klein 1995; Pine et al. 1998). Recent prospective studies confirm that anxiety disorders have an early onset in childhood and run a chronic and fluctuating course into adulthood (Costello & Angold 1995; Ferdinand & Verhulst 1995; Pine et al. 1998; Roza et al., 2003).

In the following section, we review in detail the core symptoms of three of the most common anxiety disorders: separation anxiety disorder (SAD), social phobia (SP), and generalized anxiety disorder (GAD), and discuss how these symptoms may be expressed in girls. Our focus on these three disorders derives from research documenting that the disorders share the same underlying construct of anxiety and exhibit strong associations with each other (comorbidity) both cross-sectionally and over time. These three disorders infrequently occur as isolated conditions (Kendall & Brady, 1995) and show similar familial relationships with adult anxiety and depressive disorders (Fyer, Mannuza, Chapman, Martin, & Klein, 1995; Gurley et al. 1996; Last, Hersen, Kazdin, Orvaschel, & Perrin, 1991). Finally, in child and adult studies these three conditions respond to the same treatments (psychosocial and pharmacological) with roughly the same effect size regardless of which disorder is primary and despite the high rate of comorbidity among the disorders (Gould, Buckminster, Pollack, Otto, & Yap, 1997; Gould, Otto, Pollack, & Yap, 1997). A summary of the features of obsessive-compulsive disorder (OCD), panic disorder (PD), post traumatic stress disorder (PTSD), and the phobias is also provided.

Separation Anxiety Disorder

Core Symptoms

Separation anxiety disorder (SAD) is characterized by excessive anxiety and fear concerning separation from home or from those to whom the child is attached. Given that separation anxiety is a normal developmental phenomenon for both girls and boys from approximately the age of 7 months to 6 years (Bernstein & Borchardt, 1991), the diagnosis of SAD requires that the anxiety is inappropriate for the child's age or developmental level. The child expresses fear that something catastrophic will happen to her parents or herself when they are not together, and that this will prevent them from seeing each other again. These core fears are evidenced through recurrent distress when separation is anticipated or occurs, avoidance of separation situations, and impairment in important areas of functioning. It is common for younger girls and boys with SAD to report recurrent nightmares characterized by separation themes (Bell-Dolan & Brazeal, 1993); however, nightmares are also associated with separation anxiety symptoms in adolescents (Nielsen et al., 2000).

Separation anxiety in children often results in avoidance of situations that demand being apart from parents or home. Avoidance behavior may be characterized as mild, when the child wants the parents to be available by phone during school hours or to be easily accessible when she is attending parties or other outings. The child shows hesitation about leaving home and may procrastinate during the morning routine, or incessantly question her parents about their schedules. Moderate degrees of avoidance are often characterized by refusal to attend sleepovers or outings requiring separation of several hours from the parents. Younger separation-anxious children are often very "clingy" with parents, and may follow their parents from room to room, whereas older children become reluctant to leave home or engage in peer activities in the absence of their parents (Bell-Dolan & Brazeal, 1993). Children who evidence severe avoidance behavior may refuse to attend school or to sleep in their own rooms and tend to shadow or cling to the parent(s) at all times. These children can become desperate in their attempts to contact parents, feigning illness and concocting fantastic excuses in their effort to escape or avoid the separation situation.

Related Symptoms

Both girls and boys diagnosed with SAD are more likely to report somatic complaints than children diagnosed with phobic disorders (Last, 1991). These physical symptoms progress from nonspecific complaints of stomachaches or headaches (Livingston, Taylor, & Crawford, 1988) to more serious concerns evidenced by children who vomit and experience panic attacks at separation. In a community sample, musculoskeletal pains, occurring alone and in combination with stomach aches, were associated with SAD (Egger, Costello, Erkanali, & Angold, 1999). The majority of girls with SAD reporting musculoskeletal pains were 13 years old, while most girls with SAD who did not have musculoskeletal pains were 10 years old.

Peer relations can also be affected due to the child's refusal to participate in activities away from home, although children with SAD in general are socially skilled and well liked by peers (Last, 1989). This may be particularly relevant for preadolescent girls for whom activities such as sleepovers and sleepaway camp are often critical elements of their social environment. Girls with SAD may invite their peers to their house to sleep over, but will refuse to sleep elsewhere, which may cause stress on their friendships and their family.

Academic performance can be compromised in a number of ways by separation anxiety. First, if there are frequently arguments and struggles to get the child to school, resulting in tardiness, the child may miss important information, or be too upset to learn. Also, instruction may be interrupted by repeated requests to leave class and the child's distress and preoccupation with separation concerns. In extreme form, children with SAD who refuse to attend school miss important social and academic experiences available only in the school setting (Kearney, 2001). At times, efforts are made to provide these children with tutoring and assignments to complete at home; however, repeated absences place a child at risk for failure to meet the standards for attendance set forth in state regulations. Consequently, some children are then required to repeat the academic year and, in extreme cases, are remanded to the legal system for compliance with school attendance.

Social Phobia

Core Symptoms

Social phobia is characterized by a persistent fear of one or more so-cial or performance situations in which the child feels exposed to possi-ble scrutiny. When the socially phobic child is either in social situations or anticipating them, she fears that she will be embarrassed or humil-iated or that others will laugh at her. If the fear occurs in most social situations, *DSM-IV* requires the qualifier "generalized" subtype (e.g., Hof-mann et al., 1999; Wittchen, Stein, & Kessler, 1999). Preliminary data sug-gest that the generalized subtype is the most common form of social pho-bia in children and adolescents (Beidel & Morris, 1993; Hofmann et al., 1999). Moreover, adolescents with generalized social phobia may be dis-tinguished from those with the nongeneralized form by way of an earlier age of onset, greater impairment in functioning, higher risk for the devel-opment of comorbid conditions, and a greater likelihood of earlier inhib-ited temperament or familial adversities (see Velting & Albano, 2001, for a review).

Social anxiety in its nonclinical form is common among children and adolescents, especially for girls. Studies have demonstrated that girls re-port higher levels of social anxiety than boys, particularly the social eval-uative aspect (Crick & Ladd, 1993; LaGreca & Stone, 1993; Vernberg, Abwender, Ewell, & Beery, 1992). Further, adolescent girls are more con-cerned than boys about others' judgments of their appearance and behav-ior (Rosen & Aneshensel, 1976), which likely contributes to greater social anxiety. When these fears and worries become excessive and cause sig-nificant distress and interference in the girl's life, a diagnosis of social phobia may be warranted. For example, when asked to give a presenta-tion in class, most girls would be slightly nervous, but would complete the assignment. However, the girl with social phobia might try to avoid the task by staying home from school on that day. If the child cannot com-pletely avoid the situation (i.e., school), she may speak very quietly, avoid eye contact, or even ask another child to speak for her (Beidel, 1991). Upon exposure to a social or performance situation, the child with so-cial phobia almost invariably experiences an immediate anxiety response that may take the form of a panic attack. In school situations, these chil-dren are extremely fearful of a wide range of situations including reading aloud or speaking in class, asking the teacher for help, unstructured peer encounters, gym activities, working on group projects, taking tests, and eating in the cafeteria (Beidel, Turner, & Morris, 1999; Hofmann et al., 1999). Girls and boys with social phobia are reluctant to attend extracur-ricular events such as club meetings or school dances, and need much encouragement to attend parties or similar social activities. Similar avoid-ance behavior may be observed in family situations. Social-phobic chil-dren will shrink away from extended family gatherings, avoid answering the telephone or doorbell, and are reticent when meeting friends of family members.

Related Symptoms

Peer interactions and friendships are often directly affected by a child's social anxiety. In general, children and adolescents with social phobia often have few friends, are reluctant to join group activities, endorse feelings of loneliness on self-report measures (Beidel et al., 1999; La Greca, 2001) and are considered shy and quiet by their parents and peers. Girls with high social anxiety are likely to perceive their social acceptance and romantic appeal to be low (Leary, 1990), and to have greater concerns than boys about feelings of social inadequacy (Kashani, Orvaschel, Rosenberg, & Reid, 1989), all of which may directly contribute to feelings of anxiety. Several investigators have observed impaired social skills in girls and boys with social phobia between the ages of 7 to 14 years (Beidel et al., 1999; Spence, Donovan & Brechman-Toussaint, 1999). Further, feelings of social anxiety might limit interactions with peers or inhibit dating or romantic attachments in adolescents, which serves to interfere with social functioning. Teachers may describe the youth with social phobia as a "loner." During unstructured class time, these children are typically off by themselves or in the company of one specific friend. The social-phobic adolescent lags behind peers in meeting age-specific developmental challenges such as dating and seeking employment. It is not uncommon for the parents of these adolescents to lament over not having to deal with typical teenage behavior, such as having arguments about curfews and preferring to be with friends as opposed to family members.

Children with social phobia experience physical responses to anxiety-provoking situations consistent with those of adults with social phobia (see Beidel & Morris, 1993, 1995). These physical symptoms differ from those endorsed by the child with SAD, although complaints of stomachaches and illness are common among younger children with social phobia. However, older children and adolescents become overly concerned with the physical manifestations of anxiety much like adults with social phobia. Youth with social phobia typically experience symptoms of autonomic arousal that include heart palpitations, shakiness, flushes or chills, sweating, nausea, dizziness, and headache, among others (Beidel, Christ & Long, 1991). Fears of blushing or shaking during an oral report, unsteady voice while speaking to peers, or sweating that others may notice can serve to magnify the child's social phobia.

In addition to physiological sensations, observations of children with social phobia demonstrate that their thoughts are characterized by negative self-focus and self-deprecation and are accompanied by a range of autonomic symptoms and sensations (Albano, DiBartolo, Heimberg, & Barlow, 1995; Albano, Marten, Holt, Heimberg, & Barlow, 1995; Beidel et al., 1999; Spence et al., 1999).

Avoidance of social situations may have other secondary effects on socially phobic children. For example, children and adolescents who fear being the focus of attention during meals may refuse to eat during school hours. These children may spend their lunch time in the study hall or the library, avoiding the social activity of the school cafeteria. Ironically, the attention that these children attempt to avoid often comes back in the form of "growling" stomachs caused by hunger. School avoidance or refusal is often seen in children and adolescents with social phobia (Kearney, 2001). Younger children may refuse to attend school because of fears of being teased or rejected by peers or fears of being called on by the teacher to read before the class. School refusal in the adolescent may be prompted by concerns about appearance, especially if the adolescent is required to change clothes in a locker room for gym class. Social-phobic youth go to great lengths to appear calm before their peers and to avoid any sort of attention at all costs. Therefore, children entering the middle-school years who are sensitive to negative evaluation may be particularly vulnerable to social phobia. Changing classes, using lockers, larger classrooms, and working in groups will increase the number and types of social-evaluative situations to which a child may be exposed. Hence, middle-school children who are school refusing often constitute a significant proportion of referrals to anxiety clinics. For children with significant school refusal behavior, the complications of nonattendance described for children with SAD will also apply.

Generalized Anxiety Disorder

Core Symptoms

Generalized anxiety disorder (GAD) is characterized by excessive and persistent worry that is difficult to control. The uncontrollable worry may be focused on a number of general life concerns, including the future, past behavior, and competence in areas such as sports, academics, and peer relationships. It occurs on more days than not, for at least 6 months and is accompanied by at least one physiological symptom. In *DSM-IV*, the former overanxious disorder of childhood and adolescence (OAD) was subsumed under the revised GAD and hence our understanding of the symptoms and clinical presentation of GAD in youth is based largely on studies of children with OAD. Research suggests minimal and nonsignificant differences between the *DSM-III-R* and *DSM-IV* criteria, suggesting that past research on OAD can be applied to understanding GAD in youth (e.g., Kendall & Warman, 1996; Tracey, Chorpita, Douban, & Barlow, 1997).

Gender differences in nonclinical generalized anxiety are not evident in young children but do emerge with increasing age (Spence, Rapee, McDonald, & Ingram, 2001). Girls self-report higher levels of excessive worry than boys through elementary school (Silverman, LaGreca, & Wasserstein, 1995; Spence, 1998) and during adolescence (King, Gullone, Tonge, & Ollendick, 1993). As noted previously, anxiety disorders are more prevalent in girls than boys, including generalized anxiety disorder (Anderson, Williams, McGee, & Silva, 1987; Kashani & Orvaschel, 1990; McGee, Feeham, Williams, & Anderson, 1992). However, gender differences in GAD symptoms are not well studied. Hence, the following discussion largely relates to the clinical presentation of both girls and boys with GAD.

Girls and boys with GAD are typically described as "little worriers" by adult caretakers. The most frequently reported worries of a clinical sample of GAD youth included tests or grades, natural disasters, being physically attacked, future school performance, and being bullied or scapegoated by peers (Weems, Silverman, & La Greca, 2000). These children often seem like adults because they worry about family finances (Bell-Dolan & Brazeal, 1993), keeping appointments, meeting deadlines, and adhering to rules. Because teachers and parents may value such concerns, the excessive nature of these worries may be overlooked. Children with GAD are also characterized by marked self-consciousness and require frequent reassurance from others (Eisen & Kearney, 1995; Silverman & Ginsburg, 1995; Strauss, 1990). In addition, children with GAD demonstrate cognitive distortions that are fairly continuous and not circumscribed to a particular stimulus or situation. For example, children with GAD overestimate the likelihood of negative consequences, exaggerate the predicted outcome to a catastrophic degree, and underestimate their ability to cope with less-than-ideal circumstances. Although nonreferred children also worry about low-frequency events (Silverman et al., 1995), children with GAD may not recognize that such events have a low probability of occurrence. As opposed to the number of worries, it has been found that the intensity of children's worry differentiated clinic-referred children from nonclinical controls (Muris, Meesters, Merckelbach, Sermon, & Zwakhalen, 1998; Perrin & Last, 1997; Weems et al., 2000). In fact, these studies demonstrated that nonreferred children report just as many worries as clinical samples, suggesting the intensity of worry may be the mechanism leading to a sense of uncontrollability over the worry process (Weems et al., 2000).

Related Symptoms

Children with GAD may experience worry concerning performance in school, athletics, social relationships, and similar situations, to the point of being perfectionistic (Bell-Dolan & Brazeal, 1993; Strauss, 1990). Consequently, these children place exceedingly high standards for achievement on themselves and are brutal in their self-reproach if they fail to meet these standards. In fact, worry associated with GAD persists in the absence of objective cause for concern. For example, children and adolescents with GAD who receive A's on homework and tests will continue to worry about failure or falling below some self-generated standard. These beliefs can be pervasive and can lead to feelings of hopelessness and subsequent depression. Headaches, stomachaches, muscle tension, sweating, and trembling as the most commonly reported physical complaints of children with OAD or GAD (Eisen & Engler, 1995), although the muscle tension symptom appears to be infrequently endorsed by both children and their parents (Tracey et al., 1997). In a large community sample, headaches, alone and concurrent with stomach aches, were associated with the diagnosis of GAD (Egger et al., 1999). Accordingly, many children with GAD are referred for treatment by their pediatricians or by gastrointestinal specialists (Bell-Dolan & Brazeal, 1993). In addition to physiological symptoms, disturbing dreams are also associated with GAD in adolescents, especially girls (Nielsen et al., 2000).

Additional Anxiety Diagnoses

Obsessive Compulsive Disorder

Obsessive compulsive disorder (OCD) is characterized by the presence of recurrent and intrusive obsessions or repetitive behaviors (compulsions) that are present for more than 1 hour per day and cause either considerable distress or marked impairment in functioning for affected individuals (American Psychiatric Association, 1994). Children and adolescents report similar symptoms to adults, including obsessions concerning germs, sexual images, religiosity, and violence. Compulsions may involve checking, washing, arranging, or repetitive actions. Children with OCD may engage in excessive grooming and washing activities and take exorbitant amounts of time to complete homework assignments. Although rituals and preferences are not uncommon from a developmental perspective, the content of these behaviors in youth with OCD are unusual and do not dissipate with time. Female adolescents have been observed presenting with more compulsions, more symptoms overall, and greater impairment than male adolescents (Berg et al., 1989; Maggini et al., 2001; Valleni-Basile et al., 1994).

Panic Disorder

Panic disorder (PD) is assigned as a diagnosis when an individual experiences the occurrence of at least one uncued, unexpected panic attack, followed by a minimum of 1 month of persistent fear of future attacks, worry about the meaning of the panic attacks, or a significant change in behavior due to the attacks. Panic attacks are characterized by a number of physiological symptoms such as shortness of breath, sweating, palpitations or racing heart, chest pain or discomfort, dizziness or unsteady feelings, trembling or shaking, and cognitive symptoms such as fear of losing control, going crazy, or fear of dying. Panic attacks and panic disorder are more common among adolescents than children (Hayward, Killen, Hammer, & Litt, 1992; Ollendick, Mattis, & King, 1994). In fact, panic disorder appears more common among female than male adolescents (Kearney & Allan, 1995), and this prevalent sex difference appears to continue through adulthood. Throughout childhood and adolescence, panic attacks in females are associated with advanced pubertal development (Hayward et al., 1992). The association of pubertal status and the occurrence of panic symptoms will be discussed later in this chapter.

Specific Phobia

Specific phobia (SP) is a condition characterized by an exaggerated and persistent fear of circumscribed objects or situations. These stimuli must be unrelated to fears of embarrassment or humiliation (social anxiety) or fears of having a panic attack (panic disorder). Exposure to the stimulus or situation may result in a cued, situationally bound panic attack. Typically, phobic stimuli are either avoided or endured with distress. To assign the diagnosis in children and adolescents, the fear must persist for a minimum of 6 months and cause marked interference in functioning or distress (APA, 1994). Common childhood phobias include heights, darkness, loud noises, insects, dogs and other small animals, medical and dental visits, and thunderstorms (King et al., 1993; Strauss & Last, 1993). Studies of children with phobic disorders consistently find a higher prevalence among females in community and clinical samples (Anderson et al., 1987; Marks, 1988; Ollendick, King, & Frary, 1989; Strauss & Last, 1993).

Post Traumatic Stress Disorder

Post Traumatic Stress Disorder (PTSD) is unique among the anxiety disorders in that its genesis is the result of exposure to an extremely traumatic event such as natural or man-made disasters, war, motor vehicle accidents, life-threatening illnesses (e.g., cancer) physical assault, kidnapping, or abuse. The traumatic event must be potentially life threatening to the child or another person, and the child must have either personally experienced or witnessed the event, observed the event occurring to someone (e.g., witness to spousal abuse), or heard about the event happening to someone close to the child (e.g., learned of a tragic death of a parent, such as in the World Trade Center attack). Symptoms of PTSD fall into three broad categories: reexperiencing symptoms include frightening thoughts, images, and dreams about the event, and feeling as though the event was occurring again. Numbing or avoidance symptoms involve constriction of affect, avoidance of activities reminiscent of the event (e.g., refusal to ride in cars following a traumatic motor vehicle accident), failure to recall aspects of the trauma, and refusal to speak about the event. Finally, hyperarousal symptoms include temper outbursts, exaggerated startle response, irritability, sleep disturbance, concentration disturbance, and somatic complaints. There are wide developmental variations in the expression of PTSD symptoms in youth. Younger children may engage in repetitive play that is quite specific to the event, or complain about diffuse nightmares that may or may not bear any direct relation to the trauma. Children may also respond with varying degrees of disorganized or agitated behavior, helplessness, and intense fear. Girls tend to report more dissociative symptoms than boys, although mothers rate the presence of these symptoms higher for boys than girls (Rossman, Bingham, & Emde, 1997). In some cases girls and younger children report more PTSD symptoms than boys (Green et al., 1991; Lonigan, Shannon, Finch, Daugherty, & Taylor, 1991), while in others boys report more symptoms than girls (Burke, Borus, Burns, Millstein, & Beasley, 1982; Rossman et al., 1997). The nature of these discrepant findings is unclear.

COMORBID AND ASSOCIATED FEATURES

Several commonalities exist across anxiety disorders in associated features. For example, somatic complaints and peer problems that may not be part of diagnostic criteria are common, as are comorbid conditions, and situational and contextual factors. These are reviewed next.

Associated Characteristics

Community samples of youth with anxiety disorders reveal associations between anxiety and somatic symptoms, particularly for girls. As noted previously, children and adolescents with anxiety disorders report high rates of somatic complaints, such as headaches, stomachaches, and musculoskeletal pains. For example, The Great Smoky Mountains Study, a longitudinal study of the development of psychiatric conditions and the need for mental health services in youth, found in a sample of 1,013 children that girls who met criteria for an anxiety disorder had a three times greater rate of headaches than girls who were not anxious (34.1% vs. 10%) (Egger, Angold, & Costello, 1998). Interestingly, girls with headaches who had anxiety disorders missed less school and took less medication than girls with headaches without anxiety disorders. Also, girls with depression reported more frequent headaches and more severe effects of headaches on their lives than girls with anxiety disorders. An additional study using this sample found 60% of girls with an anxiety disorder reported one or more somatic complaints, compared with 12.1% of girls without an anxiety disorder (Egger et al., 1999). Specifically, stomachaches and musculoskeletal pains in girls were associated with anxiety disorders, particularly for SAD and GAD. Interestingly, girls with anxiety disorders reported stomachaches occurring alone at the same rate as girls without an anxiety disorder, but had a significantly higher rate of stomach aches and headaches occurring together than girls without an anxiety disorder. Stomach aches and musculoskeletal pains occurring together were also associated with having an anxiety disorder. Anxiety disorders were not, however, associated with frequency or duration of stomach aches nor of restriction of activities due to musculoskeletal aches and pains. It was noted by the investigators that girls with an anxiety disorder had a 2.6 times greater prevalence of headaches, nearly 100 times greater prevalence of stomach aches and headaches occurring simultaneously, and 3.4 times greater prevalence of musculoskeletal pains than girls without an anxiety disorder. In comparison, for boys, there was a nonsignificant trend toward an association between anxiety disorders and stomach aches. Thus, girls with anxiety disorders tend to experience somatic complaints at a higher rate than males with anxiety disorders, and also at a higher rate than nonanxious male and female peers.

As indicated earlier, anxiety, particularly social anxiety, is often associated with decreased peer interactions and lower social competence in girls. A recent study of peer victimization, global self-worth, and anxiety suggests an effect of victimization on anxiety levels in girls. Grills and Ollendick (2002) examined self-report ratings of anxiety, peer victimization, and global self-worth in 279 sixth-grade students. Consistent with the literature, girls reported more anxiety than boys. For both boys and girls, a significant positive correlation was found between ratings of peer victimization and general anxiety. Significant negative correlations were found between global self-worth and the victimization and anxiety factors. Girls experienced peer victimization and negative global self-worth to a greater extent than boys. Also, for girls, but not for boys, global self-worth mediated the relationship between peer victimization and self-reported. These findings suggest that for girls but not boys, peer victimization negatively influences girls' opinions of themselves, which, in turn, may cause increased anxiety. Due to their greater emotional investment in friendships and peer status, girls may be more likely to internalize negative feedback from peers during victimization. In contrast, boys might externalize peer victimization experiences and develop negative views of their peers, rather than of themselves. This external attribution for blame may serve to protect boys from anxiety.

Comorbid Conditions

The issue of comorbidity in childhood anxiety disorders plays a critical role in the understanding of childhood anxiety more generally (e.g., Caron & Rutter, 1991). Early research attention was given to the comorbidity of childhood anxiety disorders in an investigation by Last, Strauss, and Francis (1987). Using DSM-III diagnostic criteria, the investigators examined the cooccurrence of diagnoses in an outpatient population of 73 children. The results demonstrated that OAD children demonstrated the highest rate of comorbidity, with 9% having three or more additional clinical diagnoses. In addition, children assigned principal diagnoses of OAD most frequently received social phobia or avoidant disorder as additional diagnoses. Overall, the patterns demonstrated high diagnostic comorbidity for all of the anxiety disorders studied, with additional diagnoses assigned to as many as 80% of cases for selected anxiety diagnoses (SAD, OAD, school phobia), and with additional anxiety diagnoses assigned to 100% of the children with a principal diagnosis of major depression. Studies using DSM-IV criteria, although fewer in number, find similar patterns of comorbidity as in previous DSM-III studies of the anxiety disorders. For example, in a large community sample of German adolescents, one third of the youth with specific phobias also met criteria for depressive and somatoform disorders (Essau, Conradt, & Petermann, 2000).

Associations have emerged among the individual anxiety disorders regarding patterns of associated subclinical fears and comorbid anxiety conditions. For example, children who present with SAD often report other specific fears of varying intensity, such as fears of monsters, animals, insects, and the dark (Last, 1989; Ollendick & Huntzinger, 1990). The most common fear expressed by girls and boys with SAD is of getting lost (Last, Francis, & Strauss, 1989). This fear differentiated children with SAD from children diagnosed with overanxious disorder and those with a "phobia of school" (Last et al., 1989). Approximately one third of children with SAD present with a concurrent GAD that is usually secondary to the separation anxiety; and one third of children with SAD present with a comorbid depressive disorder that develops several months following the onset of SAD (Last, Strauss, & Francis, 1987). Separation-anxious children may threaten to harm themselves in attempts to escape or avoid separations; however serious suicidal symptomatology is rarely associated with SAD (Last, 1989).

Considerable attention has been paid to the comorbidity of anxiety and depressive disorders. For example, Strauss, Last, Hersen, and Kazdin (1988) examined anxiety and depression in 106 outpatient children and adolescents using *DSM-III* criteria. For children diagnosed with an anxiety disorder, comorbidity with depression was extensive (28%), and those children with comorbid anxiety and depression showed more severe anxiety symptomatology than those children with anxiety disorders alone. In a study examining the developmental characteristics of OAD, Strauss, Lease, Last, and Francis (1988) found children with overanxious disorder presenting with a high rate of concurrent anxiety and affective disorders. Younger children (aged 5–11 years) tended to present with comorbid separation-anxiety concerns and attention-deficit disorder, whereas major depression and simple (specific) phobia were more common to the older children with OAD (ages 12–19 years; Strauss, Lease, et al., 1988). Masi, Favilla, Mucci, and Millipiedi (2000) examined 108 children and adolescents with GAD, and found those with comorbid depression ($n = 55$) to report significantly more anxiety symptoms and more severe functional impairment than youth with pure GAD and no depressive comorbidity. Age, gender, and socioeconomic status did not differentiate these two groups.

In a review of the extant literature, Brady and Kendall (1992) found that 15.9–61.9% of youth identified as anxious or depressed have comoribid anxiety and depressive disorders, and that measures of anxiety and depression are highly correlated. Moreover, young children were more likely to be diagnosed only with an anxiety disorder, while older children and adolescents are more likely to show comorbidity with multiple disorders and to present as more impaired and symptomatic. This suggests not only the overlap between the latent constructs of anxiety and depression, but it also supports the possibility of a developmental progression, whereby anxiety precedes depression and leads to more detrimental outcomes (Hankin & Abramson, 2001). In the prospective, longitudinal Oregon Adolescent Depression Study, youth with a lifetime anxiety disorder ($n = 134$) demonstrated an intraanxiety comorbidity rate of 18.7% and were predominantly female, whereas the lifetime comorbidity rate between anxiety and other mental disorders (primarily major depressive disorder) was 73.1% and not associated with being female (Lewinsohn, Zinbarg, Seeley, Lewinsohn, & Sack, 1997). Further research using prospective longitudinal designs is needed to examine patterns of anxiety expression and the development of comorbid conditions as they relate to demographic and developmental factors.

Situational and Contextual Factors

As noted in the introduction of this chapter, girls are often expected to act in a deferential manner and to exhibit more fearfulness and less independent, proactive thought and fearless behavior than boys. Social reinforcement in the form of praise, attention, and tangible reward may all shape a child's tendency toward approach or avoidance of certain situations. In this regard, familial and cultural attitudes may differentially reinforce anxious withdrawal or fearless coping in female versus male children. Preschool-aged girls may be coddled and considered "cute" if they respond with tears and avoidant behavior in response to a barking small dog, whereas boys are more likely to be encouraged to pet and interact with the animal. This is probably also more often true for situations involving interacting with "rough and tumbling" aggressive peers and for engaging in risky play activities, such as climbing on the jungle gym on the playground. Similarly, parents may be more likely to tolerate the tears of a female child who sustains a scrape or minor injury during play, whereas the male child is often encouraged to "keep a stiff upper lip" and handle the injury "like a man." These types of gender bias in coping behaviors are imposed early in development and likely continue throughout the years of childhood and adolescence.

The idea that excessive or disruptive levels of anxiety develop and are expressed within an interpersonal context (Dadds, Davey & Field, 2001) was tested in a study examining the impact of parental behavior on fear acquisition in young children. Thirty toddlers aged 15–20 months were presented with a novel threat stimulus, either a toy spider or snake, simultaneously with the laboratory-induced expression of either positive or negative affect from their mothers. Results demonstrated the toddlers developed avoidance behavior of the toys following exposure to the negative expressions from their mothers (Gerull & Rapee, 2002). The children showed significantly greater avoidance of the toy when paired with the mothers' negative expression than when the mothers' affect was positive. Moreover, this difference was maintained after a 10-minute delay and paired with the mothers showing a neutral affect. Although gender differences were not observed in this study, the impact of parental models and the modeling of behavior by significant others (e.g., peers, other family members, adult authority figures) may differentially influence the development of anxiety in girls and boys through either direct or indirect pathways.

A wealth of data exists supporting the familial transmission of anxiety disorders, although the heritability of these disorders through genetic versus environmental influences is still debated (see Feigon, Waldman, Levy, & Hay, in press; Rose & Ditto, 1983; Silove, Manicavasagar, O'Connell, & Morris-Yates, 1995; Wood, McLeod, Sigman, Hwang, & Chu, 2003). The child's temperament will interact with conditioning experiences and help to shape the child's psychological strengths or vulnerabilities, including self-identity, self-concept, and cognitive style. As demonstrated by Gerull and Rapee (2002), the parent-child relationship provides a primary interpersonal context for the acquisition of the fear response for girls and boys.

As children mature and are exposed to a wider range of behavioral mod-els and contexts (e.g., teachers, peers, competitive situations, play, situa-tions requiring independent judgment), further opportunities for observing models either mastering or shrinking away from anxiety-provoking stim-uli are encountered. These observations may interact with the psycholog-ical resources of the child or adolescent (e.g., self-concept) to provide suc-cessful or negative outcomes. For example, during adolescence, girls have lower levels of self-esteem, self-worth, perceptions of physical attractive-ness, and competence in physical activities than do their same-age male peers (Allgood-Merten, Lewinsohn, & Hops, 1990; Ohannessian, Lerner, von Eye, & Lerner, 1996). When these self-perceptions are positive, ado-lescents evidence better emotional adjustment as indicated by lower levels of anxiety and depression (Allgood-Merten et al., 1990; Papini & Roggman, 1992). It may be that adolescent girls with higher levels of self-confidence and self-efficacy are more effective in managing less-than-ideal interper-sonal situations and contexts than their less confident female peers.

In addition to the family environment (Ginsburg, Siqueland, Masia-Warner, & Hedtke, 2004), peer relationships may be a critical substrate to the development of or protection from pathological anxiety states. For example, among middle-school youth, greater generalized social avoidance and distress at the beginning of the school year predicted lower levels of intimacy and companionship in adolescents' close friendships later in the year, especially for girls (Vernberg et al., 1992). LaGreca and Lopez (1998) examined the relationships among social anxiety, peer relations, friend-ships, and social functioning in a sample of 250 nonreferred adolescents enrolled in the 10th through 12th grades. Girls reported greater fear of negative evaluation from peers on the Social Anxiety Scale for Adolescents (SAS-A) and more social avoidance and distress in new situations. Girls also reported more social support from their best friends and teachers, more intimacy in close friendships, and perceptions of greater competency in their close friendships. Overall, higher social anxiety was related to less support from classmates and lower perceptions of social acceptance and romantic appeal, and these correlations were higher for girls. Adolescent girls who reported higher levels of social anxiety also reported having fewer best friends, feeling less competent in their friendships, and perceiving friendships as less supportive, less intimate, and lower in companionship. Close friendships and peer acceptance were significant predictors of social anxiety and peer acceptance consistently contributed to prediction of social anxiety even after accounting for the contribution of close friendships in girls. The authors suggest that factors that interfere with the development of close, intimate friendships (e.g., anxiety) may have greater impact on girls than boys, placing them at higher risk for impairment. A bidirectional relationship is proposed, in which social anxiety leads to peer difficulties, which in turn, contribute to increased anxiety.

Overall, the interpersonal contexts of the family and peer relationships appear to be potent mediators for the development of anxiety in vulnerable girls, with adolescence being a critical period for the expression of certain pathological anxiety conditions, most notably, social anxiety and panic.

Further research is necessary to examine why girls appear to be more vulnerable to the development of anxiety than boys within these contexts.

EPIDEMIOLOGY

Separation Anxiety Disorder

The most common of the anxiety disorders among children and adolescents, community samples indicate a prevalence rate for SAD in the range of 3–5% (Anderson et al., 1987; Kashani, Orvaschel, Rosenberg, & Reid, 1987; Lewinsohn, Hops, Roberts, Seeley, & Andrews, 1993). SAD is typically the most prevalent disorder found in clinical samples of anxious youth (Last, Francis, Hersen, Kazdin, & Strauss, 1987). In general, the peak age of onset of SAD appears to be around 7 to 9 years of age (Bird, Gould, Yager, Staghezza, Canino, 1989; Last, Perrin, Hersen & Kazdin, 1992), although the disorder is also known to develop during adolescence (Last et al., 1992). Several studies report an overrepresentation of girls with SAD (Anderson et al., 1987; Compton, Nelson, & March, 2000; Last et al., 1987), while others report an equal prevalence in girls and boys (Francis, Last, & Strauss, 1987; Last et al., 1992).

Social Phobia

The true prevalence of social phobia is largely unknown for children and adolescents, despite the disorder being the third most common mental disorder found in adults (Kessler et al., 1994). Although epidemiological studies of child and adolescent samples place the prevalence of social phobia at 1% of the general child population (Anderson et al., 1987; Kashani & Orvaschel, 1990), this is likely an underestimate due to methodological and definitional problems found in early studies (Albano et al., 2003; Beidel, Morris, & Turner, 2004). In a later study using *DSM-IV* criteria in a sample of German adolescents, the prevalence of social phobia was found to be 1.6% for youth aged 12 through 17 years (Essau, et al., 2000). The average age of onset for social phobia is early-to-middle adolescence (DeWit, Ogborne, Offord, & MacDonald, 1999; Liebowitz, Gorman, Fyer, & Klein, 1985), with 11.3 to 12.3 years reported as the average age of onset in clinical samples (Last et al., 1992; Strauss & Last, 1993). Some studies report a predominance of boys in clinical and community samples of youth with social phobia (Compton et al., 2000; Last et al., 1992, respectively), while others find more girls than boys (Beidel et al., 1999).

Generalized Anxiety Disorder

The prevalence of GAD is also difficult to estimate, as early epidemiological studies focused on the *DSM-III* (APA, 1980) and *DSM-III-R* (APA, 1984) diagnosis of overanxious disorder of childhood and adolescence

(OAD). The OAD diagnosis was notorious for having poorly defined symptoms that corresponded to symptoms of other anxiety disorders, such as social phobia or SAD. As noted previously, the criteria for OAD were revised for the *DSM-IV* and subsumed under the category of GAD. Hence, studies may have reported rates for OAD or GAD. Prevalence rates for OAD or GAD in community samples range from 2% to 19% (Anderson et al., 1987; Cohen, Cohen, & Brook, 1993; McGee et al., 1990; Werry, 1991). OAD or GAD in clinical samples is reported to range from 10% to 58% (Beitchman, Wekerle & Hood, 1987; Kendall et al., 1997; Last et al., 1987). Although one study reported symptoms of OAD present as early as at 4 years (Beitchman et al., 1987), the mean age of onset of OAD or GAD ranges from 10.8 years (Last et al., 1987) to 13.4 years (Last et al., 1987). More girls than boys are diagnosed with GAD; however, this difference does not appear until adolescence (Last et al., 1987; Kendall et al, 1997), and may be an artifact of fewer males presenting to treatment clinics (Valez, Johnson, & Cohen, 1989).

Additional Anxiety Diagnoses

Although once thought a very rare condition, OCD is reported to occur in up to 4% of youth surveyed in community samples (Flament et al., 1988; Maggini et al., 2001; Valleni-Basile et al., 1994; Zohar et al., 1992). Onset may occur earlier than 7 years; however, the mean age of onset is typically reported between 10 and 12.5 years (Leonard & Rapoport, 1991; Swedo et al., 1989; Wewetzer et al., 2001). In OCD, onset appears earlier in boys than girls; however, gender differences disappear by adolescence (Albano et al., 2003). As noted previously, panic attacks, panic disorder, and specific phobias are more common in girls than boys, and panic is often associated with female sex and advanced pubertal development (see Albano et al., 2003; Morris & March, 2004). Adolescent girls and women are consistently shown to be at higher risk for the development of PTSD than are boys and men (Hanna & Grant, 1997; Kessler et al., 1994), although there is some evidence that this is only true when PTSD is comorbid with other disorders such as major depression (Kilpatrick et al., 2003).

Social Class, Ethnicity, and Culture

Poverty and disadvantaged living conditions are associated with a range of psychosocial impairments and psychopathology across the ages. In a study of children in the rural South, Black children were three times more likely than White children to be living in poverty (Costello, Keeler, & Angold, 2001). Although exposure to poverty differed dramatically, the association between poverty and risk factors for any psychiatric disorder was roughly the same for Black and White children, with the prevalence of disorder increasing as the number of risk factors increased. This was especially true for White children. After controlling for a number of risk factors, White children living in poverty were found to be at higher risk for a psychiatric disorder than Black children. However, an excess of disorders, particularly anxiety disorders, were found for poorer children overall. When specifically examining the relationship of anxiety and anxiety disorders to sociodemographic variables in youth, Last and colleagues (1987, 1992) found 50% to 75% of their sample of children with SAD to come from low socioeconomic backgrounds (SES), and to be of lower SES than children with overanxious disorder and school phobia (Last et al., 1987).

Subclinical fears have been found to be more frequent in African American children than White children (Neal, Lilly, & Zakis, 1993). However, the number of fears and focus of the fear changes at different ages, while the observation of girls reporting more fears than boys is consistent across cultures (Albano et al., 2003). For clinical disorders, rates of SAD in children presenting to specialty clinics for anxiety disorders are equivalent between Euro-American and African American children (Perrin & Last, 1993) and between Euro-American and Hispanic American children (Ginsburg & Silverman, 1996). However, a community study of 2,384 youth aged 8 years to 19 years, found African American children reporting a higher number of SAD symptoms than White children (Compton et al., 2000). Beidel et al. (1999) found White children and African American children to have similar clinical presentations of social phobia. No specific racial or cultural patterns have emerged for GAD.

ADOLESCENT AND ADULT FEMALE OUTCOMES

Adolescence is known as the period of storm and stress, but this characterization is owed mainly to the behavior problems of boys. Indeed, adolescent girls tend to suffer with more episodic pathologies such as anxiety or depression, or milder forms of externalizing pathology such as non-aggressive types of conduct problems (Bardone et al., 1998). Bardone and colleagues (1998) examined the young adult physical health outcomes of adolescent girls diagnosed with anxiety, depression, and conduct problems. Subjects in this study were participants in the Dunedin Multidisciplinary Health and Development Study, a longitudinal investigation of children who were assessed periodically between the ages of 5 years and 21 years. For the adult outcomes study, a subsample of 459 girls (92% of the original cohort of girls) was assessed at the age of 15 years for mental health problems. Of these youth, 341 had no clinical disorder (healthy controls), 67 had an anxiety disorder, 25 presented with major depressive disorder or dysthymia, and 44 were assigned the conduct disorder diagnosis (Bardone et al., 1996). At the age of 21 years, data were collected for 470 young women (94% of the original female cohort). Results indicated that as compared to healthy controls who reported on average one medical health problem, young adult women with anxiety disorders reported, on average, two medical problems. Even when controlling for potentially confounding variables such as socioeconomic status, age at menarche, childhood health, and others, adolescent anxiety predicted more medical problems in young adulthood relative to healthy controls. In general, however, healthy controls and girls with anxiety disorders, depression self-reported fairly good health in contrast to girls with conduct disorder, who self-reported overall poor health. Girls with anxiety also did not differ in body mass index (BMI; calculated via height and weight) from healthy controls, whereas conduct disorder predicted lower BMI relative to controls. Further results from this study indicated that anxiety in adolescence did not lead to an increased risk for substance dependence disorder, tobacco dependence, or daily use of tobacco. Girls with anxiety also did not differ from healthy controls and depressed girls with regard to the number of sexual partners before the age of 21 years, risk for contracting a sexually transmitted disease, or pregnancy before the age of 21 years. It was suggested that adolescent anxiety and medical problems in adulthood may be linked through biological mechanisms, such as hyperactivation of the sympathetic nervous system. Although the results of this study suggest that this cohort of adolescents with anxiety did not view themselves as having poor overall physical health, the investigators caution that anxious girls may be encouraged to seek medical attention for any physical symptom or complaint at a higher rate than girls without anxiety disorder. If this occurs, girls at risk for anxiety may be vulnerable to developing and sustaining somatic complaints through a process of conditioning and reinforcement.

CONCEPTUALIZING ANXIETY DISORDERS IN GIRLS

As noted throughout this chapter, the extant developmental psychology literature, stemming back to the early 1920s, finds a higher prevalence of nonclinical, age-related fears in girls than boys beginning in infancy and continuing through adolescence (Albano, Causey, & Carter, 2001). Although girls evidence more subclinical fears than boys from an early age, most epidemiological studies examining the prevalence of the anxiety disorders demonstrate an equal sex ratio for these conditions until puberty (Hayward, 2003). Once pubertal development begins to advance, girls report more symptoms of anxiety disorders and are diagnosed more frequently with these disorders as compared to boys, with the possible exception of obsessive-compulsive disorder (Albano et al., 2003; Morris & March, 2004). Biological and psychosocial mechanisms have been proposed to account for this differential expression of fears, anxiety disorders, and related internalizing problems in girls.

Biological Theories

It has been suggested that the transmission of anxiety may start in utero (Halbreich, 2003). Anxiety disorders and anxiety symptoms are prevalent among pregnant women (e.g., Field et al., 2003) and are associated with a number of biological markers in the developing fetus including reduced blood flow to and increased cortisol and activity levels for the fetus (Glover, Teixeira, Gitau, & Fisk, 1999; see Halbreich, 2003). It is also suggested that mothers with high anxiety levels during pregnancy delivered babies who spend more time in deep sleep and less time in quiet and alert states (Field et al., 2003), in addition to several neurobehavioral differences including lower vagal tone and higher frontal EEG activity. The implications of these differences are not known, and Halbreich cautions that it is purely speculative and premature to assume that the mothers' anxiety during pregnancy leads to the development of anxiety disorders in the developing child. Nevertheless, neurobiological mechanisms are the focus of much attention by researchers interested in developmental psychopathology, and inhibited temperament in early childhood is one biological marker that is often associated with the later development of anxiety and anxiety disorders.

Girls who are highly behaviorally inhibited (BI) have been shown to be more likely to develop anxiety disorders than those who are uninhibited (reference for specific study). For example, whether a child's temperament is inhibited or uninhibited has been shown to be more consistent from 14 months to 7.5 years for girls than boys. Girls with anxious symptoms were significantly more fearful and subdued in the second year than girls who were not anxious. Similar, although smaller, differences were found for boys. At 7.5 years, a number of differences were found between typically inhibited girls, characterized by being highly reactive and highly fearful at 14 and 21 months, to prototypically uninhibited girls, who were low-reactive as infants and fearless at 14 and 21 months.

These findings provide preliminary support for the hypothesis that high reactivity in utero or infancy is associated with later anxiety, as evidenced through the sympathetic activation of the cardiovascular system at 7.5 years of age. To clarify, girls who had been high reactive infants were most likely to show a steady rise in heart rate as they listened to white noise gradually rising in intensity: 51% of the high-reactive girls showed an acceleratory trend, while only 26% decelerated. Among low-reactive children, 44% showed deceleration and 39% showed acceleration. Girls who showed heart rate acceleration in response to higher noise levels had been more fearful at 2 years of age than girls whose heart rate had decelerated. This relationship was only found in girls suggesting that indexes of strong sympathetic influence on the heart are more closely linked to fear and anxiety in girls, than in boys. This is also supported by the fact that only among girls was there a relation between high and stable heart rate (low heart period variability) while in a standing posture and anxious symptoms. Similarly, 57% of high-reactive girls who had high and stable heart rates on at least two of the evaluations (14 months, 21 months, 4.5 years) had anxious symptoms at 7.5 years. Although six low-reactive girls showed high and stable heart rates on at least two occasions, none developed anxious symptoms. Since no relationship was found between high and stable heart rate and later anxiety in boys, the authors hypothesize that the link between sympathetic activity on the cardiovascular system and inhibition or anxious symptoms might be stronger in girls than boys.

From a biological perspective then, certain temperamental styles evident in early life, and physiological mechanisms involved in later pubertal development, are thought to render girls more sensitive to the development and expression of anxiety during puberty (Hayward & Sanborn, 2002). For example, research suggests that pubertal stage is a strong predictor of the occurrence of panic attacks in girls, as opposed to chronological age. In a study of sixth- and seventh-grade girls, Hayward et al. (1992) found for girls aged 11 to 13 years, the frequency of panic attacks was associated with advanced pubertal stage and not associated with age. Similar results were found for symptoms of eating disorders (Killen et al., 1992) and depression (Angold, Costello, & Worthman, 1998), suggesting a possible pubertal association for internalizing disorders, in general. Further research found an association between pubertal timing and internalizing symptoms in girls (Graber, Lewinsohn, Seely, & Brooks-Gunn, 1997; Hayward, Killen, Wilson, & Hammer, 1997), suggesting that internalizing symptoms including anxiety and other problem behaviors are associated with earlier onset of puberty for some girls. Similarly, various hormonal changes that affect neurotransmitter systems and others that interact with hormones released in response to stress are also suggested as possible modulators of anxiety in girls and women (Goodyer et al., 2000; Nottleman, et al., 1987; Rubinow & Schmidt, 1996; Slap et al., 1994; Susman, Nottelmann, & Inoff-Germain, 1987). Investigators caution, however, that the mechanisms accounting for the associations between pubertal timing, hormonal activity, and psychopathology are not yet understood (Hayward & Sanborn, 2002).

Gender Role Orientation

One of the most common psychological explanations for these gender differences is that of gender role orientation. In studies of adults, feminine gender role orientation is shown to be related to increased self-report of fears, whereas male gender role orientation is associated with less fear (Carey, Dusek, & Spector, 1988; Dillon, Wolf, & Katz, 1988; Tucker & Bond, 1997). These differences are found regardless of the sex of the individual. A recent study examined these issues in a sample of 66 children who presented at an anxiety disorders clinic (Ginsburg & Silverman, 2000). The children completed the Children's Sex Role Inventory (CSRI; Boldizar, 1991) and the Fear Survey Schedule for Children- Revised (FSSC-R; Ollendick, 1983). Masculinity scores were significantly negatively correlated with overall fearfulness, fears of the unknown, fears of failure and criticism, and medical fears. Femininity was not significantly related to overall fearfulness or any specific fears. These findings suggest that children who identify with a masculine gender role may be less likely to express feelings of fear. Also, children with higher levels of masculinity may be more likely to adopt instrumental traits and less likely to avoid feared situations, thereby reducing excessive fear levels. The authors suggest that the lack of a relationship between femininity and fearfulness may be a result of a biased sample, as there were no differences on the femininity scale between boys and girls. Successful women in our culture are often described as aggressive, daring, unemotional (cf., cold), and driven to succeed. These traits are historically aligned with masculinity, and thus the association of fearlessness, an overt behavior, and masculine gender role orientation, a psychological-emotional internal construction, may be partially explained by a secular trend. In this regard, environmental influences are shaping the adoption of certain behaviors associated with success with an internalized sex role orientation geared toward the masculine end of the gender role orientation continuum.

Psychosocial Factors

Several theorists have proposed that sex differences in the expression of anxiety in adolescence result from differences in the experience of interpersonal stress and emotional reactions to stress (see Rudolph, 2002 for a review). Adolescent girls report more interpersonal stress, including negative events and problems involving family, peer, and intimate relationships, than boys (Gore, Aseltine, & Colten, 1993; Wagner & Compas, 1990). Also, adolescent girls perceive negative interpersonal events as more stressful than boys (Wagner & Compas, 1990). These differences appear to last into adulthood where women report more stress associated with their social networks, whereas men report higher levels of stress associated with work problems (Kendler, Thornton, & Prescott, 2001; Kessler & McLeod, 1984). Girls tend to the socialize in dyadic relationships, which may lead them to value intimacy, whereas boys socialize more in groups (Maccoby, 1990). Further, relationships are more central to the self-definition and identity in females than males (Gore et al., 1993; Hill & Lynch, 1983; Maccoby, 1990). Girls have a greater tendency to value close relationships and to rely on these relationships as a source of emotional support and to be concerned about maintaining friendships and being evaluated positively (Maccoby, 1990; Cross & Madson, 1997). This may explain why there is a stronger association between interpersonal loss or separation events and anxiety and depressive disorders in girls than in boys (Goodyer & Altham, 1991). Because girls rely more heavily on their peers for emotional support and intimacy than boys, disruptions in social networks and shifts in interpersonal roles are likely to create higher levels of stress for girls. These might be normative changes in peer groups, misunderstandings, or minor disagreements that occur for both boys and girls, but because they have more salience for girls, they lead to greater stress.

Rudolph and her colleagues performed a series of studies to further examine this theory in preadolescent and adolescent girls (Rudolph, 2002). In a study of 88 children and adolescents (aged 8–18 years), girls reported experiencing significantly more interpersonal stress, and specifically interpersonal conflict than boys. Further, levels of stress increased from preadolescence to adolescence in girls, while no increase was seen for boys. This finding was particularly robust for dependent stress that was generated by the child. Another study of 460 fifth to eighth graders examined children's experience of stressful experiences with peers, discriminating between disruption of close friendships versus general peer group stress. Overall, girls reported experiencing greater levels of friendship stress than boys, while boys experienced more general peer group stress than girls. Further, friendship and peer group stress were associated significantly more strongly with emotional distress in girls than boys. Using regression analyses, the authors found that friendship stress accounted for part of the gender differences in depression and anxiety. Girls demonstrated higher levels of anxiety and depression in the face of friendship stress and peer group stress than boys. Minimal gender differences in emotional distress were found in low levels of stress.

Several theories suggest that female-linked relational orientation styles are associated with high levels of interpersonal sensitivity and emphasize maintenance of harmonious relationships and concerns about social approval, while male-linked relational orientation styles are characterized by an emphasis on self-enhancement, dominance, and competition. In a study of 478 early adolescents, Rudolph and her colleagues used structural equation modeling to test a model that linked gender differences in interpersonal sensitivity with gender differences in emotional distress. Consistent with recent theories, the results showed that girls possessed higher levels of interpersonal sensitivity (increased psychological and emotional investment in relationships) than boys. Also, interpersonal sensitivity was associated with heightened emotional distress and was found to account for observed gender differences in emotional distress. Interestingly, interpersonal sensitivity also accounted for more adaptive social behavior in girls, suggesting that there is likely a trade-off of heightened sensitivity. Another study found that social anxiety predicted increased social helplessness over time in early adolescents who experienced high but not low levels of peer exclusion. Also, a high need for approval was associated more strongly with self-esteem deficits and anxiety in girls than boys. In conclusion, these studies lend support to theories suggesting the roles of stress exposure and reactivity in gender differences in emotional distress.

A Developmental Psychopathology Framework

Rather than assume an either/or approach regarding the role of psychosocial and biological factors in accounting for gender differences in the anxiety disorders, a developmental psychopathology framework provides a multifactorial and transactional model to study and understand the differential expression of anxiety pathologies in girls. Albano and Hayward (2004) outline a framework for understanding social anxiety disorder in youth that may similarly be applied to examining gender disparities for the range of anxiety disorders. Critical to this framework is the understanding that the focus or type of anxiety varies by developmental stage, that multiple factors from a variety of psychosocial and biological domains can contribute to the risk or protection from the development of anxiety, and that the various contributory factors interact in a bidirectional manner. For example, it is expected that preschool-aged girls (and boys) will evidence fears of novel situations or objects, such as of insects, the dark, separation situations, and so on. Having an inhibited temperament may predispose a child to easier expression of these normal, stage-related fears. However, one child may have a parent with a phobic or anxiety disorder, thus providing a model for fear and avoidance behavior, whereas another child may not. The absence of the parental modeling of anxiety may protect the child with a temperamental risk for anxiety at this early developmental stage, and at the very least, delay the onset of pathological fear reactions. Similarly, one child's inhibited temperament may shape parental behavior to be more overprotective whereas the child with an inquisitive and exploring temperament may shape the parents to be less hands-on with guiding her behavior (cf., Chorpita & Barlow, 1998; Rapee, 2001). Hence, the inhibited child may be kept from gaining experience in confronting anxiety-provoking situations and developing self-soothing and proactive coping behaviors, whereas the noninhibited child is free to engage in trial-and-error learning to master novel stimuli and situations. And, parental expectations may also vary depending on the gender of the child, such that their daughter is "expected" to shy away from stimuli such as insects and darkness, whereas their son is to "tough it out" and master these situations on his own. As noted by Albano and Hayward (2004), the developmental psychopathology framework seeks to examine the complex course and developmental patterns of behavior that occur across the life span. Developmental transitions, changes in biological or physical maturational, cognitive, and social emotional development, and interactions between the individual and his or her environment over time are simultaneously accounted for in this model. Indeed, from this perspective, it is expected that there are multiple pathways to developing the anxiety disorders and whether girls or boys develop anxiety or anxiety disorders results from bidirectional transactions between the individual and his or her environment.

ASSESSMENT AND TREATMENT IMPLICATIONS AND CONSIDERATIONS WITH GIRLS

Assessment Issues

In this era of manualized and empirically supported treatments for anxiety and related disorders, the issue of accurate assessment and diagnosis is paramount. Most treatment manuals are developed to target a specific anxiety disorder or cluster of co-occurring anxiety disorders. Hence, the reliable and valid identification of children and adolescents with the target disorder is essential for ensuring the best chance of success in treatment. Issues plaguing the field of diagnostic classification are well documented in textbooks on child psychpathology (Mash & Barkley, 2003) and childhood anxiety (Morris & March, 2004; Ollendick & March, 2004; Vasey & Dadds, 2001). Confounds to the accurate diagnosis of youth revolve around issues of the utility and validity of the current diagnostic classification system, limitations of various assessment modalities and measures, issues in reporter bias, and poor or little understanding of the line between normal versus clinical manifestations of anxiety, among many others. Hence, we proceed with some issues pertaining specifically to girls but recognizing that this discussion is not complete due to the enormity and complexity of the issues of assessment and diagnosis, overall.

It is recognized that the norms of several self-report measures of anxiety require higher scores for girls as compared to boys to reach the "clinical cutoff" for the disorder or construct in question. For example, the Social Anxiety Scale for Children- Revised, requires that girls receive a score of 54 or above to be considered as having "high social anxiety" whereas boys only need to score at or above 50. Similarly, the distinction of "nonsocially anxious" for girls is defined as a total score at or below 40, and for boys the score needs to fall at or below 36. These seemingly minor differences take into account that girls tend to be more socially anxious than boys across the ages and reflect sensitivity to this observed gender difference, and are not the result of gender stereotyping influencing the development of assessment items.

While it is important that assessment measures are sensitive to sex differences in detecting the level of anxiety or presence of an anxiety disorder, the nature of these differences is still not well understood. One problem that arises in assessment is whether the method of assessment results in false-positive or false-negative reports, and whether these are a function of age, gender, or other factors. Using panic attacks as an example, reviews of the literature indicate that although children and adolescents experience panic attacks (Ollendick et al., 1994), the severity and frequency of these symptoms may differ depending on the method of assessment and age of the sample. Using interview measures, lifetime prevalence rates of panic attacks in nonclinical samples have been shown to be 11.9% in ninth graders (Hayward et al., 1989) and 5.4% in sixth- and seventh-grade girls (Hayward et al., 1992). In contrast, studies of panic attack frequency using questionnaires have demonstrated prevalence rates ranging from 43% in high school students in Australia (King et al., 1993) to 60% of high school students surveyed in the United States (Warren & Zgourides, 1988). Hayward and his colleagues examined these assessment differences in a sample of 1,013 seventh- and eighth-grade girls. According to the interview, the lifetime prevalence of panic disorder was 1.7% ($n = 17$) and the lifetime prevalence of four-symptom panic attacks was 3.8% ($n = 38$). In contrast, 21.4% of subjects ($n = 217$) reported a four-symptom panic attack on the questionnaire. Further, during the interview, 9.7% of the sample ($n = 99$) reported episodes of normal fear. These subjects also scored significantly higher on depression and anxiety sensitivity measures compared to subjects who did not report normal fear episodes. Interestingly, 25% of those who indicated that they had experienced at least one panic attack on the questionnaire were found on the interview to have normal fear episodes, versus only 5% of the remaining sample had normal fear episodes. The results of this study confirm the presence of panic in a nonclinical sample and replicate previous findings that rates of panic differ significantly depending on the method of assessment. The authors suggest that the questionnaire casts a "wider net" than the interview. They also hypothesize that the questionnaire might be oversensitive in capturing normal fear episodes and that some of false-positive responses on the questionnaire might be cases of fear resulting from situations that would frighten most adolescent girls. The questionnaire does not allow for the assessment of circumstances under which panic occurs as accurately as with the interview method.

To summarize, to some degree sex differences in the expression of anxiety states are captured through gender-based norms and reflect the observation that overall, fears and anxiety are more common in girls than boys. While distinctions in clinical cutoffs respect the gender disparity, interpretation of the results of an assessment should take into account factors such as method variance. It is widely recognized that multiple informants and multiple methods are necessary for forming an accurate diagnostic or clinical picture in youth. Developmental variations, peer, cultural and familial influences, attention to reporter bias, and environmental context all contribute to forming the clinical formulation and optimal treatment plan for a youngster with anxiety.

Treatment of Anxiety in Girls

Anxiety disorders are highly treatable for the majority of youth through either cognitive behavioral therapy (Prins & Ollendick, 2003) or pharmacotherapy (Varley & Smith, 2003), and an evaluation of the relative efficacy of each monotherapy and their combination is presently in progress in a large, randomized, controlled clinical trial (J. Walkup, personal communication). Kendall's Coping Cat program (Kendall, 1990/2001) is the most well-established and disseminated treatment approach for SAD, social phobia, and GAD in youth aged 7 to 16 years. Known as "The Coping Cat," both individual and group treatment formats are found efficacious at the acute end of treatment and over the long term in a number of randomized clinical trials (see Albano & Kendall, 2002, for a review), with adaptations for greater involvement of family members also demonstrating good effectiveness (e.g., Barrett, Dadds, Rapee, & Ryan, 1996). Manuals targeting specific disorders have also been developed for school refusal behavior (Kearney & Albano, 2000a, 2000b), OCD (March & Mulle, 1998), phobias (Silverman & Kurtines, 1996, which also covers SAD, GAD, and social phobia), social phobia in children (Beidel & Turner, 1998) and adolescents (Albano et al., 1995; Hayward et al., 2000), and PTSD (March, Amaya-Jackson, Murry, & Schulte, 1998).

In addition to CBT, several studies support the use of medications, particularly the selective serotonin reuptake inhibitors (SSRIs), in the treatment of childhood anxiety disorders. Studies of children with anxiety disorders indicated good efficacy, tolerable side effects, and a good safety profile for the SSRIs (Rynn, Siqueland, & Rickels, 2001). Studies enrolling youth with GAD, SAD, and/or social phobia yielded positive results for fluoxetine (Prozac; Birmaher et al., 1994; Manassis & Bradley, 1994), fluvoxamine (Luvox; RUPP Anxiety Study Group, 2001), and sertraline (Rynn et al., 2001). Long-term effectiveness and safety of medication treatment for youth have not been examined to date, though, leading to recent concerns regarding potentially negative side effects and use of medications as the first line of treatment more generally.

Little is known about the differential response of girls and boys to either psychosocial or pharmacological treatments for anxiety disorders. The prevalence and intensity of fears at post-treatment did not differ as a function of gender in clinical trials conducted using the Kendall protocol (Treadwell, Flannery, & Kendall, 1995) group CBT for anxious youth (Silverman et al. 1999a; Beidel et al. 2000), or fluvoxamine (RUPP Anxiety Work Group, 2002). In contrast, younger children (7–10 years) and females of any age responded better than older children (11–14 years) and males to family involvement in CBT (Barrett et al. 1996), although the long-term relevance of this finding is not understood. Similarly, it is not known whether girls respond differentially to certain treatment components than boys. Egger and Burns (2004) report that girls are more likely to receive education-based clinical services for SAD, social phobia, GAD or specific phobia, as compared to boys. Clearly, in light of the differences highlighted previously concerning self-concept, rejection sensitivity, and prevalence of disorder, further research is warranted to examine whether treatments, particularly psychosocial treatments, can be tailored to meet the needs of girls and consequently, to optimize treatment response.

CONCLUDING COMMENTS

Little is understood about the nature of sex differences in the prevalence of fears and anxiety disorders in girls or the specific developmental pathways by which girls develop anxiety disorders. As noted, girls are consistently found to be more fearful at a nonclinical level from an early age. With increasing age and development, anxiety disorders become more prevalent in girls than boys, and result in a wide range of impairment in psychosocial functioning for females. Indeed, the popular and stable conception that girls and women are the weaker and more anxious sex is not yet dispelled by the extant literature examining the developmental psychopathology of anxiety.

Research illuminating the neurobiological bases for these sex differences is just coming into focus. There is the suggestion that the prenatal environment may place a child at risk for anxiety disorders. If this is so, then research must focus on the mechanisms by which this transmission occurs, and more importantly, on whether prevention and treatment services for anxious women of child-bearing potential can stop this pathway to anxiety. Temperament and pubertal mechanisms are clearly identified as biological risk factors for, or mechanisms involved in, the development of anxiety disorders in girls. Whether this occurs as an interaction or separate pathways may be irrelevant. However, partitioning out the biological mechanisms from the interaction of these factors with the response of the environment to an inhibited or developing young girl may be critical for advising parents and informing the development of gender-sensitive psychosocial treatments. The continual study of biological and psychosocial factors, from an integrated developmental psychopathology perspective, is necessary to inform our efforts to assist girls with healthy adjustment and diminish the risk for anxiety disorders across the lifespan.

REFERENCES

Achenbach, T. M., Howell, C. T., McConaughy, S. H., & Stanger, C. (1995). Six-year predictors of problems in a national sample of children and youth: I. Cross-informant syndromes. *Journal of the American Academy of Child & Adolescent Psychiatry, 34,* 336–347.

Albano, A. M., Causey, D., & Carter, B. (2001). Fear and anxiety in children. In C. E. Walker & M. C. Roberts (Eds.), *Handbook of clinical child psychology* (3rd ed., pp. 291–316). New York: Wiley.

Albano, A. M., Chorpita, B. F., & Barlow, D. H. (2003). Anxiety Disorders. In E. J. Mash & R. A. Barkley (Eds.), *Child psychopathology* (2nd ed., pp. 279–329). New York: Guilford.

Albano, A. M., DiBartolo, P. M., Heimberg, R. G., & Barlow, D. H. (1995). Children and adolescents: Assessment and treatment. In R. G. Heimberg, M. R. Liebowitz, D. A. Hope, & F. R. Schneier (Eds.), *Social phobia: Diagnosis, assessment, and treatment* (pp. 387–425). New York: Guilford.

Albano, A. M., & Hayward, C. (2004). The developmental psychopathology approach to understanding and treating social anxiety disorder. In T. H. Ollendick & J. S. March (Eds.), *Phobic and anxiety disorders: A clinician's guide to effective psychosocial and pharmacological interventions.* New York: Oxford University Press.

Albano, A. M., & Kendall, P. C. (2002). Cognitive behavioural therapy for children and adolescents with anxiety disorders: clinical research advances. *International Review of Psychiatry, 14,* 128–133.

Albano, A. M., Marten, P. A., Holt, C. S., Heimberg, R. G., & Barlow, D. H. (1995). Cognitive-behavioral group treatment for adolescent social phobia: A preliminary study. *Journal of Nervous and Mental Disease, 183,* 685–692.

Allgood-Merten, B., Lewinsohn, P. M., & Hops, H. (1990). Sex differences and adolescent depression. *Journal of Abnormal Psychology, 99,* 55–63.

American Psychiatric Association (1980). *Diagnostic and statistical manual of mental disorders* (3rd ed.). Washington, DC: Author.

American Psychiatric Association (1987). *Diagnostic and statistical manual of mental disorders* (Rev. ed.). Washington, DC: Author.

American Psychiatric Association (1994). *Diagnostic and statistical manual of mental disorders* (4th ed.). Washington, DC: Author.

Anderson J. C., Williams, S., McGee, R., & Silva, P. A. (1987). DSM-III disorders in preadolescent children: Prevalence in a large sample from the general population. *Archives of General Psychiatry, 44,* 69–76.

Angold, A., Costello, E. J., & Worthman, C. M. (1998). Puberty and depression: The roles of age, pubertal status and pubertal timing. *Psychological Medicine, 28,* 51–61.

Bardone, A. M., Moffitt, T. E., Caspi, A., Dickson, N., & Silva, P. A. (1996). Adult mental health and social outcomes of adolescent girls with depression and conduct disorder. *Development and Psychopathology, 8,* 811–829.

Bardone, A. M., Moffitt, T. E., Caspi, A., Dickson, N., Stanton, W. R., & Silva, P. (1998). Adult physical health outcomes of adolescent girls with conduct disorder, depression, and anxiety. *Journal of the American Academy of Child and Adolescent Psychiatry, 37,* 594–601.

Barrett, P. M., Dadds, M. R., Rapee, R. M., & Ryan, S. M. (1996). Family intervention for childhood anxiety: A controlled trial. *Journal of Consulting and Clinical Psychology, 64,* 333–342.

Beidel, D. C. (1991). Social phobia and overanxious disorder in school-age children. *Journal of the American Academy of Child and Adolescent Psychiatry, 30,* 545–552.

Beidel, D. C., Christ, M. A., & Long, P. J. (1991). Somatic complaints in anxious children. *Journal of Abnormal Child Psychology, 19,* 659–670.

Beidel, D. C., & Morris, T. L. (1993). Avoidant disorder of childhood and social phobia. *Child and Adolescent Psychiatric Clinics of North America, 2*, 623–638.

Beidel, D. C., & Morris, T. L. (1995). Social phobia. In J. S. March (Ed.), *Anxiety disorders in children and adolescents* (pp. 181–211). New York: Guilford.

Beidel, D. C., & Turner, S. M. (1998). *Shy children, phobic adults: Nature and treatment of social phobia.* Washington, DC: American Psychological Association.

Beidel, D. C., Turner, S. M., & Morris, T. L. (1999). Psychopathology of childhood social phobia. *Journal of the American Academy of Child and Adolescent Psychiatry, 38*, 643–650.

Beidel, D. C., Turner, S. M., & Morris, T. L. (2000). Behavioral treatment of childhood social phobia. *Journal of Consulting and Clinical Psychology, 68*, 1072–1080.

Beitchman, J. H., Wekerle, C., & Hood, J. (1987). Diagnostic continuity from preschool to middle childhood. *Journal of the American Academy of Child and Adolescent Psychiatry, 26*, 694–699.

Bell-Dolan, D., & Brazeal, T. J. (1993). Separation anxiety disorder, overanxious disorder, and school refusal. *Child and Adolescent Psychiatric Clinics of North America, 2*, 563–580.

Benjamin R. S., Costello E. J., & Warren, M. (1990). Anxiety disorders in a pediatric sample. *Journal of Anxiety Disorders, 4*, 293–316.

Berg, C., Rapoport, J. L., Whitaker, A., Davies, M., Leonard, H., Swedo, S., et al. (1989). Childhood obsessive compulsive disorder: A two-year prospective follow-up of a community sample. *Journal of the American Academy of Child and Adolescent Psychiatry, 28*, 528–533.

Bernstein, G. A., & Borchardt, C. M. (1991). Anxiety disorders of childhood and adolescence: A critical review. *Journal of the American Academy of Child and Adolescent Psychiatry, 30*, 519–532.

Bird, H. R., Gould, M. S., Yager, T., Staghezza, B., & Canino, G. (1989). Risk factors for maladjustment in Puerto Rican children. *Journal of the American Academy of Child and Adolescent Psychiatry, 28*, 847–850.

Birmaher, B., Waterman, S. G., Ryan, N., Cully, M., Balach, L., Ingram, J., et al. (1994). Fluoxetine for childhood anxiety disorders. *Journal of the American Academy of Child and Adolescent Psychiatry, 33*, 993–999.

Boldizar, J. P. (1991). Assessing sex typing and androgyny in children: The Children's Sex Role Inventory. *Developmental Psychology, 27*, 505–515.

Bourdon, K. H., Boyd, J. H., Rae, D. S., Burns, B. J. (1988). Gender differences in phobias: Results of the ECA community survey. *Journal of Anxiety Disorders, 2*, 227–241.

Brady, E. U., & Kendall, P. C. (1992). Comorbidity of anxiety and depression in children and adolescents. *Psychological Bulletin, 111*, 244–255.

Breslau, N., Davis, G. C., Andreski, P., & Peterson, E. (1991). Traumatic events and post-traumatic stress disorder in an urban population of young adults. *Archives of General Psychiatry, 48*, 216–222.

Burke J. D., Borus J. F., Burns B. J., Millstein K. H., & Beasley, M. C. (1982), Changes in children's behavior after a natural disaster. *American Journal of Psychiatry 139*, 1010–1014.

Carey, M. P., Dusek, J. B., & Spector, I. P. (1988). Sex roles, gender, and fears: A brief report. *Phobia Practice & Research Journal, 1*, 114–120.

Caron, C., & Rutter, M. (1991). Comorbidity in child psychopathology: Concepts, issues and research strategies. *Journal of Child Psychology and Psychiatry, 32*, 1063–1080.

Chorpita, B. F., & Barlow, D. H. (1998). The development of anxiety: The role of control in the early environment. *Psychological Bulletin, 124*, 3–21.

Cohen, P., Cohen, J., & Brook, J. S. (1993). An epidemiological study of disorders in late childhood and adolescence: II. Persistence of disorders. *Journal of Child Psychology and Psychiatry and Allied Disciplines, 34*, 869–877.

Compton, S. N., Nelson, A. H., & March, J. S. (2000). Social phobia and separation anxiety symptoms in community and clinical samples of children and adolescents. *Journal of the American Academy of Child & Adolescent Psychiatry, 39*, 1040–1046.

Costello, E. J., & Angold, A. (1995). Epidemiology in anxiety disorders in children and adolescents. In J. S. March (Ed.), *anxiety disorders in children and adolescents* (pp. 109–124). New York: Guilford.

Costello, E. J., Keeler, G. P., & Angold, A. (2001). Poverty, race/ethnicity, and psychiatric disorder: A study of rural children. *American Journal of Public Health, 91,* 1494–1498.

Crick, N. R., & Ladd, G. W. (1993). Children's perceptions of their peer experiences: Attributions, loneliness, social anxiety, and social avoidance. *Developmental Psychology, 29,* 244–254.

Cross, S. E., & Madson, L. (1997). Models of the self: Self- construals and gender. *Psychological Bulletin, 122,* 5–37.

Dadds, M. R., Davey, G. C. L., & Field, A. P. (2001). Developmental aspects of conditioning processes in anxiety disorders. In M. W. Vasey & M. R. Dadds (Eds.), *The Developmental Psychopathology of Anxiety* (pp. 205–230). New York, NY: Oxford University Press.

DeWit, D. J., Ogborne, A., Offord, D. R., & MacDonald, K. (1999). Antecedents of the risk of recovery from DSM-III-R social phobia. *Psychological Medicine. 29,* 569–582.

Dillon, K. M., Wolf, E., & Katz, H. (1985). Sex roles, gender, and fear. *Journal of Psychology, 119,* 355–359.

Egger, H. L., Angold, A., & Costello, E. J. (1998). Headaches and psychopathology in children and adolescents. *Journal of the American Academy of Child & Adolescent Psychiatry, 37,* 951–958.

Egger, H. L., & Burns, B. J. (2004). Anxiety disorders and access to mental health services. In T. H. Ollendick & J. S. March (Eds.), *Phobic and anxiety disorders in children and adolescents* (pp. 530–549). New York: Oxford University Press.

Egger, H. L., Costello, E. J., Erkanali, A., & Angold, A. (1999). Somatic complaints and psychopathology in children and adolescents: Stomach aches, musculoskeletal pains, and headaches. *Journal of the American Academy of Child and Adolescent Psychiatry, 38,* 852–860.

Eisen, A. R., & Engler, L. B. (1995). Chronic anxiety. In A. R. Eisen, C. A. Kearney, & C. A. Schaefer (Eds.), *Clinical handbook of anxiety disorders in children and adolescents.* Northvale, NJ: Jason Aronson.

Eisen, A. R., & Kearney, C. A. (1995). *Practitioner's guide to treating fear and anxiety in children and adolescents: A cognitive-behavioral approach.* Northvale, NJ: Jason Aronson.

Essau, C. A., Conradt, J., & Petermann, F. (2000). Frequency, comorbidity, and psychosocial impairment of specific phobia in adolescents. *Journal of Clinical Child Psychology, 29,* 221–231.

Feigon, S. A., Waldman, I. D., Levy, F., & Hay, A. D. (2001). Genetic and environmental influences on separation anxiety disorder symptoms and their moderation by age and sex. *Behavior Genetics, 31,* 403–411.

Field, T., Diego, M., Hernandez-Reif, M., Schanberg, S., Kuhn, C. R. Y., & Bendell, D. (2003). Pregnancy anxiety and comorbid depression and anger effects on the fetus and neonate. *Depression and Anxiety, 17,* 140–151.

Ferdinand R. F., & Verhulst F. C. (1995). Psychopathology from adolescence into young adulthood: An 8-year follow-up study. *American Journal of Psychiatry. 152,* 586–94.

Flament, M. F., Whitaker, A., Rapoport, J. L., Davies, M., Zeremba-Berg, C., Kalikow, K. S., et al. (1988). Obsessive compulsive disorder in adolescence: An epidemiological study. *Journal of the American Academy of Child and Adolescent Psychiatry, 27,* 764–771.

Francis, G., Last, C. G., & Strauss, C. C. (1987). Expression of separation anxiety disorder: The roles of age and gender. *Child Psychiatry and Human Development, 18,* 82–89.

Fyer, A., Mannuzza, S., Chapman, T., Martin, L., & Klein, D. (1995). Specificity in familial aggregation of phobic disorders. *Archives of General Psychiatry, 52,* 564–573.

Gerul, F. C., & Rapee, R. M. (2002). Mother knows best: Effects of maternal modeling on the acquisition of fear and avoidance behaviour in toddlers. *Behavior Research and Therapy, 40,* 279–287.

Ginsburg, G. S., & Silverman, W. K. (1996). Phobic and anxiety disorders in Hispanic and Caucasian youth. Journal of Anxiety Disorders. 10, 517–528.

Ginsburg, G. S., & Silverman, W. K. (2000). Gender role orientation and fearfulness in children with anxiety disorders. *Journal of Anxiety Disorders. 14 ,* 57–67.

Ginsburg, G. S., Siqueland, L., Masia-Werner, C., & Hedtke, K. A. (2004). Anxiety disorders in children: Family matters. *Cognitive and Behavioral Practice, 11,* 28–43.

Glover, V., Teixeira, J., Gitau, R., & Fisk, N. M. (1999). Mechanisms by which maternal mood during pregnancy may affect the fetus. *Contemporary Review of Obstetrics and Gynecology*, 1–6.

Goodyer, I. M., & Altham, P. M. E. (1991). Lifetime exit events and recent social and family adversities in anxious and depressed school-age children and adolescents: I. *Journal of Affective Disorders, 21*, 219–228.

Goodyer, I. M., Herbert, J., Tamplin, A., & Altham P. M. E. (2000). Recent life events, cortisol, dehydroepiandrosterone and the onset of major depression in high-risk adolescents. *British Journal of Psychiatry, 177*, 499–504.

Gould, R. A., Buckminster, S., Pollack, M. H., Otto, M. W., & Yap, L. (1997). Cognitive-behavioral and pharmacological treatment for social phobia: A meta-analysis. *Clinical Psychology: Science and Practice, 4*, 291–306.

Gould, R. A., Otto, M. W., Pollack, M. P., & Yap, L. (1997). Cognitive-behavioral and pharmacological treatment of generalized anxiety disorder: A preliminary meta-analysis. *Behavior Therapy, 28*, 285–305.

Gore, S., Aseltine, R. H., & Colten, M. E. (1993). Gender, social-relational involvement, and depression. *Journal of Research on Adolescence, 3*, 101–125.

Graber, J. A., Lewinsohn, P. M., Seeley, J. R., & Brooks-Gunn, J. (1997). Is psychopathology associated with the timing of pubertal development? *Journal of the American Academy of Child and Adolescent Psychiatry, 36*, 1768–1776.

Green, B. L., Korol, M., Grace, M. C., Vary, M. G., Leonard, A. C., Goldine, G. C., & Smitson-Cohen S. (1991). Children and disaster: age, gender, and parental effects on PTSD symptoms. *Journal of the American Academy of Child and Adolescent Psychiatry 30*, 945–951.

Grills, A. E., & Ollendick, T. H. (2002). Issues in parent-child agreement: The case of structured diagnostic interviews. *Clinical Child & Family Psychology Review, 5*, 57–83.

Gullone, E., & King, N. J. (1993). The fears of youth in the 1990s: Contemporary normative data. *Journal of Genetic Psychology, 154*, 137–153.

Gurley D, Cohen P, Pine DS, & Brook J (1996). Discriminating anxiety an depression in youth: A role for diagnostic criteria. *Journal of Affective Disorders, 39*, 191–200.

Halbreich, U. (2003). Anxiety disorders in women: A developmental and lifecycle perspective. *Depression and Anxiety, 17*, 107–110.

Hankin, B. L., & Abramson, L. Y. (2001). Development of gender differences in depression: An elaborated cognitive vulnerability-transactional stress theory. *Psychological Bulletin, 127*, 773–796.

Hanna, E. Z., & Grant, B. F. (1997). Gender differences in DSM-IV alcohol use disorders and major depression as distributed in the general population: Clinical implications. *Comprehensive Psychiatry, 38*, 202–212.

Hayward, C. (Ed.). (2003). *Gender differences at puberty*. New York: Cambridge University Press.

Hayward, C., Killen, J. D., Hammer, L., & Litt, I. F. (1992). Pubertal stage and panic attack history in sixth- and seventh-grade girls. *American Journal of Psychiatry, 149*, 1239–1243.

Hayward, C., Killen, J. D., Taylor, C. B. (1989). Panic attacks in young adolescents. *American Journal of Psychiatry, 146*, 1061–1062.

Hayward, C., Killen, J. D., Wilson, D. M., & Hammer, L. D. (1997). Psychiatric risk associated with early puberty in adolescent girls. *Journal of the American Academy of Child and Adolescent Psychiatry, 26*, 225–262.

Hayward, C., & Sanborn, K. (2002). Puberty and the emergence of gender differences in psychopathology. *Journal of Adolescent Health, 30 (Supp.)*, 49–58.

Hayward, C., Varady, S., Albano, A. M., Thienemann, M., Henderson, L., & Schatzberg, A. F. (2000). Cognitive-behavioral group therapy for social phobia in female adolescents: Results of a pilot study. *Journal of the American Academy of Child & Adolescent Psychiatry, 39*, 721–726.

Hill, J. P., & Lynch, M. E. (1983). The intensification of gender-related role expectations. In J. Brooks-Gunn & A. C. Petersen (Eds.), *Girls at puberty* (pp. 201–228). N ew York: Plenum.

Hofmann, S., Albano, A. M., Heimberg, R. G., Tracey, S., Chorpita, B. F., & Barlow, D. H. (1999). Subtypes of social phobia in adolescents. *Depression and Anxiety, 9*, 8–15.

Ialongo, N., Edelsohn, G., Werthamer-Larsson, L., Crockett, L., & Kellam, S. (1994). The significance of self-reported anxious symptoms in first-grade children. *Journal of Abnormal Child Psychology. 22*, 441–55.

Ialongo, N., Edelsohn, G., Werthamer-Larsson, L., Crockett, L., & Kellam, S. (1995). The significance of self-reported anxious symptoms in first grade children: Prediction to anxious symptoms and adaptive functioning in fifth grade. *Journal of Child Psychology and Psychiatry and Allied Disciplines, 36,* 427–37.

Kagan, J. (2001). Temperamental contributions to affective and behavioral profiles in childhood. In S. G. Hofmann & P. M. DiBartolo (Eds.), Social phobia and social anxiety: An integration (pp. 216–234). New York: Plenum Press.

Kashani, J. H., & Orvashel, H. (1990). A community study of anxiety in children and adolescents. *American Journal of Psychiatry, 147,* 313–318.

Kashani, J. H., Orvaschel, H., Rosenberg, T. K., & Reid, J. C. (1999). Psychopathology in a community sample of children and adolescents: A developmental perspective. *Journal of the American Academy of Child & Adolescent Psychiatry. 28,* 701–706.

Kearney, C. A. (2001). *School refusal behavior in youth: A functional approach to assessment and treatment.* Washington, DC: American Psychological Association.

Kendall, P. C. (1990). *Coping Cat Workbook.* Ardmore, PA: Workbook Publishing.

Kendall, P. C. (Ed). (2000). *Child and adolescent therapy: Cognitive-behavioral procedures* (2nd ed.) New York: Guilford.

Kearney, C. A., & Albano, A. M. (2000a). When children refuse school: A therapist's manual. San Antonio, TX: The Psychological Corporation.

Kearney, C. A., & Albano, A. M. (2000b). When children refuse school: A parent's guide. San Antonio, TX: The Psychological Corporation.

Kearney, C. A., & Allan, W. D. (1995). Panic disorder with or without agoraphobia. In A. R. Eisen & C. A. Kearney, & Schaefer, C. E. (Eds), *Clinical handbook of anxiety disorders in children and adolescents* (pp. 251–281). Northvale, NJ, US: Jason Aronson, Inc.

Kendall, P. C., & Brady, E. U. (1995). Comorbidity in the anxiety disorders of childhood. In K. D. Craig & K. S. Dobson (Eds.), *Anxiety and depression in adults and children.* Newbury Park, CA: Sage.

Kendall, P. C., Flannery-Schroeder, E., Panicelli-Mindel, S. M., Southam-Gerow, M. A., Henin, A., & Warman, M. (1997). Therapy for youths with anxiety disorders: A second randomized clinical trial. *Journal of Consulting and Clinical Psychology, 65,* 366–380.

Kendall, P. C., & Warman, M. J. (1996). Anxiety disorders in youth: Diagnostic consistency across DSM-III-R and DSM-IV. *Journal of Anxiety Disorders, 10,* 453–463.

Kendler, K. S., Thornton, L. M., & Prescott, C. A. (2001). Gender differences in the rates of exposure to stressful life events and sensitivity to their depressogenic effects. *American Journal of Psychiatry, 158,* 587–593.

Kessler, R. C., McGonagle, K. A., Zhao, S., Nelson, C. B., Hughes, M., Eshlemann, S., Wittchen, H. U., & Kendler, S. (1994). Lifetime and 12-month prevalence of DSM-III–R psychiatric disorders in the United States: Results from the National Comorbidity Study. *Archives of General Psychiatry, 51,* 8–19.

Kessler, R. C., & McLeod, J. D. (1984). Sex differences in vulnerability to undesirable life events. *American Sociological Review, 49,* 620–631.

Killen, J. C., Hayward, C., & Litt, I. F. (1992). Is puberty a risk factor for eating disorders? *American Journal of Diseases of Childhood, 146,* 323–325.

Kilpatrick, D. G., Ruggiero, K. J., Acierno, R., Saunders, B. E., Resnick, H. S., & Best, C. L. (2003). Violence and risk of PTSD, major depression, substance abuse/dependence, and comorbidity: Results from the National Survey of Adolescents. *Journal of Consulting & Clinical Psychology. 71,* 692–700.

King, N. J., Gullone, E., Tonge, B. J., & Ollendick, TH. (1993). Self-reports of panic attacks and manifest anxiety in adolescents. *Behaviour Research and Therapy, 31,* 111–116.

Klein, D. N. (1995). Diagnosis and classification of dysthymic disorder (pp. 1–19). In J. H. Kocsis & D. N. Klein, DN. (Eds), *Diagnosis and treatment of chronic depression.* NY: Guilford.

La Greca, A. M. (2001). Friends or foes? Peer influences on anxiety among adolescents. In W. K. Silverman & P. Treffers (Eds.), *Anxiety disorders in children and adolescents* (pp. 159–186). New York: Cambridge University Press.

La Greca, A. M., & Lopez, N. (1998). Social anxiety among adolescents: Linkages with peer relations and friendships. *Journal of Abnormal Child Psychology, 26,* 83–94.

La Greca, A. M., & Stone, W. L. (1993). Social Anxiety Scale for Children–Revised: Factor structure and concurrent validity. *Journal of Clinical Child Psychology, 22,* 17–27.

Last, C. G. (1989). Anxiety disorders of childhood or adolescence. In C. G. Last & M. Hersen (Eds.), *Handbook of child psychiatric diagnosis* (pp. 156–169). New York: Wiley.

Last, C. G. (1991). Somatic complaints in anxiety disordered children. *Journal of Anxiety Disorders, 5,* 125–138.

Last, C. G., Francis, G., Hersen, M., Kazdin, Alan E., & Strauss, C. C (1987). Separation anxiety and school phobia: A comparison using DSM-III criteria. *American Journal of Psychiatry, 144,* 653–657.

Last, C. G., Francis, G., & Strauss, C. C. (1989). Assessing fears in anxiety-disordered children with the Revised Fear Survey Schedule for Children (FSSC-R). *Journal of Clinical Child Psychology, 18,* 137–141.

Last, C. G., Hersen, M., Kazdin, A. E., Finkelstein, R. (1987). Comparison of DSM-III separation anxiety and overanxious disorders: Demographic characteristics and patterns of comorbidity. *Journal of the American Academy of Child & Adolescent Psychiatry, 26,* 527–531.

Last, C. G., Hersen, M., Kazdin, A., Orvaschel, H., & Perrin, S. (1991). Anxiety disorders in children and their families. *Archives of General Psychiatry, 48,* 928–934.

Last, C. G., & Perrin, S. (1993). Anxiety disorders in African-American and White children. *Journal of Abnormal Child Psychology. 21,* 153–164.

Last, C. G., Perrin, S., Hersen, M., & Kazdin, A. E. (1992). DSM-III–R anxiety disorders in children: Sociodemographic and clinical characteristics. Journal *of the American Academy of Child and Adolescent Psychiatry, 31,* 1070–1076.

Last, C. G., Strauss, C. C., & Francis, G. (1987). Comorbidity among childhood anxiety disorders. *Journal of Nervous and Mental Disease, 175,* 726–730.

Leary, M. R. (1990). Responses to social exclusion: Social anxiety, jealousy, loneliness, depression, and low self-esteem. *Journal of Social and Clinical Psychology, 9,* 221–229.

Leonard, H. L., & Rapoport, J. (1991). Obsessive–compulsive disorder. In J. M. Wiener (Ed.), *Textbook of child and adolescent psychiatry* (pp. 323–329). Washington, DC: American Psychiatric Press.

Liebowitz, M. R., Gorman, J. M., Fyer, A. J., & Klein, D. F. (1985). Social phobia: Review of a neglected anxiety disorder. *Archives of General Psychiatry. 42,* 729–736.

Lewinsohn, P. M., Gotlib, I. H., Lewinsohn, M., Seeley, J. R., & Allen, N. B. (1998). Gender differences in anxiety disorders and anxiety symptoms in adolescents. *Journal of Abnormal Psychology, 107,* 109–117.

Lewinsohn, P. M., Zinbarg, R., Seeley, J. R., Lewinsohn, M., & Sack, W. H. (1997). Lifetime comorbidity among anxiety disorders and between anxiety disorders and other mental disorders in adolescents. *Journal of Anxiety Disorders, 11,* 377–394.

Lewinsohn, P. M., Hops, H., Roberts, R. E., Seeley, John R. & Andrews, J. A. (1993). Adolescent psychopathology: I. Prevalence and incidence of depression and other DSM-III–R disorders in high school students. *Journal of Abnormal Psychology, 102,* 133–144.

Livingston, R., Taylor, J. L., & Crawford, S. L. (1988). A study of somatic complaints and psychiatric diagnosis in children. *Journal of the American Academy of Child and Adolescent Psychiatry, 27,* 185–187.

Lonigan, C. J., Shannon, M. P., Finch, A. J., Daugherty, T. K., & Taylor CM (1991). Children's reactions to a natural disaster: Symptom severity and degree of exposure. *Advances in Behavior Research and Therapy, 13,* 135–154.

Maccoby, E. E. (1990). Gender and relationships: A developmental account. *American Psychologist, 45,* 513–520.

Maggini, C., Ampollini, P., Gariboldi, S., Cella, P. L., Peqlizza, L., & Marchesi, C. (2001). The Parma high school epidemiological survey: Obsessive compulsive symptoms. *Acta Psychiatrica Scandinavica, 103,* 441–446.

Manassis, K., & Bradley, S. J. (1994). The development of childhood anxiety disorders: Toward an integrated model. *Journal of Applied Developmental Psychology, 15,* 345–366.

March, J., Amaya-Jackson, L., Murry, M., & Schulte, A. (1998). Cognitive-behavioral psychotherapy for children and adolescents with post-traumatic stress disorder following a single incident stressor. *Journal of the American Academy of Child and Adolescent Psychiatry, 37,* 585–593.

March, J., & Mulle, K. (1998). *OCD in children and adolescents: A Cognitive-behavioral treatment manual.* New York: Guilford.

Marks, I. M. (1988). Blood-injury phobia: A review. *American Journal of Psychiatry, 145,* 1207–1213.

Mash, E. J., & Barkley, R. A. (Eds.). (2003). *Child psychopathology* (2nd ed.). New York: Guilford.

Masi, G., Favilla, L, Mucci, M., & Millepiedi, S. (2000). Depressive comorbidity in children and adolescents with generalized anxiety disorder. *Child Psychiatry and Human Development, 30,* 205–215.

McGee, R., Feehan, M., Williams, S., Partridge, F. (1990). DSM-III disorders in a large sample of adolescents. *Journal of the American Academy of Child and Adolescent Psychiatry, 29,* 611–619.

Morris, T. L., & March, J. S. (Eds.). (2004). *Anxiety disordes in children and adolescents* (2nd ed.). New York: Guilford.

Muris, P., Meesters, C., Merckelbach, H., Sermon, A., & Zwakhalen, S. (1998). Worry in normal children. *Journal of the American Academy of Child and Adolescent Psychiatry, 37,* 703–710.

Neal, A. M., Lilly, R. S., & Zakis, S. (1993). What are African American children afraid of? A preliminary study. *Journal of Anxiety Disorders. 7,* 129–139.

Nielsen, T. A., Laberge, L., Paquet, J., Tremblay, R. E., Vitaro, F., & Montplaisir, J. (2000). Development of disturbing dreams during adolescence and their relation to anxiety symptoms. *Sleep, 23,* 727–736.

Nottelmann, E. D., Susman, E. J., Blue, J. H., Inoff-Germain, G., Dorn, L. D., Loriaux, D. L., et al. (1987). Gonadal and adrenal hormone correlates of adjustment in early adolescence. In R. M. Lerner, & T. T. Foch, (Eds.), *Biological-psychosocial interactions in early adolescence. Child psychology.* (pp. 303–323). Hillsdale, NJ: Lawrence Erlbaum Associates.

Ohannessian, C. M., Lerner, R. M., von Eye, A., & Lerner, J. V. (1996). Direct and indirect relations between perceived parental acceptance, perceptions of the self, and emotional adjustment during early adolescence. *Family and Consumer Sciences Research Journal, 25,* 159–183.

Ollendick, T. H. (1983). Reliability and validity of the Revised Fear Survey Schedule for Children (FSSC-R). *Behaviour Research and Therapy, 21,* 685–692.

Ollendick, T. H., & Huntzinger, R. M. (1990). Separation anxiety disorder in childhood. In M. Hersen & C. G. Last (Eds.), *Handbook of child and adult psychopathology: A longitudinal perspective* (pp. 133–149). New York: Pergamon.

Ollendick, T. H., King, N. J., & Frary, R. B. (1989). Fears in children and adolescents: Reliability and generalizability across gender, age and nationality. *Behaviour Research & Therapy, 27,* 19–26.

Ollendick, T. H., & March, J. S. (Eds.). (2004). Phobic and anxiety disorders in children and adolescents. New York: Oxford University Press.

Ollendick, T. H., Mattis, S. G., & King, N. J. (1994). Panic in children and adolescents: A review. *Journal of Child Psychology and Psychiatry and Allied Disciplines. 35,* 113–134.

Ollendick, T. H., Yang, B., Dong, Q., Xia, Y., & Lin, L. (1995). Perceptions of fear in other children and adolescents: The role of gender and friendship status. *Journal of Abnormal Child Psychology, 23,* 439–452.

Papini, D. R., & Roggman, L. A. (1992). Adolescent perceived attachment to parents in relation to competence, depression, and anxiety: A longitudinal study. *Journal of Early Adolescence, 12,* 420–440.

Perrin, S., & Last, C. G. (1997). Worrisome thoughts in children referred for anxiety disorder. *Journal of Clinical Child Psychology, 26,* 181–189.

Pigott, T. A. (1999). Gender differences in the epidemiology and treatment of anxiety disorders. *Journal of Clinical Psychiatry, 60* (Suppl 18), 4–15.

Pine, D. S. (1994). Child-adult anxiety disorders. *Journal of the American Academy of Child and Adolescent Psychiatry, 33,* 2280.

Pine, D. S., Cohen, P., Gurley, D., Brook, J., & Ma, Y. (1998). The risk for early-adulthood anxiety and depressive disorders in adolescents with anxiety and depressive disorders. *Archives of General Psychiatry, 55,* 56–64.

Prins, P. J. M., & Ollendick, T. H. (2003). Cognitive change and enhanced coping: Missing mediational links in cognitive behavior therapy with anxiety-disordered children. *Clinical Child and Family Psychology Review, 6,* 87–105.

Rapee, R. M. (2001). The development of generalized anxiety. In M. W. Vasey & M. R. Dadds (Eds.), *The developmental psychopathology of anxiety* (pp. 481–503). New York: Oxford University Press.

Rose, R. J., & Ditto, W. B. (1983). A developmental-genetic analysis of common fears from early adolescence to early adulthood. *Child Development, 54,* 361–368.

Rosen, B. C., & Aneshensel, C. S. (1976). The chameleon syndrome: A social psychological dimension of the female sex role. *Journal of Marriage & the Family, 38,* 605–617.

Rossman, B. R., Bingham, R. D., & Emde, R. N. (1997). Symptomatology and adaptive functioning for children exposed to normative stressors, dog attack, and parental violence. *Journal of the American Academy of Child and Adolescent Psychiatry, 36,* 1089–1097.

Roza, S. J., Hofstra, M. B., van der Ende, J., & Verhulst, F. C. (2003). Stable prediction of mood and anxiety disorders based on behavioral and emotional problems in childhood: A 14-year follow-up during childhood, adolescence, and young adulthood. *American Journal of Psychiatry, 160,* 2116–2121.

Rubinow, D. R., & Schmidt, P. J. (1996). Androgens, brain, and behavior. *American Journal of Psychiatry, 153,* 974–984.

Rudolph, K. D. (2002). Gender differences in emotional responses to interpersonal stress during adolescence. *Journal of Adolescent Health, 30S,* 3–13.

RUPP Anxiety Study Group (2001). Fluvoxamine for the treatment of anxiety disorders in children and adolescents. *New England Journal of Medicine, 344,* 1279–1285.

Rynn, M. A., Siqueland, L., & Rickels, K. (2001). Placebo-controlled trial of sertraline in the treatment of children with generalized anxiety disorder. *American Journal of Psychiatry, 158,* 2008–2014.

Seligman, L. D., & Ollendick, T. H. (1998). Comorbidity of anxiety and depression in children and adolescents: An integrative review. *Clinical Child and Family Psychology Review, 1,* 125–144.

Shaffer, D., Gould, M. S., Fisher, P., Trautman, P., Moreau, D., Kleinman, M., & Flory, M. (1996). Psychiatric diagnosis in child and adolescent suicide. *Archives of General Psychiatry 53* 339–348.

Silove, D., Manicavasagar, V., O'Connell, D., & Morris-Yates, A. (1995). Genetic factors in early separation anxiety: Implications for the genesis of adult anxiety disorders. *Acta Psychiatrica Scandinavia, 92,* 17–24.

Silverman, W. K., & Ginsburg, G. S. (1995). Specific phobia and generalized anxiety disorder. In J. S. March (Ed.), *Anxiety disorders in children and adolescents* (pp. 151–180). New York: Guilford.

Silverman, W. K., & Kurtines, W. M. (1996). *Anxiety and phobic disorders: A pragmatic approach.* New York: Plenum.

Silverman, W. K., Kurtines, W.M., Ginsburg, G. S., Weems, C. F., Lumpkin, P., White C., et al. (1999). Treating anxiety disorders in children with group cognitive-behavioral therapy: A randomized clinical trial. *Journal of Consulting and Clinical Psychology 67,* 995–1003.

Silverman, W. K., LaGreca, A., & Wasserstein, S. (1995). What do children worry about? Worries and their relation to anxiety. *Child Development, 66,* 671–686.

Silverman, W. K., & Nelles, W. B. (1988). The anxiety disorders interview schedule for children. *Journal of the American Academy of Child and Adolescent Psychiatry, 27,* 772–778.

Slap, G. B., Khalid, N., Paikoff, R. L., & Brooks-Gunn J. (1994). Evolving self-image, age, pubertal manifestations, and pubertal hormones: Preliminary findings in young adolescent girls. *Journal of Adolescent Health, 15,* 327–335.

Spence, S. H. (1998). A measure of anxiety symptoms among children. *Behaviour Research and Therapy, 36*, 545–566.

Spence, S. H., Donovan, C., & Brechman-Toussaint, M. (1999). Social skills, social outcomes, and cognitive features of childhood social phobia. *Journal of Abnormal Psychology, 108*, 211–221.

Spence, S. H., Rapee, R., McDonald, C., & Ingram, M. (2001). The structure of anxiety symptoms among preschoolers. *Behaviour Research and Therapy, 39*, 1293–1316.

Strauss, C. C. (1990). Anxiety disorders of childhood and adolescence. *School Psychology Review, 19*, 142–157.

Strauss, C. C., & Last, C. G. (1993). Social and simple phobias in children. *Journal of Anxiety Disorders, 7*, 141–152.

Strauss, C. C., Lease, C. A., Last, C. G., & Francis, G. (1988). Overanxious disorder: An examination of developmental differences. *Journal of Abnormal Child Psychology, 16*, 433–443.

Strauss, C. C., Last, C. G., Hersen, M., & Kazdin, A. E. (1988). Association between anxiety and depression in children and adolescents with anxiety disorders. *Journal of Abnormal Child Psychology, 16*, 57—68.

Susman, E. J., Nottelmann, E. D., & Inoff-Germain, G. (1987). Hormonal influences on aspects of psychological development during adolescence. *Journal of Adolescent Health Care, 8*, 492–504.

Swedo, S. E., Rapoport, J. L., Leonard, H.,L., Lenane, M. (1989). Obsessive-compulsive disorder in children and adolescents: Clinical phenomenology of 70 consecutive cases. *Archives of General Psychiatry, 46* , 335–341.

Tracey, S. A., Chorpita, B. F., Douban, J., & Barlow, D. H. (1997). Empirical evaluation of DSM-IV generalized anxiety disorder criteria for children and adolescents. *Journal of Clinical Child Psychology, 26*, 404–414.

Treadwell, K. R. H., Flannery-Schroeder, E. C., & Kendall, P. C. (1995). Ethnicity and gender in relation to adaptive functioning, diagnostic status, and treatment outcome in children from an anxiety clinic. *Journal of Anxiety Disorders, 9*, 373–384.

Tucker, M., & Bond, N. W. (1997). The roles of gender, sex role, and disgust in fear of animals. *Personality and Individual Differences, 22* , 135–138.

Valleni-Basile, L. A., Garrison, C. Z., Jackson, K. L., Waller, J. L., McKeown, R. E., Addy, C. L., & Cuffe, S. P. (1994). Frequency of obsessive-compulsive disorder in a community sample of young adolescents. *Journal of the American Academy of Child and Adolescent Psychiatry, 33*, 782–791.

Varley, C. K., & Smith, C. J. (2003). Anxiety disorders in the child and teen. *Pediatric Clinics of North America, 50*, 1107–1138.

Vasey, M. W., & Dadds, M. R. (Eds.). (2001). *The developmental psychopathology of anxiety.* New York: Oxford University Press.

Velting, O. N., & Albano, A. M. (2001). Current trends in the understanding and treatment of social phobia in youth. *The Journal of Child Psychology and Psychiatry and Allied Disciplines, 42*, 127–140.

Vernberg, E. M., Abwender, D. A., Ewell, K. K., & Beery, S. H. (1992). Social anxiety and peer relationships in early adolescence: A prospective analysis. *Journal of Clinical Child Psychology. 21*, 189–196.

Wagner, B. M., & Compas, B. E. (1990). Gender, instrumentality, and expressivity: Moderators of the relation between stress and psychological symptoms during adolescence. *American Journal of Community Psychology, 18*, 383–406.

Warren, R., & Zgourides, G. (1988). Panic attacks in high school students: Implications for prevention and intervention. *Phobia Practice & Research Journal. 1*, 97–113.

Weems, C. F., Silverman, W. K., & La Greca, A. M. (2000). What do youth referred for anxiety problems worry about? Worry and its relation to anxiety and anxiety disorders in children and adolescents. *Journal of Abnormal Child Psychology, 28*, 63–72.

Werry, J., S. (1991). Overanxious disorder: A review of its taxonomic properties. *Journal of the American Academy of Child and Adolescent Psychiatry. 30*, 533–544.

Wewetzer, C., Jans, T., Mueller, B., Neudoerfl, A., Buecherl, U., Remschmidt, H., et al. (2001). Long-term outcome and prognosis of obsessive-compulsive disorder with onset in childhood or adolescence. *European Child and Adolescent Psychiatry, 10*, 37–46.

Wittchen, H., Stein, M., & Kessler, R. (1999). Social fears and social phobia in a community sample of adolescents and young adults: Prevalence, risk factors, and comorbidity.
Psychological Medicine, 29, 309–323.
Wood, J. J., McLeod, B. D., Sigman, M., Hwang, W., & Chu, B. C. (2003). Parenting and
childhood anxiety: Theory, empirical findings, and future directions. *Journal of Child
Psychology and Psychiatry, 44,* 134–151.
Zohar, A. H., Ratzoni, G., Pauls, D. L., Apter, A., Bleich, A., Kron, S., et al. (1992). An epidemiological study of obsessive-compulsive disorder and related disorders in Israeli adolescents. *Journal of the American Academy of Child and Adolescent Psychiatry, 31,* 1057–
1061.

III

Behavioral Disorders

4

Attention-Deficit/ Hyperactivity Disorder in Girls

STEPHEN P. HINSHAW and DARA R. BLACHMAN

Despite a density of research on attention-deficit/hyperactivity disorder (ADHD) in the past several decades that can conservatively be described as voluminous—and despite the considerable attention and controversy that have attended to this diagnostic category in both the scientific literature and popular media (see DeGrandpre & Hinshaw, 2000)—only an extremely small proportion of relevant investigations has focused on girls. Indeed, the predominance of males in the current literature far outweighs the ratio of boys to girls with the disorder, which has been estimated to be approximately 3:1 in community samples and perhaps twice as high in clinical samples (American Psychiatric Association, 1994; Lahey, Miller, Gordon, & Riley, 1999). As a result, the field's predominant models reflect what is known largely or exclusively about males. Much of our current chapter constitutes an attempt to redress this state of affairs; we initially take up the question as to the roots of the male-predominated literature and evidentiary base in the field.

HISTORICAL BACKGROUND

First, nearly all of the developmental disorders show a male predominance (Eme, 1992). As a result, girls have tended to be neglected both scientifically and clinically, in areas of investigation beyond ADHD (e.g., conduct disorder as well; see Waschbusch, 2002). Second, there has been a general tendency for biomedical science to prioritize investigations of

STEPHEN P. HINSHAW and DARA R. BLACHMAN • University of California, Berkeley, California, 94720-1650.

disorder in male—witness, for instance, the underrepresentation of women in research on cardiovascular disease. The past decade, however, has witnessed a significant turnaround, as exemplified by the need for adequate representation of females and of both ethnic and minority individuals in all NIH grant submissions (National Institutes of Health, 1994). It is no longer adequate, ethical, or scientifically defensible to make any presumption that male manifestations of physical or mental disorder should receive research or clinical primacy.

Third, whereas most clinical literature is based on samples of individuals who have been referred for assessment and treatment, clinic-based sampling is not appropriate for inferring rates of incidence, prevalence, or comorbidity (Angold, Costello, & Erkanli, 1999; Goodman et al., 1997). In fact, as noted above, the male:female ratio regarding ADHD is lower in representative than in clinic-derived samples, so that ADHD may be more relevant to females than previously suspected (Arnold, 1996; Gaub & Carlson, 1997).

Fourth, for much of the past century, the field viewed constituent symptoms of ADHD as commensurate with aggression, and conduct problems (Hinshaw, 1987). Because boys display higher rates of these latter behavior patterns than do girls, males were preferentially selected for research investigations of the precursor syndromes to ADHD (i.e., minimal brain dysfunction, hyperkinesis, or hyperactivity). Boys were also referred clinically at higher rates than girls, because such externalizing symptomatology is salient and troubling to parents and teachers. During the 1980s and 1990s, with the development of assessment instruments that could disentangle these partially independent domains (e.g., Loney, 1987), more girls were identifiable as having ADHD. Fifth, with the appearance of the of "ADD without hyperactivity" in the third edition of the *Diagnostic and Statistical Manual of Mental Disorders* (*DSM-III*; American Psychiatric Association, 1980) and the "Inattentive type" of ADHD in the fourth edition (*DSM-IV*; American Psychiatric Association, 1994), the field recognized forms of the disorder with particular salience for females (Arnold, 1996; Lahey et al., 1994; Nadeau, Littman, & Quinn, 1999). Thus, changes in diagnostic conceptions have paved the way for increasing recognition of ADHD in females.

In addition, recent data suggest that adult manifestations (or at least self-presentations) of ADHD are strongly present in women (Arcia & Conners, 1998; Henker & Whalen, 1999; Nadeau et al., 1999). A key reason here may be the tendencies for (a) hyperactive symptomatology (initially salient in boys) to recede across development but for (b) inattentive symptoms (relatively more salient in girls) to maintain their initial levels or to decline less sharply over time (Hart et al., 1995). Thus, although we direct our attention to ADHD in childhood and adolescence, we recognize that ADHD in women is an extremely understudied issue, and one for which the salience of female manifestations is quite strong.

In sum, political awareness, sampling methods, diagnostic reconceptualizations, and attention to developmental issues have spurred the growing awareness that girls and women can and do exhibit significant and impairing symptomatology related to ADHD. Therefore, within the past decade there has been an increasing call for greater focus on female manifestations and models pertinent to this disorder (Arnold, 1996; Biederman et al., 1999; Brown, Madan-Swain, & Baldwin, 1991; McGee & Feehan, 1991; see also Berry, Shaywitz, & Shaywitz, 1985). Despite this raising of consciousness, the extant database on girls with ADHD is still limited, centering on "gender differences" or "sex differences" regarding the expression of the disorder (see, in particular, the meta-analytic reviews of Gaub & Carlson, 1997, and Gershon, 2002). That is, small and homogeneous samples or subsamples of girls with ADHD, selected in accordance with diagnostic criteria based almost exclusively on male conceptions of the disorder, have been contrasted with much larger groups of boys. Although constituting a start, such investigations typically do not illuminate the processes and mechanisms underlying symptom expression, impairment, and developmental progressions in girls with ADHD, considered in and of themselves. Indeed, mean levels of symptoms or impairments may be identical in two subgroups (e.g., boys and girls) with entirely different processes having led to such similar rates of behavior. Developmentally informative, process-oriented investigations with female samples are quite recent.

Indeed, we confess a certain level of frustration in preparing this chapter. For one thing, nearly all studies of girls with ADHD are cross-sectional in nature, and most have a largely descriptive, adevelopmental focus. Although adequate description is necessary for an understudied phenomenon, the field still lacks the kinds of models that would be most important for a thorough understanding of ADHD in girls. And, in the nearly total absence of prospective longitudinal data, the developmental course of ADHD in girls is largely unknown. There is also inconsistency in the findings that emanate from much of the current literature on several of the topics we address (e.g., comorbidities, familial/genetic underpinnings, neural mechanisms, social deficits in girls with ADHD), with investigations from different laboratories yielding contradictory results. This state of affairs reflects different sampling strategies utilized by different investigators and the lack of sophistication in paradigms for investigating females. In short, our frustration stems from a male-dominated literature, a dearth of important process-oriented investigations of girls with ADHD, and a lack of appropriate framing or conceptualization of basic issues in the field in terms of sex and gender. Our key conclusion is therefore that basic, applied, and clinical investigators need to pay far greater attention to the topic of ADHD in girls, with developmental sensitivity. When such attention is paid, a more informed chapter should emerge in subsequent editions of this book.

ADHD: BASIC ISSUES AND CONCEPTUALIZATION REGARDING GIRLS

Key Issues Regarding ADHD

Even a cursory review of ADHD is beyond the scope of this chapter (for authoritative information, see Barkley, 1998). It is a prevalent, impairing, and clinically salient developmental disorder, first evident in childhood and with a strong tendency toward persistence across the years (Hinshaw, 1994). The key symptoms fall along two dimensions: (a) inattention/disorganization and (b) hyperactivity/impulsivity, which are ubiquitous phenomena in young children, during the periods of increased demands for socialization, self-regulation, and academic performance that emerge in early to middle childhood. Thus, constituent symptoms are not rare, unusual behavior patterns are but behaviors exhibited by all young children. The key question is knowing when the behavior patterns of a given child are worthy of diagnosis.

Issues regarding sex (biological status of an individual as male or female) and gender (ascription of behavior according to sex-typed norms) are immediately apparent. That is, starting at ages 3 to 4 years, boys display higher rates of noncompliant, impulsive, and hyperactive behavior patterns than do girls (Keenan & Shaw, 1997). This sex difference in the precursors to the constituent symptomatology undoubtedly reflects both underlying biological differences and gender-based socialization patterns that interact and transact with such proclivities. Should, then, girls be compared with all-female norms when a diagnostic decision is to be made? Or should there be "sex-neutral" criteria (see general discussion in Hartung & Widiger, 1998)? Furthermore, are there uniquely "female" aspects to ADHD that are not captured in the current diagnostic algorithms? We consider these questions in the subsection on diagnostic criteria.

A diagnosis of ADHD is warranted if the symptom patterns are marked by developmental extremity, early onset (before age 7), persistence (at least 6 months' duration), and cross-situationality (i.e., displayed in multiple contexts; American Psychiatric Association, 1994). Thus, essentials of a diagnostic work-up include a thorough history of the child's development, the perspectives of parents and teachers who see the child in everyday environments, the use of normed assessment instruments, and both medical and psychosocial evaluations to rule out the many neurological and developmental conditions and patterns that may mimic ADHD—e.g., seizure disorders or response to abusive childrearing environments. Furthermore, because ADHD often presents in combination with other disorders (Angold et al., 1999), an essential part of the diagnostic process is evaluating comorbid conditions (see section on comorbidity).

Like many conditions in medicine and psychiatry (e.g., depression, hypertension), ADHD is a categorical diagnosis applied to constituent behavior patterns that are distributed continuously in the population. Even the genetic liability for ADHD, which is considerable (see below), pertains to the underlying dimensions of inattentive, hyperactive, and impulsive behaviors rather than to a diagnostic category per se (Levy, Hay, McStephen, Wood, & Waldman, 1997). Thus, the decision as to the cutoff score for ascertaining diagnosable ADHD is, as in the case of many other disorders, somewhat arbitrary, although sound clinical judgment and sound quantitative research can help to guide the decision process. For current perspectives on the dimensional versus categorical nature of child psychopathology in general, see Pickles and Angold (2003).

In terms of etiology, the core symptomatology of ADHD displays heritability estimates ranging from .7 to over .8 (see Tannock, 1998). Thus, ADHD is one of the most heritable conditions in all of psychiatry. Other risk factors include low birthweight (Mick, Biederman, Prince, Fischer, & Faraone, 2002; Whitaker et al., 1997) and maternal use of tobacco, alcohol, or illicit drugs during pregnancy (Mick, Biederman, Faraone, Sayer, & Kleinman, 2002). Whereas parenting styles or psychosocial variables are generally not believed to be causal of ADHD, they interact with underlying biological vulnerabilities to shape severity, impairment, and comorbidity (Biederman et al., 1995; Hinshaw, 1999). Again, however, the vast majority of the relevant literature on risk and etiologic factors applies to boys, not necessarily to girls.

ADHD is a disorder that persists across development in most cases (Mannuzza & Klein, 1999). The vast majority of boys diagnosed with ADHD will continue to meet criteria for diagnosis in adolescence; by adulthood, the continuity of symptomatology is lower, although recent evidence suggests far stronger persistence of the condition when multiple informants are used to appraise adult symptoms and impairment (Barkley, Fischer, Smallish, & Fletcher, 2002). Prospective data are vanishingly rare for girls, however, and the suggestion that women may equal men in terms of prevalence of ADHD in adulthood highlights the clear research need for greater understanding of female developmental trajectories.

A central issue regarding ADHD pertains to subtypes of the disorder. *DSM-IV* (American Psychiatric Association, 1994) lists three subtypes, based on the predominant symptom pattern (for conduct disorder, on the other hand, subtypes are based on age of onset; see Moffitt, 1993). (1) The Combined type, the most prevalent variant referred for clinical services, presents with high levels of both inattentive/disorganized and hyperactive/impulsive symptoms. (2) The Inattentive type (similar to the former label of "attention deficit disorder without hyperactivity" in *DSM-III*; American Psychiatric Association, 1980) features inattention but not hyperactivity/impulsivity; it appears to be the most prevalent manifestation in community samples (Wolraich, Hannah, Pinnock, Baumgaertel, & Brown, 1996). Although it has been argued that the Inattentive type is qualitatively distinct from the other subtypes (Milich, Balentine, & Lynam, 2001), evidence in this regard is mixed (see Hinshaw, 2001). (3) The rarer Hyperactive–Impulsive type is salient largely for preschoolers (see Lahey et al., 1994) and may have limited validity for older children.

Sex Differences Regarding ADHD

Despite small samples in most relevant investigations, there are now sufficient numbers of studies of girls with ADHD to warrant meta-analytic reviews on the topic of "head to head" comparisons with boys (Gaub & Carlson, 1997; Gershon, 2002). First, referral source appears to moderate a number of key meta-analytic findings. Specifically, in nonreferred or community samples, girls meeting criteria for ADHD appear to be (a) less symptomatic than boys meeting criteria for ADHD, with respect to parent and teacher ratings of both inattention and hyperactivity/ impulsivity (Gershon, 2002) and (b) less impaired than boys in terms of reading achievement, internalizing features, aggression, and peer status (Gaub & Carlson, 1997; Gershon, 2002). On the other hand, among clinic-referred individuals, female and male samples are typically indistinguishable in terms of most measures of symptomatology and impairment, with some suggestion that clinical samples of girls have *lower* IQ scores (Gaub & Carlson, 1997) and *greater* amounts of inattention (Gershon, 2002) than do clinically referred boys. Thus, girls who get referred for assessment and treatment may well be the most severely affected girls displaying the constituent symptoms. Whether sex differences truly exist is therefore clouded by the sample type investigated; clinical samples of girls may not be representative of all girls with ADHD.

Second, Gaub and Carlson (1997) point out that most sex differences that exist are small in magnitude, even if statistically significant. Especially in clinical samples, the basic similarity of boys and girls with ADHD is the most salient finding. Recently, however, Rucklidge and Tannock (2001) contrasted adolescent (a) boys and girls with ADHD and (b) comparison boys and girls with respect to both symptomatology and domains of impairment. Here, for several important variables (particularly internalizing features), the adolescent females with ADHD were *more* impaired than the adolescent males with ADHD. An implication is that, by adolescence, ADHD may carry an increasing burden for females, although (a) in the absence of prospective studies from childhood to adolescence, this assertion is premature and (b) comparing clinical samples of boys and girls is not the most valid means of ascertaining comparative rates of prevalence, comorbidity, or impairment (Angold et al., 1999). Nonetheless, if girls get referred for treatment, their levels of problematic functioning are noteworthy, a pattern that may increase with development.

Third, ADHD subtypes were, unfortunately, either not specified or were too small in numbers for separate consideration in the meta-analyses. It is essential to indicate the type of ADHD displayed by research participants, especially in examinations of girls.

We note that the three largest clinical samples of girls with ADHD in the current literature are of recent origin: (a) the 140 girls with ADHD (along with 122 matched comparison girls) of Biederman et al. (1999, 2002), aged 6–17 years; (b) the 140 girls with ADHD and 88 matched comparison girls of Hinshaw (2002b) and Hinshaw, Carte, Sami, Treuting, and Zupan (2002), aged 6–12 years; and (c) the 116 girls in the Multimodal Treatment Study of Children with ADHD, aged 7–10 years (MTA Study; MTA Cooperative Group, 1999a, 1999b). All three investigative teams have utilized multi-informant, multimethod assessment strategies to document comorbidity, associated features, and impairment in their samples; all three relied on rigorous multigated assessment strategies to pinpoint diagnoses of ADHD. In addition, the Hinshaw (2002b) and MTA Cooperative Group (1999a, 1999b) samples are diverse ethnically and socioeconomically. The key finding from these samples is that the girls show substantial impairment in terms of social, cognitive, achievement-related, and personal domains of functioning, impairment that appears comparable to that of boys with the disorder. Thus, it can no longer be argued that referred samples of girls with ADHD are clinically inconsequential or that they suffer from mild impairments.

Realizing, however, that girls with ADHD are symptomatic, impaired, and in need of clinical intervention in middle childhood or in adolescence does not inform us of the processes whereby such clinically significant problems emerge. In fact, a developmental psychopathology perspective is necessary to consider in relation to mechanisms and developmental progressions.

Developmental Psychopathology Perspective

In contrast to the static conception of psychopathology incorporated in categorical nosologies, developmental psychopathology is a discipline concerned with understanding developmental processes and mechanisms responsible for the dynamic display of symptoms, strengths, and impairments across time (e.g., Cicchetti, 1993; Cicchetti & Cohen, 1995; Rutter & Sroufe, 2000; Sroufe & Rutter, 1984). We headline several core tenets of this perspective, all of which are pertinent to the investigation of ADHD in girls. (1) Study of normal development is essential to the understanding of atypical development, and vice versa. (2) Development must be understood in terms of continuities and discontinuities over time; hence, a longitudinal perspective is essential for gaining understanding of relevant mechanisms. (3) Development proceeds by processes of interaction and transaction across underlying biological predispositions and environmental contexts (ranging from parent–child interactions to characteristics of schools, neighborhoods, and cultures); thus, psychopathology is the result of a set of dynamic processes across multiple levels of analysis (Cicchetti & Dawson, 2003). (4) Because underlying genetic mechanisms are governed by superordinate forces as much as they determine such forces (i.e., epigenesis; Gottlieb, 1998), contextual influences and transactional patterns of influence are essential to understand regarding both typical and atypical development.

Three recent conceptual and empirical syntheses highlight the importance of social context in terms of both ADHD and broader patterns of development. First, regarding normative development, Maccoby (1998) highlights the substantially different socialization patterns displayed by girls, who tend to interact in dyads or small groups, versus boys, who utilize larger physical areas and make more sporadic contact with larger numbers of peers. Such sex-specific socialization is essential to consider in future investigations of the influence of peers on the development of girls with ADHD. Second, Keenan and Shaw (1997) portray a rich web of contextual influences, interacting with both underlying biological vulnerabilities and differential maturation across the sexes, in shaping the problem behavior of young girls. In brief, whereas sex differences in temperament, aggression, inhibition, and problem behavior are virtually nonexistent during infancy and toddlerhood, boys make a "leap" with respect to hyperactivity, impulsivity, and aggression in the preschool years, whereas girls show elevations regarding internalizing symptomatology, escalating markedly during adolescence. Two hypothesized mechanisms are cited regarding such patterns: (a) girls attain developmental competence in emotional, cognitive, and social functioning earlier than boys; and (b) adults and peers socialize girls toward internalization (rather than externalization) of conflict. Third, Campbell (2002) focuses on the transactional nature of the development of externalizing behavior problems in young children. Her data (primarily on boys) show that both the severity of problematic, ADHD-related problem behavior early in development (e.g., ages 3–4) *and* the contextual influence of early disruption in the parent–child relationship are predictive of the continuity of ADHD behavior patterns.

To cover the domain of ADHD in girls, we first take up the issue of the viability of current diagnostic criteria for females and then consider epidemiology, comorbidity, impairments and associated features, developmental progressions, and underlying mechanisms/causal factors. We close with brief discussion of issues pertinent to assessment and treatment.

DIAGNOSTIC CRITERIA

The constituent behaviors for ADHD include nine symptoms related to inattention/disorganization and nine related to impulsivity/hyperactivity. Among the many considerations regarding these symptoms are (a) they are macrobehavioral in nature, selected in part for ease of rating by parents and teachers but corresponding only loosely with laboratory measures of the underlying constructs (Hinshaw, 1999), and (b) they fail to capture the underlying problems in inhibitory control increasingly believed to be the core underlying processes related to ADHD (e.g., Barkley, 1997). Such conceptual issues are beyond the scope of this chapter. The primary question is whether the current diagnostic algorithms for ADHD are valid for girls (for an excellent discussion of gender-related bias regarding diagnosis in general, see Hartung & Widiger, 1998).

As the recognition of female manifestations of ADHD has grown, the issue of sex-specific versus sex-neutral diagnostic systems has come into focus. One line of argument is that, because rates of the constituent symptomatology are lower in girls than in boys in representative samples (Gaub & Carlson, 1997; Gershon, 2002), diagnostic thresholds should be sex-specific (e.g., Barkley, 1996). That is, girls should be compared with female norms regarding cutoff scores for requisite levels of symptomatology; otherwise, girls with serious symptoms (though not as extreme as those of boys) will be missed diagnostically. Counterarguments, however, center on the contention that sex-specific cutoff scores might not yield truly impairing levels of symptomatology (Arnold, 1996; Zahn-Waxler, 1993). This is an empirical question, and sorely needed are data on the issue of whether girls identified on the basis of female norms show clear clinical impairment. A "compromise" solution, utilized by our own laboratory (Hinshaw, 2002a) and others (see Sharp et al., 1999) is to invoke sex-specific cutoff scores at the phases of recruitment and screening, to ensure that potentially diagnosable girls are not eliminated prematurely; but then to insist on uniform, sex-neutral criteria for final diagnosis, such that all girls with ADHD must meet stringent criteria on the basis of validated structured interviews, with the same algorithm as for boys.

Neither strategy, however, can deal with the contention that the items utilized for diagnosis do not cover the range of symptomatology relevant for girls. Specifically, if girls are more likely to display inattentive/disorganized symptoms (and perhaps associated internalizing symptomatology, especially in terms of depressive symptoms in adolescence) than boys, or if girls present with "hyperverbal" behavior rather than overactive motor behavior per se (Nadeau et al., 1999), then the current diagnostic criteria may fail to incorporate the types of problems uniquely presented by females. In addition, *DSM-IV* may have eliminated a subset of items relevant to inattention/disorganization—those pertinent to a "sluggish cognitive tempo" (McBurnett, Pfiffner, & Frick, 2001) such as forgetfulness, sluggishness/drowsiness, and the tendency to daydream—that potentially capture a qualitatively distinct variant of Inattentive-type ADHD and that could be pertinent to ADHD presentation in a substantial number of girls. Carlson and Mann (2002) recently contended that an inattentive subgroup based on the presence of sluggish cognitive tempo was, in fact, homogeneous and distinct from the remainder of the Inattentive type. Although girls did not predominate in this subgroup (Carlson & Mann, 2002), it is still possible that key items relevant to female presentation have been excluded from the diagnostic criteria.

Zoccolillo (1993) made a similar argument with respect to diagnostic criteria for conduct disorder, contending that girls do not display the same degree of physical aggression and violence as boys but that indirect aggression and even somatic symptoms are likely to characterize conduct-disordered girls. On the other hand, Zahn-Waxler (1993) criticized this contention, arguing that it makes no sense to "water down" the conduct disorder diagnosis with nonaggressive items that fail to capture the types of antisocial behavior at the core of the category. Should the criterion list for ADHD be expanded to include additional items relevant to females? If so, what would such items constitute? Until psychopathologists have a better grasp on the precise nature of this diagnostic category (at levels spanning neurobiology, attentional processes, and interactions with culture), it is difficult to make a priori arguments about the symptomatic bounds of ADHD.

As noted earlier, *DSM-IV* states that impairing symptoms must be displayed prior to the age of 7 years. As argued, however, by Barkley and Biederman (1997) as well as Nadeau et al. (1999), a substantial proportion of children (many of whom display primarily inattentive/disorganized symptomatology) do not come to clinical attention until middle school or later, at which time their levels of impairment are clinically significant. Such youth, who are likely to include relatively high rates of females (see following section) yet who are eliminated from consideration for diagnosis in *DSM-IV* because of late age at onset, may comprise "false negatives," unless the criterion pertaining to age of onset is reconsidered in future nosologies.

In all, the diagnostic criteria for ADHD are largely descriptive and behavioral in nature. Sex-specific norms would increase the numbers of females meeting diagnostic criteria, but it is unknown whether such norms would uncover a truly impaired set of females. Whether the item content covered by *DSM-IV* criteria is relevant for females is as much a philosophical as an empirical issue; it is possible that symptoms related to sluggish cognitive tempo may help to reveal a more homogeneous variant of the Inattentive type that is of particular relevance for girls. Finally, the 7-year age-of-onset criterion in *DSM-IV* appears to be overly restrictive for many children with primarily inattentive symptomatology, comprising a disproportionate percentage of girls.

EPIDEMIOLOGY

As reviewed authoritatively by Lahey et al. (1999), definitive data on the prevalence of ADHD are limited by the lack of a national-level investigation of child mental disorders utilizing population-based, representative samples. Partly as a result, estimates of the prevalence of ADHD vary from study to study, ranging from approximately 3–9%. The best evidence suggests that, among community samples, boys outnumber girls by a ratio of approximately 3:1 during preadolescence (see, e.g., the exemplary Canadian investigation of Offord, Boyle, & Racine, 1989; Offord et al., 1987; see also the range of estimates in Lahey et al., 1999). In clinic samples, however, the male:female ratio is considerably higher, presumably because of the stronger likelihood of referral for youth with associated aggression, which is more likely to appear in males.

Recent population-based investigations are quite consistent with the figures above. For example, Barbaresi et al. (2002) studied all children born in Rochester, Minnesota, during the 6-year period between 1976 and 1982. With the criterion of "definite" ADHD (clinical diagnosis plus supporting documentation), the overall prevalence through age 19 was 7.5%, with the relative risk for boys to girls of 3.1:1. Second, in a survey utilizing data from the National Health Interview Survey, which examined children aged 6–11 years and used parental report of the child's receipt of diagnosis, Pastor and Reuben (2002) found a boy:girl ratio for overall ADHD (including learning disabilities as well) of approximately 2.5:1. Note that the rate was nearly 3:1 when "caseness" was defined as ADHD-only, without co-occurring learning disabilities.

Unfortunately, neither report provided any information on the sex ratios for the subtypes of ADHD. In clinical samples, girls appear relatively more likely to display the Inattentive type of ADHD (e.g., Biederman et al., 2002; Lahey et al., 1994; Willcutt et al., 2002). Importantly, Willcutt et al. (2002) recently pooled data from a number of population-based investigations, providing new, less biased information on the issue of whether the sex ratio varies as a function of ADHD subtype. In brief, larger proportions of girls who surpassed symptom cutoffs for any type of ADHD met criteria for the Inattentive type (51.5% for parent report, 60.5% for teacher report) than was the case for boys (39.7 and 49.5%, respectively). The investigations under review, however, examined symptom criteria alone; whether the relative female predominance with respect to the Inattentive type would pertain to the impairment or age-of-onset criteria is unknown.

Importantly, by adolescence, the sex ratio regarding the diagnosis of ADHD in community samples is reduced to about 2:1. By early adulthood, this ratio approaches unity (Cohen et al., 1993; see also DuPaul et al., 2001, which presents self-report data from college students). Note that these are cross-sectional results. Without longitudinal data, contentions that girls are more likely to persist with or develop ADHD by adulthood are not definitive.

In summary, girls are found to be less afflicted with diagnosable ADHD than are boys utilizing current diagnostic criteria, but in childhood the disparity within representative samples (approximately 3:1) is less marked than in clinical samples of referred youth. ADHD therefore afflicts a large number of girls in terms of absolute numbers, with additional evidence that the sex ratio declines by adolescence and may actually be "even" by adulthood. Girls also appear somewhat more likely to display the Inattentive type of the disorder than are boys, meaning that an exclusive focus on the most visible and clinically salient symptoms will overlook a substantial number of girls.

COMORBIDITY

The investigation of comorbidity in developmental psychopathology is essential for both clinical and conceptual reasons (see Chapter 1 of this volume; see also Caron & Rutter, 1991; Jensen, Martin, & Cantwell, 1997). In particular, if boys and girls with ADHD have different patterns of comorbidity, then what appear to be "sex differences" in manifestations of the disorder may actually reflect differences in the comorbid conditions. Appraisal of comorbid diagnoses is thus necessary in research on both girls and boys with ADHD. A key problem, however, is that prevalence rates of comorbidity can be appraised accurately only in nonreferred samples (Angold et al., 1999), meaning that much of the evidence reported herein (largely from clinical samples) may be biased.

From recent evidence in the past two decades (Biederman et al., 1999, 2002; see also Gaub & Carlson, 1997; Gershon, 2002), girls with ADHD appear to have lower rates of comorbid disruptive behavior disorders—oppositional defiant disorder (ODD) and conduct disorder (CD)—than do boys, for whom rates of such comorbidity approach or surpass 50%. Yet one should not make the automatic assumption that girls with ADHD display such aggressive comorbidity only rarely. In fact, Hinshaw (2002b) recently showed that preadolescent girls with ADHD have high rates of ODD (over 60%) and CD (approximately 20%), at least when diagnoses are made on the basis of parent report. It may be that parents of girls with ADHD are quite sensitive to any gender-atypical defiant and aggressive behavior patterns displayed by their daughters (in fact, rates of objectively observed aggressive and antisocial behaviors were considerably lower in the Hinshaw, 2002b, investigation than they had been in prior samples of boys with ADHD). Note also that the form of aggressive behavior termed relational aggression (Crick & Grotpeter, 1995) may be particularly salient for girls, who are likely to display it at higher rates than is the case for more overt forms of aggression (see Foster, this volume).

Findings are mixed when considering internalizing patterns—that is, those marked by anxiety, depression, social withdrawal, and somatic complaints (e.g., Achenbach, 1991). The meta-analytic review of Gershon (2002) revealed significantly *higher* rates of internalizing disorders in girls with ADHD than in boys, yet the earlier meta-analysis of Gaub and Carlson (1997) revealed a *lower* rate of internalizing behavior in girls with ADHD. This latter finding, however, was moderated by referral source: nonreferred girls showed lower rates of internalizing patterns than did boys, but for referred children, the rates were equivalent between the sexes. Crucially, internalizing conditions and disorders constitute a wide array of symptoms and impairments; it is necessary to specify this broad category. For example, Biederman et al. (2002) showed that clinic-referred girls with ADHD had lower rates of comorbid major depression (15%) than did a comparable sample of clinic-referred boys with ADHD (29%). Also, Hinshaw (2002b) showed that ADHD subtype differences in rates of internalizing behavior differed according to content and source of measurement. That is, girls with the Combined versus Inattentive types of ADHD were equivalent with respect to diagnoses of depression and anxiety disorders, parent-reported internalizing symptoms, and self-reported depressive symptoms. Yet, whereas staff-rated anxiety/depression scores were higher for the Combined than the Inattentive type, objective staff observations of social withdrawal yielded higher rates for the Inattentive than the Combined girls. Overall, the story is complex; prospective investigations into adolescence and adulthood—periods of markedly increased risk for internalizing conditions in females—will provide crucial data.

In terms of learning disabilities, despite evidence that girls with ADHD display lower intelligence than do boys with ADHD, particularly in clinical samples (Gaub & Carlson, 1997; Gershon, 2002), there are no conclusive data that girls with ADHD have higher rates of diagnosable learning disabilities. In fact, Biederman et al. (2002) showed that girls with ADHD were *less* likely (12%) than comparably ascertained boys with ADHD to have discrepancy-based reading or math disabilities (30%). Interestingly, Willcutt and Pennington (2000) showed that reading disorder was significantly associated with inattentive symptoms in both boys and in girls but was associated with hyperactive–impulsive symptomatology only in boys.

Another perspective on comorbidity is provided by Neuman et al. (2001), who investigated an extremely large population sample of adolescent female twins ($N = 2904$). Through latent class analysis, they uncovered three underlying categories among these girls: one consisting of inattentive symptoms alone, a second comprising inattentive symptoms plus

ODD, and a third constituting inattentive plus hyperactive/impulsive symptoms comorbid with ODD, separation anxiety, and depressive symptoms. Patterns of comorbidity may thus be complex among girls.

Finally, we describe briefly some recent and provocative evidence regarding the possibility of higher rates of comorbid substance use disorders among girls with ADHD than among boys. Both Biederman et al. (2002), utilizing clinic-referred samples of girls and boys with ADHD, and Disney, Elkins, McGue, and Iacono (1999), investigating a large, population-based twin sample of adolescents, found that the females with ADHD had higher rates of various substance use disorders than did the males. Each set of findings should be interpreted cautiously: Biederman et al. because of potential cohort effects, as the male and female samples were ascertained at different times; Disney et al. because the larger odds ratios for girls than for boys with ADHD regarding nicotine dependence, cannabis abuse/dependence, or any substance use disorder were not significantly larger. Nonetheless, it is conceivable that girls with ADHD are at particularly high risk for the development of potentially impairing and dangerous problems with substance use and abuse. Once again, prospective, longitudinal data are necessary to discern causal pathways in this regard.

IMPAIRMENTS AND ASSOCIATED FEATURES

One of the hallmarks of ADHD is the wide range of associated impairments that tend to accompany the disorder, which include cognitive, language, and academic difficulties; conflictual relationships with adults; problematic peer relationships; poor emotion regulation; and high rates of accidental injuries, including driving related difficulties (Hinshaw, 2002a). Once again, evidence in this regard is drawn from male-dominated studies. Thus, we focus herein on girls.

As highlighted earlier, several recent, clinic-based samples of girls with ADHD have documented a range of impairments across domains. Biederman et al. (1999) reported lower intellectual functioning, academic achievement, and global assessment of functioning scores, relative to a comparison sample. In addition, the girls with ADHD experienced greater family dysfunction (higher conflict, lower cohesion) and higher levels of school-related difficulties (special classes, repeated grades, tutoring) as well as greater levels of social impairment and higher rates of "social disability" than did the comparison girls (Greene et al., 2001). Also, in an adolescent sample, Rucklidge and Tannock (2001) showed that, relative to comparison females, girls with ADHD reported greater dissatisfaction with teachers, more negative life events and greater impact of such events, more global and stable attributions for negative events, greater external locus of control, more suicidal ideation (past and current), and higher levels of self-harm. They also demonstrated lower overall IQ and achievement scores and were viewed as more impaired by parents and teachers. Thus, available evidence suggests that girls with ADHD exhibit high levels of impairment across multiple domains.

Although such descriptive studies of clinic-referred samples are useful in establishing the validity of the diagnosis of ADHD, they do not yield information as to the processes and mechanisms underlying the emergence and maintenance of such impairing problems. Thus, we now consider investigations that may begin to illuminate such processes, focusing on several key findings from our recent sample of 140 girls with ADHD and 88 matched comparison girls (Hinshaw, 2002b). Several advantages of this sample include (a) its multi-informant, multimethod assessment across a wide range of domains; (b) its utilization of strict, multigated diagnostic criteria; and (c) its socioeconomic and ethnic diversity. In addition, the naturalistic camp setting in which we observed the participants provides a minilongitudinal perspective and allows the examination of the emergence and maintenance of social processes among a group of previously unfamiliar peers. The all-female composition of the sample is consistent with the normative gender segregation of play among preadolescent children (Maccoby, 1998), affording examination of relational forms of aggression noted to be more relevant to girls' peer interactions (Crick & Grotpeter, 1995). Finally, focusing exclusively on girls provides enough statistical power to examine subtype differences (Inattentive versus Combined).

Initially, Hinshaw (2002b) reported that, relative to comparison girls, girls with ADHD had more school-related problems (special education placement, grade retention, speech/language difficulties), lower academic and cognitive performance, higher rates of authoritarian parenting, and a greater likelihood of having been adopted. At the summer camp, girls with ADHD (particularly the Combined type) displayed higher rates of peer rejection, overt aggression, relational aggression, and noncompliance; as noted earlier, girls with the Inattentive type of ADHD exhibited more observed social isolation than those with the Combined type. Importantly, nearly all of the ADHD versus comparison group differences were extremely robust to statistical control of comorbidity (see Hinshaw, 2002b), so that diagnostic group differences were not simply artifacts of additional disorders likely to be displayed by girls with ADHD. Accounting for comorbidity is essential in future research on girls with ADHD, if underlying mechanisms are to be teased apart.

We highlight our investigations of peer relationships within this sample, as the social domain has been consistently demonstrated to be one of critical importance for children with ADHD (Hinshaw & Melnick, 1995). The scant existing evidence regarding girls with ADHD suggests that they may be *more* at risk than boys with the disorder for negative peer experiences (e.g., Carlson, Tamm, & Gaub, 1997). It is likely that certain behaviors typical of children with ADHD (e.g., high activity level, disruption) are more salient and deviant in female peer groups and may therefore lead to higher levels of peer rejection. It is also possible that the peer difficulties of girls with ADHD may be related to the cognitive and language deficits in this group (see Gaub & Carlson, 1997), which may put them at a social disadvantage given the focus on verbal interchange in the social interactions of school-aged girls (Maccoby, 1998).

Findings from our sample support the contention that girls with ADHD experience far higher rates of peer rejection than do comparison girls

(Hinshaw, 2002b). Given the stability of peer rejection and the abundance of evidence demonstrating that childhood peer difficulties are related to both concurrent and future maladjustment in such areas as mental health problems, delinquency, and school failure (McDougall, Hymel, Vaillancourt, & Mercer, 2001), such high rates of peer-rejection among girls with ADHD are worthy of attention. Yet not all peer-rejected children develop adjustment related difficulties. This *multifinality* of outcomes has propelled several lines of investigation examining potential risk and protective factors and processes that may be operating among girls with poor peer experiences.

First, Thurber, Heller, and Hinshaw (2002) found that although the social goals of girls with and without ADHD did not differ, girls with ADHD offered more aggressive (both overt and relational) solutions and fewer co-operative solutions to hypothetical social scenarios. Importantly, these responses predicted peer rejection and observed social behavior at the camp. Thus, although girls with ADHD appear to have the same goals for social interactions as other girls, they are less able to consider and implement adaptive behaviors that would facilitate such positive social interactions. These findings highlight the importance of social cognitive mechanisms in the development of peer-related difficulties for girls with ADHD.

Next, Mikami and Hinshaw (2003) investigated popularity with adult staff and observations of goal-directed solitary play as potential buffers of concurrent adjustment difficulties (aggressive and anxious/depressed behavior) among peer-rejected girls. They found that, for all girls, popularity with adults predicted lower levels of aggression, whereas goal-directed solitary play predicted lower levels of anxious and depressive symptoms. The ability to engage in solitary play was a stronger predictor of lower levels of internalizing behaviors for girls with ADHD than for comparison girls, possibly because girls with ADHD typically have fewer positive social interactions in their lives outside of the peer domain (e.g., family members, teachers), rendering them more likely to receive compensatory benefit from protective mechanisms than similarly rejected girls who have other positive social experiences (Mikami & Hinshaw, 2003). This finding offers preliminary evidence for the differential operation of risk and resilience processes among girls with and without ADHD.

Another investigation focuses on participation in dyadic friendships. To set the stage, we note that a critical distinction exists between children's experiences in the peer group as a whole (i.e., rejection or acceptance) and their participation in friendships. Evidence suggests that, in addition to having a friend, both the quality of the relationship (e.g., positive and negative features) and the stability of the friendship are independently related to adjustment (Parker & Asher, 1993; Parker & Seal, 1996). Furthermore, having a stable friendship may serve as a potential buffer from short-term negative adjustment outcomes among rejected children. Understanding the role of friendship in the adjustment of girls with ADHD may be particularly critical, given their increased risk for peer rejection, the emphasis on dyadic/triadic close relationships among school-aged females (Maccoby, 1998), and preliminary evidence that friendship processes play a unique role over and above peer rejection in the development of internalizing difficulties (see Bagwell, Newcomb, & Bukowski, 1998). Furthermore, given the arduous task of improving a child's status within the peer group, dyadic friendships may provide a more manageable and fruitful area of social intervention for girls with ADHD.

In the first known examination of the friendship experiences of girls with ADHD, Blachman and Hinshaw (2002) considered friendship participation, stability, and quality. Friendships were measured through reciprocal peer nominations at the summer program. In brief, girls with ADHD were *more* likely to have *no* friends and *less* likely to have *multiple* friends than were comparison girls. Whereas girls with Combined type of ADHD demonstrated difficulties maintaining *any* stable friendships from the beginning to the middle of camp, girls with the Inattentive type exhibited difficulties keeping *more than one* consistent friendship from the middle to end of the summer. Also, among those girls with ADHD who were participating in mutual friendships, these relationships were of lower quality than those of their typically developing peers, particularly with respect to increased levels of negative features such as conflict and relational aggression. Finally, controlling for Verbal IQ and diagnostic subgroup, the number of mutual friends yielded a significant contribution to the prediction of overall peer liking and disliking at the end of the summer, particularly for girls with the Combined type of ADHD (Blachman & Hinshaw, in press). In suggesting that friendship participation is more related to peer dislike for girls with ADHD than for comparison girls, we note another developmental process that may operate differentially across clinical and nonclinical populations.

We also consider three illustrative studies examining family context. As noted earlier in the chapter, conflictual parent–child relationships are quite common in families of boys with ADHD, and such negative interactions have been implicated in the emergence of oppositional and aggressive behaviors and the maintenance of ADHD-related symptomatology (Johnston & Mash, 2001). In earlier investigations of boys diagnosed with ADHD, we found that maternal negativity displayed during parent–child interactions predicted noncompliance and stealing at our summer programs, even after statistically controlling for the boy's negative and noncompliant behavior with his mother during the interaction (Anderson, Hinshaw, & Simmel, 1994). When we investigated similar processes among girls with ADHD and their mothers, a different pattern emerged: Maternal negativity was no longer predictive of the daughter's camp externalizing (or internalizing) behavior once the girl's level of noncompliance during the interaction was controlled (Chang & Hinshaw, 2004). Yet mothers' depressive symptoms and levels of parental stress *did* predict her daughter's level of externalizing and internalizing behavior at camp, even with control of daughters' noncompliance during the interaction. It may be the case that transactional processes between mothers and daughters are subtle in nature, mediated through "internal" distress in the mother. Although preliminary, this finding highlights another underlying mechanism that may operate differentially across the sexes.

Second, we examined levels of "expressed emotion" (EE) among parents in this sample. This variable, assessed by ascertaining parental levels of criticism/hostility and overinvolvement in describing their offspring, has been linked to relapse of adolescent and adult disorders like schizophrenia and is a candidate for linkage with child psychopathology. High levels of EE (particularly the criticism/hostility component) displayed by mothers and by fathers discriminated between girls with and without ADHD, independent of comorbid disruptive behavior disorders and of ADHD subtype (Peris & Hinshaw, 2003). In other words, parents of all girls with ADHD demonstrated higher levels of EE than did parents of comparison girls. These predictions also held when independent staff ratings of ADHD-related symptomatology comprised the criterion measure. It may be the case that inattentive symptomatology (whether or not paired with hyperactivity/impulsivity) elicits negative, critical attitudes in the parents of girls with ADHD; this finding points to another dynamic in the parent–child relationship that may prove to be predictive of certain negative adjustment patterns, particularly in girls.

Third, Briscoe and Hinshaw (2004) investigated rates of documented physical and sexual abuse within this sample. As expected, given a higher rate of adoptions and the demonstrated conflictual parent–child interactions in ADHD families, girls with ADHD exhibited higher rates of having been abused (combined category of physical plus sexual abuse). More important, however, was the finding that the subgroup of girls with ADHD plus an abuse history was substantially more impaired than the remaining girls with ADHD across externalizing behavior patterns and peer rejection, measured by a variety of sources. The suggestion is that a history of trauma/abuse is critical to understanding the development of a wide range of maladaptive outcomes among a subsample of girls with ADHD.

In all, our investigations provide preliminary evidence of key underlying processes and mechanisms that appear to be related to the functioning of girls with ADHD in the domains of peer relationships (e.g., capacity for solitary play, social-cognitive processes, friendships) and family context (e.g., maternal stress and depression, hostility/criticism, history of abuse). This research provides a starting point for understanding of the functioning of girls with ADHD considered in their own right. Prospective, longitudinal studies are urgently needed to provide more rigorous tests of developmental processes and to begin to address issues of causality and directionality of effects. Indeed, we are currently engaged in a five-year follow-up study of the girls who attended our summer camps, in which we aim to examine such developmental issues.

DEVELOPMENTAL PROGRESSIONS

A recap of findings with boys is in order, given the nearly nonexistent prospective database on girls. The first round of longitudinal studies in the field documented persisting symptoms and impairment in boys initially diagnosed with MBD, hyperactivity, or hyperkinesis, but such reports were initiated before rigorous research criteria were in use, were not always prospective, and were sometimes performed without control groups (see review of Thorley, 1984). With more rigorous investigations having now occurred, the following key points are established: (a) a gradual diminution, over time, of attentional symptoms but a more rapid decline of hyperactive/impulsive symptomatology (Hart et al., 1995); (b) the persistence into adolescence of impairing, ADHD-related symptoms (that still meet criteria for diagnosis) for up to 80% of youth, with lower rates of persistence into adulthood, which vary with the source of information used to obtain adult status (Mannuzza & Klein, 1999; see also Barkley et al., 2002); (c) indicators of aggressive comorbidity, delinquency, and even antisocial personality disorder that are substantially elevated; (d) marked risk for academic dysfunction and early school termination (Barkley, 1998); and (e) several additional areas of impairment (e.g., driving accidents, employment problems, reduced self-esteem) through early adulthood.

The authoritative review of Mannuzza and Klein (1999) cites a total of *one* controlled, prospective, follow-up investigation of girls in the literature (Mannuzza & Gittelman, 1984), with a sample size of 12 (expanded to $N = 19$ in the unpublished presentation of Klein, 1990). Other prospective investigations either have not included females or have had extremely small female subsamples. Babinski, Hartsough, and Lambert (1999) have prospectively followed 75 girls with ADHD-related symptomatology in childhood, but initial ascertainment was done prior to modern *DSM* specifications. Note also that in the recent meta-analyses of Waschbusch (2002), with respect to studies of at least four years' duration focusing on the outcome domain of ADHD-related symptoms, the male N was 938 but the female N was 15.

Although ADHD and conduct disorder clearly differ, the literature on prospective studies of girls with conduct disorder may provide clues for parallel investigations of ADHD. In updating the seminal work of Olweus (1979), Frick and Loney (1999) have shown that in short-term follow-ups (<6 months), boys and girls show extremely comparable stability estimates for measures of aggression, with rs ranging from roughly .34 to .65 for both sexes. For longer follow-up periods, however, striking differences emerge, such that females show substantially lower stability. Kratzer and Hodgins (1997), for instance, found that among youth with conduct disorder between the ages of 12 and 16, 64% of the boys went on to commit a crime during a 16-year follow-up compared with only 17% of the girls. If there is generalizability from conduct problems to ADHD, it is possible that girls with ADHD will not show as much persistence as boys. On the other hand, given that inattentive symptomatology persists to a greater extent than does the hyperactive–impulsive variety (Hart et al., 1995), girls could show *more* stability than boys. Only prospective data can answer this question.

We note also that although females with adolescent conduct problems are (like males) at elevated risk for antisocial outcomes (Pajer, 1998), the specificity of prediction across time appears lower than for males (e.g., Zoccolillo, Pickles, Quinton, & Rutter, 1992). That is, whereas conduct-disordered behavior in males predicts subsequent antisocial behavior in adulthood with strong sensitivity and moderate specificity, in females the negative outcomes appear to be more disparate (Moffitt, Caspi, Rutter, & Silva, 2001). Girls with conduct problems show high risk for internalizing disorders, including depression (and suicide) as well as somatization disorders; early mortality (often from violent causes of death); low educational attainment; substance abuse; and the development of severe personal and social problems (see Pajer, 1998). Externalizing behavior in females therefore appears to show *multifinality*, whereby disparate outcomes emerge from the "same" precursor variable. Outcome measures for prospective investigations of girls with ADHD should therefore include domains of functioning well beyond ADHD or externalizing problems.

UNDERLYING MECHANISMS AND CAUSAL FACTORS

Almost without exception, the developmental, behavioral, and emotional disorders of childhood show a male predominance (Eme, 1992; Hartung & Widiger, 1998). ADHD is a clear example, even in community samples. What theoretical models or accounts could pertain here? Over the past decades, literature has appeared sporadically on the so-called gender paradox, whereby the sex with the lower prevalence of a given condition is purported to display a more severe and impairing variant of the disorder, including a higher likelihood of comorbidity and of familial/genetic risk factors (e.g., Gualtieri & Hicks, 1985; Taylor & Ounstead, 1972; see review in Eme, 1992). To explain this putative phenomenon, two key models have been proposed. (1) In the polygenetic multiple-threshold model, females have a higher threshold than males for the combination of genetic and environmental factors that constitute the liability for the disorder (Eme, 1992). In other words, it takes a greater "dose" of risk factors for the subgroup (in this case, females) with the lower overall prevalence of a given condition to emerge with disorder. Thus, females "... are predicted to be more seriously affected, to have a higher genetic loading, and to have more affected relatives" (Eme, 1992, p. 355). (2) In the constitutional variability model, on the other hand, there is greater variability of genetic risks in males than in females. Thus, there would be greater familial loading for boys than for girls. Crucially for this model, males would show mild variants of disorder, whereas females would reach diagnostic thresholds only from organic pathology (see Eme, 1992).

The only evidence in Eme (1992) relevant to ADHD emanated from James and Taylor (1990), who found evidence for lower IQ scores and higher rates of language-related and neurological problems in their clinic-referred girls with ADHD than in their boys. This finding was interpreted as consistent with a constitutional variability model, in that the neurological and language-related factors were risks for girls, but not for boys. What does more recent evidence have to say with respect to either model?

Severity

If the gender paradox is a valid proposition with regard to ADHD, there would need to be evidence for greater severity of ADHD in girls than in boys. Yet research does not favor this contention, particularly in representative samples (Gaub & Carlson, 1997; Gershon, 2002). First, as noted earlier, girls with ADHD appear to show *lower* overall rates of the constituent symptoms in the community, whereas in clinical samples severity of symptomatology seems equivalent (or perhaps higher in some instances; see Rucklidge and Tannock, 2001). Second, examinations of neuropsychological and neural deficits also do not point to evidence of greater severity among females. Indeed, in an initial report, Seidman et al. (1997) found that girls with ADHD did not reveal the same degree of impairment in terms of so-called executive functions (EF), such as response organization, planning, and set-shifting, as did comparably aged boys with the disorder. Crucially, however, the majority of girls in this study performed the neuropsychological tests while receiving stimulant medication, which is known to improve performance on such measures. In fact, a growing literature (Castellenos et al., 2000; Hinshaw et al., 2002) shows that when tested off medication, girls with ADHD do show clear EF deficits (in contrast to a matched comparison group) of moderate to large sizes. Yet these deficits are comparable in magnitude to those found for boys with ADHD; they do not appear to be more severe, as would be predicted by the gender paradox.

Furthermore, with respect to objective indicators of inattention and impulsivity, Newcorn et al. (2001) performed extensive analyses of girls and boys in the MTA sample regarding a continuous performance test (CPT). Overall, girls in the sample were *less* impulsive on the CPT than were boys; furthermore, the comorbid subgroup of girls with ADHD plus an anxiety disorder were less impulsive on this objective measure than were non-comorbid girls.

In terms of actual neural deficits, measured by means of structural magnetic resonance imaging (MRI), Castellanos et al. (2001) examined a well-characterized sample of 50 girls with ADHD, who had previously been found to exhibit comparable levels of severity and impairment as previous male samples (Sharp et al., 1999). Overall, like boys with ADHD in relation to male controls, the girls with ADHD had significantly smaller total cerebral volumes (on the order of 4%) than did comparison girls, a difference that was associated with somewhat lower IQ scores in the ADHD group. Yet other brain regions that had differed between ADHD and comparison boys did not differ for the girls. The clear exceptions were in the caudate, implicated in motor control, and in a region of the cerebellum (the posterior–inferior cerebellar vermis), which were both clearly smaller in the ADHD than in the comparison females—even with the difference in total cerebral volume statistically controlled. (These effects held when the subsample of girls who had never received stimulant medication was analyzed separately.) Furthermore, recent data on electroencephalographic (EEG) indicators between girls with ADHD and comparison girls revealed that group differences were not as large as those found between boys with ADHD and comparison boys (Clarke, Barry, McCarthy, & Selikowitz, 2001).

In conclusion, the data on neuropsychological and neural underpinnings of ADHD as well as the data on basic levels of symptomatology from representative samples do not support a stronger pattern of deficits in females than in males. Thus, the "gender paradox" itself (e.g., higher levels of severity among females with the disorder) may not be a valid hypothesis as the basis for which to support either the polygenetic multiple threshold model or the constitutional variability model.

Heritability

Despite the lack of evidence for an existing gender paradox, we can examine whether the heritability of ADHD varies by sex, which might provide information relevant to proposed theoretical models. Although ADHD symptomatology as well as the three ADHD "clusters" identified through latent class analysis (see earlier discussion of Neuman et al., 2001) were found to be extremely heritable, Rhee, Waldman, Hay, and Levy (1999) discovered, in a large population sample of Australian twins and sibling pairs, that the heritability of ADHD was extremely and comparably high in both males and females. This finding replicates earlier results reaching essentially the same conclusion (e.g., Gjone, Stevenson, & Sundet, 1996; see literature review in Rhee et al., 1999). Thus, neither the polygenetic multiple threshold model (which would posit higher heritability in girls) nor the constitutional variability model (which would posit higher heritability in boys) receives support from these data.

In terms of overall familial risk for ADHD, Faraone et al. (2000) contrasted biological relatives of (a) the clinical sample of girls with ADHD reported in Biederman et al. (1999) with (b) a comparably sized clinical sample of boys (see Biederman et al., 2002). Whereas there was substantial familial "loading" in the female ADHD sample, such that relatives had substantially higher rates of ADHD than did relatives of comparison girls, the rates of familial disorder were comparable to those found for the male ADHD sample. "Thus, the differing prevalences of ADHD between boys and girls cannot be attributed to any familial transmission model that posits that, compared with boys, girls require a greater 'dose' of familial risk factors to express ADHD" (Faraone et al., 2000, p. 1081). In other words, there was no support found for the polygenetic threshold theory suggesting a greater familial "loading" for girls with ADHD. In addition, Faraone et al. (2001) showed that the relatives of the male and female samples had comparable rates of *comorbidity* between ADHD and other disorders.

On the other hand, Smalley et al. (2000) ascertained cases through an affected sibling pair design in which at least two children in a given family had to meet criteria for ADHD. Consistent with the polygenetic multiple-threshold model, they found that the rate of ADHD in *parents* was greater for families in which at least one of the siblings with ADHD was a girl than in those with only male siblings with ADHD. Similarly, Rhee, Waldman, Hay, and Levy (2001) found that twins or siblings of female probands had higher rates of ADHD symptoms than did twins or siblings of male probands (see also Rhee et al., 1999). Thus, at least some evidence exists in support of the contention that familial loading is higher in girls with ADHD than in boys.

Nongenetic Risk Factors

With respect to nongenetic risk factors, we highlight briefly two recent investigations by Mick, Biederman, and colleagues. Although the data reveal that low birth weight (LBW; Mick, Biederman, Prince et al., 2002) and maternal use of tobacco, alcohol, and illicit drugs during pregnancy (Mick, Biederman, Faraone et al., 2002) are risk factors for ADHD—reflecting prior investigations in these areas—neither factor interacted statistically with male versus female status of the participants. Thus, girls and boys were equally likely to be influenced by LBW and by prenatal exposure to teratogens with respect to subsequent risk for ADHD. Whereas the statistical power to ascertain interaction effects in such samples is limited, the data suggest equivalence across the sexes for these risk factors, once again challenging the very notion of a gender paradox.

Conclusions

On the basis of data regarding severity of ADHD, as well as neuropsychological, neural, and nongenetic risk factors, it is not clear that a "gender paradox" actually exists. Thus, despite some inconsistencies in the literature, and despite sex comparisons that still lack optimal statistical power to reveal male versus female differences, the results cited herein support the underlying similarity of girls with ADHD to boys with ADHD regarding severity and key risk mechanisms. Although there is at least some evidence for a greater familial loading of ADHD in biological relatives of females with ADHD than males with ADHD, which would support a polygenetic multiple threshold model, the overall pattern of results is far from conclusive in this regard.

We also note that regarding conceptual models of ADHD, if it continues to be confirmed that girls with ADHD are relatively more likely to display the Inattentive type of the disorder than boys, recent models of ADHD as a disorder characterized by faulty inhibitory processes leading to predominantly impulsive behavior patterns (Barkley, 1997) may not fully apply to girls. Yet precisely which motivational, affective, and cognitive parameters are relevant to female presentations of the disorder is simply not known at present, given the paucity of research on females. Exciting developments in this regard must await additional translational research blending the best of basic research and clinical investigative methodology.

IMPLICATIONS FOR ASSESSMENT AND TREATMENT

We have space for only brief consideration of assessment and treatment issues. As for assessment, until existing diagnostic issues (e.g., sex-specific criteria or thresholds, age of onset, inclusion of "sluggish cognitive tempo" symptoms) are resolved, assessment is likely to remain a complicated enterprise for females. The most important issue here pertains to the identification and referral process. That is, girls are less likely to be referred for clinical attention, particularly if they display primarily inattentive symptoms. When girls *are* referred, it is often not until late childhood or early adolescence, and the primary concern may often be a comorbid disorder (e.g., learning problem, depression, acting-out behavior). In short, potential ADHD in girls could well be missed (Arnold, 1996; Nadeau et al., 1999). Overall, despite recent progress, awareness of the existence of ADHD in girls needs to be part of the assessor's mindset. Furthermore, teachers' knowledge of ADHD may be based largely on behavior patterns typical of the Combined type, with a resultant likelihood to identify or refer boys. Thus, teachers (as well as parents) need to be made more aware of the prototypically inattentive presentation of ADHD in girls, along with its more subtle behavioral manifestations in females.

What of the assessment and diagnostic process, once appropriate referrals have been made? First, rigorous procedures must be followed when assessing girls referred for problems potentially related to ADHD, including a thorough developmental history, information from multiple informants, and consideration of comorbid behavior patterns. Indeed, differential diagnosis of ADHD versus learning disorders or internalizing disorders may be more difficult in girls than in boys, because of the less overt nature of girls' symptomatology in many instances. Second, standard parent and teacher reports of symptoms (focused on observable behaviors that are more externalizing in nature) may not fully capture the range of symptoms and experiences of girls. Particularly during adolescence, self-report measures of symptoms should be included, particularly as female risk for depression begins to escalate. The third, and relatedly a key, goal is to understand the scope of relevant behaviors into which current diagnostic criteria could profitably be expanded. Possible domains include "sluggish cognitive tempo" (e.g., daydreaming, drowsiness/sluggishness), anxiety/depression, self-esteem, emotional sensitivity, and "hyperfocusing" behavior (see Nadeau et al., 1999).

With respect to treatment strategies and implications, the extremely limited data in the field point to a "null" conclusion with respect to male versus female differences regarding response to effective treatments. In an early investigation, Pelham, Walker, Sturges, and Hoza (1989) examined response to one dosage level of methylphenidate among a sample of 12 girls with ADHD and 12 boys with ADHD, matched for age and IQ, who attended a structured summer program. No sex differences emerged across a range of outcome measures (e.g., negative social behaviors, rule following, reading accuracy/productivity). Similarly, Barkley (1989) found no sex differences in medication response with respect to mother–child interactions.

More recently, the MTA study found that sex of participant did not moderate response to treatment across a range of study outcomes (MTA Cooperative Group, 1999b; Owens et al., 2003). Given the size and rigor of the MTA, such equivalence is striking.

Note, however, that the MTA included only the Combined type of ADHD. If it is the case that the Inattentive type of ADHD shows preferential response to relatively low dosages of stimulant medication (see Barkley, DuPaul, & McMurray, 1991, for suggestive evidence), then girls with ADHD (who appear more likely to emerge in this subtype) might tend to be over-medicated unless careful titration procedures are followed. Furthermore, additional moderator analyses from the MTA showed that children with ADHD who displayed comorbid anxiety disorders were just as likely to respond favorably to a structured behavioral intervention as to a medication regimen (MTA Cooperative Group, 1999b). Thus, accurate diagnosis of this comorbidity could well influence the decision to start with a nonpharmacologic approach as opposed to medication; clinicians should thus assess carefully for anxious symptomatology in girls with ADHD. Overall, individual differences in treatment response are extremely salient; the clinician must individually and carefully appraise treatment response in each patient, boy or girl.

More speculative treatment implications have been proposed by Nadeau et al. (1999). For example, when girls with ADHD reach adolescence, and issues of self-esteem and body image attain salience, clinicians should be aware of effects of both treatments and symptoms on eating patterns. It is also possible that group treatments may be particularly helpful for girls with ADHD, given the social support they may provide. As suggested earlier, peer-related components of intervention and promotion of friendships could also be quite salient for girls with ADHD. Yet intervention studies focused on girls are sorely needed before specific treatment strategies can be recommended with confidence.

Finally, we note the importance of sociocultural attitudes toward treatment acceptability. Provocative evidence from disparate lines of research suggests that girls (even when displaying clear ADHD symptoms) are less likely to receive stimulant medication than boys, despite its demonstrated effectiveness. Indeed, a major epidemiologic study of 9- to 16-year-olds in a rural population found that among children meeting full diagnostic criteria for ADHD, girls were less likely to be receiving stimulant medication (Angold, Erkanli, Egger, & Costello, 2000). Also, when presented with hypothetical vignettes of children's behaviors and a range of treatment options, teachers viewed medication as a less acceptable treatment option for girls, even when the presenting behaviors were identical (Pisecco, Huzenic, & Curtis, 2001). Thus, even when girls display similar levels of ADHD-related symptoms as boys, certain sociocultural beliefs may be exacerbating the underreferral and undertreatment of girls with ADHD.

In sum, we assert with confidence that ADHD does exist as a real and substantially impairing condition in girls. Furthermore, girls are likely to be underreferred, underdiagnosed, and undertreated, particularly if they exhibit only problems with inattention. They are also likely to receive "notice" later in development and fail to be recommended for pharmacologic treatment. Thus, raising professional awareness of the behavioral manifestations of inattention, utilizing self-report assessment tools, and inquiring into a broader range of behaviors and domains may prove to be useful in the assessment of girls for ADHD-related problems. Furthermore, although effective treatments currently in use are as likely to benefit girls as boys, our knowledge about assessment and treatment with girls emanates more from clinical experience than empirical evidence. Thus, systematic, empirically based investigations of the utility of various assessment methods and treatment strategies for girls are sorely needed.

SUMMARY AND CONCLUSIONS

In many respects, the literature on girls with ADHD has only begun to emerge. As we have emphasized repeatedly, data on the developmental course of ADHD in females is a pressing need for the field; the current research foundation is based largely on cross-sectional investigations of relatively small samples of girls with ADHD, homogeneous in terms of socioeconomic status and ethnicity, studied outside the usual social contexts in which girls interact and develop. As systematic examination of developmental processes occurs in female samples, the field will begin to obtain clarity regarding such pressing issues as the use of sex-specific versus sex-neutral norms, the age of onset of ADHD in females, the boundaries of ADHD-related symptomatology in girls, the viability of current ADHD subtypes for girls, and the kinds of modifications to existing treatment protocols needed for optimal efficacy and effectiveness with female populations. It will be important, as well, to advocate for large-scale epidemiologic data on ADHD in girls, utilizing diverse, representative samples and reflecting information on risk factors and correlates as well as symptoms and syndromes per se. Functional neuroimaging and molecular genetic methodologies will also need to be extended to girls with ADHD plus carefully matched comparison groups.

Overall, we hope that we have elucidated the viability of ADHD in girls as well as the importance of the topic, both clinically and conceptually. We trust that assessors, clinicians, and investigators will come to realize the necessity of considering that ADHD is a salient problem for girls and women, and we emphasize that studies of processes and mechanisms underlying symptom expression are essential for continued progress to be made (Hinshaw, 2002b). Although there is certainly a long way to go, the advances that await the field's redoubled efforts will be exciting to behold, with far-reaching implications for prevention, clinical care, and conceptual models of psychopathology. Indeed, manifestations of psychopathology and impairment in girls with ADHD should be relevant for testing the generality and generalizability of biological, psychosocial, and transactional models of the disorder that have been promoted nearly exclusively on the basis of research with boys. The coming years promise breakthroughs that will hold both clinical and conceptual relevance.

ACKNOWLEDGEMENTS. Work on this chapter was supported by National Institute of Mental Health Grants R01 MH45064 and U01 MH50461. We gratefully acknowledge the many girls, and their families, who have participated in our research projects over the years.

REFERENCES

Achenbach, T. M. (1991). *Manual for the CBCL/4–18 and Revised Child Behavior Profile.* Unpublished manuscript, University of Vermont Department of Psychiatry.

American Psychiatric Association. (1980). *Diagnostic and statistical manual of mental disorders* (3rd ed.). Washington, DC: Author.

American Psychiatric Association. (1994). *Diagnostic and statistical manual of mental disorders* (4th ed.). Washington, DC: Author.

Anderson, C. A., Hinshaw, S. P., & Simmel, C. (1994). Mother–child interactions in ADHD and comparison boys: Relationships to overt and covert externalizing behavior. *Journal of Abnormal Child Psychology, 22,* 247–265.

Angold, A., Costello, E. J., & Erkanli, A. (1999). Comorbidity. *Journal of Child Psychology and Psychiatry, 40,* 57–87.

Angold, A., Erkalni, A., Egger, H., & Costello, E. J. (2000). Stimulant treatment for children: A community perspective. *Journal of the American Academy of Child and Adolescent Psychiatry, 39,* 975–984.

Arcia, E., & Conners, C. K. (1998). Gender differences in ADHD? *Journal of Developmental and Behavioral Pediatrics, 19,* 77–83.

Arnold, L. E. (1996). Sex differences in ADHD: Conference summary. *Journal of Abnormal Child Psychology, 24,* 555–569.

Babinski, L. M., Hartsough, C. S., & Lambert, N. M. (1999). Childhood conduct problems, hyperactivity–impulsivity, and inattention as predictors of adult criminal activity. *Journal of Child Psychology and Psychiatry, 40,* 347–355.

Bagwell, C. L., Newcomb, A. F., & Bukowski, W. M. (1998). Preadolescent friendship and peer rejection as predictors of adult adjustment. *Child Development, 69,* 140–153.

Barbaresi, W. J., Katusic, S. K., Colligan, R. C., Pankratz, V. S., Weaver, A. L., Weber, K. J., et al. (2002). How common is attention-deficit/hyperactivity disorder? *Archives of Pediatric and Adolescent Medicine, 156,* 217–224.

Barkley, R. A. (1996). Attention–deficit hyperactivity disorder. In E. J. Mash & R. A. Barkley (Eds.), *Child psychopathology* (pp. 63–112). New York: Guilford.

Barkley, R. A. (1997). *ADHD and the nature of self-control.* New York: Guilford.

Barkley, R. A. (1998). *Attention deficit hyperactivity disorder: A handbook for diagnosis and treatment* (2nd ed.). New York: Guilford.

Barkley, R. A. (1989). Hyperactive girls and boys: Stimulant drug effects on mother–child interactions. *Journal of Child Psychology and Psychiatry, 30,* 379–390.

Barkley, R. A., & Biederman, J. (1997). Toward a broader definition of the age-of-onset criterion for attention-deficit–hyperactivity disorder. *Journal of the American Academy of Child and Adolescent Psychiatry, 36,* 1204–1210.

Barkley, R. A., DuPaul, G. J., & McMurray, M. B. (1991). Attention deficit disorder with and without hyperactivity: Clinical response to three dose levels of methylphenidate. *Pediatrics, 87,* 519–531.

Barkley, R. A., Fischer, M., Smallish, L., & Fletcher, K. (2002). The persistence of attention deficit/hyperactivity disorder into young adulthood as a function of reporting source and definition of disorder. *Journal of Abnormal Psychology, 111,* 279–289.

Berry, C. A., Shaywitz, B. E., & Shaywitz, S. A. (1985). Girls with attention deficit disorder: A silent minority? A report on behavioral and cognitive characteristics. *Pediatrics, 76,* 801–809.

Biederman, J., Faraone, S. V., Mick, E., Williamson, S., Wilens, T. E., Spencer, T. J., et al. (1999). Clinical correlates of ADHD in females: Findings from a large group of girls ascertained from pediatric and psychiatric referral sources. *Journal of the American Academy of Child and Adolescent Psychiatry, 38,* 966–975.

Biederman, J., Mick, E., Faraone, S. V., Braaten, E., Doyle, A., Spencer, T., et al. (2002). Influence of gender on attention deficit hyperactivity disorder in children referred to a psychiatry clinic. *American Journal of Psychiatry, 159,* 36–42.

Biederman, J., Milberger, S., Faraone, S. V., Kiely, K., Guite, J., Mick, E., et al. (1995). Family-environment risk factors for attention deficit hyperactivity disorder: A test of Rutter's indicators of adversity. *Archives of General Psychiatry, 52,* 464–470.

Blachman, D. R., & Hinshaw, S. P. (2002). Patterns of friendship among girls with attention-deficit/hyperactivity disorder. *Journal of Abnormal Child Psychology, 30,* 625–640.

Briscoe, A., & Hinshaw, S. P. (2004). *Child abuse and attention-deficit/hyperactivity disorder in girls: Effects on multiple domains of functioning.* Unpublished manuscript, University of California, Berkeley.

Brown, R. T., Madan-Swain, A., & Baldwin, K. (1991). Gender differences in a clinic referred sample of attention deficit disorder children. *Child Psychiatry and Human Development, 22,* 111–128.

Campbell, S. (2002). *Behavior problems in preschool children* (2nd ed.). New York: Guilford.

Carlson, C. L., & Mann, M. (2002). Sluggish cognitive tempo predicts a different pattern of impairment in the attention deficit hyperactivity disorder, predominantly inattentive type. *Journal of Clinical Child and Adolescent Psychology, 31,* 123–129.

Carlson, C. L., Tamm, L., & Gaub, M. (1997). Gender differences in children with ADHD, ODD, and co-occurring ADHD/ODD identified in a school population. *Journal of the American Academy of Child and Adolescent Psychiatry, 36,* 1706–1714.

Caron, C., & Rutter, M. (1991). Comorbidity in child psychopathology: Concepts, issues, and research strategies. *Journal of Child Psychology and Psychiatry, 32,* 1063–1080.

Castellanos, F. X., Giedd, J. N., Berquin, P. C., Walter, J. N., Sharp, W., Tran, T., et al. (2001). Quantitative brain magnetic resonance imaging in girls with attention-deficit/hyperactivity disorder. *Archives of General Psychiatry, 58,* 289–295.

Castellanos, F. X., Marvasti, F. F., Ducharme, J. L., Walter, J. M., Israel, M. E., Krain, A., et al. (2000). Executive function oculomotor tasks in girls with ADHD. *Journal of the American Academy of Child and Adolescent Psychiatry, 39,* 644–650.

Chang, J., & Hinshaw, S. P. (2004). *Mother–child interactions, maternal depression, and parenting stress in girls with ADHD and comparison girls.* Unpublished manuscript, University of California, Berkeley.

Cicchetti, D. (1993). Developmental psychopathology: Reactions, reflections, projections. *Developmental Review, 13,* 471–502.

Cicchetti, D., & Cohen, D. J. (Eds.). (1995). *Developmental psychopathology.* New York: Wiley.

Cicchetti, D., & Dawson, G. (Eds.). (2003). Multilevel analysis in developmental psychopathology. Special issue, *Development and Psychopathology, 15.*

Clarke, A. R., Barry, R. J., McCarthy, R., & Selikowitz, M. (2001). Age and sex effect in the EEG: Difference in the two subtypes of attention-deficit/hyperactivity disorder. *Clinical Neurophysiology, 112,* 815–826.

Cohen, P., Cohen, J., Kasen, S., Velez, C. N., Hartmark, C., Johnson, J., et al. (1993). An epidemiological study of disorders in late childhood and adolescence: I. Age- and gender-specific prevalence. *Journal of Child Psychology and Psychiatry, 34,* 851–867.

Crick, N. R., & Grotpeter, J. K. (1995). Relational aggression, gender, and social-psychological adjustment. *Child Development, 66,* 710–722.

DeGrandpre, R., & Hinshaw, S. P. (2000). Attention-deficit hyperactivity disorder: Psychiatric problem or American cop-out? *Cerebrum: The Dana Foundation Journal on Brain Sciences, 2,* 12–38.

Disney, E. R., Elkin, I. J., McGue, M., & Iacono, W. G. (1999). Effects of ADHD, conduct disorder, and gender on substance use and abuse in adolescence. *American Journal of Psychiatry, 156,* 1515–1521.

DuPaul, G. J., Schaughency, E. A., Weyandt, L. J., Tripp, G., Kiesner, J., Ota, K., et al. (2001). Self-report of ADHD symptoms in university students: Cross-gender and cross-national prevalence. *Journal of Learning Disabilities, 34,* 370–379.

Eme, R. (1992). Selective female affliction in the developmental disorders of childhood: A literature review. *Journal of Clinical Child Psychology, 21,* 354–364.

Faraone, S. V., Biederman, J., Mick, E., Doyle, A. E., Wilens, T., Spencer, T., et al. (2001). A family study of psychiatric comorbidity in girls and boys with attention-deficit/hyperactivity disorder. *Biological Psychiatry, 50,* 586–592.

Faraone, S. V., Biederman, J., Mick, E., Williamson, S., Wilens, T., Spencer, T., et al. (2000). Family study of girls with attention deficit hyperactivity disorder. *American Journal of Psychiatry, 157,* 1077–1083.

Frick, P. J., & Loney, B. R. (1999). Outcomes of children and adolescents with opposi-tional defiant disorder and conduct disorder. In H. C. Quay & A. E. Hogan (Eds.), *Handbook of disruptive behavior disorders* (pp. 507–524). New York: Kluwer Academic/ Plenum.

Gaub, M., & Carlson, C. L. (1997). Gender differences in ADHD: A meta-analysis and critical review. *Journal of the American Academy of Child and Adolescent Psychiatry, 36,* 1036–1045.

Gershon, J. (2002). A meta-analytic review of gender differences in ADHD. *Journal of Attention Disorders, 5,* 143–154.

Gjone, H., Stevenson, J., & Sundet, J. M. (1996). Genetic influences on parent-reported attention-related problems in a Norwegian general population twin sample. *Journal of the American Academy of Child and Adolescent Psychiatry, 35,* 588–596.

Goodman, S. H., Lahey, B. B., Fielding, B., Dulcan, M., Narrow, W., & Regier, D. (1997). Representativeness of clinical samples of youth with mental disorders: A preliminary population-based study. *Journal of Abnormal Psychology, 106,* 3–14.

Gottlieb, G. (1998). Normally occurring environmental and behavioral influences on gene activity: From central dogma to probabilistic epigenesis. *Psychological Review, 105,* 792–802.

Greene, R. W., Biederman, J., Faraone, S. V., Monuteaux, M. C., Mick, E., DuPre, E. P., et al. (2001). Social impairment in girls with ADHD: Patterns, gender comparisons, and correlates. *Journal of the American Academy of Child and Adolescent Psychiatry, 40,* 704–710.

Gualtieri, T., & Hicks, R. (1985). An immunoreactive theory of selective male affliction. *Be-havioral and Brain Sciences, 8,* 427–431.

Hart, E. L., Lahey, B. B., Loeber, R., Applegate, B., Green, S. M., & Frick, P. J. (1995). Develop-mental change in attention-deficit hyperactivity disorder in boys: A four-year longitudinal study. *Journal of Abnormal Child Psychology, 23,* 729–749.

Hartung, C. M., & Widiger, T. A. (1998). Gender differences in the diagnosis of mental disor-ders. *Psychological Bulletin, 123,* 260–278.

Henker, B., & Whalen, C. K. (1999). The child with attention-deficit/hyperactivity disorder in school and peer settings. In H. C. Quay & A. E. Hogan (Eds.), *Handbook of disruptive behavior disorders* (pp. 157–178). New York: Kluwer Academic/Plenum.

Hinshaw, S. P. (1987). On the distinction between attentional deficits/hyperactivity and con-duct problems/aggression in child psychopathology. *Psychological Bulletin, 101,* 443–463.

Hinshaw, S. P. (1994). *Attention deficits and hyperactivity in children.* Thousand Oaks, CA: Sage.

Hinshaw, S. P. (1999). Psychosocial intervention for childhood ADHD: Etiologic and devel-opmental themes, comorbidity, and integration with pharmacotherapy. In D. Cicchetti & S. L. Toth (Eds.), *Rochester Symposium on Developmental Psychopathology: Vol. 9. Devel-opmental approaches to prevention and intervention* (pp. 221–270). Rochester, NY: Uni-versity of Rochester Press.

Hinshaw, S. P. (2001). Is the inattentive type of ADHD a separate disorder? *Clinical Psychology: Science and Practice, 8,* 498–501.

Hinshaw, S. P. (2002a). Is ADHD an impairing condition in childhood and adolescence? In P. S. Jensen & J. R. Cooper (Eds.), *Attention-deficit hyperactivity disorder:* State of the art, best practices (pp. 5–21). Kingston, NJ: Civic Research Institute.

Hinshaw, S. P. (2002b). Preadolescent girls with attention-deficit/hyperactivity disorder: I. Background characteristics, comorbidity, cognitive and social functioning, and parenting practices. *Journal of Consulting and Clinical Psychology, 70,* 1086–1098.

Hinshaw, S. P. (2002c). Process, mechanism, and explanation related to externalizing behavior problems. *Journal of Abnormal Child Psychology, 31*, 431–445.

Hinshaw, S. P., Carte, E. T., Sami, N., Treuting, J. J., & Zupan, B. A. (2002). Preadolescent girls with attention-deficit/hyperactivity disorder: II. Neuropsychological performance in relation to subtypes and individual classification. *Journal of Consulting and Clinical Psychology, 70*, 1099–1111.

Hinshaw, S. P., & Melnick, S. (1995). Peer relationships in children with attention-deficit hyperactivity disorder with and without comorbid aggression. *Development and Psychopathology, 7*, 627–647.

James, A., & Taylor, E. (1990). Sex differences in the hyperkinetic syndrome of childhood. *Journal of Child Psychology and Psychiatry, 31*, 437–446.

Jensen, P. S., Martin, D., & Cantwell, D. P. (1997). Comorbidity in ADHD: Implications for research, practice, and *DSM-V*. *Journal of the American Academy of Child and Adolescent Psychiatry, 36*, 1065–1079.

Johnston, C., & Mash, E. J. (2001). Families of children with attention-deficit/hyperactivity disorder: Review and recommendations for future research. *Clinical Child and Family Psychology Review, 4*, 183–207.

Keenan, K., & Shaw, D. S., (1997). Developmental and social influences on young girls' early problem behavior. *Psychological Bulletin, 121*, 95–113.

Klein, R. G. (1990). *Relationship between childhood hyperactivity and adult affective, antisocial and substance use disorders*. Paper presented at the Third Annual Research Conference of the New York State Office of Mental Health, Albany, NY.

Kratzer, L., & Hodgins, S. (1997). Adult outcomes of child conduct problems: A cohort study. *Journal of Abnormal Child Psychology, 25*, 65–81.

Lahey, B. B., Applegate, B., McBurnett, K., Biederman, J., Greenhill, L., Hynd, G. W., et al. (1994). *DSM-IV* field trials for attention deficit/hyperactivity disorder in children and adolescents. *American Journal of Psychiatry, 151*, 1673–1685.

Lahey, B. B., Miller, T. L., Gordon, R. A., & Riley, A. W. (1999). Developmental epidemiology of the disruptive behavior disorders. In H. C. Quay & A. E. Hogan (Eds.), *Handbook of disruptive behavior disorders* (pp. 23–48). New York: Kluwer Academic/Plenum.

Levy, F., Hay, D., McStephen, M., Wood, C., & Waldman, I. D. (1997). Attention deficit hyperactivity disorder (ADHD): A category or a continuum? *Journal of the American Academy of Child and Adolescent Psychiatry, 36*, 737–744.

Loney, J. (1987). Hyperactivity and aggression in the diagnosis of attention deficit disorder. In B. B. Lahey & A. E. Kazdin (Eds.), *Advances in clinical child psychology* (Vol. 10, pp. 99–135). New York: Plenum.

Maccoby, E. E. (1998). *The two sexes: Growing up apart, coming together*. Cambridge, MA: Harvard University Press.

Mannuzza, S., & Gittelman, R. (1984). The adolescent outcome of hyperactive girls. *Psychiatry Research, 13*, 19–29.

Mannuzza, S., & Klein, R. G. (1999). Adolescent and adult outcomes in attention-deficit/hyperactivity disorder. In H. C. Quay & A. E. Hogan (Eds.), *Handbook of disruptive behavior disorders* (pp. 279–294). New York: Kluwer Academic/Plenum.

McBurnett, K., Pfiffner, L. J., & Frick, P. J. (2001). Symptom properties as a function of ADHD type: An argument for continued study of sluggish cognitive tempo. *Journal of Abnormal Child Psychology, 29*, 207–213.

McDougall, P., Hymel, S., Vaillancourt, T., & Mercer, L. (2001). The consequences of childhood peer rejection. In M. R. Leary (Ed.), *Interpersonal rejection* (pp. 213–247). New York: Oxford University Press.

McGee, R., & Feehan, M. (1991). Are girls with problems of attention underrecognized? *Journal of Psychopathology and Behavioral Assessment, 13*, 187–198.

Mick, E., Biederman, J., Faraone, S. V., Sayer, J., & Kleinman, S. (2002). Case–control study of attention-deficit hyperactivity disorder and maternal smoking, alcohol use, and drug use during pregnancy. *Journal of the American Academy of Child and Adolescent Psychiatry, 41*, 378–385.

Mick, E., Biederman, J., Prince, J., Fischer, M. J., & Faraone, S. V. (2002). Impact of low birth weight on attention-deficit hyperactivity disorder. *Journal of Developmental and Behavioral Pediatrics, 23*, 16–22.

Mikami, A., & Hinshaw, S. P. (2003). Buffers of peer rejection among girls with and without ADHD: The role of popularity with adults and solitary play. *Journal of Abnormal Child Psychology, 31,* 381–397.

Milich, R., Balentine, A. C., & Lynam, D. R. (2001). ADHD combined type and ADHD predominantly inattentive type are distinct and unrelated disorders. *Clinical Psychology: Science and Practice, 8,* 463–488.

Moffitt, T. E. (1993). Life-course persistent and adolescence-limited antisocial behavior: A developmental taxonomy. *Psychological Review, 101,* 674–701.

Moffitt, T. E., Caspi, A., Rutter, M., & Silva, P. A. (2001). *Sex differences in antisocial behavior.* Cambridge, England: Cambridge University Press.

MTA Cooperative Group. (1999a). Fourteen-month randomized clinical trial of treatment strategies for attention-deficit hyperactivity disorder. *Archives of General Psychiatry, 56,* 1073–1086.

MTA Cooperative Group. (1999b). Moderators and mediators of treatment response for children wth ADHD: The MTA study. *Archives of General Psychiatry, 56,* 1088–1096.

Nadeau, K., Littman, E. B., & Quinn, P. O. (1999). *Understanding girls with AD/HD.* Silver Spring, MD: Advantage Books.

National Institutes of Health. (1994). NIH guidelines on the inclusion of women and minorities as subjects in clinical research. *NIH Guide, 23*(10), 1–34.

Neuman, R. J., Heath, A., Reich, W., Bucholz, K. K., Madden, P. A. F., Sun, L., et al. (2001). Latent class analysis of ADHD and comorbid symptoms in a population sample of adolescent female twins. *Journal of Child Psychology and Psychiatry, 42,* 933–942.

Newcorn, J. H., Halperin, J. M., Jensen, P. S., Abikoff, H. B., Arnold, L. E., Cantwell, D. P., et al. (2001). Symptom profiles in children with ADHD: Effects of comorbidity and gender. *Journal of the American Academy of Child and Adolescent Psychiatry, 40,* 137–146.

Offord, D. R., Boyle, M. H., & Racine, Y. (1989). Ontario Child Health Study: Correlates of disorder. *Journal of the American Academy of Child and Adolescent Psychiatry, 28,* 856–860.

Offord, D. R., Boyle, M. H., Szatmari, P., Rae-Grant, N., Links, P. S., Cadman, D. T., et al. (1987). Ontario Child Health Study: II. Six-month prevalence of disorder and rates of service utilization. *Archives of General Psychiatry, 44,* 832–836.

Olweus, D. (1979). Stability of aggressive reaction patterns in males: A review. *Psychological Bulletin, 86,* 852–875.

Owens, E. B., Hinshaw, S. P., Kraemer, H. C., Arnold, L. E., Abikoff, H. B., Cantwell, D. P., et al. (2003). Which treatment for whom for ADHD? Moderators of treatment response in the MTA. *Journal of Consulting and Clinical Psychology, 71,* 540–552.

Pajer, K. A. (1998). What happens to "bad" girls? A review of the adult outcomes of antisocial adolescent girls. *American Journal of Psychiatry, 155,* 862–870.

Parker, J. G. & Asher, S. R. (1993). Friendship and friendship quality in middle childhood: Links with peer group acceptance and feelings of loneliness and social dissatisfaction. *Developmental Psychology, 29,* 611–621.

Parker, J. G., & Seal, J. (1996). Forming, losing, renewing, and replacing friendships: Applying temporal parameters to the assessment of children's friendships. *Child Development, 67,* 2248–2268.

Pastor, P. N., & Reuben, C. A. (2002). Attention deficit disorder and learning disability: United States, 1997–98. *National Center for Health Statistics, Vital and Health Statistics, 10*(206).

Pelham, W. E., Walker, J. L., Sturges, J., & Hoza, B. (1989). Comparative effects of methylphenidate on ADD girls and ADD boys. *Journal of the American Academy of Child and Adolescent Psychiatry, 28,* 773–776.

Peris, T., & Hinshaw, S. P. (2002). *Family dynamics and preadolescent girls with ADHD: The relationship between expressed emotion, ADHD symptomatology, and comorbid disruptive behavior.* Unpublished manuscript, University of California, Berkeley.

Pickles, A., & Angold, A. (2003). Natural categories or fundamental dimensions: On carving nature at the joints and the re-articulation of psychopathology. *Development and Psychopathology, 15,* 529–551.

Pisecco, S., Huzenic, C., & Curtis, D. (2001). The effect of child characteristics on teachers' acceptability of classroom-based behavioral strategies and psychostimulant medication for the treatment of ADHD. *Journal of Clinical Child Psychology, 30,* 413–421.

Rhee, S. H., Waldman, I. D., Hay, D. A., & Levy, F. (1999). Sex differences in genetic and environmental influences on *DSM-III-R* attention-deficit/hyperactivity disorder. *Journal of Abnormal Psychology, 108,* 24–41.

Rhee, S. H., Waldman, I., Hay, D. A., & Levy, F. (2001). Aetiology of the sex difference in the prevalence of *DSM-III-R* ADHD: A comparison of two models. In F. Levy & D. A. Hay (Eds.), *Attention, genes, and ADHD* (pp. 139–156). Philadelphia: Brunner-Routledge.

Rucklidge, J. J., & Tannock, R. (2001). Psychiatric, psychosocial, and cognitive functioning of female adolescents with ADHD. *Journal of the American Academy of Child and Adolescent Psychiatry, 40,* 530–540.

Rutter, M., & Sroufe, L. A. (2000). Developmental psychopathology: Concepts and challenges. *Development and Psychopathology, 12,* 265–296.

Seidman, L. J., Biederman, J., Faraone, S. V., Weber, W., Mennin, D., & Jones, J. (1997). A pilot study of neuropsychological function in girls with ADHD. *Journal of the American Academy of Child and Adolescent Psychiatry, 36,* 366–373.

Sharp, W. S., Walter, J. M., Marsh, W. L., Ritchie, G. G., Hamburger, S. D., & Castellanos, F. X.(1999). ADHD in girls: Clinical comparability in a research sample. *Journal of the American Academy of Child and Adolescent Psychiatry, 38,* 40–47.

Smalley, S. L., McGough, J. J., Delhomme, M., Newdelman, J., Gordon, E., Kim, T., et al. (2000). Familial clustering of symptoms and disruptive behavior disorders in multiplex families with attention-deficit/hyperactivity disorder. *Journal of the American Academy of Child and Adolescent Psychiatry, 39,* 1135–1143.

Sroufe, L. A., & Rutter, M. (1984). The domain of developmental psychopathology. *Child Development, 55,* 17–29.

Tannock, R. (1998). Attention deficit hyperactivity disorder: Advances in cognitive, neurobiological, and genetic research. *Journal of Child Psychology and Psychiatry, 39,* 65–99.

Taylor, D. C., & Ounsted, C. (1972). The nature of gender differences explored through ontogenetic analysis of sex ratios in the disease. In C. Ounsted & D. C. Taylor (Eds.), *Gender differences: Their ontogeny and significance* (pp. 215–240). London: Churchill Livingstone.

Thorley, G. G. (1984). Review of follow-up and follow-back studies of childhood hyperactivity. *Psychological Bulletin, 96,* 116–132.

Thurber, J., Heller, T., & Hinshaw, S. P. (2002). The social behaviors and peer expectations of girls with ADHD and comparison girls. *Journal of Clinical Child and Adolescent Psychology, 31,* 443–452.

Waschbusch, D. (2002). A meta-analytic examination of comorbid hyperactive-impulsive-attention problems and conduct problems. *Psychological Bulletin, 128,* 118–150.

Whitaker, A. H., Van Rossem, R., Feldman, J. F., Schonfeld, I. S., Pinto-Martin, J. A., Torre, C., et al. (1997). Psychiatric outcomes in low-birth-weight children at age 6 years. Relation to neonatal cranial ultrasound abnormalities. *Archives of General Psychiatry, 54,* 847–856.

Willcutt, E. G., Lahey, B. B., Pennington, B., Carlson, C. L., Nigg, J. T., & McBurnett, K. (2002). *Validity of attention-deficit/hyperactivity disorder.* Unpublished manuscript, University of Denver Department of Psychology.

Willcutt, E. G., & Pennington, B. F. (2000). Comorbidity of reading disability and attention-deficit/hyperactivity disorder: Differences by gender and subtype. *Journal of Learning Disabilities, 33,* 179–191.

Wolraich, M. L., Hannah, J. N., Pinnock, T. Y., Baumgaertel, A., & Brown, J. (1996). Comparison of diagnostic criteria for attention deficit hyperactivity disorder in a county-wide sample. *Journal of the American Academy of Child and Adolescent Psychiatry, 35,* 319–324.

Zahn-Waxler, C. (1993). Warriors and worriers: Gender and psychopathology. *Development and Psychopathology, 5,* 79–89.

Zoccolillo, M. (1993). Gender and the development of conduct disorder. *Development and Psychopathology, 5,* 65–78.

Zoccolillo, M., Pickles, A., Quinton, D., & Rutter, M. (1992). The outcome of childhood conduct disorder: Implications for defining adult personality disorder and conduct disorder. *Psychological Medicine, 22,* 971–986.

5

Aggression and Antisocial Behavior in Girls

SHARON L. FOSTER

Until the 1990s, childhood aggression was generally thought to be the province of males. Theories and research developed either based mostly on male samples or without regard to gender. Since 1990, however, researchers have focussed considerably more interest on antisocial behavior in girls. Some have questioned whether definitions of aggression should be constrained to examinations of harm to people and property, or should be expanded to include intentional harm to relationships (e.g., Bjorkqvist, 1994; Crick & Grotpeter, 1995). Others have recognized that even if girls generally display lower rates of physical aggression and delinquency than boys, substantial numbers of girls show antisocial behavior at some point in their lives. For whatever the reason, research on aggression that focuses specifically on girls has begun to emerge.

This literature, although much smaller than the vast body of research on boys, is exciting for various reasons. First, a few longitudinal studies with large samples of girls have begun to show how antisocial girls' development does and does not accord with prevailing theories and data based mainly on boys. Second, many contemporary researchers have begun to realize that the mechanisms that create and maintain antisocial behavior will best be illuminated in the context of normative female development, and by attending to factors that may be particularly salient for girls and young women.

This chapter provides an overview of current research on aggression and antisocial behavior in female children and adolescents. I begin by overviewing the varying definitions of aggression and antisocial behavior that have undergirded research in this area. I then turn to an examination of problems that occur concurrently with antisocial behavior in girls, and

SHARON L. FOSTER • Alliant International University, San Diego, California, 92131-1799.

look at what is known about the developmental course of aggression in females. I also examine theories and data on the mechanisms that may be involved in the development and maintenance of aggression and antisocial behavior.

A few words on gender differences are warranted here. I mention gender differences in prevalence, comorbidity, and predictors of aggression throughout this chapter, largely because (a) much of the literature on antisocial behavior in females has compared boys and girls, and (b) gender differences in prevalence may reflect potentially important differences in causes and processes of antisocial behavior in males and females. These processes may be far more important in understanding aggression than are differences in rates of behavior per se (Rutter, Caspi, & Moffitt, 2003). In other words, the focus of research on aggression in girls should be on understanding mechanisms involved in the development of antisocial behavior, and on linking particular processes to maladaptive outcomes. This can be done in the context of studying gender differences, but if so, the aim of these studies should be to examine either (a) factors that mediate or explain gender differences, or (b) gender as a moderator of process–outcome relationships, rather than whether males and females differ in mean levels of antisocial behavior or risk factors. Studies that look only at girls can also produce information important to understanding processes that promote healthy and maladaptive development in females. Both approaches to research on girls' aggression are important.

DEFINITIONS AND PREVALENCE RATES

Antisocial behavior has been studied under various guises, the most prominent of which have been aggression, conduct disorder, and delinquency. The term "aggression" generally refers to harmful behavior (or threats of harmful behavior) judged to be intentional and directed toward others or their property (see Coie & Dodge, 1998, for extended discussion). Although early research tended to operationalize aggression in ways that varied widely, current researchers distinguish between types of aggression in more precise ways. Two related distinctions that are particularly important for understanding aggression among girls are overt versus relational aggression and direct versus indirect aggression.

The distinction between overt and relational aggression derives from the type of harm inflicted on the victim: overt aggression involves harm to one's body or possessions (physical aggression) or to one's self esteem (verbal aggression). Relational aggression refers to harm done to individuals' social relationships, and includes such acts as intentional social exclusion, telling others not to be friends with someone, and threatening to withdraw one's friendship if the friend does not accede to the perpetrator's wishes. Direct and indirect aggression are similar to overt and relational aggression: Direct aggression refers to harmful acts aimed directly at the victim, whereas indirect aggression involves harmful acts done in a way that avoids direct confrontation with the victim (Underwood, 2003). Thus, hitting would be a form of direct aggression, whereas spreading untrue rumors would be a form of indirect aggression. Much but not all relational aggression is indirect. There are exceptions, however: Threatening to break up with a boyfriend or girlfriend to the person's face would be direct aggression, but would also be relational in nature.

Research on relational aggression substantiates its inclusion as a legitimate form of aggression in several ways: (a) children view the behavior as harmful (Crick, Bigbee, & Howes, 1996); (b) victims of relational aggression, like victims of overt aggression, express heightened loneliness and depression (Crick & Bigbee, 1998; Crick & Grotpeter, 1996); and (c) relational and overt aggression emerge as separate but correlated factors in samples that include both boys and girls, with *r*s about .5–.6 when peer nomination measures are used (Crick & Grotpeter, 1995; see Crick et al., 1999, for review) and an estimated *r* of about .45 on the basis of a brief maternal report measure (Vaillancourt, Brendgen, Boiven, & Tremblay, 2003). In girl-only samples, it is not uncommon for relational and overt aggression peer nomination items to load on a single factor (Crain, Finch, & Foster, in press; Elenbaas, 1995), perhaps because of restricted range on overt aggression items (Vaillancourt et al., 2003).

Most studies of the prevalence of antisocial behavior focus on gender differences, concluding that males are more antisocial than females, particularly when physical aggression is examined. At the same time, sizable populations of antisocial girls exist, with prevalence rates that vary depending on the type of harmful or antisocial behavior being addressed and the age of the girls.

Aggression

Research on overt and direct aggression generally shows boys to be more directly/overtly aggressive than girls (e.g., Bjorkqvist, Lagerspetz, & Kaukiainen, 1992; Crick & Grotpeter, 1995). This difference is even more pronounced when physical aggression is studied separately from verbal aggression (see Bjorkqvist, 1994, and Hyde, 1984, for reviews). There are two exceptions to this general finding, however. Prior to about age 4, sex differences in physical aggression (e.g., hitting, biting) are rare (see Keenan & Shaw, 1997, for review), particularly among children with older siblings (Tremblay et al., 1999). The second exception is in romantic relationships, where boys and girls appear to be equally physically aggressive (Moffitt, Caspi, Rutter, & Silva, 2001; see also Wolfe, Scott, & Crooks, this volume).

Verbal aggression has been less widely studied than physical aggression. Results regarding gender differences have been mixed (see Underwood, 2003, for review), possibly because definitions of verbal aggression have varied widely.

Findings regarding relational aggression are also mixed. Some investigators have found relational aggression to be more common among preschool (Crick, Casas, & Mosher, 1997), grade-school (Crick & Grotpeter, 1995), and teenage (Miller & Foster, 2003) girls than boys in the United States, although others have found no gender differences between girls and boys (e.g., Rys & Bear, 1997). Occasionally peers rate boys higher than girls in relational aggression (e.g., David & Kistner, 2000). Similarly, peers generally rate Finnish school-age girls and adolescents to be more indirectly aggressive than boys (e.g., Lagerspetz, Bjorkqvist, & Peltonen, 1988; Salmivalli, Kaukiainen, & Lagerspetz, 2000), but this gender difference was reversed among Italian middle-school children (Tomada & Schneider, 1997), and Hart and colleagues found no gender differences in Russia with preschoolers (Hart, Nelson, Robinson, Olson, & McNeilly-Choque, 1998). A more consistent finding is that peers and teachers rate girls higher on average on relational than on physical aggression (see Underwood, 2003, for review). Thus, when girls choose to inflict harm on their peers, it is more likely to be done in ways that damage relationships than by attempting physical harm.

Unfortunately, population-based epidemiological data specifically addressing the prevalence of physical, verbal, and relational aggression at different ages are not to our knowledge available. Survey data on bullying shed some light on the prevalence of these problems, although rates vary widely across countries and depend upon the way bullying is defined and assessed (Wolke, Woods, Stanford, & Schultz, 2001). In one extensive study of over 6,000 students in England, Whitney and Smith (1993) indicated that 12% of girls aged 8–11 and 6% aged 11–16 reported that they bullied others "sometimes" or more; 4% of the younger girls and 1% of the older girls reported bullying once a week or more. This study, like many others, included both direct and indirect aggression in the definition of bullying given to participants and did not differentiate between them. In one study that assessed these types of behavior separately, Wolke, Woods, Bloomfield, et al. (2000) identified 6- to 9-year-old girls in the UK who reported they engaged in relationally and overtly aggressive behaviors at least every week. They found that 5.3% of girls would be classified as relational bullies, and 9% would be classified as overtly aggressive bullies. Because of self-serving biases in self-reports of aggression (Osterman et al., 1994), these data may underestimate the number of girls who engage in high rates of relationally and overtly aggressive behavior.

Conduct Disorder

Other investigations of antisocial behavior have focused on Conduct Disorder (CD), a diagnostic category of the *DSM-IV* (American Psychiatric Association, 1994). To be formally diagnosed with CD, a child or teen must show persistent violations of the rights of others or societal rules and norms, as indicated by at least 3 of 15 behaviors. Among the general types of behaviors included in this list of antisocial behaviors are the following: physical aggression toward people or animals (e.g., cruelty to animals, weapon use, theft involving confrontation with the victim), threats, property damage, theft, lies, running away, frequent truancy prior to age 13, and staying out all night. Possibly because so many of these behaviors explicitly involve physical aggression (8 of 15, including physical aggression against property), many more boys are diagnosed with CD than girls.

Estimates based on epidemiological samples in the UK and US range from 2 to 4 boys to each girl, averaged across wide age groups (Moffitt et al., 2001). Despite these gender differences, the *DSM-IV* cites prevalence rates of 2 to 9% for females under the age of 16. Among girls, CD is more frequent after the onset of puberty than before (Zoccolillo, 1993).

Antisocial behavior is also sometimes equated with delinquency, defined as violation of laws. Delinquency is sometimes assessed via arrest or conviction rates, a risky enterprise for girls because some evidence suggests that girls and boys may be treated differently by the justice system (e.g., girls are more likely to have cases handled informally and are less likely to be adjudicated; Hoyt & Scherer, 1998). Although this could be due to different sorts of offenses, some differences in treatment appear when their offenses are similar (e.g., females are more likely to be arrested for status offenses than males; Hoyt & Scherer, 1998). In addition, delinquency typically involves drug- and alcohol-related offenses (including consumption) as well as aggressive acts (e.g., assault), which means that samples of delinquent girls are likely to contain large numbers of substance users who may or may not engage in aggression or other antisocial acts.

Self-report data from epidemiological studies indicate that rates of delinquency are generally higher among boys than girls, although the degree to which the genders differ depends on the type of offense. Here I focus on crimes not involving substance use; Andrews describes research on girls' substance use in detail in this volume. Violent and property offenses are much more common among boys than girls, whereas the gender gap is narrower for other offenses (e.g., status offenses). Snyder (2001) presented data on children under the age of 13 who were arrested in the United States in 1997 for various crimes. Females constituted only 14 and 9% of those arrested for violent offenses and aggravated assault, respectively, and 26% of those arrested for property crimes (mostly due to involvement in larceny [31%] rather than burglary [12%]). Larger percentages of females were among those arrested for running away from home (48%) and offenses against the family (type not specified; 37%).

Among adolescents, the pattern is similar. Snyder, Sickmund, and Bilchuk (1999) reported data based on 1997 statistics from the National Longitudinal Survey of Youth, which involved interviews with a large nationally representative US sample of youth ages 12–16. These data indicated that 8% of females (compared with 16% of males) reported having committed assault within the last year; 11% of females (20% of males) had destroyed property; and 3% of females (7% of males) admitted having stolen something worth over $50. In contrast, 11% of females (vs. 10% of males) reported that they had run away from home at some time in the past. One in 20 (5%) females reported having been arrested once or more in their lives. Rates for assault were somewhat higher among Black (12%) and Hispanic (10%) than White females (7%); rates for property damage and theft were virtually identical among females in these three racial/ethnic groups.

Different ways of defining antisocial behavior clearly overlap to some degree, with the clearest area of overlap being that overt aggression, CD and delinquency all can include physical aggression. The degree to which these definitions include antisocial behaviors other than physical aggression is important both in understanding the population being investigated and in examining gender differences. This is because gender differences are most pronounced with physical aggression but are sometimes less apparent in other forms of antisocial behavior (Silverthorn & Frick, 1999). Gender differences depend on the type of CD being examined, with child-onset conduct problems showing a 10:1 male:female ratio, versus a 1.5:1 male:female ratio for adolescent-onset conduct problems (Moffitt et al., 2001). In addition, CD prevalence rates in girls reflect the prevailing criteria used for diagnosis at the time the study was done: as these criteria have changed, so has the prevalence of CD in girls (Zoccolillo, Tremblay, & Vitaro, 1996).

Formal diagnostic criteria for Conduct Disorder do not include the more subtle forms of social harm included under the relational or indirect aggression rubric. Nor are these activities illegal, so measures of delinquency do not assess these forms of harm. Because of this, and because the study of relational and indirect aggression is fairly recent, most theories and studies of aggression and delinquency in girls have implicitly or explicitly focused on types of antisocial behavior in which physical aggression plays a large role. Thus, most of the literature I survey in this chapter comes from that tradition. Where similar theories and constructs have been studied with relational or indirect aggression, I include those findings as well.

COMORBIDITY

Findings regarding the problems that cooccur with aggression among girls depend to some extent on how aggression or antisocial behavior is defined, the age(s) at which girls are assessed, and whether assessments are cross-sectional or longitudinal. Most studies of comorbidity look at mental health diagnoses that occur concurrently with Conduct Disorder using cross-sectional designs. As with studies of prevalence of antisocial behavior, many studies of comorbidity compare girls with boys. In these comparisons, it is crucial to consider the fact that base rates of the disorders that co-occur with CD vary by gender (Zoccolillo, 1993). For example, one would expect higher rates of comorbidity between CD and affective disorders among girls than boys in adolescence (but not necessarily in earlier years) because CD is more common generally among boys whereas affective disorders are more common among girls.

Among girls, the occurrence of concurrent problems is the rule, not the exception. In one of the largest and most ambitious studies of girls' antisocial behavior to date, Moffitt et al. (2001) followed a sample that began with 1,661 children born in Dunedin, New Zealand. They collected data regularly until the children were 21. Moffitt et al. examined the lifetime prevalence of any diagnosable disorder (besides CD) among the 72 girls who met criteria for CD at one or more assessment points. Almost all (93%) of these girls (and 88% of CD boys) met criteria for one or more disorder at one or more assessment points.

Among boys, the most common comorbid diagnosis with CD is Attention-Deficit/Hyperactivity Disorder (ADHD). Among girls diagnosed with CD, ADHD is also more common than would be expected given its base rate among girls generally. Offord, Alder, and Boyle (1986) found that 56.3% of girls between the ages of 4 and 11 who met the criteria for CD also met criteria for ADD. Moffitt et al. (2001) examined the numbers of males and females diagnosed with CD at any time point prior to age 21 in their longitudinal study, finding much lower rates: 23% of CD males and 9% of CD females also met the criteria for ADHD at age 11, 13, or 15. Although both males' and females' risk for ADHD was higher if they had a CD diagnosis than if they did not, the difference in risk did not differ for males and females when the differential base rates for the disorders were taken into account. These studies have not considered whether comorbidity rates for girls might vary depending on the subtype of ADHD: Hinshaw and Blachman (2004) suggest that the Inattentive ADHD subtype (characterized by problems with organization and attention) may be more common in girls than the Combined subtype (which includes both attentional and impulsivity/overactivity difficulties), whereas for boys, the opposite may be true.

Moffitt et al. also found that 72% of girls diagnosed with CD in their study met criteria for depression or dysthymia at some point between ages 11 and 21. Similarly, 72% met criteria for an anxiety disorder during the same period. Both percentages were higher than would be expected by chance for adolescent females. These findings parallel those of others showing elevated rates of depressive and anxiety disorders among CD girls and teens (Loeber & Keenan, 1994; Zoccolillo & Rogers, 1991). Furthermore, Moffitt et al. (2001) found that CD in adolescence predicted depression in adult women, but that depression in girlhood did not predict CD in adolescence. These results have not been consistent across investigators, samples, and time frames, however (Loeber & Keenan, 1994), so the sequencing of these problems has not been firmly established.

Moffitt et al. (2001) also reported other disorders that occurred more commonly than would be expected in light of their base rates in girls. Alcohol and marijuana dependence at ages 18 or 21 was reported by 31 and 27% of the girls diagnosed with CD at some point in the study (compared with 11 and 4% among girls not diagnosed), a finding quite consistent with those of others who have studied drug and alcohol use in combination with CD and delinquency (Huizinga, Loeber, & Thornberry, 1993; Loeber & Keenan, 1994). CD girls were also at elevated risk for eating disorders at ages 18–21, although eating disorders were fairly uncommon (found in 9% of CD girls and 1% of non-CD girls).

Despite the fact that gender differences in comorbidity rates show patterns related to gender differences in the disorders being investigated, rates of comorbidity among girls diagnosed with CD are still higher than would be expected given chance occurrence of each of the disorders. Because Moffitt et al.'s (2001) data are from a community sample, these findings are not an artifact of different patterns of referral of boys and girls for clinical services. The "gender paradox" hypothesis (Eme, 1992) explains these findings by postulating that although CD is relatively uncommon among girls, those girls who meet criteria for CD are likely to be particularly severely afflicted. Thus, they may have a greater number of comorbid problems than would be expected by chance. One explanation for this is that genetic and biological factors may better protect girls against developing antisocial behavior than boys, requiring greater adversity or more serious risk factors to push girls over the threshold into serious levels of antisocial behavior.

Proponents of the gender paradox hypothesize that girls will show more serious forms of CD or more comorbidity than boys. On the basis of their review of the literature, Loeber and Keenan (1994) suggested that a gender paradox for CD in girls does exist. However, they drew data from many studies that did not directly compare rates of comorbidity in boys and girls statistically after controlling for different rates of the disorders in the two sexes. Moffitt et al. (2001) used appropriate statistical controls and found little evidence that girls who met criteria for CD at some time during childhood and adolescence were more likely to have comorbid diagnoses than boys after base rates of the disorders were taken into account statistically. In addition, Moffitt et al. examined whether boys and girls had different thresholds of risk for developing Conduct Disorder by looking at whether girls with CD had more troubled family backgrounds, neuropsychological problems, difficult temperaments, IQs, or peer relations problems than boys. Of the 45 analyses they conducted, only two showed that girls with CD had higher scores on the risk variable than boys, about what would be expected by chance. Thus, their analyses failed to support the gender paradox. Instead, their findings suggested that many risk factors operate similarly in boys and girls. Boys are exposed to higher levels of risk, and that this differential exposure explains much of the variance in sex differences in antisocial behavior.

Although studies of relational aggression are less numerous than studies of overt conduct problems, these indicate that relational aggression is associated with several other concurrent difficulties. Like overt aggression, relational aggression has been linked to peer rejection in both mixed-sex and all-girl samples in the United States and Europe (Crick & Grotpeter, 1995; Elenbaas, 1995; Tomada & Schneider, 1997). In girl-only samples, relational aggression has been associated with low rates of teacher- and peer-reported prosocial behavior (Crain, 2002; Crick et al., 1999; Osantowski, 2001). Among studies examining boys and girls as a group, children who are high on peer-reported relational aggression relative to their classmates also received relatively high scores on teacher reports of internalizing and externalizing problems and themselves reported more feelings of loneliness, depression, and isolation than their classmates (Crick, 1996; Crick & Grotpeter, 1995). In girl-only samples, relationships between relational aggression and internalizing problems have not always replicated, although relational aggression correlates highly with indicators of overt aggression (Crick & Bigbee, 1998; Osantowski, 2001). Relationships between relational aggression and other comorbid difficulties associated with overt aggression in females have not been examined, but would be likely to be similar (at least in community samples), given the strong relationship between overt and relational aggression in girls assessed in school settings.

DEVELOPMENTAL COURSE

Continuity and Stability

Tremblay and colleagues (1999) distinguish between continuity and stability in aggressive behavior. Continuity occurs when those high in aggression at one point in time remain so at a later point and is generally shown by correlations in rates of behavior over time. Stability, in Tremblay et al.'s view, involves the question of whether the frequency with which individual children engage in aggression changes over time—for example, do girls hit others more often at age 2 than at age 6?

Tremblay et al. (1999) provided data on stability which indicated that—according to mothers' reports—the percentage of girls (and boys) who kicked, hit, or bit either "sometimes" or "often" declined in a linear fashion from ages 2 to 11. Nonetheless, most studies of girls have examined continuity of aggression or antisocial behavior. Moffitt et al. (2001) provided the most comprehensive data on this issue based on the Dunedin sample. From ages 5–15, two-year correlations based on parent reports of antisocial behavior ranged from .5 to .7; two-year correlations based on teacher reports ranged from .3 to .5 for ages 5–13. Over longer time periods, correlations were more modest, as would be expected. Parent reports of antisocial behavior at age 5, for example, correlated . 41 with parent reports at age 13; the correlation was .17 for teacher reports. Continuity of self-report during adolescence was even less; girls' self-reports over 2-year intervals from age 11–21 ranged from .15 to .63; girls' self-reported antisocial behavior at age 11 was unrelated to reports at age 15 ($r = .08$) and 19 ($r = -.02$).

The fact that correlations among rates of overt aggression are less than perfect is due in part to the fact that individual girls' rates of aggression can change over time: some girls desist and others begin to aggress despite an earlier history of low rates of antisocial behavior. One way to examine this is to look at patterns in the evolution of antisocial behavior to identify different trajectories or patterns of change over time. Côté, Zoccolillo, Tremblay, Nagin, and Vitaro (2001) examined patterns of continuity and change in a sample of almost 900 girls (one group randomly sampled to be representative of Quebec, supplemented with a second group rated high by a parent or teacher on externalizing behaviors in kindergarten), using teacher ratings of disruptive behavior collected yearly when girls were of ages 6 to 12. They identified four trajectory groups. The largest group (57%) showed very low levels of disruptive behaviors across childhood. A second group (32%) showed "medium" levels, a third group (10%) higher levels, and the fourth and rarest group (1%) showed consistent high rates of disruption. Interestingly, all groups showed at least slight declines over time.

Côté et al. (2001) also determined whether girls met criteria for a CD diagnosis in adolescence (average age, 15.7 years). The two groups of girls with the highest rates of disruptive behavior had a significantly higher likelihood of being diagnosed than girls in the other two groups. This amounted, however, to a 1 in 12 chance of being diagnosed with CD if the girl had been consistently disruptive, versus a 1 in 49 chance if the girl had shown consistently low rates of disruptive behavior.

These findings illustrate three important points. First, although a history of childhood antisocial behavior increases the risk of subsequent adolescent antisocial behavior, many girls who are quite disruptive as youngsters do not develop CD—at least as it is currently diagnosed—as adolescents. The same is true when girls are younger at the point of diagnosis: using data drawn from the sample just described, Zoccolillo et al. (1996) found that only 3 of 74 girls who scored high on antisocial behavior in kindergarten by *both* a teacher and a parent met criteria for CD at age 10. Similarly, Moffitt and Caspi (2001) identified 39 girls (of a community sample of 445 females in New Zealand) with high levels of antisocial behavior shown in at least three of four assessments between the ages of 5 and 11. Of these, only 6 (15%) showed serious problems with delinquent behavior at ages 15–18.

Second, the persistent and cross-situational *absence* of disruptive, aggressive behavior over time appears in particular to predict continued lack of problems with antisocial behavior. Zoccolillo et al. (1996) found that not a single girl (of 80) that both a parent and a teacher rated low in antisocial behavior in kindergarten met criteria for CD at age 10, regardless of whether *DSM-III-R* or *DSM-III* criteria were used. Similarly, Stattin and Magnusson (1989) found that between 92 and 96% of females who received the lowest teacher ratings on measures of overt aggression at age 10 had no criminal contacts (arrests or convictions) at age 26; 100% of females with the lowest teacher ratings at age 13 had no criminal contacts.

The third point to emerge from these studies is that despite the fact that some girls show patterns of disruptive and aggressive behavior that do not seem to culminate in continued serious overt aggression into adolescence, a small number of girls do persist. This is important because both Patterson DeBaryshe, & Ramsey, (1989) and Moffitt (1993) have posited that there are two types of delinquent boys. "Early starter" or "childhood-onset" delinquents show high rates of problem behavior in childhood, which continue into adolescence and adulthood. In contrast, "adolescence-limited" delinquents only begin to show problems with aggression and law breaking in the teen years, and are more likely to desist as they become adults. Among girls, early starters who also show antisocial behavior in adolescence can be identified, but these are rare. Moffitt and Caspi (2001) identified only 6 out of a sample of 445 girls followed longitudinally from age 5 to 18. This is not because there are no overtly aggressive young girls, however. As noted above, many girls desist at least to some extent as they grow older.

Fergusson and Horwood (2002) also examined trajectories of antisocial behavior in a large sample of girls (630 began the study), focusing on violent behavior and property damage reported yearly from ages 12–21. Their study included teacher reports of aggression averaged for ages 8, 9, and 10. They identified five trajectories. These trajectories applied equally well to males and females, although numbers of males and females in each trajectory group differed. Females were most likely to belong to a group that had low rates of offending over the entire time period (75%) and to a group characterized by low rates of aggression during childhood that rose in early adolescence, peaked at about age 13, and had relatively low risk from age 17 on (the early onset adolescence-limited group; 21% of females). Smaller numbers of females fell into groups characterized by onset of violence and property damage in mid- or late adolescence. Similar to Moffitt and Caspi's findings, the smallest group of females was the chronic offender (early starter) group ($n = 8$ of 461).

Little is known about the stability and continuity of relational aggression. Some data do speak to these issues, however. Relational aggression has been found to be relatively stable among grade-school girls over a 3–6-month period, with correlations ranging from .68 to .82 (Crick, 1996; Tomada & Schneider, 1997). Vaillancourt et al. (2003) reported stability coefficients of .54 for indirect aggression over a two-year period and .45 over a four-year period, based on maternal reports collected for children ages 7–11. In addition, Cairns, Cairns, Neckerman, Ferguson, and Gariepy (1989) found increases from 4th- to 10th-grade in children's reports of conflicts in which social alienation featured prominently, suggesting that the frequency of relational aggression increases from grade school to early adolescence. Because this research area is so new, longitudinal work involving measures of relational aggression is only beginning, so data examining trajectories are not available.

Prognosis

High rates of overt aggression and antisocial behavior in middle childhood predict later problems in adolescence. One consistent and troubling finding is that aggressive girls are at risk for early sexual activity, teenage pregnancy, and early childbearing (Huizinga et al., 1993; Moffitt et al., 2001; Serbin, Peters, McAffer, & Schwartzman, 1991; Underwood, Kupersmidt, & Coie, 1996; Woodward & Fergusson, 1999; Zoccolillo & Rogers, 1991). This is particularly disturbing because early parenthood is a risk factor for behavior problems in the offspring. Furthermore, women who meet criteria for CD at any time prior to age 18 have an increased risk for pairing up with antisocial males in serious relationships, and such pairing amplifies the probability their own antisocial behavior will continue into adulthood (Moffitt et al., 2001).

Aggression and antisocial behavior in young girls are also associated with academic difficulties, including teacher concerns about the girl (Pulkkinen & Pitkänen, 1993) and suspension from school by grade 6 (Ialongo, Vaden-Kiernan, & Kellam, 1998). It is less clear whether aggression in grade school predicts academic problems in adolescence (Pulkinnen & Pitkanen, 1993). Nonetheless, antisocial behavior among adolescent girls is associated with low grades in adolescence (Pulkinnen & Pitkanen, 1993) and with later academic difficulties, including leaving school prematurely and being less likely than peers to seek university education (Cairns, Cairns, & Neckerman, 1989; Moffitt et al., 2001; Pajer, 1998). Not surprisingly, given their lack of education, antisocial girls are more likely than others to be supported by welfare as young women (Moffitt et al., 2001).

Adolescent antisocial behavior is also associated with a variety of romantic relationship difficulties for young women, including poor heterosexual relationship quality and likelihood of being involved in a physically abusive relationship (Moffitt et al., 2001; Pajer, 1998). A significant number of girls (in the range of 25–50%, according to Pajer's, 1998, review of the literature) diagnosed with CD or labeled as delinquent in adolescence also go on to engage in criminal behavior as adults. Many of these young women experience problems in multiple domains of functioning.

Alternative Developmental Pathways

Investigators have raised some concerns about whether the developmental pathways to antisocial behavior posited for boys also characterize girls (Crick & Zahn-Waxler, 2003). Possibly the most dominant description of the development of delinquency in boys involves two pathways to delinquency—"childhood-onset" or "early starter" and "adolescent-limited" or "late starter," Moffitt (1993) and Patterson et al. (1989), speculate that different sets of factors propel boys toward antisocial behavior that begins in childhood versus adolescence. For example, Moffitt suggested that the childhood-onset pathway is characterized by many environmental and biological risk factors. In contrast, she hypothesized that children in the adolescence-limited pathway experience relatively few risk factors in childhood. Instead, peer influences coupled with excessive wishes for adult autonomy contribute to antisocial behavior that emerges for the first time at puberty or in midadolescence.

Moffitt and Caspi (2001) propose that childhood-onset and adolescence-limited pathways—and their developmental antecedents—also apply to girls (Moffitt et al., 2001), with the caveat that the adolescent pathway is much more typical of girls than the child-onset pathway. Like Moffitt and Caspi (2001), Silverthorn and Frick (1999) concluded that most antisocial girls do not develop conduct-related problems until adolescence. Unlike Moffitt and Caspi, however, these authors believe that girls who develop antisocial behavior in the teen years have the same sorts of backgrounds that characterize early-onset boys, such as coercive family interaction patterns, problems with impulse control, and cognitive impairment. Because they hypothesized that these girls' problematic antisocial behaviors do not emerge until the adolescent years, Silverthorne and Frick (1999) posited a "delayed onset" pathway for girls. Silverthorn, Frick, and Reynolds (2001) provided data from incarcerated boys and girls (about 60% of whom were African American) indicating that very few girls reported antisocial behavior or police contact prior to age 10, and that delayed-onset girls were similar to early-onset boys and significantly worse than adolescence-onset boys in impulse control, as would be predicted by their theory. Their study did not assess a full range of risk variables, however, and was also limited by the small samples of early- and adolescence-onset boys ($n = 11$ and 13, respectively).

In a more comprehensive, larger-scale study with a community sample, Moffitt and Caspi (2001) pitted the early/late-starter model against the delayed-onset model proposed by Silverthorn and Frick (1999) using the data from the Dunedin study. They found that although early starter girls were quite rare (only 6; 1% of their sample), they resembled the early starter boys: They had difficult temperaments, showed undercontrolled and overactive behavior at an early age, had lower than average IQs, and lived in households characterized by disrupted parenting and conflict. In contrast, girls who became delinquent in adolescence (but not earlier) resembled late-starter boys. Both late-starter girls and late-starter boys differed from early-starter boys in the same ways, suggesting that variables that contribute to adolescence-onset delinquency are similar for boys and girls. I review these variables in a later section of this chapter.

Despite their differences, all of these views share the notion that middle childhood is less problematic for girls than for boys. Silverthorn and Frick postulate that this is because girls experience a number of protective factors prior to puberty that are less prevalent among boys, including adult and peer socialization practices that discourage overt aggression, encourage better academic achievement, and more adaptive hormonal regulation. Keenan and Shaw (1997) describe additional factors that may inhibit the development of overt aggression during early and middle childhood. These include girls' more rapid physical, linguistic, and social development, particularly in early childhood. In a related vein, Eme and Kavanaugh (1995) suggested that girls are more resistant to biological and environmental stressors than males. All of these factors could protect girls from developing antisocial behavior problems.

As Crick and Zahn-Waxler (2003) point out, other investigators have voiced the concern that researchers may have underestimated the prevalence of serious problems among preadolescent girls because they have not defined and assessed externalizing behavior problems that are particularly relevant to females (e.g., Bjorkqvist et al., 1992; Crick & Grotpeter, 1995; Feshbach, 1969). According to some of these authors, girls' externalizing difficulties in middle childhood may be as prevalent as those of boys, but take a different form. Specifically, girls may be more likely to harm others' social relationships than they are to act out physically. Because relationally aggressive behaviors have not traditionally been the focus of clinical or academic attention, they are often not included in measures of girls' externalizing problems, making girls appear less antisocial than boys. Consistent with this perspective, some empirical evidence suggests that gender differences in aggression during middle childhood disappear when the aggression category being examined includes relational or indirect aggression as well as overt aggression (e.g., Cairns et al., 1989; see Crick et al., 1999, for review).

MECHANISMS IN THE DEVELOPMENT OF ANTISOCIAL BEHAVIOR IN GIRLS

Differences between boys and girls in the type and amount of antisocial behavior they display suggests that the mechanisms involved in the development of these behaviors may differ for the two genders. Researchers have offered several hypotheses to help explain gender differences in antisocial behavior (Mears, Ploeger, & Warr, 1998). Some hypothesize that risk and protective factors may operate similarly for males and females, but boys and girls have different rates of exposure to each (e.g., Moffitt et al., 2001). Others speculate that girls and boys might be affected to different degrees by the same levels or types of risks (Mears et al., 1998), with biological factors and gender-related socialization being the usual factors invoked to explain differential response to the same factors in girls and boys.

Regardless of which set of explanations best captures the development of aggression in girls, explorations of mechanisms involved in the development of antisocial behavior in girls must be considered in a transactional context. No risk or protective factor operates in a vacuum; influences on girls' development are multiply interdependent. Furthermore, risk and protective factors unfold and may change over time as girls mature and encounter new developmental challenges, norms, and influences. In addition, girls bring biological propensities to their interactions with adults and peers and as a result may face different social and instrumental challenges and respond to them in different ways. These challenges occur in the context of social groups—families, peer groups, schools—that exist within broader social contexts such as neighborhoods and cultures that also influence proximal determinants of girls' behavior.

Interactions among girls' skills, biological factors, environmental constraints and opportunities, social groups and culture, and reactions of others in girls' day-to-day lives all shape the cognitive, affective, and behavioral skills girls develop and use to manage their lives. Although I consider variables implicated in antisocial behavior in the next section of this chapter one at a time, they likely work in interaction. Furthermore, the specific nature of important mechanisms likely varies depending on the girl's stage of development and the contexts in which she grows up.

Biological Mechanisms

Genetic Factors

Parental problems (depression and other psychiatric problems, parental criminality) are associated with antisocial behavior in adolescence in both boys and girls (Fergusson & Horwood, 2002; Moffitt et al., 2001). Parental difficulties are also common in clinic samples: Webster-Stratton

(1996) found, for example, that 37.5% of girls ages 3–7 referred for treatment of oppositional and conduct problems had some alcohol/drug abuse, or criminal history in their immediate family.

This does not necessarily imply a genetic component to girls' aggression: parents who themselves have behavioral or emotional difficulties also have poorer parenting skills than their less distressed counterparts (Capaldi, DeGarmo, Patterson, & Forgatch, 2002). More compelling evidence comes from Cronk et al.'s (2002) study examining 1,093 pairs of monozygotic (identical) and 855 pairs of dizygotic (fraternal) female twins. Conduct problem symptoms reported by mothers correlated .88 for the monozygotic twins, compared with .66 for the dizygotic girls. Heritability estimates for CD symptoms were still moderate after controlling for measures of the extent to which the twins had similar friends and classes, important potential environmental influences on the development of antisocial behavior. Jacobson, Prescott, and Kendler (2002) reported similar findings based on twins' retrospective reports of antisocial behavior. Twin studies that have examined girls and boys separately all support some genetic contribution to antisocial behavior in girls, although estimates of the relative contributions of genetics versus shared environment vary, as do the presence and magnitude of gender differences in heritability (Eley, Lichtenstein, & Moffitt, 2003; Eley, Lichtenstein, & Stevenson, 1999; Jacobson et al., 2002). These differences may be due to the source of information about antisocial behavior (self-report versus parent report); whether the authors use a measure that assesses aggressive antisocial behavior, nonaggressive antisocial behavior, or a combination (Eley et al., 1999, 2003); and whether antisocial behavior is assessed in childhood or adolescence (Jacobson et al., 2002).

Hormonal Factors

The consistent gender differences in overt aggression have led many researchers to speculate on the role of hormones that differentiate males and females, particularly testosterone. Testosterone levels have been inconsistently related to aggression among adolescent males and females (see Coie & Dodge, 1998, Volavka, 1995, and Zoccolillo, 1993, for reviews). In addition, recent evidence suggests that changes in testosterone over the course of the day may be more strongly related to disruptive behavior in girls than overall testosterone levels, but this relationship only emerged after controlling for pubertal status (Granger et al., 2003). Further complicating the picture are findings that engaging in aggression or conflict can increase testosterone, challenging assumptions about the direction of causation (Coie & Dodge, 1998).

Inconsistent evidence suggests that cyclical fluctuations in the menstrual cycle may be associated with increased propensity for aggression and criminality among adult women (Volavka, 1995). Whether this occurs in adolescence is not clear, nor are the hormonal mechanisms that might be involved.

Maturation Rate

Early puberty relative to peers also is a risk factor for onset of Conduct Disorder among girls in adolescence. Although this could be a result of hormonal changes, it is more likely the result of interactions among hormonal changes, their physical consequences, and the characteristics of the girl's environment. The environment in which this early development occurs is important: Caspi, Lynam, Moffitt, and Silva (1993) found that early-maturing girls were at risk for later CD if enrolled in mixed-sex schools, but not in all-girl schools. This may be because their older appearance makes girls more attractive to boys, particularly deviant males, and girls in all-female schools are less likely to encounter these boys than girls in mixed-sex schools. As described later, involvement with antisocial males is particularly risky for girls.

Cognitive and Affective Mechanisms

IQ and Executive Functioning

Correlational studies show that externalizing behavior problems are associated with lower IQ scores among girls at age 8 (Woodward & Fergusson, 1999). Some longitudinal evidence suggests that as a group, both boys and girls who were delinquent at ages 13–15 had lower IQs at ages 7–13 than their nondelinquent counterparts (White, Moffitt, & Silva, 1989). Other evidence suggests that girls in community samples who develop conduct problems as teenagers after relatively low rates of problems as youngsters do not necessarily show neurocognitive deficits (Moffitt & Caspi, 2001).

The most severely troubled girls, however, may be particularly likely to display cognitive deficits: Giancola, Mezzich, and Tarter (1998) examined girls with and without a psychoactive substance abuse disorder; 79% of those with substance abuse problems also met the criteria for CD. Girls completed a battery of tests assessing executive functioning, generally defined as higher order cognitive skills (e.g., planning, reasoning) involved in self-regulation and goal-oriented activity. Scores on the battery predicted between 1 and 10% of the variance in different measures of aggression and delinquency, even after socioeconomic status, age, and rates of drug use had been controlled.

Distorted and Deficient Social Cognition

Various theories and studies link distorted and deficient cognitive processing to aggression in childhood and adolescence. One comprehensive cognitive theory of aggressive behavior is the Social Information Processing (SIP) model, as reformulated by Crick and Dodge (1994). The SIP model hypothesizes that children who are aggressive show maladaptive processing at one or more of several steps involved in managing one's social interactions: encoding and interpreting social cues, selecting goals for one's interactions with others, accessing possible responses to the situation, evaluating and selecting responses, and enacting behavior choices. Crick and Dodge (1994) hypothesize that these cognitive responses are proximal contributors to aggression: they occur in specific social situations and increase the likelihood the child will respond to that situation with aggression.

Although many studies have examined SIP mechanisms, most of these have either focused solely on boys or have not had sufficient statistical power to detect differences between aggressive boys and girls if such differences in fact exist (Crick & Dodge, 1994). A few have examined relatively large mixed-sex samples, however, and found that gender did not moderate the relationship between social information processing variables and overt aggression. Specifically, compared with less aggressive peers, overtly aggressive children attribute more hostile intent to peers in ambiguous provocation situations (Crick, 1995; Crick, Grotpeter & Bigbee, 2002) and view themselves as particularly capable of responding aggressively (Dodge, Lochman, Harnish, Bates, & Pettit, 1997). They are also more likely than nonaggressive peers to report they would behave aggressively in hypothetical problem situations and to evaluate aggressive responses more positively (Dodge et al., 1997; Slaby & Guerra, 1988).

For girls, these cognitive biases may be most evident in extremely aggressive samples: Slaby and Guerra (1988) compared the social cognition of 11th- and 12th-grade teenagers rated by teachers as high and low in aggression with the cognitions of boys and girls in a maximum-security juvenile facility. On 4 of the 12 information-processing variables, not one of the highly aggressive high school girls endorsed biased views. In contrast, the aggressive high school boys and institutionalized boys and girls all showed similar and higher rates of biased cognition.

Findings regarding social information processing mechanisms and relational aggression (RA) have been mixed. Crick and colleagues (Crick, 1995; Crick et al., 2002) found that boys and girls high in relational aggression reported more hostile attribution bias than less aggressive peers in relational provocation situations. In three studies of girl-only samples, however, Crain et al. (in press) and Osantowski (2001) failed to replicate this finding. Neither Crick and Werner (1998) nor Crain et al. (in press) found children's evaluations of the likely outcomes of RA in hypothetical situations to correlate with the child's relationally aggressive behavior as reported by peers. Furthermore, Crain et al. (in press) found that relationship-focused goals, instrumental goals, or likelihood of selecting relational aggression as a strategy were not associated with relational aggression in the peer group. Together these findings raise the possibility that cognitive processes associated with relational aggression in girls might differ from those involved in overt aggression.

Bandura and colleagues (Bandura, 1999; Bandura, Caprara, Barbaranelli, Pastorelli, & Regalia, 2001) have proposed that somewhat different cognitive mechanisms might be involved in aggression. Specifically, they propose that certain cognitive practices disinhibit aggressive conduct. These "moral disengagement" processes include justifying the aggressive act as serving worthwhile purposes, minimizing one's role in the harm caused by the aggression, and blaming the victim for provoking the aggression. Bandura et al. (2001) examined self-reports of moral disengagement among Italian children at age 11 and found that they were linked with self-reports of delinquency at age 11 and 13. Importantly, the relationships between moral disengagement and delinquency were virtually identical when the data were examined separately by gender. Data also suggested that moral disengagement was linked to delinquent behavior through reports of "ruminative affectivity" in both boys and girls. Ruminative affectivity refers to the tendency to be preoccupied with grievances and need for vengeance, and to be easily aroused to anger. These mechanisms have not to date been examined with relational aggression.

Empathy

Empathy has also been suggested as a protective factor for the development of aggression, in part because boys and girls often differ on levels of empathy in ways that parallel gender differences in overt aggression. Two early studies found that measures of empathy were associated with overt aggression for elementary school boys but not for girls (Bryant, 1982; Feshbach & Feshbach, 1969), suggesting that empathy might be protective only for boys. Several later studies, however, looked at older samples and clearly distinguished between the affective (e.g., responding emotionally to others' needs) and cognitive aspects (e.g., ability to take the perspective of the other) of empathy. All of these found that affective but not cognitive components of empathy correlated negatively with overt aggression among adolescents (e.g., Carlo, Raffaelli, Laible, & Mayer, 1999; Cohen & Strayer, 1996; Lafferty & Foster, 2004). Furthermore, measures of affective empathy mediated or partially mediated gender differences in overt (Carlo et al., 1999; Lafferty & Foster, 2004) and relational aggression (Lafferty & Foster, 2004). Although these findings suggest that emotional responsivity may play a role in protecting against aggression in both boys and girls (at least in adolescence), more research focused specifically on girls is needed.

Social Mechanisms

Demographic Factors

Girls at risk for the development of aggression and delinquency come disproportionately from disadvantaged circumstances. Their mothers are more likely than the mothers of nonaggressive girls to be young when the girls are born (Moffitt et al., 2001; Woodward & Fergusson, 1999) and to be single, poor, and have limited education (Woodward & Fergusson, 1999). As they grow up, girls who meet criteria for CD in adolescence are more likely than their non-CD counterparts to live in low-income single-parent households and to experience caretaker changes during their childhoods (Moffitt et al., 2001). All of these factors can contribute to parental stress and disrupted parenting. As is the case with boys, living in poor neighborhood can also limit the quality of girls' educational experiences, which may be particularly problematic because of the poor academic skills of some girls at risk.

Family

Problematic family interactions in childhood and adolescence feature prominently in theories of male aggression and delinquency. Among factors strongly implicated in the development of aggression in boys are inconsistent parenting; harsh, ineffective discipline strategies; poor parental supervision (particularly during the preadolescent and adolescent years); and low rates of parental positive involvement with the boy (see Wasserman & Seracini, 2001, for review).

Unfortunately, the extensive research that has elucidated these factors—particularly Patterson and colleagues' detailed observations of families that have documented the microsocial processes of poorly functioning families—has been done with boys. The limited research with girls, however, suggests that some of the same family factors may contribute to aggression and conduct problems in girls. Webster-Stratton (1996) found that parents of girls versus boys ages 3–7 referred to a clinic for behavior problems did not differ in their observed patterns of interactions, suggesting that parenting of difficult boys and girls is quite similar. In addition, rates of mother negativity and criticism correlated significantly with observed conduct problems in the home and with teacher reports of conduct problems among clinically referred girls ages 3 to 7. Father negativity was unrelated to girls' observed conduct problems but was significantly correlated with conduct problems among boys, suggesting that maternal parenting may be a particularly salient factor at least in maintaining girls' overt aggression. McFayden-Ketchum, Bates, Dodge, and Pettit (1996) similarly found that observed maternal aversive responses to child misbehavior and low rates of affection were associated with relatively high teacher ratings of aggressive and disruptive behavior among kindergarten girls.

How coercive parenting affects changes in aggression over time is less clear. McFayden-Ketchum et al. (1996) found that maternal aversive responding to girls' misbehavior predicted increases in aggression in the classroom from kindergarten to Grade 3 for boys, but predicted *decreases* for girls who showed high rates of aggression in kindergarten. On the other hand, Moffitt and colleagues (2001) found that mothers' reports of harsh and inconsistent parent discipline at ages 7 and 9 predicted later conduct problems in girls in adolescence, suggesting that parenting practices may have cumulative effects over time. Different samples, measurement strategies, ages of girls, and analytic techniques could contribute to the discrepant findings. Nonetheless, the effects of different parenting disciplinary practices on girls clearly warrant further study, particularly using observational methods.

Parent–child conflict has been consistently related to aggression and delinquency in girls. Conflict has been associated with externalizing problems in girls aged 8–11 (Jaycox & Repetti, 1993; Woodward & Fergusson,

1999) and delinquency in adolescent females (Cernkovich & Giordano, 1987). Moffitt et al. (2001) also found conflict reported by mothers at ages 7 and 9 to differentiate girls with and without a diagnosis of Conduct Disorder in adolescence. Girls who met criteria for CD also reported less trust and communication with parents during adolescence than non-CD girls.

Among boys, parental monitoring is an important correlate of aggressive and delinquent behavior, with findings suggesting that parental monitoring limits boys' exposure to deviant peers, which in turn reduces proximal influences on antisocial behavior (Dishion, French & Patterson, 1995). Barrera, Biglan, Ary, and Li (2001) found that conflictual family relationships and parental monitoring related to both association with deviant peers and to a problem behavior cluster (drug use, antisocial behavior, poor academic performance) in large samples of 7th-grade Hispanic, Native American, and Caucasian girls. Similarly, Cernkovich and Giordano (1987) found that parent disapproval of peers significantly related to delinquency for both White and non-White girls aged 12–19; parental control and monitoring were also important for non-White females.

Very little is known about family patterns related to relational or indirect aggression. Hart et al. (1998) found that mother reports of coercive parenting related significantly but only weakly to teacher reports of relational aggression among Russian preschool girls; reports of paternal coercion and parental responsiveness were unrelated to relational aggression. Crick et al. (1999) describe unpublished research suggesting that children's relational aggression is associated with parent use of both relational and physical aggression, children's reports that they desire closeness with their parents, and fathers' use of withdrawal of affection as a control tactic. These data suggest that parents may model use of relationally harmful tactics in a climate that encourages close relationships, thus potentially increasing the salience of relational harm for children.

Underwood (2003) also speculates that gender differences in parent socialization of expressions of emotion may play a role in the emergence of relational aggression and the suppression of physical aggression. She reviews research indicating that parents (and teachers) respond to anger in girls in ways that would decrease its future occurrence (e.g., ignoring). At the same time, parents talk more with girls than with boys about emotion, and girls are more prone to empathy and guilt than boys, all of which may protect against the development of overt aggression and lead girls to aggress in more indirect and covert ways. Whether these parent socialization practices correlate negatively with measures of relational and overt aggression in girls, however, remains to be investigated.

Exposure to Trauma

Dodge, Pettit, Bates, and Valente (1995) linked physical abuse in young childhood with later externalizing behavior in Grades 3 and 4 in a mixed-sex sample, even after controlling for demographic factors and exposure to violence in the community. Interestingly, their data also suggested that physical abuse was associated with dysfunctional social information processing patterns, and that these cognitions mediated the relationship between abuse and later behavior problems. Whether the trauma of abuse per se is the culprit here, or whether abuse is a proxy for high rates of harsh and inconsistent discipline—also linked to aggression and CD in girls—is not clear, however.

Some data suggest that adjudicated delinquent female adolescents have experienced particularly high rates of exposure to sexual and other forms of abuse (McCabe, Lansing, Garland, & Hough, 2002; Silverthorn et al., 2001; see also Hoyt & Scherer, 1998, for review). This relationship could result from the fact that some girls repeatedly exposed to trauma run away from home and then must engage in criminal activities to survive on the streets (Cauce, Stewart, Whitbeck, Paradise, & Hoyt, this volume; Hoyt & Scherer, 1998). Importantly, however, not all females who come into contact with the juvenile justice system display aggression or conduct problems, raising questions about whether abuse is uniquely associated with aggressive behavior or rather increases the likelihood of apprehension for illegal activity more generally. For example, McCabe et al. (2002) found that only 38% of their representative sample of adjudicated adolescent females met diagnostic criteria for CD.

Peer-Group Factors

One of the most robust findings in the peer relations literature is that overt aggression correlates positively with rejection by peers in early and middle childhood in mixed-gender samples (see Newcomb, Bukowski, & Pattee, 1993, for review) and in all-girl samples (Fergusson, Woodward, & Horwood, 1999; Moffitt et al., 2001). This is particularly true for girls in settings where overt aggression is relatively infrequent, although aggressive girls are reasonably well accepted in mixed-sex classrooms where aggression occurs frequently (Stormshak et al., 1999).

The relationship between overt aggression and rejection does not necessarily mean that overtly aggressive girls are friendless. Overtly aggressive girls are likely to belong to social networks, but these networks are likely to contain similarly aggressive girls (Cairns, Cairns, Neckerman, Gest, & Gariepy, 1988). This has led to the general speculation that aggression promotes rejection, which in turn decreases a child's affiliation with prosocial peers and increases interaction with peers with similarly poor social skills. Current findings suggest, however, that affiliation with deviant peers may be driven more by the child's externalizing problems than by rejection, at least in later childhood and adolescence: antisocial girls (and boys) may both be rejected *and* seek out interactions with others who are like them— i.e., act in disruptive and aggressive ways (Fergusson et al., 1999; Laird, Jordan, Dodge, Pettit, & Bates, 2001). The deviant peer group presumably influences the aggressive child in ways that support continued acting out and delinquent behavior.

Supporting the final portion of this contention are robust findings that bullying (Salmivalli, Lappalainen, & Lagerspetz, 1998) and delinquency (e.g., Giordino, 1978; Moffitt et al., 2001) in adolescence are strongly related to similar behavior in teens' immediate peer groups for both boys and girls. The role of deviant peers may differ depending on whether a girl shows externalizing problems prior to menarche: Caspi et al. (1993) showed that the risk associated with early puberty for girls without prior conduct problems was almost entirely explained by exposure to delinquent peers. For girls with prior externalizing problems, early maturation and exposure to delinquent peers operated additively.

Among adolescent girls, affiliation with boys seems to be particularly risky. Delinquent girls report more opposite-sex friendships than do non-delinquent girls (Claes & Simard, 1992; Giordino, 1978); this may be more true for White than Black girls (Giordino, 1978). When asked about the context in which their offenses occur, delinquent girls most often reported being with a group of males and females (Giordino, 1978). Because most measures used to assess the deviance of teens' peer groups do not distinguish between male and female peers, it is possible that the associations between peer deviance and antisocial behavior in adolescence for girls are due to affiliation with deviant male, not female, peers. Consistent with this speculation are findings that girls in mixed-sex middle schools are exposed to more delinquent peers than are girls in same-sex schools (Caspi et al., 1993).

Peer factors associated with relational aggression in children and teens resemble those associated with overt aggression, but with some notable differences as well. As is the case with overt aggression, relationally aggressive girls are particularly likely to be disliked by peers in grade school (e.g., Crick & Grotpeter, 1995; Rys & Bear, 1997) and high school (e.g., Miller, Foster, Kruger, & Weltsch, 2001; Salmivalli et al., 2000). Some relationally aggressive girls are liked by at least some of their peers, however. Controversial girls—those who are liked by many but also disliked by many—are rated as high or higher in relational aggression than are rejected girls (Crick & Grotpeter, 1995; Elenbaas, 1995; Miller et al., 2001), and the majority of relationally aggressive girls have at least one reciprocal friend (Rys & Bear, 1997).

Underwood (2003) takes a broad view of dynamics of the peer environment that could suppress physical aggression and encourage relational aggression in girls. She describes the "Two Cultures Theory," which postulates that gender differences are influenced in part by the differences between boys' and girls' peer interactions, particularly in middle childhood. Observational research shows that during this period, girls and boys play predominantly in same-sex groups of children. These groups engage in different activities and differ in size, composition, and language use. Maccoby (1998) summarizes these differences. Although specifics vary depending on the age of the girl, girls' peer groups are smaller (dyads and triads), and involve more turn-taking and collaborative dialogue than boys'. Girls' groups are relatively less focused on establishing dominance hierarchies and on competitive activities. In middle childhood conflict occurs less often in female than male peer groups. Compared with boys, girls handle conflict more with compromise, indirect expressions of anger, or attempts to understand the other's position.

By implication, then, girls' peer groups encourage a focus on close relationships. Excessive emphasis on intimacy and exclusivity in relationships could promote manipulation of relationships among girls who are easily threatened by friendship loss, creating a breeding ground for understanding how to harm others through relational means. The limited research on relationally aggressive girls' friendships supports some of these hypotheses. In grade school, relationally aggressive girls report more intimacy in their friendships and greater desire for exclusivity than do girls who are not relationally aggressive. They are also more relationally aggressive with their friends (Grotpeter & Crick, 1996). High school girls appear to be more selective in how they direct their relational aggression: Miller (2001) found that peer nominations of relational aggression in the peer group, self- and friend reports of relational aggression in friendships, and self-report of relational aggression in romantic relationships related only weakly. Relational aggression within friendships and romantic relationships was, however, related to greater jealousy and desire for an exclusive relationship as well as to more reported negative interactions within the relationship. These data suggest that relational aggression in middle childhood and adolescence may be particularly fueled by threats to intimacy, closeness, and exclusiveness in friendships and romantic relationships.

Although these speculations are appealing, Underwood (2003) cautions against wholescale adoption of the Two Cultures Theory as an explanatory framework for understanding relational aggression, in part because it is not clear that girls are consistently more relationally aggressive than boys, or that girls' friendship networks generally are more exclusive or smaller than boys. At the same time, Underwood points out that many of the gender-related mechanisms of peer socialization implied by Two Cultures Theory have not been tested directly as potential contributors to relational aggression in females. These mechanisms include peer suppression of direct expressions of negative affect, conversational content that focuses on relationships, opportunities to observe relational aggression in the peer group, and exposure to and pressure to conform to gender stereotypes.

IMPLICATIONS AND FUTURE DIRECTIONS

Although many questions remain about the nature, conceptualization, and developmental course of aggression and conduct problems in females, much important new knowledge has emerged in the last decade. The most important findings come from studies that look either at all-girl samples or that examine gender as a moderator in samples that are large enough to have the statistical power to detect interactions between gender and other variables.

Several conclusions emerge from this research. First, although the prevalence of aggression and related conduct problems among girls is less than among boys, aggression is a serious problem for many girls, associated with concurrent and prospective difficulties. Second, differences between girls and boys in rates of problem behavior depend on the type of antisocial behavior being assessed. Third, factors that promote antisocial behavior vary to some extent for males and females, with both commonalities and differences. Fourth, models of social cognition and ways of characterizing developmental trajectories that have worked well for understanding the development of antisocial behavior in males may or may not capture the development of girls' aggression. Fifth, mechanisms that promote and inhibit the development of antisocial behavior in young girls may differ from mechanisms involved in antisocial behavior in adolescence, underscoring the need for a developmental focus on patterns of antisocial behavior as they change over time.

Research indicates that girls display some antisocial behavior (e.g., violent physical aggression) much less often than boys, whereas the gender gap narrows with other antisocial behaviors (e.g., verbal aggression; theft). These findings have spurred considerable controversy about how formal classification schemes—most notably, the *DSM*—should define "conduct disorders." Zoccolillo (1993) recommended the development of gender specific criteria for CD, arguing that many girls with serious conduct problems go undiagnosed because of the large number of CD criteria that involve overt aggression. He proposed that this could be done by (a) using a lower threshold for diagnosis of CD for females than males or (b) assigning the same proportion of males and females to "deviant" groups, based on within-gender norms.

Zoccolillo's recommendations to establish diagnostic criteria that more closely "equalize" the number of diagnosed males and females by lowering the number of criteria required for diagnosis has been criticized on both conceptual and empirical grounds. From a conceptual perspective, Zahn-Waxler (1993) argued that gender differences in rates of CD are the product of true differences in the ways boys and girls are socialized, and that different rates of CD in boys and girls should be expected, not masked with different thresholds for diagnosis. From an empirical perspective, Moffitt et al. (2001) argued that if Zoccolillo's recommendation is correct, females with elevated but subclinical levels of CD symptoms (according to current criteria) should experience the same negative outcomes as a group of males that meet the current diagnostic criteria. To test this, they identified females who would be labeled "CD" if the threshold for diagnosis were lowered, then compared them with a group of males who met the current criteria. They found that the subclinical females had considerably better outcomes in a number of domains than the comparison males. In contrast, females and males who met the *same* criteria (i.e., exceeded the same cutoff score) did not differ for the most part in outcomes.

Zoccolillo (1993) also proposed that different criteria might be developed for use with girls—criteria that are more sensitive to girls' patterns of behavior. This recommendation would not require changing the cutoff for diagnosis. Instead, the CD criteria could be broadened to make them more applicable to girls. Less scholarly attention has focused on this recommendation, although the most likely candidates for modified criteria involve relational and indirect aggression. Research on relational and indirect aggression indicates that many females (and males) inflict pain on others and violate social rules in troubling ways that do not involve physical harm. Although these acts are not illegal, children victimized by relational aggression share much in common with victims of overt aggression, suggesting that both types of behavior may produce comparable harm in victims (e.g., Crick & Bigbee, 1998). Consistent, planful acts of exclusion (and other forms of relational aggression) seem to meet the spirit of the *DSM-IV* overview of CD as involving behaviors "in which the basic rights of others . . . are violated" (p. 90), if basic "rights" are conceptualized as freedom from intentional physical, emotional, or relational harm or abuse. Yet many of the *DSM-IV* criteria involving aggression focus on physical harm. Given the many parallels between relational and overt aggression in children, extending the CD criteria to capture persistent infliction of relational as well as physical harm seems warranted.

At the same time, it is important to establish at what point and in what forms relational aggression becomes a clinically significant problem. Many studies have established cutoffs for "high" levels of relational aggression by selecting the top 10–20% of a group of children (e.g., Crick & Grotpeter, 1995). It is not clear, however, that this indicates anything other than the fact that a child is high in aggression relative to his or her classroom peers. Assessment tools need to develop specific cutoff scores indicating problematic levels of relational aggression. These cutoffs should be anchored to indicators of important negative outcomes to provide empirical guidelines for distinguishing between the occasional gossip and the relational bully.

Several other areas warrant increased attention in studies of girls. Keenan, Loeber, and Green (1999) point to the need to examine whether treatments for overt aggression and CD are equally effective for boys and girls. In addition, randomized controlled trials evaluating treatments to reduce relational forms of aggression are sorely needed. Keenan et al. (1999) also point to the need to examine factors related to gender that may serve as protective factors mitigating against the development of conduct problems, with a particular focus on girls' experiences and lives at different points in development.

Greater integration of literatures on aggression, conduct disorder, and delinquency would advance our understanding of the development of these overlapping ways of categorizing antisocial behaviors in girls. At the same time, investigators should direct more attention to finer-grained evaluations of particular forms of antisocial behavior (e.g., physical aggression versus verbal aggression versus relational aggression; violent versus nonviolent delinquency) to determine similar and unique contributors to each. In addition, the nature of the sample of girls used to study antisocial behavior is important: correlates of antisocial behavior in incarcerated or institutional samples of girls often are much more pronouncedly negative than the same correlates in girls identified as antisocial in community samples. For example, differences between boys and girls may differ depending on whether antisocial girls and boys are from community versus incarcerated samples (e.g., Slaby & Guerra, 1988; Moffitt & Caspi, 2001, versus Silverthorn et al., 2001). This may indicate that trajectories that lead to serious criminal behavior differ from those that lead to less deviant behavior among girls. Alternatively, the likelihood of placing girls and boys outside the home may differ. For example, perhaps only the most troubled or difficult to manage girls from the worst environments are removed from their homes for treatment or incarceration. If this were the case, gender differences in incarcerated samples would be confounded with gender-linked processes involved in determining how youth are handled in the judicial system. Whether or not this proves to be the case, it is important to realize that conclusions based on community versus incarcerated samples of girls may differ and need to be reconciled.

It is also important for theories and research alike to consider the fact that although girls are generally less physically aggressive than boys, males and females are equally physically aggressive in romantic relationships (see Wolfe et al., this volume). The prevalence of physical aggression in romantic relationships suggests that both boys and girls are more likely to aggress physically in romantic relationships than in other contexts, with the discrepancy across contexts being more pronounced for females than for males. Physical and genetic differences between males and females alone cannot account for these findings, as these factors do not change across contexts. Nor can gender socialization theories, at least as they currently are framed. What factors suppress physical aggression in so many settings for females, but allow it in the context of intimate relationships? Frameworks that permit more contextualized understanding of aggressive behavior in both males and females will be required to explain this seeming paradox.

Finally, it is important for investigators to look at risk and protective factors involving different forms of aggression and antisocial behavior in different ethnic and racial groups. Much of what we know about the longitudinal course of girls' aggression comes from studies conducted in Scandinavia, Canada, and New Zealand; data from the United States are beginning to emerge (Brody et al., 2003). Although the international nature of this body of literature is laudable, limits on generalizability may exist. Studies of psychological factors involved in girls' aggression in US populations for the most part pay scant attention to issues of ethnicity and social class, perhaps due to sample size limitations. At the same time, more explicit explorations of consistencies and differences in factors related to girls' aggression across cultural and economic groups have the potential to reveal important facts about contextual factors that influence development, and how these translate into transactional processes that influence girls' development.

REFERENCES

Bandura, A. (1999). Moral disengagement in the perpetration of inhumanities. *Personality and Social Psychology Review, 3,* 193–209.

Bandura, A., Caprara, G. V., Barbaranelli, C., Pastorelli, C., & Regalia, C. (2001). Sociocognitive self-regulatory mechanisms governing transgressive behavior. *Journal of Personality and Social Psychology, 80,* 125–135.

Barrera, M., Jr., Biglan, A., Ary, D. V., & Li, F. (2001). Replication of a problem behavior model with American Indian, Hispanic, and Caucasian youth. *Journal of Early Adolescence, 21,* 133–157.

Bjorkqvist, K. (1994). Sex differences in physical, verbal, and indirect aggression: A review of recent research. *Sex Roles, 30,* 177–188.

Bjorkqvist, K., Lagerspetz, K. M. J., & Kaukiainen, A. (1992). Do girls manipulate and boys fight? Developmental trends in regard to direct and indirect aggression. *Aggressive Behavior, 18,* 117–127.

Broidy, L. M., Nagin, D. S., Tremblay, R. E., Bates, J. E., Brame, B., Dodge, K. A., et al. (2003). Developmental trajectories of childhood disruptive behaviors and adolescent delinquency: A six-site, cross-national study. *Developmental Psychology, 39,* 222–245.

Bryant, B. K. (1982). An index of empathy for children and adolescents. *Child Development, 53,* 413–425.

Cairns, R. B., Cairns, B. D., & Neckerman, H. J. (1989). Early school dropout: Configurations and determinants. *Child Development, 60,* 1437–1452.

Cairns, R. B., Cairns, B. D., Neckerman, H. J., Ferguson, L. L., & Gariepy, J. (1989). Growth and aggression: Childhood to early adolescence. *Developmental Psychology, 25,* 320–330.

Cairns, R. B., Cairns, B. D., Neckerman, H. J., Gest, S. D., & Gariepy, J. (1988). Social networks and aggressive behavior: Peer support or peer rejection? *Developmental Psychology, 24,* 815–823.

Capaldi, D., DeGarmo, D., Patterson, G. R., & Forgatch, M. (2002). Contextual risks across the early life span and association with deviant behavior. In J. B. Reid, G. R. Patterson, & J. Snyder (Eds.), *Antisocial behavior in children and adolescents: A developmental analysis and model for intervention* (pp. 123–145). Washington, DC: American Psychological Association.

Carlo, G., Raffaelli, M., Laible, D. J., & Mayer, K. A. (1999). Why are girls less physically aggressive than boys? Personality and parenting mediators of physical aggression. *Sex Roles, 40,* 711–729.

Caspi, A., Lynam, D., Moffitt, T. E., & Silva, P. A. (1993). Unraveling girls' delinquency: Biological, dispositional and contextual contributions to adolescent misbehavior. *Developmental Psychology, 29,* 19–30.

Cauce, A. M., Stewart, A., Whitbeck, L. B., Paradise, M., & Hoyt, D. R. (2004). Girls on their own: Homelessness in female adolescents. In D. J. Bell, S. L. Foster, & E. J. Mash (Eds.), *Handbook of behavioral and emotional problems in girls* pp. 439–522. New York: Kluwer Academic/Plenum Publishers.

Cernkovich, S., & Giordano, P. (1987). Family relationships and delinquency. *Criminology, 25,* 295–319.

Claes, M., & Simard, R. (1992). Friendship characteristics of delinquent adolescents. *International Journal of Adolescence and Youth, 3,* 287–301.

Cohen, D., & Strayer, J. (1996). Empathy in conduct-disordered and comparison youth. *Developmental Psychology, 32,* 988–998.

Coie, D. C., & Dodge, K. A. (1998). Aggression and antisocial behavior. In W. Damon & N. Eisenberg (Eds.), *Handbook of child psychology: Vol. 3. Social, emotional, & personality development* (5th ed., pp. 779–862). New York: Wiley.

Côté, S., Zoccolillo, M., Tremblay, R. E., Nagin, D., & Vitaro, F. (2001). Predicting girls' conduct disorder in adolescence from childhood trajectories of disruptive behaviors. *Journal of the American Academy of Child and Adolescent Psychiatry, 40,* 678–684.

Crain, M. M. (2002). *The relationship of intent attributions, goals and outcome expectancies to relationally aggressive behavior in pre-adolescent girls.* Unpublished doctoral dissertation, Alliant International University, San Diego, CA.

Crain, M. M., Finch, C. L., & Foster, S. L. (in press). The relevance of the social information processing model for understanding relational aggression in girls. *Merrill-Palmer Quarterly.*

Crick, N. R. (1995). Relational aggression: The role of intent attributions, feelings of distress, and provocation type. *Development and Psychopathology, 7,* 313–322.

Crick, N. R. (1996). The role of relational aggression, overt aggression, and prosocial behavior in the prediction of children's future social adjustment. *Child Development, 67,* 2317–2327.

Crick, N. R., & Bigbee, M. A. (1998). Relational and overt forms of peer victimization: A multiinformant approach. *Journal of Consulting and Clinical Psychology, 66*, 337–347.

Crick, N. R., Bigbee, M. A., & Howes, C. (1996). Gender differences in children's normative beliefs about aggression: How do I hurt thee? Let me count the ways. *Child Development, 67*, 1003–1014.

Crick, N. R., Casas, J. F., & Mosher, M. (1997). Relational and overt aggression in preschool. *Developmental Psychology, 33*, 579–588.

Crick, N. R., & Dodge, K. A. (1994). A review and reformulation of social information processing mechanisms in children's social adjustment. *Psychological Bulletin, 115*, 74–101.

Crick, N. R., & Grotpeter, J. K. (1995). Relational aggression, gender, and social-psychological adjustment. *Child Development, 66*, 710–722.

Crick, N. R., & Grotpeter, J. K. (1996). Children's treatment by peers: Victims of relational and overt aggression. *Development and Psychopathology, 8*, 367–380.

Crick, N.R., Grotpeter, J. K., & Bigbee, M. A. (2002). Relationally and physically aggressive children's intent attributions and feelings of distress for relational and instrumental peer provocations. *Child Development, 73*, 1134–1142.

Crick, N. R., Werner, N. E., Casas, J. F., O'Brien, K. M., Nelson, D. A., Grotpeter, J. K., et al. (1999). Childhood aggression and gender: A new look at an old problem. In D. Bernstein (Ed.), *Nebraska Symposium on Motivation* (Vol. 45, pp. 75–141). Lincoln, NE: University of Nebrasha Press.

Crick, N. R., & Werner, N. E. (1998). Response decision processes in relational and overt aggression. *Child Development, 69*, 1630–1639.

Crick, N. R., & Zahn-Waxler, C. (2003). The development of psychopathology in females and males: Current progress and future challenges. *Development and Psychopathology. 15*, 719–742

Cronk, N. J., Slutske, W. S., Madden, P. A. E., Bucholz, K. K., Reich, W., & Heath, A. (2002). Emotional and behavioral problems among female twins: An evaluation of the equal environments assumption. *Journal of the American Academy of Child and Adolescent Psychiatry, 41*, 829–837.

David, C. F., & Kistner, J. A. (2000). Do positive self-perceptions have a "dark side?" Examination of the link between perceptual bias and aggression. *Journal of Abnormal Child Psychology, 28*, 327–337.

Dishion, T. J., French, D. C., & Patterson, G. R. (1995). The development and ecology of antisocial behavior. In D. Cicchetti & D. J. Cohen (Eds.), *Developmental Psychopathology Vol. 2: Risk, disorder, and adaptation* (pp. 421–471). New York: Wiley.

Dodge, K. A., Lochman, J. E., Harnish, J. D., Bates, J. E., & Pettit, G. S. (1997). Reactive and proactive aggression in school children and psychiatrically impaired chronically assaultive youth. *Journal of Abnormal Psychology, 106*, 37–51.

Dodge, K. A., Pettit, G. S., Bates, J. E., & Valente, E. (1995). Social information-processing patterns partially mediate the effect of early physical abuse on later conduct problems. *Journal of Abnormal Psychology, 104*, 632–643.

Elenbaas, D. M. (1995). *Types of aggression and their relationship to sociometric status in preadolescent girls.* Unpublished doctoral dissertation, California School of Professional Psychology, San Diego, CA.

Eley, T. C., Lichtenstein, P., & Moffitt, T. E. (2003). A longitudinal behavioral genetics analysis of the etiology of aggressive and nonaggressive antisocial behavior. *Development and Psychopathology, 15*, 383–402.

Eley, T. C., Lichtenstein, P., & Stevenson, J. (1999). Sex differences in the etiology of aggressive and nonaggressive antisocial behavior: Results from two twin studies. *Child Development, 70*, 155–168.

Eme, R. F. (1992). Selective female affliction in the developmental disorders of childhood: A literature review. *Journal of Clinical Child Psychology, 21*, 354–364.

Eme, R. F., & Kavanaugh, L. (1995). Sex differences in conduct disorder. *Journal of Clinical Child Psychology, 24*, 406–426.

Fergusson, D. M., & Horwood, L. J. (2002). Male and female offending trajectories. *Development and Psychopathology, 14*, 159–177.

Fergusson, D. M., Woodward, L. J., & Horwood, L. J. (1999). Childhood peer relationship problems and young people's involvement with deviant peers in adolescence. *Journal of Abnormal Child Psychology, 27*, 357–370.

Feshbach, N. D. (1969). Sex differences in children's modes of aggressive responses towards outsiders. *Merrill-Palmer Quarterly, 15*, 249–258.

Feshbach, N. D., & Feshbach, S. (1969). The relationship between empathy and aggression in two age groups. *Developmental Psychology, 1*, 102–107.

Giancola, P. R., Mezzich, A. C., & Tarter, R. E. (1998). Disruptive, delinquent, and aggressive behavior in female adolescents with a psychoactive substance use disorder: Relation to cognitive functioning. *Journal of Studies on Alcohol, 59*, 560–566.

Giordino, P. C. (1978). Girls, guys and gangs: The changing social context of female delinquency. *The Journal of Criminal Law and Criminology, 69*, 126–132.

Granger, D. A., Shirtcliff, E. A., Zahn-Waxler, C., Usher, B., Klimes-Dougan, B., & Hastings, P. (2003). Salivary testosterone diurnal variation and psychopathology in adolescent males and females: Individual differences and developmental effects. *Development and Psychopathology, 15*, 431–449.

Grotpeter, J. K., & Crick, N. R. (1996). Relational aggression, overt aggression, and friendship. *Child Development, 67*, 2328–2338.

Hart, C. H., Nelson, D. A., Robinson, C. C., Olson, S. F., & McNeilly-Choque, M.-K. (1998). Overt and relational aggression in Russian nursery-school-age children: Parenting style and marital linkages. *Developmental Psychology, 34*, 687–697.

Hinshaw, S. P., & Blachman, D. R. (2004). Attention-Deficit/Hyperactivity Disorder in girls. In D. J. Bell, S. L. Foster, & E. J. Mash (Eds.), *Handbook of behavioral and emotional problems in girls* pp. 117–147. New York: Kluwer Academic/Plenum Publishers.

Hoyt, S., & Scherer, D. G. (1998). Female juvenile delinquency: Misunderstood by the juvenile justice system, neglected by social science. *Law and Human Behavior, 22*, 81–107.

Huizinga, D., Loeber, R., & Thornberry, T. P. (1993). Longitudinal study of delinquency, drug use, sexual activity, and pregnancy among children and youth in three cities. *Public Health Reports, 106*, 90–96.

Hyde, J. S. (1984). How large are gender differences in aggression? A developmental meta-analysis. *Developmental Psychology, 20*, 722–736.

Ialongo, N. S., Vaden-Kiernan, N., & Kellam, S. (1998). Early peer rejection and aggression: Longitudinal relations with antisocial behavior. *Journal of Developmental and Physical Disabilities, 10*, 199–213.

Jacobson, K. C., Prescott, C. A., & Kendler, K. S. (2002). Sex differences in the genetic and environmental influences on the development of antisocial behavior. *Development and Psychopathology, 14*, 395–416.

Jaycox, L. H., & Repetti, R. L. (1993). Conflict in families and the psychological adjustment of preadolescent children. *Journal of Family Psychology, 7*, 344–355.

Keenan, K., Loeber, R., & Green, S. (1999). Conduct disorder in girls: A review of the literature. *Clinical Child and Family Review, 2*, 3–19.

Keenan, K., & Shaw, D. (1997). Developmental and social influences on young girls' early problem behavior. *Psychological Bulletin, 121*, 95–113.

Lafferty, J. A., & Foster, S. L (March 2004). *The relationships between gender, empathy, and aggressive behaviors among early adolescents.* Paper presented at the Society for Research on Adolescence, Baltimore, MD.

Lagerspetz, K. M., Bjorkqvist, K., & Peltonen, T. (1988). Is indirect aggression typical of females? Gender differences in aggressiveness in 11- to 12-year-old children. *Aggressive Behavior, 14*, 403–414.

Laird, R. D., Jordan, K. Y., Dodge, K. A., Pettit, G. S., & Bates, J. E. (2001). Peer rejection in childhood, involvement with antisocial peers in early adolescence, and the development of externalizing behavior problems. *Development and Psychopathology, 13*, 337–354.

Loeber, R., & Keenan, K. (1994). The interaction between conduct disorder and its comorbid conditions: Effects of age and gender. *Clinical Psychology Review, 14*, 497–523.

Maccoby, E. (1998). *The two sexes: Growing up apart, coming together.* Cambridge, MA: The Belknap Press of Harvard University Press.

McCabe, K. M., Lansing, A. E., Garland, A., & Hough, R. (2002). Gender differences in psychopathology, functional impairment, and familial risk factors in adjudicated delinquents. *Journal of the American Academy of Child and Adolescent Psychiatry, 41*, 860–867.

McFayden-Ketchum, S. A., Bates, J. E., Dodge, K. A., & Pettit, G. S. (1996). Patterns of change in early childhood aggressive–disruptive behavior: Gender differences in predictions from elary coercive and affectionate mother–child interactions. *Child Development, 67*, 2417–2433.

Mears, D. P., Ploeger, M., & Warr, M. (1998). Explaining the gender gap in delinquency: Peer influence and moral evaluations of behavior. *Journal of Research in Crime and Delinquency, 35*, 251–266.

Miller, D. R. (2001). *Friendship and romantic relationship features among relationally aggressive adolescent girls*. Doctoral dissertation, Alliant International University.

Miller D. R., & Foster, S. L. (2003). *Relational aggression and characteristics of adolescent friendships and romantic relationships*. Manuscript in preparation. Alliant International University.

Miller, D. R., Foster, S. L., Kruger, A., & Weltsch, M. (2001). *Measurement and correlates of relational and physical aggression in adolescence*. Minneapolis: Society for Research in Child Development.

Moffitt, T. E. (1993). Adolescence-limited and life-course-persistent antisocial behavior: A developmental taxonomy. *Psychological Review, 100*, 674–701.

Moffitt, T. E., & Caspi, A. (2001). Childhood predictors differentiate life-course persistent and adolescence-limited antisocial pathways among males and females. *Development and Psychopathology, 13*, 355–375.

Moffitt, T. E., Caspi, A., Rutter, M., & Silva, P. A. (2001). *Sex differences in antisocial behavior.* New York: Cambridge University Press.

Newcomb, A. F., Bukowski, W. M., & Pattee, L. (1993). Children's peer relations: A meta-analytic review of popular, rejected, neglected, controversial, and averaged sociometric status. *Psychological Bulletin, 113*, 99–128.

Offord, D. R., Alder, R. J., & Boyle, M. H. (1986). Prevalence and sociodemographic correlates of Conduct Disorder. *American Journal of Social Psychiatry, 6*, 272–278.

Osantowski, J. (2001). *The social cognitions associated with relational aggression and depression in preadolescent girls*. Unpublished doctoral dissertation, California School of Professional Psychology, San Diego, CA.

Osterman, K., Bjorkqvist, K., Lagerspetz, K. M. J., Kaukiainen, A., Huesmann, L. R., & Fraczek, A. (1994). Peer and self-estimated aggression and victimization in 8-year-old children from five ethnic groups. *Aggressive Behavior, 20*, 411–428.

Pajer, K. (1998). What happens to "bad girls?" A review of the adult outcomes of antisocial adolescent girls. *American Journal of Psychiatry, 155*, 862–870.

Patterson, G. R., DeBaryshe, B. D., & Ramsey, E. (1989). A developmental perspective on antisocial behavior. American Psychologist, *44*, 329–335.

Pulkkinen, L., & Pitkänen, T. (1993). Continuities in aggressive behavior from childhood to adulthood. *Aggressive Behavior, 19*, 249–263.

Raine, A. (2002). Biosocial studies of antisocial and violent behavior in children and adults. *Journal of Abnormal Child Psychology, 30*, 311–326.

Rutter, M., Caspi, A., & Moffitt, T. E. (2003). Using sex differences in psychopathology to study causal mechanisms: Unifying issues and research strategies. *Journal of Child Psychology and Psychiatry, 44*, 1092–1115.

Rys, G. S., & Bear, G. G. (1997). Relational aggression and peer relations: Gender and developmental issues. *Merrill-Palmer Quarterly, 43*, 87–106.

Salmivalli, C., Kaukiainen, A., & Lagerspetz, K. (2000). Aggression and sociometric status: Do gender and type of aggression matter? *Scandinavian Journal of Psychology, 41*, 17–24.

Salmivalli, C., Lappalainen, M., & Lagerspetz, K. (1998). Stability and change of behavior in connection with bullying in schools: A two-year follow-up. *Aggressive Behavior, 24*, 205–218.

Serbin, L. A., Peters, P. L., McAffer, V. J., & Schwartzman, A. E. (1991). Childhood aggression and withdrawal as predictors of adolescent pregnancy, early parenthood, andenvironmental risk for the next generation. *Canadian Journal of Behavioural Science, 23,* 318–331.

Silverthorn, P., & Frick, P. J. (1999). Developmental pathways to antisocial behavior: The delayed-onset pathway in girls. *Development and Psychopathology, 11,* 101–126.

Silverthorn, P., Frick, P. J., & Reynolds, R. (2001). Timing of onset and correlates of severe conduct problems in adjudicated girls and boys. *Journal of Psychopathology and Behavioral Assessment, 23,* 171–181.

Slaby, R. G., & Guerra, N. G. (1988). Cognitive mediators of aggression in adolescent offenders: 1. Assessment. *Developmental Psychology, 24,* 580–588.

Snyder, H. N. (2001). Epidemiology of official offending. In R. Loeber & D. P. Farrington (Eds.), *Child delinquents: Development, intervention, and service needs* (pp. 25–46). Thousand Oaks, CA: Sage.

Snyder, H. N., Sickmund, M., & Bilchuk, S. (1999). *Juvenile offenders and victims: 1999 national report.* Office of Juvenile Justice and Delinquency Prevention. Retrieved from http://www.ncjrs.org/html/ojjdp/nationalreport99/toc.html., October 30, 2002.

Stattin, H., & Magnusson, D. (1989). The role of early aggressive behavior in the frequency, seriousness, and types of later crime. *Journal of Consulting and Clinical Psychology, 57,* 710–718.

Stormshak, E. A., Bierman, K. L., Bruschi, C., Dodge, K. A., Coie, J. D., & Conduct Problems Prevention Research Group. (1999). The relation between behavior problems and peer preference in different classroom contexts. *Child Development, 70,* 169–182.

Tomada, G., & Schneider, B. H. (1997). Relational aggression, gender, and peer acceptance: Invariance across culture, stability over time, and concordance among informants. *Developmental Psychology, 33,* 601–609.

Tremblay, R. E., Japel, C., Perusse, D., McDuff, P., Boivin, M., Zoccolillo, M., et al. (1999). The search for the age of "onset" of physical aggression: Rousseau and Bandura revisited. *Criminal Behavior and Mental Health, 9,* 8–23.

Underwood, M. K. (2003). *Social aggression among girls.* New York: Guilford.

Underwood, M. K., Kupersmidt, J. B., & Coie, J. D. (1996). Childhood peer sociometric status and aggression as predictors of adolescent childbearing. *Journal of Research on Adolescence, 6,* 201–223.

Vaillancourt, T., Brendgen, M., Boiven, M., & Tremblay, R. (2003). A longitudinal confirmatory factor analysis of indirect and physical aggression: Evidence of two factors over time? *Child Development, 74,* 1628–1638.

Volavka, J. (1995). *Neurobiology of violence.* Washington, DC: American Psychiatric Press.

Wasserman, G. A., & Seracini, A. M. (2001). Family risk factors and interventions. In R. Loeber & D. P. Farrington (Eds.), *Child delinquents: Development, intervention, and service needs* (pp. 165–189). Thousand Oaks, CA: Sage.

Webster-Stratton, C. (1996). Early-onset conduct problems: Does gender make a difference? *Journal of Consulting and Clinical Psychology, 64,* 540–551.

White, J. L., Moffitt, T. E., & Silva, P. A. (1989). A prospective replication of the protective effects of IQ in subjects at high risk for juvenile delinquency. *Journal of Consulting and Clinical Psychology, 57,* 719–724.

Whitney, I., & Smith, P. K. (1993). A survey of the nature and extent of bullying in junior/middle and secondary schools. *Educational Research, 35,* 3–25.

Wolfe, D. A., Scott, K., & Crooks, C. (2004). Dating and relationship violence among adolescent girls. In D. J. Bell, S. L. Foster, & E. J. Mash (Eds.), *Handbook of behavioral and emotional problems in girls* pp. 381–414. New York: Kluwer Academic/Plenum Publishers.

Wolke, D., Woods, S., Bloomfield, L., & Karstadt, L. (2000). The association between direct and relational bullying and behaviour problems among primary school children. *Journal of Child Psychology and Psychiatry, 48,* 989–1002.

Wolke, D., Woods, S., Stanford, K., & Schultz, H. (2001). Bullying and victimization of primary school children in England and Germany: Prevalence and school factors. *British Journal of Psychology, 92,* 673–697.

Woodward, L. J., & Fergusson, D. M. (1999). Early conduct problems and later risk of teenage pregnancy in girls. *Development and Psychopathology, 11,* 127–141.

Zahn-Waxler, C. (1993). Warriors and worriers: Gender and psychopathology. *Development and Psychopathology, 5,* 79–89.

Zoccolillo, M. (1993). Gender and the development of conduct disorder. *Development and Psychopathology, 5,* 65–78.

Zoccolillo, M., & Rogers, K. (1991). Characteristics and outcome of hospitalized adolescent girls with conduct disorder. *Journal of the American Academy of Child and Adolescent Psychiatry, 30,* 973–981.

Zoccolillo, M., Tremblay, R., & Vitaro, F. (1996). DSM-III-R and DSM-III criteria for Conduct Disorder in preadolescent girls: Specific but insensitive. *Journal of the American Academy of Child and Adolescent Psychiatry, 35,* 461–470.

6

Substance Abuse in Girls

JUDY A. ANDREWS

Substance use and abuse in girls encompasses using tobacco (primarily cigarettes), drinking alcohol, smoking marijuana, and using other illicit drugs. Although there is co-occurrence among the use of substances, with some similarity in causes and consequences, each substance is unique, with a unique developmental trajectory and a unique set of predictors. In general, boys engage in more binge drinking and use marijuana and other illicit drugs more frequently than girls (Johnston, O'Malley, & Bachman, 2002). Boys also report more problems (i.e., missed school or work) associated with substance use than girls (Johnston et al., 2002). In addition, although boys initiate alcohol and cigarette use at a younger age than girls, girls quickly catch up, so that use is similar in the late teens and young adulthood. Further, more girls use prescribed psychoactive substances than boys throughout adolescence (Johnston et al., 2000).

Despite the known gender differences in use and abuse of substances, the literature is sparse on this subject. Studies that have guided theoretical frameworks developed to understand the etiology of substance use have often been based on male samples (e.g., Loeber, Keenan, & Zhang, 1997; Patterson, Reid, & Dishion, 1992). Other studies have not investigated gender differences (e.g., Bentler, 1992; Newcomb & Bentler, 1988), or have analyzed findings for males and females separately (e.g., Jessor, Jessor, & Finney, 1973), with no attempt at comparison. Gender differences are inferred if an effect is significant for one gender, but not the other (e.g., Ensminger et al. 1982). More recent work has explored the moderating effects of gender by directly examining interactions of the proposed risk factor and gender (Moffitt, Caspi, Rutter, & Silva, 2001). This latter work and those similar to it are the most fruitful in identifying and understanding the processes explaining gender differences. In this chapter, I will summarize the literature regarding gender differences in the prevalence,

JUDY A. ANDREWS • Oregon Research Institute, Eugene, Oregon, 97403.

comorbidity, and developmental course of substance use and the etiology of substance use, with particular emphasis on findings regarding girls and young women.

CURRENT PREVALENCE OF SUBSTANCE USE: GENDER DIFFERENCES

Gender differences vary developmentally and across specific substances. Two longitudinal community-based studies that assessed use of substances among children as early as first grade showed that although prevalence is low, the use of alcohol and cigarettes among boys significantly exceeds girls in the early elementary years (Andrews, Tildesley, Duncan, Hops, & Severson, 2003; Andrews & Tildesley, 2003; Cohen, Brownell, & Felix, 1990). Yet, by sixth (Andrews et al., in press) or seventh grade (Cohen et al., 1990), girls' cigarette use exceeds that of boys, and their alcohol use and marijuana use exceeds boys' use by eighth grade. Data from cross-sectional studies also support the gender disparity in the early years, which disappears as the child ages. Regional studies (Grady, Snow, & Kessen, 1986; Johnson, Arria, Borges, Ialongo, & Anthony, 1995) suggest a higher prevalence of alcohol, smokeless tobacco and marijuana use among elementary school-age boys as compared to girls. Data from the Cardiovascular Health in Children and Youth Study (Harrell, Bangdiwala, Deng, Webb, & Bradley, 1998) showed that while third through ninth grade boys had a higher prevalence of experimental smoking than girls across the same grades, differences were significant only in the early grades.

Studies spanning early to mid adolescence (ages 11 to 17) show mixed results, which may be culture dependent. In the Great Smokey Mountain Study (GSMS; Costello, Erkanli, Federman, & Angold, 1999), conducted in the rural southeast of the United States, boys were more likely than girls to use chewing tobacco, cannabis, snuff, and crack cocaine in their lifetime. Nonetheless, there were no gender differences in the use of other substances or in substance abuse or dependence. In a study conducted among school children in the north of England, Gilvarry, McCarthy, and McArdle (1995) showed that whereas more boys than girls drank daily (22% vs. 17%), more girls than boys smoked daily (12% vs. 8%), and occasionally (13% vs. 11%). National data from the National Household Survey on Drug Abuse (DHHS, SAMHSA, 2000), based on 12 to 17 year olds, do not show gender differences in the use of alcohol or marijuana. Boys, however, have a higher prevalence than girls of heavy drinking, smokeless tobacco, and illicit drug use (other than marijuana), throughout adolescence. According to the 2001 Monitoring the Future Study (Johnston, O'Malley & Bachman, 2002b), a national study assessing 8th, 10th and 12th graders showed little difference in prevalence among 8th and 10th graders in 2001. However, among 12th graders, the 30-day prevalence of smoking was 30% for boys and 29% for girls. The prevalence of binge drinking among boys was 36% versus 24% for girls and the 30-day prevalence of marijuana use was 26%

for boys and 19% for girls. The daily prevalence of marijuana use was 8% for boys and 4% for girls. Data from community based representative samples of older adolescents show gender differences in prevalence of substance use disorders favoring males. Lewinsohn, Hops, Roberts, Seeley, and Andrews (1993), in an epidemiological study of over 1500 Oregon high school students, showed a higher point prevalence among boys in substance use disorders, in general, and a higher lifetime prevalence among boys in the cannabis dependence and abuse. Although the prevalence of alcohol use across genders was similar, boys used it more frequently and in greater quantities than did girls (Lewinsohn, Rhode, & Seeley, 1996). Cohen et al. (1993), reporting on a sample of high school students, showed a 20% prevalence rate of alcohol abuse among boys as compared to a 10% rate among girls. Compared to alcohol, the prevalence of marijuana abuse and other drug abuse was low, with rates somewhat higher for boys for marijuana use. Both national (Windle, 1990) and community studies (Moffitt et al., 2001) show that boys report proportionately more drug and alcohol-related offenses than do girls.

National epidemiological studies either have been conducted solely with adults or have presented combined results for older adolescents and young adults (e.g., the Epidemiological Catchment Area studies, Robins, Helzer, & Przybeck, 1986). Therefore, Kandel (2000) used data from the National Household Survey on Drug Abuse from 1991, 1992, and 1993 (USDHHS, 1993; 1995a; 1995b) to obtain estimates of substance dependence among adolescents, according to *DSM-IV* criteria. In contrast to the community studies, her results show gender differences favoring girls. A higher, albeit nonsignificant, proportion of girls were dependent on marijuana and three times as many girls than boys were dependent on cocaine.

Thus, together these studies suggest that although boys initiate substance use earlier than girls, girls' use increases faster over time relative to boys. By late adolescence, there are no gender differences in cigarette, marijuana, or regular alcohol use. Gender differences favoring boys remain for heavy drinking, smokeless tobacco, and illicit drug use, abuse and dependence, with the exception of cocaine dependence. The finding that girls' substance use increases faster in late childhood and early adolescence than does boys' use stresses the importance of identifying factors that may influence girls' use as they transition into and through adolescence.

Historical Context

Prior to World War II, the prevalence of smoking, drinking, and other substance use was much lower among girls than boys. However, as noted above, this gender discrepancy for the use of several substances has disappeared in recent times. Johnson and Gerstein (1998) charted the proportion of individuals under the age of 21 who used alcohol, cigarettes, and other drugs by birth cohort, beginning in 1919 and ending in 1975. Their estimates are based on the retrospective report of respondents from the 1991, 1992, and 1993 National Household Survey on Drug Abuse (DHHS, SAMHSA, 1991, 1992, 1993), a national survey based on a probability sample of individuals living in households or noninstitutional group quarters.

In general, the proportion reporting under-age regular alcohol use increased with birth cohort, under-age daily cigarette use decreased, and use of marijuana, cocaine, or hallucinogens increased. Across substances, the magnitude of the gender difference in prevalence decreased dramatically. For example, from 1919 to 1929, the proportion reporting under-age regular alcohol use was 45% for boys and 11% for girls, and daily cigarette use was 59% for boys and 19% for girls. From 1971 to 1975, the proportion reporting under-age regular alcohol use was 63% for boys and 49% for girls, and daily cigarette use was 31% for boys and 34% for girls. Prior to 1941, few individuals reported using illicit substances before they were 21. From 1941 to 1945, the proportion reporting marijuana use was 11% for boys and 3% for girls. This proportion increased dramatically for both genders to 52% of the boys and 50% of the girls from 1971 to 1975. Thus, from 1919 through 1975 the overall prevalence of use of alcohol and illicit substances among those under age 21 had increased for both genders, with a dramatic increase in the use of all substance for girls resulting in a narrowing of the gender gap in use of substances.

The Monitoring the Future Study (Johnston, O'Malley, & Bachman, 2002) has assessed the prevalence of substance use among 12th graders in schools across the United States annually since 1975. Data from these assessments show that substance use has decreased across both genders since 1975. However, the decrease in use among boys is much larger than the decrease among girls, resulting in small or no current gender discrepancies in current prevalence.

It is essential to understand the reasons for this increase in substance use and abuse among girls over the past 50 years. The historical context, together with changes in etiological factors affecting substance use in girls, is a potential contributor. During this period in history, women adopted typically male roles (e.g., that of bread winner) with increasing frequency. In addition, the discrepancy between men and women in political and economic power has decreased. Unfortunately, women have also engaged in more health-risk behaviors, such as substance use, that have traditionally been males' domain. The media has strengthened the association between the liberalization of women and substance use, particularly cigarette use (e.g., the popular cigarette advertisement of the 1990s, "You've come a long way baby!"). Alternatively, as substance use has become more normative and acceptable for girls, they may be less hesitant to report their use. Thus, through the years, girls' self-report of use may have become more reflective of their actual use. Although a portion of the increase could be due to a reporting bias in the early years, it is unlikely to account for all of the dramatic changes seen over that period. Unquestionably girls' substance use has increased dramatically since the 1920s.

Assessment Issues

Diagnostic Criteria for Abuse and Dependence

According to *DSM-IV* criteria (APA, 1994) substance dependence or abuse is a maladaptive pattern of use leading to significant impairment or distress. To meet the criteria for dependence, three or more symptoms must be present. These symptoms include tolerance, withdrawal, use of more of the drug than intended, a persistent desire or unsuccessful effort to control use, spending a great deal of time in activities necessary to obtain the substance, and continued use despite recurrent problems associated with use. According to *DSM-IV*, a diagnosis of abuse requires one of the following four symptoms, recurrent use interfering with role obligations at school or home, recurrent use in physically hazardous situations, recurrent substance-related legal problems, and continued use despite recurrent social or interpersonal problems. A diagnosis of abuse is preempted by dependence if the individual has ever met the diagnostic criteria for dependence.

Age-Related Issues

Although the specific *DSM* criteria for dependence and abuse were developed for adults, these criteria are used for both adolescents and adults. However, symptoms may vary depending on whether the user is a child, adolescent, or an adult (Newcomb & Bentler, 1989). Compared to adults, adolescents typically use substances in a social context, use them more episodically than adults, use greater quantities, and more frequently binge (Bailey, Martin, Lynch & Pollock, 2000). This variance affects the occurrence of symptoms. For example, episodic, binge drinking is less likely to result in withdrawal. For children, occasional or regular use of drugs prior to puberty may be considered abuse, if the use of the substance interferes with developmental tasks or has psychological or physiological consequences (Newcomb & Bentler, 1989). Thus, abuse or dependence may well be based on varying symptoms depending on the child's age.

Gender-Related Issues

Symptoms of abuse and dependence may also vary by gender. Several investigators have questioned the validity of some *DSM* criteria for the diagnosis of abuse in girls and women (Haver, 1986). For example, adolescent girls tend to have a lower occurrence of recurrent use associated with legal problems and in hazardous situations than do boys (Wagner, Lloyd, & Gil, 2002). In contrast, in a clinical sample of adolescent inpatients, girls reported more symptoms of dependence, in particular more alcohol and polysubstance withdrawal symptoms, than did adolescent boys (Stewart & Brown, 1995). Thus, a diagnosis of abuse or dependence may consist of varying symptoms across the two genders. These gender differences in symptom prevalence could affect the relative prevalence of a diagnosis of abuse and dependence. However, the notion of gender-specific criteria for abuse and dependence has yet to be explored.

Reliability of Self-Report

The assessment of substance use, abuse and dependence is based on self-report. Studies have demonstrated reliability of self-report of substance use by children (Henrickson & Jackson, 1999), and adolescents (Henly & Winters, 1989) and the reliability of restrospective recall of age of first use by adolescents and adults (Johnson & Mott, 2001) across genders. However, the reliability of self-report of symptoms of abuse and dependence has yet to be investigated.

Comorbidity

Several studies, including those based on clinical and community samples, report on a relation between substance use disorders (SUD) and other disorders in adolescence, particularly conduct disorders (CD), and mood disorders.

Association of SUD with CD

While some studies show male-female differences in comorbidity between SUD and CD, not all studies do so. Additionally, gender-related differences in comorbidity may vary across specific substances. Using a clinical sample of substance abusers, Hovens and colleagues (Hovens, Cantwell, & Kiriakos, 1994) showed that 91% of males had a diagnosis of CD, while only 55% of the females did. Brady and colleagues (Brady, Grice, Dustan, & Randall, 1993) replicated this gender difference. However, Bukstein and colleagues (Bukstein, Glancy, & Kaminer, 1992; Clark et al., 1997), using samples of adolescents diagnosed with a substance use disorder, reported no gender difference in the relation between those with SUD and those with CD. Brown and colleagues (Brown, Gleghorn, Schuckit, Myers, & Mott, 1996) reported that while boys with SUD displayed significantly more behaviors associated with a *DSM-III-R* diagnosis of conduct disorder than girls, frequency of occurrence of each behavior was similar across gender.

In community epidemiological studies, Rhode and colleagues (Rhode, Lewinsohn & Seeley, 1996), reporting on data from the Oregon Adolescent Depression Project showed no gender differences in the co-occurrence of problem alcohol use and conduct disorders. However, Costello and associates (Costello, Angold, Burns, Stangl et al., 1996), reporting data from the Great Smokey Mountain Study (GSMS) showed that among those with behavior disorders, the incidence of smoking and cannabis use and abuse was higher for girls than boys. Reporting on data from the Dunedin, New Zealand, longitudinal cohort study, Henry and associates (Henry et al., 1993) showed that for both genders substance use was concurrently related to conduct disorders at age 15. A further examination of specific substances showed that symptoms of conduct disorder were concurrently related to cigarette and marijuana use for both boys and girls. For girls only symptoms of conduct disorder were related to the concurrent use of substances for purposes of self-medication.

Association of SUD with Mood Disorders

In general, clinical studies have shown a higher co-occurrence of affective disorders and substance abuse among girls than boys. With adolescent in-patient SUD samples, both Bukstein et al. (1992) and Deykin, Buka, and Zeena (1992) reported a higher prevalence of Major Depressive Disorder (MDD) among girls than boys. Similarly, among adolescents diagnosed with alcohol dependence, Clark et al. (1997) showed a higher incidence of MDD and Post-Traumatic Stress Disorder among girls than boys. However, in community samples, gender differences are shown less often. Henry et al. (1993) reporting data from the Dunedin study showed that symptoms of depression were concurrently related to substance use for both boys and girls. However, for girls only, symptoms of depression were concurrently related to the use of substances for the purpose of self-medication. In the Great Smokey Mountain Study (Costello et al., 1999), there was no gender difference in the co-occurrence between depression and substance use disorders. Thus, the gender ratio of comorbidity between SUD and MDD is higher among clinical samples diagnosed with SUD than among community samples.

Association of SUD with Other Disorders

The comorbidity of substance use disorders with eating disorders, suicide attempts, and child sexual abuse, is particularly relevant to girls, because these latter disorders are more prevalent in girls (Andrews & Lewinsohn, 1992; Molnar, Buka & Kessler, 2001; Wichstrom, 2000). Studies suggest comorbidity between substance use and purging anorexia and bulimia, but not restrictive anorexia (Carcos et al., 2001; See Mitchell, Pyle, Specker & Hanson, 1992, for review). Data from epidemiological studies show that adolescent suicide attempts co-occur with substance use disorders (Andrews & Lewinsohn, 1992; Wichstrom, 2000) and child sexual abuse is related to the subsequent onset of substance use disorders (Molnar, Buka, & Kessler, 2001).

Order of Disorders

In the Great Smokey Mountain Study (Costello et al., 1996), there were no gender differences in the order of onset of comorbid disorders. In all cases, according to *DSM-IV* criteria, the onset of attention deficit hyperactivity disorder, conduct disorder, oppositional defiant disorder, anxiety disorder, and depressive disorder, occurred in early to mid childhood, well before the onset of SUD. In contrast, the onset of depression was generally one year after first reports of alcohol use, and two years after first reports of smoking. In the Dunedin study, Henry et al. (1993) showed that, for boys only, symptoms of depression and conduct disorder prospectively predicted substance use. Among young adult women diagnosed with eating disorders, the eating disorder predated the substance use disorder twice as often as vice versa. Women whose eating disorder predated their substance use disorder were more likely to have an earlier onset of the eating disorder and more likely to have other types of comorbid pathology than women whose substance use disorder predated the eating disorder (Wiseman et al., 1999).

Developmental Course and Outcomes

The literature has consistently identified early initiation of substance use, including experimental use, as the strongest predictor of subsequent problem use and abuse (Andrews, Hops, Ary, Tildesley, & Harris, 1993; Gruber, DiClemente, Anderson, & Lodico, 1996; Hawkins et al., 1997; Kandel, 1984; Kandel & Raveis 1989; Kaplan et al., 1986; Stein et al., 1987). For example, youth who begin drinking by age 13 are twice as likely to become alcoholics as those who begin drinking at age 17 and five times more likely than those who begin at age 21 (Grant & Dawson, 1997). Similarly, those who start smoking earlier, smoke more heavily in adulthood and have more difficulty quitting (Chassin, Presson, & Sherman, 2000). Evidence suggests that the time between age of first use and dependence and abuse may be shorter for girls than boys. For example, although girls initiate alcohol use at a later age than do boys, onset of alcohol abuse or dependence is on average earlier for girls than boys (Lewinsohn et al., 1996). This relation suggests that girls may become dependent on substances more easily than boys.

Gender Differences in Cessation and Relapse

Not only do girls become dependent on substances more easily than do boys, evidence suggests that girls have more difficulty quitting the use of substances and may relapse more easily. Although the majority of the data supporting this contention are from intervention trials, at least one community-based longitudinal study shows that girls who are dependent on alcohol relapse more easily than boys (Lewinsohn et al., 1996). Although not all adolescent substance abuse trials show gender differences (e.g., Latimer, Newcomb, Winters, & Stinchfield, 2000; Winters, Stinchfield, Opland, Weller, & Latimer, 2000), those that do show that the intervention is less effective with girls than boys (e.g., Latimer, Winters, Stinchfield, & Traver, 2000; Flay, Allred, & Ordway (2001); Holsten, 1980).

Most individuals smoke for 15 to 20 years before they quit smoking (Pierce & Gilpin, 1996), thus information on tobacco cessation in young girls is limited. Research suggests that tobacco cessation may be difficult for adult women, however. Women make successful quit attempts less frequently than men and relapse more frequently than men (Blake et al., 1989; Swan, Ward, Carnelli, & Jack, 1993; Ward, Klesges, Zbikowski, Bliss, & Garvey, 1997). This gender difference could be due to at least two factors. First, a review of the psychobiology of smoking suggests that nicotine has anti-depressant properties and chemicals in cigarettes function as MAO-inhibitors. Thus, abrupt cessation may cause a rebound effect, increasing depression and anxiety immediately following cessation. Women may relapse to cope with this negative affect (Carmody, 1989). Burgess et al. (2002) showed that among women in an intervention program with a history of major depression, those who had increased symptoms of depression after cessation were most likely to relapse. There is some evidence that antidepressants such as buproprion or Zyban can aid smoking cessation and prevent relapse (Skaar et al., 1997), possibly by reducing symptoms of depression during the cessation process. Second, some women tend to gain weight following tobacco cessation (Williamson et al., 1991). Buproprion has also been shown to decrease weight gain following tobacco cessation (Ahluwalia et al., 2002).

Physiological Effects

The pharmacological effects of the use of substances may vary by gender. Research suggests gender differences in the physiological effects of similar amounts of alcohol, which could in part be due to the gender differences in body weight and tissue composition (Dunne, 1988; Jones & Jones, 1976). Women given the same amount of ethanol have higher blood alcohol levels than men (Jones & Jones, 1976), perhaps due to the higher concentration of body water in men. In addition, women may absorb much more of alcohol consumed than men (Frezza et al., 1990). These physiological differences could contribute to gender differences in the time between first alcohol use and abuse and dependence.

Health Consequences

These physiological differences may also result in serious health consequences. The majority of health consequences associated with adolescent use occurs in adulthood, following long-term use. Gender differences are noted in these health effects. Women are not only at risk for all the smoking-related diseases demonstrated in men, but women smokers also have higher rates of osteoporosis and experience earlier menopause (USDHHS, 1989). Evidence suggests that the health consequences of alcohol use may be more deleterious for women than men (Collins, 1993) and several consequences are specific to women. Growing evidence suggests that the pathological effects of alcohol consumption (e.g., liver cirrhosis) may develop more rapidly in women (Blume, 1992). Among women, alcohol use has also been associated with adverse cardiovascular outcomes and breast cancer risk (Hill, 1995).

ETIOLOGICAL FACTORS

To understand the processes that contribute to gender differences in substance use it is necessary to a) identify gender differences in the level of etiological factors and b) to examine the differential relation between potential etiological factors and substance use. This review addresses both of these issues.

Several researchers have postulated developmental pathways to substance abuse that parallel changes in antisocial behavior from early adolescence to young adulthood (e.g., Moffitt, 1997; Patterson, DeBaryshe, & Ramsey, 1989). These pathways may help to explain the increase in substance use in early adolescence among girls. For example, Moffitt (Moffitt, 1997; Moffitt et al., 2001) and Patterson (Patterson et al., 1989) have proposed two developmental trajectories describing the development of antisocial behavior, including substance use. The life course persistent trajectory is characterized by early onset and is maintained throughout life. Moffitt and her colleagues (2001) found that this pathway is more characteristic of boys than of girls. However, the second pathway, termed "adolescent limited," is more characteristic of girls (Moffitt et al., 2001). In this pathway, substance use reaches a peak in adolescence and then declines in young adulthood. Similarly, Silverthorn and Frick (1999) proposed a "delayed onset" pathway that characterizes the relatively late onset of antisocial behavior in girls.

Studies have shown empirical links between childhood behaviors, such as childhood aggression, underachievement and poor social skills (Brook, Whiteman, Finch, & Cohen, 1995; Clayton, 1991; Kellam et al., 1983; Ensminger, Brown, & Kellam, 1982; Hops, Davis, & Lewin, 1999; Severson, Andrews, & Walker, 2003) and early substance initiation and heavy or problem use in adolescence. These factors also predict the life-course persistent trajectory of antisocial behavior. The higher prevalence of these early childhood behaviors among boys than girls (Johnson, Arria, Borges, Ialongo, & Anthony, 1995; Grady, Gersick, Snow, & Kessen, 1986) may partially explain the gender differences favoring boys in onset of substance use and heavy alcohol use and illicit substance abuse and dependence later in adolescence or adulthood. According to Silverthorn and Frick (1999), these early problem behaviors may also be linked to the late onset of antisocial behaviors in girls. The challenge is to understand the mechanisms through which these early childhood behaviors are linked to the substance use of girls later in adolescence.

Genetic Influences

Family studies, particularly coupled with genetic epidemiological analyses, have shown evidence for a genetic influence on substance abuse (Crabbe, 2002). Further, genetics may partially explain the comorbidity among substance use disorders, such as alcoholism and smoking (Rose, 1995). Several investigators have suggested reward-deficiency pathways of addiction (e.g., through dopaminergic, opioidergic, seratonergic, and cholinergic receptors) that are common across substances and could have a genetic link (Robinson & Berridge, 2000; 2001; Koob & LeMoal, 2001).

There is some evidence for gender specificity in the heritability of substance use. For example, Type II alcoholism, which is characterized by early onset, violence, and criminality, is largely limited to males (Cloninger,

1987). However, the metho[...]
outcome. For example, pop[...]
bility across genders of the h[...]
Kendler, 1999). In contrast, t[...]
of alcohol abuse, limited onl[...]
Further analysis of the heri[...]
this gender-limited finding [...]
(Prescott & Kendler, 2000).

An extensive literature [...]
wherein the environment mod[...]
"different genotypes respond [...]
(Crabbe, 2002, p. 447). For [...]
the risk of displaying a genetic[...]
protect an individual from dis[...]
gender in the effect of gene-e[...]
example, Cadoret, Rigg[...] d Stewart (2000),
in a summary of t[...] eractions in antisocial beha[...] their sample,
but not the [...]optees of biological pare[...]ese authors
showed that [...]l personality, symptoms[...]re related
to the number [...]who were
at genetic risk fo[...] factors
protected them fr[...]e psychopathology of the[...]arent
factors" contributed [...]ohol
and substance abuse.

Biological Influences

Pubertal Maturation

Early biological maturat[...] ppears particularly problematic for the young girl (Stattin & Magnusson, 1990). The physical appearance of these girls may lead others, including parents, to treat them as more mature, which can be problematic if their physical maturity outpaces their social maturity. Both early maturing girls and fast maturing girls are more likely to associate with older friends and male friends (Silbriesen, Kracke, & Nowack, 1992; Stattin & Magnusson, 1990) and are more likely to have friends who approve of their use (Silbriesen & Kracke, 1997). Early maturing girls are more likely to engage in behaviors that are more normative for older adolescents, including substance use (Magnusson, Stattin, & Allen, 1986; Stattin & Magnusson, 1990), reporting particularly high levels of consumption (Aro & Tarpale, 1987; Peterson, Graber, & Sullivan, 1990; Stattin & Magnusson, 1990). For example, Magnusson, Stattin and Allen (1985) showed that early maturing girls tended to be truant, smoke marijuana, and get drunk more often in mid adolescence than did later maturing girls. The association with older peer groups mediated differences between biological age groups. These differences leveled out in late adolescence as late maturing girls caught up with earlier maturing girls in their substance use. Early maturation also affects girls' body image (Peterson & Crockett, 1985; Siegel, Yancey, Aneshensel, & Schuler, 1999), as a partial result of increase in body mass, and is related to the self-report of depressive symptoms (Alsaker, 1992). These factors could partially mediate the relation between early pubertal development and substance use.

Hormonal Influences

The biological changes associated with puberty are particularly influential in the pre to early adolescent years (Buchanan, Eccles, & Becker, 1992) and could affect the substance use of the adolescent girl through their effect on emotional levels and risk taking. Estradiol begins to show significant increases at about 9 or 10 years of age (Apter, 1980) and may have early influences on the pre-adolescents' and adolescents' behavior. Estradiol, in the absence of progesterone, may have arousal and excitatory properties. Girls may thus turn to substance use as a form of self-medication. Low levels of testosterone concentrations are produced by girls in pre-adolescence and increase over the maturational period, but at a slower rate than estradiol. Testosterone concentrations have been correlated with sensation seeking, disinhibition and impulsivity (Booth, Johnson, & Granger, 1999; Daitzman & Zuckerman, 1980), risk factors for substance use and other problem behaviors (Zuckerman, 1993).

Cultural Influences

Cross-cultural comparisons of substance use among women have been limited to smoking. A review by Aghi, Asma, Yeong, and Vaithinathan (2001), shows a large variation across countries in the prevalence of cigarette smoking among women. In the mid-1990s, the global prevalence of smoking among women was 12% with national prevalence ranging from 3% in China to 35.5% in Norway. Whereas in low-income countries the prevalence of smoking among women is low, the prevalence of smoking among men is high. In general, women in low-income countries have traditional values, which may affect their smoking initiation. It is hoped that the liberalization of women's roles in these countries will not affect their health behaviors.

National surveys showing ethnic differences in girls' substance use suggest cultural differences within the US in substance use. Prevalence estimates vary across regions of the country and across communities, as well as across racial or ethnic groups. For example, according to a review conducted by Oetting and Beauvais (1990), using data from the annual Monitoring the Future study, Mexican American girls who have recently emigrated from Mexico tend to try marijuana less frequently and have a lower rate of being drunk than male Mexican Americans or Anglos or

Hispanics who have been in this country for several generations. Oetting and Beauvais (1990) attribute this difference to "Marianisma," the attitude that traditional female adolescents should be innocent. This attitude is presumably lost with acculturation.

Psychosocial Factors

The psychosocial factors related to substance use and abuse among girls include both environmental and intrapersonal factors. In adolescence, both the family (Glynn, 1981) and peer group (Brook et al., 1992) play central roles in the etiology of substance use. Intrapersonal factors related to antisocial behavior, such as early aggression (Brook et al., 1992; Kellam et al., 1983), low academic achievement (Kandel & Raveis, 1989); and emotional distress of the adolescent (Kaplan et al., 1986; Newcomb et al., 1987) predict substance use. In addition, stress and coping (Wills, Sandy, & Yaeger, 2002), body image (Klesges, Meyers, Klesges & LaVasque, 1989) and the propensity to take risks (Wills et al., 2000) are related to the etiology of use. Whereas these factors are predictive across genders, some are particularly salient to the prediction of substance use in girls. These latter factors will be the focus of this review.

Familial Influences

After reviewing the literature, Glynn (1981) concluded that parent use of a specific substance was the most powerful influence on the adolescent's initiation of that substance. Although the literature suggests that mothers and fathers may influence boys and girls differently, these gender differences are not conclusive. For example, whereas some studies suggest that the substance use of boys, as compared to girls, is more influenced by their father's substance use (e.g., Wilks et al., 1989) other studies suggest that fathers' substance use influences girls more than boys (Andrews, Hops, & Duncan, 1997; Hops, Duncan, Duncan, & Stoolmiller, 1996). The developmental literature (e.g., Maccoby, 1990) supports this latter finding, also suggesting that fathers' influence may, in general, be stronger for girls than for boys.

A meta-analysis (Pollock, Schneider, Gabrielli, & Goodwin, 1987) suggested that sons and daughters of male alcoholics and daughters of female alcoholics are more likely than children of nonalcoholics to become alcoholic at some point in their lives. More recent work by Chassin, Curran, Hussong, & Colder (1996) suggests a mechanism for this finding. These researchers showed that paternal alcoholism was associated with adolescent reports of negative affect and stress, which in turn were associated with escalation of substance use over time. Negative affect is more prevalent among adolescent girls than boys (Lewinsohn et al., 1993) and the influence of these variables on substance use may be stronger for girls (Windle, 1992). Thus, although not conclusive, results suggest that both parents might influence girls' substance use and that the influence might be both direct and indirect, through negative affect and stress.

Peer Influences

At puberty, girls become more intensely involved in their same-sex peer relationships and their interest in boys increases (Steinberg, 1987). Larson and Richards (1991) used a time sampling study and found that girls increased the amount of time spent with peers from childhood to adolescence, while time with family decreased. Substance use onset can be conceptualized as a social phenomenon, most likely to occur within the context of a peer group, with or without peer pressure (Friedman et al., 1985). For example, Barton and associates (Barton, Chassin, Presson, & Sherman, 1982) describe smoking as a shared activity with an important socializing function for youth. Some evidence suggests that delinquent activities, such as substance use, are more likely to occur in a peer context among girls than boys (Emler, Reicher, & Ross, 1997). Thus, association with peers, particularly peers of the opposite gender, may put girls at risk for subsequent initiation of substance. Supporting this contention, Swan and colleagues (1990) showed that among girls, participation in organized social activities and spending time with opposite-gender friends were associated with increased odds of smoking initiation.

The adolescent literature has consistently shown similarity in substance use between peers (e.g., Ennett & Bauman, 1991, 1994; Urberg, Degirmenciouglu, & Pilgrim, 1997). This similarity typically has been attributed to both selection, or choosing a friend that is similar to oneself, and socialization, wherein the peer influences the substance use of the adolescent. Results from longitudinal studies with both adolescents and young adults have shown the effects of both socialization (Andrews, Tildesley, Hops, & Li, 2002; Ennett & Bauman, 1994, Schulenberg et al., 1999; Wills & Cleary, 1999) and selection (Ennett & Bauman, 1994) across substances. Results from adolescent studies investigating gender differences on the effects of peer influences on substance use have been mixed. However, when gender differences were found, the effect of peer influence was stronger for girls than boys (Billy & Udry, 1985; Berndt & Keefe, 1995; Duncan, Duncan, & Hops, 1994; Kandel, 1978).

Images of Substance Users

Our current data from the Oregon Youth Substance Use project (Andrews et al., 2003) suggest that first through eighth grade girls have a more positive image of substance users than boys of a similar age. Girls were more likely than boys to think that kids who use substances were popular, exciting, and cool. Andrews, Hampson, Tildesley and Peterson (2002) showed that these positive images predicted initiation of cigarettes for girls, and initiation of alcohol for both genders. Popularity is particularly important for adolescent girls (Rutter, 1979) and girls may strive to achieve these positive images. Research suggests that the self-image or aspiring image of girls is similar to their image of substance users (Aloise-Young & Hennigan, 1996). The consistency between these self or aspired images and positive images of smokers predict intention to smoke in the future (Burton et al., 1989; Norman & Tedeschi, 1989), which in turn is related to subsequent initiation (Andrews et al., 2002). These positive images of substance users can most likely be attributed partially to the media. As an example, cigarette advertising targeting women portrays women as thin, stylish, glamorous, sophisticated, sexually attractive, athletic, liberated, and independent (Kaufman & Nichter, 2001).

Body Image

A review of the literature on the relation between smoking and body weight (Klesges, Meyers, Klesges & LaVasque, 1990) showed a covariation between smoking and body weight and a prospective relation between quitting smoking and weight gain, particularly for women (Williamson et al., 1991). Further, weight concerns predict initiation of smoking among adolescent girls, but not boys (French, Perry, Keib, & Fulkerson, 1994). The image that girls strive for is also changing. Wiseman et al. (1992) have shown that the sociocultural image of a desirable body shape has become increasingly lean over the past two decades.

Stress and Coping

Several theorists have noted that adolescent girls report more negative life events than boys (Compas & Wagner, 1991; Simmons et al., 1987) and experience more family conflict and peer relationship difficulties (Rudolph & Hammen, 1999). Further, several studies show a relation between stressful life events (Wills, 1986; 1990; Wills, Sandy, & Yaeger, 2002) and adolescent substance use, particularly for girls (Windle, 1992).

Some theorists suggest that adolescents use substances to regulate their emotional responses to stress (Labouvie, 1986). Recent research suggests that this behavior in girls may be reinforced by actual reduction in stress. In an interesting double-blind study, File, Fluck, and Leahy (2001) exposed participants to moderate stress that significantly increased ratings of anxiety, discontent, and aggression. Nicotine reduced these psychological effects in women, while enhancing these effects in men. Thus, this study suggests that, for girls, self-medication through smoking actually reduces anxiety.

Risk Taking

Risk taking or sensation seeking refers to the tendency to seek new experiences, particularly those that involve high emotional reactivity (Cloninger et al., 1987). This dimension has been related to escalation in substance use in adolescence (Wills et al., 2000). A meta-analysis conducted by Byrnes and colleagues (Byrnes, Miller, & Schafer, 1999) shows that boys tend to take more risks than girls, across activities. Although boys may be more likely than girls to take risks, some studies suggest that girls' substance use is more related to risk-taking than is boys' use. For example, Simon, Sussman, Dent, Burton, and Flay (1995) showed that risk-taking significantly predicted initiation of smoking in early adolescence for both genders, but the effect was stronger for girls than boys.

Theories of Substance Use

Problem Behavior Theory

According to Jessor's (1987) Problem Behavior Theory, substance use is a part of an underlying "problem behavior syndrome," along with antisocial behavior and conduct disorders. Sexually risky behavior and academic failure have also been included in the constellation of problem behaviors. According to these theorists, alcohol use, particularly heavy use, is the primary substance use that covaries with other problem behaviors. Data from several studies suggest that boys are more antisocial than girls from an early age onward across nations (e.g., Moffitt et al., 2001). Thus, the tenets of Problem Behavior Theory may be more applicable for explaining substance use among boys than girls. Risk factors that have been identified within this theoretical framework predict life course persistent antisocial behavior, which is more typical of males than of females.

Nevertheless, for some girls, substance use can be considered as part of a "problem behavior syndrome" in which, as with boys, substance use clusters with other problem behaviors. For example, research suggests that the antisocial behavior of girls places them at risk for subsequent substance use. Severson, Andrews, and Walker (2003) recently showed that overt aggression identified by teachers in fourth and fifth grade predicting smoking initiation by seventh and eighth grade for both males and females. Duncan and Tildelsey (1996) investigated the influence of four types of antisocial behaviors on changes in alcohol, cigarettes, and marijuana use in the subsequent year by gender and showed that, for girls only, aggressive behavior predicted increased involvement in cigarettes and alcohol use, whereas for both genders, rule violations predicted increased involvement in all three substances. There is also some suggestion of a higher co-occurrence of substance use and sexual risk-taking for girls than for boys. For example, among youth admitted for substance abuse treatment, a significantly higher proportion of girls reported engaging in sexual risk related behaviors than boys (Pugatch et al., 2000).

Social Process Theories

Within the framework of social learning theory (Bandura, 1977), children and adolescents model the substance use of those they view as important in their lives or those they admire. Thus, within this framework, the substance use of both family members and the peer group (or a "wanabe" peer group) are contributing factors to the substance use of the girl. Empirical support for the effect of parental substance use on their child's use is substantial for both genders (Glynn, 1981; Andrews, et al., 1993). There is some evidence that the influence of peers on the substance use of girls is more than that of boys, particularly in the early to mid adolescent years (Billy & Udry, 1985; Duncan, Duncan, & Hops, 1994). Within the social learning framework, the influence of peers could be a contributing factor to the substantial increase in initiation of substance use among girls during the transition to adolescence.

According to the social interactional theory (e.g., Brook et al., 1990; Cairns et al., 1985; Dishion, 1990; Patterson et al., 1992), conflict in the home and conflictual family interactions, along with poor parental monitoring, lead to an association with deviant peers and subsequent antisocial behavior, including substance use. Social interactional theory may partially explain the increase in substance use among girls during adolescence. Research suggests an increase in parent and adolescent conflict in early adolescence (Montemayor, 1983), particularly with the same-gender parent (Steinberg, 2001). Several studies suggest more conflict between early maturing girls and their parents, primarily the mother, than between early maturing boys (Savin-Williams & Small, 1986) or late maturing girls (Crocket & Peterson, 1987; Steinberg, 1987) and their parents.

The decrease in parental monitoring accompanying the transition to adolescence (Parke & Bhavnagri, 1989), along with maturation and subsequently an initiation of dating and heterosexual relationships (Peterson, 1987), puts girls at particular risk since they may associate with male peers who use substances (Patterson et al., 1992). Girls who begin dating generally date older boys who may participate in activities with them that are more normative for these older adolescents. Girls who mature early are at particular risk since they experience more family conflict and associate with older male peers (Stattin & Magnusson, 1990).

Cognitively-Based Theories

Two theoretical frameworks have related cognitions to subsequent health behavior, including substance use. Within the Theory of Reasoned Action (Ajzen & Fishbein, 1980) and the Theory of Planned Behavior (Ajzen, 1988), attitudes and subjective norms (or normative beliefs) are assumed to influence health behavior change. Attitudes can be interpreted as beliefs about the outcomes of the behavior or evaluation of the behavior. Subjective norms are operationalized as beliefs about the extent to which other people are engaging in that behavior. In the Prototype or Willingness model (Gibbons & Gerrard, 1995), the prototype or image of substance users predicts subsequent use. These models are intended to describe the etiology of substance use in both boys and girls. However, as noted above, since girls have more positive images of substance users than boys, and these images are related to smoking initiation only for girls, these theories may be more useful in predicting substance use among girls. Further research examining the theoretical relations between social images and substance use as a function of gender is needed.

Stress-Related Theories

Wills and colleagues (Wills, 1986; 1990; Wills et al., 2002) have developed a model wherein perceived stress is related to subsequent substance use. They posit that individuals with ineffective coping skills use substances as a form of self-medication in reaction to stress. This model seems particularly applicable to girls and may provide an explanation for the increase in substance use in girls as they transition to adolescence. Changes accompanying the transition to adolescence occur in every contextual domain of girls' lives, and some girls may perceive these changes as stressful events. They include change in school environment (Eccles et al., 1993); change in parental restrictiveness and monitoring (Peterson, 1985; Savin-Williams & Small, 1986; Parke & Bhavnagri, 1989); an increase in the salience of the peer group (Steinberg & Silverburg, 1986), along with a decrease in the salience of the family (Steinberg & Silverburg, 1986) and an increase in parental conflict (Montmeyor, 1983); an increase in adolescent autonomy (Steinberg, 1988); initiation of dating and heterosexual relationships (Peterson, 1987); changes in sex-role expectations (Brooks-Gunn, 1987); weight gain, accompanied by a decrease in body image (Siegel, Yancey, Aneshensel, & Schuler, 1999); and the onset of menarche, which can be particularly stressful for girls who are unprepared (Brooks-Gunn, 1987; Brooks-Gunn & Ruble, 1982). Further, pubertal maturation may "sensitize" females to the effects of negative life events (Cyranowski et al., 2000) so that the effect of these different life events may be experienced differently as a function of the pubertal development of the young girl.

Reviews of the literature (e.g., Compas, 1987; Compas & Wagner, 1991) regarding the occurrence and impact of these changes in late childhood and early to mid adolescence suggest that these events, and the timing of them, may combine to put some individuals at risk for the development of substance use as well as other problem behaviors. Girls, in particular, appear to experience a greater number of negative life events during this age span (Compas & Wagner, 1991; Simmons, Bergeson, Carolton-Ford & Blyth, 1987). Interestingly, the nature of negative events experienced by girls may change from preadolescence to adolescence. Rudolph and Hammen (1999) reported that pre-adolescent girls (as compared to boys and adolescent girls) experienced the highest level of independent stress (i.e., events that the person was not responsible for bringing about) and conflict within the family context. In contrast, adolescent girls experienced the highest levels of interpersonal stress, especially parent-child conflict and peer relationship difficulties. These stressful events may put girls at risk for the use of substances, particularly if they have ineffective coping strategies for dealing with this stress.

Comparisons Across Theories

Across all theoretical perspectives, contextual influences including the peer and family are central to the etiology of substance use. Within problem behavior theory, peer and family influences are both distal and proximal predictors of problem behavior (Jessor, 1987). Social process, cognitive-based, and stress theories all propose specific models through which peers and family members influence the etiology of substance use. For example, in social process models, family influences are hypothesized to moderate the effect of peers on substance use. In cognitive-based models, the girls' perceptions of peers' behavior (i.e., normative beliefs) and their perceptions or images of substance users are hypothesized to predict subsequent use. In stress models, the stressful changes in girls' family, peer and contextual environment, in general, are hypothesized to indirectly influence the use of substances through self-medication, mediated by depressive symptoms. The similarities among these theoretically derived models emphasize the necessity of an integrated model of substance use, incorporating components across theories, to examine the etiology of substance use in girls.

CONCLUSIONS

Current cultural norms in North America put girls at great risk for substance use as they transition to adolescence. Because substance use, particularly the use of cigarettes, alcohol, and marijuana, has become increasingly normative for girls over the past 50 years, girls have initiated use earlier and thus are more at risk for dependence and abuse. The longer duration of use in conjunction with greater physiological effects of substance use puts girls at high risk for negative health consequences.

It is somewhat unnerving that currently girls' self report of use surpasses that of boys by the eighth grade. Further, data derived from national studies show that adolescent girls' dependence on cannabis is higher than that of boys. If the historical trend continues, girls' abuse and dependence on other substances could also surpass that of boys.

The design of effective prevention and intervention programs targeting girls' substance use is thus imperative. Although research regarding the etiology of substance use among girls is just beginning, findings suggest factors to incorporate into these programs. Whereas a broad program aimed at changing antisocial behavior in general may be an appropriate substance use prevention program for boys, this review suggests that programs targeting girls may often need to be less broad and more specific. For example, programs specifically for early maturing girls are needed. One approach to prevention of substance use in girls is to improve girls' emotional well being and to teach them effective coping skills for the new situations they encounter as they transition to adolescence. These skills could potentially prevent the use of substances as a form of self-medication in response to the stress associated with adolescence. Prevention programs targeting girls could also focus on the social aspects of substance use. Components of these programs could focus on changing perceived acceptability of substance use among peers and decrease positive images of substance users.

Further research focusing on girls is needed to understand the historical and developmental increase in substance use among girls. This review suggests a central role of depressive symptoms in explaining the etiology of substance use in girls. Perhaps the findings that girls become dependent on substances faster than boys, are less responsive to treatment, and are more likely to relapse are related to the more frequent occurrence of depressive symptoms among girls. Although preliminary research lends support to this hypothesis, further research is needed to explore the relation between depression and substance use and abuse. Next, the exploration of if and why the liberalization of women's rights and the attainment of masculine roles affect the substance use of girls is needed. Finally, investigation of the transition to adolescence among girls requires further attention. An integrated approach combining both biological and psychosocial factors is necessary. An understanding of the stresses that girls face as they transition into and through adolescence could further guide the etiology of substance use in girls during this period.

ACKNOWLEDGEMENTS. This work was supported by the National Institute of Drug Abuse, DA10767 and DA03706. The author gratefully acknowledges the assistance of Ms. Christine Lorenz in the preparation of this manuscript and Dr. Anne Simons for her contributions to the section on pubertal maturation and stress.

REFERENCES

Aghi, M., Asma, S., Yeong, C. C., & Vaithinathan, R. (2001). Initiation and maintenance of tobacco use. In J. M. Samet & S. Y. Yoon (Eds.), *Women and the tobacco epidemic* (pp. 49–68). Geneva: World Health Organization.

Ahluwalia, J. S., Harris, K. J., Catley, D., Okuyemi, K. S., & Mayo, M. S. (2002). Sustained-release bupropion for smoking cessation in African Americans: A randomized controlled trial. *Journal of the American Medical Association, 288*, 468–474.

Ajzen, I. (1988). *Attitudes, personality and behavior.* New York: Open University Press.

Ajzen, I., & Fishbein, M. (1980). *Understanding attitudes and predicting social behavior.* Englewood Cliffs, NJ: Prentice Hall.

Aloise-Young, P. A., & Hennigan, K. M. (1996). Self-image, the smoker stereotype and cigarette smoking: Developmental patterns from fifth through eighth grade. *Journal of Adolescence, 19*, 163–177).

Alsaker, F. D. (1992). Pubertal timing, overweight, and psychological adjustment. *Journal of Early Adolescence, 12*, 396–419.

American Psychiatric Association. (1994). *Diagnostic and statistical manual of mental disorders (4th edition),* Washington, DC: Author.

Andrews, J. A., Hampson, S. H., Tildesley, E., & Peterson, M. (May, 2002). *The prospective relation between cognitions and use of cigarettes and alcohol: An elementary school sample.* Poster presented to Society for Prevention Research, Seattle, WA.

Andrews, J. A., Hops, H., Ary, D., Tildesley, E., & Harris, J. (1993). Parental influence on adolescent substance use: Specific and non-specific effects. *Journal of Early Adolescence, 13*, 285–310.

Andrews, J. A., Hops, H., & Duncan, S. C. (1997). Adolescent modeling of parent substance use: The moderating effect of the relationship with the Parent. *Journal of Family Psychology, 11*, 259–270.

Andrews, J. A., & Lewinsohn, P. M. (1992). Suicidal attempts among older adolescents: Prevalence and co-occurrence with psychiatric disorders, *Jounral of the American Academy of Child and Adolescent Psychiatry, 31*, 655–662.

Andrews, J. A., & Tildesley, E. A. (2003). *Intentions and use of alcohol, tobacco, marijuana and inhalants among 1st through 8th graders.* Paper presented at the Society for Research in Child Development, Tampa, Florida.

Andrews, J. A., Tildesley, E., Duncan, S., Hops, H., & Severson, H. H. (2003). Elementary children's behaviors and attitudes regarding substance use. *Journal of Clinical Child Psychology, 32*, 556–567.

Andrews, J. A., Tildesley, E., Hops, H., & Li, F. (2002). The influence of peers on young adult substance use. *Health Psychology, 21,* 349–357.

Annis, J. M., & Liban, C. D. (1980). Alcoholism in women: Treatment modalities and outcomes. In O. J. Kalant (Ed.), *Alcohol and drug problems in women: Research advances in alcohol and drug problems* (pp. 385–422). New York: Plenum.

Apter, D. (1980). Serum steroids and pituitary hormone in female puberty: A partly longitudinal study. *Clinical Endocrinology, 12,* 107–120.

Aro, H., & Taipale, V. (1987). The impact of timing of puberty on psychosomatic symptoms among fourteen to sixteen-year-old Finnish girls. *Child Development, 58,* 261–268.

Bailey, S. L., Martin, C. S., Lynch, K. G., & Pollock, N. K. (2000) Reliability and concurrent validity of DSM-IV subclinical symptom ratings for alcohol use disorders among adolescents. *Alcoholism, Clinical and Experimental Research, 24,* 1795–1802.

Bandura, A. (1977). *Social learning theory.* Englewood Cliffs, NJ: Prentice-Hall.

Barton, J., Chassin, L., Presson, C. C., & Sherman, S. J. (1982). Social image factors as motivators of smoking initiation in early and middle adolescence. *Child Development, 53,* 1499–1511.

Bentler, P. M. (1992). Etiologies and consequences of adolescent drug use: Implications for prevention. *Journal of Addictive Diseases, 11,* 47–61.

Berndt, T. J., & Keefe, K. (1995). Friends' influence on adolescents' adjustment to school. *Child Development, 66,* 1312–1329.

Billy, J. O., & Udry, J. R. (1985). The influence of male and female best friends on adolescent sexual behavior. *Adolescence, 20,* 21–32.

Blake, S. M., Klepp, K.-I., Pechacek, T. F., Folsom, A. R., Luepker, R. V., Jacobs, D. R., & Mittelmark, M. B. (1989). Differences in smoking cessation strategies between men and women. *Addictive Behaviors, 14,* 409–418.

Blume, S. B. (1992). Alcohol and other drug problems in women. In J. H. Lowinson, P. Ruiz, R. B. Millman, & J. G. Langrod (Eds.), *Substance abuse: A comprehensive textbook* (2nd ed., pp. 794–807). Baltimore, MD: Williams and Wilkins.

Booth, A., Johnson, D., & Granger, D. A. (1999). Testosterone and men's depression: The role of social factors. *Journal of Health and Social Behavior, 40,* 130–140.

Brady, K. T., Grice, D. E., Dustan, L., & Randall, C. (1993). Gender differences in substance use disorders. *American Journal of Psychiatry, 150,* 1707–11.

Brook, J. S., Brook, D. W., Gordon, A. S., Whiteman, M., & Cohen, P. (1990). Childhood precursors of adolescent drug use: A longitudinal analysis. *Genetic, Social and General Psychology Monographs, 116,* 195–213.

Brook, J. S., Cohen, P., Whiteman, M., & Gordon, A. S. (1992). Psychosocial risk factors in the transition from moderate to heavy use or abuse of drugs. In M. Glantz & R. Pickens (Eds.), *Vulnerability to drug abuse* (pp. 359–388). Washington, DC: American Psychological Association.

Brook, J., Whiteman, M., Finch, S., & Cohen, P. (1995). Aggression, intrapsychic distress, and drug use: Antecedent and intervening processes. *Journal of the American Academy of Child and Adolescent Psychiatry, 34,* 1076–1084.

Brooks-Gunn, J. (1987). Pubertal processes and girls' psychological adaptation. In R. M. Lerner & T. T. Foch (Eds.), *Biological–psychosocial interactions in early adolescence* (pp. 123–153). Hillsdale, NJ: Erlbaum.

Brooks-Gunn, J., & Ruble, D. N. (1982). The development of menstrual-related beliefs and behaviors during early adolescence. *Child Development, 53,* 1567–1577.

Brown, S. A., Gleghorn, A. A., Schuckit, M. A., Myers, M. G., & Mott, M. A. (1996). Conduct disorder among adolescent alcohol and drug abusers. *Journal of Studies on Alcohol, 57,* 314–324.

Buchanan, C. M., Eccles, J. S., & Becker, J. B. (1992). Are adolescents the victims of raging hormones: Evidence for activational effects of hormones on moods and behavior at adolescence. *Psychological Bulletin, 111,* 62–107.

Bukstein, O. G., Glancy, L. J., & Kaminer, Y. (1992). Patterns of affective comorbidity in a clinical population of dually diagnosed adolescent substance abusers. *Journal of the American Academy of Child and Adolescent Psychiatry, 31,* 1041–1045.

Burgess, E. S., Brown, R. A., Kahler, C. W., Niaura, R. S., Miller, I. W., Goldstein, M. G., & Abrams, D. B. (2002). Patterns of change in depressive symptoms during smoking cessation: Who's at risk for relapse. *Journal of Consulting and Clinical Psychology, 70,* 356–361.

Burton, D., Sussman, S., Hansen, W. B., Johnson, C. A., & Flay, B. R. (1989). Image attributions and smoking intentions among seventh grade students. *Journal of Applied Social Psychology, 19,* 656–664.

Byrnes, J. P., Miller, D. C., & Schafer, W. D. (1999). Gender differences in risk taking: A meta-analysis. *Psychological Bulletin, 125,* 367–383.

Cadoret, R. J., Riggins-Caspers, K., Yates, W. R., Troughton, E. P., & Stewart, M. A. (2000). Gender effects in gene–environment interactions in substance abuse. In E. Frank (Ed.), *Gender and its effects on psychopathology* (pp. 253–279). Washington, DC: American Psychiatric Press, Inc.

Cairns, R. B., Perrin, J. E., & Cairns, B. D. (1985). Social structure and social cognition in early adolescence: Affiliative patterns. *Journal of Early Adolescence, 5,* 339–355.

Carmody, T. P. (1989). Affect regulation, nicotine addiction, and smoking cessation. *Journal of Psychoactive Drugs, 21*(3), 331–342.

Chassin, L., Presson, C. C., & Sherman, S. J. (2000). The natural history of cigarette smoking from adolescence to adulthood in a midwestern community sample: Multiple trajectories and their psychosocial correlates. *Health Psychology, 19,* 223–231.

Chassin, L., Curran, P. J., Hussong, A. M., & Colder, C. R. (1996). The relation of parent alcoholism to adolescent substance use: A longitudinal follow-up study. *Journal of Abnormal Psychology, 105,* 70–80.

Clark, D. B., Pollock, N., Bukstein, O. G., Mezzich, A. C., Bromberger, J. T., & Donovan, J. E. (1997). Gender and comorbid psychopathology in adolescents with alcohol dependence. *Journal of the American Academy of Child and Adolescent Psychiatry, 36,* 1195–1203.

Clayton, R. R., Voss, H. L., Robbins, C., & Skinner, W. F. (1986). Gender differences in drug use: An epidemiological perspective. In B. A. Ray & M. C. Braude (Eds.), *Women and drugs: A new era for research.* (NIDA Monograph 65, DHHS Publication (ADM) 86-1447; pp. 80–99). Washington, DC: Superintendent of Documents, U.S. Government Printing Office.

Cloninger, C. R. (1987). Neurogenetic adaptive mechanisms in alcoholism. *Science, 236,* 410–416.

Cohen, P., Cohen, J., Kasen, S., Velez, C. N., Hartmark, C., Johnson, J., Rojas, M., Brook, J., & Streuning, E. L. (1993). An epidemiological study of disorders in late childhood and adolescence: I. Age- and gender-specific prevalence. *Journal of Child Psychology and Psychiatry, 34,* 851–867.

Cohen, R. Y., Brownell, K. D., & Felix, M. R. J. (1990). Age and sex differences in health habits and beliefs of schoolchildren. *Health Psychology, 9,* 208–224.

Collins, R. L. (1993). Women's issues in alcohol use and cigarette smoking. In J. S. Baer, G. A. Marlatt, & R. J. McMahon (Eds.), *Addictive behaviors across the life span* (pp. 274–306). Newbury Park: Sage.

Compas, B. E. (1987). Stress and life events during childhood and adolescence. *Clinical Psychology Review, 7,* 275–302.

Compas, B. E., & Wagner, B. M. (1991). Psychosocial stress during adolescence: Intrapersonal and interpersonal processes. In M. E. Colton & S. Gore (Eds.), *Adolescent stress: Causes and consequences* (pp. 67–85). New York: Walter de Gruyter, Inc.

Costello, E. J., Erkanli, A., Federman, E., & Angold, A. (1999). Development of psychiatric comorbidity with substance abuse in adolescents: Effects of timing and sex. *Journal of Clinical Child Psychology, 28,* 298–311.

Costello, E. J., Angold, A., Burns, B. J., Erkanli, A., Stangl, D. K., & Tweed, D. L. (1996). The Great Smoky Mountains Study of Youth: Goals, design, methods, and the prevalence of DSM-III-R disorders. *Archives of General Psychiatry 53*(12), 1129–1136.

Crabbe, J. C. (2002). Genetic contributions to addiction. *Annual Review of Psychology, 53,* 435–462.

Cyranowski, J., Frank, E., Young, E., & Shear, K. (2000). Adolescent onset of the gender difference in lifetime rats of major depression. *Archives of General Psychiatry, 57,* 21–27.

Daitzman, R., & Zuckerman, M. (1980). Disinhibitory sensation seeking, personality and gonadal hormones. *Personality and Individual Differences, 1,* 103–110.

Deykin, E. Y., Buka, S. L., & Zeena, T. H. (1992). Depressive illness among chemically dependent adolescents. *American Journal of Psychiatry, 149,* 1341–1347.

Dishion, T. J. (1990). The peer context of troublesome child and adolescent behavior. In P. Leone (Ed.), *Understanding troubled and troubling youth: Multidisciplinary perspective* (pp. 128–153). Newbury Park, CA: Sage.

Duncan, T. E., Duncan, S. C., & Hops, H. (1994). The effect of family cohesiveness and peer encouragement on the development of adolescent alcohol use: A cohort-sequential approach to the analysis of longitudinal data. *Journal of Studies on Alcohol, 55,* 588–599.

Duncan, S. C., & Tildesley, E. (1996, March). *Adolescent substance use types of deviance and gender: A lagged analysis using GEE.* Poster presented at the annual meeting of the Society for Research on Adolescence, Boston, MA.

Dunne, F. (1988). Are women more easily damaged by alcohol than men? *British Journal of Addiction, 83*(10), 1135–1136.

Eccles, J. S., Midgley, C., Wigfield, A., Buchanan, C. M., Reuman, D., Flanagan, C., & Mac Iver, D. (1993). Development during adolescence: The impact of stage–environment fit on young adolescents' experiences in school and in families. *American Psychologist, 48,* 90–101.

Emler, N., Reicher, S., & Ross, A. (Eds.). (1997). The social context of delinquent conduct. *Journal of Child Psychology and Psychiatry, 28,* 99–109.

Ennett, S. T., & Bauman, K. E. (1991). Mediators in the relationship between parental and peer characteristics and beer drinking by early adolescents. *Journal of Applied Social Psychology, 18,* 289–314.

Ennett, S. T., & Bauman, K. E. (1994). The contributions of influence and selection to adolescent peer group homogeneity: The case of adolescent cigarette smoking. *Journal of Personality and Social Psychology, 67,* 653–663.

Ensminger, M. E., Brown, C. H., & Kellam, S. G. (1982). Sex differences in antecedents of substance use among adolescents. *Journal of Social Issues, 38,* 25–42.

File, S. E., Fluck, E., & Leahy, A. (2001). Nicotine has a calming effects on stress-induced mood changes in females, but enhances aggressive mood in males. *International Journal of Neuropsychopharmacology, 4,* 371–376.

Flay, B. R., Allred, C. G., & Ordway, N. (2001). Effects of the Positive Action program on achievement and discipline: Two matched-control comparisons. Prevention-Science. 2, 71–89.

Friedman, L. S., Lichtenstein, E., & Biglan, A. (1985). Smoking onset among teens: An empirical analysis of initial situations. *Addictive Behaviors, 10,* 1–13.

French, S. A., Perry, C. L., Leon, G. R., & Fulkerson, J. A. (1994). Weight concerns, dieting behavior, and smoking initiation among adolescents: A prospective study. *American Journal of Public Health, 84,* 1818–1820.

Frezza, M., De Padova, C., Pozzato, G., Terpin, M., Baraona, E., & Lieber, C. S. (1990). High blood alcohol levels in women: The role of decreased gastric alcohol dehydrogenase and first-pass metabolism. *New England Journal of Medicine, 322,* 95–99.

Gibbons, F. X., & Gerrard, M. (1997). Health images and their effects on health behavior. In B. P. Buunk & F. X. Gibbons (Eds.), *Health, coping, and well-being: Perspective from social comparison theory* (pp. 63–94). Mahwah, NJ: Erlbaum.

Gibbons, F. X., & Gerrard, M. (1995). Predicting young adults' health-risk behavior. *Journal of Personality and Social Psychology, 69,* 505–517.

Gilvarry, E., McCarthy, S., & McArdle, P. (Eds.). (1995). Substance use among schoolchildren in the north of England. *Drug and Alcohol Dependence, 37,* 255–259.

Glynn, T. J. (1981). From family to peer: A review of transitions of influence among drug-using youth. *Journal of Youth and Adolescence, 10,* 363–383.

Grady, K., Gersick, K. E., Snow, D. L., & Kessen, M. (1986). The emergence of adolescent substance use. *Journal of Drug Education, 16*(3), 203–220.

Grant, B. F., & Dawson, D. A. (1997). Age at onset of alcohol use and its association with DSM-IV alcohol abuse and dependence: Results from the National Longitudinal Alcohol Epidemiologic Survey. *Journal of Substance Abuse, 9,* 103–10.

Gruber, E., DiClemente, R. J., Anderson, M. M., & Lodico, M. (Eds.). (1996). Early drinking onset and its association with alcohol use and problem behavior in late adolescence. *Preventive Medicine, 25*(59), 293–300.

Harrell, J. S., Bangdiwala, S. I., Deng, S., Webb, J. P., & Bradley, C. (1998). Smoking initiation in youth: The roles of gender, race, socioeconomics, and developmental status. *Journal of Adolescent Health, 23,* 271–279.

Hawkins, J. D., Graham, J. W., Maguin, E., Abbott, R. D., Hill, K. G., & Catalano, R. F. (1997). Exploring the effects of age alcohol use initiation and psychosocial risk factors on subsequent alcohol misuse. *Journal of Studies on Alcohol, 58,* 280–290.

Henricksen, L., & Jackson, C. (1999). Reliablity of children's self-reported cigarette smoking. *Addictive Behaviors, 24,* 271–277.

Henly, G. A., & Winters, K. C. (1989). Development of psychosocial scales for the assessment of adolescents involved with alcohol and drugs. *International Journal of the Addictions, 24,* 973–1001.

Henry, B., Feehan, M., McGee, R., Stanton, W., Moffitt, T. E., & Silva, P. (1993). The importance of conduct problems and depressive symptoms in predicting adolescent substance use. *Journal of Abnormal Child Psychology, 21,* 469–480.

Hill, S. Y. (1995). Mental and physical health consequences of alcohol use in women. *Recent Developments in Alcohol, 12,* 181–197.

Holsten, F. (1980). Repeat follow up studies of 100 young Norwegian drug abusers. *Journal of Drug Issues, 10,* 491–504.

Hops, H., Davis, B., & Lewin, L. (1999). The development of alcohol and other substance use: A gender study of family and peer context. *Journal of Studies on Alcohol, 13,* 22–31.

Hops, H., Duncan, T. E., Duncan, S. C., & Stoolmiller, M. (1996). Parent substance use as a predictor of adolescent use: A six-year lagged analysis. *Annals of Behavioral Medicine, 18*(3), 157–164.

Hovens, J. G. F. M., Cantwell, D. P., & Kiriakos, R. (1994). Psychiatric comorbidity in hospitalized adolescent substance abusers. *Journal of the American Academy of Child and Adolescent Psychiatry, 33,* 476–483.

Jang, K. L., Livesley, J. W., & Vernon, P. A. (1997). Gender-specific etiological differences in alcohol and drug problems: A behavioral genetic analysis. *Addiction, 92,* 1265.

Jessor, R. (1987). Problem behavior theory, psychosocial development, and adolescent problem drinking. *British Journal of Addiction, 82,* 331–342.

Jessor, R., Jessor, S. L., & Finney, J. (1973). A social psychology of marijuana use: Longitudinal studies of high school and college youth. *Journal of Personality and Social Psychology, 26,* 1–15.

Johnson, E. O., Arria, A. M., Borges, G., Ialongo, N., & Anthony, J. C. (Eds.). (1995). The growth of conduct problem behaviors from middle childhood to early adolescence: Sex differences and the suspected influence of early alcohol use. *Journal of Studies on Alcohol, 56*(6), 661–671.

Johnson, R. A., & Gerstein, D. R. (1998). Initiation of use of alcohol, cigarette, marijuana, cocaine, and other substances in US birth cohorts since 1919. *American Journal of Public Health, 88,* 27.

Johnson, T. P., & Mott, J. A. (2001). The reliability of self-reported age of onset of tobacco, alcohol and illicit drug use. *Addiction, 96,* 1187–1198.

Johnston, L. D., O'Malley, P. M., & Bachman, J. G. (2002a). *Monitoring the Future national results on adolescent drug use: Overview of key findings 2001.* Rockville, MD: U.S. Department of Health and Human Services.

Johnston, L. D., O'Malley, P. M., & Bachman, J. G. (2002b). *Monitoring the Future national survey results on drug use, 1975–2001.* Rockville, MD: U.S. Department of Health and Human Services.

Johnston, L. D., O'Malley, P., & Bachman, J. G. (2000). *Monitoring the Future, national survey results on drug use, 1975–1999: Vol. 1: Secondary school students.* Bethesda, MD: National Institute of Drug Abuse.

Johnston, L. D., O'Malley, P. M., & Bachman, J. G. (1996). *National survey results on drug use from The Monitoring the Future study 1975–1995: Vol. 1: Secondary students.* Rockville, MD: U.S. Department of Health and Human Services.

Jones, B. M., & Jones, M. K. (1976). Women and alcohol: Intoxication, metabolism, and the menstrual cycle. In M. Greenblatt & M. A. Schuckit (Eds.), *Alcohol problems in women and children* (pp. 103–136). New York: Grune & Stratton.

Kandel, D. B. (2000). Gender differences in the epidemiology of substance dependence in the United States. In E. Frank (Ed.), *Gender and its effects on psychopathology* (pp. 231–252). Washington, DC: American Psychiatric Press, Inc.

Kandel, D. B. (1984). Marijuana users in young adulthood. *Archives of General Psychiatry, 41,* 200–209.

Kandel, D. B. (1978). Homophily, selection, and socialization in adolescent friendships. *American Journal of Sociology, 84,* 427–436.

Kandel, D. B., & Raveis, V. H. (1989). Cessation of illicit drug use in young adulthood. *Archives of General Psychiatry, 46*(2), 109–116.

Kaplan, H. B., Martin, S. S., Johnson, R. J., & Robbins, C. A. (1986). Escalation of marijuana use: Application of a general theory of deviant behavior. *Journal of Health and Social Behavior, 27,* 44–61.

Kaufman, N. J., & Nichter, M. (2001). The marketing of tobacco to women: Global perspectives. In J. M. Samet & S. Y. Yoon (Eds.), *Women and the tobacco epidemic* (pp. 69–98). Geneva: World Health Organization.

Kellam, S. G., Simon, M. B., & Ensminger, M. E. (1983). Antecedents in first grade of teenage substance use and psychological well-being: A ten-year community-wide prospective study. In D. F. Ricks & B. S. Dohrenwend (Eds.), *Origins of psychopathology* (pp. 17–42). Cambridge, MA: Cambridge University Press.

Klesges, R. C., Meyers, A. W., Klesges, L. M., & La Vasque, M. E. (1989). Smoking, body weight, and their effects on smoking behavior: A comprehensive reivew of the literature. *Psychological Bulletin, 106,* 204–230.

Koob, G. F., & LeMoal, M. (2001). Drug addiction, dysregulation of reward, and allostasis. *Neuropsychopharmacology, 24,* 97–129.

Labouvie, E. W. (1986). Alcohol and marijuana use in relation to adolescent stress. *The International Journal of the Addictions, 21,* 333–345.

Larson, R., & Richards, M. H. (1991). Daily companionship in late childhood and early adolescence: Changing developmental contexts. *Child Development, 62,* 284–300.

Latimer, W. W., Newcomb, M., Winters, K. C., & Stinchfield, R. D. (2000). Adolescent substance abuse treatment outcome: The role of substance abuse problem severity, psychosocial and treatment factors. *Journal of Consulting and Clinical Psychology, 68,* 684–696.

Latimer, W. W., Winters, K. C., Stinchfield, R., & Traver R. E. (2000). Demographic, individual and interpersonal predictors of adolescent alcohol and marijuana use following treatment. *Psychology of Addictive Behaviors, 14,* 162–173.

Lewinsohn, P. M., Hops, H., Roberts, R. E., Seeley, J. R., & Andrews, J. A. (1993). Adolescent psychopathology: I. Prevalence and incidence of depression and other DSM-III-R disorders in high school students. *Journal of Abnormal Psychology, 102,* 133–144.

Lewinsohn, P. M., Rhode, P., & Seeley, J. R. (1996). Alcohol consumption in high school adolescents: Frequency of use and dimensional structure of associated problems. *Addiction, 91,* 375–390.

Loeber, R., Keenan, K., & Zhang, Q. (1997). Boys' experimentation and persistence in developmental pathways toward serious delinquency. *Journal of Child and Family Studies, 6,* 321–357.

Maccoby, E. E. (1990). Gender and relationships: A developmental account. *American Psychologist, 45,* 513–520.

Magnusson, D., Stattin, H., & Allen, V. A. (1986). Differential maturation among girls and its relevance to social adjustment: A longitudinal perspective. In D. L. Featherman & R. M. Loerner (Eds.), *Life-span development and behavior* (Vol. 7, pp. 135–172), New York: Academic Press.

Magnusson, D., Stattin, H., & Allen, V. L. (1985). Biological maturation and social development: A longitudinal study of some adjustment processes from mid-adolescence to adulthood. *Journal of Youth and Adolescence, 14,* 267–283.

Mezzich, A. C., Moss, H., Tarter, R. E., & Wolfenstein, M. (1994). Gender differences in the pattern and progression of substance use in conduct disordered adolescents. *American Journal on Addiction, 3,* 289–295.

Moffitt, T. E. (1997). Adolescence-limited and life-course-persistent offending: A complementary pair of developmental theories. *Developmental theories of crime and delinquency* (pp. 11–54). New Brunswick, NJ: Transaction.

Moffitt, T. E., Caspi, A., Rutter, M., & Silva, P. A. (2001). *Sex differences in antisocial behaviour: Conduct disorder, delinquency, and violence in the Dunedin Longitudinal Study.* New York: Cambridge University Press.

Molnar, B. E., Buka, S. L., & Kessler, R. C. (2001). Child sexual abuse and subsequent psychopathology: Results from the Natiaonl Comorbidity Survey. *American Journal of Public Health, 91,* 753–760.

Newcomb, M. D., & Bentler, P. M. (1988). *Consequences of adolescent drug use: Impact on the lives of young adults* (pp. 285). Newbury Park, CA: Sage.

Newcomb, M. D., & Bentler, P. M. (1989). Substance use and abuse among children and teenagers. *American Psychologist, 44,* 242–248.

Norman, N. M., & Tedeschi, J. T. (1989). Self-presentation, reasoned action, and adolescents: Decisions to smoke cigarettes. *Journal of Applied Social Psychology, 19,* 543–558.

Oetting, E. R., & Beauvais, F. (1990). Adolescent drug use: Findings of national and local surveys. *Journal of Consulting and Clinical Psychology, 58,* 385–394.

Parke, R. D., & Bhavnagri, N. (1989). Parents as managers of children's peer relationships. In D. Belle (Ed.), *Children's social networks and social supports* (pp. 241–259). New York: Wiley.

Patterson, G. R., DeBaryshe, B. D., & Ramsey, E. (1989). A developmental perspective on antisocial behavior. *American Psychologist, 44,* 329–336.

Patterson, G. R., Reid, J. B., & Dishion, T. J. (1992). *A social interactional approach: IV. Antisocial boys.* Eugene OR: Castalia.

Peterson, A. C. (1987). The nature of biological–psychosocial interactions: The sample case of early adolescence. In R. M. Lerner & T. T. Foch (Eds.), *Biological–psychosocial interactions in early adolescence: A life-span perspective* (pp. 35–61). Hillsdale, NJ: Erlbaum.

Peterson, A. (1985). Pubertal development as a cause of disturbance: Myths, realities, and unanswered questions. *Genetic Psychology Monographs, 111,* 207–231.

Peterson, A. C., & Crockett, L. (1985). Pubertal timing and grade effects on adjustment. *Journal of Youth and Adolescence, 14,* 192–206.

Peterson, A. C., Graber, J. A., & Sullivan, P. (1990, March). *Pubertal timing and adjustment in adolescence: Variations in effects.* Paper presented at the Third Biennial Meeting of the Society for Research in Adolescence, Atlanta, GA.

Pierce, J. P., & Gilpin, E. A. (1996). How long will today's new adolescent smoker be addicted to cigarettes? *American Journal of Public Health, 86,* 253–256.

Pugatch, D., Ramratnam, M., Strong, L., Feller, A., Levesque, B., & Dickinson, B. P. (2000). Gender differences in HIV risk behaviors among young adults and adolescents entering a Massachusetts detoxification center. *Substance Abuse, 21,* 79–86.

Pollock, V. E., Schneider, L. S., Gabrielli, W. F., & Goodwin, D. W. (1987). Sex of parent and offspring in the transmission of alcoholism: A meta-analysis. *Journal of Nervous and Mental Disease, 175*(11), 668–673.

Prescott, C. A., & Kendler, K. S. (2000). Influence of ascertainment strategy on finding sex differences in genetic estimates from twin studies of alcoholism. *American Journal of Medical Genetics, 96,* 754–761.

Prescott, C. A., Aggen, S. H., & Kendler, K. S. (1999). Sex differences in the sources of genetic liability to alcohol abuse and dependence in a population-based sample of U.S. twins. *Alcoholism, Clinical, and Experimental Research, 23,* 1136–1144.

Robins, L. N., Helzer, J. E., & Przybeck, T. (1986). Substance abuse in the general population. In J. E. Barrett, & R. M. Rose, (Eds.), *Mental disorders in the community: Progress and challenge.* (Proceedings of the American Psychopathological Association, Vol. 42, pp. 9–31). New York: Guilford.

Robinson, T. E., & Berridge, K. C. (2000). The psychology and neurobiology of addiction: An incentive-sensitization view. *Addiction, 95*(Suppl. 2), S91–S117.

Robinson, T. E., & Berridge, K. C. (2001). Incentive-sensitization and addiction. *Addiction, 96,* 103–114.

Rhode, P., Lewinsohn, P. M., & Seeley, J. R. (1996). Psychiatric comorbidity with problematic alcohol use in high school adolescents. *Journal of the American Academy of Child and Adolescent Psychiatry, 35,* 101–109.

Rose, R. J. (1995). Genes and human behavior. *Annual Review of Psychology, 46,* 625–654.

Rudolph, K. D., & Hammen, C. (1999). Age and gender as determinants of stress exposure, generation, and reactions in youngsters: A transactional perspective. *Child Development, 70,* 660–677.

Rutter, M. (1979). Maternal deprivation, 1972–1978: New findings, new concepts, new approaches, *Child Development, 50,* 283–305.

Rutter, M. (1988). Epidemiological approaches to developmental psychopathology. *Archives of General Psychiatry, 45,* 486–495.

Savin-Williams, R. C., & Small, S. A. (1986). The timing of puberty and its relationship to adolescent and parent perceptions of family interactions. *Developmental Psychology, 22,* 342–347.

Schulenberg, J., Maggs, J. L., Dielman, T. E., Leech, S. L., Kloska, D. D., Shope, J. T., & Laetz, V. B. (1999). On peer influences to get drunk: A panel study of young adolescents. *Merrill Palmer Quarterly, 45*(1), 108–142.

Severson, H. H., Andrews, J., & Walker, H. M. (2003). Early intervention to reduce substance use. In D. Romer (Ed.), *Reducing adolescent risk: Toward an integrated approach* (pp. 132–138). Thousand Oaks, CA: Sage.

Siegel, J. M., Yancey, A. K., Aneshensel, C. S., & Schuler, R. (1999). Body image, perceived pubertal timing, and adolescent mental health. *Journal of Adolescent Health, 25,* 155–165.

Silbereisen, R. K., & Kracke, B. (1997). Self-reported maturational timing and adaptation in adolescence. In J. Schulenberg & J. L. Maggs (Eds.), *Health risks and developmental transitions during adolescence.* Cambridge: Cambridge University Press.

Silbereisen, R. K., & Kracke, B. (1997). Self-reported maturational timing and adaptation in adolescence. In J. Schulenberg & J. L. Maggs (Eds.), *Health risks and developmental transitions during adolescence.* Cambridge University Press: Cambridge.

Silverthorn, P., & Frick. P. J. (1999). Developmental pathways to antisocial behavior: The delayed-onset pathway in girls. *Development and Psychopathology, 11,* 101–126.

Simmons, R. G., Burgeson, R., Carolton-Ford, S., & Blyth, D.A. (1987). The impact of cumulative change in early adolescence. *Child Development, 58,* 1220–1234.

Simon, T. R., Sussman, S., & Dent, C. W. (1995). Prospective correlates of exclusive or combined adolescent use of cigarettes and smokeless tobacco: A replication-extension. *Addictive Behaviors, 20,* 517–524.

Simon, T. R., Sussman, S., Dent, C. W., Burton, D., & Flay, B. (1995). Prospective correlates of exclusive or combined adolescent use of cigarettes and smokeless tobacco: A replication-extension. *Addictive Behaviors, 20*(4), 517–524.

Skaar, K. L., Tsoh, J. Y., McClure, J. B., Cinciripini, P. M., Friedman, K., Wetter, D. W., et al. (1997). Smoking cessation: 1. An overview of research. *Behavior Medicine, 23*(1), 5–13.

Spooner, C., & Hall, W. (Eds.). (2002). Preventing drug misuse by young people: We need to do more than 'just say no.' *Addiction, 97,* 478–481.

Stattin, H., & Magnusson, D. (1990). *Pubertal maturation in female development.* Hillsdale, NJ: Erlbaum.

Stein, J. A., Newcomb, M. D., & Bentler, P. (1987). An 8-year study of multiple influences on drug use and drug use consequences. *Journal of Personality and Social Psychology, 53,* 1094–1105.

Steinberg, L. D. (1987). The impact of puberty on family relations: Effects of pubertal status and pubertal timing. *Developmental Psychology, 23,* 451–460.

Steinberg, L. D. (1988). Reciprocal relations between parent–child distance and pubertal maturation. *Developmental Psychology, 24,* 122–128.

Steinberg, L., & Silverburg, S. (1986). The vicissitudes of autonomy in early adolescence. *Child Development, 57,* 841–851.

Stewart, D. G., & Brown, S. A. (2001). Withdrawal and dependence symptoms among adolescent alcohol and drug abusers. *Addiction, 90,* 627–635.

Swan, G. E., Carmelli, D., Rosenman, R. H., Fabsitz, R. R., & Christian, J. C. (1990). Smoking and alcohol consumption in adult male twins: Genetic heritability and shared environmental influences. *Journal of Substance Abuse, 2*(1), 39–50.

Swan, G. E., Ward, M. M., Carmelli, D., & Jack, L. M. (1993). Differential rates of relapse in subgroups of male and female smokers. *Journal of Clinical Epidemiology, 46*(9), 1041–1053.

Urberg, K. A., Degirmencioglu, S. M., & Pilgrim, C. (1997). Close friend and group influence on adolescent cigarette smoking and alcohol use. *Developmental Psychology, 33*(5), 834–844.

U.S. Department of Health and Human Services. (1989). *Reducing the health consequences of smoking: 25 years of progress. A report of the Surgeon General* (DHHS Publication No. (CDC) 89-8411). Washington, DC: U.S. Department of Health and Human Services, Public Health Service, Centers for Disease Control, Center for Chronic Disease Prevention and Health Promotion, Office on Smoking and Health.

U. S. Department of Health and Human Services. (2000). *National Household Survey on Drug Abuse: Main findings: 1998.* Rockville, MD: DHHS/SAMHSA, National Household Survey.

U. S. Department of Health and Human Services. (1995). *National Household Survey on Drug Abuse: Main Findings: 1993.* Rockville, MD: DHHS/SAMHSA.

U. S. Department of Health and Human Services. (1995). *National Household Survey on Drug Abuse: Main findings: 1992.* Rockville, MD: DHHS/SAMHSA.

U. S. Department of Health and Human Services. (1993). *National Household Survey on Drug Abuse: Main findings: 1991.* Rockville, MD: DHHS/SAMHSA.

Ward, K. D., Klesges, R. C., Zbikowski, S. M., Bliss, R. E., & Garvey, A. J. (1997). Gender differences in the outcome of an unaided smoking cessation attempt. *Addictive Behaviors, 22,* 521–533.

Wichstrom, L. (2000). Predictors of adolescent suicide attempts: A nationally representative longitudinal study of Norwegian adolescents. *Journal of the American Academy of Child and Adolescent Psychiatry, 39,* 603–610.

Wills, J., Callan, V. J., & Austin, D. A. (Eds.). (1989). Parent, peer and personal determinants of adolescent drinking. *British Journal of Addiction, 84,* 619–630.

Wills, T. A., Sandy, J. M., & Yaeger, A. M. (2002). Stress and smoking in adolescence: A test of directional hypotheses. *Health Psychology, 21*(2), 122–130.

Wills, T. A., Sandy, J. M., & Yaeger, A. (2000). Temperament and adolescent substance use: An epigenetic approach to risk and protection. *Journal of Personality, 68*(6), 1127–1151.

Wills, T. A. (1986). Stress and coping in early adolescence: Relationships to substance use in the urban school samples. *Health Psychology, 5,* 503–529.

Wills, T. A. (1990). Stress and coping factors in the epidemiology of substance use. In L. T. Kozlowski, H. M. Annis, H. D. Cappell, F. B. Glaser, M. S. Goodstadt, Y. Israel, H. Kalant, E. M. Sellers, & E. R. Vingillis (Eds.), *Research Advances in Alcohol and Drug Problems* (Vol. 10, pp. 215–250). New York: Plenum.

Wills, T. A., & Cleary, S. D. (1999). Peer and adolescent substance use among 6th–9th graders: Latent growth analyses of influence versus selection mechanisms. *Health Psychology, 18*(5), 453–463.

Windle, M. (2002). Alcohol use among adolescents. *The Prevention Researcher, 9*(3), 1–3.

Windle, M. (1992). A longitudinal study of stress buffering for adolescent problem behaviors. *Developmental Psychology, 28,* 522–530.

Windle, M. (1990). A longitudinal study of antisocial behaviors in early adolescence as predictors of late adolescent substance use: Gender and ethnic group differences. *Journal of Abnormal Psychology, 99,* 86–91.

Winters, K. C., Stinchfield, R. D., Opland, E. , Weller, C., & Latimer, W. W. (2000). The effectiveness of the Minnesota Model approach in the treatment of adolescent drug abusers. *Addiction, 95,* 601–612.

Wiseman, C. V., Gray, J. J., Mosiman, J. E., & Ahrens, A. H. (Eds.), (1992). Cultural expectations of thinness in women: An update. *International Journal of Eating Disorders, 11*(85), 85–89.

Wiseman, C. V., Sunday, S. R., Halligan, P., Korn, S., Brown, C., & Halmi, K. A. (1999). Substance dependence and eating disorders: Impact of sequence on comorbidity. *Comprehensive Psychiatry, 40,* 332–336.

Zuckerman, M. (1993). P-impulsive sensation seeking and its behavioral, psychophysiological biochemical correlations . *Neuropsychobiology, 28,* 30–36.

IV

Developmental and Learning Disorders

7

Pervasive Developmental Disorders in Girls

KATHLEEN KOENIG and KATHERINE D. TSATSANIS

Pervasive developmental disorders are a group of conditions sharing as their common features impairment in social reciprocity, developmental disturbances affecting communication, and manifestation of restricted and repetitive behaviors. Autism is the prototypical pervasive developmental disorder, and others include Asperger's Disorder, Rett's Disorder, Childhood Disintegrative Disorder, and Pervasive Developmental Disorder-Not Otherwise Specified (PDD-NOS). Critical to understanding these conditions is appreciation of the developmental nature of the impairment, such that a lack of mastery in particular social developmental tasks early in life has implications for mastery of other more complex social challenges (Koenig, Tsatsanis, & Volkmar, 2001). Delays in the emergence of language, as well as deviant language use, impair the development of sophisticated communication strategies and the capacity for self-regulation. In addition, restricted interests or repetitive verbalizations and behaviors serve to socially isolate the affected individual to a greater extent as development progresses.

Research on pervasive developmental disorders (PDDs) more frequently involves affected boys exclusively, because approximately four males are affected for every one affected female (Fombonne, 1999). Affected boys are more readily ascertained for research participation; when girls are also included, their numbers are typically too small to permit separate sex-specific analyses. A further consideration is that research results regarding neurobiological mechanisms and the efficacy of intervention are generalizable to a wider population of affected children if boys are studied. However,

KATHLEEN KOENIG • Yale University, New Haven, CT, 06520-7900.
KATHERINE D. TSATSANIS • Harvard Medical School, Cambridge, Massachusetts, 02138.

greater effort to identify and study affected girls should be made, since this may provide crucial clues to the genetic and neurobiological mechanisms involved in the disorder (Leibenluft, 1996). For all psychiatric disorders, variation in presentation between the sexes within a disorder can provide important information regarding pathophysiology (Kelly, Ostrowski, & Wilson, 1999). In addition, intervention approaches may vary for subsets of children with the disorder, and these subsets may include division by sex.

In this chapter, we describe the current research findings on pervasive developmental disorders in girls, including epidemiology and diagnostic issues, etiologic considerations, possible differences in clinical presentation and developmental trajectory between girls and boys with the disorder, and assessment and intervention implications. Very little research directly addresses the factors relevant to the assessment, diagnosis, and treatment of girls with PDDs. Thus, we identify social-communicative and behavioral markers for which there are sex differences in typical children so that the impact of these sex differences as they apply to girls with PDDs will be evident.

This chapter is focused on girls with autism and Pervasive Developmental Disorder-Not Otherwise Specified, because most of the extant literature is centered on these two, more common, diagnoses within the spectrum of pervasive developmental disorders. Little has been written about girls with Asperger's Disorder, so that the discussion of characteristic behaviors of girls and possible differences in presentation between the sexes is necessarily brief. Childhood Disintegrative Disorder is an extremely rare condition and no differences in presentation between girls and boys have been described. Rett's Disorder is a rare developmental condition that has been described, until recently, only in girls. As such, we present some relevant features of this disorder, but refer the interested reader to Hagberg (1993) for a more extensive discussion.

EPIDEMIOLOGIC AND DIAGNOSTIC CONSIDERATIONS

The disparity in prevalence between males and females with autism and related conditions has provoked three overarching questions. First, is this disparity an accurate representation of a differential occurrence of the disability in males and females, or does this reflect insensitivity in the current diagnostic system, which fails to encompass differences in presentation between the sexes? Second, are girls with autism spectrum conditions more impaired in terms of intellectual functioning, social disability, or adaptive functioning as a group than boys with these conditions? And third, if the disparity accurately reflects the true prevalence, what neuropathological mechanisms explain this differential?

The criteria for autism have changed considerably with subsequent editions of the Diagnostic and Statistical Manual of Mental Disorders (*DSM-IV*; American Psychiatric Association, 1994) and the International Classification of Diseases (WHO, 1993) (Fombonne & Tidmarsh, 2003). Since the existing definition of a disorder governs who is included for study, addressing the questions outlined above through a comparison of studies over time becomes problematic. One must make comparisons between epidemiological or phenomenological data, while also considering what criteria were used to determine eligibility for the study.

Currently, autism is diagnosed if a child meets criteria in three symptom clusters, and if the onset of symptoms was before 3 years of age (American Psychiatric Association, 1994). The first cluster is impairment in socially reciprocal behavior, for example, poor eye contact, lack of interest in people, or a lack of social relationships. Impairment in communication ability, the second cluster, may take the form of delayed or deviant language use, or poor conversational skills. The third cluster, restricted or repetitive behaviors, includes motor or vocal stereotypies, perseverative behavior, or narrowly focused, usual interests that dominate the individual's life.

Asperger's Disorder is diagnosed in individuals who show social impairment and restricted interests. Early formal language skills develop normally and patterns of restricted behavior take the form of all-absorbing preoccupation with a particular area of interest. Lorna Wing (1981a) described Asperger's Disorder in girls and in mentally retarded individuals as well, but more recent reports have described the condition as most frequently seen in nonretarded males (Klin & Volkmar, 2003). Overall, a lack of consensus among researchers and clinicians regarding the definitive characteristics of persons with Asperger's Disorder has impeded progress in epidemiological and phenomenological studies, and currently no information on Asperger's Disorder as it presents in girls is available (Fombonne & Tidmarsh, 2003; Klin & Volkmar, 2003).

Rett's Disorder is characterized by apparent normal health at birth, with normal achievement of developmental milestones for at least the first 6 months of life. Before 3 years of age, stereotypic hand movements (hand wringing) develop, along with gait abnormalities and loss of early language (Hagberg, 1993). Head growth deceleration is noted, mental retardation becomes evident, and social interest may decline. At the time that Rett's Disorder was included in *DSM-IV*, it was believed to occur only in girls. Subsequent to the identification of the MECP2 gene, which plays a role in Rett's Disorder, variants of the syndrome have been reported in males with mutations of MECP2 (Amir et al., 1999; Schwartzman et al., 1999). Diagnosis is made through genetic testing; assessment and intervention focus on the neuromuscular and communication deficits for affected children, and should be undertaken by clinicians experienced with this rare disorder.

Childhood Disintegrative Disorder (CDD) is characterized by a severe regression in development following at least 2 years of normal maturation, with motor, social, and language milestones achieved on time (Volkmar, Klin, Marans, & Cohen, 1997). Social interest declines, and language and communication skills are lost. Toileting skills may deteriorate as well. Stereotypic behaviors develop, and these children become indistinguishable from children with classic autism. The hallmark of CDD is the extended period of normal development before regression. This feature lies in contrast to autism, in which language, with few exceptions, does not develop in the usual time frame. Finally, the diagnosis of Pervasive Developmental Disorder-Not Otherwise Specified (PDD-NOS) is used to designate individuals with characteristics of PDD who do not meet criteria for any specific PDD. However, this diagnosis in no way denotes a single clinical entity (Towbin, 1997).

DSM-IV diagnostic criteria for the pervasive developmental disorders were based on field trials involving over 900 children at multiple sites worldwide. Special efforts were made to include females with higher intelligence scores, in order to provide for adequate coverage of the range of syndrome expression for males and females (Volkmar et al., 1994). This effort to guard against sex bias in the development of the diagnostic criteria was critical, because efforts to identify affected girls and to clarify what sex differences might exist in syndrome expression will be confounded if diagnostic criteria are based on syndrome expression in boys only. In the *DSM-IV* field trials, the ratio of boys to girls with autism was 4.4:1, while for all other PDDs the ratio was 3.7:1.

The difference in prevalence between males and females with autism or pervasive developmental disorders is consistently noted, from the earliest epidemiological studies to the most recent (Fombonne, 2001; Lotter, 1966). In an extensive review of epidemiological studies using rigorous case finding methods, Fombonne (1999) reported that male:female ratios for autism varied from 16:1 to 2:1 with a median male:female ratio of 2.6:1 and a mean male:female ratio of 3.8:1. Males were disproportionately represented in the normal band of intellectual functioning, (i.e., "high-functioning"). Two recent, epidemiological surveys of autism and related conditions reported similar ratios (Fombonne, 2001; Yeargin-Allsop et al., 2003).

Research that considers the sex ratio in PDDs has consistently conveyed that girls with PDD are, on average, "lower functioning" than boys with PDD, although the use of this term has been inconsistent. In most studies, "low functioning" refers to intellectual functioning in the range of mental retardation, but some investigators have used it to describe neurological impairment or social impairment. A need for clarity in the use of this term is highlighted when one considers how intellectual functioning, for example, may influence the manifestation of other features of the disorder.

If symptoms of social disability are considered apart from the presence or degree of mental retardation, will differences in presentation between males and females with the disorder significantly impact prevalence as currently reported? Volkmar, Szatmari, and Sparrow (1993) noted that if a greater degree of mental retardation leads directly to more autistic-like behaviors, then controlling for IQ in studies of sex differences is appropriate, in order to examine differences in behavior apart from those impacted by level of intelligence. However, if the pathology or vulnerability that results in the different rates of occurrence in males versus females induces mental retardation and also induces autistic-like behavior as separate entities, then controlling for intelligence will restrict the sample, limiting the possibilities for discovering the way sex may interact with the manifestation of autistic-like behavior.

A comparison of the existing studies of sex differences in pervasive developmental disorder highlights the way in which different results are obtained when factors such as intelligence, degree of social or communication disability, or restricted and repetitive behaviors are considered (Table 1). Two small studies addressed whether differences exist in the presentation of autistic symptoms between the sexes by matching girls and boys for IQ, and choosing the highest functioning children for study, thus eliminating the confound of mental retardation (McLennan, Lord, & Schopler, 1993; Pilowsky, Yirmiya, Shulman & Dover, 1998). McLennan et al. showed that males displayed greater deviance in early social development, reciprocal social interaction, and early communication deficits, whereas females showed more impairment in social interaction during adolescence as compared with males. Moreover, males showed more restricted and repetitive behaviors related to play as compared with females, consistent with Lord, Schopler, and Revicki's 1982 study. Pilowsky et al. (1998) failed to replicate these findings, but lack of appropriate subject matching prevents interpretation of their data.

Of interest when considering how girls and boys with autism are identified, Wing and Gould (1979) reported no differences in the sex ratio by severity of social impairment. In their sample the ratio of boys to girls was equal in each category: mild, moderate, or severe social impairment, yet boys were 15 times more likely to be diagnosed with autism at the time of the study than girls. That is, while the girls in the study showed social impairment that was not better or worse than boys, the girls were not assigned the diagnosis of autism in equal proportion.

As noted in Table 1, sex differences in social or play behavior can be identified in children with PDDs. However, clinicians may not be aware of these differences. Koop and Gilberg (1992) described six girls with social and communicative deficits of the autistic type, and restricted and repetitive behaviors, all identified by 2 years of age. Each child had an IQ score above 60 yet none had been diagnosed with autism until after the age of 6 years. It is not clear why these girls were not diagnosed with autism since they met the diagnostic criteria; however, one wonders if a bias operates during differential diagnosis, in which girls who appear autistic as compared with the "prototype" established for autistic boys receive an autism diagnosis, and girls who do not fit the prototype are given other, various diagnoses.

In summary, it cannot be stated that girls, as a rule, are more severely affected than boys in terms of social and communicative impairment, because it is difficult to separate out the effects of low cognitive functioning from the symptoms of the social disability (Lord et al., 1982). In fact, the modest literature available supports the view that although girls with strictly defined autism may appear to be lower functioning overall, *when IQ is controlled*, the symptom presentation can be different across sex. Particularly in the category of PDD-NOS, where symptoms show a great deal more variability, this would likely be true. If girls show a variable phenotype, and this phenotype is poorly described, then that cohort of girls with PDD-like impairments may be excluded from epidemiological studies or

Table 1. Studies of sex differences in pervasive developmental disorders

Study	Sample	N (M: F)	Intelligence considered?	Social & Communicative behavior considered?	Restricted and Repetitive behavior considered?	Differences
Wing & Gould (1979)	E	132 2.7:1	Yes	Yes	Yes	No differences in presentation between males and females with autism
Tsai, Stewart & August (1981)	C	102 3.25:1	Yes	No	No	No differences in IQ score between males and females. Females showed more neurological symptoms than males.
Tsai & Beisler (1983)	C	75 2.26:1	Yes	Yes	No	Females showed lower IQ scores and social scores than males. No assessment of social or communicative behavior with control for IQ
Lord, Schopler, & Revicki (1982)	C	478 4.2:1	Yes	Yes	Yes	Males showed higher IQ scores and better social functioning than females. Males showed more frequent and unusual visual interests With control for IQ score, males showed less appropriate, more routinized play as compared with females.
Volkmar, Szatmari, & Sparrow (1993)	C	273 3.63:1	Yes	Yes	Yes	Males showed higher IQs and better social functioning than girls, while girls showed more autistic symptomatology. Adaptive behavior scores were equal. When IQ was controlled, sex differences were not observed
McLennen, Lord, & Schopler (1993)	R	21 males 21 females	Yes	Yes	Yes	In this IQ-matched sample, males showed more deviance in social and communicative behavior, but females showed more social deviance after the age of 12 years than males. Males showed more restricted and repetitive behavior.
Pilowsky, Yirmiya, Shulman, & Dover (1998)	R	18 males 18 females	Yes	Yes	Yes	Sample not appropriately matched for intelligence, females showed significantly lower IQ scores. No meaningful sex differences reported.

*E = Epidemiological sample, C = Clinic sample, R = Research sample.

not referred for clinical consultation (Wing, 1981b). Elucidation of symptoms of impairment not due to low cognitive functioning and identifying sex-specific differences in social or communicative behavior are critical for understanding the mechanisms underlying autism spectrum disorders.

ETIOLOGY OF SEX DIFFERENCES IN PERVASIVE DEVELOPMENTAL DISORDERS

A number of hypotheses have been proposed to explain the uneven sex ratio in pervasive developmental disorders. Each has some empirical foundation, but none fully explain the phenomenon and further investigation is needed.

Liability/Threshold Model

Tsai, Stewart, and August (1981) suggested a multifactorial mode of inheritance, in which all genetic and environmental factors relevant to an autism diagnosis are normally distributed and represented by one variable, liability. The distribution of liability would be equal in both sexes, but the threshold for impairment would be different, with males showing comparable vulnerability at lower levels of liability. In this model, the less frequently affected sex (females) would be more severely impaired when affected, and would have more relatives with autism spectrum conditions. In the small clinic sample considered by these authors, females with autism did have more affected first-degree relatives. However, this finding has not been borne out in subsequent, large epidemiological family studies (Pickles et al., 1995; Szatmari et al., 2000).

Greater Variability Model

An alternative hypothesis is that males show greater variability in the measurable characteristics relevant for these disorders, so that males will be more likely to show some features of the disorder if these characteristics are affected to any degree (Wing, 1981b). Females, on the other hand, show less variability so the magnitude of an insult would have to be much greater in order to produce impairment comparable to that seen in a male. If females show an advantage in social or communicative functioning, this could mitigate against the development of a serious impairment (Wing, 1981b).

Constantino and Todd (in press) showed that typical females display fewer subthreshold characteristics of autism than typical males. Using the Social Reciprocity Scale, a measure validated previously with respect to differentiating healthy typically developing children, children with nonautism spectrum psychiatric conditions, and children with PDDs (Constantino, Przybeck, Friesen, & Todd, 2000), the investigators showed that typically developing females had 25% fewer *autistic-like* features than typically developing males. In addition, heritability estimates were substantially higher for males than females, and no evidence of sex-specific genetic influences was noted in the model. The authors proposed that either the phenotypic expression of the impairment in females is *different* due to reduced contribution of both genetic and environmental influences or females are more *sensitive to environmental influences* such that early social experiences have a mitigating effect on the full expression of the disorder. Neither of these possibilities has been fully explored.

Brain Differences Model

Baron-Cohen and Hammer (1997) have advanced the hypothesis that autism is an "extreme form of the male brain," based on the view that males in the general population show better logical or mathematical and visual-perceptual skills than females, and females show better verbal and social-emotional skills. While this view in no way explains the insult that causes PDDs, it is reasonable to consider sex differences in brain structure and function as a contributing factor to the unequal prevalence of PDDs in males versus females.

A critical concept underlying the study of sexual dimorphisms of the human brain is that these differences represent dimorphisms in brain circuitry (Pilgrim & Hutchison, 1994). Gonadal and adrenal hormones play a significant role in the organization of the mammalian brain, with effects that are more widespread than altering sexually dimorphic structures involved in reproductive function. In particular, the limbic system, including the hypothalamus, hippocampus, amygdala, cingulate cortex, septum, and the orbitofrontal cortex are strongly influenced by the actions of androgens and estrogens in the developing fetus (McEwen, Alves, Bulloch, & Weiland, 1998). These structures are of particular relevance in neurodevelopmental disorders in which emotional and social functioning is paramount; abnormal functioning of the limbic system is a prominent theory of etiology in pervasive developmental disorders (Schultz, Romanski, & Tsatsanis, 2000).

Hormonal influences in the development of gender-specific behavior in nonhumans and humans are well documented (Halpern, 2000). Numerous studies in which pre- and postnatal alterations of hormone levels in humans have been manipulated (due to pathological processes) show differences in reproductive behavior, exploratory behavior, spatial learning, rough and tumble play, visual discrimination learning, and social behavior (Collaer & Hines, 1995; Ehrhardt et al., 1989). Masculizing effects of hormones are seen in a greater tendency toward rough and tumble play, enhanced visual-spatial abilities, and preferences for different toys, playmates, and activities. These findings are interesting in light of the kind of play that is typical of children with autism, which includes a focus on rough and tumble (sensory-motor) play, visual manipulation of objects, and visual-spatial kinds of materials (puzzles, computer programs, manipulatives). Whether these play preferences are equally true for affected males and females is unknown.

Studies of nonhuman primates and humans support a role for medial temporal structures, particularly the hippocampus and amygdala, in cognition, emotion, and learning (Bachevalier, 1994). In humans, the amygdala and hippocampus, structures previously noted to be key for processing social information, show differences in maturational patterns in males and females (Giedd et al., 1996). Variability in the maturational patterns of these structures in males and females may impact their relative vulnerability during critical periods of development.

Differences in the characteristics of these structures across gender are likely to influence neuronal circuitry as well. Gender differences are noted in the activation of the amygdala while experiencing sadness or perceiving affect in faces (Kilgore, Oki & Yurgelun-Todd, 2001; Schneider, Habel, Kessler, Salloum & Posse, 2000). In addition, an initial study of hippocampal volumes between autistic persons and controls showed no differences; however, the variance of the reported volumes in females showed an effect size of more than one standard deviation greater for the right hippocampus when females with autism and controls were compared (Piven, Bailey, Ranson & Ardut, 1998). Unfortunately, separate analyses by gender could not be conducted, and the difference in effect size disappeared when male and female participants were combined. A second structural MRI study showed reduced hippocampal and amygdala volumes in autistic males versus controls (Aylward et al., 1999). These studies, taken together, suggest possible differences in size or in neural circuitry for the processing of emotion between the sexes, which has implications for social functioning.

Differences such as these may be critical in understanding sex differences in social behavior since responding to the social environment requires *appreciation of the emotional significance of the verbalizations and facial expression of others*, and *making appropriate associations between these signals and past events*. An advantage in these skills for females may contribute to competency in the social domain, and reduce or protect against the pathological processes activated in the development of PDD. In this regard, greater exploration of sex differences in social and communicative behavior, and of the mechanisms that regulate repetitive or restricted behavior in typically developing children provides the framework for interpreting the constellation of symptoms in pervasive developmental disorders.

SEX DIFFERENCES IN SOCIAL, COMMUNICATIVE, AND REGULATORY BEHAVIORS: IMPLICATIONS FOR SEX DIFFERENCES IN PERVASIVE DEVELOPMENTAL DISORDERS

Implicit when considering sex differences in PDDs is the view that meaningful and clinically relevant sex differences in social, communicative, and regulatory behavior are found in normal children and adults (Wing, 1981b). Early work on this topic implied that although some sex differences in cognition were noted using experimental paradigms, the significance of these differences was minimal or confined to circumscribed and potentially irrelevant domains (Maccoby & Jacklin, 1974). Subsequent work, broadening the field to include studies of social behavior, language development and communication style, and self-regulatory behavior suggests many sex-specific differences that impact the day-to-day functioning of males and females across various contexts (Ervin-Tripp, 2001; Halpern, 2000; Karmiloff & Karmiloff-Smith, 2001; Kimura, 2000; McClure, 2000). These differences serve as the foundation for understanding how pervasive developmental disorders may manifest differently in girls versus boys, and what issues may be most salient for assessing and treating girls with this disorder.

Social Development

Though social interest and socially reciprocal behavior are an integral part of human behavior across all cultures, a universally accepted, invariant sequence of social developmental stages is not identified; nor is there an exhaustive inventory of the specific components that comprise competent social behavior. Research on empathy, pro-social behavior, understanding of other's minds, and recognition of facial expressions and nonverbal communicative cues have enhanced our understanding of why and how people express interest in relationships with others from the earliest days of life. An extensive review of this literature is beyond the scope of this chapter, but we do describe several components of social behavior in which sex differences are noted in order to lay the foundation for discussion about how these differences may contribute to presentation of symptoms in social disability and how intervention efforts may be affected by these differences.

The existing literature regarding sex differences in various components of social behavior and social functioning is considerable and at times conflicting, as conceptual framework, methods, and sample characteristics vary. For example, the expression of anger within a social context can be investigated from a neurobiological vantage point, with measurement of the intensity of "felt" emotion, (i.e., physiological response), or from a social-contextual vantage point, taking into account the display rules appropriate for each sex. Whereas females may experience angry feelings as intensely as males, their overt expression of anger may be muted (Grossman & Wood, 1993). Thus, sex differences in the expression of this emotion may be reported differently depending on how the question is framed and studied.

These differences in conceptual framework and methods are critical with regard to investigation in pervasive developmental disorders. Given that a defining feature of pervasive developmental disorders is impairment in socially reciprocal behavior, context plays a significant role in determining the extent of disability. The limitations imposed by neurobiological deficits in social perception and integration of this information interfere with feedback from the social environment being received or understood.

In some cases, differences in context may mask the magnitude of the disability, while other contexts may accentuate the disability.

Recognizing Faces and Interpreting Nonverbal Communicative Cues

The ability to recognize faces, interpret facial expressions, and encode and decode nonverbal communicative cues is critical for effective social functioning. In typically developing children, face and affect recognition skills emerge in the first months of life, and there may be a critical window between 2 and 6 months during which exquisite sensitivity to these stimuli result in fine tuning of the face recognition system (Acerra, Burnod, & de Schonen, 2002; de Haan, 2001; Le Grand, Mondloch, Maurer, & Brent, 2001). Across the life span, females show better face recognition, affect recognition, and skill at decoding nonverbal communicative cues in comparison with males (see McClure, 2000 for a comprehensive review). The origin of this advantage is not known although metabolic and maturational differences in relevant brain regions between males and females during a critical period of development may be implicated (De Courten-Myers, 1999; Grachev and Apkarian, 2000).

Persons with autism show difficulty in recognizing faces and facial expressions (Braverman, Fein, Lucci, & Waterhouse, 1989; Klin et al., 1999; Ozonoff, Pennington, & Rogers, 1990). Sex differences in these skills have not been systematically investigated in this population thus far. If typically developing girls show better skill with faces and nonverbal communicative cues than boys, then two outcomes are possible for girls with PDDs. The female advantage in face skills and nonverbal decoding skills could mitigate against deficits in such a way that affected girls show less impairment than affected boys overall. Alternatively, if affected girls show comparable impairment to affected boys, then the girls studied may be *more* impaired than the boys studied relative to their normally developing same sex peers. Social relationships, as opposed to activity-based interests, are primary for girls during school age and adolescent years, and the consequences of these deficits for an affected girl may be quite severe.

Empathy

Empathy is an important component of competent social behavior, and the development of empathic responses has been particularly well studied across the life span, and in typical and clinical populations (Eisenberg & Fabes, 1995; Eisenberg et al., 1995). The capacity for empathy shows genetic influence and empathic responses are noted in children as young as at 2 years of age (Zahn-Waxler, Radke-Yarrow, Wagner, & Chapman, 1992). As children develop, they become more attuned to others' feelings, and more adept at intervening in situations in which an empathic response is required. From the preschool years onward, girls demonstrate more frequent and competent empathic responses to distress situations as compared with boys (Brown & Dunn, 1996; Eisenberg & Fabes, 1995;

Eisenberg et al., 1996). Females report greater intensity of vicariously experienced emotion in response to the distress of others, and physiological measures confirm this finding (Brown & Dunn, 1996; Zahn-Waxler,
Cole, Welsh, & Fox, 1995). Females may display emotions more readily
than males due to early socialization patterns in which "display rules" are
taught to babies by mothers, who reinforce different patterns of display
depending on the sex of the child (Malatesta & Haviland, 1982).

Lack of empathic response to others is a frequently noted deficit in
social interaction found in pervasive developmental disorders, particularly
autism. Sigman and Ruskin (1999) found that children with autism were
less likely to look at or respond to an adult who had appeared to injure
him or herself, as compared to children with developmental delays. It is
possible that lack of empathic responsiveness in persons with autism is
impacted by decreased attention to people, difficulty in reading facial expressions and nonverbal, social-emotional cues, as well as deficits in the
ability to think abstractly, resulting in an inability to represent another's
perspective symbolically, and consequently, an inability to experience another's emotions vicariously.

No data exist that address sex differences in empathy in children with
pervasive developmental disorders. As with facial expressions and nonverbal cues, an advantage in empathic ability could mitigate against more severe impairment, or girls with impairment in empathic ability may appear
more impaired relative to their same-sex peers, in comparison to impaired
boys and their same-sex peers.

Taking Another's Perspective

A host of studies in the developmental literature have tracked the
emergence of perspective-taking or "theory of mind," which refers to the
process by which children develop the sense that other people have
thoughts, intentions, motivations and emotions, and that these are largely
responsible for behavior (Baron-Cohen et al., 2000). This initial understanding, termed "first-order theory of mind," emerges between 3 and 4
years of age. More sophisticated "second-order theory of mind" skills entail understanding that one may act on one's belief about another's belief.
The development of the theory of mind (ToM) skills has been linked to language competency and the emergence of a coherent sense of self; these
skills are thought to underlie competent social behavior.

Theory of mind (ToM) skills appear to have cognitive and affective components, and competent perspective taking in social situations requires
the effective integration of these components. Several studies (Bosacki,
2000; Cutting & Dunn, 1999) have found that school-age and preadolescent girls and women show superior skill in perspective-taking and mental
state attribution as compared with boys and men, but others have reported
nonsignificant effects (Jenkins & Astington, 1996). While language ability
is clearly related to theory of mind skills in young children, other individual characteristics that may contribute to the development of these skills,
particularly in the affective domain, are not identified. For example, skill in

interpretation of nonverbal communicative cues might assist girls in taking another's perspective.

Persons with autism may have difficulty with theory of mind tasks (Baron-Cohen et al., 2000). With regard to sex differences, Nydén, Hjelmquist, and Gilberg (2001) found that girls with PDDs performed more poorly on a theory of mind task than boys with PDD, and suggested that girls may be more impaired in terms of social understanding than is immediately apparent. These data are preliminary, however, since the study relied on a very small sample, and the influence of general problem-solving ability was not examined in detail.

Research on the impact of teaching ToM skills to increase socially competent behavior is far from conclusive (Hadwin, Baron-Cohen, Howlin, & Hill, 1996; Ozonoff & Miller, 1995). Whether this is because teaching strategies have not been aimed toward generalization, or because ToM skills comprise only a small fraction of those skills needed for socially competent behavior is not clear. Nevertheless, since superiority in ToM tasks has been demonstrated in typically developing girls, the opportunity to examine components of this skill in relation to that demonstrated in boys may be relevant for developing more successful interventions.

Understanding of Context and Mores of Sex-Specific Groups

A crucial issue for the development of appropriate social skills is developing awareness and understanding of appropriate cultural and sex-specific conduct. This requires observation of contextual factors in social situations, along with an ability to model one's behavior after others with respect to language, communicative gestures, and other social communicative behaviors. For example, girls tend to socialize in dyads, and play is more cooperative and marked by companionship rather than competition during activities, as compared with boys (Crombie, 1988; Underwood, Hurley, Johanson, & Mosley, 1999). Social roles for boys include active, aggressive behavior for the communication of needs and wants, and girls are more likely to exhibit passive, nonverbal means of communication (Von Klitzing, Kelsay, Emde, Robinson, & Schmitz, 2000). Girls' play is more sedentary and more likely to involve verbal interaction, while boys' play is often more physical, loosely organized, competitive, and peer oriented (Benenson, Morash, & Petrakos, 1998; Huston, Carpenter, Atwater, & Johnson, 1986).

Differences in social styles between the sexes influence task demands in social situations (Benenson et al., 1993). Boys may need to negotiate in social situations involving more participants, which requires monitoring multiple interactions simultaneously and dealing with the unpredictability of a group. These demands can overwhelm children with PDDs, who function best in one-to-one interactions, in which the behavior of their social partner may be somewhat predictable. Affected girls may be able to function more effectively in early dyadic relationships with their same-sex peers, because although verbal skills are required, multiple, competing social demands are limited.

Individuals who fail to recognize these implicit contextual and sex-specific cues are more likely to stand out from others with respect to social behavior, and become less adept at appreciating what behaviors will help to ensure the acceptance of others. Deficits in these abilities are commonly observed in both males and females with PDDs likely because these skills require abstract thinking and an ability to generalize. McLennan et al. (1993) noted that, after the age of 10 years, autistic females showed more impairment in friendships than autistic males, and suggested that changes in social task demands for pubescent and adolescent girls made sustaining friendships more difficult. No data suggest that females with PDD show any advantage with respect to these skills, so affected females are as likely as males to appear odd in social situations, and are vulnerable to being ostracized socially.

The Development of Language and Communication Skills

Research regarding differences in formal language development show few differences between boys and girls, although girls speak earlier and have a greater lexicon as compared with boys during the early period of language learning, possibly due to girls' greater control over the articulatory apparatus (Karmiloff & Karmiloff-Smith, 2001). Research regarding language comprehension differences has yielded mixed results, with some studies claiming a female advantage while others report no differences. Other work to date shows a female advantage in social initiation and responsiveness using language (Hannah & Murachver, 1999; Thompson & Moore, 2000). While a female advantage in verbal fluency is noted throughout development, this advantage is slight, and some have argued that it has virtually no impact on differences in language use overall (Halpern, 2000). Moreover, these differences seem to be attenuated by the time of entry into school, so that no differences are noted between the sexes in formal language skills in later childhood. Of course, this would be expected since standardized tests are designed to minimize sex differences. Despite these data, sex differences in select aspects of verbal ability may be meaningful for some populations, particularly those groups in which language skills are delayed or deviant (Morisset, Barnard, & Booth, 1995).

More critical than the results of formal language testing is how language is used in social situations. It is here that sex differences impact social functioning. Differences in topic selection and communication style are noted between the sexes from the preschool years onward, and these stylistic differences progress throughout the school age years into adolescence (Anderson & Leaper, 1998; Raffaelli & Duckett, 1989). Beginning in preschool, girls talk more about emotions than boys and these differences remain stable as development progresses (Cervantes & Callanan, 1998). While the evidence is conflicting, some research shows that mothers speak more about emotions to girls than to boys during the period of language learning, and this may impact understanding of the causes of emotional states (Cervantes & Callanan, 1998). These differences may be part of a general approach toward gender socialization, in which the importance of interpersonal relatedness and emotional expressivity is emphasized for girls as opposed to boys.

These sex differences in language use reflect the very different social goals of males and females over the course of development (Hannah & Murachver, 1999). For boys and men, close relationships are typically established through a focus on object- and activity-related themes, such as hobbies, sports, or events. Conversation is likely to reflect these themes. In contrast, for girls and women, relationships are established through the sharing of thoughts and emotions, as well as the sharing of activities, and conversation is more likely to be focused on social themes. These sex differences in language use in the service of the development of relationships are found in children with mental retardation as well as nonretarded children (Wilkinson & Murphy, 1998).

For individuals with pervasive developmental disorders, appreciating these topic and communicative-style differences between the sexes is difficult, and deficits in understanding will be reflected in awkward, inefficient communication with others. Older girls with pervasive developmental disorders may have more difficulty establishing relationships through conversation than similarly affected boys. Boys and men may be able to converse with others with respect to hobbies or events, although the more informal kinds of communication, such as joking or teasing, may elude them. For girls, conversation regarding social themes may be nearly impossible to sustain, and informal conversation may be lacking as well. In this regard, same-sex socialization for adolescent girls with PDDs may present increasing challenges.

Regulation of Restricted and Repetitive Behaviors

Restricted and repetitive behaviors observed in pervasive developmental disorders may take the form of repetitive movements, such as hand and finger mannerisms, body rocking, spinning or pacing, or other repetitive movements of the whole body. Self-stimulatory behaviors, such as repetitive vocalizations or strategies to obtain visual stimulation, for example, watching objects spin, are included as well. Compulsive behavior is seen as well as "insistence on sameness" or a restricted repertoire of behaviors. For higher-functioning persons with autism, interests that are unusual in their focus and intensity may be noted, such as an interest in electric fans or in numbers associated with radio stations. While repetitive behaviors occur in nonautistic persons with developmental delay as well, there are a number of behaviors that are specific to autism, particularly compulsive behaviors (Bodfish, Symons, Parker, & Lewis, 1999).

The etiology of these symptoms in PDDs is not understood. The most prominent of the hypotheses regarding these behaviors is that they are employed by persons with PDDs to regulate internal states of arousal, or that repetitive behavior which begins during infancy is maintained in some form because the sensory feedback is in and of itself reinforcing (Turner, 1999). A corollary to these hypotheses has been that individuals with the lowest cognitive abilities engage in repetitive behavior with greater frequency than higher-functioning individuals. This appears accurate with respect to persons with mental retardation, but the data do not support this link for persons with autism (Bodfish et al., 2000; Turner, 1999). What is most clear is that the range of restricted and repetitive behaviors observed in these disorders likely has multiple determinants. Each of these hypotheses is considered here with respect to sex differences in order to consider how these behaviors may be different between males and females with PDDs or how differences may elucidate the pathophysiology of these behaviors.

The development of stereotypic behavior to regulate internal states of arousal is pertinent to the study of sex differences since boys show much more difficulty regulating these states as infants and young children as compared to girls (Kochanska, Murray, & Harlan, 2000). As infants and young babies, boys show a lower tolerance for stimuli, they are more easily upset, show more difficulty using self-soothing strategies, and take longer to recover when upset as compared with girls (Weinberg, Tronick, Cohn, & Olsen, 1999). As toddlers, boys show greater proneness toward anger and a higher activity level as compared with girls, while girls show greater inhibitory control (Goldsmith, Buss, & Lemery, 1997). If the development of some repetitive behaviors occurs as an attempt to regulate internal states, one would expect that boys with PDD would show significantly more of these behaviors than girls with PDD of the same age and cognitive, communicative, and social impairment. A number of studies have shown this to be the case. Boys with autism show more abnormal movements than girls (Tsai et al., 1981), and more unusual body and object use (Lord et al., 1982; Volkmar et al., 1988).

With respect to the development of repetitive behavior in autism, one must consider that repetitive movements and ritualistic behavior occur in typically developing young babies and young children. Exploration of the sensory aspects of the environment is the earliest form of play for young babies, and the development of rituals for daily behavior is a normal aspect of development in toddlers and preschool children (Evans et al., 1997). However, as development progresses, the focus on sensory aspects of the environment is replaced by interest in cause and effect, and then symbolic kinds of play. For children with autism, impairment in conceptual thinking abilities may constrain their ability to develop more sophisticated forms of play. Sensory stimulation may serve as the only form of play available to these children.

The development of rituals for daily living in young children (e.g., needing to always have a particular color cup or needing to get dressed in a particular sequence) is most prominent at approximately 2 years of age. These rituals are thought to provide the child with a sense of control and security as they become increasingly exposed to novel people and activities (Evans, Gray, & Leckman, 1998). As children develop an understanding of how events occur in their world, tight adherence to ritualistic behaviors seems to abate in most typically developing children by about 4 years of age. For children with PDDs, it is conceivable that these behaviors might continue well beyond this age precisely because the children do not develop an increased understanding of the world around them. Limited comprehension of language, impaired expressive communication abilities, and reduced capacity to think abstractly will impede the child's ability to increase his understanding of how and why events occur as they do. Thus, a change in routine, for example, from one route for driving to school to another, may be perceived as confusing and disturbing to a child with PDD.

With respect to sex differences, Evans et al. (1997) did not find that girls and boys differed in the number or type of routines and ritualistic behavior during early childhood. If these behaviors are equivalent in type and intensity in typical children, this raises the question of whether boys with PDDs tend to rely on these behaviors for stimulation or to reduce arousal to a greater degree as development progresses, whereas girls are more easily able to reduce their reliance on these behaviors. This question is unexplored and awaits further research. At present, implications for intervention would not be different between boys and girls. Intervention typically takes the form of using comprehensive behavioral strategies to reduce or replace these behaviors.

IMPLICATIONS FOR ASSESSMENT AND TREATMENT

No neurobiological marker exists for the identification of pervasive developmental disorders. Diagnosis of a PDD is best made by a clinician with special expertise in this area. Difficulties in social functioning are seen in a variety of childhood disorders including learning disabilities, language disorders, mental retardation, attention deficit hyperactivity disorder, and anxiety disorders. Since the social difficulties that occur as part of these disorders can become compounded over the course of development, in some situations the symptoms of social impairment observed in a particular child may create diagnostic confusion, particularly when the child is seen at only one point in time. However, in PDD the *quality* of social relatedness is markedly different from the quality of relatedness seen in other disorders. Experience with this population in a clinical setting will help the clinician make these crucial distinctions.

There are a number of screening instruments and more extensive diagnostic instruments available to assist with diagnosis. Standardization samples for these instruments typically included more boys than girls, at a ratio of approximately 3:1 (Table 2). The screening instruments have not been designed as an exhaustive inventory of all possible manifestations of symptomatology, therefore clinicians should approach the "cut-off" score for categorical diagnosis thoughtfully, since some children may be significantly impaired in one domain; for example, the social domain, yet not meet criteria in another domain, for example, restricted and repetitive behaviors. With regard to the assessment of girls, impairment may manifest differently. For example, while social impairment may be significant, the presence of restricted interests and repetitive behavior may not be as prominent. In this situation it would be important to err on the side of caution, and refer the child for more extensive assessment, since other, more subtle signs of impairment may become evident over time.

Table 2. Instruments used in the assessment of pervasive developmental disorders

Instrument	Purpose	Standardization sample	Comments
Autism Behavior Checklist (ABC) [Krug, Avrick, & Almond, 1980]	Screening	2,000 children No data on sex ratio of sample provided	Checklist of 57 items sampling a range of behaviors associated with autism, completed by parents. Scores of 67 or above support an autism diagnosis.
Childhood Autism Rating Scale (CARS) (Schopler, Reichler, De Vellis, & Daly, 1980)	Screening	500 children M:F ratio = 3:1	Completed by the clinician during direct observation of the child. Scores are totaled to indicate severe, moderate, or mild autism, or not autistic.
Checklist for Autism in Toddlers (CHAT) (Baron-Cohen, Cox, Baird, Swettenham, Nightengale, Morgan, Drew & Charman, 1996)	Screening	160,000 children M:F ratio = 1.05:1	Nine items asked of parents and five items completed by caregivers to identify children at risk. Sensitivity of 38% and specificity of 98%.
Autism Diagnostic Interview-R (ADI-R) (Lord, Rutter & LeCouteur, 1994)	Diagnostic Interview	M:F ratio = 3:1	Completed by trained interviewer. Scores are assigned to individual items and an algorithm is derived which predicts the likelihood of an autism or PDD spectrum diagnosis.
Autism Screening Questionnaire (ASQ) (Berument, Rutter, Lord, Pickles, & Bailey, 1999)	Screening	200 individuals M:F ratio for autism = 2.8:1, M:F ratio for other PDDs = 6.7:1	Males showed higher overall scores in the category of "other PDDs" (not autism).
Autism Diagnostic Observation Schedule—G (ADOS-G) (Lord, Risi, Lambrecht, Cook, Leventhal, DiLavore, Pickles, & Rutter (2000).	Diagnostic Assessment	250 children Male: Female ratio = 3.33:1	Behavior is rated with respect to that observed in pervasive developmental disorders, particularly autism and PDD-NOS. An algorithm is derived which predicts an autism or PDD-NOS diagnosis.

The most extensive diagnostic instruments available are the Autism Diagnostic Interview—Revised (ADI-R) (Lord, Rutter, & Le Couteur, 1994) and the Autism Diagnostic Observation Schedule—Generic (ADOS-G) (Lord, Risi, Lambrecht, Cook, & Leventhal, 1994). The ADI-R is an extensive developmental interview designed to separate children with developmental delays from those with pervasive developmental disorders. Initial studies to establish validity of the instrument included only one female for every four-to-seven boys (Le Couter et al., 1989), and a more recent study with a sex ratio of 4:1 did not consider sex differences in presentation (Lord et al., 1997). While these ratios mirror current epidemiological statistics, broader coverage of syndrome presentation in girls would be preferable.

The Autism Diagnostic Observation Schedule—Generic is a play or semistructured interview session in which the examiner uses structured "presses" to evoke social and communicative behavior from the participant (Lord et al., 1994). The ADOS-G is unique in that the use of tasks to promote social interaction allows the examiner to observe the quality of impairment, rather than relying on third-party report. Initial studies used in the development of this instrument included many fewer girls than boys (Lord et al., 1994). The disparity in sex ratio resulted in significant sex-by-symptom domain score effects, which the authors suggested was due to unequal sample sizes as opposed to real differences in symptom presentation.

At the present time, there is no body of gender-specific research or clinical information to guide in the assessment of girls with pervasive developmental disorders, or those suspected of having a pervasive developmental disorder. The clinician must rely on the best practices for assessment for children with PDDs, incorporating knowledge of sex differences in social and communicative behavior as they apply to the particular child (see Volkmar & Cohen, 1997). Assessment must include developmental history with parents, in addition to direct assessment of the child with respect to social and communicative behavior. Ultimately, the judgment regarding the quality of the social or communicative impairment is based on the clinician's ability to elicit these behaviors and compare them to normative behavior in children of the same age and sex. Since these normative behaviors differ with respect to sex, the assessment will be informed by greater knowledge regarding these differences.

Most germane to the identification of girls with pervasive developmental disorders is that diagnostic assignment should be made with a heightened sensitivity to the fact that sex differences in social and communicative context may make a difference in the way symptoms are manifest. The quality and severity of impairment should be considered in the context of the child's social world, as well as in comparison to other children for whom the diagnosis has been established. In this way, one guards against using a mental "prototype" for diagnosis that has been constructed based on experience with affected boys only.

Evaluation should include either a play session for younger children, or an interview for more verbally adept children. Cognitive evaluation is important, and instruments should be chosen that minimize language abilities, since this is an area of weakness for all children with PDDs. For a more comprehensive review of assessment procedures see Sparrow (1997). With regard to sex differences, the clinician should keep in mind the different uses of communication in boys versus girls, and determine the extent to which the child conforms to these communication styles and topics. Evaluation of the use of eye contact, recognition of facial expressions and nonverbal cues, ability to take the perspective of the other, empathy, and recognition of contextual cues and appropriate behavior for one's sex and age should be included.

A careful developmental history will assist the clinician to make judgments regarding social interests and communicative skills. In particular, the clinician should consider the multiple social contexts in which the child functions when making judgments about the appropriateness of social or communicative behavior. Adaptive functioning is important to consider, and the child's social skills, and daily living skills need to be examined with regard to the level of cognitive functioning.

With respect to repetitive and restricted behaviors, it is possible that affected girls will not show these behaviors to the same degree or intensity as affected boys; thus it is critical to assess a girl's social and communication abilities thoroughly in order to avoid missing girls with severe a social and communication disability who do not show the more obvious unusual behaviors or restricted interests. These deficits will need to be clearly documented to secure services for girls in particular, since they may not display the kinds of disruptive behavior that would ordinarily bring a child to the attention of school personnel.

All children with PDDs should be assessed with respect to comorbid conditions, and the clinician should be aware that obsessive-compulsive disorder and depression are frequently noted in children with PDDs, particularly in adolescents (Martin, Scahill, Klin & Volkmar, 1999). It is possible that these increased affective and anxiety symptoms occur as the affected individual becomes more aware of the ways in which they are different from their peers. With regard to girls, depression is a particular risk, especially post-puberty.

With regard to intervention, sex-specific responses should be considered. For example, in an open-label study of fluvoxamine for the treatment of compulsive behaviors in children and adolescents with PDDs, girls responded significantly better as compared with boys (Martin, Koenig, Anderson, & Scahill, 2003). This ad hoc finding was consistent with two reports of higher female versus male response rates in adult patients treated with SSRIs for depression (Kornstein et al., 2000) and posttraumatic stress disorder (Davidson, Rothbaum, van der Kolk, Sikes, & Farfel, 2001). These findings highlight the need to explore differential responses to treatment between males and females for the purpose of maximizing intervention and elucidating neurobiological mechanisms.

Beyond these preliminary differences in medication response, there are no data to support differences in the intervention approach between girls and boys with PDDs. In designing a treatment plan for a girl with a PDD, it is important to adapt established behavioral or environmental strategies with regard to differences in how the child might learn, or how the child might be expected to behave in particular situations. Social skills training, including teaching pragmatic communication skills, reading of social skills, and developing social relationships should be designed with sex-specific behaviors in mind, given the age of the child. Appropriate social behavior for teenage boys and girls in same-sex or mixed-sex groups is very different, and these kinds of subtle differences will not be apparent to an adolescent with a PDD.

In summary, understanding the way sex differences may affect intervention in persons with PDD is very limited at this juncture. Constantino and Todd (in press) have suggested that girls may be more amenable to environmental influences with respect to the molding of social behavior. These data are preliminary but are highlighted here because as work progresses in this area, relevant information may be gleaned with respect to intervention in girls.

FUTURE DIRECTIONS

It is interesting to note that despite the startling disparity in prevalence between girls and boys with pervasive developmental disorders, this topic has been the subject of a very modest body of research. Early on in the history of the research of these disorders, so little was understood regarding genetic and brain mechanisms that it is likely that the pursuit of an understanding of the role of sex differences in the etiology of the disorder was considered less of a priority than identifying fundamental mechanisms common to all affected persons. At present, however, progress in epidemiology, neurobiology, and phenomenology in the study of pervasive developmental disorders has reached a critical point in which more subtle questions can and should be addressed. Moreover, given the large body of psychological and biological literature regarding sex differences in typically developing children, these questions can be pursued in the context of a broader framework.

With regard to girls and boys with these disorders, differences in presentation need to be examined more rigorously. Identified girls should always be considered with respect to typically developing girls of the same age and cognitive ability, not to typically developing or affected boys. If sex differences have no real impact on the presentation of the disorder, this strategy should not change the outcome of case identification and incidence rates to any great degree.

Clear evidence of structural and functional differences in the brain between males and females lends support to the view that sex-specific behavior could impact the manifestation of symptoms and the developmental trajectory in PDD. Future research in functional brain imaging should consider these sex differences in the investigation of all structures and circuitry relevant to social or communication processing, and in the processes involved in the regulation of restricted and repetitive behaviors.

These studies need to be conducted with an appreciation that a lack of a sex difference in the size of a structure, or even the size or number of cells within a region, does not rule out the possibility of developmentally programmed sex differences in neurochemistry or in the neuroanatomy of synaptic connections (McEwen, 1999). The temporal sequence of the influence of sex hormones on the growth and development of the brain should be considered as well, as that may be informative regarding a critical period during fetal development during which particular insults might occur (Pilgrim & Hutchison, 1994).

Related to sex differences in neurobiology, differential response to intervention in girls as compared to boys should be explored. As work in psychopharmacology has shown in several disorders, females and males may show a different response to a particular class of medications. Similarly, responses to other kinds of intervention, specifically behavioral intervention are conceivable, although much work needs to be done to clarify this issue. Overall, the exploration of sex differences in pervasive developmental disorders will only enrich the existing body of knowledge regarding the pathophysiology of the disorder, and the best methods for intervention.

ACKNOWLEDGEMENTS. The authors would like to acknowledge the help and support of the following individuals: Fred Volkmar, M.D., Robert Schultz, Ph.D., Andrés Martin, M.D., Elena Grigorenko, Ph.D., James Leckman, M.D., Ami Klin, Ph.D., Robert Koenig, Ph.D., Tammy Babitz, M.A., and Rosalind Oti, B.S.

REFERENCES

Acerra, F., Burnod, Y., & de Schonen, S. (2002). Modelling aspects of face processing in early infancy. *Developmental Science, 5,* 98–117.

American Psychiatric Association. (1994). *Diagnostic and Statistical Manual of Mental Disorders.* Washington, DC: American Psychiatric Association.

Amir, R. E., Van de Veyver, I., Wan, M., Tran, C., Franke, U., & Zoghbi, H. Y. (1999). Rett syndrome is caused by mutations in X linked MECP2, encoding methyl-CpG-binding protein 2. *Nature Genetics, 23,* 185–188.

Anderson, K. J., & Leaper, C. (1998). Meta-analyses of gender effects on conversational interruption: Who, what, when, where, and how. *Sex Roles, 39,* 225–252.

Aylward, E. H., Minshew, N. J., Goldstein, F., Honeycutt, N. A., Augustine, A. M., Yates, K. O., et al. (1999). MRI volumes of amygdala and hippocampus in non-mentally retarded autistic adolescents and adults. *Neurology, 53,* 2145–2150.

Bachevalier, J. (1994). Medial temporal lobe structures and autism: A review of clinical and experimental findings. *Neuropsychologia, 32,* 627–648.

Baron-Cohen, S., Cox, A., Baird, G., Swettenham, J., Nightengale, N., Morgan, K., et al. (1996). Psychological markers in the detection of autism in infancy in a large population. *British Journal of Psychiatry, 168,* 158–163.

Baron-Cohen, S., & Hammer, J. (1997). Is autism an extreme form of the "male brain?" *Advances in Infancy Research, 11,* 193–217.

Baron-Cohen, S., Tager-Flusberg, H., & Cohen, D. J. (2000). *Understanding other minds: Perspectives from autism* (2nd ed.). Oxford: Oxford University Press.

Benenson, J. F. (1993). Greater preference among females than males for dyadic interaction in early childhood. *Child Development, 64,* 544–555.

Benenson, J. F., Morash, D., & Petrakos, H. (1998). Gender differences in emotional closeness between preschool children and their mothers. *Sex Roles, 38*, 975–985.

Berument, S. K., Rutter, M., Lord, C., Pickles, A., & Bailey, A. (1999). Autism Screening Questionnaire: Diagnostic validity. *The British Journal of Psychiatry, 175*, 444–451.

Bodfish, J. W., Symons, F. J., Parker, D. E., & Lewis, M. (2000). Varieties of repetitive behavior in autism: Comparisons to mental retardation. *Journal of Autism and Developmental Disorders, 30*, 237–243.

Bosacki, S. L. (2000). Theory of mind and self-concept in preadolescents: Links with gender and language. *Journal of Educational Psychology, 92*, 709–717.

Braverman, M., Fein, D., Lucci, D., & Waterhouse, L. (1989). Affect comprehension in children with pervasive developmental disorders. *Journal of Autism and Developmental Disorders, 19*, 301–315.

Brown, J. R., & Dunn, J. (1996). Continuities in emotion understanding from three to six years. *Child Development, 67*, 789–802.

Cervantes, C. A., & Callanan, M. A. (1998). Labels and explanations in mother-child emotion talk: Age and gender differentiation. *Developmental Psychology, 34*, 88–98.

Collaer, M. L. & Hines, M. (1995). Human behavioral sex differences: A role for gonadal hormones during early development? *Psychological Bulletin, 118*, 55–107.

Constantino, J. N., Przybeck, T., Friesen, D., & Todd, R. D. (2000). Reciprocal social behavior in children with and without pervasive developmental disorders. *Journal of Developmental and Behavioral Pediatrics, 21*, 2–11.

Constantino, J. N., & Todd, R. D. (2003). Autistic traits in the general population: A twin study. 60, 524–530.

Crombie, G. (1988). Gender differences: Implications for social skills assessment and training. *Journal of Clinical Child Psychology, 17*, 116–120.

Cutting, A., & Dunn, J. (1999). Theory of mind, emotion understanding, language and family background: Individual differences and interrelations. *Child Development, 70*, 853–865.

Davidson, J. R., Rothbaum, B. O., van der Kolk, B. A., Sikes, C. R., & Farfel, G. M. (2001). Multicenter, double-blind comparison of sertraline and placebo in the treatment of posttraumatic stress disorder. *Archives of General Psychiatry 58*, 485–92.

De Courten-Myers, G. (1999). The human cerebral cortex: Gender differences in structure and function. *Journal of Neuropathology and Experimental Neurology, 58*, 217–226.

de Haan, M. (2001). The neuropsychology of face processing during infancy and childhood. In C. A. Nelson & M. Luciana (Eds.), *Handbook of developmental cognitive neuroscience.* Cambridge, MA: MIT Press.

Eisenberg, N., & Fabes, R. A. (1995). The relation of young children's vicarious emotional responding to social competence, regulation, and emotionality. *Cognition and Emotion, 9*, 203–228.

Eisenberg, N., Fabes, R. A., Karbon, M., Murphy, B. C., Carlo, G., & Wosinski, M. (1996). Relations of school children's comforting behavior to empathy- related reactions and shyness. *Social Development, 5*, 330–351.

Eisenberg, N., Fabes, R. A., Murphy, B., Maszk, P., Smith, M., & Karbon, M. (1995). The role of emotionality and regulation in children's social functioning—A longitudinal-study. *Child Development, 66*, 1360–1384.

Ehrhardt, A., Meyer-Bahlburg, H. F. L., Rosen, L. R., Feldman, J. F., Veridiano, N. P., Elkin, E. J., et al. (1989). The development of gender-related behavior in females following prenatal exposure to diethylstilbestrol (DES). *Hormones and Behavior, 23*, 526–541.

Ervin-Tripp. (2001). The place of gender in developmental pragmatics: cultural factors. *Research on Language and Social Interaction, 34*, 131–147.

Evans, D., Gray, F. L., & Leckman, J. (1998). The rituals, fears and phobias of young children: Insights from development, psychopathology and neurobiology. *Child Psychiatry and Human Development, 29*, 261–276.

Evans, D., Leckman, J., Carter, A., Reznick, J. S., Henshaw, D., King, R., et al. (1997). Ritual, habit, and perfectionism: The prevalence and development of compulsive-like behaviors in normal young children. *Child Development, 68*, 58–68.

Fombonne, E. (1999). The epidemiology of autism: A review. *Psychological Medicine, 29*, 769–786.

Fombonne, E. (2001). Prevalence of pervasive developmental disorders in the British Nationwide Survey of Child Mental Health. *Journal of the American Academy of Child and Adolescent Psychiatry, 40*, 820–827.

Fombonne E, & Tidmarsh L. (2003). Epidemiologic data on Asperger's disorder. *Child and Adolescent Psychiatric Clinics of North America 12*, 15–21.

Giedd, J. N., Snell, J. W., Lange, N., Rajapakse, J. C., Casey, B. J., Kozuch, P. L., et al. (1996). Quantitative magnetic resonance imaging of human brain development: ages 4–18. *Cerebral Cortex, 6*, 551–560.

Goldsmith, H. H., Buss, K. A., & Lemery, K. S. (1997). Toddler and childhood temperament: Expanded content, stronger genetic evidence, new evidence for the importance of environment. *Developmental Psychology, 33*, 891–905.

Graachev, I. D., & Apkarian, A. V. (2000). Chemical heterogeneity of the living brain: A proton MR spectroscopy study on the effects of sex, age, and brain region. *Neuroimage, 11*, 554–563.

Grossman, M., & Wood, W. (1993). Sex differences in intensity of emotional experience: A social role interpretation. *Journal of Personal and Social Psychology, 65*(5), 1010–1022.

Hadwin, P., Baron-Cohen, S., Howlin, P. & Hill, K. (1997). Does teaching theory of mind have an effect on the ability to develop conversation in children with autism? *Journal of Autism & Developmental Disorders, 27*, 519–537.

Hagberg. (1993). Rett syndrome: clinical peculiarities and biological mysteries. *Acta Paediatrica, 84*, 971–976.

Halpern, D. F. (2000). *Sex differences in cognitive abilities* (3rd ed.). Mahwah, NJ: Erlbaum.

Hannah, A., & Murachver, T. (1999). Gender and conversational style as predictors of conversational behavior. *Journal of Language and Social Psychology, 18*, 153–174.

Huston, A. C., Carpenter, C. J., Atwater, J. B., & Johnson, L. M. (1986). Gender, adult structuring of activities, and social behavior in middle childhood. *Child Development, 57*, 1200–1209.

Jenkins, J., & Astington, J. (1996). Cognitive factors and family structure associated with theory of mind development in young children. *Developmental Psychology, 32*, 70–78.

Karmiloff, K., & Karmiloff-Smith, A. (2001). Learning about the meaning of words. *In* K. Karmiloff & A. Karmiloff-Smith (Eds.), *Pathways to language from fetus to adolescent.* Cambridge, MA: Harvard University Press.

Kelly, S. J., Ostrowski, N. L., & Wilson, M. A. (1999). Gender differences in brain and behavior: Hormonal and neural bases. *Pharmacology, Biochemistry, and Behavior, 64*, 655–664.

Kilgore, W. D., Oki, M., Yugelun-Todd, D. A. (2001). Sex specific developmental changes in amygdala response to affective faces. *Neuroreport, 12*, 427–433.

Kimura, D. (2000). *Sex and cognition.* Cambridge, MA: MIT Press.

Klin, A., Sparrow, S., de Bildt, A., Cicchetti, D. V., Cohen, D. J., & Volkmar, F. (1999). A normed study of face recognition in autism and related disorders. *Journal of Autism and Developmental Disorders, 29*, 499–508.

Klin A., & Volkmar F. R. (2003). Asperger syndrome: Diagnosis and external validity. *Child & Adolescent Psychiatric Clinics of North America, 12*, 1–13.

Kochanska, G., Murray, K. T., & Harlan, E. T. (2000). Effortful control in early childhood: Continuity and change, antecedents and implications for social development. *Developmental Psychology, 36*, 220–232.

Koenig, K., Tsatsanis, K. D., & Volkmar, F. (2001). Neurobiology and genetics of autism. In J. A. Burack, T. Charman, N. Yirmiya, & P. R. Zelazo, (Eds.), *The development of autism: Perspectives from theory and research.* Mahwah, NJ: Erlbaum.

Koop, S., & Gilberg, C. (1992). Girls with social deficits and learning problems: Autism, atypical asperger syndrome or a variant of these conditions. *European Child and Adolescent Psychiatry, 1*, 89–99.

Kornstein, S. G., Schatzberg, A. F., Thase, M. E., Yonkers, K. A., McCullough, J. P., Keitner, G. I., et al. (2000), Gender differences in treatment response to sertraline versus imipramine in chronic depression. *American Journal of Psychiatry 157*, 1445–1452.

Krug, D. A., Avrick, J., & Almond, P. (1980). Behavior checklist for identifying severely hand-icapped individuals with high levels of autistic behavior. *Journal of Child Psychology and Psychiatry, 21,* 221–229.

Le Couteur, A., Rutter, M., Lord, C., Rios, P., Robertson, S., Holgrafer, M., et al. (1989). Autism Diagnostic Interview: a standardized investigator based instrument. *Journal of Autism and Develomental Disorders, 19,* 363–387.

Le Grand, R., Mondloch, C. J., Maurer, D., & Brent, H. P. (2001). Neuroperception—Early visual experience and face processing. *Nature, 410,* 890–890.

Leibenluft, E. (1996). Sex is complex. *American Journal of Psychiatry, 153,* 969–972.

Lord, C., Pickles, A., McLennan, J., Rutter, M., Bregman, J., Folstein, S., Fombonne, E., Leboyer, M. & Minshew, N. (1997). Diagnosing autism: Analysis of data from the Autism Diagnostic Interview. *Journal of Autism and Develomental Disorders, 27,* 501–517.

Lord, C., Risi, S., Lambrecht, L., Cook, E. H., Leventhal, B. L. DiLavore, P. C., Pickles, A., & Rutter, M. (2000). The Autism Diagnostic Observations Schedule-Generic: A standard measure of social and communication deficits associated with the spectrum of autism. *Journal of Autism and Developmental Disorders, 30,* 205–223.

Lord, C., Rutter, M., & Le Couteur, A. (1994). Autism Diagnostic Interview–Revised: A revised version of a diagnostic interview for caregivers of individuals with possible pervasive de-velopmental disorders. *Journal of Autism and Develomental Disorders, 24,* 659–685.

Lord, C., Schopler, E., & Revicki, D. (1982). Sex differences in autism. *Journal of Autism and Developmental Disorders, 12,* 317–330.

Lotter, V. (1966). Epidemiology of autistic conditions in young children: I. Prevalence. *Social Psychiatry, 1,* 124–137.

Maccoby, E. E., & Jacklin, C. N. (1974). *The psychology of sex differences.* Stanford, CA: Stanford University Press.

Malatesta, C. Z., & Haviland, J. M. (1982). Learning display rules: The socialization of emotion expression in infancy. *Child Development, 53,* 991–1003.

Martin, A., Koenig, K., Anderson, G., & Scahill, L. (2003). Low-dose fluvoxamine treatment of children and adolescents with pervasive developmental disorders: A prospective, open-label study. *Journal of Autism and Pervasive Developmental Disorders, 33,* 77–85.

Martin, A., Scahill, L., Klin, A., & Volkmar, F. R. (1999). Higher-functioning pervasive develop-mental disorders: Rates and patterns of psychotropic drug use. *Journal of the American Academy of Child and Adolescent Psychiatry, 38,* 1–9.

McClure, E. (2000). A meta-analytic review of sex differences in facial expression processing and their development in infants, children, and adolescents. *Psychological Bulletin, 126,* 424–453.

McEwen, B. (1999). Permanence of brain sex differences and structural plasticity of the adult brain. *Proceedings of the National Academy of Science, 96,* 7128–7130.

McEwen, B. S., Alves, S. E., Bulloch, K., & Weiland, N. G. (1998). Clinically relevant basic sci-ence studies of gender differences and sex hormone effects. *Psychopharmacology Bulletin, 34,* 251–259.

McLennan, J. D., Lord, C., & Schopler, E. (1993). Sex differences in higher functioning people with autism. *Journal of Autism and Developmental Disorders, 23,* 217–227.

Morisset, C. E., Barnard, K. E., & Booth, C. L. (1995). Toddlers' language development: Sex differences within social risk. *Development Psychology, 31,* 851–865.

Nydén, A., Hjelmquist, E, & Gillberg, C. (2000). Autism spectrum and attention-deficit in girls. Some neuropsychological aspects. *European Child and Adolescent Psychiatry, 9,* 180–185.

Ozonoff, S., & Miller, J. N. (1995). Teaching theory of mind: A new approach to social skills training for individuals with autism. *Journal of Autism and Developmental Disorders, 25,* 415–433.

Ozonoff, S., Pennington, B., & Rogers, S. J. (1990). Are there emotion perception deficits in young autistic children? *Journal of Child Psychology and Psychiatry, 31,* 343–361.

Pickles, A., Bolton, P., MacDonald, H., Bailey, A., Le Couteur, A., Sim, C.-H., et al. (1995). Latent-Class analysis of recurrence risk for complex phenotypes with selection and mea-surement error: A twin and family history study of autism. *American Journal of Human Genetics, 57,* 717–726.

Pilgrim C, & Hutchison JB. (1994). Developmental regulation of sex differences in the brain: Can the role of gonadal steroids be redefined? *Neuroscience 60*, 843–855.

Pilowsky, T., Yirmiya, N., Shulman, C., & Dover, R. (1998). The Autism Diagnostic Interview-Revised and the Childhood Autism Rating Scale: Differences between diagnostic systems and comparison between genders. *Journal of Autism and Developmental Disorders, 28*, 143–151.

Piven, J., Bailey, J., Ranson, B. J. & Ardnt, S. (1998). No difference in hippocampus volume detected on magnetic resonance imaging in autistic individuals. *Journal of Autism and Developmental Disorders, 28*, 105–110.

Raffaelli, M., & Duckett, E. (1989). "We were just talking...": Conversations in early adolescence. *Journal of Youth and Adolescence, 18*, 567–582.

Schneider F, Habel U, Kessler C, Salloum JB, & Posse S. (2000). Gender differences in regional cerebral activity during sadness. *Human Brain Mapping, 9*, 226–238.

Schopler, E., Reichler, R. J., De Vellis, R. F., & Daly, K. (1980). Toward objective classification of Childhood Autism: Childhood Autism Rating Scale (CARS). *Journal of Autism and Developmental Disorders, 10*, 91–103.

Schultz, R. T., Romanski, E., & Tsatsansis, K. D. (2000). Neurofunctional models of Asperger's syndrome. In A. Klin, F. R. Volkmar, & S. Sparrow (Eds.), *Asperger syndrome* (pp. 172–209). New York: Guilford Press.

Schwartzman, J. S., Zatz, M., Vasquez, L. R., Grimes, R. R., Koiffman, C. P., Fridman, C., et al. (1999). Rett syndrome in a boy with a 47, XXY karotype (letter). *American Journal of Human Genetics, 64*, 1781–1785.

Sigman, M., & Ruskin, E. (1999). Continuity and change in the social competence of children with autism, Down syndrome, and developmental delays. *Monographs for the Society for Research in Child Development, Serial, 256, 64*.

Sparrow, S. (1997). Developmentally based assessments. In D. J. Cohen & F. R. Volkmar (Eds.), *Handbook of autism and pervasive developmental disorders* (2nd ed., pp. 441–447). New York: Wiley.

Szatmari, P., MacLean, J. E., Jones, M., Bryson, S. E., Zwaigenbaum, L., Bartolucci, G., et al. (2000). The familial aggregation of the lesser variant in biological and nonbiological relatives of PDD probands: A family history study. *Journal of Child Psychology and Psychiatry 41*, 579–586.

Thompson, R. B., & Moore, K. (2000). Collaborative speech in dyadic problem solving: Evidence for preschool gender differences in early pragmatic development. *Journal of Language and Social Psychology, 19*, 248–255.

Tsai, L. Y., & Beisler, J. M. (1983). The development of sex differences in infantile autism. *British Journal of Psychiatry, 142*, 373–378.

Tsai, L., Stewart, M. A., & August, G. (1981). Implication of sex differences in the familial transmission of infantile autism. *Journal of Autism and Developmental Disorders, 11*, 165–173.

Towbin, K. (1997). Pervasive developmental disorder not otherwise specified. In D. Cohen & F. Volkmar (Eds.), *Handbook of autism and pervasive developmental disorders* (2nd ed.). New York: Wiley.

Turner, M. (1999). Annotation: Repetitive behavior in autism: A review of psychological research. *Journal of Child Psychology and Psychiatry, 40*, 839–849.

Underwood, M. K., Hurley, J. C., Johanson, C. A., & Mosley, J. E. (1999). An experimental, observational investigation of children's responses to peer provocation: Developmental and gender differences in middle childhood. *Child Development, 70*, 1428–1446.

Vogel, S. (1990). Gender differences in intelligence, language, visual-motor abilities, and academic acheivement in students with learning disabilities: A review of the literature. *Journal of Learning Disabilities, 23*, 44–52.

Volkmar, F., Cicchetti, D., Dykens, E., Sparrow, S., Leckman, J., & Cohen, D. (1988). An evaluation of the Autism Behavior Checklist. *Journal of Autism and Developmental Disorders, 18*, 81–97.

Volkmar, F., & Cohen, D. J. (Eds.). (1997). *Handbook of autism and pervasive developmental disorders* (2nd ed.). New York: Wiley.

Volkmar, F., Klin, A., Marans, W. & Cohen, D. (1997). Childhood disintegrative disorder. In Volkmar, F. & Cohen, D. J. (Eds.), (1997). *Handbook of autism and pervasive developmental disorders* (2nd ed.). New York: Wiley.

Volkmar, F., Klin, A., Siegel, B., Szatmari, P., Lord, C., Campbell, M., et al. (1994). Field trial for autistic disorder in DSM-IV. *American Journal of Psychiatry, 151,* 1361–1367.

Volkmar, F. R., Szatmari, P., & Sparrow, S. S. (1993). Sex differences in pervasive developmental disorders. *Journal of Autism and Developmental Disorders, 23,* 579–591.

Von Klitzing, K., Kelsay, K., Emde, R. N., Robinson, J., & Schmitz, S. (2000). Gender-specfic characteristics of 5-year-olds' play narratives and associations with behavior ratings. *Journal of the American Academy of Child and Adolescent Psychiatry, 39,* 1017–1023.

Weinberg, M. K., Tronick, E. Z., Cohn, J. F., & Olsen, K. L. (1999). Gender differences in emotional expressivity and self-regulations during early infancy. *Developmental Psychology, 35,* 175–188.

Wilkinson, K. M., & Murphy, N. A. (1998). References to people in the communications of female and male youths with mental retardation. *Research in Developmental Disabilities, 19,* 201–224.

Wing, L. (1981a). Asperger's syndrome: A clinical account. *Psychological Medicine, 11,* 115–129.

Wing, L. (1981b). Language, social, and cognitive impairments in autism and severe mental retardation. *Journal of Autism and Develomental Disorders, 11,* 31–44.

Wing, L., & Gould, J. (1979). Severe impairments of social interactions and associated abnormalities in children: Epidemiology and classification. *Journal of Autism and Development Disorders, 9,* 11–29.

World Health Organization. (1992). *The Tenth Revision of the International Classification of Diseases and Related Health Problems (ICD-10).* Geneva: WHO.

Yeargin-Allsopp, M., Rice, C., Karapurkar, T., Doernberg, N., Boyle, C., & Murphy, C. (2003). Prevalence of autism in a US metropolitan area. *Journal of the American Medical Association, 289,* 87–89.

Zahn-Waxler, C., Cole, P., Welsh, J., & Fox, N. A. (1995). Psychophysiological correlates of empathy and prosocial behaviors in preschool children with behavior problems. *Developmental Psychopathology, 7,* 27–48.

Zahn-Waxler, C., Radke-Yarrow, M., Wagner, E., & Chapman, M. (1992). Development of concern for others. *Developmental Psychology, 28,* 126–136.

8

Problems of Girls and Young Women with Mental Retardation (Intellectual Disabilities)

ROBERT M. HODAPP and ELISABETH M. DYKENS

The issues of girls and young women—or even of sex differences in general—within mental retardation are woefully underexplored. To this day, we continue to lack even the most basic information about the course, associated features, and links of mental retardation to emotional or behavioral problems or other psychiatric diagnoses in girls. In specific areas, researchers and practitioners are uncertain whether the "usual" sex-difference findings concerning behavioral or emotional problems also show themselves when children have intellectual disabilities. Yet at the same time, we have enough glimmerings to proclaim the importance of this area for future work.

The task before us, then, involves outlining the territory for a more fully developed field centered on the problems of girls and young women with mental retardation. This chapter begins by assessing what is known about sex differences in general in the mental retardation-intellectual disabilities field and why we know so little. From there we examine specific issues related to girls and young women with maladaptive behavior or psychopathology and within several different genetic mental retardation syndromes, before discussing several issues that may be unique to mental retardation. We then end this chapter with some ideas about critical next steps.

ROBERT M. HODAPP and ELISABETH M. DYKENS • John F. Kennedy Center & Peabody College, Vanderbilt University, Nashville, TN 37235

THE PROBLEMS OF GIRLS WITH MENTAL RETARDATION: WHAT WE KNOW, WHAT WE DO NOT KNOW, AND WHY

Before reviewing what is known about girls and sex differences in mental retardation, two distinctions are necessary. The first involves mental retardation per se versus mental retardation plus other psychiatric conditions. In all definitional manuals (e.g., *DSM*, ICD), mental retardation is diagnosed on the basis of three criteria: (1) intellectual abilities that are significantly below average (usually, IQ < 70); (2) significant impairments in adaptive behavior (as defined by the Vineland or other tests of adaptive behavior); and (3) beginning during the childhood years (American Psychiatric Association, 1994).

In this sense, then, mental retardation itself is technically a psychiatric diagnosis, and most individuals have mental retardation alone, with no other formal *DSM* diagnosis. In contrast, as many as 40% of persons with mental retardation have significant behavioral or emotional problems that may lead them to be "dually diagnosed," that is, to have both mental retardation and one or more additional psychiatric problems.

A second distinction involves how to subtype individuals with mental retardation: by degree of impairment versus by the cause of mental retardation. Until recently, most behavioral research in mental retardation has looked at children or adults at different levels of functioning—the mild, moderate, severe, or profound levels historically used in mental retardation research. In contrast to this degree-of-impairment approach, we and others have advocated examining children who have different causes for their mental retardation (Dykens & Hodapp, 2001; Hodapp & Dykens, 1994). Thus, one might examine any domain of behavior in children with Down syndrome, or with Prader-Willi syndrome, or with any of the 1,000+ genetic disorders of mental retardation.

To this day, compared to an approach based on etiology, the degree-of-impairment approach continues to be more common in mental retardation research. At last check, approximately 80 to 90% of all behavioral studies in the major mental retardation journals did not separate out their subjects by their cause of mental retardation. At the same time, however, such a state of affairs may be changing. In a recent review, we noted that the numbers of behavioral research articles on certain genetic syndromes increased greatly from the 1980s to the 1990s (Dykens & Hodapp, 2001; Hodapp & Dykens, 2004). Although different factors account for the rising numbers in different syndromes, behavioral researchers are increasingly considering etiology as important.

Current Knowledge

Given these two caveats, we now examine some basic sex-difference issues in mental retardation. We here examine individuals with mental retardation in general (who may or may not be dually diagnosed), and adopt a "non-etiological" strategy. In later sections, we explore sex differences among those individuals with mental retardation who have severe behavior problems or psychopathology and begin to take genetic etiology into account.

Prevalence

It is now commonly accepted that more males than females are found in the population with mental retardation. *DSM-IV* (American Psychiatric Association, 1994) notes that "Mental retardation is more common among males, with a male-to-female ratio of approximately 1.5:1" (p. 44). Such differences in prevalence rates are seen as well in recent studies. In Stromme and Hagberg's (2000) prevalence study of a county surrounding Oslo, Norway, males exceeded females by a ratio of 1.3 to 1, and other studies also show a 20% to 40% excess in males versus females. This overabundance of males can be seen at both the more severe and more mild levels of mental retardation, and across studies performed many years apart and with differing methodologies (Roeleveld, Zielhuis, & Gabreels, 1997).

Why such discrepancies exist is less clear. At present, some combination of three or more reasons seems likely. First, it has long been known that a sizeable percentage of the retarded population is due to X-linked mental retardation (Dykens, Hodapp, & Finucane, 2000). Fragile X syndrome, the most commonly occurring of many X-linked mental retardation conditions, is the second most common genetic disorder (after Down syndrome) and the most common hereditary disorder associated with mental retardation. Although we describe fragile X syndrome later in this chapter, more boys than girls are affected. Partly due to the prevalence of fragile X syndrome and other X-linked disorders, then, more males than females have mental retardation.

Second, boys—as opposed to girls—may be more susceptible to various organic insults. In one recent study, Lary and Paulozzi (2001) found that overall prevalence rates of major defects at birth was 3.9% for boys, 2.8% for girls. This pattern of "boys over girls" occurred for virtually all defect conditions. As a general rule, then, the central nervous system of males seems more susceptible to a wide range of prenatal and postnatal insults (McLaren & Bryson, 1987).

A final possibility concerns differential rates of ascertainment. Oswald, Cutinho, Best, and Nguyen (2001) recently examined the impact of several socio-demographic characteristics on the identification of minority students as having mental retardation. Using U.S. Department of Education data, they found interesting effects of gender and of gender by ethnicity. As expected, girls were less often identified as having mental retardation than were boys. Within the entire group of girls, however, the odds ratios were strongly affected by ethnicity. Using Caucasian girls as the standard (1.0 odds ratio), Hispanic girls were equally likely to be identified as having mental retardation (1.01), compared to African American girls, who were 2.58 times more likely to be identified. Although the exact workings of both mild organic insults and of ethnicity remain unclear, both add to X-linked mental retardation to result in higher rates of boys compared to girls with mental retardation.

Course, Familial Patterns, and Other Associated Features

Sex differences have rarely been studied for most issues of behavioral functioning in mental retardation. To our knowledge, no studies compare girls and boys on, for example, the changing rates of intellectual, adaptive, or linguistic development over time. And few examine whether girls or boys might react differently to any type of intervention—educational, psychotherapeutic, or pharmacological. Although, as we discuss below, a few studies have examined sex differences in maladaptive behavior or psychopathology, even in that area there is a scarcity of good studies. For all these areas, the assumption throughout has been that females and males are the same.

Are Girls with Mental Retardation Truly Not Studied?

As our conclusion about the field's inattention to girls may be overly strong, we decided to test our views by turning to two sources: general handbooks and recent studies published in two of the field's main journals.

The main handbook chosen for review was the latest edition of *Ellis' Handbook of Mental Deficiency, Psychological Theory, and Research* (MacLean, 1997). *Ellis' Handbook*, now edited by William MacLean, is generally recognized as the main handbook in the mental retardation field. Its third edition contains 16 chapters covering definition and classification, emotion, behavior genetics, developmental approaches, prevention and early intervention, rigidity, cognitive competence, attention, information processing, motor skills, social intelligence, communication-language, family adaptation, and severe behavior problems. But in looking through each chapter and the book's table of contents, sex differences are absent. The handbook's index also does not provide a single entry for sex differences, gender differences, females, girls, males, or boys.

Other handbooks similarly show inattention to the problems of girls and to the issue of sex differences more generally. No chapter is devoted to girls in the *Handbook of Mental Retardation and Development* (Burack, Hodapp, & Zigler, 1998), and that handbook provides only a few mentions of any studies of girls or of sex or gender differences (e.g., Bybee & Zigler, 1998). One finds the identical situation in the *Handbook of Mental Retardation*. Although the most recent (second) edition was published in 1991 (Matson & Mulick, 1991), no chapters are devoted to the problems of girls or to sex differences. As in other handbooks, the index of the *Handbook of Mental Retardation* also shows no entries for girls, women, sex or gender differences.

A second measure involves published articles in the main behavioral research journals themselves. Here we examined research articles published in the field's two main research journals, the *American Journal on Mental Retardation* and the British-based *Journal of Intellectual Disability Research*, over the 5-year period from January, 1997 to December, 2001. As shown in Table 1, sex differences are routinely ignored in most studies published in these two journals. Overall, only about a quarter of the

Table 1. Reporting of gender distribution and differences in studies published in the two main research journals in the mental retardation field, 1997–2001

Content Area	American Journal on Mental Retardation			Journal of Intellectual Disability Research		
	Reported and Analyzed	Reported, Not Analyzed*	No Mention	Reported and Analyzed	Reported, Not Analyzed*	No Mention
Health-Physical	7 (23%)	21 (70%)	2 (7%)	21 (48%)	14 (32%)	9 (20%)
Mental Health	8 (22%)	26 (72%)	2 (6%)	15 (28%)	30 (56%)	9 (17%)
Family	12 (43%)	16 (57%)	0 (0%)	2 (15%)	5 (38%)	6 (46%)
Social-Emotional	8 (24%)	21 (64%)	4 (12%)	3 (10%)	26 (87%)	1 (3%)
Treatment-Intervention	8 (22%)	25 (69%)	3 (8%)	12 (32%)	16 (42%)	10 (26%)
Cognitive & Other Skills	11 (20%)	33 (60%)	11 (20%)	3 (12.5%)	18 (75%)	3 (12.5%)
Total	54 (24.7%)	142 (65.1%)	22 (10.1%)	56 (27.6%)	109 (53.7%)	38 (18.7%)

*Reported, Not Analyzed = No. of female and male participants noted, but no subsequent analyses reported for sex differences.

articles report analyzing for sex differences, with some subfields higher or lower. Across both journals, sex differences are rarely examined in studies of cognitive and other skills, social-emotional functioning, mental health, or treatment-intervention.

Why Such Inattention to Girls or to Sex Differences?

Although we cannot know for certain, we here provide three tentative, and not mutually exclusive, answers.

1. *Overshadowing.* In the early 1980s, Reiss and Szyszko (1983) proposed the concept of "diagnostic overshadowing." Their hypothesis was that, because an individual had been diagnosed with mental retardation, the person was less likely to receive other psychiatric diagnoses. We here borrow the overshadowing idea to explain the scarcity of studies on girls with mental retardation or on sex differences in general.

   Overshadowing may be occurring in two senses. First, the very diagnosis of mental retardation may be overshadowing all other personal characteristics, including one's age and gender. A second, related sense of overshadowing concerns the perceptions of mental retardation as a solely cognitive disorder. As Zigler (1971) has argued for many years, persons with mental retardation are "whole persons"; they are more than their intellectual deficits. Naturally, gender is among the most important of these other-than-intellectual characteristics, yet one that seems routinely overlooked in most behavioral research on this population.

2. *Small size of field.* Although a part of many disciplines, mental retardation has historically constituted a small, less salient portion of every field. Consider, for example, the membership of Division 33 of the American Psychological Association, the division on Mental Retardation and Developmental Disabilities. That division currently lists 712 members overall (including paid continuing members, new members, fellows, and lifetime members). In contrast, several of the divisions dealing with clinical psychology have over 5,000 total members (e.g., Division 13—Society of Consulting Psychology—5, 397; Division 42—Individuals in Independent Practice—5,854), and those dealing with educational (15) or school (16) psychology are also larger (1,880 and 1,949, respectively). Although a few divisions are also small, Division 33 is among the smaller of APA's 53 divisions. Similarly, the main conference for behavioral researchers, the annual Gatlinburg Conference on Mental Retardation and Developmental Disabilities (sponsored by the National Institutes of Child Health & Human Development), generally has approximately 150–200 attendees.

   This small contingent of active researchers struggles to "do it all." Small subsets of researchers thus examine various aspects of testing, diagnosis, and classification; language, cognition, and adaptive behavior; maladaptive behavior and psychopathology; behavior modification and applied behavior analysis; mother-child interaction, families, siblings, and peers; early intervention, schooling, transitions, group homes, and vocational functioning; functioning in different etiological groups; aging and (in Down syndrome) Alzheimer's disease; and a variety of other issues. In their efforts to cover all of these diverse and pressing issues, the problems of girls or young women with mental retardation have almost always taken a back seat.

3. *No existing subfield.* In psychology and related fields, the making of new fields oftentimes seems tied to the activities of specific individuals over a period of several decades. Indeed, individuals who have created subfields can be identified in most every branch of psychology. In developmental psychology, the idea that children and mothers mutually affect one another (i.e., interactionism) was championed over many years by Richard Bell (1968). Similarly, Maccoby and Jacklin (1974) highlighted the issue of gender differences in development. So too do "field-makers" exist in mental retardation; witness Zigler's (1969) developmental approach to mental retardation, and Menolascino (1970) helping to found the entire subdiscipline of dual diagnosis.

At present, no one has yet launched the subfield of girls and young women with mental retardation, or, more generally, of sex differences in the behavior of persons with mental retardation. As a result, such differences—if examined at all—have been relegated to a secondary role. As in many disciplines or subdisciplines, then, the need persists for an identified person or group to put the subfield "on the map" of important topics within mental retardation behavioral research.

GIRLS AND MALADAPTIVE BEHAVIOR—DUAL DIAGNOSIS

For many reasons, we know precious little about the mental health of girls with intellectual disabilities. First, from very the beginning of the "dual diagnosis" field, researchers and clinicians have spent extraordinary time and energy "selling" the idea that people with intellectual disabilities actually suffered from psychiatric disorders, as opposed to having behavioral problems or psychiatric symptoms as a by-product of a low IQ. While this "diagnostic overshadowing" continues today, knowledge about dual diagnosis has spread, in part due to increased awareness in training programs, and in part due to the advocacy of such groups as the National Association for Dual Diagnosis (NADD).

Second, as most persons with mental retardation now live in community settings, it is no longer necessary to compare the effects of, say, institutions versus group homes, on clients' maladaptive behavior or psychopathology. In this sense, dual diagnosis studies can now begin to look more at personal characteristics of individuals; residential status is no longer the primary "independent variable" of dual diagnosis studies.

Third, the field is still going through growing pains in terms of how to best measure psychopathology in persons with mental retardation. Some studies have thus focused on the goodness of fit between traditional nosologies such as the *DSM* or ICD systems, and the unique characteristics of those with intellectual disabilities (e.g., Sovner, 1986). A flurry of psychometric work has resulted in novel rating scales and checklists of psychopathology normed on persons with mental retardation (e.g., Aman & Singh, 1994; Einfeld & Tonge, 1992; Reiss, 1988). Across these types of measures, additional concerns arise regarding the most appropriate or "best" informant, as many persons with mental retardation are unable to identify or express the onset, frequency, and duration of various symptoms. Indeed, the mental retardation field has only now begun to ask who are the best informants for which types of symptoms (e.g., Moss, Prosner, Ibbotson, & Goldberg, 1996).

These three earlier concerns aside, a few studies have reported occasional gender results, even if researchers did not set out with the aim of examining differences in psychopathology across boys versus girls. Two general themes regarding gender emerge from this scant literature.

(1) *Sex differences in overall psychiatric prevalence rates of boys versus girls.* Based on both epidemiological and clinical samples, more males than females with mental retardation are diagnosed with psychiatric disorders. A population-based study in Norway found that boys with mental retardation were 1.6 times as likely to receive a psychiatric diagnosis than were girls (Stromme & Diseth, 2000). In an earlier epidemiological sample of 149 Swedish adolescents, Gillberg, Persson, Grufman, and Themner (1986) found that boys with mental retardation were 2.9 times as likely as girls with mental retardation to have a psychiatric diagnosis. A similarly high ratio of 2.5-to-1 for boys to girls was reported in a psychiatric clinic sample of 233 child patients (Hardan & Stahl, 1997). In contrast, sampling children in five counties of New South Wales, Einfeld and Tonge (1996) did not find that gender was a significant predictor of psychiatric "caseness" of children with mental retardation. Such contradictory findings are likely attributable to a host of subject and measurement issues (Dykens, 2000).

(2) *Sex differences in rates of problems and symptoms.* Findings are also contradictory when examining most all types of specific problems. One agreed-upon finding, however, is that males more often have autism and autism spectrum disorders than females, with an average male-to-female ratio of 3.8-to-1 (see Fombonne, 1999 for a review).

Beyond this robust finding, however, data are equivocal. For example, no gender differences were found between internalizing and externalizing types of symptoms among children with mental retardation residing in New South Wales (Einfeld & Tonge, 1996), as assessed by the well-normed

Developmental Behaviour Checklist (Einfeld & Tonge, 1992). Yet increased hyperactivity among boys was reported by Gillberg et al. (1986) using global behavioral observations. More recently, Brown, Aman and Haver-camp (2002) examined over 600 school-aged children receiving special education services for mental retardation in Ohio. Boys greatly exceeded girls on the Hyperactivity Scale of the Aberrant Behavior Checklist (Aman & Singh, 1994), another tool designed specifically for persons with mental retardation. Similarly, Dykens and Kasari (1997) found elevated aggressive scores on Achenbach's Child Behavior Checklist in a small sample of boys with mixed causes for their delay. Finally, as assessed in record reviews that included *DSM-III-R* diagnoses, poor concentration and aggression were seen more often in boys versus girls with mental retardation who received treatment for behavioral problems (Hardan & Stahl, 2000). Thus, while girls seem to show fewer externalizing symptoms, such has not always been the case. More refined studies are needed to sort out these discrepancies, in part by also taking age, type of intellectual disability, and other subject variables into account.

Findings regarding internalizing types of symptoms are also contradictory. Although adolescent girls have higher levels of internalizing problems than males in the general population (e.g., Werry, 1990), findings in those with mental retardation are not so clear-cut. Depression has been more frequently studied in adult women with intellectual disability as opposed to girls; across all studies, strong effects are found for level of cognitive impairment, not for gender. Thus, across both males and females, people with higher IQs are more likely to receive a diagnosis of depression than their lower functioning counterparts (Hardan & Stahl, 1997; Meins, 1993; Reynolds & Baker, 1988).

Such differences across IQ levels highlight an ongoing debate as to rates of depression and other internalizing problems in persons with intellectual disabilities. Persons with intellectual disabilities may be more prone to showing symptoms related to action versus thought, as well as symptoms that involve turning-against-others versus turning-against-the-self (Glick & Zigler, 1995). If so, then internalizing problems such as depression may be less frequently diagnosed than behavioral disorders in the intellectually disabled population (Jacobson, 1990). Alternatively, symptoms of depression may be altered or masked in this group, and several leaders in the field have recently developed consensus-based alternative diagnostic criteria for depression in this population (Szymanski, et al., 1998). While previous studies find that from 5% to 15% of those with mental retardation suffer from an affective illness (see Dykens, 2000 for a review), these figures may increase when criteria are used that have been adapted and validated specifically for this population.

The types and rates of anxiety disorders among girls with mental retardation have also just begun to be examined. In a study of over 1,000 Dutch children with intellectual disability, Dekker, Nunn, and Koot (2002) found a modest elevation among girls on the anxiety scale of the Developmental Behaviour Checklist. Gender differences in specific fears have been consistently found, with girls with (or without) intellectual disability showing more fears than their male peers with (or without) intellectual disability (Gullonne, Cummins, & King, 1996; Gullone, King, & Cummins, 1996). Aside from fears, then, it is unclear to what extent girls with intellectual disabilities show the age-related increases in anxiety disorders seen in their counterparts without cognitive deficits.

PROBLEMS OF GIRLS AND YOUNG WOMEN WITH SPECIFIC GENETIC SYNDROMES

An additional, intriguing perspective involves genetic mental retardation disorders. Although few studies have yet been performed that focus specifically on girls or on sex differences in most genetic syndromes, syndrome-specific behaviors show interesting twists pertaining to girls and young women. We here examine such possibilities in three genetic mental retardation syndromes.

Fragile X Syndrome

Second only to Down syndrome as a prevalent genetic form of mental retardation, fragile X syndrome is one of the few genetic mental retardation syndromes that is passed down from one generation to the next as a sex-linked condition. In most sex-linked conditions, females themselves are unaffected; by having two X chromosomes, the unaffected X buffers the female from the effects of the affected X chromosome. Thus, in most sex-linked conditions, females are (unaffected) carriers of an affected X, which they can then pass along to (on average, half of) their subsequent offspring. Daughters then themselves become unaffected carriers and males, having only one X chromosome, upon receiving an affected X chromosome show hemophilia, color blindness, or other sex-linked conditions.

In fragile X syndrome, however, the situation is more complicated. Here the disorder itself involves an "amplification" of a three-base chemical sequence (cytosine-cytosine-guanine, or CGG) along a certain portion of the X chromosome. Thus, instead of having the usual 6 to 50 copies of CGG at a specific portion of the X-chromosome, the affected individual has over 200, thus adversely affecting the production of a specific protein (FMR1 protein). In addition, a "pre-mutation" can also occur in which the individual has from 50 to 200 CGG repeats. Individuals with a premutation—male or female—are not themselves affected, but they can pass along that X chromosome to their offspring. To complicate matters further, fragile X premutations are unstable in female carriers, making it likely that, when these women pass along the affected X chromosome to their sons or daughters, the offspring will have X chromosomes with over 200 CGG repeats.

As a general rule, males with fragile X syndrome show characteristic cognitive profiles, as well as hyperactivity, social withdrawal, anxiety, and attention deficits (see Dykens et al., 2000 for a review). These males may also manifest perseverative speech and behaviors, stereotypies, and tactile defensiveness. For girls, the clinical picture is more variable, though often somewhat less severe. Females are less often affected with mental retardation, but girls and women generally show similar albeit less severe problems with social anxiety, shyness, gaze aversion, and inattention (Lachiewicz & Dawson, 1994; Sobesky, Porter, Pennington, & Hagerman, 1995). Even compared to other mothers of children with disabilities, more of these carrier females show depressive features (Thompson et al., 1994), and relatively weak interpersonal skills are also often evident.

Over the past few years, studies have increasingly demonstrated that the degree of cognitive impairment in this disorder—for both boys and girls—relates to the extent of fragile X protein (FMR1P) produced. Fully affected males with mental retardation produce virtually no FMR1P protein (Tassone et al., 1999); in contrast, males who produce some FMR1P generally have higher IQs. A similar effect appears to be operating in girls with fragile X syndrome. For both boys and girls, however, the amount of protein has yet to be linked to the presence or degree of maladaptive behavior or psychopathology.

Such a complicated pattern produces life-changing clinical issues for several groups of girls and young women. Having a premutation on one of their X chromosomes, unaffected carriers are likely to pass along a fully mutated X chromosome (i.e., over 200 CGG repeats) to half of their offspring. These women, then, must deal with the psychological consequences of having "caused" their child to either be a carrier or to have mental retardation.

Over the past few years, researchers have begun to assess the effects of screening programs on unaffected carrier girls and young women. In one set of studies, McConkie-Rosell, Spiridigliozzi, Sullivan, Dawson, and Lachiewicz (2000, 2001, 2002) looked at issues of genetic testing in 42 women at risk for being carriers of fragile X syndrome. These women filled out the Tennessee Self-Concept Scale (Roid & Fitts, 1988) and a visual analogue scale about the effects of genetic testing; they were also interviewed about genetic testing and their desire for telling and testing their own children. Women were examined both before testing and 6 months after testing, when roughly half (N = 20) had known for 6 months that they were indeed fragile X carriers, while half (N = 22) now knew that they were not carriers.

Findings across these studies reflect the complicated nature of genetic testing and of knowledge of carrier status for both the women and their children. Since no participant knew whether she was—or was not—a carrier at the first testing, carriers and noncarriers did not differ in their self-concepts at Time 1. At Time 2, 6 months later, the self-concepts of the now-identified carriers had not changed, but that of the noncarriers had improved. Several noncarrier mothers now mentioned that "I do not feel anxiety as far as having children", that [I am} "relieved I dodged the bullet" and that "I'm just thankful that I'm negative" (McConkie-Rosell et al., 2000, p. 340).

Both carrier and noncarrier mothers also held clear ideas as to when to tell and to test their children for the child's carrier status. At Time 1, mothers felt that they themselves would have wanted to know that fragile X ran in their families when mothers were 18 years old. In contrast, mothers thought that the best age for their daughters to know was about 14. Mothers felt that genetic testing should be performed at about 15 years old, and mothers who, at Time 2, knew that they were indeed carriers wanted even earlier testing, at about 13 years old for both daughters and sons. Over the entire sample, mothers split themselves into four age groups as to when their children should be told that they were potential carriers and then genetically tested: before age 10 years (child years); aged 10 to 13 years (pre-teen); aged 14 to 17 years (teen); and after the age of 18 years (adult). Mothers who wanted their children told and tested when children were below 10 years of age cited the need for many years until adulthood for the child to adjust. In contrast, mothers who opted for later ages felt that their child's beginning sexual activities and relationships made telling and testing optimal during pre-teen, teen, or adult years.

Williams Syndrome

A second genetic disorder featuring interesting issues for girls and young women is Williams syndrome. Williams syndrome affects about 1 in 20,000 individuals, and is caused by a micro-deletion on one of the chromosome 7's that include the gene for elastin (Ewart et al., 1993). Children with this syndrome generally show mild-to-moderate levels of mental retardation (IQs in the 1950s and 1960s), hyperacusis (i.e., extremely sensitive hearing), cardiovascular disease, and hypercalcemia (see Pober & Dykens, 1996). Characteristic facial features are generally described as attractive, appealing, and "elfin-like," with full lips and cheeks, wide and long philtrum (under nose), and puffy areas around the eyes (Dykens et al., 2000). These children also show relative strengths in language (Mervis, Morris, Bertrand, & Robinson, 1999), as well as in auditory processing and in some areas of music (Lenhoff, 1998). In contrast, many children with Williams syndrome perform especially poorly on a variety of visuo-spatial tasks (Udwin & Yule, 1991; Udwin, Yule & Martin, 1987).

Although such cognitive-linguistic profiles have received the most attention, two other behavioral characteristics may relate more to girls and young women. The first involves personality. Children with Williams syndrome tend to be overly friendly, affectionate, engaging, and charming. Although such sociability might be considered a strength, these children are often considered uninhibited and indiscriminate in their sociability. In one study of 36 children aged 4-to-10 years, Gosch and Pankau (1997) found that parents considered 82% to be overly friendly toward strangers. Similarly, Davies, Udwin, and Howlin (1998) noted that 94% of adults with Williams syndrome were considered socially disinhibited, with 59% engaging in inappropriate touching, hugging, and kissing others.

As might be expected from their mental retardation, high levels of language, and social disinhibition, children and young adults with Williams syndrome may be at fairly high risk for sexual exploitation and abuse. In Davies et al.'s (1998) study of adults, 10% of their sample had reported sexual assaults to police, and an additional 10% made allegations of assault that had not been reported. In studies of nonretarded children, the rates for girls of childhood sexual abuse are generally about double the rates for boys (Cutler & Nolen-Hoeksema, 1991). Although no data currently exist concerning the prevalence of sexual abuse in girls as opposed to boys with Williams syndrome, they may be at higher risk than boys with this syndrome, or than girls or boys with other types of mental retardation.

A second issue concerns fears and anxiety. Children with Williams syndrome show heightened anxiety and a wide variety of fears. Consider a recent study that identified those fears reported by 50% or more of children with Williams syndrome versus with other types of mental retardation (Dykens, 2003). A majority of participants with mental retardation (but not Williams syndrome) reported only two commonly occurring fears, of their parents getting sick and of getting a shot or injection. In contrast, more than half of the group with Williams syndrome endorsed 41 different fears. Such fears ran the gamut. Some involved interpersonal issues like being teased (92%), getting punished (85%), or getting into arguments with others (85%). Others involved such physical issues as injections (90%), being in a fire or getting burned (82%), or getting stung by a bee (79%). Still others related to these children's hyperacusis or clumsiness (loud noises—sirens, 87%; falling from high places, 79%; thunderstorms, 78%).

There also seems to be an interaction between gender and age in the number and severity of fears. Specifically, girls with Williams syndrome become increasingly fearful as they got older, whereas boys did not. Comparing 6–12-year children to adolescents or adults aged 13–18 and 18+ years, Dykens (2003) found that adolescent girls and adult women became more fearful overall, particularly as concerns their fears of injury and of animals. In terms of both their own anxiety and sexual exploitation by others, girls and young women with Williams syndrome present intriguing, and so far underexplored, problems.

Prader-Willi Syndrome

Occurring in 1 in every 10,000 to 15,000 births, Prader-Willi syndrome is caused by missing genetic material from chromosome 15 derived from the father. In approximately two-thirds of cases, such missing material comes about from a deletion on the paternally derived chromosome 15 (i.e., the deletion form); in most of the remainder, from receiving two chromosome 15s from the mother (the uniparental disomy form). Prader-Willi syndrome results in mild-borderline mental retardation (average IQ = 70), better simultaneous (i.e., Gestalt, holistic) processing than sequential (i.e., serial, step-by-step) processing, short stature, and a host of physical-medical problems (Dykens & Cassidy, 1996). Such problems include hypogonadism and incomplete pubertal development in both males and females. With few exceptions, females do not have periods and are generally infertile.

Overall, however, the disorder's most noted characteristics pertain to emotional or behavioral problems. Prader-Willi syndrome may be the only genetic mental retardation syndrome associated with severe, life-threatening, hyperphagia (i.e., excessive eating). Such hyperphagia, generally considered the hallmark of the syndrome (Holm et al., 1993), begins sometime during the 2 to 5 year period and continues throughout life (Dykens & Cassidy, 1996). Hyperphagia seems due to an impaired ability to feel satiated after eating (Holland, Treasure, Coskeran, & Dallow, 1995). As a result, many persons with this disorder feel an incessant need to search for, forage, and hoard food. If such behaviors are left unchecked, extreme obesity can result, along with associated heart and circulatory problems. To this day, the majority of early deaths in Prader-Willi syndrome result from diabetes, high blood pressure, and other health problems associated with extreme obesity (Dykens & Cassidy, 1996).

In addition to hyperphagia and obesity, many of these children also show obsessions and compulsions. Comparing individuals with Prader-Willi syndrome to same-aged nonretarded persons diagnosed with obsessive-compulsive Disorder (OCD), Dykens, Leckman and Cassidy (1996) found few group differences on behaviors such as hoarding objects (e.g., toiletries, paper, pens); ordering and arranging objects by color, size, or shape, or until they were "just right," needing to say or tell things; or redoing behaviors (e.g., tying and untying shoes). Across 100 individuals with Prader-Willi syndrome, 94% showed obsessions (thoughts) and 71% showed compulsions (behaviors; Dykens et al., 2000). Joined with overeating (98%) and temper tantrums (88%), these children demonstrate extremely high levels of maladaptive behavior (Dykens & Kasari, 1997; Dykens & Cassidy, 1996).

How, exactly, does Prader-Willi syndrome intersect with clinical or life concerns for girls and young women? At present we cannot say for certain, but several connections seem likely. The first pertains to girls' self-images. More than boys and men, how one looks–including one's weight and attaining the "ideal" body—is probably a more salient issue for female as opposed to male adolescents in American society. In Prader-Willi syndrome, however, adolescent girls and young women are most often short (average adult height is 4'10"; Cassidy, 1984) and relatively obese. What, then, are the self-images of these adolescents and young women?

Although no studies directly address such questions, the connection between one's weight and feelings may be more complicated than originally thought. Specifically, parents and professionals working with this population have long assumed that, if only children and adults with the disorder could get their weight under control, they would be happier. Unfortunately, an individual's degree of obesity (i.e., the body mass index, or one's weight relative to one's height) may negatively correlate with maladaptive behavior. Less obese individuals therefore show more—not less—distressful affect and confused and distorted thinking, anxiety, sadness, fearfulness, and crying (Dykens & Cassidy, 1995). Why such negative relations exist is unclear, although one possibility might relate to the disappointment people feel when, even though they have worked so hard to slim down, many of their interpersonal and other life problems persist.

Another intriguing possibility concerns nurturance. Anecdotally, parents and professionals note that many children and adults with

Prader-Willi syndrome possess a strong propensity to nurture others. It is common, for example, for adolescents and young adults with Prader-Willi syndrome to be highly protective of their household pets and to desire to work with animals or with babies and children in day care centers. In Dykens and Rosner's (1999) study comparing personality in persons with Prader-Willi syndrome, with Williams syndrome, and with heterogeneous causes for their mental retardation, the group with Prader-Willi syndrome was rated much higher on the item "has strong maternal/paternal instincts."

At present, it remains unclear how increased feelings of nurturance might relate to other issues in girls and young women with Prader-Willi syndrome. What, for example, do these girls and young women think about sexual and relationship issues? If, given their strong feelings of nurturance, many women with the syndrome desire to get married and have families, how do such feelings coexist in females who generally do not marry, are not sexually active, and cannot have children?

Themes Across Syndromes

In contemplating how specific genetic disorders relate to concerns of girls and young women, most problems seem to arise at the intersection of etiology-related characteristics and specific, societally endorsed sex roles. With the sole exception of fragile X syndrome, girls are not differently affected than boys. Both boys and girls with Williams syndrome are oftentimes overly friendly, disinhibited, and anxious and fearful. Both boys and girls with Prader-Willi syndrome have hyperphagia and may be highly nurturant.

Instead, the problems relate more to how these etiology-related behaviors and characteristics play themselves out in everyday interactions. Thus, our assumption is that sexual exploitation more often occurs because girls with Williams syndrome are mentally retarded, verbal, and socially disinhibited—even as boys may show similar characteristics. Similarly, given common sex-role expectations in modern Western societies, girls (as opposed to boys) with Prader-Willi syndrome should show extra problems with self-image due to their obesity, and may become more frustrated by being nurturant yet unable to bear and raise children. Studies are now needed that directly test these hypotheses.

ADDITIONAL ISSUES SPECIFIC TO MENTAL RETARDATION

So far, we have mostly focused on the problems of girls or women with mental retardation themselves, and mostly on the presence or effects of emotional or behavioral problems. Two additional, intriguing issues also pertain to mental retardation. In the first, we examine women with mental retardation as parents; in the second, the concerns of the typically developing girls and young women who are sisters to a sibling with mental retardation.

Women with Mental Retardation as Mothers

Historically, professionals have denigrated women with mental retardation who bear children. During the early years of the 20th century, a strong eugenics movement even called for the sterilization of such women, a practice that occurred in California and several other American states.

Fortunately, in modern times much of the hysteria has dissipated concerning women with mental retardation parenting children. Still, questions remain as to how many women with mental retardation are having children; how adequate their mothering is and which factors predispose such women to be good or bad parents; and whether women with mental retardation can be helped to become good parents.

The first, epidemiological question, is probably the most difficult to answer. Due in part to conflicting definitions of mental retardation and to the stigma attached to getting help, no one knows just how many women with mental retardation are currently mothers (Whitman, Graves, & Accardo, 1987). Holburn, Perkins, and Vietze (2001) estimate that the number of parents with mental retardation in the United States is likely between 1.5 and 2 million, that these numbers include far more women than men as parents, and that these parents tend to have two or three children. From large follow-up studies of numerous families over many years, approximately one-quarter of the offspring of parents with mental retardation will themselves have mental retardation (Feldman, 1994).

In contrast to earlier views, women with mental retardation can, but do not always, provide adequate mothering. To the extent that these women have difficulties in the mothering role, problems relate to both mental retardation and to associated issues. In terms of mental retardation, various studies note that an IQ level below 60 is a significant risk factor for poor parenting, with specific problems including dealing with novel parenting situations, exercising good parental judgment, and effectively monitoring their child's behaviors.

But in addition to these intrinsic problems, other barriers also make harder these women's effective parenting. In describing the "typical" parent with mental retardation, Holburn et al. (2001) conclude: "that parent is a women, she is single, and she is poor" (p. 182). Many of these women are also socially isolated, with poor or nonexistent social support systems (Booth & Booth, 1994). As a result, few have good role models of effective parenting. In addition, many suffer from psychopathology or other problems that make more difficult their learning of parenting skills. In one study, for example, of nine mothers with mental retardation in an intervention program, four also had depression, psychosomatic problems, or a history of being abused (Tymchuk & Andron, 1992). Parenting more than two children seems especially stressful, and mothers with mental retardation have more difficulties when their children show behavioral or other problems (Whitman & Accardo, 1990).

Fortunately, women with mental retardation can be helped to become effective parents. Some of this help may consist of having a single, supportive person to lean on; throughout this literature, there is talk of unpaid help provided by a supportive person who does not have mental retardation. In addition, a wide variety of behaviorally oriented programs have been tried to increase parenting skills. Although both maintenance and generalization can sometimes be problematic, such programs do appear to be reasonably successful (Feldman, 1994).

Sisters of Children with Mental Retardation

Until about 20 years ago, most studies examining families of children with mental retardation featured what might be termed a "problem-based" focus (see Hodapp, 2002 for a review). Within this context, the nonretarded, typically developing siblings of children with mental retardation were thought to be "at risk" for poor psychological adjustment. Girls—especially the oldest girl in the family—were considered at especially high risk (Lobato, 1983).

In line with recent reevaluations of the effects of the child with mental retardation on the family, two reappraisals have occurred concerning siblings. The first reappraisal concerning all siblings is that growing up with a brother or sister with mental retardation can be both good and bad. Pooling 79 effect sizes across 25 studies performed from 1972 to 1979, Rossiter and Sharpe (2001) found only a small (albeit significant) negative impact for these siblings. Negative effects were more often noted in studies that used direct observation or parent report, less often when studies employed the self-reports of the siblings themselves. Across studies, the single most often found "negative indicator" was increased depression in siblings of children with mental retardation. In contrast, compared to siblings of typically developing children, siblings of persons with mental retardation scored significantly higher on measures of positive social functioning. Finally, when studies examined children aged 13 years or less (as opposed to teenagers or adults), negative effects were more often seen for the siblings of children with mental retardation.

A second reappraisal concerns girls. In the Rossiter and Sharpe (2001) study, no sex differences were noted. Other, more recent studies have also generally not found sex differences on most measures. Overall, as a group, girls do not seem to be more adversely affected than boys from being a sibling to a child with mental retardation.

Still, the belief persists that some female siblings may suffer. Most researchers have pointed to the oldest daughter as being particularly prone to depression or other problems (Lobato, 1983). But in order to understand this negative influence—if indeed it occurs—one must consider how it might work. Essentially, faced with caring for a child with mental retardation, mothers (usually the primary caregivers) often need help in caring for the child with mental retardation or their other children, and in performing various household tasks. Since in American society women are typically responsible for caring for children and for household upkeep in general, these mothers might turn to their oldest daughters. As a result, these daughters would never have been allowed to be children during their childhood years, eventually becoming resentful and depressed (Lobato, 1983).

Further, such gender-based responsibilities might even continue into adulthood. In one of the few large-scale, longitudinal studies of aging families of offspring with mental retardation, Seltzer, Begun, Seltzer, and Krauss (1991) found that the most involved sibling, as reported by the mother, was more likely to be a sister as opposed to a brother. In addition, Orsmond and Seltzer (2000) found that sisters, as opposed to brothers, were more knowledgeable about the skills and needs of their sibling with mental retardation, and engaged in more frequent discussions about these issues with parents. Sisters also reported more contact and more "doing things together" with their adult brother or sister with disabilities. Upon the declining health of the mother, sisters even increased their time and activities with their sibling with mental retardation. Considered from this perspective of "gendered relationships" of sisters in American society, then, the problem is not intrinsic to being the oldest daughter per se, but instead to the effects of being the oldest daughter in a family holding particular views and expectations of that daughter's duties.

GIRLS WITH MENTAL RETARDATION OR INTELLECTUAL DISABILITIES: A LOOK TO THE FUTURE

In considering the problems of girls and young women with mental retardation—and even of typically developing sisters of siblings with mental retardation—we are struck by how little the field currently knows. We are struck by the many gaps that exist in our knowledge of girls and young women with mental retardation, and how rarely studies even bother to probe for sex differences. Even when problems are indeed specific to girls and young women—as in several genetic disorders and in women with mental retardation as mothers—studies often seem incomplete, explanations speculative.

Still, in the spirit of moving the field forward, we end this chapter by identifying several areas badly in need of further study. Each of these areas might be considered as connections to subfields that have yet to receive systematic attention.

Connections to Sub-Cultures and Sub-Groups

As noted above, many of the problems encountered by girls and young women with mental retardation relate to social and cultural concerns. Specifically, mothers with mental retardation are at risk because they are sometimes unable to meet societal expectations for mothering, as well as because of poverty, social isolation, and the lack of appropriate role models and social supports. Girls with Williams syndrome may face heightened levels of exploitation because their indiscriminate sociability and relatively high verbal abilities make them more vulnerable in present-day society. Similarly, the connections of weight and self-esteem arise in Prader-Willi syndrome because of the interplay of the syndrome and societal norms and expectations.

Each such issue leads to questions concerning subgroups within our society. As any pollster knows, members of any society's population differ one from another. In this country, Americans differ in terms of their social class, their race and ethnicity, their levels of education, their religions, even in terms of the region that one calls home. Yet how such diversity affects the concerns of girls and young women with mental retardation has rarely been studied. How, for example, are girls with mental retardation treated in homes of different ethnicities, or social classes, or religions? At present, we do not know.

Connections to Biology

In most examinations of girls and young women, the question of biology—particularly the role of hormones—figures prominently. Such questions concern hormonal levels and effects on both general and reproductive health, on mood, and even on aging.

To date, few such examinations have been performed for girls and young women with mental retardation. Granted, there have been a few studies on when puberty begins for girls with several genetic mental retardation syndromes, and of the effects of certain drugs on the beginning, ending, or regularity of menstruation. In addition, the effects of early versus later physical maturation remain unclear in this population, even as, in typically developing children, physically early maturers (or either sex) seem more field dependent, whereas late maturers are more field independent (Waber, 1977). Yet it remains unclear how such developmental processes work in mental retardation or in specific syndromes. How, for example, might visuo-motor skills, anxiety, or other behaviors in Williams syndrome relate to the timing of pubertal changes in girls (or boys)? Such connections to biology are almost invariably missing in most studies on girls and young women with mental retardation.

Connections to Development

In her several decades of work on self-image, Susan Harter repeatedly finds a change in the self-images of girls versus boys. Overall, females as opposed to males report more unfavorable self-perceptions of their physical appearance and of their athletic competence. But such sex differences first arise during the early pubertal years. As Harter (1999) notes, "In middle childhood, girls and boys feel equally good about their appearance; however, by the end of high school, females' scores are dramatically lower than males' scores" (p. 258).

A similar, possibly related finding concerns the rates of depression in females versus males. On average, girls and women seem about twice as likely as boys and men to become clinically depressed sometime during their lives (Wolk & Weissman, 1995). Such sex differences in prevalence rates mainly begin during the 10-to-15-year period, as do marked increases in female (as opposed to male) depressive symptoms not associated with full-blown depression (Garber, Keiley, & Martin, 2002). Granted, the 10-to-15-year period is one involving many changes, both psychosocial and biological in nature. But, as Frank and Young (2000) argue, hormonal changes—particularly involving oxytocin—may also be involved. This hormone, which in females relates to sexual drive, affiliative drive, and maternal instincts, has also been mentioned in connection with compulsive behavior in Prader-Willi syndrome (Dykens, Leckman, & Cassidy, 1996). But it remains unclear whether changing female-to-male ratios of depression during this period even occur in females with mental retardation or with Prader-Willi syndrome.

Connections to Intervention

Historically, many fields have minimized the importance of intervening to help the emotional or behavioral problems of children with mental retardation. Such neglect arose for a variety of reasons. As noted earlier, psychiatric issues in this population were often overshadowed by the person's mental retardation. In addition, in prior years advocates for persons with mental retardation tried hard to distinguish mental retardation from mental illness, thereby hoping to avoid the stigma attached to the latter group.

More recently, however, a host of interventions have begun to "come online" for persons with mental retardation. Approaches range from sophisticated behavior modification techniques (Singh, Osborne, & Huguenin, 1996), to psychopharmacology, managing the environment, psychotherapy, and supportive counseling (Rush & Frances, 2000). Several of these approaches have also been refined for persons with specific genetic mental retardation disorders, particularly as concerns psychotherapeutic approaches and vocational choices (Dykens & Hodapp, 1997), as well as etiology-related suggestions for special education (Hodapp & Fidler, 1999; Hodapp & Ricci, 2002). To date, however, no specific suggestions have arisen for girls as opposed to boys with either mental retardation or with particular mental retardation syndromes.

Although we end this chapter with four suggestions for future work, we appreciate that one could generate other, equally compelling lists of future directions. Yet the bottom line remains: The problems of girls and young women with mental retardation constitute an important, albeit underexplored, topic for research and intervention.

REFERENCES

Aman, M. G., & Singh, N. N. (1994). *Aberrant Behavior Checklist—Community supplementary manual.* East Aurora, NY: Slosson Educational Publications.

American Psychiatric Association (1994). *Diagnostic and statistical manual of mental disorders* (4th ed.). Washington, DC: Author.

Bell, R. Q. (1968). A reinterpretation of the direction of effects in studies of socialization. *Psychological Review, 75,* 81–95.

Booth, T., & Booth, W. (1994). Working with parents with mental retardation: Lessons from research. *Journal of Developmental and Physical Disabilities, 6,* 23–41.

Brown, E. C., Aman, M. G., & Havercamp, S. M. (2002). Factor analysis and norms for parent ratings on the Aberrant Behavior Checklist—Community for young people in special education. *Research in Developmental Disabilities, 23,* 45–60.

Burack, J. A., Hodapp, R. M., & Zigler, E. (Eds.). (1998). *Handbook of mental retardation and development.* Cambridge UK: Cambridge University Press.

Bybee, J., & Zigler, E. (1998). Outerdirectedness in individuals with and without mental retardation: A review. In J. A. Burack, R. M. Hodapp, & E. Zigler (Eds.). *Handbook of mental retardation and development* (pp. 434–461). Cambridge: Cambridge University Press.

Cassidy, S. B. (1984). Prader-Willi syndrome. *Current Problems in Pediatrics, 14,* 1–55.

Cutler, S. E., & Nolen-Hoeksema, S. (1991). Accounting for sex differences in depression through female victimization: Childhood sexual abuse. *Sex Roles, 24,* 425–438.

Davies, M., Udwin, O., & Howlin, P. (1998). Adults with Williams syndrome. *British Journal of Psychiatry, 172,* 273–276.

Dekker, M. C., Nunn, R., & Koot, H. M. (2002). Psychometric properties of the revised Developmental Behaviour Checklist scales in Dutch children with intellectual disability. *Journal of Intellectual Disability Research, 46,* 61–75.

Dykens, E. M. (2000). Psychopathology in children with intellectual disability. *Journal of Child Psychology and Psychiatry, 41,* 407–417.

Dykens, E. M. (2003). Anxiety, fears and phobias in persons with Williams syndrome. *Journal of Developmental Neuropsychology, 23,* 291–316.

Dykens, E. M., & Cassidy, S. B. (1995). Correlates of maladaptive behavior in children and adults with Prader-Willi syndrome. *American Journal of Medical Genetics, 60,* 546–549.

Dykens, E. M., & Cassidy, S. B. (1996). Prader-Willi syndrome: Genetic, behavioral, and treatment issues. *Child and Adolescent Psychiatry Clinics of North America, 5,* 913–927.

Dykens, E. M., & Hodapp, R. M. (1997). Treatment issues in genetic mental retardation syndromes. *Professional Psychology: Research and Practice, 28,* 263–270.

Dykens, E. M., & Hodapp, R. M. (2001). Research in mental retardation: Toward an etiologic approach. *Journal of Child Psychology and Psychiatry, 42,* 49–71.

Dykens, E. M., Hodapp, R. M., & Finucane, B. M. (2000). *Genetics and mental retardation syndromes: A new look at behavior and interventions.* Baltimore, MD: Paul H. Brookes.

Dykens, E. M., & Kasari, C. (1997). Maladaptive behavior in children with Prader-Willi syndrome, Down syndrome, and nonspecific mental retardation. *American Journal on Mental Retardation, 102,* 228–237.

Dykens, E. M., Leckman, J. F., & Cassidy, S. B. (1996). Obsessions and compulsions in Prader-Willi syndrome. *Journal of Child Psychology and Psychiatry, 37,* 995–1002.

Dykens, E. M., & Rosner, B. A. (1999). Refining behavioral phenotypes: Personality-motivation in Williams and Prader-Willi syndromes. *American Journal on Mental Retardation, 104,* 158–169.

Einfeld, S. L., & Tonge, B. J. (1992). *Manual for the Developmental Behaviour Checklist: Primary carer version.* Sydney, Australia: School of Psychiatry, University of New South Wales.

Einfeld, S. L., & Tonge, B. J. (1996). Population prevalence of psychopathology in children and adolescents with intellectual disability: II. Epidemiological findings. *Journal of Intellectual Disability Research, 40,* 99–109.

Ewart, A. K., Norris, C. A., Atkinson, D., Jin, W., Sternes, K., Spallone, P., et al. (1993). Hemizygosity at the elastin locus in a developmental disorder, Williams syndrome. *Nature Genetics, 5,* 11–16.

Feldman, M. A. (1994). Parenting education for parents with intellectual disabilities: A review of outcome studies. *Research in Developmental Disabilities, 15,* 299–332.

Fombonne, E. (1999). The epidemiology of autism: A review. *Psychological Medicine, 29,* 769–786.

Frank, E., & Young, E. (2000). Pubertal changes and adolescent challenges: Why do rates of depression rise precipitously for girls between ages 10 and 15 years? In E. Frank (Ed.), *Gender and its effects on psychopathology* (pp. 85–112). Washington, DC: Psychiatric Press.

Garber, J., Keiley, M. K., & Martin, N. C. (2002). Developmental trajectories of adolescents' depressive symptoms: Predictors of change. *Journal of Consulting & Clinical Psychology, 70*, 79–95.

Gillberg, C., Persson, E., Grufman, M., & Themner, U. (1986). Psychiatric disorders in mildly and severely mentally retarded urban children and adolescents: Epidemiological aspects. *British Journal of Psychiatry, 149*, 68–74.

Glick, M., & Zigler, E. (1995). Developmental differences in the symptomatology of psychiatric inpatients with and without mild mental retardation. *American Journal on Mental Retardation, 99*, 407–417.

Gosch, A., & Pankau, R. (1997). Personality characteristics and behavior problems in individuals of different ages with Williams syndrome. *Developmental Medicine and Child Neurology, 39*, 527–533.

Gullone, E., Cummins, R. A., & King, N. J. (1996). Self-reported fears: A comparison study of youths with and without an intellectual disability. *Journal of Intellectual Disability Research, 40*, 227–240.

Gullone, E., King, N. J., & Cummins, R. A. (1996). Fears of youth with mental retardation: Psychometric evaluation of the Fear Survey Schedule for Children-II (FSSC-II). *Research in Developmental Disabilities, 17*, 269–284.

Hardan, A., & Sahl, R. (1997). Psychopathology in children and adolescents with developmental disorders. *Research in Developmental Disabilities, 18*, 369–382.

Harter, S. (1999). *The construction of the self: A developmental perspective.* New York: Guilford.

Hodapp, R. M. (2002). Parenting children with mental retardation. In M. Bornstein (Ed.), *Handbook of parenting.* Vol. 1: *How children influence parents* (2nd ed., pp. 355–381). Hillsdale, NJ: Erlbaum.

Hodapp, R. M., & Dykens, E. M. (1994). Mental retardation's two cultures of behavioral research. *American Journal on Mental Retardation, 98*, 675–687.

Hodapp, R. M., & Dykens, E. M. (2004). Studying behavioural phenotypes: Issues, benefits, challenges. In E. Emerson, C. Hatton, T. Parmenter, & T. Thompson (Eds.), *International handbook of applied research in intellectual disabilities* (pp. 203–220). Sussex, UK: Wiley.

Hodapp, R. M., & Fidler, D. J. (1999). Special education and genetics: Connections for the 21st century. *Journal of Special Education, 33*, 130–137.

Hodapp, R. M., & Ricci, L. A. (2002). Behavioural phenotypes and educational practice: The unrealized connection. In G. O'Brien & O. Udwin (Eds.), *Behavioural phenotypes in clinical practice* (pp. 137–151). London: MacKeith.

Holburn, S., Perkins, T., & Vietze, P. (2001). The parent with mental retardation. *International Review of Research in Mental Retardation, 24*, 171–210.

Holland, A. J., Treasure, J., Coskeran, P., & Dallow, J. (1995). Characteristics of the eating disorder in Prader-Willi syndrome: Implications for treatment. *Journal of Intellectual Disability Research, 39*, 373–381.

Holm, V., Cassidy, S. B., Butler, M. G., Hanchett, J. M., Greenswag L. R., Whitman, B. Y., et al. (1993). Prader-Willi syndrome: Consensus diagnostic criteria. *Pediatrics, 91*, 398–402.

Jacobson, J. W. (1990). Do some mental disorders occur less frequently among persons with mental retardation? *American Journal on Mental Retardation, 94*, 596–602.

Lachiewicz A. M., & Dawson, D. V. (1994). Behavior problems of young girls with fragile X syndrome: Factor scores on the Connors parent questionnaire. *American Journal of Medical Genetics, 51*, 364–369.

Lary, J. M., & Paulozzi, L. J. (2001). Sex differences in the prevalence of human birth defects: A population-based study. *Teratology, 64*, 237–251.

Lenhoff, H. M. (1998). Insights into the musical potential of cognitively impaired people diagnosed with Williams syndrome. *Music Therapy, 16*, 33–36.

Lobato, D. (1983). Siblings of handicapped children: A review. *Journal of Autism & Developmental Disorders, 13*, 347–364.

MacLean, W. E., Jr. (Ed.) (1997). *Ellis' handbook of mental deficiency, psychological theory and research* (3rd ed.). Mahwah, NJ: Erlbaum.

Maccoby, E. E., & Jacklin, C. N. (1974). *The psychology of sex differences.* Stanford, CA: Stanford University Press.

Matson, J. L., & Mulick, J. A. (Eds.) (1991). *Handbook of mental retardation* (2nd ed.). New York: Pergamon.

McConkie-Rosell, A., Spiridigliozzi, G. A., Sullivan, J. A., Dawson, D. V., & Lachiewicz, A. M. (2000). Carrier testing in fragile X syndrome: Effect on self-concept. *American Journal of Medical Genetics, 92,* 336–342.

McConkie-Rosell, A., Spiridigliozzi, G. A., Sullivan, J. A., Dawson, D. V. & Lachiewicz, A. M. (2001). Longitudinal study of the carrier testing process for fragile X syndrome: Perceptions and coping. *American Journal of Medical Genetics, 98,* 37–45.

McConkie-Rosell, A., Spiridigliozzi, G. A., Sullivan, J. A., Dawson, D. V. & Lachiewicz, A. M. (2002). Carrier testing in fragile X syndrome: When to tell and test. *American Journal of Medical Genetics, 110,* 36–44.

McLaren, J., & Bryson, S. E. (1987). Review of recent epidemiological studies of mental retardation: Prevalence, associated disorders, and etiology. *American Journal on Mental Retardation, 92,* 243–254.

Meins, W. (1993). Assessment of depression in mentally retarded adults: Reliability and validity of the Children's Depression Inventory (CDI). *Research in Developmental Disabilities, 14,* 299–312.

Menolascino, F. J. (1970). *Psychiatric approaches to mental retardation.* New York: Basic Books.

Mervis, C. B., Morris, C. A., Bertrand, J., & Robinson, B. F. (1999). Williams syndrome: Findings from an integrated program of research. In H. Tager-Flusberg (Ed.), *Neurodevelopmental disorders* (pp. 65–110). Cambridge, MA: MIT Press.

Moss, S., Prosser, B., Ibbotson, B., & Goldberg, D. (1996). Respondent and informant accounts of psychiatric symptoms in a sample of patients with learning disability. *Journal of Intellectual Disability Research, 40,* 457–465.

Orsmond, G. I., & Seltzer, M. M. (2000). Brothers and sisters of adults with mental retardation: Gendered nature of the sibling relationship. *American Journal on Mental Retardation, 105,* 486–508.

Oswald, D. P., Cutinho, M. J., Best, A. B., & Nguyen, N. (2001). Impact of sociodemographic characteristics on identification rates of minority students as having mental retardation. *Mental Retardation, 39,* 351–367.

Pober, B. R., & Dykens, E. M. (1996). Williams syndrome: An overview of medical, cognitive, and behavioral features. *Child and Adolescents Psychiatric Clinics of North America, 5,* 929–943.

Reiss, S. (1988). *Reiss screen for maladaptive behavior.* Chicago: International Diagnostic Systems.

Reiss, S., & Szyszko, J. (1983). Diagnostic overshadowing and professional experience with mentally retarded persons. *American Journal of Mental Deficiency, 87,* 396–402.

Reynolds, W. M., & Baker, J. A. (1988). Assessment of depression in persons with mental retardation. *American Journal on Mental Retardation, 93,* 93–103.

Roeleveld, N., Zielhuis, G. A., & Gabreels, F. (1997). The prevalence of mental retardation: A critical review of recent literature. *Developmental Medicine and Child Neurology, 39,* 125–132.

Roid, G., & Fitts, W. (1988). *Tennessee self-concept scale.* Los Angeles: Western Psychological Services.

Rossiter, L., & Sharpe, D. (2001). The siblings of individuals with mental retardation: A quantitative integration of the literature. *Journal of Child and Family Studies, 10,* 65–84.

Rush, A. J. & Frances, A. (Eds.). (2000). Treatment of psychiatric and behavioral problems in mental retardation. Special issue of the *American Journal on Mental Retardation, 105*(3), 159–228.

Seltzer, G. B., Begun, A., Seltzer, M. M., & Krauss, M. W. (1991). Adults with mental retardation and their aging mothers: Impacts of siblings. *Family Relations, 40,* 310–317.

Singh, N. N., Osborne, J. G., & Huguenin, N. H. (1996). Applied behavioral interventions. In J. W. Jacobson & J. A. Mulick (Eds.), *Manual of diagnosis and professional practice in mental retardation* (pp. 341–353). Washington, DC: American Psychological Association.

Sobesky, W. E., Porter, D., Pennington, B. F., & Hagerman, R. J. (1995). Dimensions of shyness in fragile X females. *Developmental Brain Dysfunction, 8,* 280–292.

Sovner, R. (1986). Limiting factors in the use of the DSM-III criteria with mentally ill/mentally retarded persons. *Psychopharmacology Bulletin, 22,* 1055–1059.

Stromme, P., & Diseth, T. H. (2000). Prevalence of psychiatric diagnoses in children with mental retardation: Data from a population-based study. *Developmental Medicine and Child Neurology, 42,* 266–270.

Stromme, P., & Hagberg, G. (2000). Aetiology in severe and mild mental retardation: A population-based study of Norwegian children. *Developmental Medicine and Child Neurology, 42,* 76–86.

Szymanski, L. S., King, B. H., Goldberg, B., Reid, B. H., Tonge, B. J., & Cain, N. (1998). Diagnosis of mental disorders in people with mental retardation. In S. Reiss & M. G. Aman (Eds.), *Psychotropic medications and developmental disabilities: The international consensus handbook.* Columbus, OH: Nisonger Center, Ohio State University.

Tassone, F., Hagerman, R. J., Ikle, D. N., Dyer, P. N., Lampe, N., Willemsen, R., et al. (1999). FMRP expression as a potential prognostic indicator in fragile X syndrome. *American Journal of Medical Genetics, 84,* 250–261.

Thompson, N. M., Gulley, M. L., Rogeness, G. A., Clayton, R. J., Johnson, C., Hazelot, B., et al. (1994). Neurobehavioral characteristics of CGG amplification status in fragile X females. *American Journal of Medical Genetics, 54,* 378–383.

Tymchuk, A. J., & Andron, L. (1992). Project parenting: Child interactional training with mothers who are mentally handicapped. *Mental Handicap Research, 5,* 4–32.

Udwin, O., & Yule, W. (1991). A cognitive and behavioral phenotype on Williams syndrome. *Journal of Clinical and Experimental Neuropsychology, 13,* 232–244.

Udwin, O., Yule, W., & Martin, N. (1987). Cognitive abilities and behavioral characteristics of children with idiopathic infantile hypercalcaemia. *Journal of Child Psychology and Psychiatry, 28,* 297–309.

Waber, D. P. (1977). Biological substrates of field dependence: Implications of the sex difference. *Psychological Bulletin, 84,* 1076–1087.

Werry, J. S. (1990). Classification and epidemiology. In B. J. Tonge, G. D. Burrows, & J. S. Werry (Eds.), *Handbook of studies on child psychiatry* (pp. 71–82). Amsterdam: Elsevier.

Whitman, B. Y., & Accardo, P. (1990). *When a parent is mentally retarded.* Baltimore, MD: Paul Brookes.

Whitman, B. Y., Graves, B., & Accardo, P. (1987). Mentally retarded parents in the community: Identification method and needs assessment survey. *American Journal on Mental Deficiency, 91,* 636–638.

Wolk, S. I., & Weissman, M. M. (1995). Women and depression: An update. In J. Oldham, & M. Riba (Eds.), *American Psychiatric Press review of psychiatry* (Vol. 14, pp. 227–259). Washington, DC: American Psychiatric Press.

Zigler, E. (1969). Developmental versus difference theories and the problem of motivation. *American Journal of Mental Deficiency, 73,* 536–556.

Zigler, E. (1971). The retarded child as a whole person. In H. E. Adams & W. K. Boardman (Eds.), *Advances in experimental clinical psychology* (pp. 47–121). Oxford: Pergamon.

9

LEARNING DISORDERS IN GIRLS

ARLENE R. YOUNG

Learning disorders are among the most common of all childhood neuro-developmental disorders with an estimated prevalence of between 3% and 10 percent of the school-aged population (American Psychiatric Association 2000). Estimates of prevalence vary across studies, however, with rates as high as 20% reported by some (e.g., Smith, 1998). In addition to their relative frequency, these disorders are of clinical and research importance because of their potentially negative impact on numerous other domains of functioning including social, emotional, and vocational outcomes (for a review see Willcutt & Pennington, 2000). As in many areas of developmental psychopathology, much of what is known about learning disorders is based on samples made up primarily of affected boys. This disproportionate overrepresentation of boys in many research samples has important consequences for our understanding of the nature of learning disorders, associated conditions, and effective interventions for girls. This chapter focuses on girls with LD and reviews the reasons why girls are typically underrepresented in most LD samples. The potential implications of this phenomenon as well as research focusing on girls with learning disorders are also reviewed.

Much of this discussion will focus on reading disorder (RD), a specific type of learning disorder. This is because approximately 80% of children with LD have primary difficulties in the area of reading either in isolation or in combination with difficulties in other academic areas (Mash & Wolfe, 2002). Consequently, the majority of research and virtually all of the large-scale, epidemiological research studies have focused on children with RD or on undifferentiated learning disordered groups of which the most are children who have RD. When a particular study speaks to

ARLENE R. YOUNG, PH.D. • Simon Fraser University, Burnaby, British Columbia, V5A 1S6.

other types of learning disorder, this will be indicated in the discussion below.

LEARNING DISORDERS IN GIRLS

Diagnostic Criteria and Issues of Definition

The task of defining and establishing diagnostic criteria for LD has a long and contentious history and remains an area of considerable debate. A central feature of most definitions is the notion of unexpected academic underachievement in one or more areas. The underachievement is most often attributed to intrinsic, neurobiologically based, learner characteristics. One often-cited definition of LD in the United States is that of the National Joint Committee on Learning Disabilities (NJCLD, 1994). This definition states that:

> Learning disabilities is a general term that refers to a heterogeneous group of disorders manifested by significant difficulties in the acquisition and use of listening, speaking, reading, writing, reasoning, or mathematical abilities. These disorders are intrinsic to the individual, presumed to be due to central nervous system dysfunction, and may occur across the life span. Problems in self-regulatory behaviors, social perception, and social interaction may exist with learning disabilities but do not by themselves constitute a learning disability. Although learning disabilities may occur concomitantly with other handicapping conditions (for example, sensory impairment, mental retardation, social and emotional disturbance) or with environmental influences (such as cultural differences, insufficient/inappropriate instruction, psychogenic factors), it is not the result of these conditions or influences. [pp. 65–66]

Another frequently used definition, especially in clinical settings, is the *DSM-IV-TR* definition (APA, 2000) which includes three specific types of learning disorder based on the specific academic skill area affected including reading disorder, mathematics disorder, and disorder of written expression. The main features of the *DSM-IV-TR* diagnostic criteria are listed as follows:

- Achievement in the specific academic area (reading, mathematics, writing), as measured by individually administered standardized tests, is substantially below that expected for the person's chronological age, measured intelligence, and age-appropriate education.
- The disturbance in criterion A significantly interferes with academic achievement or activities of daily living that require the ability.
- If a sensory deficit is present, the difficulties in achievement are in excess of those associated with the deficit.

Despite the popularity and wide acceptance of the definitions outlined above, the set of diagnostic criteria is far from universal. An ongoing area of debate, for example, involves the use of ability (i.e., IQ) scores as a predictor of expected level of achievement (e.g., Fletcher, Francis, Rourke, Shaywitz, & Shaywitz, 1993; Siegel, 1992, 2003). The possibility of gender bias resulting from using IQ-achievement definitions of reading disability is discussed in greater detail below.

Learning Disability Subtypes

Attempts to subtype patterns of relative strengths and weaknesses has had a long history given the heterogeneity of LD and the observation that certain groups of LD children share common cognitive and behavioral characteristics (e.g., Bakker, 1979; Lovett, 1984; Satz, 1990). Rourke and his colleagues identified three major LD subtypes based on specific patterns of neuropsychological strengths and weaknesses. These include a subtype labeled Basic Phonological Processing Disorder, evidenced by relatively poor psycholinguistic skills but well-developed visual-spatial and nonverbal problem-solving skills. The second subtype, called Nonverbal Learning Disability (NLD), is typified by problems in visual-spatial organization and nonverbal problem solving. Finally, the third subtype, referred to as Output Disorder, is described as one in which word finding and expressive language is problematic but additional difficulties in output in writing of words and written arithmetic are noted (for a review see Rourke, 2000; Rourke & Del Dotto, 1994). Much of Rourke's work focuses on identifying the cognitive, academic, and psychosocial characteristics of the NLD subtype.

Despite this impressive body of work, few studies have examined the relations between gender and the cognitive, academic, or psychosocial characteristics and developmental outcomes in this group of LD youngsters. Further, the prevalence and incidence of NLD in general and in girls is particular is unclear as no large-scale, epidemiological studies have been reported. Differences in the definition and diagnostic criteria for the disorder also contribute to the current uncertainty regarding the incidence of NLD among girls. Considerably more is known, however, about the most cited academic deficit associated with NLD, mathematics disability (MD), and this literature is briefly outlined below.

Mathematics Disability

In contrast to the prolific literature on reading disability, research on mathematics disability (MD) is still in its formative years. Recent prevalence estimates in school-aged populations from a variety of countries range from 3% to 6.5% (Lyon, 1996; Neumarker, 2000; Shalev, Auerbach, Manor, & Gross-Tsur, 2000). This prevalence, based primarily on research and school-based samples, clearly exceeds the 1% estimated prevalence cited for the diagnosis in the *DSM-IV-TR* (APA, 2000) that is based on clinical studies. Interestingly, the usual predominance of boys with developmental disabilities is not evident as boys and girls are equally represented in MD. While no consensus regarding the etiology of MD has been reached, both genetic predisposition (Alarcon, DeFries, Gillis Light, & Pennington, 1997; Shalev, Manor, & Kerem, 2001) and structural brain abnormalities have received empirical support. The etiology of MD and mathematics achievement problems in general may vary by gender, however, as social factors, such as, parent, teacher, and peer influences have been shown to contribute to gender differences in mathematics achievement and attitudes across the normal continuum (e.g., Goldin, 2000; Tocci & Engelhard, 1991) and in MD (Shalev et al., 2000). Further, the pattern of neurocognitive strengths and weaknesses of individuals with specific arithmetic difficulties proposed by Rourke and colleagues (e.g., poor nonverbal skills relative to verbal skills) may be a fitting model for boys but not necessarily for girls. This possibility is raised by a large, prospective study by Share, Moffitt, and Silva (1988) in which girls with specific arithmetic disability did not differ from controls in either language or nonlanguage measures while boys with specific arithmetic disability replicated Rourke's predicted pattern of reverse strengths and weaknesses from boys with language-based LD. These results again speak to the need for more large-scale studies examining the potentially unique patterns of strengths and weaknesses among NLD or MD girls.

Reading Disability

Differences in prevalence of reading disability in girls compared with boys.   The most typical gender ratio of children with RD in school or clinical referrals is 3:1 favoring boys. This ratio varies considerably across studies, however, ranging from 2:1 up to 15:1 depending on the specifics of a given sample (Adelman & Vogel, 1990; Finucci & Childs, 1981; J. Stevenson, 1992). In keeping with the prevalence of boys identified as RD by school systems and clinical facilities, research samples that are drawn from these sources typically include far fewer girls than boys (Fletcher & Satz, 1984) or entirely male samples (Silva, McGee, & Williams, 1985). Thus, much of what we know about the characteristics of children with learning disabilities is based on research samples that are predominantly male.

Prevalence rates and diagnostic criteria for reading disability. The widely accepted notion that males are much more likely than females to develop reading disabilities was challenged in a study by Shaywitz, Shaywitz, Fletcher, and Escobar (1990), in which they compared the prevalence of RD in boys and girls when research-based (ability-achievement discrepancy in test results) versus school-based criteria (identified as RD by school system) were applied. The sample consisted of 445 grades 2 and 3 children (235 girls and 210 boys) drawn from a stratified random sample from the Connecticut Longitudinal Study. Results indicated that while there was no significant gender difference in the prevalence of RD using research-based criteria, the school-based criteria identified 2 to 4 times more boys than girls. A subsequent large, epidemiological study by Flynn and Rahbar (1994), reported similar results with roughly equal proportions of boys and girls failing at reading according to test results but boys outnumbering girls by teacher-identified criteria by a ratio of 2:1.

These findings have prompted some to argue that the higher prevalence of males in LD samples is an artifact of referential and diagnostic biases. In contrast, others (Badian, 1999; Rutter & Yule, 1975), report higher incidence of males in research identified samples. To date, the most comprehensive study addressing this issue is that of Flannery, Liederman, Daly, and Schultz (2000). Flannery et al. reported on a sample of children identified as RD using objective test data (N = 1405) taken from a total sample of over 32,000 children in an exceptionally large, prospective study (the National Collaborative Perinatal Project). Given that the children were recruited for the study when their mothers were pregnant, the sample is free of ascertainment bias. Results indicated that RD was more prevalent in boys irrespective of the racial or economic differences or severity of the disorder. On average, boys exceeded girls by at least 2:1. Flannery et al. concluded that male vulnerability to RD is not an artifact of (1) ascertainment bias, (2) the IQ-based discrepancy technique of diagnosis, (3) greater heterogeneity of reading performance in males, or (4) sex differences in behaviours such as inattention or overactivity. It should be noted, however, that despite this rather compelling evidence sex differences in prevalence of RD, the sex ratio of children referred for special reading services greatly exceeds 2:1. Thus, while reading disability does appear to be more prevalent in boys than girls, it is clear that boys are overdiagnosed while girls are underdiagnosed in both school and clinical settings.

Explanations for the gender difference in the incidence of LD can be roughly grouped into three main themes: biological, behavioral, and artifactual. The following sections provide very brief overviews of each of these explanations and the implications for girls with LD.

Biological explanations. In addition to LD, boys outnumber girls in a wide array of neuro-developmental disorders including mental retardation, (Richardson, Katz, & Koller, 1986), Tourettes' syndrome, cerebral palsy, speech and language disorders, autism (Fombonne, 1999; Gualtieri & Hicks, 1985; Volkmar & Klin, 2000), and attention deficit hyperactivity disorder (ADHD) (Szatmari, 1992). Theories about the mechanisms underlying male vulnerability to LD in general and RD in particular are varied and include differential rates of maturation, chromosomal factors, threshold differences for genetic vulnerability or birth complications, gestational hormones, and maternal immune response to the male fetus (e.g., Hugdahl, 1993; Tallal & Fitch, 1993). Geschwind and Behan (1982) and later Geschwind and Galaburda (1985a; 1985b; 1985c) proposed that fetal testosterone affects on cerebral lateralization could account for many of the associations between neuro-developmental disorders, learning and language problems, immune disorders, and anomalous dominance (e.g., left-handedness) often associated with LD. Very briefly, the Geschwind–Galaburda model posits that individual differences in testosterone levels are a common source of differences in the developing brain and immune systems. In particular, prenatal testosterone levels, determined primarily through the H-Y antigen that determines maleness, slows the growth of the posterior region of the left hemisphere. This left hemisphere growth delay is, in turn, associated with "anomalous dominance" evidenced by mixed or left-handedness, and a lack of the more typical strong, left hemisphere dominance for language (see also Finucci & Childs, 1981; Galaburda, Sherman, Rosen, Aboitiz, & Geschwind, 1985; Kelley, 1993; McManus & Bryden, 1991; Tallal & Fitch, 1993). While predictably more common in boys, girls may also be exposed to atypically high levels of progestogens *in utero* or may have increased tissue sensitivity to testosterone, which theoretically results in higher effective prenatal testosterone levels.

Critiques of the Geschwind–Galaburda model have focused primarily on lower-than-predicted levels of immune disorders and anomalous dominance (as evidenced by left-handedness) in the population of children with developmental learning disorders (e.g., Bishop, 1990; Locke & Macaruso, 1999; Satz & Soper, 1986). Nevertheless, the model provides a major impetus for research into interuterine factors affecting fetal brain development that will ultimately speak to gender differences in vulnerability to developmental learning disorders.

Genetic explanations.   Converging evidence amassed over the past three decades leaves virtually no doubt that genetics plays a major, though not exclusive role in the etiology of reading disorders (for an excellent review see Grigorenko, 2001). Three types of research methodology have demonstrated the heritability of reading disorders including (1) family studies (DeFries, Olson, Pennington, & Smith, 1991; Wolff & Melngailis, 1994), (2) twin studies (Brooks, Fulkner, & DeFries, 1990; DeFries, Fulkner, & LaBuda, 1987; Gayán & Olson, 1999; Wadsworth, Knopik, & DeFries, 2000), and (3) molecular genetic studies (Cardon et al., 1994; Grigorenko et al., 1997; Morris et al., 2000). Given the widely reported sex differences in prevalence of RD, considerable interest has been raised regarding the possibility of different genetic etiology across genders. In particular, it has been speculated that there may be a greater genetic influence on reading for females than males (Finucci & Childs, 1981).

One of the most comprehensive examinations of possible gender differences in the genetic etiology of RD has been conducted by the twin studies from the Colorado Reading Project and the Colorado Learning Disabilities Research Center (DeFries, 1989; DeFries et al., 1987, 1991). Earlier studies that reported on twin pairs in this continually expanding data set, were suggestive of possible gender differences but limitations in sample size made definitive statements difficult. In a more recent study from this research group (Wadsworth et al., 2000), the largest sample to date including 206 identical, 59 same-sex fraternal, and 117 opposite-sex fraternal twins with at least one member with RD was examined for possible gender differences. Results revealed no differences in the magnitude of genetic factors for males and females. Nevertheless, in this and other publications regarding gender difference in the genetics of RD (e.g., Knopik, DeFries, & Alarcon, 1998) the possibility is raised that, while the magnitude of genetic influences may be similar, sex-specific genetic influences may vary. This possibility is yet to be studied.

Behavioral explanations. The notion that teacher-initiated referrals to special education classes are prompted, in part, by classroom behavior problems is both intuitively reasonable and empirically supported. In the Connecticut Longitudinal Study, for example, Shaywitz and colleagues (1990), reported that teachers rate normal boys as significantly higher than normal girls in activity level and behavior problems. Similarly, the school-identified RD children in the Shaywitz et al. study were rated by teachers as significantly higher in these two behavioral descriptions than the research-identified RD group. These findings suggest that the behavior problems may be influential in determining whether reading-disabled children are and are not identified by their schools. In particular, children with cooccurring behavior problems are most likely to be identified as RD within the school setting. Similar results are reported by numerous other studies (e.g., Andrews, Wisniewski, & Mulick, 1997; Mirkin, 1982). The established gender differences in both activity level and behavior problems may well account for the differentially high referral rates for boys. Attention deficit hyperactivity disorder (ADHD), which frequently cooccurs with RD, is known to be more common in boys in both clinical and community samples (Barkley, 1997; McGee et al., 1990).

The pedagogical challenge of managing children with both academic and behavioral problems in a standard classroom setting undoubtedly contributes to differential referral of children who are comorbid for ADHD and RD to special education classes. Thus, teachers may overlook girls who are struggling academically but are less likely to evidence behavioral problems. Given limited resources, they may be less inclined to refer well-behaved girls for assessment and educational intervention than boys who are demonstrating a similar level of academic difficulty.

Gender bias as statistical artifact. Finally, the difference in incidence of RD for boys versus girls may reflect a bias resulting from the IQ-discrepancy definition. In particular, because boys tend to have lower reading achievement scores than girls, especially in the primary grades (e.g., Phillips, Norris, & Osmond, 2002) and the IQ-discrepancy formula is based on predicted achievement from gender-pooled norms, the predicted level of achievement will be systematically overestimated for boys and underestimated for girls. If shown to be true, this statistical artifact will result in boys being overidentified as RD while girls will be more likely to be missed. This hypothesis was examined by Share and Silva (2003) in a sample of over 900, 11-year-old children. RD groups were identified using regression equations predicting reading from IQ for gender-separate and gender-combined groups. RD children were identified as those whose reading scores were greater than 1.5 standard errors below the prediction. Predicted reading scores for the boys were overestimated by approximately 3 points while those of the girls were underestimated by the same amount. This prediction bias meant that an additional 23 boys were identified as RD while 16 girls were excluded from the definition when gender-combined versus separate gender norms were used.

Thus, these findings reinforce the need for caution in interpreting findings about gender differences in LD as girls with more severe LD are most likely to be identified given ascertainment biases inherent in school-based or clinical samples (Adelman & Vogel, 1990; Berry, Shaywitz, & Shaywitz, 1985) and systematic biases inherent in IQ-discrepancy diagnoses.

Characteristics of LD in Girls

Core Cognitive Characteristics

Research accumulated over the past two decades leaves little doubt that a core cognitive feature of RD is an underlying deficit in a specific aspect of language processing referred to as phonological awareness (e.g., Stanovich & Siegel, 1994; Vellutino & Scanlon, 1987; Wagner et al., 1997). Phonological awareness refers to the ability to recognize and manipulate the sound structure of language. No consistent gender differences in phonological awareness have been reported and both boys and girls with RD appear equally impaired in this regard. There are, however, other areas of cognitive functioning in which boys and girls do differ and these areas are highlighted below for normally achieving and children with LD. Much of this information is drawn from a comprehensive review of gender differences in students with LD by Vogel (1990) and reviews of sex differences in cognition of normally achieving adults (Halpern, 1997; Kimura, 1999). Most studies of gender differences in intelligence of normally developing individuals report that males and females do not differ on overall composite scores of cognitive ability across the age span (e.g., Lawson, Inglis, & Tittemore, 1987). When specific areas of ability are examined, females have been shown to have slightly higher verbal abilities while males show a similar advantage in nonverbal areas (Adelman & Vogel, 1990). The magnitude of the differences is typically small, however, and there is substantial overlap of performance between the genders (e.g., Hyde & Linn, 1988; Tittemore, Lawson, & Inglis, 1985). Within the nonverbal domain, the most notable and robust differences are noted in large differences in favor of males for certain spatial abilities (orientation, mental rotation, and visualization) as well as motor skills, especially when targeting (e.g., hitting a target) is required (Kimura, 1999). These differences are particularly apparent following puberty (Adelman & Vogel, 1990; Kimura, 1999). Females have been shown to perform better than males on some visual-motor tasks including fine motor tasks and perceptual speed tasks (Halpern, 1997; Kimura, 1999).

Gender patterns in the performance for students with LD have shown some important differences from those of the normally developing population. In particular, females with LD have been shown to have lower IQ scores (including FSIQ, VIQ, and PIQ) than males with LD (Adelman & Vogel, 1990; Vogel & Walsh, 1987). In addition, females tend to be referred for special services at older ages than their male counterparts (Vogel, 1990). These findings have important clinical and theoretical implications as in order to be identified within the school system as LD, a girl needs to wait longer and to demonstrate more severe cognitive and academic problems than do boys. This speaks to potentially limited generalizability of findings related to the characteristics of system-identified females and outcomes in adulthood. Notably absent are studies of the cognitive, social, and vocational characteristics of higher-functioning girls with LD.

An examination of gender patterns across various areas of cognitive functioning has shown that unlike their male counterparts, girls with LD have a relative strength on the Coding subtest of the Wechsler intelligence scales (Wechsler, 1981, 1991) (for a review see Adelman & Vogel, 1990). This subtest assesses the ability to rapidly copy a series of novel visual symbols coupled with numbers. Associated processing abilities include attentional skills, visual-motor coordination, handwriting speed, and verbal-encoding among other abilities (e.g., Sattler, 2001). The relative strength in girls on the Coding subtest is notable because this subtest is often cited among groupings of subtests known to be the most difficult for LD children. Such groupings include the Arithmetic, Coding, Information and Digit Span, often given the acronym (ACID) (e.g., Kaufman, 1994) and the Symbol Search, Coding, Arithmetic, and Digit Span subtests (Prifitera & Dersh, 1993). In fact, although not recommended (e.g., see Beitchman & Young, 1997), it is not uncommon for clinicians to look for a characteristic relative weakness in this grouping of subtests when diagnosing LD. The relative strength for females both with and without LD on the Coding subtest, therefore, could contribute to lower rates of identification by clinicians using these patterns of subtest scores based on predominantly male samples.

Social Functioning and Peer Acceptance

The notion that LD may have implications beyond academic performance has gained considerable attention in the literature. The work of Bryan (1974, 1976; Bryan & Bryan, 1990; Bryan, Sullivan-Burstein, & Mathur, 1998; Wong & Donahue, 2002), for example, has drawn attention to the social difficulties of children with LD. The underlying cause of these difficulties has also been explored. For example, considerable evidence has accrued indicating that children with LD have difficulty processing social and emotional cues as well as processing other kinds of information and that these processing deficits impact their social performance (e.g., Ochoa & Olivarez, 1995; Pearl, 1992; Swanson, 1996; Swanson & Malone, 1992). Additionally, over 20 years of research has consistently shown that students with LD have lower peer status than non-LD students (Ochoa & Olivarez, 1995). This finding is consistent despite the heterogeneity of the LD population and differences in measures used to assess peer status or social performance (Vaughn, Hogan, Kouzekanani, & Shapiro, 1990). But what, if anything, is known about the social functioning of girls with LD?

As with other areas of functioning discussed thus far, this issue has received relatively little attention to date in the research literature. Notable exceptions, however, include a study by Wong and Wong (1980) in which the social perspective-taking or role-taking ability of students with

LD was examined. They found that girls but not boys with LD showed lower perspective-taking skills than their non-LD peers. There is also some evidence that LD girls may be rated more negatively by peers than males with LD. Bryan (1974, 1976) for example, found that the groups most likely to be rated negatively by peers were girls with LD and white students with LD. These findings hint at the possibility that girls with LD may suffer more stigma and loss of social status than boys given that they appear to differ more markedly from gender-based social expectations of performance. Further research, especially studies that draw on community rather than system-identified samples of girls with LD are needed to clarify these intriguing findings.

Common Comorbidities

The extent to which children and adults with learning disorders evidence emotional and psychiatric difficulties has been of long-standing research and clinical interest. It has been shown, for example, that children with RD have more social and emotional problems than their non-RD peers (Beitchman & Young, 1997). This overlap is particularly well established in the area of externalizing disorders including attention problems, disruptive behavior disorders, and conduct disorder and this association is higher in boys than girls (Hinshaw, 1992; Smart, Sanson, & Prior, 1996; Willcutt & Pennington, 2000). The overlap among various disorders, including LD, ADHD, and mood and behavioral disorders is so substantial, in fact, that some (Kaplan, Dewey, Crawford, & Wilson, 2001) have questioned the validity of the term comorbidity, arguing instead, that commonly overlapping conditions all reflect various aspects of atypical brain development. Setting this argument aside for the purpose of this review, a small body of research has identified some areas in which gender differences affect the overlap between LD and other disorders. Girls have been shown, for example, to be more severely affected than boys as indicated by a higher number of cooccurring disorders and more severe forms of learning or language disorders (Gualtieri & Hicks, 1985; Kaplan et al., 2001; Tirosh & Cohen, 1998).

Attention Deficit Hyperactivity Disorder and LD

Attention deficit hyperactivity disorder (ADHD) and RD cooccur more frequently than can be accounted for by chance, with comorbidity rates of 25% to 40% reported (Dykman & Ackerman, 1991; Semrud-Clikeman et al., 1992). Research examining the overlap of attention deficit disorder both with hyperactivity (ADDH) and without (ADDWO) in both clinical (Barkley, DuPaul, & McMurray, 1990; Goodyear & Hynd, 1992; Marshall, Hynd, Handwerk, & Hall, 1997; Semrud-Clikeman et al., 1992) and community samples (Willcutt & Pennington, 2000) has shown the strongest relationship between ADDWO and RD. Given the predominance of males in both RD and ADHD samples, especially when clinically or school-based, most studies do not have the statistical power to examine gender differences in the association between ADHD and RD.

The study by Willcutt and Pennington (2000) is a clear exception, however, as they reported on the overlap between these disorders in the large twin study data set gathered through the Colorado Learning Disabilities Research Center (Alarcon et al., 1997; DeFries et al., 1991). In all, 494 twins with RD (223 girls, 271 boys) and 373 non-RD twins (189 girls, 184 boys) were assessed using standardized and well-validated diagnostic techniques to determine whether or not they met criteria for *DSM-IV* ADHD diagnoses including the Predominantly Inattentive, Hyperactive/Impulsive, or Combined types. Results of the study revealed that for girls, the association between RD and ADHD was limited to the inattentive subtype while boys with RD exhibited a higher prevalence of all ADHD symptoms and were more likely to meet criteria for all subtypes. Further, while the boy-to-girl ratio for their entire, community-based sample was 1.22 to 1 (consistent with many other community samples described earlier (Shaywitz et al., 1990), the gender ratios for the combination of RD and hyperactive or inattentive symptoms was much higher for boys than for girls (3.76 to 1). These findings are of note for several reasons. First, they provide additional support for the role of disruptive, hyperactive behavior in bringing attention to boys with learning difficulties. Second, they speak to a possible reason why girls may go unrecognized unless careful academic assessment and tracking is pursued. In particular, a typical feature of the inattentive subtype is lack of engagement and participation in tasks, especially in group settings. In contrast to their more behaviorally prominent male counterparts, girls with both RD and ADHD are likely to fade into the background in a classroom setting. Thus, those that may be most in need of identification and remediation may be easily overlooked.

Mood and Anxiety Disorders

There is a growing body of evidence to suggest that children, adolescents, and adults with LD are more likely to experience depression (Colbert, Newman, Ney, & Young, 1982; Goldstein, Paul, & Sanfilippo-Cohen, 1985; Hall & Haws, 1989; Huntington & Bender, 1993; D. T. Stevenson & Romney, 1984; Wright-Strawderman & Watson, 1992) and anxiety (Boetsch, Green, & Pennington, 1996; Gregg, Hoy, King, Moreland, & Jagota, 1992; Huntington & Bender, 1993) than those without LD (Willcutt & Pennington, 2000). While both anxiety disorders and depression are more common among females than males in the general population, especially in adolescence and adulthood (Kessler, McGonagle, & Zhao, 1994; Lewinsohn, Clarke, Seeley, & Rohde, 1994), females with LD have higher rates of depression than their non-LD peers. A possible explanation for this increased risk is provided by a study by Heath and Wiener (1996) in which they examined the relationships between nonacademic self-perceptions (social, athletic, physical appearance, and behavioral conduct) and depression in children with and without LD. They found that lower self-perceived social acceptance was related to depression only for students with LD. Furthermore only females with LD showed a relationship between lower self-perception of physical appearance and depression. Thus, in keeping with the earlier reported findings of lower peer acceptance ratings for girls with LD than boys with LD or non-LD children (Bryan, 1974, 1976), girls with LD appear to be at particular risk for depression, especially when they experience rejection by their peers.

Developmental Course and Outcomes

Results of numerous studies conducted over the past 15 years have revealed some consistent findings regarding adult outcomes in individuals with LD (e.g., Young et al., 2002). Specifically, academic difficulties tend to persist into adulthood; individuals with LD are at greater risk for unemployment or underemployment, and at increased risk for emotional adjustment difficulties during adulthood (Blackorby & Wagner, 1996; Maughan & Hagell, 1998; Sitlington & Frank, 1993; Vogel & Adelman, 1992; Wagner, 1992; White, 1992). In all of these domains, women with LD have been shown to do less well than men with LD or women without LD (Levine & Edgar, 1994; Levine & Nourse, 1998; Maughan & Hagell, 1998; Sitlington & Frank, 1990; Wagner, 1992).

Rojewski (1999) reported on the findings of the National Educational Longitudinal Study (1988–1994), a large, U.S. nationally representative, longitudinal study of adolescents and young adults looking at educational, vocational, and personal development. In this study, LD was identified based on parent reports of the child receiving special education services. Results revealed that while men with LD tended to fare less well than men without LD in high school completion rates and career aspirations, women with LD performed markedly below both women without LD and men with LD. In particular, 68% of women with LD graduated from high school compared with 91.9% of women without LD and 80% of men with LD. Women with LD were also six times more likely to be unemployed than men with LD in the 2-year post-secondary, follow-up period. Higher rates of unemployment and underemployment for women with LD have been confirmed in other studies (Adelman & Vogel, 1990, 1993; Fourqurean, Meisgeir, Swank, & Williams, 1991; Haring, Lovett, & Smith, 1990; Levine & Edgar, 1994; Miller, Snider, & Rzonca, 1990; Scuccimarra & Speece, 1990; Sitlington & Frank, 1990). Rojewski concluded that "The combined effects of being a woman and experiencing LD had a substantial negative effect on career choice and attainment" (p. 548).

A particularly striking finding from the National Longitudinal Transition Study reported by Wagner (1992) is that women with disabilities (including but not limited to LD) were five times more likely to be parenting at an early age than women without disabilities. Further, these women were more likely to be single parenting. Similar findings were reported by Levine and Edgar (Cardon et al.) in a study of two cohorts of graduates of special education programs and those from regular education programs within Washington State 1, 2, 6, and 7 years after high school graduation. Thus, for females with LD, the combined impact of early parenthood, lower high school completion rates, and lower vocational status represent a heavy burden that apparently exceeds that of men with LD.

These findings, while replicated across several studies, should, nonetheless, be interpreted with some caution. First, all of the studies described are based on system-identified populations (i.e., those referred for assessment or participation in special education programs in the school system). As noted earlier in the discussion of Vogel's (1990) findings, females identified in this way are more severely impaired than males as indicated by lower IQs and poorer academic achievement. Thus, these outcomes may be overly pessimistic and may not reflect those of the broader distribution of the female LD population. Other factors leading to identification within the school setting, such as comorbid conditions, may also play a role in these negative outcomes. Some support for this possibility is apparent in a study of adult outcomes in 48 women with LD and their non-LD sisters (Goodman, 1987). The children followed in this study were treated in a private center and were classified as middle-to-high in SES. Contrary to the negative outcomes cited earlier, the clients with LD and their sisters showed few differences in outcome and both groups were faring well in vocational, educational, and self-esteem outcomes. This was especially true after the age of 25 years. The mean age of the participants in Goodman's study were 37 years. This presents another potential caution in interpreting the negative results from other studies that typically measure outcomes at much younger ages. It is possible that girls with LD show a slower rate of transition into adult roles or their progress is disrupted by early parenting. Nonetheless, they may eventually perform at higher levels than is apparent during the first few years after high school. Thus, while the findings to date indicate significantly greater risks for poor outcomes in girls with LD, they may present an overly pessimistic view than is warranted in the larger population of females with LD. Later age at diagnosis may also play a role in the relatively poorer outcomes for girls. Nevertheless, these findings speak to specific areas of concern, especially within the system-identified, LD population.

Assessment and Treatment Implications

Girls with LD identified through the school system have been shown to be older and more severely impaired than boys as evidenced by lower IQs and more severe academic achievement deficits (Adelman & Vogel, 1990). Additionally, they are more likely to have internalizing rather than externalizing behavioral problems. Taken together, these gender differences mean that girls with LD are less likely to receive early access to assessment and treatment than boys. This has important implications as persistent learning problems, in particular reading problems, have long-term negative consequences. In addition to limitations in academic achievement, persistent reading problems have a negative impact on general cognitive development (Cunningham & Stanovich, 1998) and verbal reasoning abilities (Stanovich, 1986). Over the past decade, early identification and intervention has been repeatedly shown to have the greatest benefit with declining returns apparent with later intervention (for a review see Torgesen, 2000). In the Connecticut Longitudinal Study, for example, where children's reading skills were followed from kindergarten through grade 12, children identified as LD after grade 2 rarely caught up with their peers (Shaywitz et al., 1999). In general, older poor readers respond less to intervention than younger poor readers. Thus, girls who tend to go unnoticed for a longer period of time are at greater risk for chronic learning problems with their associated potentially debilitating social and vocational implications.

What then can be done to reduce these risks? The answer appears to lie in changing the currently held practice of identifying and intervening only after children show continued academic failure or relying on teacher nomination of children at risk. In a recent report by a group of well-established, learning disability researchers (Lyon et al., 2001), far-reaching changes were called for in the development of prevention and early intervention programs to address these issues. While these researchers addressed their comments to learning-disabled children in general and did not refer to gender differences, their recommendations provide guidelines that have important implications for girls with LD. Specifically, they recommend changes in the definition of LD including discarding the IQ-achievement criterion and excluding children because of inadequate instruction, cultural, and social factors and replacing this with evidence-based definitions that specify the precise characteristics of children who have LD in specific academic areas. These characteristics have already been recognized to a large extent in the identification of phonological processing problems central to RD but similar efforts are needed for other academic areas including mathematics, and written expression. Lyon et al. (2001) also argue for including a student's response to well-designed and well-implicated intervention programs as a part of LD identification criteria. In terms of prevention and early intervention they recommend wide-scale improvements to teacher education and the adoption of evidence-based, intensive intervention programs for at-risk children within the regular classroom setting. Wide-scale screening to identify children who are not progressing in the various academic areas would, under this revised approach, be administered by classroom teachers in each of the first few years following school entry. Special educators who are now involved in direct instruction of the relatively few children identified and withdrawn from the regular classroom would instead be involved in developing activities related to prevention. This restructuring of educational policy, while potentially helpful to all students with LD and at risk for LD, may be particularly efficacious in identifying and intervening with at risk girls who so often go unnoticed in the current system. As such, they offer exciting possibilities of educational practice and research.

Finally, given the apparently more pessimistic adult outcomes for girls with LD than boys, intervention needs to focus not only on promoting academic gains but on targeting social and emotional needs as well. Nonacademic factors shown to predict a more positive outcome include self-awareness, perseverance, and emotional stability (Raskind, Goldberg, Higgins, & Herman, 1999) and these factors should be addressed in programming for girls with LD.

Future Directions

This examination of current literature on the manifestations and outcomes of LD in females clearly reveals the need for prospective research using community rather than system-based samples. Only through such research can the outcomes and differential risks for girls with LD be accurately identified and evaluated. In addition, more research is needed into LD in girls in areas outside of reading disorder. Of particular interest are the outcomes in girls with mathematics disorders or with nonverbal learning disorders. The interplay between social and emotional functioning in girls with these latter types of LD are also areas of future research that have, to date, been less researched despite important practice and theoretical implications. As noted in the earlier section, however, regardless of the outcomes of these community samples, early, preventive interventions for all students at risk, but especially for girls who tend to be less easily identified in the school setting, offers the most potentially beneficial focus for future clinical and research directions.

REFERENCES

Adelman, P. B., & Vogel, S. A. (1990). College graduates with learning disabilities: Employment attainment and career patterns. *Learning Disabilities Quarterly, 13,* 154–166.

Adelman, P. B., & Vogel, S. A. (1993). Issues in the employment of adults with learning disabilities. *Learning Disabilities Quarterly, 16,* 219–232.

Alarcon, M., DeFries, J. C., Gillis Light, J., & Pennington, B. F. (1997). A twin study of mathematics disability. *Journal of Learning Disabilities, 30,* 617–623.

Andrews, T. J., Wisniewski, J. J., & Mulick, J. A. (1997). Variables influencing teachers' decisions to refer children for school psychological assessment services. *Psychology in the Schools, 34,* 239–244.

American Psychiatric Association (APA) (2000). *Diagnostic and statistical manual of mental disorders* DSM-IV-TR *(Text Revision).* Washington, DC: Author.

Badian, N. A. (1999). Reading disability defined as a discrepancy between listening and reading comprehension: A longitudinal study of stability, gender differences, and prevalence. *Journal of Learning Disabilities, 32,* 138–148.

Bakker, D. J. (1979). Hemispheric specialization and stages in the learning to read process. *Bulletin of the Orton Society, 23,* 84–100.

Barkley, R. (1997). Attention-deficit/hyperactivity disorder. In E. Mash & L. Terdal (Eds.), *Assessment of childhood disorders,* (3rd ed., pp. 71–129). New York: Guilford.

Barkley, R., DuPaul, G. J., & McMurray, M. B. (1990). A comprehensive evaluation of attention deficit disorder with and without hyperactivity. *Journal of Consulting and Clinical Psychology, 58,* 775–789.

Beitchman, J. H., & Young, A. R. (1997). Learning disorders with a special emphasis on reading disorders: A review of the past 10 years. *Journal of the American Academy of Child and Adolescence Psychiatry, 36,* 1020–1032.

Berry, C., Shaywitz, S. E., & Shaywitz, B. A. (1985). Girls with attention deficit disorder: A silent minority? A report on behavioral and cognitive characteristics. *Pediatrics, 76,* 801–809.

Bishop, D. V. M. (1990). *Handedness and developmental disorder.* Oxford: Blackwell Scientific.

Blackorby, J., & Wagner, M. (1996). Longitudinal postschool outcomes of youth with disabilities: Findings form the National Longitudinal Transition Study. *Exceptional Children, 62,* 399–413.

Boetsch, E. A., Green, P. A., & Pennington, B. F. (1996). Psychosocial correlates of dyslexia across the lifespan. *Development and Psychopathology, 8*, 539–562.

Brooks, A., Fulkner, D. W., & DeFries, J. C. (1990). Reading performance and general cognitive ability: A multivariate genetic analysis of twin data. *Personality and Individual Differences, 11*, 141–146.

Bryan, T. (1974). Peer popularity of learning disabled children. *Journal of Learning Disabilities, 7*, 621–625.

Bryan, T. (1976). Peer popularity of learning disabled children: A replication. *Journal of Learning Disabilities, 9*, 307–311.

Bryan, T., & Bryan, J. (1990). Social factors in learning disabilities: An overview. In H. L. Swanson & B. Keogh (Eds.), *Learning disabilities: Theroretical and research issues* (pp. 131–138). Hillsdale, NJ: Erlbaum.

Bryan, T., Sullivan-Burstein, K., & Mathur, S. (1998). The influence of affect on social-information processing. *Journal of Learning Disabilities, 31*, 418–426.

Cardon, L. R., Smith, S. D., Fulkner, D. W., Kimberling, W. J., Pennington, B. F., & DeFries, J. C. (1994). Quantitative trait locus for reading disability on chromosome 6. *Science, 266*, 276–279.

Colbert, P., Newman, B., Ney, P., & Young, J. (1982). Learning disabilities as a symptom of depression in children. *Journal of Learning Disabilities, 15*, 333–336.

Cunningham, A. E., & Stanovich, K. E. (1998). What reading does for the mind. *American Educator, 22*, 8–15.

DeFries, J. C. (1989). Gender ratios in children with reading disability and their affected relatives. *Journal of Learning Disabilities*, 544–545.

DeFries, J. C., Fulkner, D. W., & LaBuda, M. C. (1987). Evidence for a genetic aetiology in reading disability in twins. *Nature, 329*, 537–539.

DeFries, J. C., Olson, R. D., Pennington, B. F., & Smith, S. D. (1991). Colorado Reading Project: An update. In D. Duane & D. Gray (Eds.), *The reading brain: The biological basis of dyslexia.* Parkton, MD: York Press.

Dykman, R. A., & Ackerman, P. T. (1991). ADD and specific reading disability: Separate but often overlapping disorders. *Journal of Learning Disabilities, 24*, 96–103.

Finucci, J. M., & Childs, B. (1981). Are there really more dyslexic boys than girls? In A. Ansara, N. Geschwind, A. Galaburda, M. Albert & N. Gartrell (Eds.), *Sex differences in dyslexia* (pp. 1–9). Towson, MD: Orton Dyslexia.

Flannery, K. A., Liederman, J., Daly, L., & Schultz, J. (2000). Male prevalence for reading disability is found in a large sample of Black and White children free from ascertainment bias. *Journal of the International Neuropsychological Society, 6*, 433–442.

Fletcher, J. M., Francis, D. J., Rourke, B. P., Shaywitz, S. E., & Shaywitz, B. A. (1993). Classification of learning disabilities. In G. R. Lyon, D. B. Gray, J. F. Kavanagh, & N. A. Krasnegor (Eds.), *Better understanding learning disabilities* (pp. 27–55). Baltimore: Paul H. Brookes.

Fletcher, J. M., & Satz, P. (1984). Test-based versus teacher-based predictions of academic achievement: A three-year longitudinal follow-up. *Journal of Pediatric Psychology, 9*, 193–203.

Flynn, J. M., & Rahbar, M. H. (1994). Prevalence of reading failure in boys compared with girls. *Psychology in the Schools, 31*, 66–71.

Fombonne, E. (1999). The epidemiology of autism: A review. *Psychological Medicine, 29*, 769–786.

Fourqurean, J. M., Meisgeir, C., Swank, P. R., & Williams, R. E. (1991). Correlates of post-secondary employment outcomes for young adults with learning disabilities. *Journal of Learning Disabilities, 24*, 400–405.

Galaburda, A. M., Sherman, G. P., Rosen, G. D., Aboitiz, F., & Geschwind, N. (1985). Developmental dyslexia: Four consecutive patients with cortical anomalies. *Annals of Neurology, 18*, 222–233.

Gayán, J., & Olson, R. K. (1999). Reading disability: Evidence for a genetic etiology. *European Child and Adolescence Psychiatry, 8*(Suppl. 3), 52–55.

Geschwind, N., & Behan, P. (1982). Left-handedness: Association with immune disease, migraine, and developmental learning disorder. *Proceedings of the National Academy of Science, 79*, 5097–5100.

Geschwind, N., & Galaburda, A. (1985a). Cerebral lateralization: Biological mechanisms, associations, and pathology: I. A hypothesis and a program for research. *Archives of Neurology, 42,* 5428–5459.

Geschwind, N., & Galaburda, A. (1985b). Cerebral lateralization: Biological mechanisms, associations, and pathology: II. A hypothesis and a program for research. *Archives of Neurology, 42,* 521–552.

Geschwind, N., & Galaburda, A. (1985c). Cerebral lateralization: Biological mechanisms, associations, and pathology: III. A hypothesis and a program for research. *Archives of Neurology, 42,* 634–654.

Goldin, G. A. (2000). Affective pathways and representation in mathematical problem solving. *Mathematical Thinking and Learning, 2,* 209–219.

Goldstein, P., Paul, G. G., & Sanfilippo-Cohen, S. (1985). Depression and achievement in subgroups of children with learning disabilities. *Journal of Applied Developmental Psychology, 6,* 263–275.

Goodman, N. C. (1987). Girls with learning disabilities and their sisters: How are they faring in adulthood? *Journal of Clinical Child Psychology, 16,* 290–300.

Goodyear, P., & Hynd, G. W. (1992). Attention-deficit disorder with (ADD/H) and without (ADD/WO) hyperactivity: Behavioral and neuropsychological differentiation. *Journal of Clinical Child Psychology, 21,* 273–305.

Gregg, N., Hoy, C., King, M., Moreland, C., & Jagota, M. (1992). The MMPI-2 profile of adults with learning disabilities in university and rehabilitation settings. *Journal of Learning Disabilities, 25,* 386–395.

Grigorenko, E. L. (2001). Developmental dyslexia: An update on genes, brains, and environments. *Journal of Child Psychology, Psychiatry and Allied Disciplines, 42*(1), 91–125.

Grigorenko, E. L., Wood, F. B., Meyer, M. S., Hart, L. A., Speed, W. C., Shuster, A., et al. (1997). Susceptibility loci for distinct components of developmental dyslexia on chromosomes 6 and 15. *American Journal of Human Genetics, 60,* 27–39.

Gualtieri, T., & Hicks, R. (1985). An immunoreactive theory of selective male affliction. *Behavioral and Brain Sciences, 8,* 427–431.

Hall, C. W., & Haws, D. (1989). Depressive symptomatology in learning disabled and non-learning disabled students. *Psychology in the Schools, 26,* 359–364.

Halpern, D. F. (1997). Sex differences in intelligence: Implications for education. *American Psychologist, 52,* 1091–1102.

Haring, K. A., Lovett, D. L., & Smith, D. D. (1990). A follow-up study of recent special education graduates of learning disabilities programs. *Journal of Learning Disabilities, 23,* 108–113.

Heath, N. L., & Wiener, J. (1996). Depression and nonacademic self-perceptions in children with and without learning disabilities. *Learning Disability Quarterly, 19,* 34–44.

Hinshaw, S. P. (1992). Externalizing behavior problems and academic underachievement in childhood and adolescents: Causal relationships and underlying mechanisms. *Psychological Bulletin, 111,* 127–155.

Hugdahl, K. (1993). Functional brain asymmetry, dyslexia, and immune disorders. In A. Galaburda (Ed.), *Dyslexia and development: Neurobiological aspects of extra-ordinary brains* (pp. 133–154). Cambridge, MA: Harvard University Press.

Huntington, D. D., & Bender, W. N. (1993). Adolescents with learning disabilities at risk? Emotional well-being, depression, suicide. *Journal of Learning Disabilities, 26,* 159–166.

Hyde, J. S., & Linn, M. C. (1988). Gender difference in verbal ability: A meta-analysis. *Psychological Bulletin, 194,* 53–69.

Kaplan, B. J., Dewey, D. M., Crawford, S. G., & Wilson, B. N. (2001). The term comorbidity is of questionable value in reference to developmental disorders: Data and theory. *Journal of Learning Disabilities, 34,* 555–565.

Kaufman, A. S. (1994). *Intelligent testing with the WISC-III.* New York: Wiley.

Kelley, D. B. (1993). Androgens and brain development: Possible contributions to developmental dyslexia. In A. M. Galaburda (Ed.), *Dyslexia and development: Neurological aspects of extra-ordinary brains* (pp. 21–41). Cambridge, MA: Harward University Press.

Kessler, R. C., McGonagle, K. A., & Zhao, S. (1994). Lifetime and 12-month prevalence of DSM-III-R psychiatric disorders in the United States: Results from the National Comorbidity study. *Archives of General Psychiatry, 51,* 8–19.

Kimura, D. (1999). *Sex and cognition.* Cambridge, MA: MIT Press.

Knopik, V. S., DeFries, J. C., & Alarcon, M. (1998). Gender differences in cognitive abilities of opposite-sex and same-sex twin pairs with reading disability. *Annals of Dyslexia, 46,* 241–257.

Lawson, J. S., Inglis, J., & Tittemore, J. A. (1987). Factorially defined verbal and performance IQs derived from the WISC-R: Patterns of cognitive ability in normal and learning disabled children. *Personality and Individual Differences, 8,* 331–341.

Levine, P., & Edgar, E. (1994). An analysis by gender of long-term postschool outcomes for youth with and without disabilities. *Exceptional Children, 61,* 282–300.

Levine, P., & Nourse, S. (1998). What follow-up studies say about postschool life for young men and women with learning disabilies: A critical look at the literature. *Journal of Learning Disabilities, 31,* 212–233.

Lewinsohn, P. M., Clarke, G. N., Seeley, J. R., & Rohde, P. (1994). Major depression in community adolescents: Age at onset, episode duration and time to recurrence. *Journal of the American Academy of Child and Adolescence Psychiatry, 33,* 809–818.

Locke, J. L., & Macaruso, P. (1999). Handedness in developmental dyslexia: Direct observation of a large sample. *Journal of Neurolinguistics, 12,* 147–156.

Lovett, M. W. (1984). A developmental perspective on reading dysfunction: Accuracy and rate criteria in the subtyping of dyslexic children. *Brain and Language, 22,* 67–91.

Lyon, G. R. (1996). Learning disabilities. In E. J. Mash & R. A. Barkley (Eds.), *Child psychopathology* (pp. 390–435). New York: Guilford.

Lyon, G. R., Fletcher, J. M., Shaywitz, S. E., Shaywitz, B. A., Torgesen, J. K., Wood, F. B., et al. (2001). Rethinking learning disabilities. In J. C. E. Finn, A. J. Rotherham & C. R. Hokanson (Eds.), *Rethinking special education for a new century* (pp. 259–287). Washington, DC: Thomas B. Fordham Foundation and Progressive Policy Institute.

Marshall, R., Hynd, G. W., Handwerk, M., & Hall, J. (1997). Academic underachievement in ADHD subtypes. *Journal of Learning Disabilities, 30,* 635–642.

Mash, E. J., & Wolfe, D. A. (2002). *Abnormal child psychology* (2nd ed.). Belmont, CA: Wadsworth.

Maughan, B., & Hagell, A. (1998). Poor readers in adulthood: Psychosocial functioning. In M. E. Hertzig & E. A. Farber (Eds.), *Annual progress in child psychiatry and child development, 1997* (pp. 171–191). Philadelphia: Brunner/Manzel.

McGee, R., Feehan, M., Williams, S., Partridge, F., A., S. P., & Kelly, J. (1990). DSM-III disorders in a large sample of adolescents. *Journal of the American Academy of Child and Adolescence Psychiatry, 29,* 611–619.

McManus, I. C., & Bryden, M. P. (1991). Geschwind's theory of cerebral lateralization: Developing a formal, causal model. *Psychological Bulletin, 110,* 237–253.

Miller, R. J., Snider, B., & Rzonca, C. (1990). Variables related to the decision of young adults with learning disabilities to participate in post-secondary education. *Journal of Learning Disabilities, 23,* 349–354.

Mirkin, P. (1982). *Direct and repeated measurement of academic skills: An alternative to traditional screening, referral, and identification of learning disabled students* (ERIC Document Reproduction Service No. ED 224 191). Washington, DC: Office of Special Education and Rehabilitative Service.

Morris, D. W., Robinson, L., Turic, D., Duke, M., Webb, V., Milham, C., et al. (2000). Family-based association mapping provides evidence for reading disability on chromosome 15q. *Human Molecular Genetics, 9,* 843–848.

Neumarker, K.-J. (2000). Mathematics and the brain: Uncharted territory? *European Child and Adolescence Psychiatry, 9,* 2–10.

NJCLD. (1994). Learning disabilities issue on definition. In *Collective perspectives on issues affecting learning disabilities: Position papers and statements* (pp. 61–66). Austin, TX: PRO-ED.

Ochoa, S. H., & Olivarez, A. (1995). A meta-analysis of peer ratings sociometric studies of pupils with learning disabilities. *The Journal of Special Education, 29,* 1–19.

Pearl, R. (1992). Psychological characteristics of learning disabled students. In N. N. Singh & I. L. Beale (Eds.), *Learning disabilities: Nature, theory, and treatment* (pp. 96–125). New York: Springer-Verlag.

Phillips, L. M., Norris, S. P., & Osmond, W. C. (2002). Relative reading achievement: A longitudinal study of 187 children. *Journal of Educational Psychology, 94,* 3–13.

Prifitera, A., & Dersh, J. (1993). Base rates of WISC-III diagnostic subtest patterns among normal, learning-disabled, and ADHD samples. In B. A. Bracken & R. S. McCallum (Eds.), *Journal of Psychoeducational Assessment Monograph Series, Advances in Psychoeducational Assessment: Wechsler Intelligence Scale for Children-Third Edition* (pp. 43–55). Germantown, TN: Psychoeducational Corporation.

Raskind, M. H., Goldberg, R. J., Higgins, E. L., & Herman, K. L. (1999). Patterns of change and predictors of success in individuals with learning disabilities: Results from a twenty-year longitudinal study. *Learning Disabilities Research and Practice, 14*(1), 35–49.

Richardson, S., Katz, M., & Koller, H. (1986). Sex differences in number of children administratively classified as mildly mentally retarded: An epidemiological review. *American Journal of Mental Deficiency, 91* (250–256).

Rojewski, J. W. (1999). Occupational and educational aspirations and attainment of young adults with and without LD 2 years after high school completion. *Journal of Learning Disabilities, 32*(6), 533–552.

Rourke, B. P. (2000). Neuropsychological and psychosocial subtyping: A review of investigations within the University of Windsor Laboratory. *Canadian Psychology, 41*(1), 34–51.

Rourke, B. P., & Del Dotto, J. E. (1994). *Learning disabilities: A neuropsychological perspective* (Vol. 30). Thousand Oaks, CA: Sage.

Rutter, M., & Yule, W. (1975). The concept of specific reading retardation. *Journal of Child Psychology, Psychiatry and Allied Disciplines, 16,* 181–197.

Sattler, J. M. (2001). *Assessment of children: Cognitive applications.* San Diego: CA: Jerome M. Sattler.

Satz, P. (1990). Developmental dyslexia: An etiological reformulation. In G. T. Pavlidis (Ed.), *Perspectives on dyslexia. Vol. 1: Neurology, Neuropsychology and Genetics* (pp. 3–26). New York: Wiley.

Satz, P., & Soper, H. V. (1986). Left-handedness, dyslexia, and autoimmune disorder: A critique. *Journal of Clinical and Experimental Neuropsychology, 8,* 453–458.

Scuccimarra, D. J., & Speece, D. L. (1990). Employment outcomes and social integration of students with mild handicaps: The quality of life two years after high school. *Journal of Learning Disabilities, 23,* 213–218.

Semrud-Clikeman, M., Biederman, J., Sprich-Buckminster, S., Lehman, B., Faraone, S. V., & Norman, D. (1992). Comorbidity between ADDH and LD: A review and report in a clinically referred sample. *Journal of the American Academy of Child and Adolescence Psychiatry, 31,* 439–448.

Shalev, R. S., Auerbach, J., Manor, O., & Gross-Tsur, V. (2000). Developmental dyscalculia: Prevalence and prognosis. *European Child and Adolescence Psychiatry, 9,* 58–64.

Shalev, R. S., Manor, O., & Kerem, B. (2001). Developmental dyscalculia is a familial disability. *Journal of Learning Disabilities, 34,* 59–65.

Share, D. L., Moffitt, T. E., & Silva, P. (1988). Factors associated with arithmetic-and-reading disability and specific arithmetic disability. *Journal of Learning Disabilities, 21*(5), 313–320.

Share, D. L., & Silva, P. (2003). Gender bias in IQ-discrepancy and post-discrepancy definitions of reading disability. *Journal of Learning Disabilities, 36,* 4–14.

Shaywitz, S. E., Fletcher, J. M., Holahan, J. M., Schneider, A. E., Marchione, K. E., Stuebing, K. K., et al. (1999). Persistence of dyslexia: the Connecticut Longitudinal Study at Adolescents. *Pediatrics, 104,* 1351–1359.

Shaywitz, S. E., Shaywitz, B. A., Fletcher, J. M., & Escobar, M. D. (1990). Prevalence of reading disability in boys and girls: Results of the Connecticut Longitudinal Study. *Journal of the American Medical Association, 264,* 998–1002.

Siegel, L. S. (1992). An evaluation of the discrepancy definition of dyslexia. *Journal of Learning Disabilities, 22,* 469–478, 486.

Siegel, L. S. (2003). IQ-discrepancy definitions and the diagnosis of LD. *Journal of Learning Disabilities, 36,* 2–3.

Silva, P., McGee, R., & Williams, S. (1985). Some characteristics of 9-year-old boys with general reading backwardness or specific reading retardation. *Journal of Child Psychology, Psychiatry, 26,* 407–421.

Sitlington, P. L., & Frank, A. R. (1990). Are adolescents with learning disabilities successfully crossing the bridge into adult life? *Learning Disability Quarterly, 13,* 97–111.

Sitlington, P. L., & Frank, A. R. (1993). *Iowa statewide follow-up study: Adult adjustment of individiuals with learning disabilities three vs. one year out of school* (ERIC ED368132). Des Moines: Iowa State Department of Education.

Smart, D., Sanson, A., & Prior, M. (1996). Connections between reading disability and behavior problems: Testing temporal and causal hypotheses. *Journal of Abnormal Child Psychology, 14,* 363–383.

Smith, C. R. (1998). *Learning disabilities: The interaction of learner, task, and setting* (4th edition). Boston: Allyn and Bacon.

Stanovich, K. E. (1986). Matthew effects in reading: Some consequences of individual differences in the acquisition of literacy. *Reading Research Quarterly, 21,* 360–407.

Stanovich, K. E., & Siegel, L. S. (1994). Phenotypic performance profile of children with reading disabilities: A regression-based test of the phonological-core variable-difference model. *Journal of Educational Psychology, 86,* 24–53.

Stevenson, D. T., & Romney, D. M. (1984). Depression in learning disabled children. *Journal of Learning Disabilities, 17,* 579–582.

Stevenson, J. (1992). Identifying sex differences in reading disability: Lessons from a twin study. *Reading and Writing: An Interdisciplinary Journal, 4,* 307–326.

Swanson, H. L. (1996). Meta-analysis, replication, social skills, and learning disabilities. *The Journal of Special Education, 30,* 213–221.

Swanson, H. L., & Malone, S. (1992). Social skills and learning disabilities: A meta-analysis of the literature. *Social Psychology Review, 21,* 427–443.

Szatmari, P. (1992). The epidemiology of attention-deficit hyperactivity disorders. In G. Weiss (Ed.), *Child and adolescence psychiatric clinics of North America: Attention-deficit hyperactivity disorder* (pp. 361–372). Philadelphia: Saunders.

Tallal, P., & Fitch, R. H. (1993). Hormones and cerebral organization: Implication for development and transmission of language and learning disabilities. In A. M. Galaburda (Ed.), *Dyslexia and development: Neurobiological aspects of extra-ordinary brains* (pp. 168–186). Cambridge, MA: Harvard University Press.

Tirosh, E., & Cohen, A. (1998). Language deficit with attention-deficit disorder: A prevalent comorbidity. *Journal of Child Neurology, 13,* 493–497.

Tittemore, J. A., Lawson, J. S., & Inglis, J. (1985). Validation of a learning disability index derived from a principal components analysis of the WISC-R. *Journal of Learning Disabilities, 18,* 449–454.

Tocci, C., & Engelhard, G. (1991). Achievement, parental support, and gender difference in attitudes toward mathematics. *Journal of Educational Psychology, 84,* 280–286.

Torgesen, J. K. (2000). Individual differences in response to early interventions in reading: The lingering problem of treatment resisters. *Learning Disabilities Research & Practice, 15,* 55–64.

Vaughn, S., Hogan, A., Kouzekanani, K., & Shapiro, S. (1990). Peer acceptance, self-perceptions, and social skills of learning disabled students prior to identification. *Journal of Educational Psychology, 82,* 101–106.

Vellutino, F., & Scanlon, D. (1987). Phonological coding, phonological awareness, and reading ability: Evidence from a longitudinal and experimental study. *Merrill-Palmer Quarterly, 33,* 321–363.

Vogel, S. A. (1990). Gender differences in intelligence, language, visual-motor abilities, and academic achievement in students with learning disabilities: A review of the literature. *Journal of Learning Disabilities, 23,* 44–52.

Vogel, S. A., & Adelman, P. B. (1992). The success of college students with learning disabilities: Factors related to educational attainment. *Journal of Learning Disabilities, 25,* 430–441.

Vogel, S. A., & Walsh, P. C. (1987). Gender differences in cognitive abilities of learning-disabled females and males. *Annals of Dyslexia, 37,* 142–165.

Volkmar, F. R., & Klin, A. (2000). Pervasive developmental disorders. In B. J. Sadock & V. A. Sadock (Eds.), *Comprehensive textbook of psychiatry* (Vol. II). Philadelphia: Lippincott.

Wadsworth, S. J., Knopik, V. S., & DeFries, J. C. (2000). Reading disability in boys and girls: No evidence for a differential genetic etiology. *Reading and Writing: An Interdisciplinary Journal, 13,* 133–145.

Wagner, M. (1992). *Being female—A secondary disability? Gender differences in the transition experiences of young people with disabilities* (ERIC Document Reproduction Service No. ED 341228). Menlo Park, CA: SRI International.

Wagner, M., Torgesen, J. K., Rashotte, C. A., Hecht, S. A., Barker, T. A., Burgess, S. R., et al. (1997). Changing relations between phonological processing abilities and word-level reading as children develop from beginning to skilled readers: A 5-year longitudinal study. *Developmental Psychology, 33,* 468–479.

Wechsler, D. (1981). *Manual for the Wechsler Adult Intelligence Scale* (Rev. ed.). San Antonio, TX: The Psychological Corporation.

Wechsler, D. (1991). *Manual for the Wechsler Intelligence Scale for Children* (3rd ed.). San Antonio, TX: The Psychological Corporation.

White, W. J. (1992). The postschool adjustment of persons with learning disabilities: Current status and future projections. *Journal of Learning Disabilities, 25,* 448–456.

Willcutt, E. G., & Pennington, B. F. (2000). Comorbidity of reading disability and attention-deficit/hyperactivity disorder: Differences by gender and subtype. *Journal of Learning Disabilities, 33,* 179–191.

Wolff, P. H., & Melngailis, I. (1994). Family patterns of developmental dyslexia. *American Journal of Medical Genetics (Neuropsychiatric Genetics), 54,* 122–131.

Wong, B. Y., & Donahue, M. L. (Eds.). (2002). *The social dimensions of learning disabilities: Essays in honor of Tanis Bryan.* Mahwah: NJ: Erlbaum.

Wong, B. Y., & Wong, R. (1980). Role-taking skills in normal achieving and learning disabled children. *Learning Disability Quarterly, 3,* 11–18.

Wright-Strawderman, C., & Watson, B. L. (1992). The prevalence of depressive symptoms in children with learning disabilities. *Journal of Learning Disabilities, 25,* 258–264.

Young, A. R., Beitchman, J. H., Johnson, C., Douglas, L., Atkinson, L., Escobar, M., et al. (2002). Young adult academic outcomes in a longitudinal sample of early identified language impaired and control children. *Journal of Child Psychology and Psychiatry, 43,* 635–645.

10

Gender Identity Disorder in Girls

KENNETH J. ZUCKER

Understanding gender identity *disorder* first requires an explication of what is meant by gender identity. As a psychological construct, gender identity has been conceptualized with respect to both cognitive and affective parameters. At the cognitive level, gender identity has been defined as the child's ability to accurately discriminate females from males and then to identify her or his own gender status correctly—a task considered by some to be the first "stage" in gender constancy development, of which the "end state" is the knowledge of gender invariance (Fagot, 1995; Kohlberg, 1966; Slaby & Frey, 1975). Most recently, Martin, Ruble, and Szkrybalo (2002) suggested that this rather crude, first-stage developmental acquisition be referred to as the *basic self-labeling* of gender identity, which most children appear to master some time between the ages of 2 and 3 years. With greater reliance on nonverbal assessment techniques, a number of studies have shown that, prior to this time frame, there is evidence that infants and young toddlers, perhaps as early as 6 months of age, are sensitive to various perceptual features that are reliably correlated with biological sex, such as voice and hairstyle (reviewed in Martin et al., 2002, pp. 917–922). Sensitivity to these and other kinds of perceptual cues (e.g., clothing style) are likely related to the subsequent emergence of basic self-labeling of gender identity.

At the affective level, Stoller (1964) originally used the term *core gender identity* to describe a young child's developing "fundamental *sense* of belonging to one sex" (p. 453, emphasis added) (see also Fagot & Leinbach, 1985). Various observers have noted that children tend to take great pride in announcing to the world that they are girls or boys and will take great offense if they are miscategorized by others. Research derived from social

KENNETH J. ZUCKER • Centre for Addiction and Mental Health–Clarke Division, Toronto, Ontario M5T 1R8.

identification theory (Tajfel, 1981) has shown that mere categorization of individuals into different social groups is associated with greater liking for the in-group, relative to the out-group, perceived similarity to the in-group, and perceptions that the in-group is better than the out-group. Thus, it is not surprising that young children, as early as 3 years (Yee & Brown, 1994), show clear evidence of an affective bias for their own gender (Egan & Perry, 2001; Ruble & Martin, 1998).

The importance of affect in studying gender identity differentiation can also be gleaned from the developmental literature that has examined the distinction between children's expressed or observed gender role preferences and their knowledge (or stereotypes) concerning gender roles. For example, there is evidence that as children grow older, they become more flexible regarding behaviors considered appropriate for the female or male social role; thus, older children are more willing to concede that both girls and boys can engage in certain activities or are able to work in certain occupational roles (e.g., doctor and nurse). Yet, children's actual gender role preferences remain considerably more sex-dimorphic over time (see, e.g., Serbin, Powlishta, & Gulko, 1993).

It is primarily with regard to affect that the term gender identity disorder (GID) can best be positioned. For example, the term *gender dysphoria* began to be used in the early 1970s to describe patients, particularly adults, who felt so unhappy about their biological status as females or males that they sought out surgical sex reassignment (Fisk, 1973). At the same time, clinicians working with children who expressed the strong desire to be of the other sex also noted the importance of affect that surrounded early gender identity development (e.g., Green, 1974; Stoller, 1968). Thus, the focus of this chapter is on girls who experience a great deal of discontent and unhappiness about being girls and who have the strong desire to become a member of the opposite sex.

HISTORICAL CONTEXT

In the 19th century European literature on sexology, there were several accounts of adults who struggled with a sense of profound discomfort about what we now term their gender identity (Hoenig, 1985). Subsequently, Hirschfeld (1923) coined the term *transsexual* (see also Cauldwell, 1949). Hirschfeld's term was popularized by Benjamin (1966), an endocrinologist who played a pivotal role in humanizing the modern clinical care of adults with gender dysphoria (Memorial for Harry Benjamin, 1988).

A turning point in the recognition of transsexualism as a clinical phenomenon was the publication of the Christine Jorgensen case (a male-to-female transsexual) by the Danish endocrinologist, Hamburger (1953). Although there had been other personal and scientific reports along the same lines, including accounts of the first patients who received sex-reassignment surgery (e.g., Hoyer, 1933), the Jorgensen case helped crystallize the notion that adults' discontent with their gender identity might impel them to seek radical physical transformations. For various reasons, transsexualism in adult males was more commonly described than in adult females, but in recent decades considerably more work has appeared on gender dysphoria in females (e.g., Cromwell, 1999; Devor, 1997; Halberstam, 1998; Lothstein, 1983; Pauly, 1974a, 1974b; Prosser, 1998; Stoller, 1972), strengthening the view that intense gender dysphoria occurred in both sexes.

Several summary accounts have made the case that the wish to become a member of the opposite sex is not a novelty of 20th century social life in the West (reviewed in Zucker & Bradley, 1995). Perhaps the novelty lies in the availability of hormonal and surgical techniques for transforming aspects of biological sex to conform to the felt psychological state (Hausman, 1992). This last point is particularly relevant to biological females, in that although contrasex hormones have been available for both sexes for decades, surgical advances and refinements in phalloplasty have lagged behind vaginoplasty because of greater technical problems (Hage, 1996).

The relevance of the adult syndrome of transsexualism to the study of children became apparent from life history interviews, which indicated that the patient's gender dysphoria, or discontent, often originated in childhood. As was the case for adults, the early reports on apparent GID in children focused predominantly, if not exclusively, on boys (Green & Money, 1960); however, with the establishment of specialized gender identity clinics for children and adolescents, it became apparent that girls could also struggle quite intensely with gender identity issues.

A DEVELOPMENTAL PSYCHOPATHOLOGY FRAMEWORK

Sroufe (1990) has argued that adaptational failure must be defined with respect to normative developmental tasks. Thus, if one seeks to understand why some girls develop a sense of substantial distress regarding their gender identity, it is of great importance to understand how the vast majority of girls develop a more positive sense of being female. In many respects, the study of sex differences in psychosexual differentiation (e.g., with regard to gender identity, gender role behavior (masculinity-femininity), and sexual orientation) shares some clear similarities with the model that links developmental psychology and psychopathology. In the general population of males and females, these behavioral components show, on average, very strong sex differences: most females have a female gender identity and most males have a male gender identity; most females have a feminine gender role behavioral pattern and most males have a masculine gender role pattern; and most females are erotically attracted to males and most males are erotically attracted to females (Collaer & Hines, 1995).

Although no one has attempted to formally document the extent of these behavioral differences by meta-analysis and the effect size metric (Cohen, 1988), I have little doubt that the effects would be quite large. Thus, there is a great deal of room to study the source of these differences, which can include both biological and psychosocial mechanisms. It could be argued, therefore, that understanding the mechanisms that underlie psychosexual differentiation in females might inform us about similar mechanisms in males.

Of course, it should also be recognized that there are important within-sex variations on these parameters. For example, although there are typically large mean sex differences in children's gender role behavioral preferences (e.g., toy interests, occupational aspirations), one can still detect within-sex variability (always greater in girls than in boys) (see, e.g., Liben & Bigler, 2002). Along similar lines, heterosexual and homosexual women and heterosexual and homosexual men differ substantially in their recalled patterns of childhood sex-typed behavior, as reviewed in a meta-analytic study by Bailey and Zucker (1995). Thus, such within-sex variations can also be studied with regard to biological and psychosocial processes, for which there also might be common underlying mechanisms.

DESCRIPTION OF THE DISORDER IN GIRLS

Core Symptoms

Girls diagnosed with GID show both a strong preference for sex-typed behaviors more characteristic of the opposite sex and a rejection or avoidance of sex-typed behaviors more characteristic of their own sex. More importantly, they also express a strong desire to be of the opposite sex and often verbalize their unhappiness about being a girl. The central clinical issue concerns the degree to which a pattern of behavioral signs is present, since this pattern is the basis for inference on the extent to which a girl is cross-gender-identified.

In its full form, the clinical picture includes at least six characteristics: (a) a frequently stated desire to be a boy or an insistence that she is a boy; in addition, some girls may insist on adopting a boy's name (e.g., "Aaron" instead of "Erin"); (b) verbal or behavioral expressions of anatomic dysphoria (e.g., stating a desire to have a penis; urinating in the standing position in order to enhance the fantasy of having male genitalia); (c) an intense aversion to wearing stereotypical feminine clothing and an insistence on wearing stereotypical masculine clothing; in addition, many girls will request or insist that their hair be cut very short so that they look like boys; (d) a preference for male roles in fantasy play and an avoidance of female roles in fantasy play; (e) a preference for stereotypical masculine toys and activities and an avoidance of stereotypical feminine toys and activities; and (f) a preference for boys as playmates and an avoidance or dislike of girls as playmates.

In adolescence, the clinical picture begins to resemble the "end state" of gender dysphoria as one might observe it in adult women with GID. Thus, adolescent girls with GID will, like their child counterparts, report a strong desire to be a boy and indicate extreme distress about the physical manifestations of a feminizing puberty (e.g., with regard to breast development and menstruation). Many adolescent girls with GID will attempt to conceal their breast development (e.g., by wearing layers of t-shirts or by binding their breasts with tape), report an interest in taking contra-sex hormones to masculinize their physical development, and express a strong desire for physical sex reassignment (mastectomy and phalloplasty). Many adolescent girls with GID attempt to "pass" socially as boys (e.g., when introducing themselves to new people, upon entry into a new school).

Age of Onset

At the time of assessment, parents sometimes remark that their daughter had behaved in a cross-gendered manner "since day one." Upon questioning, what parents usually mean is that their daughter displayed cross-gender behaviors once they were old enough to engage in specific sex-dimorphic activities (e.g., toy play, dress-up play). Most typically, this is during the toddler and preschool years (2–4 years), which correspond to the developmental time period in which normative behavioral sex differences pertaining to gender identity and gender role first emerge (Martin et al., 2002; Ruble & Martin, 1998). It is common, for example, for parents to report that during these years their daughters began to reject wearing stereotypical feminine clothing. In some cases, this coincides with the girl's gender self-labeling as a boy or the expression of the wish to be a boy. In other cases, particularly in girls who are less verbally expressive, the marked aversion toward normative feminine clothing, at least in retrospect, was the first behavioral sign of gender identity conflict. The preference of these girls for a masculine style of dress does not simply result from a desire for more comfortable clothing (e.g., slacks or sweatpants, which many girls wear in social settings for this reason), but appears to be associated with the marked distress about being a girl. Some parents report that asking their daughters to wear stereotypical feminine clothing on special occasions (e.g., when going to church or to a family function) gives rise to intense, catastrophic temper tantrums.

Related Features

As noted earlier, many of the girls will demand that their hair be cut extremely short, which results in the phenotypic social appearance of a boy; indeed, it is common for girls with GID to be perceived by others as boys because of their hair style and clothing style.

In two studies, we examined formally the phenotypic physical appearance of 12 girls with GID compared to 12 clinical control and 10 normal control girls. At the time of assessment (mean age, 6.6 years), we took colored photographs of the girls in a seated position, typically from the waist up. In the first study (Fridell, Zucker, Bradley, & Maing, 1996), university students, masked to the girls' group status, were asked to rate the photographs with regard to five adjectives, four of which had a feminine connotation (attractive, beautiful, cute, pretty, and ugly), on a response scale that ranged from 1 to 5 ("not all descriptive" to "highly descriptive"). Compared to the control girls, the girls with GID were rated as significantly less attractive, beautiful, cute, and pretty, but they did not differ significantly on the rating of ugly. In the second study (McDermid, Zucker, Bradley, &

Maing, 1998), university students rated the same photographs with regard to four adjectives that had a masculine connotation: handsome, masculine, rugged, and tomboyish. On all four adjectives, the girls with GID had significantly higher ratings than the controls.

EPIDEMIOLOGY

Prevalence

The prevalence of GID in girls has not been formally studied by epidemiological methods. Nevertheless, Meyer-Bahlburg's (1985) characterization of GID as a "rare phenomenon" is not unreasonable. For example, Bakker, van Kesteren, Gooren, and Bezemer (1993) inferred the prevalence of GID in adult women in the Netherlands—1 in 30,400 women—from the number who received "cross-gender" hormonal treatment at the main adult gender identity clinic in that country.

This approach, however, suffers from at least two limitations: First, it relies on the number of biological females who attend specialty clinics serving as gateways for hormonal and surgical sex reassignment, which may not see all gender-dysphoric women. In the United States, this may be even more true nowadays as the number of university or hospital-based gender identity clinics has dwindled, with a concomitant increase of paraprofessional supports and search for care within sexual and gender minority communities. Second, the assumption that GID in girls will persist into adulthood is not necessarily true (see Developmental Course and Outcomes). It is likely, therefore, that the prevalence of GID is higher in girls than it is in women.

Another approach to the estimate of prevalence borrows from normative studies of girls in whom specific cross-gender behaviors were assessed (see, e.g., Zucker, 1985, pp. 87–95). For example, one source of information comes from the widely used Child Behavior Checklist (CBCL) (Achenbach & Edelbrock, 1983), a parent-report behavior problem questionnaire with excellent psychometric properties. It contains two items (out of 118) that pertain to cross-gender identification: "behaves like opposite sex" and "wishes to be of opposite sex." On the CBCL, ratings are made on a 3-point scale (0 = *not true*; 1 = *somewhat or sometimes true*, and 2 = *very true or often true*). As reported by Zucker, Bradley, and Sanikhani (1997), among nonreferred girls (ages 4–11 years), 8.3% received a rating of a 1 and 2.3% received a rating of a 2 for the item "behaves like opposite sex," but only 2.5% received a rating of a 1 and 1.0% received a rating of a 2 for the item "wishes to be of opposite sex." In another analysis of these data, we noted that only two of 398 girls (< 1%) received a rating of a 2 on both of these items (Zucker & Bradley, 1995).

In one study that relied on behavioral observation of cross-gender behavior, Fagot (1977) attempted to identify statistically preschool girls with "moderate" levels of cross-gender behavior. Such girls were defined as obtaining preference scores for opposite-sex activities that were at least 1 SD above the mean of the opposite sex and preference scores for same-sex activities that were at least 1 SD below the mean of their own sex. Based on this criterion, 5 (4.9%) of 101 girls displayed moderate cross-gender preferences.

The main problem, however, with this type of data is that it does not identify adequately patterns of cross-gender behavior that would be of use in determining "caseness." Thus, such data may be best viewed as screening devices for more intensive evaluation.

Sex Differences in Referral Rates

Consistently, it has been observed that boys are referred more often than girls for concerns regarding gender identity. In our own clinic, we have had a referral ratio of 5.75:1 (N = 358) of boys to girls based on consecutive referrals from 1975 to 2000 (Cohen-Kettenis, Owen, Kaijser, Bradley, & Zucker, 2003). In the Cohen-Kettenis et al. study, we had comparative data from children evaluated at the sole gender identity clinic for children in Utrecht, The Netherlands. Although the sex ratio was significantly lower at 2.93:1 (N = 130), it still favored referral of boys over girls.

How might this disparity be best understood? One possibility is that the sex difference in referral rates reflects a true sex difference in prevalence. Unfortunately, because good data on prevalence are lacking, it is not possible at this time to test this hypothesis. Another possibility is that social factors play a role in accounting for the disparity. For example, it is well established that parents, teachers, and peers are less tolerant of cross-gender behavior in boys than in girls (Fagot, 1985), which might result in a sex-differential in clinical referral (for review, see Zucker & Bradley, 1995). Weisz and Weiss (1991) devised a "referability index" (RI), which reflected the frequency with which a child problem, adjusted for its prevalence in the general population, resulted in a clinic referral. All 118 items from the CBCL were analyzed in a comparison of clinic-referred and nonreferred children. Among parents in the United States, the 20 most referable problems (e.g., vandalism, poor schoolwork, attacks people) appeared to be relatively serious. In contrast, the 20 least referable problems (e.g., bragging, teases a lot, likes to be alone) appeared less so. Weiss (personal communication, March 4, 1992) indicated that, for boys, the CBCL item "wishes to be of opposite sex" had a high RI of 91 of 118 (i.e., in the upper quartile) and "behaves like opposite sex" had an RI of 80 of 118. For girls, the RI was lower: 55 of 118 for "wishes to be of opposite sex" and 14 of 118 for "behaves like opposite sex."

Weisz and Weiss's (1991) study, along with studies from the normative literature, led us to predict that referred girls would display more extreme cross-gender behavior than referred boys, which might account therefore, at least in part, for the disparity by sex in referral rates. Both Zucker et al. (1997) and Cohen-Kettenis et al. (2003) provided data that supported this prediction, suggesting that girls may need to display more cross-gender behavior than boys before a referral is initiated. This higher threshold for referral appeared consistent with the fact that, in both the Toronto and

Utrecht clinics, girls were referred, on average, about 10 months later than were boys (M age, 8.1 years vs. 7.3 years, respectively), a significant difference, despite the fact that the girls showed, on average, higher levels of cross-gender behavior than the boys. However, it is important to note that the sexes did not differ in the percentage who met the complete DSM criteria for GID; thus, there was no gross evidence for a sex difference in false-positive referrals.

As noted above, the greater tolerance in the culture for cross-gender behavior in girls than in boys might affect referral rates as well as the timing of referral. In the Cohen-Kettenis et al. (2003) study, we found that on a CBCL-derived measure of poor peer relations, boys in both clinics had significantly more impaired ratings than did the girls although the mean ratings for both sexes were significantly higher than that of unaffected siblings (unpublished data). Given that girls with GID do not have peer relationships that are deemed as problematic as that of boys with GID, this may result in somewhat less pressure to seek out a clinical evaluation.

Another factor that could affect sex differences in referral rates pertains to the relative salience of cross-gender behavior in boys versus girls. For example, it has long been observed that the sexes differ in the extent to which they display sex-typical behaviors; when there is significant between-sex variation, it is almost always the case that girls are more likely to engage in masculine behaviors than boys are likely to engage in feminine behaviors (e.g., Cole, Zucker, & Bradley, 1982; Sandberg, Meyer-Bahlburg, Ehrhardt, & Yager, 1993). Thus, the base rates for cross-gender behavior, at least within the range of normative variation, may well differ between the sexes. In our analysis of the two CBCL gender items (see above), we found that more mothers of girls gave ratings of either a 1 or a 2 than did mothers of boys; however, these differences were statistically significant only for the rating of a 1 for the item "Behaves like opposite sex" (Zucker et al., 1997). Thus, it appears that the sex differences occur only with regard to mild displays of cross-gender behavior.

Social Class, Ethnicity, and Culture

The association of GID with demographic variables, such as social class and ethnicity, and with culture has been examined to varying degrees. In our clinic, girls with GID are represented in all socioeconomic groups, as defined by Hollingshead's (1975) Four-Factor Index of Social Status, and this was also the case in the child sample from The Netherlands reported in Cohen-Kettenis et al. (2003). In a study in which we compared our child and adolescent patients (Zucker, Owen, Bradley, & Ameeriar, 2002), we found that the child patients (N = 358, of whom 53 were girls) were significantly more likely to come from a higher social class background than did the adolescent patients (N = 72, of whom 31 were girls). In the same sample, we also found that the child patients were more likely to be Caucasian than were the adolescent patients (83.0% vs. 65.3%). The child patients were also more likely to speak English as their first language and to be born in Canada than were the adolescent patients. Unfortunately, we do not know if these child-adolescent differences in demographics are unique to youngsters with GID or would be characteristic of clinic-referred youngsters in general who are seen from the same catchment area.

With regard to culture, there is certainly a considerable amount of evidence that GID occurs in both Western and non-Western cultures although there has been much more written about the apparent similarity in phenomenology with regard to adults than with regard to children (see, e.g., Herdt, 1994; Kulick, 1998; Newman, 2002; Tucker & Keil, 2001). With regard to biological females, one example from the cross-cultural record pertains to the so-called Albanian sworn virgins. As described by Young (2000), the Balkan sworn virgin is a traditional role in which a female-born person becomes a social man, fulfilling all social and political functions of men except marriage and procreation, generally assuming the new identity at or before puberty, and swearing lifelong chastity and celibacy. Some of these individuals are reported to have shown signs of girlhood masculinity from an early age, in a manner that bears a striking similarity to the phenomenology of GID as reported in modern Western cultures. It is less clear, however, whether or not the surface similarity in behavior reflects an underlying common etiology or is an example of equifinality, that is, different starting points leading to the same outcome (Cicchetti & Rogosch, 1996).

DSM DIAGNOSTIC CRITERIA FOR GENDER IDENTITY DISORDER

The diagnosis of gender identity disorder for children made its first appearance in the third edition of the *Diagnostic and Statistical Manual of Mental Disorders* (*DSM-III*; American Psychiatric Association, 1980). Modifications to the criteria were made in both the revised third (*DSM-III-R*; American Psychiatric Association, 1987) and fourth editions (*DSM-IV*; American Psychiatric Association, 1994, 2000). Table 1 shows the criteria as they appear in the *DSM-IV*.

Diagnostic Issues

Over the years, there has been debate in the literature regarding the merit in operationalizing diagnostic criteria for several child psychiatric disorders, such as Conduct Disorder and Attention-Deficit/Hyperactivity Disorder, *without* consideration of possible sex differences in core features and phenomenology (e.g., Biederman et al., 2002; Zahn-Waxler, 1993; Zoccolillo, 1993; see also Widiger, 1998). Interestingly, the *DSM* criteria for GID have always contained some differences by sex; indeed, it is the only

Table 1. DSM-IV Diagnostic Criteria for Gender Identity Disorder

A. A strong and persistent cross-gender identification (not merely a desire for any perceived cultural advantages of being the other sex). In children, the disturbance is manifested by at least four (or more) of the following:

1. repeatedly stated desire to be, or insistence that he or she is, the other sex
2. in boys, preference for cross-dressing or simulating female attire; in girls, insistence on wearing only stereotypical masculine clothing
3. strong and persistent preferences for cross-sex roles in make-believe play or persistent fantasies of being the other sex
4. intense desire to participate in the stereotypical games and pastimes of the other sex
5. strong preference for playmates of the other sex

B. Persistent discomfort with his or her sex or sense of inappropriateness in the gender role of that sex. In children, the disturbance is manifested by any of the following: in boys, assertion that his penis or testes are disgusting or will disappear or assertion that it would be better not to have a penis, or aversion toward rough-and-tumble play and rejection of male stereotypical toys, games, and activities; in girls, rejection of urinating in a sitting position, assertion that she has or will grow a penis, or assertion that she does not want to grow breasts or menstruate, or marked aversion toward normative feminine clothing.

C. The disturbance is not concurrent with a physical intersex condition.

D. The disturbance causes clinically significant distress or impairment in social, occupational, or other important areas of functioning.

Reprinted with permission of the American Psychiatric Association. Only criteria for children are listed.

diagnosis in the DSM reserved for children that includes this consideration in the criteria themselves (for a review of these differences in *DSM-III* and *DSM-III-R*, see Zucker, 1982, 1992).

From *DSM-III* to *DSM-IV*, the diagnostic criteria for GID have become more similar for girls and boys; for example, it can be seen in Table 1 that the Point A criteria are almost identical for the two sexes. Of note, the proviso that the "...strong and persistent cross-gender identification" as "...not being merely a desire for any perceived cultural advantages of being the other sex" was present only for girls in *DSM-III* and *DSM-III-R*, but in *DSM-IV* is present for both sexes.

The rationale for this proviso is controversial. As noted by Zucker (1992), this exclusion rule presented a couple of difficulties. First, it makes an etiological or motivational assumption, namely, that one type of desire is based on a perception of cultural bias, whereas at least one other unspecified type is not. Although this distinction might have relevance for parameters such as natural history and response to treatment, it is unclear why it should be used diagnostically. Clinically, there is evidence that both girls and boys with GID will often explain their desire to be of the opposite sex with regard to perceptions of "cultural" difference between the sexes (e.g., boys don't have to wear dresses, are stronger, have better toys; girls get to wear lipstick and prettier clothes, are not yelled at as much, do not play rough). Unfortunately, the DSM does not provide clear guidelines as to how this exclusion criterion should be operationalized and, to my knowledge, no empirical study has addressed its clinical utility or validity.

In both sexes, the Point B criterion can be met by one of two criteria. One element pertains to the concept of "anatomic dysphoria," that is, the child's discomfort with her or his sexual anatomy. Although the behavioral criteria appear to reflect the phenomenology as it is observed in clinical practice, there has been very little in the way of systematic empirical research that documents its prevalence, including sex differences, in children referred for gender identity concerns. Clinically, it has been my impression that its occurrence is less common among children than it is among adolescents, for whom severe anatomic dysphoria is almost always present, as it is in adults.

The second element pertains to the rejection of same-sex attributes. For boys, it refers to an aversion toward rough-and-tumble play *and* a rejection of various stereotypical masculine toys, games, and activities. For girls, it refers only to a marked aversion toward normative feminine clothing. In part, these distinctions appeared to be based on sex differences in phenomenology. For example, although boys with GID often prefer to engage in cross-dressing (e.g., during fantasy play), they appear to show less resistance or discomfort in wearing gender-typical clothing than do girls in social settings (e.g., at school or special occasions, such as going to church).

Reliability and Validity

Can the DSM diagnosis of GID be made reliably? To date, no study has formally examined this question with regard to the current criteria. One earlier reliability study of the *DSM-III* criteria obtained kappas of .89 and .80 for the Point A and Point B criteria, respectively (both $ps < .001$), based on 36 consecutive referrals of children to our gender identity clinic (Zucker, Finegan, Doering, & Bradley, 1984).

Zucker and Bradley (1995) studied the validity of the *DSM-III* criteria by comparing gender-referred children who met the complete DSM criteria with those children who were subthreshold for the diagnosis on a number of sex-typed measures, including parent-report, play observations, and projective tests. It should be noted that, by and large, the children who did not meet the complete *DSM-III* criteria showed at least some characteristics of cross-gender-identification and were not necessarily inappropriate referrals. The results showed that the *DSM-III* subgroup showed significantly more cross-gender behavior or less same-gender behavior than the non-*DSM-III* subgroup on 11 of 17 measures; thus, there seemed to be at least some behavioral differences between the two diagnostic subgroups in the degree of same-sex-typed or cross-sex-typed behavior, even after controlling for demographic variables that also differed between the two subgroups.

The discriminant validity of the DSM criteria has also been studied by comparing gender-referred children with three control groups (siblings, clinical controls, and normal controls) utilizing various measures of sex-typed behavior. As reviewed elsewhere (Zucker, 1992; Zucker & Bradley, 1995), the proband-control differences have been statistically significant on all measures studied to date, with very minimal differences among the controls.

As one example of this type of assessment technique, we developed a 12-item structured Gender Identity Interview for Children (Zucker et al., 1993). Factor analysis identified two factors, which were labeled "Cognitive Gender Confusion" and "Affective Gender Confusion," respectively. Cutoff scores of any three or four deviant responses yielded high specificity rates (88.8% and 93.9%, respectively), but lower sensitivity rates (54.1% and 65.8%, respectively). The following responses were obtained from a 5-year-old girl with GID (IQ = 101):

Interviewer (I): Are you a girl or a boy? [Cog][1]
Child (C): Boy.
I: Are you a girl? [Cog]
C: No, a boy.
I: When you grow up, will you be a daddy or a mommy? [Cog]
C: Daddy.
I: Could you ever grow up to be a mommy? [Cog]
C: No.
I: Are there any good things about being a girl?
C: Yes.
I: Tell me some of the good things about being a girl.
C: You disturb boys. Girls can distract you. It's your job.
I: Are there any things that you don't like about being a girl? [Aff]
C: No.
I: Do you think it is better to be a girl or a boy? [Aff]
C: Boy.
I: Why?
C: Because they have bald hair. Can do tricks with other boys and stuff.
I: In your mind, do you ever think that you would like to be a boy? [Aff]
C: Yes.
I: Can you tell me why?
C: Because I like to. Because boys are so special.
I: In your mind, do you ever get mixed up and you're not really sure if you are a girl or a boy? [Aff]
C: Yes.
I: Tell me more about that
C: A boy could do everything over girls. I really am a boy.
I: Do you ever feel more like a boy than like a girl? [Aff]
C: Yes.
I: Tell me more about that.
C: Because I feel like being a boy.
I: . . . In your dreams, are you a girl, a boy, or sometimes a girl and sometimes a boy? [Aff]

[1]Questions that loaded on the Cognitive Gender Confusion (Cog) or Affective Gender Confusion (Aff) factors, respectively. The question "Are there any good things about begin a girl?" had factor loadings of < .30 on both factors and thus was not included on either.

C: Both.
I: Tell me about the dreams in which you're a boy.
C. (No elaboration).
I: Do you ever think that you really are a boy? [Aff]
C. Yes.
I: Tell me more about that.
C. Because...

For the questions comprising the Cognitive Gender Confusion factor, this youngster had "deviant" responses on all four, well above the mean of 0.50 for the gender-referred probands and the mean of 0.05 in the controls in Zucker et al. (1993). For the seven questions comprising the Affective Gender Confusion factor, there were six "deviant" responses, also well above the mean of 2.9 for the gender-referred probands and the mean of 0.9 in the controls.

Differential Diagnosis

An understudied aspect of the DSM criteria pertains to their ability to distinguish girls with GID from girls commonly referred to as *tomboys* (see, e.g., Bailey, Bechtold, & Berenbaum, 2002; Green, Williams, & Goodman, 1982). As defined by the Merriam-Webster's Collegiate Dictionary (1993), a tomboy is "a girl who behaves in a manner usually considered boyish" (see also Thorne, 1986, 1993; Yamaguchi & Barber, 1995). Note that this definition does not include reference to gender dysphoria (or gender identity), but only to culturally defined gender-role related behaviors.

In a study in which children were recruited by newspaper ads, Bailey et al. (2002) compared girls nominated by their parents as "tomboys" to their sisters and brothers on several measures pertaining to gender identity and gender role preferences. Compared to their sisters, the tomboys were significantly more masculine on all measures, with effect sizes ranging from .40 to 2.80. Although brothers were more masculine than tomboys, the differences were much less substantial.

Unfortunately, no study has made a direct comparison of girls who, say, by parent report, meet the diagnostic criteria for GID versus girls who are nominated by their parents as tomboys, but who do not meet the DSM criteria for GID. Indeed, it is possible that in the Bailey et al. (2002) study the sample consisted of both types of girls, thus obscuring potentially important differences between them (see also Berenbaum & Bailey, 2003).

Judgments of Persistence

A clinical-diagnostic issue that cuts across all editions of the DSM pertains to judgments of behavioral persistence. For example, the A criterion requires a clinical judgment in determining what qualifies as a "repeatedly stated desire to be...the other sex" or "strong and persistent preferences for cross-sex roles in make-believe play..." What criteria should clinicians utilize in deciding whether the desire to change sex is persistent or that

Table 2. Maternal Ratings of Specific Sex-Typed Behaviors in Girls with Gender Identity Disorder and Female Controls

	Group	
	Gender Identity Disorder	Controls
Wish to be opposite sex[a]	(N = 50)	(N = 188)
Frequently/Every day	44.0%	0.0%
Once-in-a-while	26.0%	1.1%
Very rarely	14.0%	0.5%
Never	16.0%	98.4%
Dress-up play[b]	(N = 29)	(N = 163)
Same-sex	10.3%	92.0%
Equally	6.9%	5.5%
Cross-Sex	82.8%	2.5%
Roles in fantasy play[c]	(N = 38)	(N = 169)
Same-sex	15.8%	95.3%
Equally	15.8%	3.6%
Cross-Sex	68.4%	1.1%
Favorite playmates[d]	(N = 50)	(N = 187)
Same-sex	10.0%	65.2%
Equally	34.0%	32.1%
Cross-Sex	56.0%	2.7%

NOTE: Controls consisted of three groups of girls: siblings, clinic-referred, and nonreferred ("normals"). Nonreferred controls provide a baseline with which to compare the other groups. Clinic-referred controls provide a test of specificity, that is, whether or not the behavior of the index clinical group is specific to that group or characteristic of clinical populations in general. Siblings provide some control for both genetic and shared environmental influences. Preliminary analyses showed no differences among the three types of controls, so their data were collapsed. Same-sex and cross-sex categories combined the response options of *Usually* and *Always*. For dress-up play, role play, and playmates there was a *Not applicable* option (e.g., "doesn't dress up). Children whose mother endorsed this option had their data excluded from these analyses; hence, the Ns varies from item to item. The four items are from a 16-item parent-report questionnaire (Johnson et al., 2004).
[a] $\chi^2(3) = 148.7$, $p < .001$
[b] $\chi^2(2) = 129.6$, $p < .001$
[c] $\chi^2(2) = 136.0$, $p < .001$
[d] $\chi^2(2) = 105.9$, $p < .001$

cross-gender behaviors are strong? To some extent, the answer to this question hinges on what is known about the prevalence and intensity of such behaviors in the general population. Unfortunately, there is really no "gold standard" for the clinician to use (as there might be, for example, in the use of a laboratory test to diagnose a physical disorder, such as juvenile diabetes) and the *DSM-IV* does not provide explicit guidelines for addressing this matter. Of course, this is a problem not unique to the diagnosis of GID.

Table 2 provides an illustration of how this matter can be studied empirically. It shows maternal questionnaire ratings of specific sex-typed behaviors relevant to the DSM criteria for gender-referred girls and three comparisons groups of girls (siblings, clinic-referred, and nonreferred). For the wish to be of the opposite sex, even the response option of "very rarely" appears to distinguish gender-referred girls from control girls. For dress-up play, roles in fantasy play, and peer preference, a cross-sex preference appears to work well as a reasonable cut point.

Table 3. Maternal Ratings of Behavioral Disturbance on the Child Behavior Checklist of Girls with Gender Identity Disorder (GID) and Female Siblings

Measures	GID (N = 60)		Siblings (N = 142)	
	M	*SD*	*M*	*SD*
No. Elevated Narrow-Band Scales	2.35	2.79	.73	1.47
Number of Items	35.95	20.15	22.59	16.03
Sum of Items	45.92	29.17	27.36	21.81
Internalizing T	60.60	12.09	52.73	11.37
Externalizing T	60.62	13.61	52.00	10.92
Age (years)	7.99	2.77	7.72	2.91
Social Class	41.00	15.35	44.58	14.74
Marital Status				
Both Parents	N 38		103	
Other	N 22		39	

NOTE: For one proband and her two sisters, the mother did not read English, so she could not complete the CBCL. The father could read English, so his data were used. CBCL data for two other probands were not available.
$p < .001$ for the GID-sibling comparisons on all five CBCL measures.

ASSOCIATED BEHAVIOR PROBLEMS

The assessment of associated behavior problems in girls with GID has been largely restricted to standardized parent- and teacher-report questionnaires. In our clinic, we have utilized the parent- and teacher versions of the CBCL. In the original standardization of the CBCL, factor analysis was performed on six sex-by-age groupings (4–5 years, 6–11 years, and 12–16 years). Two broadband factors were identified, termed Internalizing and Externalizing, respectively. Across the six groups, there were also common and unique narrow-band factors (see Achenbach & Edelbrock, 1983).

CBCL Data on Girls with Gender Identity Disorder

Table 3 presents maternal-report data for 60 gender-referred girls and 142 female siblings (of both our female and male probands) for five CBCL indices of disturbance.[2] On all five indices, the gender-referred girls had significantly higher levels of behavioral disturbance (all *ps* < .001). Within each group, the Internalizing T and Externalizing T scores did not differ significantly from each other. Paternal-report data (N = 35 for the gender-referred girls; N = 108 for the siblings) also yielded significant

[2]As noted earlier, there are two items on the CBCL that specifically pertain to cross-gender behavior (Item 5: "behaves like opposite sex" and Item 110: "wishes to be of opposite sex."). It has also been our experience that certain other items on the CBCL are endorsed in a manner that reflect the child's cross-gender-identification. For example, a parent might endorse Item 84 ("strange behavior") and then provide an example such as "thinks she's a boy." For all of the analyses reported here, these items were scored as 0's to avoid any artificial inflation of the disturbance indices.

between-group differences (all $ps < .001$). CBCL data were also reported by Cohen-Kettenis et al. (2003) on 33 girls with GID from the Netherlands. The degree of behavior problems was similar to the Toronto sample, thus establishing a replication of the findings in an independent sample.

CBCL ratings were available from 143 fathers of the 202 girls and the mother-father correlations were significant for all five indices (rs ranged from .58 to .62, all $ps < .001$, one-tailed). The strength of these correlations was consistent with many other studies that have assessed the concordance of parent ratings (Achenbach, McConaughy, & Howell, 1987; Duhig, Renk, Epstein, & Phares, 2000). Ratings on the Teacher's Report Form (Achenbach & Edelbrock, 1986) were available for 41 of the GID girls and the mother-teacher correlations were significant for four of the five indices (rs ranged from .26 to .49, all $ps < .05$, one-tailed). Although these correlations were lower than the mother-father ratings, they tended to be somewhat higher than those reported in the literature (see Achenbach et al., 1987).

Table 4 presents the CBCL data as a function of two age groupings, 3–5 and 6–12 years, respectively.[3,4] The 3–5-year-old girls with GID had substantially lower disturbance ratings than did their 6–12-year-old counterparts, whereas the female siblings in the two age groupings did not. In the 3–5-year-old group, the girls with GID had a significantly higher Internalizing T score than did the female siblings, with age covaried ($p < .05$), but did not differ significantly on the remaining four indices. In contrast, the 6–12-year-old girls with GID had significantly higher levels of disturbance than the female siblings on all five indices, with social class covaried (all $ps < .001$). Table 4 also shows the CBCL data for girls from the standardization sample. For the 3–5-year-old age group, the girls with GID had scores that were, on average, closer to those of the nonreferred than to the referred sample. In contrast, the 6–12-year-old girls with GID had scores that were, on average, closer to the referred than to the nonreferred sample.

Of the 19 3–5-year-old girls with GID, 5 (26.3%) had a total behavior problem score in the clinical range, compared to 7 (16.6%) of 42 female siblings, a nonsignificant difference, $\chi^2(1) < 1$. In contrast, 27 (65.8%) of 41 girls aged 6–12 years with GID had scores in the clinical range compared to only 24 (24.0%) of 100 female siblings, $\chi^2(1) = 20.29$, $p < .001$. The percentage of 6–12-year-old girls with GID with a total behavior problem score in the clinical range was significantly higher than their 3–5-year-old counterparts ($\chi^2[1] = 6.64$, $p < .01$), but there was no corresponding age effect for the female siblings, $\chi^2(1) < 1$.

Of the eight CBCL narrow-band scales (Figure 1), the 3–5-year-old girls with GID had significantly higher T scores than the female siblings on two:

[3]Several girls in each group were 3 years old. Their CBCL profiles were computed using the norms for 2- to 3-year-olds (Achenbach, Edelbrock, & Howell, 1987) and were prorated to adjust for the smaller number of items on the questionnaire. For the narrow-band factors (see Figure 1), data from girls whose mothers completed the 2–3-year-old CBCL were not included.

[4]Several girls in each group were 12-year-olds. Their CBCL profiles were computed using the norms for 12- to 16-year-olds, but for the narrow-band factors (see Figure 2) were recalculated using the norms for 6- to 11-year-olds.

Table 4. Maternal Ratings of Behavioral Disturbance on the CBCL for Girls with Gender Identity Disorder, Female Siblings, and the Standardization Sample

| | 4–5 years | | | | | | | |
| Measures | Gender Identity Disorder ($n = 19$) | | Siblings ($n = 42$) | | Nonreferred ($n = 100$) | | Referred ($n = 100$) | |
	M	SD	M	SD	M	SD	M	SD
No. elevated narrow-band scales	0.9	2.2	0.4	0.9	–	–	–	–
Number of items	29.0	20.1	24.1	16.0	–	–	–	–
Sum of items	34.4	25.3	29.3	21.9	25.2	17.1	58.8	29.1
Internalizing T	55.0	13.9	48.6	10.2	50.8	10.5	66.5	11.3
Externalizing T	52.0	12.4	48.1	8.9	49.8	8.7	61.5	12.8
Age (in years)	5.0	0.7	4.1	1.1	–	–	–	–
Social class	44.6	12.9	40.8	16.3	–	–	–	–
Marital status								
Both parents	15 (n)		31 (n)		–	–	–	–
Mother only/ reconstituted	4 (n)		11 (n)		–	–	–	–

| | 6–11 years | | | | | | | |
| | Gender Identity Disorder ($n = 41$) | | Siblings ($n = 100$) | | Nonreferred ($n = 100$) | | Referred ($n = 100$) | |
	M	SD	M	SD	M	SD	M	SD
No. elevated narrow-band scales	3.0	2.8	0.9	1.6	–	–	–	–
Number of items	39.2	19.6	22.0	16.1	–	–	–	–
Sum of items	51.2	29.6	26.5	21.8	19.9	14.2	58.4	26.2
Internalizing T	63.2	10.3	54.5	11.4	51.3	9.1	67.0	9.1
Externalizing T	64.6	12.4	53.6	53.6	51.0	9.4	68.1	9.5
Age (years)	9.4	2.2	9.3	1.9	–	–	–	–
Social class	39.3	16.2	46.2	13.8	–	–	–	–
Marital status								
Both parents	23 (n)		72 (n)		–	–	–	–
Mother only/ reconstituted	18 (n)		28 (n)		–	–	–	–

NOTE: Data for the nonreferred and referred samples from Achenbach and Edelbrock (1983, Appendix D, pp. 213–214).

Social Withdrawal ($p < .025$) and Sex Problems ($p < .01$). With the exception of the Somatic Complaints narrow band, the 6–12-year-old girls with GID had significantly higher T scores than the female siblings on the other eight narrow-band scales (ps ranged from $< .001$ to $.05$) (Figure 2).

Predictors of Behavior Problems

In the Cohen-Kettenis et al. (2003) study, we examined the predictors of CBCL behavior problems in girls with GID using the sum of items rated as a 1 or a 2 as the criterion variable. Eight predictor variables were entered into the regression equation: Clinic (Toronto vs. Utrecht),

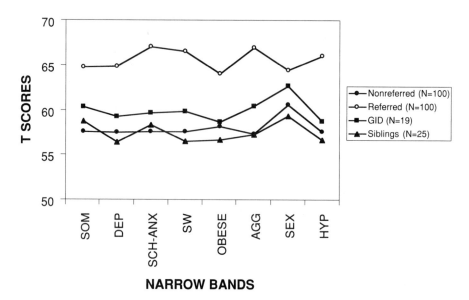

Figure 1. Narrow-band factors on the CBCL for 4- to 5-year-old girls. SOM, Somatic complaints; DEP, Depressed; SCH-ANX, Schizoid or anxious; SW, Social withdrawal; OBESE, Obese; AGG, Aggressive; SEX, Sex problems; HYP, Hyperactive.

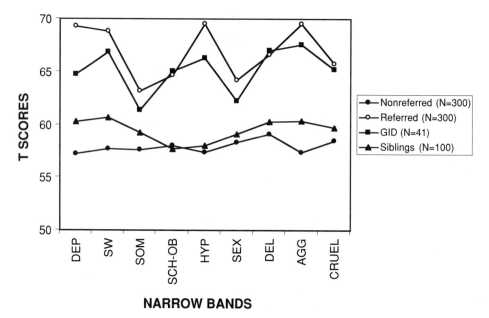

Figure 2. Narrow-band factors on the CBCL for 6- to 11-year-old girls. DEP, Depressed; SW, Social withdrawal; SOM, Somatic complaints; SCH-OB, Schizoid-obsessive; HYP, Hyperactive; SEX, Sex problems; DEL, Delinquent; AGG, Aggressive; CRUEL, Cruel.

age, full-scale IQ, social class, parent's marital status, diagnostic status (whether or not the girl met the complete DSM criteria for GID or was sub-threshold), the two CBCL gender items (see Footnote 2), and a 3-item CBCL-derived composite Peer Relations Scale. Of these eight variables, three were statistically significant: the Peer Relations Scale ($R^2 = .246$), the two CBCL gender items ($R^2\Delta = .148$), and full-scale IQ ($R^2\Delta = .053$), all $ps < .025$. Thus, girls who had poorer peer relations, more cross-gender behavior, and a lower IQ had more behavioral problems on the CBCL.

In Cohen-Kettenis et al. (2003), the regression analysis did not detect an age effect for either girls or boys. It is likely that the age effect noted above (3–5-year-olds vs. 6–12-year-olds) was washed out by the influence of the Peer Relations Scale, suggesting that poor peer relations functions as a mediating variable. This is consistent with the extant literature on children's reactions to cross-gender behavior in their peers, namely that social ostracism becomes more salient in older rather than younger children.

CBCL data on adolescent girls with GID suggest not only a continuation of behavioral difficulties, but an intensification. In Zucker et al. (2002), adolescent girls with GID had significantly more behavioral problems than their child counterparts, with effect sizes ranging from .55 to .93, even after covarying for demographic differences (e.g., IQ, social class, etc.). Moreover, their scores on our CBCL-derived measure of poor peer relations were significantly higher. Although these are cross-sectional data, they suggest that the developmental trajectory for clinic-referred girls with gender identity problems worsens over time, with an increase in co-occurring general behavior problems.

Summary

Overall, the CBCL data showed that girls with GID were, in general, more disturbed than their female siblings. This finding parallels our data on boys with GID compared to their male siblings (Zucker & Bradley, 1995). In the 6–12-year-old group with GID, they were more disturbed than were the nonreferred girls in the CBCL standardization sample, but this difference was not as apparent in the 3–5-year-old group. The patterning of behavioral disturbance indicated a mixture of both internalizing and externalizing symptomatology, which contrasts with our data on boys with GID, who showed a predominance of internalizing symptomatology (Zucker & Bradley, 1995).

Although we have successfully identified some correlates of CBCL behavioral problems in girls with GID, more work is required. For example, it might be useful to carry out more formal DSM-oriented structured psychiatric interviews to map the CBCL data to categorical diagnoses. Moreover, more refined analyses are required to elaborate upon the domain-specific areas of impairment, including relations with parents and peers (e.g., experiences of victimization) and functioning within the school environment.

ETIOLOGY

Both biological and psychosocial theories (and, more narrowly, hypotheses) have been developed to account for both between- and within-sex variations in psychosexual differentiation. In this section, I will provide a selective overview of these theories, including a summary of the empirical database, with an emphasis on studies most relevant to understanding GID in girls.

Biological Mechanisms

Five parameters are commonly used to classify a person's biological sex: chromosomal sex, gonadal sex (ovaries vs. testis), hormonal sex, the internal reproductive structures, and the external genitalia (Migeon & Wisniewski, 1998). Over the past couple of decades, there has also been an interest in the possibility that the human brain has sex-dimorphic characteristics, but the existence of such putative anatomic and functional properties has not, as of yet, been part of any formal taxonomic system in classifying humans as female or male (or as a third "intersex," more commonly known as hermaphrodites).

For over 40 years now, the most prominent biological hypothesis that has guided research on psychosexual differentiation pertains to the role of prenatal sex hormones (and, in some lower animals, perinatal sex hormones). The classic version of the theory posits that prenatal exposure to androgens (a male-typical hormone) both masculinizes and defeminizes postnatal sex-dimorphic behavior (Collaer & Hines, 1995; Meyer-Bahlburg, 1984). In part, the theory draws on literally thousands of experimental studies of lower animals in which the effects of the manipulation of the prenatal and perinatal hormonal milieu is evaluated with regard to species-specific sex-dimorphic behaviors (for reviews, see Dixson, 1998; Wallen & Baum, 2002). If the theory has plausibility for the human situation, then variations in postnatal sex-dimorphic behavior should be related to variations in exposure to prenatal sex hormones.

Given that female and male fetuses are clearly exposed to different amounts of prenatal androgen (Smail, Reyes, Winter, & Faiman, 1981), which, in turn, affect the sex-dimorphic differentiation of the external genitalia and the CNS, perhaps it is this variation that accounts for the large sex differences that are observed with regard to gender identity, gender role, and sexual orientation. The theory would also posit that within-sex variation in exposure to prenatal sex hormones might explain within-sex variation in postnatal sex-dimorphic behaviors. Critics, however, have noted that because most females and males are "reared" or socialized as girls and boys, respectively, the influence of biological and psychosocial factors are usually perfectly confounded.

For this reason, many studies have examined the psychosexual differentiation of children born with physical intersex conditions in which it is known that the prenatal sex hormone milieu is altered in a sex-atypical manner. One such condition, which affects both genetic females and males, is congenital adrenal hyperplasia (CAH). In genetic females, this inherited, autosomal recessive disorder results in the excessive production of adrenal androgens, which causes ambiguous or fully masculinized external genitalia. Postnatally, feminizing surgery can normalize the appearance of the external genitalia and, since 1950, cortisone replacement therapy has been used to normalize the malfunctioning endocrine system which, in theory, essentially shuts down the excessive production of adrenal androgen, which blocks further postnatal masculinization of the genitalia. Treated CAH, then, has been used as a model "experiment of nature" in which the effects of abnormal prenatal hormone exposure on postnatal sex-dimorphic behavior can be observed.

The results of this research appear to show effects consistent with the prenatal hormone hypothesis. Girls with CAH show more masculinized gender role behavior and their sexual orientation, in adulthood, appears to be shifted away from the female-typical pattern of sexual attraction to males, with most studies finding higher rates of a bisexual sexual orientation, particularly in fantasy. Gender identity appears least affected although the differentiation of a male gender identity (including gender change later in life) occurs at a rate than is higher than one would expect based on population baserates (for reviews, see Collaer & Hines, 1995; Meyer-Bahlburg, 2001; Zucker, 1999).

Regarding GID in girls and women, the main problem with the model is that there is no compelling evidence of a gross prenatal hormonal anomaly since the genitalia are invariably normal. On the surface, then, it would appear that there is no clear indication of a masculinized prenatal hormonal milieu; however, over the past couple of decades, new research on lower animals has shown that it is possible to manipulate the prenatal hormonal environment and cause sex-dimorphic behavioral effects, but leave the structure of the external genitalia intact.

In female rhesus macaques (*Macaca mulatta*), for example, Goy, Bercovitch, and McBrair (1988) were able to induce behavioral masculinization in the absence of genital masculinization by varying the timing of exogenous injections of testosterone propionate during the pregnancy. From an interpretive point of view, this methodology is of interest because it eliminates a possible confound—that the masculinized behavior is, in part, a function of how the social group reacts to the anomalous genitalia of the female offspring. Goy et al. found that early-exposed females, who were genitally masculinized, showed increased rates of maternal- and peer-mounting (male-typical behaviors) and lowered rates of grooming of their own mothers (a female-typical behavior) compared to normal females but did not differ from normal females in their rates of rough play. In contrast, late-exposed females, who were not genitally masculinized, showed increased rates of rough play and peer-mounting but did not differ from normal females in their rates of maternal-mounting. The mothers of the early-exposed females were more likely to inspect their genitalia than were the mothers of normal females, but the mothers of the late-exposed females were not. Goy et al. concluded that "the individual behavior traits that are components of the juvenile male role are independently regulated by the organizing actions of androgen and have separable critical periods" (p. 552). The association between prenatal androgen exposure and increased rates of some male-typical behaviors, despite the absence of genital masculinization, suggests that there can be a *dissociation* of morphological and behavioral effects in nonhuman primates. This clearly opens the possibility that similar mechanisms operate in human females.

As a result of this work, researchers have sought to identify sex-dimorphic behavioral markers that might be affected by more subtle variations in the prenatal hormonal milieu, that is, variations that do not affect the configuration of the external genitalia. Table 5 summarizes some selected domains that have relied on this model. These include "normative" variation in prenatal exposure to testosterone (T), that is, variation that does not affect the external genitalia, prenatal maternal stress, dermatoglyphics, functional aspects of the auditory system, handedness, sibling sex ratio and birth order, and temperament.

As one example, Hines et al. (2002a) measured prenatal levels of T and sex-hormone binding globulin (SHBG) in blood samples from pregnant women, who produced 337 female and 342 male offspring. At the age of 3.5 years, gender role behavior was assessed using the Pre-School Activities Inventory, a standardized parent-report measure. Higher levels of prenatal T were related linearly to gender role behavior in girls, but not boys. No gender role effects were found for variations in SHBG. Girls classified as behaviorally "masculine" had higher maternal prenatal T than girls classified as behaviorally "feminine" at the order of .35 SD; however, it should be noted that the amount of variance in the gender role behavior of the girls related to maternal T was only 2%.

The results of this study suggest that T from the maternal system passes into the developing female fetus and has a modest effect on postnatal sex-dimorphic behavior, consistent with the prenatal hormonal hypothesis. An alternative interpretation is that variation in prenatal T levels is genetically influenced; thus, it is possible that mothers with relatively high T have daughters with relatively high T, because of a genetic predisposition that is passed from mother to daughter. In this case, the fetus's own T could masculinize her development.

Unfortunately, very little biologically informed research has been conducted on girls with GID. For example, although there is some evidence that women with a homosexual sexual orientation are more likely to have lesbian sisters than women with a heterosexual sexual orientation (see Table 5 for references), no formal studies have examined whether or not girls with GID have an excess of sisters who are also GID or have a higher rate of a homosexual sexual orientation. In our clinic, none of the girls with GID had sisters who were also GID. There have also been no studies of girls with GID in which rates of GID or a homosexual sexual orientation have been ascertained in parents or first-degree relatives (e.g., aunts and uncles).

The one domain for which we have some data concerns activity level (AL), a commonly accepted dimension of temperament, for which there is some evidence of a genetic basis and possibly prenatal hormonal influences. AL as a predisposing factor has long been considered of relevance, since it shows a rather strong sex difference, with boys having a higher AL than girls (Eaton & Enns, 1986). Socially interactive rough-and-tumble (RT) play, another sex-dimorphic behavior (DiPietro, 1981), bears some similarity to AL, in that it is often characterized by high energy expenditure.

Table 5. Recent Biological Research on Psychosexual Differentiation in Females

Domain	Behavioral Traits	Results	Selected References
Molecular genetics	Sexual Orientation	No linkage between Xq28 markers and sexual orientation	Hu et al. (1995)
Behavior genetics: Twin studies	Gender Role; Sexual Orientation	Conflicting evidence for greater concordance in MZ > DZ twins for sexual orientation; evidence for heritability of gender role behavior	Bailey, Dunne, and Martin (2000); Bailey, Pillard, Neale, and Agyei (1993)
Behavior genetics: Family studies	Sexual Orientation	Lesbians have higher rate of homosexual brothers and sisters than heterosexual women	Bailey and Benishay (1993)
Prenatal sex hormones	Gender Role	Variation in maternal prenatal testosterone significantly associated with daughters' gender role preference at age 3.5 yrs	Hines et al. (2002a)
Prenatal maternal stress	Gender Role; Sexual Orientation	Little evidence for an association between prenatal maternal stress and gender role or sexual orientation	Ellis and Cole-Harding (2001); Hines et al. (2002b)
Dermatoglyphics	Gender identity; sexual orientation	Conflicting evidence that measures of fingerprint patterns are related to gender identity; some evidence that the ratio of finger length (2nd digit:4th digit) is masculinized in lesbians	Green and Young (2000); Lippa (2003); Slabbekoorn, van Goozen, Sanders, Gooren, and Cohen-Kettenis (2000); Williams et al. (2000)
Otoacoustic emissions and auditory evoked potentials	Sexual orientation	Masculinized in lesbians	McFadden (2002)
Handedness	Gender identity; sexual orientation	Increased rates of left-handedness or nonconsistent right-handedness in women with GID and lesbians	Green and Young (2000); Lalumière, Blanchard, and Zucker (2000)
Sibling sex ratio and birth order	Gender identity; gender role; sexual orientation	Girls with GID early-born; no effects of birth order in lesbians; no alteration in sibling sex ratio (ratio of brothers:sisters) in lesbians	Blanchard (1997); Zucker et al. (1998)
Temperament: activity level	Gender identity; gender role	Girls with GID have a higher activity level than control girls	Zucker and Bradley (1995)

NOTE: These references do not include studies of girls and women with physical intersex conditions (for review of those studies, see Zucker, 1999).

Using a 17-item factor (labeled Activity Level/Extraversion) from a parent-report measure, we found that girls with GID had a significantly higher AL than control girls (a combined sample of female siblings, clinical controls, and normal controls), with an effect size of .74, whereas boys with GID had a significantly lower AL than control boys; indeed, the girls with GID had a significantly higher AL than the boys with GID, whereas for the controls, the typical sex difference was observed. Indeed, the AL of the GID girls was comparable to that of the control boys (Zucker & Bradley, 1995).

It appears from these data that AL and RT are important characteristics associated with GID in both girls and boys. Regarding biological factors, there is some evidence that AL has a genetic basis (e.g., Willerman, 1973). AL also appears to be related to hormonal factors, as judged, for example, by studies of girls with CAH (Ehrhardt & Baker, 1974; Pasterski, 2002). In a study of 7,018 children from the National Collaborative Perinatal Project, Eaton, Chipperfield, and Singbeil (1989) found that early borns were more active than later borns, which is of interest in light of our finding that girls with GID are, on average, early born (Zucker, Lightbody, Pecore, Bradley, & Blanchard, 1998) whereas boys with GID are later born (Blanchard, Zucker, Bradley, & Hume, 1995). As noted by Eaton et al. (1989), the relation between AL and birth order could be accounted for by prenatal hormone differences within a sibship.

Regarding social influences on AL, Eaton et al. (1989) noted that changes within the family could also be important; for example, older siblings are more verbally and physically aggressive than younger siblings (e.g., Abramovitch, Corter, Pepler, & Stanhope, 1986) and parents may be less tolerant of high AL when they have several children. Thus, it is conceivable that aspects of the social environment exacerbate or attenuate the expression of AL (see, e.g., Fagot & O'Brien, 1994). There is also some evidence that certain highly physical activities are perceived by children as more appropriate for the masculine social role (Pellett & Harrison, 1992) and that children are more active when engaged in masculine play behavior (O'Brien & Huston, 1985).

From a more clinical perspective, various hypotheses can be entertained regarding how a child's proclivity for active play and behavior could affect social relations, particularly with peers. For example, a high-active girl with GID may find the typical play behavior of other girls to be incompatible with her own behavioral style, which would make it difficult for her to enjoy the activities of a female peer group. Similarly, an interest in RT play may increase the likelihood that a girl will develop social affiliations with boys rather than girls, again on the grounds of behavioral compatibility (e.g., Martin & Fabes, 2001; Serbin, Moller, Gulko, Powlishta, & Colburne, 1994).

The research reviewed here and summarized in Table 5 suggests that there may well be biological factors that predispose to within-sex variation in psychosexual differentiation in females. I use the verb "predispose" to argue that these biological factors act in such a manner to attenuate or exacerbate the patterning of sex-dimorphic behaviors because it is fairly clear that these influences leave a lot of the variance unexplained (cf. Wallen, 1996). For example, in our own research we have found that, on some measures, girls with GID show more masculinized sex-dimorphic behavior than a comparison group of prenatally androgenized girls with various types of intersex conditions (Zucker, Allin et al., 2003). Thus, it is of note that girls with GID, without an apparent prenatal hormonal anomaly, showed *more*, not less, cross-gender behavior, including cross-gender identity, than girls with such an anomaly. This suggests that additional factors are required to account for the behavioral outcome; however, because both the GID girls and intersex girls showed more cross-gender behavior than controls, it is also an illustrative example of the concept of equifinality, that is, different starting points leading to the same outcome (Cicchetti & Rogosch, 1996).

Psychosocial Mechanisms

Psychosocial factors can be considered with regard to predisposing, precipitating, and perpetuating or maintaining factors. To merit causal status, psychosocial factors would need to influence the onset of cross-gender behaviors and feelings. A multifactorial model of causality can, however, also entertain perpetuating factors, which can exacerbate any type of predisposing factor, including biological influences. Unfortunately, there has been little in the way of systematic research on psychosocial factors, so the material reviewed here relies primarily on systematic clinical observations.

Girls with GID are invariably assigned to the female sex at birth. Thus, unlike in the case of some physical intersex conditions, in which there can be prolonged uncertainty about gender assignment (Meyer-Bahlburg, 2001), this does not appear to be an operative mechanism in girls with GID. During the first few years of life, some clinicians and researchers have suggested that a predisposing factor might be related to the girl's difficulty in forming a secure attachment to the mother, thus inhibiting subsequent same-sex gender identification (Stoller, 1972). Zucker and Bradley (1995) presented some data suggesting that severe maternal psychiatric difficulties during this time period may be contributory. Of 26 girls who had been assessed at that time, 10 (38.4%) had mothers who were, or had been, in outpatient treatment, and of these mothers, two had also been inpatients (as it turned out, two other mothers were admitted as inpatients after we had assessed their daughters). Based on clinical interview data, 20 (76.9%) of the mothers had histories of depression. Although many of these mothers had been depressed prior to the birth of their daughters, they were all depressed when their daughter was in her infancy or toddler years. Eleven of the 26 mothers met criteria for Axis II personality disorders.

On this basis, it was argued that the girls had difficulty in forming an emotional connection to their mothers and attachment assessments suggested that the most common type of pattern was of the Avoidant subtype (unpublished data). In some instances, it seemed that the girl either failed to identify with her mother (or deidentified from her) because she perceived her as weak, incompetent, or helpless. In fact, many of the mothers devalued their own efficacy and regarded the female gender role with disdain. For example, one couple, when the wife became pregnant for a second time (the proband was the couple's first-born), stated that they intended to obtain an amniocentesis and that they would abort the fetus if it was female, but keep it if it was male. In a smaller number of cases, it seemed that significant medical illness or a "difficult temperament" during infancy had impaired the girl's relationship with her mother.

Six of the mothers had a history of severe and chronic sexual abuse of an incestuous nature. The femininity of these mothers had always been clouded by this experience, which rendered them quite wary about men and masculinity and created substantial dysfunction in their sexual lives. In terms of psychosocial transmission, the message to the daughters seemed to be that being female was unsafe.

Another factor of importance is the GID girl's experience of severe paternal or male sibling aggression. Such aggression had been directed at the mother, at the girl, or at both. Such aggression occurred in 12 of the 26 families. In these cases, the classic mechanism of "identification with the aggressor" seemed relevant to the girl's cross-gender identification, which is consistent with the clinical observation that many girls with GID are preoccupied with power, aggression, and protection fantasies. In one family, the father's chronic anger was described by the mother as resulting in a kind of "Stockholm syndrome," that is, the phenomenon in which the hostage identifies with the hostage taker. In another family, a girl was subjected to severe physical abuse by her father and by his sons from previous liaisons. Eventually, her father's current partner shot him in the face. While in residential care, the girl was chronically fearful that her father would eventually find her and wanted a gun and a penis in order to protect both herself and her mother from him. In another case, a girl, at the age of 4 years, developed the fantasy of becoming a boy after her mother was killed by a boyfriend. When assessed at the age of 9 years, she reasoned that if she were a boy, she would be stronger and thus might have been able to save her mother. Thus, these types of experiences seem to fuel the "fantasy solution" of becoming a boy for protective purposes.

In terms of perpetuating factors, many parents of girls with GID will report a period of time in which the cross-gender behavior was tolerated or encouraged, often being viewed as "only a phase." Thus, during the preschool years, when gender identity is in a phase of consolidation (Martin et al., 2002), many girls with GID appear to grow up in an environment that enhances their fantasies of being boys. As noted earlier, many girls with GID have a masculine phenotypic physical appearance (based on hair-style and clothing style), which often results in significant others in the social environment (e.g., peers) perceiving them as boys, which may also function as a perpetuating factors. Lastly, we have shown that girls with GID appear to show a developmental lag in gender constancy acquisition (Zucker et al., 1999), which may contribute to their difficulty in consolidating a female gender identity.

DEVELOPMENTAL COURSE AND OUTCOME

Retrospective studies of adult women with GID invariably indicate an early childhood-onset of cross-gender behavior and feelings (Blanchard & Freund, 1983; Devor, 1997). Given the outcome, it is apparent that such behaviors and feelings persisted. The vast majority of women with GID are sexually attracted to biological females and thus, with regard to their birth sex, have a homosexual sexual orientation.[5] Adult women with GID who are sexually attracted to biological males have been less well studied, but they appear to have been less masculine during girlhood (Chivers & Bailey, 2000). On average, adult women with a homosexual sexual orientation recall more masculine sex-typed behavior in childhood than do women with a heterosexual sexual orientation, with a mean effect size of .96 (Bailey & Zucker, 1995). No studies of women with a homosexual sexual orientation have, however, retrospectively assessed the percentage who may have met criteria for GID in childhood. In the literature, there is a general consensus that adult women with GID were, on average, more likely to be cross-gendered during childhood than lesbians (Blanchard & Freund, 1983); however, it is likely that there is overlap between these two groups of women, particularly with regard to those lesbians who, in adulthood, self-identify as "butch" as opposed to "femme" (Lee, 2001; Singh, Vidaurri, Zambarano, & Dabbs, 1999; Tortorice, 2002).

From a prospective perspective, the psychosexual differentiation of girls with GID can probably best be examined with regard to three broad types of outcomes, as assessed in adolescence and adulthood: (1) persistence of GID, with a cooccuring homosexual sexual orientation; (2) desistance of GID, with a cooccurring homosexual sexual orientation; and (3) desistance of GID, with a cooccurring heterosexual sexual orientation.

So, what do we know about the long-term psychosexual differentiation of girls with GID? Studies of adolescent samples of girls with GID, like adult samples, suggest persistence based on retrospective data (Cohen-Kettenis & van Goozen, 1997; Zucker & Bradley, 1995), but because the phenomenology in adolescence appears more closer to that seen in adults, this is not particularly surprising. At present, we have only a scattering of data from samples of girls with GID followed prospectively from childhood.

Green (1979) reported on the adolescent or young adulthood outcome of four girls who were seen in childhood: one was transsexual, with a homosexual sexual orientation; the remaining three did not have apparent GID; of these, two reported a heterosexual sexual orientation in fantasy (but were not sexually active), and the other reported no sexual feelings. More recently, Cohen-Kettenis (2001) reported preliminary data on a sample of 18 girls first seen in childhood (mean age at assessment, 9 years; range, 6–12 years) and who had now reached adolescence. Of these, eight (44.4%)

---

[5]In this context, a homosexual sexual orientation is used with respect to the person's birth sex. The vast majority of adolescent and adult female transsexuals are erotically attracted to heterosexual biological females and experience their sexual attraction to women as heterosexual, in line with their identity as males (see Chivers & Bailey, 2000).

requested sex reassignment, and all had a homosexual sexual orientation (Cohen-Kettenis, personal communication, February 1, 2003). Thus, the rate of persistence, at least into adolescence, was high.

In my own clinic, from a total sample of 60 girls, we have, to date, outcome data on eight girls, originally assessed at a mean age of 9 years (range, 3–12 years) and followed-up at a mean age of 20 years (range, 15–28 years) (for a description of the assessment procedure, see Zucker & Bradley, 1995). Of these eight girls, three had persistent GID (at follow-up ages of 17, 17, and 24 years, respectively), two of whom had a homosexual sexual orientation and the third was asexual. Of the remaining five girls, three had a homosexual sexual orientation and two had a heterosexual sexual orientation, none of whom had co-occurring gender dysphoria.

Although these data are preliminary, it appears that there is a range of outcomes, but it is clear that the rates of GID and a homosexual sexual orientation without cooccurring gender dysphoria are likely to be higher than the base rates of these two aspects of psychosexual differentiation in an unselected population of women. At present, the database on girls with GID is simply insufficient to predict with any degree of certainty outcome for individual cases.

Little is known about the general long-term psychologic or psychiatric adaptation of girls with GID. In our own clinic, adolescents with GID had substantially higher rates of disturbance on the CBCL than did children with GID, with effect sizes ranging from .55 to .93, even after controlling for demographic differences (Zucker, Owen et al., 2002), suggesting that persistent GID is associated with greater co-morbidity.

IMPLICATIONS FOR TREATMENT AND PREVENTION

The prevention and treatment of GID has often aroused controversy, and the clinician must consider a variety of complex ethical and social issues (reviewed in Zucker, 2001). For example, some critics take the position that GID is not a disorder at all, but merely an extreme example of "gender nonconformity" and that the diagnosis simply reinforces societal stereotypes about gender-related behavior (e.g., Bartlett, Vasey, & Bukowski, 2000; Bem, 1993; Moore, 2002). This type of criticism raises, of course, a host of complex questions pertaining to fundamental assumptions about the defining features of "normal" versus "abnormal" and the distinction between mere variation from the norm and disorder (see, e.g., Zucker & Bradley, 1995, pp. 52–59).

If, however, the primary goal of treatment is to alleviate the suffering of the individual, a developmental perspective is essential. The data reviewed here and elsewhere (e.g., Cohen-Kettenis & van Goozen, 1997) suggest that persistent gender dysphoria, at least when it continues into adolescence, is unlikely to be alleviated in the majority of cases by psychological means, and thus is likely best treated by hormonal and physical contra-sex interventions, particularly after a period of living in the cross-gender role indicates that this will result in the best adaptation for the adolescent female (Smith, van Goozen, & Cohen-Kettenis, 2001). In childhood, however, where the possibility of greater plasticity in outcome is more likely, many clinicians take the position that a trial of psychological treatment, including individual therapy and parent counseling, is warranted (for review of various intervention approaches, see Zucker, 2001). At present, however, systematic studies of treatment efficacy have not been carried out on girls with GID, so the relative success of such interventions remains unknown.

FUTURE DIRECTIONS

In this chapter, I have provided an overview of the literature on GID in girls. Since GID first appeared in the *DSM-III* in 1980, considerable advances have been made in some areas. For example, the phenomenology of GID in girls is now well described and extant assessment procedures are available to conduct a thorough and competent diagnostic evaluation. Like other psychiatric disorders of childhood, it is apparent that complexity, not simplicity, is the guiding rule-of-thumb in any effort to make sense of the origins of GID. It appears that both biological and psychosocial factors contribute to the disorder's genesis and maintenance and we are making some progress in identifying specific markers of both processes; however, compared to boys, the empirical literature on its origins has been relatively understudied and much remains to be learned. We are only beginning to obtain data on the "natural history" of girls with GID, particularly when carried out from a prospective standpoint, and almost nothing in the way of empirical research has been carried out with regard to psychological interventions. Like many other childhood psychiatric disorders, research on girls with GID has lagged behind research on boys and it is hoped that this chapter will contribute to a more comprehensive understanding of those girls who struggle so intensely with their feelings about being female.

REFERENCES

Abramovitch, R., Corter, C., Pepler, D. J., & Stanhope, L. (1986). Sibling and peer interaction: A final follow-up and a comparison. *Child Development, 57*, 217–229.

Achenbach, T. M., & Edelbrock, C. (1983). *Manual for the Child Behavior Checklist and Revised Child Behavior Profile*. Burlington, VT: University of Vermont, Department of Psychiatry.

Achenbach, T. M., & Edelbrock, C. (1986). *Manual for the Teacher's Report Form and Teacher Version of the Child Behavior Profile*. Burlington, VT: University of Vermont Department of Psychiatry.

Achenbach, T. M., Edelbrock, C., & Howell, C. T. (1987). Empirically based assessment of the behavioral/emotional problems of 2- and 3-year-old children. *Journal of Abnormal Child Psychology, 15*, 629–650.

Achenbach, T. M., McConaughy, S. H., & Howell, C. T. (1987). Child/adolescent behavioral and emotional problems: Implications of cross-informant correlations for situational specificity. *Psychological Bulletin, 101*, 213–232.

American Psychiatric Association. (1980). *Diagnostic and statistical manual of mental disorders* (3rd ed.). Washington, DC: Author.

American Psychiatric Association. (1987). *Diagnostic and statistical manual of mental disorders* (3rd ed., rev.). Washington, DC: Author.

American Psychiatric Association. (1994). *Diagnostic and statistical manual of mental disorders* (4th ed.). Washington, DC: Author.

American Psychiatric Association. (2000). *Diagnostic and statistical manual of mental disorders* (4th ed., Text rev.). Washington, DC: Author.

Bailey, J. M., Bechtold, K. T., & Berenbaum, S. A. (2002). Who are tomboys and why should we study them? *Archives of Sexual Behavior, 13,* 333–341.

Bailey, J. M., & Benishay, D. S. (1993). Familial aggregation of female sexual orientation. *American Journal of Psychiatry, 150,* 272–277.

Bailey, J. M., Dunne, M. P., & Martin, N. G. (2000). Genetic and environmental influences on sexual orientation and its correlates in an Australian twin sample. *Journal of Personality and Social Psychology, 78,* 524–536.

Bailey, J. M., & Zucker, K. J. (1995). Childhood sex-typed behavior and sexual orientation: A conceptual analysis and quantitative review. *Developmental Psychology, 31,* 43–55.

Bakker, A., van Kesteren, P. J. M., Gooren, L. J. G., & Bezemer, P. D. (1993). The prevalence of transsexualism in the Netherlands. *Acta Psychiatrica Scandinavica, 87,* 237–238.

Bartlett, N. H., Vasey, P. L., & Bukowski, W. M. (2000). Is gender identity disorder in children a mental disorder? *Sex Roles, 43*(11/12), 753–785.

Bem, S. L. (1993). *The lenses of gender: Transforming the debate on sexual inequality.* New Haven, CT: Yale University Press.

Benjamin, H. (1966). *The transsexual phenomenon.* New York: Julian Press.

Berenbaum, S. A., & Bailey, J. M. (2003). Effects on female gender identity of prenatal androgens and genital appearance: Evidence from girls with congenital adrenal hyperplasia. *Journal of Clinical Endocrinology and Metabolism, 88,* 1102–1106.

Biederman, J., Mick, E., Faraone, S. V., Braaten, E., Doyle, A., Spencer, T., et al. (2002). Influence of gender on attention deficit hyperactivity disorder in children referred to a psychiatric clinic. *American Journal of Psychiatry, 159,* 36–42.

Blanchard, R. (1997). Birth order and sibling sex ratio in homosexual versus heterosexual males and females. *Annual Review of Sex Research, 8,* 27–67.

Blanchard, R., & Freund, K. (1983). Measuring masculine gender identity in females. *Journal of Consulting and Clinical Psychology, 51,* 205–214.

Blanchard, R., Zucker, K. J., Bradley, S. J., & Hume, C. S. (1995). Birth order and sibling sex ratio in homosexual male adolescents and probably prehomosexual feminine boys. *Developmental Psychology, 31,* 22–30.

Cauldwell, D. O. (1949). Psychopathia transsexualis. *Sexology, 16,* 274–280.

Chivers, M. L., & Bailey, J. M. (2000). Sexual orientation of female-to-male transsexuals: A comparison of homosexual and nonhomosexual types. *Archives of Sexual Behavior, 29,* 259–278.

Cicchetti, D., & Rogosch, F. A. (1996). Equifinality and multifinality in developmental psychopathology. *Development and Psychopathology, 8,* 597–600.

Cohen, J. (1988). *Statistical power analysis for the social sciences* (2nd ed.). Hillsdale, NJ: Erlbaum.

Cohen-Kettenis, P. T. (2001). Gender identity disorder in DSM? [Letter to the editor]. *Journal of the American Academy of Child and Adolescent Psychiatry, 40,* 391.

Cohen-Kettenis, P. T., Owen, A., Kaijser, V. G., Bradley, S. J., & Zucker, K. J. (2003). Demographic characteristics, social competence, and behavior problems in children with gender identity disorder: A cross-national, cross-clinic comparative analysis. *Journal of Abnormal Child Psychology, 31,* 41–53.

Cohen-Kettenis, P. T., & van Goozen, S. H. M. (1997). Sex reassignment of adolescent transsexuals: A follow-up study. *Journal of the American Academy of Child and Adolescent Psychiatry, 36,* 263–271.

Cole, H. J., Zucker, K. J., & Bradley, S. J. (1982). Patterns of gender-role behaviour in children attending traditional and non-traditional day-care centres. *Canadian Journal of Psychiatry, 27,* 410–414.

Collaer, M. L., & Hines, M. (1995). Human behavioral sex differences: A role for gonadal hormones during early development? *Psychological Bulletin, 118,* 55–107.

Cromwell, J. (1999). *Transmen and FTMs: Identities, bodies, genders, and sexualities.* Urbana, IL: University of Illinois Press.

Devor, H. (1997). *FTM: Female-to-male transsexuals in society.* Bloomington, IN: Indiana University Press.

DiPietro, J. A. (1981). Rough and tumble play: A function of gender. *Developmental Psychology, 17,* 50–58.

Dixson, A. F. (1998). *Primate sexuality: Comparative studies of the prosimians, monkeys, apes, and human beings.* Oxford: Oxford University Press.

Duhig, A. M., Renk, K., Epstein, M. K., & Phares, V. (2000). Interparental agreement on internalizing, externalizing, and total behavior problems: A meta-analysis. *Clinical Psychology: Science and Practice, 7,* 435–453.

Eaton, W. O., Chipperfield, J. G., & Singbeil, C. E. (1989). Birth order and activity level in children. *Developmental Psychology, 25,* 668–672.

Eaton, W. O., & Enns, L. R. (1986). Sex differences in human motor activity level. *Psychological Bulletin, 100,* 19–28.

Egan, S. K., & Perry, D. G. (2001). Gender identity: A multidimensional analysis with implications for psychosocial adjustment. *Developmental Psychology, 37,* 451–463.

Ehrhardt, A. A., & Baker, S. W. (1974). Fetal androgens, human central nervous system differentiation, and behavior sex differences. In R. C. Friedman, R. M. Richart, & R. L. Vande Wiele (Eds.), *Sex differences in behavior* (pp. 33–51). New York: Wiley.

Ellis, L., & Cole-Harding, S. (2001). The effects of prenatal stress, and of prenatal alcohol and nicotine exposure, on human sexual orientation. *Physiology and Behavior, 74,* 213–226.

Fagot, B. I. (1977). Consequences of moderate cross-gender behavior in preschool children. *Child Development, 48,* 902–907.

Fagot, B. I. (1985). Beyond the reinforcement principle: Another step toward understanding sex role development. *Developmental Psychology, 21,* 1097–1104.

Fagot, B. I. (1995). Psychosocial and cognitive determinants of early gender-role development. *Annual Review of Sex Research, 6,* 1–31.

Fagot, B. I., & Leinbach, M. D. (1985). Gender identity: Some thoughts on an old concept. *Journal of the American Academy of Child Psychiatry, 24,* 684–688.

Fagot, B. I., & O'Brien, M. (1994). Activity level in young children: Cross-age stability, situational influences, correlates with temperament, and the perception of problem behaviors. *Merrill-Palmer Quarterly, 40,* 378–398.

Fisk, N. (1973). Gender dysphoria syndrome (the how, what, and why of a disease). In D. Laub & P. Gandy (Eds.), *Proceedings of the second interdisciplinary symposium on gender dysphoria syndrome* (pp. 7–14). Palo Alto, CA: Stanford University Press.

Fridell, S. R., Zucker, K. J., Bradley, S. J., & Maing, D. M. (1996). Physical attractiveness of girls with gender identity disorder. *Archives of Sexual Behavior, 25,* 17–31.

Goy, R. W., Bercovitch, F. B., & McBrair, M. C. (1988). Behavioral masculinization is independent of genital masculinization in prenatally androgenized female rhesus macaques. *Hormones and Behavior, 22,* 552–571.

Green, R. (1974). *Sexual identity conflict in children and adults.* New York: Basic Books.

Green, R. (1979). Childhood cross-gender behavior and subsequent sexual preference. *American Journal of Psychiatry, 136,* 106–108.

Green, R., & Money, J. (1960). Incongruous gender role: Nongenital manifestations in prepubertal boys. *Journal of Nervous and Mental Disease, 131,* 160–168.

Green, R., Williams, K., & Goodman, M. (1982). Ninety-nine "tomboys" and "non-tomboys": Behavioral contrasts and demographic similarities. *Archives of Sexual Behavior, 11,* 247–266.

Green, R., & Young, R. (2000). Fingerprint asymmetry in male and female transsexuals. *Personality and Individual Differences, 29,* 933–942.

Green, R., & Young, R. (2001). Hand preference, sexual preference, and transsexualism. *Archives of Sexual Behavior, 30,* 565–574.

Hage, J. J. (1996). Metaidioplasty: An alternative phalloplasty technique in transsexuals. *Plastic and Reconstructive Surgery, 97,* 161–167.

Halberstam, J. (1998). *Female masculinity.* Durham, NC: Duke University Press.

Hamburger, C. (1953). The desire for change of sex as shown by personal letters from 465 men and women. *Acta Endocrinologica, 14,* 361–375.

Hausman, B. L. (1992). Demanding subjectivity: Transsexualism, medicine, and the technologies of gender. *Journal of the History of Sexuality, 3,* 270–302.

Herdt, G. (Ed.). (1994). *Third sex, third gender: Beyond sexual dimorphism in culture and history.* New York: Zone Books.

Hines, M., Golombok, S., Rust, J., Johnston, K. J., Golding, J., and the Avon Longitudinal Study of Parents and Children Study Team. (2002a). Testosterone during pregnancy and gender role behavior of preschool children: A longitudinal, population study. *Child Development, 73,* 1678–1687.

Hines, M., Johnston, K. J., Golombok, S., Rust, J., Stevens, M., Golding, J., et al. (2002b). Prenatal stress and gender role behavior in girls and boys: A longitudinal, population study. *Hormones and Behavior, 42,* 126–134.

Hirschfeld, M. (1923). Die intersexuelle konstitution. *Jahrbuch für Sexuelle Zwischenstufen, 23,* 3–27.

Hoenig, J. (1985). The origin of gender identity. In B. W. Steiner (Ed.), *Gender dysphoria: Development, research, management* (pp. 11–32). New York: Plenum.

Hollingshead, A. B. (1975). *Four factor index of social status.* Unpublished manuscript, Department of Sociology, Yale University, New Haven, CT.

Hoyer, N. (1933). *Man into woman.* New York: Dutton.

Hu, S., Pattatucci, A. M. L., Patterson, C., Li, L., Fulker, D. W., Cherny, S. S., et al. (1995). Linkage between sexual orientation and chromosome Xq28 in males but not in females. *Nature Genetics, 11,* 248–256.

Johnson, L. L., Bradley, S. J., Birkenfeld-Adams, A. S., Kuksis, M. A. R., Maing, D. M., Mitchell, J. N., & Zucker, K. J. (2004). A parent-report gender identity questionnaire for children. *Archives of Sexual Behavior, 33,* 105–116.

Kohlberg, L. (1966). A cognitive-developmental analysis of children's sex-role concepts and attitudes. In E. E. Maccoby (Ed.), *The development of sex differences* (pp. 82–173). Stanford, CA: Stanford University Press.

Kulick, D. (1998). *Travesti: Sex, gender, and culture among Brazilian transgendered prostitutes.* Chicago: University of Chicago Press.

Lalumiére, M. L., Blanchard, R., & Zucker, K. J. (2000). Sexual orientation and handedness in men and women: A meta-analysis. *Psychological Bulletin, 126,* 575–592.

Lee, T. (2001). Trans(re)lations: Lesbian and female to male transsexual accounts of identity. *Women's Studies International Forum, 24,* 347–357.

Liben, L. S., & Bigler, R. S. (2002). The developmental course of gender differentiation. *Monographs of the Society for Research in Child Development, 67*(2, Serial No. 269).

Lippa, R. A. (2003). Are 2D:4D finger-length ratios related to sexual orientation? Yes for men, no for women. *Journal of Personality and Social Psychology, 85,* 179–188.

Lothstein, L. M. (1983). *Female-to-male transsexualism: Historical, clinical, and theoretical issues.* Boston: Routledge.

Martin, C. L., & Fabes, R. A. (2001). The stability and consequences of young children's same-sex peer interactions. *Developmental Psychology, 37,* 431–446.

Martin, C. L., Ruble, D. N., & Szkrybalo, J. (2002). Cognitive theories of early gender development. *Psychological Bulletin, 128,* 903–933.

McDermid, S. A., Zucker, K. J., Bradley, S. J., & Maing, D. M. (1998). Effects of physical appearance on masculine trait ratings of boys and girls with gender identity disorder. *Archives of Sexual Behavior, 27,* 253–267.

McFadden, D. (2002). Masculinizing effects of the auditory system. *Archives of Sexual Behavior, 31,* 99–111.

Memorial for Harry Benjamin. (1988). *Archives of Sexual Behavior, 17,* 1–31.

Merriam Webster's Collegiate Dictionary (10th ed.). (1993). Springfield, MA: Merriam-Webster.

Meyer-Bahlburg, H. F. L. (1984). Psychoendocrine research on sexual orientation: Current status and future options. *Progress in Brain Research, 61,* 375–398.

Meyer-Bahlburg, H. F. L. (1985). Gender identity disorder of childhood: Introduction. *Journal of the American Academy of Child Psychiatry, 24,* 681–683.

Meyer-Bahlburg, H. F. L. (2001). Gender and sexuality in classic congenital adrenal hyperplasia. *Endocrinology and Metabolism Clinics of North America, 30,* 155–172.

Migeon, C. J., & Wisniewski, A. B. (1998). Sexual differentiation: From genes to gender. *Hormone Research, 50,* 245–251.

Moore, S. M. (2002). *Diagnosis for a straight planet: A critique of gender identity disorder for children and adolescents in the DSM-IV.* Unpublished doctoral dissertation, The Wright Institute, Berkeley, CA.

Newman, L. K. (2002). Sex, gender and culture: Issues in the definition, assessment and treatment of gender identity disorder. *Clinical Child Psychology and Psychiatry, 7,* 352–359.

O'Brien, M., & Huston, A. C. (1985). Activity level and sex-stereotyped toy choice in toddler boys and girls. *Journal of Genetic Psychology, 146,* 527–533.

Pasterski, V. L. (2002). *Development of gender role behaviour in children: Prenatal hormones and parental socialisation.* Unpublished doctoral dissertation, City University, London, UK.

Pauly, I. B. (1974a). Female transsexualism: Part I. *Archives of Sexual Behavior, 3,* 487–507.

Pauly, I. B. (1974b). Female transsexualism: Part II. *Archives of Sexual Behavior, 3,* 509–526.

Pellett, T. L., & Harrison, J. M. (1992). Children's perceptions of the gender appropriateness of physical activities: A further analysis. *Play and Culture, 5,* 305–313.

Prosser, J. (1998). *Second skins: The body narratives of transsexuality.* New York: Columbia University Press.

Ruble, D. N., & Martin, C. L. (1998). Gender development. In W. Damon (Series Ed.) and N. Eisenberg (Vol. Ed.), *Handbook of child psychology. Vol. 3: Social, emotional, and personality development* (5th ed., pp. 933–1016). New York: Wiley.

Sandberg, D. E., Meyer-Bahlburg, H. F. L., Ehrhardt, A. A., & Yager, T. J. (1993). The prevalence of gender-atypical behavior in elementary school children. *Journal of the American Academy of Child and Adolescent Psychiatry, 32,* 306–314.

Serbin, L. A., Moller, L. C., Gulko, J., Powlishta, K. K., & Colburne, K. A. (1994). The emergence of gender segregation in toddler playgroups. In C. Leaper (Ed.), *Childhood gender segregation: Causes and consequences* (pp. 7–17). San Francisco: Jossey-Bass.

Serbin, L. A., Powlishta, K. K., & Gulko, J. (1993). The development of sex typing in middle childhood. *Monographs of the Society for Research in Child Development, 58*(2, Serial No. 232).

Singh, D., Vidaurri, M., Zambarano, R. J., & Dabbs, J. M. (1999). Lesbian erotic role identification: Behavioral, morphological, and hormonal correlates. *Journal of Personality and Social Psychology, 76,* 1035–1049.

Slabbekoorn, D., van Goozen, S. H. M., Sanders, G., Gooren, L. J. G., & Cohen-Kettenis, P. T. (2000). The dermatoglyphic characteristics of transsexuals: Is there evidence for an organizing effect of sex hormones? *Psychoneuroendocrinology, 25,* 365–375.

Slaby, R. G., & Frey, K. S. (1975). Development of gender constancy and selective attention to same-sex models. *Child Development, 46,* 849–856.

Smail, P. J. Reyes, F. I., Winter, J. S. D., & Faiman, C. (1981). The fetal hormone environment and its effect on the morphogenesis of the genital system. In S. J. Kogan & E. S. E. Hafez (Eds.), *Pediatric andrology* (pp. 9–20). Hague, The Netherlands: Martinus Nijhoff.

Smith, Y. L. S., van Goozen, S. H. M., & Cohen-Kettenis, P. T. (2001). Adolescents with gender identity disorder who were accepted or rejected for sex reassignment surgery: A prospective follow-up study. *Journal of the American Academy of Child and Adolescent Psychiatry, 40,* 472–481.

Sroufe, L. A. (1990). Considering normal and abnormal together: The essence of developmental psychopathology. *Development and Psychopathology, 2,* 335–347.

Stoller, R. J. (1964). The hermaphroditic identity of hermaphrodites. *Journal of Nervous and Mental Disease, 139,* 453–457.

Stoller, R. J. (1968). Male childhood transsexualism. *Journal of the American Academy of Child Psychiatry, 7,* 193–209.

Stoller, R. J. (1972). Etiological factors in female transsexualism: A first approximation. *Archives of Sexual Behavior, 2,* 47–64.

Tajfel, H. (1981). *Human groups and social categories*. Cambridge: Cambridge University Press.

Thorne, B. (1986). *Crossing the gender divide: What "tomboys" can teach us about processes of gender separation among children*. Unpublished manuscript, Department of Sociology, Michigan State University, East Lansing, MI.

Thorne, B. (1993). *Gender play: Girls and boys in school*. New Brunswick, NJ: Rutgers University Press.

Tortorice, J. L. (2002). *Written on the body: Butch/femme lesbian gender identity and biological correlates*. Unpublished doctoral dissertation, Rutgers, The State University of New Jersey, New Brunswick.

Tucker, J. B., & Keil, H. H. J. (2001). Can cultural beliefs cause a gender identity disorder? *Journal of Psychology and Human Sexuality, 13*(2), 21–30.

Wallen, K. (1996). Nature needs nurture: The interaction of hormonal and social influences on the development of behavioral sex differences in rhesus monkeys. *Hormones and Behavior, 30*, 364–378.

Wallen, K., & Baum, M. J. (2002). Masculinization and defeminization in altricial and precocial mammals: Comparative aspects of steroid hormone action. *Hormones, Brain and Behavior, 4*, 385–423.

Weisz, J. R., & Weiss, B. (1991). Studying the "referability" of child clinical problems. *Journal of Consulting and Clinical Psychology, 59*, 266–273.

Widiger, T. A. (1998). Invited essay: Sex biases in the diagnosis of personality disorders. *Journal of Personality Disorders, 12*, 95–118.

Willerman, L. (1973). Activity level and hyperactivity in twins. *Child Development, 44*, 288–293.

Williams, T. J., Pepitone, M. E., Christensen, S. E., Cooke, B. M., Huberman, A. D., Breedlove, N. J., et al. (2000). Finger-length ratios and sexual orientation. *Nature, 404*, 455–456.

Yamaguchi, L., & Barber, K. (Eds.). (1995). *Tomboys! Tales of dyke derring-do*. Los Angeles, CA: Alyson Publications.

Yee, M., & Brown, R. (1994). The development of gender differentiation in young children. *British Journal of Social Psychology, 33*, 183–196.

Young, A. (2000). *Women who become men: Albanian sworn virgins*. Oxford: Berg.

Zahn-Waxler, C. (1993). Warriors and worriers: Gender and psychopathology. *Development and Psychopathology, 5*, 79–89.

Zoccolillo, M. (1993). Gender and the development of conduct disorder. *Development and Psychopathology, 5*, 65–78.

Zucker, K. J. (1982). Childhood gender disturbance: Diagnostic issues. *Journal of the American Academy of Child Psychiatry, 21*, 274–280.

Zucker, K. J. (1985). Cross-gender-identified children. In B. W. Steiner (Ed.), *Gender dysphoria: Development, research, management* (pp. 75–174). New York: Plenum.

Zucker, K. J. (1992). Gender identity disorder. In S. R. Hooper, G. W. Hynd, & R. E. Mattison (Eds.), *Child psychopathology: Diagnostic criteria and clinical assessment* (pp. 305–342). Hillsdale, NJ: Erlbaum.

Zucker, K. J. (1999). Intersexuality and gender identity differentiation. *Annual Review of Sex Research, 10*, 1–69.

Zucker, K. J. (2001). Gender identity disorder in children and adolescents. In G. O. Gabbard (Ed.), *Treatments of psychiatric disorders* (3rd ed., Vol. 2) (pp. 2069–2094). Washington, DC: American Psychiatric Press.

Zucker, K. J., Allin, S., Babul-Hirji, R., Bradley, S. J., Chitayat, D., Khoury, A. E., et al. (2003). Assessment of gender identity and gender role behavior: A comparison of girls with gender identity disorder, girls exposed prenatally to gender-atypical levels of androgens, and control girls [Abstract]. *The Endocrinologist, 13*, 291.

Zucker, K. J., & Bradley, S. J. (1995). *Gender identity disorder and psychosexual problems in children and adolescents*. New York: Guilford.

Zucker, K. J., Bradley, S. J., Kuksis, M., Pecore, K., Birkenfeld-Adams, A., Doering, R. W., et al. (1999). Gender constancy judgments in children with gender identity disorder: Evidence for a developmental lag. *Archives of Sexual Behavior, 28*, 475–502.

Zucker, K. J., Bradley, S. J., Lowry Sullivan, C. B., Kuksis, M., Birkenfeld-Adams, A., & Mitchell, J. N. (1993). A gender identity interview for children. *Journal of Personality Assessment, 61,* 443–456.

Zucker, K. J., Bradley, S. J., & Sanikhani, M. (1997). Sex differences in referral rates of children with gender identity disorder: Some hypotheses. *Journal of Abnormal Child Psychology, 25,* 217–227.

Zucker, K. J., Finegan, J. K., Doering, R. W., & Bradley, S. J. (1984). Two subgroups of gender-problem children. *Archives of Sexual Behavior, 13,* 27–39.

Zucker, K. J., Lightbody, S., Pecore, K., Bradley, S. J., & Blanchard, R. (1998). Birth order in girls with gender identity disorder. *European Child & Adolescent Psychiatry, 7,* 30–35.

Zucker, K. J., Owen, A., Bradley, S. J., & Ameeriar, L. (2002). Gender-dysphoric children and adolescents: A comparative analysis of demographic characteristics and behavioral problems. *Clinical Child Psychology and Psychiatry, 7,* 398–411.

V

Stress and Negative Life Events

11

Physical Abuse and Neglect in Girls

SANDRA T. AZAR

The experience of physical abuse or neglect is a complex event that may trigger social, emotional, and physical consequences. It can also be invested with cognitive meaning about the self, others, and one's place in the world. These transactional problems typically occur within a dysfunctional family setting and tend to be nested in larger societal problems (e.g., poverty), both of which may contribute to girls' reactions. Unlike the literature in other areas of family violence (domestic violence or sexual abuse), work on physical abuse and neglect has remained relatively silent on the topic of gender. Interestingly, it is also only recently that their potential differential and interactive effects with other forms of family violence have been explored (Hennessy, Rabideau, Cicchetti, & Cummings, 1994; Hughes, Parkinson, & Vargo, 1989).

Unlike most of the other "disorders" discussed in this volume, our traditional diagnostic systems such as *DSM-IV* (American Psychiatric Association, 1994) have not elevated "symptoms" that occur in response to child maltreatment to specific diagnostic status (except where it is included as a source of Post Traumatic Stress Disorder). In part, this is due to the fact that children's reactions are heterogeneous and symptoms, if they appear, cross diagnostic boundaries. Also, the locus of disorder is the family system, rather than the girl involved. That is, if a "disorder" is involved, it involves the behavior of a person or persons who is/are her caregiver(s), the transactions within the girl's family, the context in which these transactions take place (e.g., poverty, minority status, high crime neighborhood), and societal reactions to these events in her life.

Why then have a chapter in a book about psychopathology on this topic? Girls do have reactions that warrant treatment and these reactions

SANDRA T. AZAR • The Pennsylvania State University, University Park, Pennsylvania, 16802.

require a well-specified treatment plan that is particularly sensitive to the systemic issues involved. This chapter will attempt to frame the clinical issues involved with physical abuse and neglect of girls in historical and sociocultural contexts and to articulate the nature of the experience of these forms of child maltreatment with these larger contexts in mind. Girls' problems cannot be decontextualized in clinical work. Girls who experience physical abuse or neglect (or both) cannot be discussed without talking about parents and families. These are often targets of treatment. Given that the focus of this text is on females and most of what we know about perpetrators of physical abuse and neglect has been learned from studying mothers, this chapter will focus on the characteristics of female perpetrators and partners of perpetrators, as well as victims.

Neglecting male victims and ignoring male perpetrators, however, may have problematic consequences. First, there is potential for stereotyping of victim status as a female role. Although this status may have some utility in the "healing" process (e.g., it may mobilize women), it may have negative effects (e.g., be less useful in the later phases of recovery; not allow males to disclose their abuse to avoid this role delineation). More important, in contrast to sexual abuse, both sexes are physically victimized and neglected with equal frequency.

Problems also exist with writing about abuse and neglect as a problem perpetrated by women. It has been viewed this way too often in the literature—mothers who have gone awry, done the unspeakable, and harmed their children. Intense media coverage of a psychiatrically impaired mother, Andrea Yates, who killed her children, testifies to the depth of reactions society has to women who behave in a manner so out of their "instinctually" driven role (Mailcall, 2001). Indeed, anger itself (a potential antecedent of physical abuse) has been described as an "outlaw emotion" in women (Brown, 1998). This chapter should not contribute to the mother blaming so prevalent in clinical psychology. To this end, men's role as perpetrators must be discussed and the etiological role of larger contextual factors that affect women most, such as poverty, requires consideration. As many children are killed at the hands of male caretakers as female ones (Administration on Children, Youth, and Families [ACYF], 2001a). So, at least when it comes to more dire consequences, men are equally as culpable. Couple this fact with the higher involvement of men in perpetrating other forms of family violence (domestic violence, sexual abuse), and a picture emerges of their playing as strong, if not stronger, a role in exposing children to violence. Also, based on incidence data, males are the more common perpetrator of physical abuse (Sedlak & Broadhurst, 1996). In addition, even though neglect is more often "perpetrated" by females, there may be a bias in who is labeled (i.e., it is still seen as *women's* responsibility to monitor, to feed, and to care for children). Yet, poverty which is often linked to neglect is a "problem" visited on women and children, more than men. Also, this economic status may result from failures on males' parts (e.g., not paying child support; http://www.census.gov/apsd/www/statbrief/sb95_16.pdf; http://www.futureofchildren.org/information2827/information_show.

htm?doc_id=75562) or society's ambivalence in supporting mothering as a "job" (e.g., tighter restrictions on welfare funds). As one considers women's involvement in maltreatment, all of this must be kept in mind.

With these points made, I will turn to the task at hand—what do we know about physical child abuse and neglect as it relates to girls and what are the implications of this knowledge for how we intervene clinically and form social policy? What are the characteristics of women who engage in physical abuse or extreme omissions in child care and what are the contextual factors that may play a role? Also, because maltreatment is a transactional problem, are there gender-based factors that influence how female children respond to this experience? Finally, for both halves of the dyad, how should we intervene with girls and their mothers when they are involved in child maltreatment, and are there gendered "responses" clinicians and society may make that may do further harm?

HISTORICAL AND SOCIOCULTURAL CONTEXT

Historical context is especially relevant in understanding maltreatment and its impact on girls. Five domains are relevant: (a) changes in the valuing of children; (b) the value attached to girls and minority girls in particular; (c) changes in societally defined parental responsibilities; (d) the gendered nature of these responsibilities; and (e) extended families' and society's role in supporting mothers. Girls react to maltreatment in the context of the entire picture of girls' sense of value and being worthy of care. This historical context may help us to understand women as perpetrators and girls as victims from a much broader lens and prevent perpetuating historically based and gendered mythology in our practice.

The passage of abuse reporting laws in the 1960s was the culmination of a long historical shift in the value of children, and in parents' responsibilities to them. Children went from being seen as nothing more than chattel to possessing rights of their own that are independent of those decided upon by parents (Zelizer, 1985). In ancient times, for example, children were their fathers' property and could be given away to pay off debts (Kadushin, 1967). Later, children were seen as having labor value (working on farms or caring for elderly; Mason, 1994). This is still the case in countries whose economy is more agriculturally based and where there are no other means of old-age security (Kagitcibasi, 1982). Daughters in particular are socialized to provide such elder care. This fact may be relevant for girls living in poverty and girls from immigrant families in today's society. Greater child care duties may be viewed normatively by the girls themselves and their families, but may border on parental neglect in some cases.

Historically, girls have been less valued, a situation that may still be true among immigrant populations. For example, at many points in history girl babies were abandoned more readily than boy babies, and girls were given less education (e.g., in colonial America, most boys could sign their name by the late 1700s, whereas less than half of the females could).

Even today, in many societies from which US immigrant families come preference for male children is stronger than that for female ones (e.g., Arnold & Kuo, 1984; Crawford & Unger, 2004; Keller & Zach, 2002). The deference given to males, for example, is especially strong in Hispanic culture and Hispanic girls' self-esteem has in at least one large study been shown to be lower than that of Hispanic boys (American Association of University Women, 1991).

The state's interest in protecting children has also shifted over time. At first, parents had complete control over them, with little state intervention, except in extreme situations (i.e., the murdering of a child). Societal protection emerged first historically around goals of economic self-sufficiency and religious training. In colonial America, for instance, the state intervened if children were not brought up to be productive members of society (e.g., for girls, this meant being trained in domestic work). Fathers were punished if this training did not occur. Beyond this, however, not much else was required of parents (Mason, 1994).

By the late 1800s, the sentimental value of children increased, as did women's rights and views of mothers' roles began to change. Up until then, courts favored fathers, giving them child custody should a marriage end. In this period, women's role as mothers became glorified and they began to be favored in the custody of younger children. With this, however, also came a greater responsibility to mothers for children's outcomes.

Private agencies' efforts emerged at this time to support women who were parenting alone. Yet, the support was so meager that women either still needed to work to support families or had to give children up either temporarily or permanently to the care of others (e.g., relatives, institutions) or both (Chase-Lansdale & Vinovskis, 1995). Society did not see itself as being in the business of subsidizing the "work" of mothers.

Gradually, larger scale public funding began for the "deserving" poor (e.g., workman's compensation to families of disabled workers, widows' pensions, Aid to Dependent Children (ADC)). Funding for children, however, still did not support the mothers who cared for them. It did not occur until the mid-1900s (ADC became Aid to Families with Dependent Children). This formal supporting of caregiving marked a change in state involvement in parenting, although it remains somewhat ambivalent, as is evident in US welfare reforms in the mid 1990s that shortened mothers' stay on welfare, limited its lifetime use, and required them to work (Personal Responsibility and Work Opportunity Reconciliation Act of 1996).

Structural changes in families have also lessened informal support available to parents. In the past responsibility for the functions of parenting were distributed throughout the extended family, rather than vested solely in two adults as it is today. Grandmothers and aunts, often alternative caregivers, are more often working today and thus are not available to take on extra duties. Also, family mobility has meant many no longer live near their extended family. The parenting dyad has also changed (Shiono & Quinn, 1994). There have been sharp rises in divorce and single parenthood, especially among minorities who are overrepresented in child-protective samples. Noncustodial fathers often fail to provide economic and physical support after divorce, leaving women to provide and care for children alone.

One might see physical abuse and neglect in part as a consequence of this narrowing of responsibility for the function of parenting which has resulted in increases in the potential for failure. Because mothers carry out most of the elements of parenting, especially in lower-SES homes, their social, cognitive, and behavioral skills are more often put to the test, as opposed to fathers' (e.g., noticing signs of illness, monitoring of child safety). Deficiencies, if they exist, become more apparent with fewer resources and the tasks become far more overwhelming and, for some, impossible. With a rise in beliefs in "child centeredness," mothers not only must provide for survival needs, but also more intangible and psychological needs. They must put their own needs aside. This may be especially problematic for young women whose own developmental task has been emphasized as being self-focused exploration and experimentation, which would compete with meeting the needs of children. It is no wonder early parenting is linked with maltreatment. Finally, despite society's wanting maternal self-sufficiency, a mother who works and often leaves her child with relatives may be viewed with suspicion (e.g., can this mother parent independently?).

For families on welfare, a group overrepresented in child protection samples, the tasks of supporting one's family have become more complex. New programs tie support to mothers' working. Work means new tasks are added as single mothers attempt to organize their own and their children's lives around the work world. For example, although child care supports are provided, that support may not fit with the schedules of evening and weekend work and may be lost with slight increases in income above thresholds. Loss of child care may mean older daughters are left to care for siblings or makeshift care arrangements are made—in some cases, leaving girls vulnerable (e.g., unemployed boyfriends of mother providing care). Living in poverty and attempting to raise children, therefore, becomes like playing an action video game at the most advanced level with one hand tied behind one's back and dangers popping out from all directions.

Welfare families are not the only ones coping with economic stress and greater burden. Many two-parent families in which both parents work fall below the poverty line and more women are working outside the home, juggling the responsibilities of multiple roles. Little in the way of state child care support is provided.

In sum, parenting has changed over time in terms of who was seen as "responsible" for children (moving from fathers to mothers) and what these responsibilities were. In addition, the more psychological role parents are expected to play today, the state's ambivalence in providing appropriate levels of support to caregivers, structural changes in the family, and contextual strains such as in poverty (e.g., stigma, lack of resources, high-crime neighborhoods) are a backdrop against which to see maltreatment and this backdrop is crucial to devising contextually sensitive treatments. These pressures have a gendered quality and disproportionately affect minorities, who tend to be in the lower economic strata of US society. Failure to acknowledge the impact of these pressures may lead to biases and ineffectiveness in our intervention efforts.

Recent History, Child Abuse Statutes and Research

Child physical abuse rose in public consciousness in the United States in the 1960s, when states passed statutes requiring reporting of suspected harm to children. Initial interest focused on infants and their physical needs and potential for injury. Concerns later widened to older children, the emotional needs of children, and a greater concern with the careful monitoring of children and the nature of the environments in which they live. For example, exposure to domestic violence is now seen as maltreatment in some states. Psychology entered the field with these shifts in concern.

The science surrounding maltreatment, however, has been driven by politics. Societal reactions have been dominated by emotion (Azar, Fantuzzo, & Twentyman, 1984). This has meant rapid development of interventions without adequate definition of the phenomenon of maltreatment, theory building, and understanding of the origins of abuse (Plotkin, Azar, Twentyman, & Perri, 1981). With little science to act as a foundation, the field accepted societal perspectives that such parents' behaviors were aberrations and placed less emphasis on the idea of a complex interaction of causal factors. Interventions were funded with little evaluation of their outcomes. When interventions were later evaluated, poor outcomes were found.

Although the complexity of etiology has received acceptance by researchers (Azar, 1986; Belsky, 1980; Sameroff & Chandler, 1975), society has persisted in seeing maltreating parents as different from others. This has continued to keep the field mired in a categorical view (i.e., parents who maltreat must be damaged—attachment problems, personality disordered, or substance abusers—rather than responding to a high level of burdens with little support) and continues to color intervention efforts. Research on sequelae with children has also been mired in a "presence/absence" view of abuse/neglect rather than attending to the complex array of factors associated with maltreatment that may contribute to child outcome (dimensions of the maltreatment, family and community reactions, contextual factors).

THE BASICS: DEFINITIONS AND EPIDEMIOLGY

Definitions of maltreatment are socially determined to a certain extent. Rather than the early definitions that focused on physical outcomes (e.g., bruises, broken bones), maltreatment has come to be defined by researchers as specific acts judged by a mixture of community values and professional expertise to be inappropriate or damaging (Garbarino & Giliam, 1980). Such a definition is "socially mediated" and allows for a narrow versus a broad continuum in thinking about impact (e.g., demonstrable harm vs. endangerment) and actions (e.g., from failure to supervise to threatening a child with a knife).

With more focus on a developmental psychopathology perspective of outcomes in children, even broader definitions have emerged, including seeing maltreatment as part of a more general breakdown in caregiver capacities. Here, the focus is on parents, adult development (their repertoire of care giving and life skills), and the parent–child relationship, as well as environmental and child-based factors that may tax parents' capacities and disrupt parent–child transactions (Azar, 1986; Azar, Barnes, & Twentyman, 1988). Child abuse/neglect are seen as being on a continuum with normal parenting (i.e., as part of a cluster of behaviors at one end of normal parenting practices that lead to negative child outcomes; Azar, 1986; Azar et al., 1988). As a corollary, children's experiences with it might also be viewed as on a continuum with, and in the context of, other socialization and family experiences to which they are exposed more generally. From a developmental psychopathology perspective, the clustering and timing of these experiences with others make for better or worse outcomes, not just a single event such as an incident of abuse (Sameroff & Chandler, 1975). Thus, to truly understand the impact on girls' developmental trajectory, one must view maltreatment in this transactional context and not in isolation. For girls, this context includes gender expectations and pressures that are visited upon females in US society. Within some ethnic and racial groups, the effects of discrimination must also be considered. As will be seen later, this broader perspective contrasts with more categorical legal views. Both are important to consider, in that the latter identifies a child for treatment and the former helps frame interventions chosen and how they are carried out.

The Use of Legal Categories and Other Dimensions to Consider in Case Formulation

In formulating cases, there is pressure to think in terms of legally defined categorization of abuse/neglect, but other dimensions may be crucial to consider as well. The legally identified categories of neglect and physical abuse are umbrellas for a heterogeneous set of events occurring to girls. For example, Zuravin (1991) defined 13 types of behaviors included in neglect: supervisory neglect, refusal or delay in providing health or mental health care, custody refusal or related neglect, abandonment/desertion, failure to provide a home, personal hygiene, housing hazards or sanitation, nutritional neglect, and educational neglect. Some definitions of neglect also include emotional neglect (a marked indifference to children's need for affection, attention, and emotional support), as well as exposure to chronic or extreme spousal abuse. Emotional abuse has been seen as both central to all maltreatment and as a distinct entity. It includes acts that are psychologically damaging to children (e.g., rejecting, terrorizing, degrading; Brassard, Germain, & Hart, 1987). Although somewhat less heterogeneous, physical abuse can include everything from restraining a child inappropriately (e.g., locking in closets for long periods) to beating with an electric cord, breaking bones, or threatening with a gun or knife. Clearly, such heterogeneity has been difficult to capture in a single theory of

etiology and makes understanding the impact of abuse on girls more difficult. The emotionally abusive aspects of both forms of maltreatment may
be most relevant to clinical work with victims and which require special
consideration in thinking about girls' cognitive, emotional, and social reactions. For example, females are said to be more relationally oriented
(Markus & Oyserman, 1989) and thus, damaging interpersonal experiences may have a deeper meaning to self for girls than for boys.

Unfortunately, there is no consensus regarding the level at which these
parenting difficulties become maltreatment. Neglect may be particularly
subject to such definitional problems (e.g., what is adequate supervision?
And, do girls differ from boys in how much they need?). Developmental
stage of the girl matters (e.g., neglectful behavior for an infant may not
be so for an adolescent). Given there are gender-based trajectories for the
development of various capacities, effects may also have differential pathways depending upon *when* maltreatment occurs. For example, girls develop perspective-taking capacities earlier than boys and empathy is more
highly emphasized in girls' than in boys' socialization. Girls may, therefore,
expend more energy than males do in trying to understand the abuser when
abuse occurs earlier in life. Girls' skills may make them better able than
males to de-center from the idea that they play a role in the cause of the
maltreatment. In contrast, girls also experience father's rejection in adolescence more strongly (Kavanagh & Hops, 1994) and thus, physical and
emotional maltreatment in the teen years may have greater repercussions.

Girls' special care needs (e.g., chronic illness) may also define whether
harm occurs or not. Some omissions of care may be labeled as risk producing, which otherwise would not be. How chronically an omission needs
to occur before it is considered neglectful has also not been addressed
well.

Types of maltreatment often co-occur and over multiple reports, many
cases appear to move from one type to another (English, Marshall, &
Orme, 1999). Co-occurrence may mean greater environmental stress. For
instance, a girl who grows up in a home that is chaotic and marked by poor
hygiene, and who is left with an inappropriate babysitter who molests her is
exposed to greater risk than a girl who has a parent who reacts one time by
hitting her for destroying a treasured object. Gender may be important also
in what combinations appear. Females are overrepresented among sexual
abuse cases and thus, if there are interactive effects of sexual abuse coupled with neglect or physical abuse, girls will be more likely to show these
effects. Also, some forms of neglect early in life may have physical effects in
areas affecting females only, such as the consequences of early malnutri-
tion or lead poisoning on reproductive health. Physical abuse and neglect
have also been associated with heightened rates of certain disorders more
common among females (e.g., eating disorders, borderline personality disorder; Zanarini et al., 2000). The specific pathways by which this occurs are
unknown as yet. There may be critical periods where abuse may lead more
easily to these disorders; the context of the maltreatment may be important in determining the outcome (e.g., family versus nonfamily perpetrator
or some complex interactions among other factors may increase risk).

Other attributes of maltreatment may also be important (e.g., severity, frequency, age of child; Cicchetti & Barnett, 1991) in formulating clinical responses. For example, physical abuse that occurs at points of girls' pushes for autonomy (e.g., terrible two's) may have different parent-based antecedents than when it occurs across all of childhood. The latter may indicate anger control deficits and the former may signal more pervasive problems. Each of these would have more narrow or more pervasive effects. Similarly, the different antecedents may have different effects for boys and girls. For example, females have traditionally been socialized to be generally more dependent on others than are males (Condry, Condry, & Pogatshnik, 1983; Mitchell, Obradovich, Herring, & Tromborg, 1992, Thompson, 1999). Thus, excessively punishing girls' autonomy-related behavior may further direct them toward passivity. Some evidence suggests that physical punishment, which some see on a continuum with physical abuse, is more commonly engaged in by mothers with sons in early years and by father with daughters in teen years (Wauchope & Straus, 1987). This suggests that risk prevention might need to be gender-specific by age.

One last factor discussed recently would be the meaning that girls themselves attribute to their experiences (Azar & Bober, 1999). It has been suggested that girls may incorporate into schema regarding the self, others, and the world elements of their maltreatment that influence their later functioning (Janoff-Bulman, 1992). The girl's own views may be the best predictor of outcome (e.g., in sexual abuse, it has been found that self-blame predicts severity of outcomes; Wyatt & Newcomb, 1990). The entire parenting context may temper the meaning to her. Harsh treatment that is predictable and occurs within a context of otherwise positive parenting may not have the same meaning than if it occurs at erratic moments and in the absence of other "saving graces" in the relationship. As noted earlier, the effects of parental rejection, lack of care, and active physical abuse may have different meaning for girls and boys. The gender of the perpetrator may also influence meaning. For example, Olsen, (2000) found that women reporting emotional neglect by fathers during childhood were more likely than males to be more sensitive to relational slights (i.e., social triggers were more likely to be antecedents for anger and aggression). No effects were found for emotional maltreatment by mothers.

Finally, as noted earlier, parenting practices are socioculturally situated and definitions of maltreatment need to give greater recognition to diverse pathways to parental fitness and meeting children's needs. Cultures vary in their treatment and valuing of women. Thus, some parental behaviors labeled as mistreatment in US society may have very different social meaning and "acceptability" for girls from some immigrant cultures. Our parenting theories are based on narrow samples (e.g., middle and upper class, European American parents; Azar & Cote, 2002; Chao, 1997). Current frames for judging parenting capacities need not be abandoned, but care should be taken in accepting their universal utility and a "functional" approach to judging practices may be required. This would involve differentiating parenting practices that are cultural universals from ones requiring more local definition (Korbin, 1994). For example, in many cultures, females act as caregivers for siblings. This is normative and an important source of self-esteem. In contrast, such caretaking may be viewed as bordering on neglectful behavior in US society.

Socioeconomic status may also be relevant. Child maltreatment most often is identified in the lower-SES groups (Pelton, 1994). Yet, negative behavioral outcomes are more common when physical abuse and neglect occur in higher-SES groups than in lower groups (Eckenrode, Laird, & Doris, 1993; Trickett, Aber, Carlson, & Cicchetti, 1991). These effects, however, do not differ by gender.

For the purposes of this chapter, physical abuse and neglect will be broadly defined as transactional problems nested within the broader context of a disturbed repertoire of parenting responses. They signal a breakdown of socialization processes, where parents function at the periphery of what is culturally considered normative parenting. Viewing maltreatment this way opens up the idea that the occurrence of physical abuse or neglect is just the tip of an iceberg of a cluster of parenting practices. To understand it, we need to understand the nature and the development of the capacities to parent and the factors affecting their trajectory (Azar, 2002). The environmental pressures placed on parents that may detract from the capacity to parent, the social network of supports provided, and societal supports and valuing of their role all play a part in the successful operation of parenting. Gender and socialization of gender roles are also important. The societal expectations placed on the parents of each gender may play themselves out differently. For example, the resources available to men and women in US society differ, as does the investment expected of them in parenting. Single parenting is more common among women, and their cognitive and behavioral skills are more often put to the test. Society plays a role in that it may or may not reduce the burden (e.g., welfare reform; legal pressure on deadbeat dads to pay child support).

Physical Child Abuse and Neglect Statistics: Women as Perpetrators and Girls as Victims

The National Incidence Study in Child Abuse and Neglect, a community-based survey, found that women are seen as responsible for 87% of neglect (Sedlak & Broadhurst, 1996). This is congruent with the fact women are typically the primary caretaker and are "the primary persons held accountable for any omissions and/or failings in caretaking" (p. 6–10). In contrast, abuse overall tends to be slightly more often perpetrated by males (58% of physically abused children). Somewhat similar findings occur in other studies (71.0% of neglect by females; for physical abuse, 51.9% by females; Way, Chung, Jonson-Reid, & Drake, 2001).

Child victim rates for males and females are almost identical. Overall, 11.2 male children and 12.8 female children per 1,000 children were abused and neglected in 1999 (ACYF, 2001a). Differences exist in sexual abuse where girls are more prevalent. Therefore, if this form is coupled with other forms, girls are more likely to be victims in identified samples.

There are some gender differences by age. Rates of physical abuse for males were highest in the 4- to 7-year-old and 8- to 11-year-old ranges and for females, it was highest in the 12- to 15-year-old range in 1999. These peaks in rates parallel the rates of physical punishment in the general population (Wauchope & Strauss, 1987). The youngest age ranges have the highest rates of neglect (ages 0–3; 11.5 males and 11.0 females per 1,000 children), with almost no gender differences across all ages. African Americans and Native Americans had rates of abuse and neglect at least double those of Caucasians. Rates for Hispanics were slightly higher than those for Whites. Poverty, discrimination, and other factors (parenting practices/norms) may explain these differences.

When it comes to child fatalities, perpetrators are considerably younger than maltreaters in general—e.g., in 1998, 62.3% were younger than age 30 compared with 38.7% in this age category for maltreatment more generally (ACYF, 2000). Men and women are almost equally responsible for fatalities. At the same time, the rate of mothers' involvement as the sole perpetrator in fatalities is lower. Parental age in general also plays a role. Under the age of 50, females are more often the perpetrators, but the pattern reverses after age 50. This parallels use of physical discipline, where fathers are more likely to use punishment with teenagers and mothers are more likely to use it with young children (Wauchope & Strauss, 1987). Gender patterns differ also when it comes to victims; in 1999, slightly more males were killed (56.7%) compared with females (43.3%) (ACYF, 2001b). Victims of physical and sexual abuse, compared with those of general neglect and medical neglect, were more often maltreated by a male parent acting alone. Neglect is by far the most common cause of fatalities (34.9%; with physical abuse, 27.8%, and combined abuse/neglect, 22.2%).

Recidivism

Maltreatment in general has high levels of recidivism both when perpetrators are in and out of treatment. Estimates range from 20 to 70% (Williams, 1983). Neglect in one study was found to be 44% more likely to re-occur than physical abuse in the 6 months following a report. Recidivism also shows a high level of cross-occurrence of forms of maltreatment. One study showed higher recidivism for female than male perpetrators (28 to 35% greater risk of being re-reported for child maltreatment), as well as greater crossover recidivism (Way et al., 2001). Neglect was often coupled over time with other forms of maltreatment for female perpetrators. Way et al. (2001) caution, as noted earlier, that women tend to be labeled as the neglector within the family, even if there is more than one parent figure available. If first reported for another form of maltreatment, women tended to be re-reported for neglect (25.6% of those first reported for sexual abuse and 27.7% of those first reported for physical abuse were reported later for neglect). Neglect may be easier to substantiate and thus, the label may be used to keep a case in the system when other forms of maltreatment are suspected but not proven. Also, as will be seen later in this chapter, biased processes may operate in social service agencies to foster the labeling of women. Poor neighborhood residency increased risk of recidivism in this study, but Way et al. did not examine whether female perpetrators were more often from such neighborhoods than males. Given the feminization of poverty, this may account for the gender findings. The higher stresses associated with poverty may be more common among women and may also produce the recidivism. Nonetheless, these patterns of maltreatment need to be considered in intervention planning.

Child gender also predicts recidivism (Fryer & Miyoshi, 1994), with females having more re-abuse/re-neglect. This differs by type of maltreatment, with neglect the most often re-occurring. Possibly biases in seeing females as more vulnerable leads to re-labeling of cases in order to keep them open in the system. During treatment, recidivism continues to be high, in most studies ranging from 28 to 87%. Clinicians must be vigilant regarding re-occurrences. Monitoring child safety is crucial.

UNDERSTANDING OUTCOMES IN GIRLS WHO ARE PHYSICALLY ABUSED AND NEGLECTED

As emphasized above, maltreatment needs to be understood in the context of transactions between parents and children and within the family setting as a whole. This necessitates reviewing briefly the characteristics of mothers who maltreat their children and the interactions that have been found to be typical within such families before a discussion of girls' outcomes can occur. Such a discussion is crucial as well because it has implications for intervention directed at parents and the family, as well as at girls.

Abusive and neglectful parents and their children exhibit disturbances that are not necessarily captured by diagnostic labels. A more useful framework is to think about domains of functioning that are problems for the parent and might also result in negative outcomes in the child. Studies have identified cognitive and behavioral problems and a set of contextual factors that characterize mothers who maltreat. As will be seen, these deficit areas and the nature of family interactions closely foreshadow the nature of victim outcomes. That is, because parents and the family play important roles in socializing both social behaviors and modeling and facilitating cognitive abilities, deficits here are recapitulated in the offspring. Much of what we know is based on studies with mothers and thus, we do not know if these domains apply to fathers as well.

For mothers, five areas are high probability candidates for intervention: interpersonal and emotional disturbances, cognitive disturbances, social skills problems, stress-coping difficulties, and anger control problems. These same five areas appear to be areas of concern for abused and neglected girls (Azar & Bober, 1999; Azar & Twentyman, 1986). In some cases, specific diagnosable difficulties may also need to be targeted as they may act as setting events or as triggers for abuse (e.g., parental drug abuse, child oppositional defiant disorder) or neglect (e.g., substance abuse). Each area will be discussed first for the parent and then their implications for the family environment across the periods of childhood will be outlined, finishing with a discussion of outcomes found among physically abused and neglected girls.

Disturbances in Abusive Mothers

The most pervasive disturbance seen in abusive mothers is a variety of *parenting skill deficits*. Mothers who maltreat tend to engage in less overall interaction and use more negative, coercive, and rigid control tactics (Bousha & Twentyman, 1984; Burgess & Conger, 1978; Oldershaw, Walters, & Hall, 1989). They also show deficits in areas vital for children's development. For example, they use explanation less than nonmaltreating mothers when disciplining (Barnes & Azar, 1990; Trickett & Kuczynski, 1986), which is crucial for the development of empathy and social perspective taking. More fine-tuned disturbances in responsiveness and sensitivity to infant/toddler cues have also been found (see Azar et al., 1988, for a detailed review). Given the importance placed on interpersonal sensitivity in females, the impact of such poor modeling of these capacities may have radiating effects upon girls' later functioning.

Social cognitive problems have also been found (Azar, 1989; Milner, 1993a). Physically abusive and neglectful mothers have been shown to have poorer problem-solving ability in child rearing and other situations, to make more negative attributions to children, and to judge child misbehavior more harshly in some domains (Azar, Robinson, Hekimian, & Twentyman, 1984; Chilamkurti & Milner, 1993; Hansen, Pallotta, Tishelman, & Conaway, 1989; Larrance & Twentyman, 1983). They also appear to have more unrealistic expectations regarding what is appropriate child behavior (Azar et al., 1984; Azar & Rohrbeck, 1986) and to have subtle interpersonal discrimination problems leading to poorer "tracking" of child behavior (Wahler & Dumas, 1989). Abusers also appear to be lower in cognitive flexibility (Robyn & Fremouw, 1996). These difficulties have been shown to vary together and to be linked to more coercive and ineffective parenting (Azar et al., 1999; Barnes & Azar, 1990; Dix, Ruble, & Zambarano, 1989). Such parenting techniques have been linked to child self-regulation (Patterson, 1982; Brody & Ge, 2001).

These cognitive biases may operate differently for girls and boys. One study, using a discipline diary methodology, found that mothers with more unrealistic expectations of children were less likely to report education as a goal of discipline with males as opposed to females than mothers who had fewer such expectations (Barnes & Azar, 1990). This may reflect less interest in engaging in socializing sons as opposed to daughters and may have its roots in more aversive and helplessness-producing interactions with men more generally. These mothers may see their sons as dispositionally impervious to interventions as they view the other males in their lives. If girls incorporate such beliefs, it may lead to problems in their interactions with males. These mothers, however, may be more invested in interventions with daughters as opposed to sons.

Contributing further to a negative child rearing environment are maternal deficits that interfere with self-regulating behavior both within and outside the family. Maltreating mothers appear to have difficulties *managing stress* and experience some events as more stressful than nonabusive parents. For example, they show greater physiological arousal in response to both child-related stimuli (Frodi & Lamb, 1980; Wolfe, Fairbanks, Kelly, & Bradlyn, 1983) and non–child-related events (Casanova, Domanic, McCanne, & Milner, 1992) and show poorer ability to inhibit impulsive behavior (Rohrbeck & Twentyman, 1986). As a result, they may respond aggressively to behaviors that would not provoke such responses in others (*anger-management problems*).

A final area of disturbance involves both a lack of social resources and *social skills deficits.* Social supports are important buffers against stress (e.g., provide instrumental help, information, feedback). Physically abusing mothers have smaller social support networks than nonabusing ones (Salzinger, Kaplan, & Artemyeff, 1983), tend to view themselves as more isolated (Newberger, Hampton, Marx, & White, 1986), tend to show poorer interpersonal problem solving in peer and partner interactions (Hansen et al., 1989), and tend to overattribute responsibility for aversive behavior to others (Miller & Azar, 1996). Thus, interpersonal difficulties may characterize mothers' social transactions. Indeed, those with more pervasive interpersonal problems show poorer outcomes in treatment (Szykula & Fleischman, 1985). Mothers provide important modeling of social capacities and affective regulation. Social and self-regulatory capacities are expected in females, and the lack of a facilitating environment for developing these skills may be especially detrimental to girls.

Other problems such as substance abuse (Famularo, Stone, Barnum, & Wharton, 1986), neurological problems (Elliot, 1988), and low intellectual functioning (e.g., in neglectful mothers in particular; Schilling & Schinke, 1984) have been cited as characterizing abusive and neglectful mothers. Intergenerational transmission of abuse has also been noted, although this link has been questioned (Widom, 1989). It is estimated that between 25 and 35% of maltreated girls grow up to abuse their children (Kaufman & Zigler, 1987). This may vary by type (e.g., lower rates for neglect; Starr, MacLean, & Keating, 1991). Clearly, such experiences foster disturbed relationship patterns (e.g., "scripts" for parenting, Azar, 1990; Zeanah & Zeanah, 1989), placing the next generation at risk and thus, may need attention in girls.

Child maltreatment is not solely a person-based problem, although it is persons with whom clinicians intervene. Life stress, downturns in the economy (e.g., high unemployment rates), poverty, and social isolation are all contextual factors linked to higher levels of physical abuse and neglect. These may have etiological significance or may increase child risk (or both). For example, although the stresses of poverty may in part account for the occurrence of neglect (e.g., poor medical care, poor nutrition), they also provide a context for thinking about girls' reactionsFor example, gender egalitarian roles may be less prevalent in lower-SES groups and thus, low-SES maltreated girls may also experience being less valued in other arenas of their lives. This may be especially true for girls from certain minority groups that cluster in the lower strata of US society. Lower-SES status also means poorer health care, schools, and resources that might act as buffers to abuse experiences or that may exacerbate their negative impact. Negative social forces require social policy actions and macro-level intervention strategies (e.g., welfare/health care reform).

Shelter data suggest a high co-occurrence of partner aggression with child maltreatment. Physical child abuse is committed at high rates by both batterers (between 47 and 54%) and victims of battering (between 28 and 35%; Saunders, 1994). Recidivism in domestic violence also appears to be high. Rates of cessation over 2-year periods have been shown to be only 20% (Quigley & Leonard, 1996) to 40% (Aldarondo & Sugarman, 1996). Thus, it may be a constant in some girls' lives. Data has shown negative psychological effects of exposure to domestic violence on children, some of which are gender-specific. Higher levels of both internalized and externalized behavioral problems have been found, although variations in outcomes depend upon child age, gender, appraisal of the conflict, level of involvement in disputes, and the co-occurrence of other violence such as child abuse (Fantuzzo, 1999; Margolin, 1998). Little work has been done on ethnic/racial effects.

In retrospective report studies, growing up in a domestically violent home has been associated with a heightened probability of being in domestically violent relationships for women (Kalmuss, 1984; Ehrensaft et al., 2003), including dating aggression (in mid- to late adolescence) and marital violence. Thus, young women exposed to such models of relationships may internalize this as an acceptable part of couple life. Indeed, a study by O'Leary, Malone, and Tyree (1994) found that women in stably violent relationships tended to discount the meaning of the aggression toward them, which suggests some kind of "habituation" to being treated badly. Although this long-term outcome may not be at the fore of clinicians' work with girls exposed to child maltreatment, work on changing gender stereotypes and distorted elements of relationship schema might be fruitful areas. Wolfe et al. (1997) have developed a prevention program in this area that targets adolescents' gender stereotypes and the development of positive male–female relationships. Along with distorted relational schema, some have suggested that automatized sources of aggression may develop when chronic and high levels of violence exposure occur (Todorov & Bargh, 2002). Thus, the co-occurrence of domestic violence in abusive families may in part explain the self-regulation difficulties described in children exposed to physical abuse that are described below. Displays of aggression, problematic for both genders, may be less tolerated in females than males. Interventions with mothers, therefore, should also incorporate work around domestic violence, along with targeting maltreatment. Clearly, reducing children's exposure to violence is crucial, rather than trying to repair damage once exposure has occurred.

This discussion of domestic violence highlights the importance of a systemic view in treatment. Subtle and not-so-subtle disturbances in girls' family system and social context may shift their trajectory in later life, setting them up for approaching later developmental tasks at a disadvantage. The next section attempts to broaden our lenses further to family interactions within maltreating families across girls' development.

A Systemic Developmental View of the Family Interactions of Physically Abused and Neglected Girls

Maltreatment develops against the backdrop of the tasks all families face across children's development (Azar & Siegel, 1990). For example, maltreatment that emerges in adolescence may be related to unique cues that emerge during this period (e.g., developing sexuality); whereas physical abuse that occurs in the late preschool years and re-emerges in adolescence may be related to the tensions of increasing autonomy demands made by children during both these periods. Such developmental changes in girls (i.e., autonomy seeking) being met with abuse may have far-reaching effects beyond the direct impact of violence.

In parenting of infants and toddlers, the transition to parenthood becomes a relevant issue. Infants pose many demands and the birth of children may heighten pre-existing interpersonal inadequacies. Girls at this age are especially physically vulnerable. The potentially maltreating parent may not be prepared for parenting (e.g., poor role models in her life). Pregnancy and birth may be marked by crises (e.g., unplanned pregnancy; being pushed out of the parental home) or be the result of other deficits such as heightened risk-taking behavior. Maltreating parents begin their parenting earlier than nonmaltreating ones (National Research Council, 1993). Yet, parenting at a young age is not a risk factor in and of itself. Rather the economic hardships associated with it may heighten risk (e.g., failure to complete an education; poverty). For all women, assuming the role of parent is associated with expectations (e.g., how one will share tasks with one's partner) which are often violated (i.e. one's partner does not act as expected). These violated expectancies coupled with the strains of new parenthood may lead to greater levels of stress for women in particular (Kalmuss, Davidson, & Cushman, 1992).

Social isolation characterizes maltreating mothers (Salzinger et al., 1983). Mothers may experience this more strongly as they have been socialized to rely on social supports more than males. Negative mood states may occur, which have been associated with parenting disturbances (e.g., lowered interaction with children, irritability). Indeed, disturbances in family interaction have been found in abusive families in this age period (e.g., insensitive caregiving) that may set the stage for later difficulties. Triggers for abuse during this period may include prolonged crying, feeding and sleep problems, and soiling (Herrenkohl, Herrenkohl, & Egolf, 1983). When aversive child behavior occurs, parents may mistakenly believe that babies need discipline and that shaking them is better than striking them. This can lead to "shaken baby syndrome" (intracranial bleeding, brain swelling, or damage to the blood vessels of the eyes).

Prematurity, poor nutrition, and inadequate prenatal care may increase infants' caretaking needs during this period. Prematurity is more characteristic of early-age parenting and in and of itself is associated with negative cognitive and behavioral childhood outcomes even if maltreatment does not occur. Parental disturbances (stress, depression) may lead to poorer monitoring of children. As toddlers become more mobile, environmental risks and lack of supervision may result in injuries.

The social relationship disturbances found in abused children may have their roots in this period (i.e., attachment problems; Azar et al., 1988; Cicchetti, 1989). Infants and toddlers may come to experience their world as one upon which they cannot depend (e.g., for food, safety, nurturance), affecting basic trust of others, and setting the stage for the interpersonal difficulties seen in girls later. Also, because of infants' vulnerability, foster care placement may be more likely at this age, leading to additional instability in a period of life when stability is crucial.

Interventions aimed at increasing parental supports in the transition to the role may be useful during this period. "Well baby" visits for all parents, common in other countries, would provide state support to prevent maltreatment. Prevention efforts that have targeted cognitive distortions have shown promise during this age period (Bugenthal et al., 2002), as well as ones that target broad areas of parental life and aim to improve their overall well-being, as well as parenting behaviors (Olds, Henderson, Chamberlin, & Tatelbaum, 1986).

Increases in children's abilities to operate autonomously, which occur during the preschool and school ages, may result in behaviors that could be perceived by all parents as oppositional. Indeed, the use of physical punishment peaks at age 4 for parents more generally (Wauchope & Straus, 1987). Mothers need child management and social cognitive skills, both of which are areas of deficit for maltreaters. Mothers spend more time with children in these early years and thus, they are subjected to oppositional behavior more often, perhaps increasing their risk of responding in frustration. Parents who have low frustration tolerance or have cognitive biases toward attributing this oppositional behavior as intended to annoy them may be particularly vulnerable to physical abuse during this period.

Although data are limited, termination of parental rights and placement for adoption appears to occur most often during this period (i.e., at age 4; Sedlak, 1991). Adoptions that take place later than this carry risk of disruption (Rosenthal, 1993), resulting in further distress to children. Little is known regarding the effects of such disruptions or adoption more generally on girls' long-term functioning. Clinicians working with adopted children may not even attend to the history of maltreatment and mistakenly focus their attention entirely on the adoptive family's relationships.

The heightened autonomy seen during middle childhood may also mislead neglectful mothers to expect girls to engage in more self-care and parental need fulfillment (e.g., being left home alone, caring for siblings). Injuries due to house fires where children are unsupervised may occur during this period (Dubowitz, 1991). After-school hours for working mothers may present particular risks. Child care is harder to find during these hours and so children may be left home alone. After-school programs do not exist in all communities or may be too costly. Poor nutrition and fatigue due to a lack of a structured routine and added household burdens may influence girls' school performance and social behavior.

Sexual abuse is usually initiated during this period. Ages 4 to 9 are especially high-risk years. Perpetrators may exploit girls' desire to please adults at this point in development (Gelinas, 1983). Because sexual abuse co-occurs with abuse and neglect for girls, this also must be considered in treatment planning.

The adolescent years have received less attention, except for sexual abuse. Rates of *identified* physical abuse and neglect appear lower during this period, but, based on community surveys, in reality may be just as high (Sedlak & Broadhurst, 1996). Maltreated children may exhibit behavior that fosters labeling them during this period as runaways, truant, delinquent, or oppositional defiant, as opposed to seeing parents' behavior as problematic. Screening for maltreatment needs to be considered in such cases.

Triggers for physical abuse during adolescence may have to do with the shift in allegiance to peers and the need for parents to adjust to emerging sexuality. The socially isolated mother may find the shift to peers particularly difficult, as adolescent girls spend more time with their parents than do teenage boys. Also, with younger-aged parenting, mothers may be dating at the time their teenage daughters are and thus, potential rivalry may emerge (Obeidallah & Burton, 1999). Adolescents' focus on identity formation may make them particularly susceptible to the effects of emotional maltreatment (e.g., name calling, belittling). Perception of rejection by fathers is associated with higher levels of antisocial behavior in girls (Kavanagh & Hops, 1994). Communication training and work on negotiation skills may be crucial during this period. Mothers may need help with social skills to develop alternative means of support. Targeting perspective-taking skills may reduce some of the tension in the parent–child relationship during this period.

Neglect may take different forms during adolescence. Educational neglect (truancy), poor nutrition, and lack of supervision may be especially prominent and may influence long-term health and adjustment. Also, lack of supervision may make teenagers more vulnerable to sexual abuse. It has been suggested that perpetrators may be more likely to use force during this period (Gelinas, 1983), which may result in more trauma symptoms. Antisocial behavior has also been associated with less parental supervision (Dishion & Andrews, 1995). Dating violence has been said to occur in high numbers of teen relationships and for young women who come from abusive *and* domestically violent homes, there may be greater risk. Prevention work in this area may be especially useful.

In summary, it is crucial to take a systemic/developmental view of families in understanding and treating physical abuse and neglect. Relevant intervention targets are dependent on the parent's stage of adult development and mastery of the parenting tasks and on the salient developmental tasks the child must accomplish at particular ages. Clinical interventions need to be sensitive to the gendered nature of the burdens mothers have throughout girls' development and consider ways to alleviate these. Mothers' own adult developmental needs and tasks, as well as her own relationships, should be given attention. Also, interventions need to be sensitive to girls' greater connectedness to others across development and the manner in which physical abuse and neglect may place particular strains on girls' accomplishment of developmental tasks. Furthermore, the impact that parental emotional maltreatment, lack of supervision, and selective punishment of appropriate behaviors (autonomy seeking) may have on girls' developmental trajectory needs to be considered. Outcomes found in children and teenagers are discussed in the next section.

THE IMPACT OF PHYSICAL ABUSE AND NEGLECT ON GIRLS' DEVELOPMENT

The overview of maternal disturbances and of the nature of the family of abused and neglected children illustrate why predicting girls' outcomes in response to physical abuse and neglect is very complex and no single pattern has been identified. A bidirectional interaction of several factors determine child outcome, with both parent and child contributing to transactions that shape it (Azar et al., 1988; Cicchetti & Carlson, 1989; Parke & Collmer, 1975). Furthermore, outcomes may not only relate to the maltreatment experience(s), but also to contextual factors associated with it (e.g., domestic violence, violent neighborhoods, poverty) or society's responses to it (e.g., foster care), or both. These other factors may have additive effects (Hennessy et al., 1994), and/or their effects may overshadow those of the maltreatment. Finally, debate in the field varies between those trying to link specific outcomes to specific forms of maltreatment and those arguing for the global stress effects, irrespective of type.

Contributing to the confusion are methodological problems. Many studies do not differentiate abused (both physical and sexual) from neglected samples, making it more difficult to document specific effects. Also, although the impact of physical abuse alone has received some attention, research on the effects of neglect has been particularly "neglected." The few studies that exist either vary as to which types of neglect are a focus or do not define what the label includes. Some make physical, medical, and emotional neglect one group; but others do not.

Most studies of sequelae of maltreatment during childhood and adulthood either do not report or even examine gender differences. Typically, when the interaction between gender and maltreatment status is examined, no differences are found. The few that have found some interactive effects between maltreatment and gender used clinical samples and employed retrospective reports. They also included in their samples individuals who have experienced sexual abuse. Gender-based sequelae are more clear in this form of maltreatment. Retrospective studies also tended to employ larger samples, which may account for greater sensitivity to detect male/female differences. On the other hand, because clinical samples have gender biases built into them, their findings may not be representative (e.g., females who are in the juvenile court system may be more distressed than those who are not). In the discussion below, places where boys and girls differ in their response to maltreatment will be noted. Examples of both global problems observed and ones that may be more specific to particular forms of maltreatment will be outlined below. Although difficulties are discussed separately, they are intrinsically linked. For example, health issues may lead to attention problems, resulting in lower academic performance.

It should be noted that even if general gender differences do not exist in response to child abuse and neglect, the reactions of others to the negative outcomes that do occur may differ. For example, heightened aggression may be better tolerated by others in males than in females. Cultural expectations for more mature interpersonal responses in women are deeply ingrained.

Finally, interactions with other socio-demographic factors have rarely been examined. Because of the different place in US society of diverse ethnic/racial groups and confounds of minority status with poverty, differences might be expected. As suggested earlier, being a minority girl, living in poverty and dealing with discrimination both within one's subcultural group and outside of it may have interactive effects with the experience of maltreatment. Minority girls may, for example, experience heightened values conflict between their own culture's and that of the middle class White culture's (e.g., for Latina girls, expectations to be self-sacrificing, to remain at home and care for siblings vs. the expectations at school). Such conflicts coupled with a sense of being unvalued that may result from maltreatment may make minority girls who are maltreated prime candidates for the kind of internalizing that leads to the depression.

Maltreatment may leave physical, social, and/or emotional "scars," which, for some girls, have little in the way of observable consequences and for others, severely affect functioning. This continuum of impact and multi-determined outcomes need to be considered carefully when making clinical decisions. Also, the global indicators found in outcome studies may not tell us about more fine-grained vulnerabilities. On the other hand, clinicians may be too ready to see such children as troubled and overlook strengths. It is important to distinguish among girls' ability to adjust, vulnerability to stressors, and difficulties coping with stressors (effort required to achieve good outcomes; Farber & Egeland, 1987).

Five areas of development may be negatively affected by physical abuse and neglect and deserve clinical attention (Azar, Lauretti, & Loding, 1998): (a) physical health, (b) cognitive functioning and academic performance, (c) emotional and social development, (d) stress management, and (e) anger control and other self-regulation capacities. As noted earlier, these parallel disturbances are found in maltreating parents, suggesting they are "socialized" within the disturbed interaction patterns of maltreating families.

Although it seems intuitive that maltreatment might negatively affect *physical health* and well-being, little research has examined this. Consequences of physical abuse can include trauma, such as bruises, burns, and skeletal, head, and internal injuries. It can leave lasting effects (e.g., neuropsychological deficits, disabilities), resulting in the need for further coping on the child's part (e.g., ongoing medical care, adjusting to a disability), as well as for their biological, foster-care, or adoptive families. These can also influence children's social interaction (e.g., dealing with being stared at by peers because of scars). In some cases, these may affect girls more—for example, the importance placed on attractiveness for females. Although younger children may be more physically vulnerable, teenagers' health should not be ignored. Lack of monitoring may affect nutrition and sleep level, both of which may make them more vulnerable to illness. Furthermore, it may allow risk-taking behavior to occur (e.g., substance abuse, early sexual behavior) that might expose girls to other health risks (e.g. STDs) and prematurely assuming adult roles (i.e., early pregnancy). Some data exist suggesting hormonal effects in girls (earlier puberty) exposed to sexual abuse, and this might be expected with other forms of maltreatment, given comorbidity (Trickett & Putnam, 1993).

Neglected girls and boys may suffer the most physical consequences because of undernourishment, lack of medical and dental care, and parental failures to monitor and supervise the child. Failure to thrive, for example, can result from neglect and can have long-term effects. Lack of supervision may account for burns/deaths due to house fires. Anemia due to poor nutrition can cause apathy and lead to poor school performance. One review of research indicated that neglected children show lower levels of a growth hormone, which leads to delays in physical growth (Kaplan, Pelcovitz, & LaBruna, 1999), and another reported delays in motor development (Wright, 1994). Finally, although causality is not clear, emotional abuse can produce physical complaints due to chronic anxiety (e.g., stomach aches, headaches). Failures in health care may also exacerbate existing health problems. Dubowitz (1991) gives the example of asthma. Proper treatment of asthma may keep a child free of symptoms and out of the hospital. Clearly, health-screening is crucial, as is targeting parental health care skills (Gershater-Molko & Lutzker, 1999).

Developmental effects are numerous. Children must direct energy typically used for developmental growth into protection from abusive parents and for basic survival with neglectful ones, resulting in multiple *lags in cognitive, social, and emotional development*. School-aged and adolescent neglected and physically abused children have consistently been found to have lower IQ scores (e.g., Perez & Widom, 1994; Widom, 1998), verbal intelligence (e.g., Wright, 1994), reading and math scores (e.g., Perez & Widom, 1994), language development (Cahill, Kaminer, & Johnson, 1999) and memory than comparison children (e.g., Wright, 1994). Neglect is more strongly associated with poor achievement than is abuse (e.g., Cahill et al., 1999; Kaplan et al., 1999). More school behavior problems occur among neglected/abused children than matched controls (e.g., truancy, suspension, or expulsion; Perez & Widom, 1994; Powers, Eckenrode, & Jaklitsch, 1990). These difficulties appear to persist into adulthood (Perez & Widom, 1994). Abuse and neglect are associated with significantly fewer years of schooling, lower employment rates, and higher levels of menial and semiskilled occupations (e.g., Widom, 1998). Careful cognitive and academic assessment is needed. One study indicated physically abused girls behave differently during assessments They showed higher levels of eye contact without verbalization and were lower in negative demanding behavior compared with abused boys and nonabused girls (Trickett, 1993). This is suggestive of coping differences during stressful situations, such as hypervigilance and being constricted. Academic skills, school attendance, and behaviors leading to school suspensions may all be targeted in treatment.

The largest body of research on sequelae of maltreatment has focused on *emotional and social difficulties*. During infancy and early childhood, maltreated children show greater dependency, tend to have insecure attachment relationships, and show little concern for their peers' distress (Azar & Bober, 1999; Carlson, Cicchetti, Barnett, & Braunwald, 1989; George & Main, 1980). Abused boys and girls also show problems in emotional development, including lower self-esteem, disturbances in healthy conceptions of self, mood, trust in others, and in basic emotional skills (e.g., recognition and expression of emotion; Azar et al., 1988; Wolfe, 1987). Rutter (1979) found that children deprived of primary caregivers in infancy (emotional neglect) were overly friendly with strangers, sought attention and were clingy toward adults, and were inept in social behavior at school (i.e., attention-seeking, restlessness, disobedience, unpopularity). Such children also engage less in interaction with peers (Cahill et al., 1999) and have more conflictual relationships with friends and fewer reciprocal friendships than controls (Kaplan et al., 1999). Given gendered socialization in US society, such social disturbances may be particularly problematic for females, resulting in peer rejection and/or male adult exploitation.

Social problems seen in maltreated girls may vary with age. Attachment difficulties and unresponsiveness have been observed in male and female infants and toddlers (Carlson et al., 1989; Crittendon, 1985); whereas poor social skills (e.g., empathy, perspective taking, poor problem solving) are found among older girls and boys (Barahal, Waterman, & Martin, 1981; George & Main, 1980; Haskett, 1990). A study by Salzinger, Kaplan, Pelcovitz, Samit, and Krieger (1984) suggests physically abused girls and boys may evidence social cognitive distortions. The maltreated 8- to 12-year-olds they studied identified specific peers as being "friends," who by their own reports did not even like the target child. Noteworthy, however, in this study was the fact that 13 of the 87 abused children were rated as popular with peers, suggesting resiliency. This may stem from having alternative social support during development or from an early period of competency that acts as a foundation for later adjustment (Farber & Egeland, 1987).

Problems persist into adolescence and to adulthood including depression, isolation, loneliness, and higher divorce and separation rates (Cook, 1991; Loos & Alexander, 1997; Melchert, 2000; Naar-King, Silvern, Ryan, & Sebring, 2002; Powers et al., 1990; Widom, 1998). As noted earlier, heightened rates of certain disorders are more common among females (e.g., eating disorders, borderline and multiple personality disorder; Zanarini et al., 2000). Abuse is associated with elevated PTSD symptoms, although this is more common in sexual abuse (Naar-King et al., 2002).

At least one study (a 20-year follow-up of a group of abused and neglected children), however, found females to be more resilient than males across a larger number of domains of functioning. Resilience was defined by meeting criteria for success across six of eight domains of functioning including employment, homelessness, education, social activity, psychiatric disorder, substance abuse, and criminal behavior (both self-reported and official arrests; McGloin & Widom, 2001). Indeed, 22% of abused and neglected children followed into young adulthood met the criteria for resilience, again cautioning against an automatic assumption of psychopathology. It may be that buffers exist in girls' lives that do not for males. These resources need to be identified for individual girls and enhanced. However, it also needs to be considered that even if "bottom line" outcomes are not as bad for females as for males, the cost required to achieve them may still be great.

Maltreated children experience significant stress, which may be chronic and impact the development of *stress-management skills and anger control*. Girls may develop coping strategies that work in their maladaptive homes (e.g., dissociation), but that do not serve them well outside the family. Stress and anger management and other self-regulation capacities, therefore, also require attention. Numerous self-regulation difficulties, such as overly compliant or aggressive, demanding and rageful behaviors, are shown by maltreated children (Fantuzzo, 1990; Widom, 1989). Overly compliant behavior may help girls to avoid confrontations with parents. On the other hand, aggressive behavior may be caused by continual frustration of their needs and modeling of aggressive responses to frustration.

Maltreated girls and boys show more negative emotions and behaviors (i.e., anger, fear, or physical attack), more avoidance and noncompliance (Wright, 1994), and more conduct disorder (Rutter, 1979) than their peers. Their play shows more developmental delays and more antisocial, disruptive, aggressive, and conflict themes (Wright, 1994). Abuse and neglect have been linked to delinquent behavior, including fighting, stealing, skipping school, and traffic violations, among adolescents (Brown, 1984; Mak, 1994). They have also been associated with heightened risk-taking behaviors such as early sexual activity and teenage parenthood (Kaplan et al., 1999; Wright, 1994) and in adulthood, with an increased risk of alcohol abuse (Widom, 1998). Adults neglected or abused as children are more likely than controls to be arrested as a juvenile or adult, to be arrested for violent crimes, and to be diagnosed with antisocial personality disorder (Cahill et al., 1999; Widom, 1998). Subtle gender differences may occur in the antecedents of problematic behavior that are worthy of further study. For example, Olsen, 2000 found emotional neglect to predict hypersensitivity to social slights in adult females as opposed to males. It also predicted heightened levels of aggression. Aggressive girls are at higher risk for problems with their own offspring (Pajer, 1998) and thus, relational interventions may be crucial to stop later "developmental" failures.

IMPLICATIONS FOR ASSESSMENT AND TREATMENT OF ABUSED AND NEGLECTED CHILDREN

The above discussion suggests that intervention must be done at multiple levels: with the individual girl, her parents, and family. Interventions may also need to involve the major community contexts in which the maltreated girl lives and other institutional settings that intervene in her life (e.g., child protection system, juvenile courts, schools, and court system). Space limitations do not allow a detailed discussion of intervention into the familial and parenting setting, and the literature on individual treatment of girls who have been physically abused and neglected is almost nonexistent at this point. Clearly, each of the domains of functioning outlined as deficit areas for parents and for girls have interventions associated with them (see Azar, 1989, and Azar & Wolfe, 1998, for further details on parenting interventions). Nonetheless, *unique* elements/adaptations may be *specific* to addressing the abuse and neglect experiences and characteristics of the individuals/families involved. The following discussion of parenting interventions will provide a general case formulation framework, risk assessment strategies, and adaptations needed in treatment for maltreating mothers who are often low in cognitive functioning, are often involuntary clients, and are subject to multiple stressors. For female victims, treatment will be discussed that might increase coping and appropriate social interactions inside and outside the family. The gendered nature of systemic responses to child maltreatment will also be outlined and improvements in strategies considered.

Issues in Treating Mothers

Global frameworks designed to assess parenting skills and family functioning provide a starting point for assessment. Tymchuk's (1998) model of assessment covers basic child care needs in four areas: (a) fundamental knowledge and skills (including effective coping strategies, grooming and hygiene skills, meal planning and finance management, ability to create and maintain a support network; cognitive stimulation skills); (b) health-related knowledge and skills (e.g., knowledge of common health problems, illnesses and medicines, ability to recognize and evaluate severity of symptoms, ability to recognize and prevent life-threatening emergencies); (c) safety-related knowledge and skills (e.g., knowledge of potential dangers in the home and in the community); and (d) mutual parent–child enjoyment capacities (e.g., playing together, reading to the child). Assessment of family functioning can also be guided by the McMaster's model's three tasks families must accomplish (Epstein, Bishop, & Baldwin, 1982): (a) basic tasks that involve survival needs (food, shelter); (b) developmental tasks that involve adjusting to family members' shifting development needs and fostering their progress; and (c) emergency tasks, which involve capacities to handle emergencies. To meet these tasks, capacities in six areas are needed: problem solving, behavioral control, affective responsiveness, affective involvement, communication, and adequate distribution of family roles. A cognitive–behavioral model for assessment emphasizes the five domains of parent's skill deficits described earlier across all areas of functioning (Azar & Twentyman, 1986; Azar, Lauretti, & Loding, 1998).

For neglect, many of the areas to be assessed (e.g., cleanliness) are personal and clinicians should be careful about the timing and attitude with which assessment is done. Also, although the diversity of maternal behavior has long been understood by sociobiologists (Hrdy, 1999), there are still strong societal beliefs that parenting comes "naturally" (e.g., maternal instinct), and mothers may approach treatment with a sense of "damage" or at least a perception the clinician will see them that way. Evaluation needs to occur in a trust-building, normalizing, and relationship-enhancing manner ("If any of these questions feel too personal, please let me know," "I ask these questions of all parents that I see"; see Azar & Soysa, 2000). Parents also prefer assessment that focuses on their skills rather than deficits. This may be especially important in that such families are often involuntary clients and are lower in SES, both of which have been associated with high attrition rates from treatment. Careful engagement with clients is crucial to maintaining them in treatment and affecting changes. (More will be said about treatment processes later.)

Literacy is a problem for parents. Use of self-report measures requires reading items to insure understanding and education in how to use Likert scales. Performance-based evaluation, including task analyses (breaking skills into small steps), live role-plays, and use of visual prompts to solicit cognitive and behavioral capacities (e.g., enactment of a grease fire and parents' response to it to assess emergency skills) may also be necessary with more limited parents. Finally, clinicians need to be sensitive to variation in cultural practices and tolerance for the intrusion of outsiders in family life.

Ongoing risk assessment, crucial to working with family violence, should involve an examination of current level of risk in areas noted in past CPS reports. This narrows the areas to be assessed in depth, with a broader screening in other areas. Consultation with others regarding child health and school attendance and performance also is useful. Repeated failures to make appointments or small cues that emerge in interacting with the family need follow-up (e.g., a young child repeatedly answers the phone and reports the parent is not available to talk may indicate children being left home alone or parental substance abuse). Risk protocols exist for physical abuse (e.g., Child Abuse Potential Inventory; Milner, 1986), but not neglect. If necessary, foster care may be required to insure child safety and allow treatment to proceed. Ongoing evaluation of stress level is also needed, as it may act as a setting event for abuse or neglect to occur. Issues such as the occurrence of domestic violence, housing instability, increases in child care issues, and other matters associated with poverty and maltreatment all may need a rapid response during treatment.

Issues in Treatment of Girls

A thorough assessment of the child's functioning is required along with assessing the match of parental skills to the girl's needs. This can focus on the five child areas outlined earlier. Given the heterogeneity of outcomes, assessment might start with a standard assessment and include screening issues related to specific forms of neglect (e.g., examining school records for attendance; lead paint poisoning screening), supplemented where needed with more detailed evaluations. Broad- and narrow-band (e.g., attentional problems; trauma) screening instruments can be employed. Because parents may distort child difficulties, reports of others (foster parents, teachers) and self-reports (with older children) might be solicited.

A multidisciplinary approach is essential (Azar & Wolfe, 1998; Hansen & Warner, 1992), including medical, behavioral, neurological, educational, and speech evaluations with children. Health-screening instruments might provide a starting point here (see Dubowitz, 1991, for measures). If specific areas of deficit are found, more focused assessment can occur (e.g., for nutritional neglect, growth patterns). An assessment of special needs should also be done. Child skills and contextual stresses might be examined directly and through parents' and others' reports (e.g., teachers), using behavioral problem checklists, and might provide insight into the parenting difficulties. The child's functioning needs to be considered across contexts. Discrepancies in functioning may hint at environmental contingencies that negatively affect the child and which, if the parent is unable to protect against them, may bode poorly for the children's development. For example, for children with attentional problems, a highly chaotic environment would be detrimental to performing adequately. Areas to consider are the consistency, quality, and content of the care required (e.g., does the child have special psychological or medical needs, such as care and monitoring of a chronic illness, regular injections, medication, dietary restrictions?), special safety needs (e.g., does the child engage in self-injurious behaviors requiring constant monitoring?); needs for stability/structure; and needs for higher than typical caregiver patience and responsiveness (e.g., where the child exhibits high rates of oppositional behavior or, in contrast, is highly passive) (Azar et al., 1998).

This highlights the need to evaluate parent–child match. The level of a parent's capacities might not place a *well-functioning* child at risk, but would endanger a child who has *intensive medical care or other special needs*. For instance, an asthmatic child needs a cleaner home than the average child. Parenting disabled children requires adaptations including efforts to understand the child's disability, behaviors, and needs; continuing behavior management; and long-term cooperation with medical/educational caregivers. Parents must advocate in multiple settings (e.g., with schools to provide an optimal learning setting). Teachers, pediatricians, and child therapists are sources of data regarding parents' advocacy ability.

As noted earlier, child-focused treatment outcome work with maltreated children is quite limited. Therapeutic day care and foster care provide safety and foster developmental skills (Ayoub, 1991; Culp, Heide, & Richardson, 1987). Recently, a few published studies have examined skills training (e.g., social skills; Fantuzzo, Stovall, Schachtel, Goins, & Hall, 1987) and treatment of PTSD symptoms (Deblinger, McLeer, & Henry, 1990). Fantuzzo and colleagues (1987), for example, have used peer and teacher prompting techniques to improve the social skills of abused preschoolers. Interestingly, perhaps because of victims' relationship history with adults, peers were superior to teachers. In work with children evidencing PTSD, Lipovksy (1991) emphasizes education, facilitation of emotional expression, anxiety control, and controlled exposure to memories. Stress management, anger control training, and remedial academic work may also be useful.

A number of issues must be considered in doing child treatment. First, safety should be a priority. Therapy will be of little use if the child must continue to devote energy to concerns regarding harm. If the child remains in parental custody, concurrent work with parents should be required. Concurrent work with foster or adoptive parents may also be useful to help them cope with the children's response to their past maltreatment and regarding separation issues from family of origin. Given girls' socialization toward connectedness, these may be greater for females. Second, although the heterogeneity of child problems seen makes it difficult to suggest universal treatment targets, reduction of aversive child behaviors (e.g., opposition, aggression, wetting the bed) that may act as triggers for maltreatment and would be viewed most negatively in females might be the first order of business. Efforts should then be directed to increasing adaptive behaviors (e.g., social skills). Trauma symptoms (e.g., dissociation), which are most likely in girls who have been exposed to multiple forms of maltreatment, may also be a high priority, as they may interfere most with functioning. Common themes to which therapists need to be sensitive include problems with trust, anticipation of rejection, feelings of loss, and fear of adults.

Systemic Interventions

How cases are handled may affect girls. Clinicians, agency staff, and courts may recapitulate the relationships females have within maltreating families, leading to further bad modeling. Work on parenting and in child maltreatment has noted potential for bias in dealing with poor women. Biases include the tendency to see them as hopeless, helpless, and despicable (Azar, 1996; Farmer & Owen, 1998; Milner, 1993b) and must be considered by clinicians as they work with maltreated girls and their families.

Biases have also been discussed and begun to be documented in all phases of the child protection system (CPS) as well: in decision-making, intervention, and outcomes of systems interventions (Farmer & Owen, 1998; Milner 1993b). In one small-scale British study of cases, Farmer and Owen (1998) found that mothers were underincluded in offers of services and overincluded in efforts aimed at control. Mothers who had parenting difficulties were not given priority in services and passed over for allocation of services. This was true even when mothers demonstrated high initiation rates for requests for services. In an examination of the CPS system, Milner (1993b) also reported that physically abusing mothers were more likely to have their cases substantiated than were physically abusing men. Farmer and Owen (1998) found similar results. In over three-quarters of their small sample (77%) of cases where mothers were held responsible for physical abuse, the case was substantiated; in contrast fewer than half (48%) were substantiated when a father, stepfather, or male cohabitee was held responsible. The single-parent status of the mothers in this study (much more common in US society) may have been responsible for this gender difference. In another study conducted in Western Australia, more children from single-female-headed households than two-parent ones were placed in foster care at the point of investigation (Thorpe, 1994). Women in two-parent families may be seen as better able to protect their children, reflecting biases against single parenthood. An alternative explanation is that social service departments may be less willing to intervene in situations where fathers are seen as unwilling or more threatening (Miller & Fisher, 1992; O'Hagan, 1997, cited by Farmer & Owen, 1998). The latter case would mirror the relationship women may have with such men within the family.

Gender enters into later actions in CPS as well. Farmer and Owen (1998) found that even if the father was the perpetrator of abuse, in two-parent families, case discussion, assessments, and intervention quickly shifted to mother's capacities. Again, potential gender biases may be responsible (e.g., mothers being the one who are seen as "responsible" for child care; female caseworkers shying away from working with belligerent men). In any case, such actions and greater scrutiny may leave women feeling stigmatized and blamed. Fathers may also more easily "opt out" without consequences, for example, by being "unavailable" when home visits are scheduled or not appear for treatment visits with the child. Farmer and Owen (1998) in their ethnographic study of cases found that in the cases where the father was the perpetrator of physical abuse and the couple did not separate, the focus of intervention shifted to mother early. Despite father's behavior being an initial focus of the case, subsequent reviews ignored it and continued the focus on mothers.

On the basis of studies of perceptions of procedural fairness, the lower rates of providing services requested by these women and these other systems-based biases may produce greater noncompliance with services that are offered as the case progresses. Such noncompliance is a predictor of later termination of parental rights (Jellinek et al., 1992). Overall, these system actions may intensify gender roles present already in the family (i.e., mothers bearing the burden of child care alone; men not being held accountable), increase stress on mothers, and perhaps alienate them from their children. Ultimately, the impact will be felt by children. Given aggressive males' documented tendency to blame others for their negative behavior (e.g., ascribing it to negative intent in others) and the professionals' response to mothers (either overt blaming and/or pressure for them to be responsible for "fixing" the situation), girls may get the impression they themselves or their mothers are responsible for the behavior of males and thus, men are not culpable. This reinforcing of biased gendered schema is problematic for girls' later functioning.

Implications for mental health clinicians are clear. Biases may enter into our work as well. Mothers may be seen as more workable, more available, and "more responsible" for care of children and we may neglect to attend to men's role in the difficulties. We too may fear the threat of violence in work with fathers. This models for girls a biased view of their problems and does harm to their views of their mothers (she alone is responsible for their basic needs) and to their view of themselves as responsible for the abusive behavior.

CONCLUSIONS

This chapter has emphasized the importance of attending to systemic issues in dealing with abuse and neglect of girls and the need to tailor interventions so as not to lose sight of historical and sociopolitical factors affecting parental role distributions, the value placed on children and women in particular, visions of poor and minority families, and the pressures faced by the maltreating family both from within and without in US society. The clinician is cautioned to guard against recapitulating the biases in society and disturbed interaction patterns seen within the maltreating family. Physical abuse and neglect occurs within relationships and it is these relationships that need to be targeted for intervention. Sociologists have argued that family violence is associated with lower hierarchical status within social groups. Within this framework, clinicians/caseworkers must take care to use their status/power wisely to assist family change without replicating structures with which the mother and daughter must grapple in their everyday life. This is important in the treatment of girls who have encountered maltreatment, especially those who are from diverse backgrounds. They themselves have experienced lack of care and abuse, but have a high likelihood of observing their most closely allied role model, their mothers, also not being treated with respect and at times abused by others (e.g., battering partner, difficult welfare office encounters, etc.). A global sense of lack of worth, helplessness, and acceptance of one's role as victim may work against treatment efficacy. In addition, careful attention to the other pressures encountered by girls and their families may also be crucial (e.g., economic strain, domestic violence, dating violence, etc.). Finally, many issues raised in this chapter require social policy changes to improve the environments in which such girls live and allow them greater safety and services if maltreatment is identified. For example, the impact of welfare reform on maltreatment rates has been examined. Patterns of leaving welfare rolls (either returning to work or exceeding the time limits of participation) have in fact been linked to increases in maltreatment rates, with parents who are later leavers having significantly higher rates (Ovwigho, Leavitt, & Born, 2003).

REFERENCES

Administration for Children, Youth, and Families. (2000). *Child maltreatment 1998. Reports from the states to the National Center on Child Abuse and Neglect.* Washington, DC: U.S. Department of Health and Human Services.

Administration on Children, Youth, and Families. (2001a). *10 years of reporting on child maltreatment.* Washington, DC: U.S. Department of Health and Human Services.

Administration for Children, Youth, and Families. (2001b). *Child maltreatment 1999. Reports from the states to the National Center on Child Abuse and Neglect.* Washington, DC: U.S. Department of Health and Human Services.

Aldarondo, E., & Sugarman, D. B. (1996). Risk marker analysis of the cessation and persistence of wife assault. *Journal of Consulting and Clinical Psychology, 64,* 1010–1019.

American Association of University Women. (1991). *Shortchanging girls, shortchanging America.* Washington, DC: Author.

American Psychiatric Association. (1994). *Diagnostic and statistical manual of mental disorders* (4th ed.) . Washington, DC: Author.

Arnold, F., & Kuo, E. C. (1984). The value of daughters and sons: A comparative study of the gender preferences of parents. *Journal of Comparative Family Studies, 15,* 299–318.

Ayoub, C. (1991). Physical violence and preschoolers: The use of therapeutic day care in the treatment of physically abused children and children from violent families. *The Advisor, 4,* 1–18.

Azar, S. T. (1986). A framework for understanding child maltreatment: An integration of cognitive behavioral and developmental perspectives. *Canadian Journal of Behavioral Science, 18,* 340–355.

Azar, S. T. (1989). Training parents of abused children. In C. E. Shaefer & J. M. Briesmeister (Eds.), *Handbook of parent training* (pp. 414–441). New York: Wiley.

Azar, S. T. (1990, November). *"Parenting" risk in adolescents with a history of abuse.* Paper presented at the annual meeting of the Association for the Advancement of Behavior Therapy, San Francisco.

Azar, S. T. (1996). Cognitive restructuring of professionals' schema regarding women parenting in poverty. *Women & Therapy, 18,* 147–161.

Azar, S. T. (2002). Adult development and parenting. In J. Demick (Ed.), *Adult development* (pp. 391–416). New York: Sage.

Azar, S. T., Barnes, K. T., & Twentyman, C. T. (1988). Developmental outcomes in physically abused children: Consequences of parental abuse or the effects of a more general breakdown in caregiving behaviors? *Behavior Therapist, 11,* 27–32.

Azar, S. T., & Bober, S. (1999). Children of abusive families. In W. K. Silverman & T. H. Ollendick (Eds.), *Developmental issues in the clinical treatment of children and adolescents* (pp. 371–392). Boston: Allyn & Bacon.

Azar, S. T., & Cote, L. (2002). Sociocultural issues in the evaluation of the needs of children in custody decision-making. *International Journal of Law & Psychiatry, 25,* 193–217.

Azar, S. T., Fantuzzo, J., & Twentyman, C. T. (1984). An applied behavioral approach to child maltreatment: Back to basics. *Advances in Behavior Research and Therapy, 6,* 3–11.

Azar, S. T., Lauretti, A., & Loding, B. (1998). The evaluation of parental fitness in termination of parental rights cases. *Clinical Child and Family Psychology Review, 1,* 77–99.

Azar, S. T., Povilaitis, T., Johnson, E., Breton, S., Ferraro, M. H., & Soysa, C. (1999, April). *Maternal expectations, problem solving and discipline and synchrony: A test of social cognition model.* Paper presented at the meeting of the Society for Research in Child Development, Albuquerque, NM.

Azar, S. T., Robinson, D. R., Hekimian, E., & Twentyman, C. T. (1984). Unrealistic expectations and problem solving ability in maltreating and comparison mothers. *Journal of Consulting and Clinical Psychology, 52,* 687–691.

Azar, S. T., & Rohrbeck, C. A. (1986). Child abuse and unrealistic expectations: Further validation of the Parent Opinion Questionnaire. *Journal of Consulting and Clinical Psychology, 54,* 867–868.

Azar, S. T., & Siegel, B. (1990). Behavioral treatment of child abuse: A developmental perspective. *Behavior Modification, 14,* 279–300.

Azar, S. T., & Soysa, K. (2000). How do I assess a caregiver's parenting attitudes, knowledge, and level of functioning? In H. Dubowitz & D. De Panfilis (Eds.), *The handbook of child protection* (pp. 308–313), New York: Sage.

Azar, S. T., & Twentyman, C. T. (1986). Cognitive behavioral perspectives on the assessment and treatment of child abuse. In P. C. Kendall (Ed.), *Advances in cognitive behavioral research and therapy* (Vol. 5, pp. 237–267). New York: Academic Press.

Azar, S. T., & Wolfe, D. A. (1998). Child abuse and neglect. In E. G. Mash & R. A. Barkley (Eds.), *Behavioral treatment of childhood disorders* (2nd ed., pp. 501–544), New York: Guilford.

Barahal, R. M., Waterman, J., & Martin, H. P. (1981). The social cognitive development of abused children. *Journal of Consulting and Clinical Psychology, 49,* 508–516.

Barnes, K. T., & Azar, S. T. (1990, August). *Maternal expectations and attributions in discipline situations: A test of a cognitive model of parenting.* Paper presented at the annual meeting of the American Psychological Association, Boston.

Belsky, J. (1980). Child maltreatment: An ecological integration. *American Psychologist, 35,* 320–335.

Bousha, D., & Twentyman, C. T. (1984). Abusing, neglectful and comparison mother–child interactional style. *Journal of Abnormal Psychology, 93,* 106–114.

Brassard, M. R., Germain, R., & Hart, S. N. (1987). *Psychological maltreatment of children and youth.* New York: Pergamon.

Brody, G., & Ge, X. (2001). Linking parenting processes and self regulation to psychological functioning and alcohol use during early adolescence. *Journal of Family Psychology, 15,* 82–94.

Brown, L. M. (1998). *Raising their voices: The politics of girls' anger.* Boston: Harvard University Press.

Brown, S. E. (1984). Social class, child maltreatment, and delinquent behavior. *Criminology, 22,* 259–278.

Bugenthal, D. B., Ellerson, P. C., Lin, E. K., Rainey, B., Kokotovic, A., & O'Hara, N. (2002). A cognitive approach to child abuse prevention. *Journal of Family Psychology, 16,* 243–258.

Burgess, R. L., & Conger, R. D. (1978). Family interaction in abusive, neglectful and normal families. *Child Development, 49,* 1163–1173.

Cahill, L. T., Kaminer, R. K., & Johnson, P. G. (1999). Developmental, cognitive, and behavioral sequelae of child abuse. *Child and Adolescent Psychiatric Clinics of North America, 8,* 827–843.

Carlson, V. Cicchetti, D., Barnett, D., & Braunwald, K. G. (1989). Finding order in disorganization: Lessons from research on maltreated infants' attachments to their caregivers. In D. Cicchetti & V. Carlson (Eds.), *Child maltreatment* (pp. 494–528). New York: Cambridge University Press.

Casanova, G. M., Domanic, J., McCanne, T. R., & Milner, J. S. (1992). Physiological responses to non-child-related stressors in mothers at risk for child abuse. *Child Abuse and Neglect, 16,* 31–44.

Chao, R. (1997, April). *The "meaningfulness" of our most familiar constructs: Research on parenting for ethnically diverse populations.* Paper presented at the meeting of the Society for Research in Child Development, Washington, DC.

Chase-Lansdale, P. L., & Vinovskis, M. S. (1995). Whose responsibility? An historical analysis of the changing roles of mothers, fathers, and society. In P. L. Chase-Lansdale, and J. Brooks-Gunn (Eds.), *Escape from poverty. What differences does it make?* (pp. 11–37). New York: Cambridge University Press.

Chilamkurti, C., & Milner, J. S. (1993). Perceptions and evaluations of child transgressions and disciplinary techniques in high- and low-risk mothers and their children. *Child Development, 64,* 31–44.

Cicchetti, D. (1989). How research on child maltreatment has informed the study of child development. In D. Cicchetti & V. Carlson (Eds.), *Child maltreatment* (pp. 377–431). Cambridge: Cambridge University Press.

Cicchetti, D., & Barnett, D. (1991). Toward the development of a scientific nosology of child maltreatment. In D. Cicchetti & W. Grove (Eds.), *Thinking clearly about psychology* (pp. 346–377). Minneapolis: University of Minnesota Press.

Cicchetti, D., & Carlson, V. (1989). *Child maltreatment: Theory and research on the causes and consequences of child abuse and neglect.* Cambridge: Cambridge University Press.

Condry, S. M., Condry, J. C., & Pogatshnik, L. W. (1983). Sex differences: A study of the eye of the beholder. *Sex Roles, 9,* 697–704.

Cook, D. A. (1991). College students from emotionally neglectful homes. *New Directions for Student Services, 54,* 77–90.

Crawford, M., & Unger, R. (2004). *Women and gender.* Boston: McGraw-Hill.

Crittenden, P. M. (1985). Maltreated infants: Vulnerability and resilience. *Journal of Child Psychology & Psychiatry, 26,* 85–96.

Culp, E., Heide, J. S., & Richardson, M. T. (1987). Maltreated children's developmental scores: Treatment versus nontreatment. *Child Abuse and Neglect, 11,* 29–34.

Deblinger, E., McLeer, S. V., & Henry, D. (1990). Cognitive behavioral treatment for sexually abused children suffering from post traumatic stress: Preliminary findings. *American Academy of Child and Adolescent Psychiatry, 29,* 747–752.

Dishion, T. J., & Andrews, D. W. (1995). Preventing escalation in problem behaviors with high risk young adolescents. *Journal of Consulting and Clinical Psychology, 3,* 538–548.

Dix, T., Ruble, D. N., & Zambarano, R. J. (1989). Mothers' implicit theories of discipline: Child effects, parent effects, and the attribution process. *Child Development, 60,* 1373–1391.

Dubowitz, H. (1991). The impact of child maltreatment on health. In R. H. Starr and D. A. Wolfe (Eds.), *The effects of child abuse and neglect* (pp. 278–294). New York: Guilford.

Eckenrode, J., Laird, M., & Doris, J. (1993). School performance and disciplinary problems among abused and neglected children. *Developmental Psychology, 29,* 53–62.

Ehrensaft, M. K., Cohen, P., Brown, J., Smailes, E., Chen, H., & Johnson, J. G. (2003). Intergenerational transmission of partner violence: A 20-year prospective study. *Journal of Consulting and Clinical Psychology, 71,* 741–753.

Elliot, F. A. (1988). Neurological Factors. In V. B. Vantlasselt, R. L. Morison, A. S. Bellack, & M. Hersen (Eds.), *Handbook of Family Violence* (pp. 359–382). New York: Plenum.

English, D. J., Marshall, D. B., & Orme, M. (1999). Characteristics of repeated referrals to child protective services in Washington State, WA, U.S. *Child Maltreatment, 4,* 297–307.

Epstein, N. B., Bishop, D. S., & Baldwin, L. M. (1982). McMaster model of family functioning. In F. Walsh (Ed.), *Normal family processes* (pp. 115–141). New York: Guilford.

Famularo, R., Stone, I., Barnum, R., & Wharton, R. (1986). Alcoholism and severe child maltreatment. *American Journal of Orthopsychiatry, 56,* 481–485.

Fantuzzo, J. W. (1999). Prevalence and effects of child exposure to domestic violence. *The Future of Children. Domestic Violence and Children, 9,* 21–32.

Fantuzzo, J. W., Stovall, A., Schachtel, D., Goins, C., & Hall, R. (1987). The effects of peer social initiations on the social behavior of withdrawn maltreated preschool children. *Journal of Behavior Therapy and Experimental Psychiatry, 18,* 357–363.

Farber, E. A., & Egeland, B. (1987). Invulnerability among abused and neglected children. In E. J. Anthony & B. J. Cohler (Eds.), *The invulnerable child* (pp. 253–288). New York: Guilford.

Farmer, E., & Owen, M. (1998). Gender and the child protection process. *The British Journal of Social Work, 28,* 545–564.

Frodi, A. M., & Lamb, M. (1980). Child abuser's responses to infant smiles and cries. *Child Development, 51,* 238–241.

Fryer, G. E., & Miyoshi, T. J. (1994). A survival analysis of the revictimization of children: The case of Colorado. *Child Abuse & Neglect, 18,* 1063–1071.

Garbarino, J., & Giliam, G. (1980). *Understanding abusive families.* Lexington, MA: Lexington.

Gelinas, D. J. (1983). The persisting negative effects of incest. *Psychiatry, 46,* 312–332.

George, C., & Main, M. (1980). Social interactions of young abused children: Approach, avoidance and aggression. *Child Development, 50,* 306–318.

Gershater-Molko, R. M., & Lutzker, J. R. (1999). Child neglect. In R. T. Ammerman & M. Hersen (Eds.), *Assessment of family violence* (pp. 157–183). New York: Wiley.

Hansen, D. J., Pallotta, G. M., Tishelman, A. C., & Conaway, L. P. (1989). Parental problem-solving skills and child behavior problems: A comparison of physically abusive, neglectful, clinic, and community families. *Journal of Family Violence, 4,* 353–368.

Hansen, D. J., & Warner, J. E. (1992). Child physical abuse and neglect. In R. T Ammerman and M. Hersen (Eds.), *Assessment of family violence* (pp. 123–147). New York: Wiley.

Haskett, M. E. (1990). Social problem-solving skills of young physically abused children. *Child Psychiatry and Human Development, 21,* 109–118.

Hennessy, K., Rabideau, G., Cicchetti, D., & Cummings, E. M. (1994). Responses of physically abused and nonabused children to different forms of inter-adult anger. *Child Development*, 65, 815–828.

Herrenkohl, R. C., Herrenkohl, E. C., & Egolf, B. P. (1983). Circumstances surrounding the occurrence of child maltreatment. *Journal of Consulting and Clinical Psychology*, 51, 424–431.

Hrdy, S. B. (1999). *Mother nature: Maternal instincts and how they shape the human species.* New York: Ballantine Books.

Hughes, H. M., Parkinson, D., & Vargo, M. (1989). Witnessing spouse abuse and experiencing physical abuse: A "double whammy"? *Journal of Family Violence*, 4, 197–209.

Janoff-Bulman, R. (1992). *Shattered assumptions: Toward a new psychology of trauma.* New York: Free Press.

Jellinek, M. S., Murphy, J. M., Poitrast, F., Quinn, D., Bishop, S. J., & Goshko, M. (1992). Serious child mistreatment in Massachusetts: The course of 206 children through the courts. *Child Abuse & Neglect*, 16, 179–185.

Kadushin, A. (1967). *Child welfare services.* New York: Macmillian.

Kagitcibasi, C. (1982). Old-age security value of children. Cross-national socioeconomic factors. *Journal of Cross Cultural Psychology*, 13, 29–42.

Kalmuss, D. (1984). The intergenerational transmission of marital aggression. *Journal of Marriage and the Family*, 46, 11–19.

Kalmuss, D., Davidson, A., & Cushman, L. (1992). Parenting expectations, experiences, and adjustment to parenthood. *Journal of Marriage and the Family*, 54, 516–526.

Kaplan, S. J., Pelcovitz, D., & LaBruna, V. (1999). Child and adolescent abuse and neglect research. *Journal of the American Academy of Child & Adolescent Psychiatry*, 38, 1214–1222.

Kaufman, J., & Zigler, E. (1987). Do abused children become abusive parents? *American Journal of Orthopsychiatry*, 57, 186–192.

Kavanagh, K., & Hops, H. (1994). Good girls? Bad boys? Gender and development as contexts for diagnosis and treatment. *Advances in Clinical Child Psychology*, 16, 45–79.

Keller, H., & Zach, U. (2002). Gender and birth order as determinants of parental behaviour. *Journal of Behavioral-Development*, 26, 177–184.

Korbin, J. E. (1994). Sociocultural factors in child maltreatment. In G. B. Melton and F. D. Barry (Eds.), *Protecting children from abuse and neglect* (pp. 182–223). New York: Guilford.

Larrance, D. T., & Twentyman, C. T. (1983). Maternal attributions in child abuse. *Journal of Abnormal Psychology*, 92, 449–457.

Lipovsky, J. A. (1991). Posttraumatic stress disorder in children. *Family and Community Health*, 14, 42–51.

Loos, M. E., & Alexander, P. C. (1997). Differential effects associated with self-reported histories of abuse and neglect in a college sample. *Journal of Interpersonal Violence*, 12, 340–360.

Mailcall. (2001, July 23). Motherhood's darkest moment. *Newsweek*, 2001.

Mak, A. S. (1994). Parental neglect and overprotection as risk factors in delinquency. *Australian Journal of Psychology*, 46, 107–111.

Markus, H., & Oyserman, D. (1989). Gender and thought: The role of the self-concept. In M. Crawford & M. Gentry (Eds.), *Gender and thought: Psychological perspectives* (pp. 100–127). Harrisonburg, VA: RR. Donnelley.

Margolin, G. (1998). Effects of domestic violence. In P. K. Trickett & C. J. Shellenbach (Eds.), *Violence against children in the family and the community* (pp. 57–102). Washington, DC: APA.

Mason, M. (1994). *From father's property to children's rights.* New York: Columbia Unversity Press.

McGloin, J., & Widom, C. S. (2001). Resilience among abused and neglected children grown up. *Development and Psychopathology*, 13, 1021–1038

Melchert, T. P. (2000). Clarifying the effects of parental substance abuse, child sexual abuse, and parental caregiving on adult adjustment. *Professional Psychology: Research and Practice*, 31, 64–69.

Miller, L. R., & Azar, S. T. (1996). The pervasiveness of maladaptive attributions in mothers at-risk for child abuse. *Family Violence and Sexual Abuse Bulletin, 12,* 31–37.

Miller, L. B., & Fisher, T. (1992). Some obstacles to the effective investigation and registration of children at risk: Issues gleaned from a worker's perspective. *Journal of Social Work Practice, 6,* 129–140.

Milner, J. S. (1986). *The Child Abuse Potential Inventory* (2nd ed.). Webster, NC: Psytec.

Milner, J. S. (1993a). Social information processing and physical child abuse. *Clinical Psychology Review, 13,* 275–294.

Milner, J. S. (1993b). A disappearing act. *Critical Social Policy, 13,* 48–63.

Mitchell, G., Obradovich, S., Herring, F., & Tromborg, C. (1992). Reproducing gender in public places: Adults' attention to toddlers in three public locales. *Sex Roles, 26,* 323–330.

Naar-King, S., Silvern, V., Ryan, V., & Sebring, D. (2002). Type and severity of abuse as predictors of psychiatric symptoms in adolescence. *Journal of Family Violence, 17,* 133–149.

National Research Council. (1993). *Understanding child abuse and neglect.* Washington, DC: National Academy Press.

Newberger, E. H., Hampton, R. L., Marx, T. J., & White, K. M. (1986). Child abuse and pediatric social illness. *American Journal of Orthopsychiatry, 56,* 589–601.

Obeidallah, D. A., & Burton, L. M. (1999). Affective ties between mothers and daughters in adolescent childbearing families. In M. J. Cox & J. Brooks-Gunn (Eds.), *Conflict and cohesion in families. Causes and consequences* (pp. 37–49). Mahweh, NJ: Erlbaum.

O'Hagan, K. (1997). The problem of engaging men in child protection work. *British Journal of Social Work, 27,* 25–42.

Oldershaw, L., Walters, G. C., & Hall, D. K. (1989). A behavioral approach to the classification of different types of abusive mothers. *Merrill-Palmer Quarterly, 35,* 255–279.

Olds, D. L., Henderson, C. R., Chamberlin, R., & Tatelbaum, R. (1986). Preventing child abuse and neglect: A randomized trial of nurse home visitation. *Pediatrics, 78,* 65–78.

O'Leary, D. K., Malone, J., & Tyree, A. (1994). Physical aggression in early marriage: Pre-relationship and relationship effects. *Journal of Consulting and Clinical Psychology, 62,* 594–602.

Olsen, N., (2000). Exploring the relationships among perceptions of childhood emotional neglect, perceptions of inequity in current relationships, and relationally triggered anger incidents. Masters thesis, Clark University.

Ovwigho, P. C., Leavitt, K. L., & Born, C. E. (2003). Risk factors for child abuse and neglect among former TANF families. *Children and Youth Services Review, 25,* 139–163.

Pajer, K. A. (1998). What happens to "bad" girls? A review of the adult outcomes of antisocial adolescent girls. *American Journal of Psychiatry, 155,* 862–870

Parke, R. D., & Collmer, C. W. (1975). Child abuse: An interdisciplinary analysis. In E. M. Hetherington (Ed.), *Review of child development research* (Vol. 5, pp. 509–590). Chicago: University of Chicago Press.

Patterson, G. R. (1982). *Coercive family processes.* Eugene, OR: Castlia.

Pelton, L. H. (1994). The role of material factors in child abuse and neglect. In G. B. Melton, & F. D. Barry (Eds.), *Protecting children from abuse and neglect: Foundations for a new national strategy* (pp. 131–181). New York: Guilford.

Perez, C. M., & Widom, C. S. (1994). Childhood victimization and long-term intellectual and academic outcomes. *Child Abuse & Neglect, 18,* 617–633.

Personal Responsibility and Work Opportunity Reconciliation Act of 1996. *Public Law 104–193,* section 103,110 Stat. 2113.

Plotkin, R. C., Azar, S. T., Twentyman, C. T., & Perri, M. G. (1981). A critical evaluation of the research methodology employed in the investigation of causative factors of child abuse and neglect. *International Journal of Child Abuse and Neglect, 1,* 449–455.

Powers, J. L., Eckenrode, J., & Jaklitsch, B. (1990). Maltreatment among runaway and homeless youth. *Child Abuse & Neglect, 14,* 87–98.

Quigley, R. M., & Leonard, K. E. (1996). Desistance of husband aggression in the early years of marraige. *Violence and Victims, 11,* 355–370.

Robyn, S., & Fremouw, W. J. (1996). Cognitive and affective styles of parents who physically abuse their children. *American Journal of Forensic Psychology, 14,* 63–79.

Rohrbeck, C. A., & Twentyman, C. T. (1986). A multimodal assessment of impulsiveness in abusing, neglectful, and nonmaltreating mothers and their preschool children. *Journal of Consulting and Clinical Psychology, 54,* 231–236.

Rosenthal, J. A. (1993). Outcomes of adoption of children with special needs. *The Future of Children, 3,* 77–88.

Rutter, M. (1979). Maternal deprivation 1972–1978. *Child Development, 50,* 283–305.

Sameroff, A. J., & Chandler, M. J. (1975). Reproductive risk and the continuum of caretaking casualty. In D. Horowitz, M. Hetherington, S. Scarr, S. Salapatek, & G. Siegel (Eds.), *Review of child development research* (Vol. 4, pp. 187–243). Chicago: University of Chicago Press.

Salzinger, S., Kaplan, S., & Artemyeff, C. (1983). Mother's personal social networks and child maltreatment. *Journal of Abnormal Psychology, 92,* 68–72.

Salzinger, S., Kaplan, S., Pelcovitz, D., Samit, C., & Krieger, R. (1984). Parent and teacher assessment of children's behavior in child maltreating families. *Journal of the American Academy of Child Psychiatry, 23,* 458–464.

Saunders, D. G. (1994). Child custody decisions in families experiencing woman abuse. *Social Work, 39,* 51–59.

Schilling, R. F., & Schinke, S. P. (1984). Maltreatment and mental retardation. *Perspectives and Progress in Mental Retardation, 1,* 11–22.

Sedlak, A. J., & Broadhurst, D. B. (1996). *Third National Incidence Study of child abuse and neglect. Final report.* Washington, DC: U.S. Department of Health and Human Services.

Shiono, P. H., & Quinn, L. S. (1994). Epidemiology of divorce. *The Future of Children, 4,* 15–28.

Starr, R. H., MacLean, D. J., & Keating, D. P. (1991). Life span developmental outcomes of child maltreatment. In R. Starr & D. A. Wolfe (Eds.), *The effects of child abuse and neglect* (pp. 1–32). New York: Guilford.

Szykula, S. A., & Fleischman, M. J. (1985). Reducing out of home placements of abused children: Two controlled studies. *Child Abuse & Neglect, 9,* 277–284.

Thompson, R. B. (1999). Gender differences in preschoolers' help-eliciting communication. *Journal of Genetic Psychology, 160,* 357–368.

Thorpe, D. (1994). *Evaluating child protection.* Buckingham: Open University Press.

Todorov, A., & Bargh, J. A. (2002). Automatic sources of aggression. *Aggression and Violent Behavior, 7,* 53–68

Trickett, P. K. (1993). Maladaptive development of school-aged physically abused children: Relationships with the childrearing context. *Journal of Family Psychology, 7,* 134–147.

Trickett, P. K., Aber, J. L., Carlson, V., & Cicchetti, D. (1991). Relationship of socioeconomic status to the etiology and developmental sequelae of physical child abuse. *Developmental Psychology, 27,* 148–158.

Trickett, P. K., & Kuczynski, L. (1986). Children's misbehaviors and parental discipline strategies in abusive and nonabusive families. *Developmental Psychology, 22,* 115–123.

Trickett, P. K., & Putnam, F. W. (1993). Impact of child sexual abuse on females: Toward a developmental, psychobiological integration. *Psychological Science, 4,* 81–87.

Tymchuk, A. J. (1998). The importance of matching educational interventions to parent needs in child maltreatment. In J. R. Lutzker (Ed.), *Handbook of child abuse research and treatment* (pp. 421–448). New York: Plenum.

Wahler, R. G., & Dumas, J. E. (1989). Attentional problems in dysfunctional mother–child interactions: An interbehavioral model. *Psychological Bulletin, 105,* 116–130.

Wauchope, B. A., & Straus, M. A. (1987, July). *Age, class, and gender differences in physical punishment and physical abuse of American children.* Paper presented at the National Conference of Family Violence Research, Durham, NH.

Way, I., Chung, S., Jonson-Reid, M., & Drake, B. (2001). Maltreatment perpetrators: A 54-month analysis of recidivism. *Child Abuse & Neglect, 25,* 1093–1108.

Widom, C. S. (1989). Does violence beget violence? A critical examination of the literature. *Psychological Bulletin, 106,* 3–28.

Widom, C. S. (1998). Childhood victimization. In D. P. Dohrenwend (Ed.), *Adversity, stress, and psychopathology* (pp. 81–94). Oxford: Oxford University Press.

Williams, G. (1983). The urgency of authentic prevention. *Journal of Clinical Child Psychology, 12,* 312–319.

Wolfe, D. A. (1987). *Child abuse: Implications for child development and psychopathology.* Newbury Park, CA: Sage.

Wolfe, D. A., Fairbanks, J. A., Kelly, J. A., & Bradlyn, A. S. (1983). Child abusive parents' physiological responses to stressful and non-stressful behavior in children. *Behavioral Assessment, 5,* 363–371.

Wolfe, D. A., Wekerle, C., Reitzel-Jaffe, D., Grasley, C., Pittman, A., & MacEachran, A. (1997). Interrupting the cycle of violence. In D. A. Wolfe, R. J. McMahon, & R. D. Peters (Eds.), *Child abuse. New directions in prevention and treatment across the lifespan* (pp. 102–129). Thousand Oaks, CA: Sage.

Wright, S. A. (1994). Physical and emotional abuse and neglect of preschool children: A literature review. *Australian Occupational Therapy Journal, 41,* 55–63.

Wyatt, G. E., & Newcomb, M. (1990). Internal and external mediators of sexual abuse in childhood. *Journal of Consulting and Clinical Psychology, 60,* 167–173.

Zanarini, M. C., Frankenburg, F. R., Reich, B. D., Marino, M. F., Lewis, R. E., Williams, A. A., & Khera, G. S. (2000). Biparental failure in the childhood experiences of borderline patients. *Journal of Personality Disorders, 14,* 264–273.

Zeanah, C. J., & Zeanah, P. D. (1989). Intergenerational transmission of maltreatment: Insights from attachment theory and research. *Psychiatry, 52,* 177–196.

Zelizer, V. A. (1985). *Pricing the priceless children.* New York: Basic Books.

Zuravin, S. J. (1991). Research definitions of child physical abuse and neglect. In R. H. Starr and D. A. Wolfe (Eds.), *The effects of child abuse and neglect: Issues and research* (pp. 100–128). New York: Guilford.

12

The Consequences of Child Sexual Abuse for Female Development

PENELOPE K. TRICKETT, DAWN A. KURTZ, and JENNIE G. NOLL

Only in about the last two decades have people realized that the sexual abuse of children in America occurs frequently. Prior to that time sexual abuse, and especially familial sexual abuse or incest, was viewed as very rare. The National Center of Child Abuse and Neglect (NCCAN) sponsored three national incidence studies that were published in 1980 (Burgdorf, 1980), 1988 (NCCAN, 1988), and 1996 (NCCAN, 1996). All of these studies examined the annual incidence of child maltreatment in a representative sample of counties across the United States. Sexual abuse was one of four types of maltreatment examined and was defined as, "The . . . use, persuasion, . . . or coercion of any child to engage in . . . any sexually explicit conduct . . . or the rape, . . . statutory rape, molestation, prostitution, or other form of sexual exploitation of children, or incest with children" (NCCAN, 1996). The Third National Incidence and Prevalence Study (NCCAN, 1996) documented that each year approximately 300,000 children are recognized (by public agencies such as protective service and mental health agencies and the schools) as being sexually abused. This is a rate of between five and seven per thousand American children known to be sexually abused each year. It represents an increase in recognized cases of child sexual abuse of more than 100% from 1988 (NCCAN, 1988) and of more than 600% from 1980 to 1996 (NCCAN, 1996).

A number of prevalence studies suggest even higher rates than are suggested by this work on annual incidence. In separate studies, for example,

PENELOPE K. TRICKETT, DAWN A. KURTZ, and JENNIE G. NOLL • University of Southern California, Los Angeles, California, 90089-0411.

Russell (1986) and Finkelhor and his colleagues (1990) report prevalence rates between 27% and 38%. Other prevalence studies have reported rates ranging from a low of 6% to a high of 62% (Peters et al., 1986). Prevalence rates should be higher than annual incidence rates, because they represent cumulative childhood experiences and because they include more than just those cases recognized by official agencies. Usually retrospective prevalence studies indicate that in the majority of cases the abuse was never reported to authorities (Russell, 1986). Some recent reports claim that yearly estimates of reported childhood sexual abuse rose steadily in the 1980s, peaking in the early 1990s and, due to changes in protective service procedures and policy as well as increased prevention and criminal justice efforts, have been declining ever since (Jones, Finkelhor, & Kopiek, 2001). Even if substantiated cases of childhood sexual abuse appear to be on the decline, the fact remains sexual abuse occurs more frequently than previously realized, though it cannot be stated with certainty how frequently it occurs.

These incidences and prevalence studies have also identified other characteristics of sexual abuse of particular relevance to this chapter. First, in contrast to other forms of abuse and neglect where males and females are equally likely to be victims, in almost all reports of sexual abuse females are found to be the victims more often than males, the ratio being approximately four to one. Second, for female victims as compared with males, the abuser is more likely to be a relative or family friend and thus occurs within a family context that has implications for development. Third, as indicated in Figure 1, sexual abuse occurs across childhood from infancy through adolescence. For females the average age at onset of the abuse is between 7 and 8 years of age and the mean duration is about two years. (For male victims, the peak age at onset is prior to puberty,

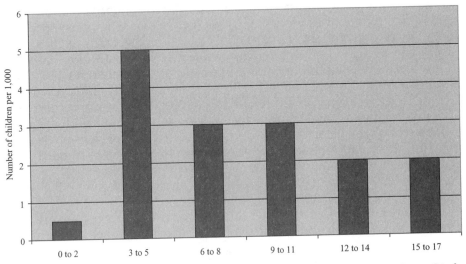

Figure 1. Age differences in sexual abuse (adapted from 3rd National Incidence Study, NCCAN, 1996)

as for females, but the duration of the abuse tends to be less; Burgdorf, 1980; NCCAN, 1988). It is important to consider sexual abuse as a *repeated* trauma, rather than a one time event (Putnam & Trickett, 1993). Fourth, poverty is associated with the likelihood of sexual abuse making victims thus vulnerable to the pernicious effects of both poverty and abuse.

In sum, girls are sexually abused more often than boys and more often by a family member than boys are. The sexual abuse frequently occurs prior to puberty and, on average, occurs repeatedly over an extended period of time. Furthermore, girls who are sexually abused are more likely to be poor, an additional developmental risk factor. Taken together, all these features suggest that sexual abuse of girls is likely to have adverse developmental consequences during childhood, adolescence, and adulthood. In particular it has been hypothesized that sexual abuse of girls may have both psychological and psychobiological effects because of the stress or trauma involved that (1) may affect the transition (and perhaps even timing) of puberty and (2) may be exacerbated by poor or disrupted family support that can be critical for development in adolescence and beyond. (See Trickett & Putnam, 1993, for an in-depth examination of this developmental, psychobiological perspective.)

The purpose of this chapter is to examine what is known about the developmental consequences of sexual abuse for female development. Research on the effects of sexual abuse has proliferated in recent years and a number of reviews of this research have previously been published (see, e.g., Beitchman, Zucker, Hood, daCosta, & Akman, 1991; Beitchman, Zucker, Hood, daCosta, Akman, & Cassavia, 1992; Kendall-Tackett, Williams, & Finkelhor, 1993; Trickett & McBride-Chang, 1995; Trickett & Putnam, 1998). This chapter updates these prior reviews with an emphasis on where the cumulative knowledge about the impact of sexual abuse now stands and where the field is, or should be, heading.

Prior to beginning this review, a few caveats are in order. With a very few notable exceptions, research on sexual abuse has used two basic designs. Each has some inherent limitations. First, short-term or acute impact has been assessed using cross-sectional designs in samples of children and adolescents after sexual abuse has been officially identified or disclosed. Second, long-term impact has been assessed using retrospective designs in samples of adults who report themselves to have been abused as children. There are few longitudinal studies and even fewer that have followed sexually abused children for more than one or two years or across developmental stages. While cross-sectional designs can provide knowledge on developmental processes and change, most of the cross-sectional studies concerning child abuse have not been designed carefully enough to do so. In fact, a number do not consider age or developmental stage as a variable even when samples include participants who range widely in age.

This is a particular difficulty with cross-sectional designs in the area of child sexual abuse because aspects of the abuse can easily be confounded with the age or developmental stage of the research participants. For example, the type of abuse and its frequency or duration are likely to differ depending on whether the child is three, or eight, or twelve. A cross-sectional design usually does not allow one to disentangle these factors.

Retrospective designs also have some inherent limitations. The most serious problem concerns the distortions of memory which can occur with the passage of time and with experience (see, for example, Brewin, Andrews, & Gotlib, 1993). In the area of child sexual abuse this is particularly problematic for two reasons. First, sexual abuse has been shown to affect memory under certain circumstances as yet not fully understood. In some cases it has been shown to be associated with amnesias and other types of forgetting (see, e.g., Feldman-Summers, & Pope, 1994; Putnam & Carlson, 1993; Williams, 1994). Some also express concerns that "false memories" of sexual abuse experiences can be induced under certain circumstances (see, e.g., Loftus, 1994). A second related problem with the use of retrospective designs in studies of the impact of child sexual abuse on adults is that the information used to classify a research subject as "abused" is based entirely on that person's memory and perceptions, which is quite different from the way this classification takes place in the studies involving children. In studies involving children, samples almost always come from an agency (such as a county child protective services agency), which determines the presence of abuse based on a number of sources of evidence including, but not limited to, self-report.

Although these characteristics of the adult studies can be viewed as problematic, it is important to review this research because it provides the main extant evidence on the long term effects of child sexual abuse. In addition, these studies as a group have strengths as well. They are quite varied when it comes to sampling strategy, drawing from large and not so large community samples, university samples, and samples coming from professional organizations (e.g., nurses). In general, the samples are larger than the child studies (with sample sizes most often in the hundreds), so they do not share the statistical power problems which some of the smaller child studies have.

As noted earlier, there are few long-term longitudinal studies, In fact only two have been identified, both of which are ongoing. One of these is being conducted by Widom (see, e.g., Widom, 1989; Widom & Kuhns, 1996; McGloin & Widom, 2001). This study employed a large number of abused and neglected male and female children (over 600, approximately 100 of whom were sexually abused) and a particularly well-matched comparison group (over 500; same sex, race, date of birth (+/− 1 week), or same class in the same elementary school for older children). Participants were followed up approximately 20 years after their childhood victimization and assessed across a wide range of domains of functioning including cognitive, emotional, psychiatric, social and interpersonal, occupational and general health, (see Table 2). This study has many strengths, but also suffers some shortfalls including a large attrition rate (over 25% over 20 years), a relatively broad definition of what constituted childhood sexual abuse (e.g., from "assault and battery with intent to gratify sexual desires" to "fondling or touching in an obscene manner", to "sodomy" and "incest"), and, in many cases, single item, dichotomous outcome variables (e.g., promiscuity is defined as "having had sex with 10 or more people within any single year"). Regardless of these problems, there is no doubt that this study has broadened our knowledge of the long-term consequences of sexual abuse and has underscored the importance of following victims through development and assessing a broad range of outcomes.

The second longitudinal study, initiated by Putnam and Trickett (see, e.g., Putnam & Trickett, 1993; Trickett & Putnam, 1993), consists of a sample of approximately 160 females, half of whom were sexually abused by a family member and half of whom are a demographically similar comparison group. At the inception of the study, these participants ranged from 6 to 16 years of age (mean age = 11). To date, five assessments have been completed and the sixth is underway. The focus of this study has been on the psychobiological correlates of sexual abuse and on the impact on important developmental tasks as the young women transition from childhood, to adolescence, to young adulthood. Many cross-sectional and longitudinal findings of this study and the Widom study are included in Tables 1 and 2.

Besides the limitations stemming from the research designs employed, the extant research on child sexual abuse has other shortcomings. Detailing many of these is beyond the scope of this paper (see the reviews previously cited or the National Research Council (1993) publication on research knowledge on child abuse and neglect). A few of these shortcomings need to be described, because they affected how the present review was conducted and how the conclusions can be interpreted. First, many studies on sexual abuse, especially early ones, did not include an appropriate control or comparison group. This is a basic flaw given the clear research evidence that many of the outcome measures of interest in child abuse research are adversely influenced by poverty or low social class status and thus without an appropriate comparison group, one cannot distinguish between abuse effects and poverty effects (see Trickett, Aber, Carlson, & Cicchetti, 1991). For the present review, only studies with an appropriate comparison group have been considered. That is, studies with no comparison group are not reviewed, nor are those which compare groups of abused children to test norms, or those which have a clinical comparison group only (e.g., studies which compare abused psychiatric patients with nonabused psychiatric patients only). A further requirement for inclusion is that evidence was provided that the groups are comparable on relevant demographic characteristics, especially SES, or statistical methods were used to control the differences.

Another problem with the extant research is that the definition and description of the sexual abuse experienced by the research participants has been inconsistent and, in some cases, too sketchy to allow the reader to understand what it is, exactly, that the child experienced. Sexual abuse differs from other forms of child maltreatment in that it varies more in terms of whether parents (or parent figures) or persons other than a parent are the

Table 1. Summary of Research Findings on the Impact of Sexual Abuse—Early and Middle to Late Childhood

	Early Childhood	Middle to Late Childhood
Physical/Motor Development	Enuresis (esp. girls) (1) Somatic complaints (esp. boys; 1)	Genital abnormalities (3) Enuresis (4) Elevated, disregulated cortisol (5,6) Increased catecholamines (20) Immunological problems (17) Not greater somatic complaints (2) More physical problems (19)
Social/Emotional Developmental	Innappropriate sexual behavior (1,2) Internalizing problems-anxiety, social withdrawal (1,2)	Inappropriate sexual behavior and sexual activity (3,7,8,9) Internalizing (esp. depression) and externalizing (esp. aggression, conduct disorder) problems (2,4,10,19) Dissociation (11,19) Anxiety (18) Anxiety higher initially but not at follow-up (12) Anxiety and PTSD not higher (4) Small and unsatisfactory peer networks (13) Classroom behavior problems (14) Lower self-concept (12,19)
Cognitive/Academic Development	Developmental delay (1)	Not lower grades but lower overall academic performance and more learning problems (teacher ratings; 14) Low overall academic performance (15) Not lower grades and test scores (school records; 16) Attention Deficit Hyperactive Disorder (ADHD; 4)

[1]White, Halpin, Strom, & Santilli, 1988; [2]Friedrich, Beilke, & Urquiza, 1987; [3]Kolko, Moser, & Weldy, 1990; [4]Trickett & Putnam, 1991; [5]DeBellis, Chrousos, Dorn, Burke, Helmers, & Kling, et al. 1994; [6]Putnam & Trickett, 1991; [7]Deblinger, McLeer, Atkins, Ralphe, & Foa, 1989; [8]Einbender & Friedrich, 1989; [9]Goldston, Turnquist, & Knutson, 1989; [10]McBride-Chang, Trickett, Horn, & Putnam, 1992; [11]Putnam, Helmers, & Trickett, 1993; [12]Mannarino, Cohen, Smith, & Moore-Motily, 1991; [13]Helmers, Everett, & Trickett, 1991; [14]Trickett, McBride-Chang, & Putnam, 1994; [15]Tong, Oates, & McDowell, 1987; [16]Eckenrode, Laird, & Doris, 1993; [17]DeBellis, Burke, Trickett, & Putnam, 1996; [18]Nash, Hulsey, Sexton, Harralson, & Lambert, 1993; [19]Trickett, Noll, Reiffman, & Putnam 2001; [20]DeBellis, Lefter, Trickett, & Putnam, 1994.

perpetrators. In some research, samples are limited to intrafamilial abuse (which includes perpetrators who are parents as well as non-parental figures such as uncles or older siblings). In other cases, extrafamilial cases are also included. Also, in some studies, the participants experience a wide variety of different types of sexual abuse from indecent exposure to repeated violent rape. For some studies, it is unclear what types of sexual abuse are included.

Almost all of the research on sexual abuse has had samples that are all female or that are overwhelmingly female (e.g., 10% male). A third limitation

Table 2. Summary of Research Findings on the Impact of Sexual Abuse—Adolescence and Adulthood

	Adolescence	Adulthood
Physical/Motor Development	Elevated, disregulated cortisol (2,3) Increased catecholamines (26) Immunological dysfunction (27) No somatic complaints (28) Long-term health problems (e.g. digestive problems; 29*) More doctors visits/hospitalizations (29*) More rapid pubertal growth (pubic hair only; 57) Higher Body Mass Indices (BMI) (58) No difference in age at menarche (58)	Somatic complaints (12)
Social/Emotional Development	Internalizing and externalizing problems (1,4,5) More aggressive and more depression/withdrawn behaviors (single perpetrator abuse only; 59) Suicidal or self-injurious behavior (10) More male peers in social network (6) Earlier sexual activity, including coitus, and more sexual partners (11) Illegal acts, running away (10) Depression (30) Dissociation (biological father abuse only) (59) Revictimization (e.g. unwanted sexual contact) (32) Eating disturbance (e.g. weight dissatisfaction, purging behavior; 33) No difference in purging behavior when controlling family dysfunction (34) Less preoccupation with sex & increased use of birth control when happy with males in social network (35) Higher abortion rate when physically active with boyfriend in childhood (35)	Alcohol and/or drug abuse (13,14) DSM-III diagnosis of antisocial personality, affective and anxiety disorders (14) Depression (15,16,37,38,39,40,41,42) Anxiety (16,17,18,38,43) High Global Severity Index and symptomatology of depression, anxiety, and psychoticism (12,19) Poor social adjustment, more social isolation, interpersonal problems (20,40,43) More marriage disruption and dissatisfaction with sex (21,44) Maladaptive sexual adjustment relative to physical abuse victims (22) No difference in sexual dysfunction or dissatisfaction (19,41) More preoccupation with sex, younger at 1st voluntary intercourse, lower birth control efficacy (45) Revictimization (e.g., rape, battering; 17,23,46,56) Child rearing problems (24,25) Increased prostitution (47,48) Teen pregnancy (45,49) No teen pregnancy (48,50) Suicidal ideation/self-harm (51,56)

(Continued)

Table 2. (*Continued*)

	Adolescence	Adulthood
		Dissociation (41,52)
		Reluctance to disclose sexual information to partner (53)
Cognitive/Academic Development	Not lower grades but lower overall academic performance, and learning problems (7)	Poor short-term memory (54) Lower IQ (55)
	Not lower grades and test scores (school records; 9)	
	Lower IQ & school achievement (4)	
	Lower overall academic performance (8)	
	Lower scores on crystallized & fluid ability (36)	

*Covers period from late adolescence to early adulthood.
[1]Trickett & Putnam, 1991; [2]DeBellis, Chrousos, Dorn, Burke, Helmers, & Kling, et al. 1994; [3]Putnam & Trickett, 1991; [4]Einbender & Friedrich, 1989; [5]McBride-Chang, Trickett, Horn, & Putnam, 1992; [6]Helmers, Everett, & Trickett, 1991; [7]Trickett, McBride-Chang, & Putnam, 1994; [8]Tong, Oates, & McDowell, 1987; [9]Eckenrode, Laird, & Doris, 1993; [10]Kendall-Tackett, Williams, & Finkelhor, 1993; [11]Wyatt, 1988; [12]Greenwald, Leitenberg, Cado, & Tarran, 1990; [13]Peters, 1988; [14]Stein, Golding, Siegel, Burnam, & Sorenson, 1988; [15]Mullen, Romans-Clarkson, Walton, & Herbison, 1988; [16]Sedney & Brooks, 1984; [17]Fromuth, 1986; [18]Murphy, Kilpatrick, Amick-McMullen, Veronen, Paduhovich, & Best, et al. 1988; [19]Fromuth & Burkhart, 1989; [20]Harter, Alexander, & Neimeyer, 1988; [21]Finkelhor, Hotaling, Lewis, & Smith, 1989; [22]Briere, & Runtz, 1990; [23]Russell, 1986; [24]Cole, Woolger, Power, & Smith, 1992; [25]Burkett, 1991; [26]DeBellis, Lefter, Trickett, & Putnam, 1994; [27]DeBellis, Burke, Trickett, & Putnam, 1996; [28]Friedrich, Beilke, & Urquiza, 1987; [29]Sickel, Noll, Moore, Putnam, & Trickett, 2002; [30]Lipovsky, Saunders, & Murphy, 1989; [31]Putnam, Helmers, & Trickett, 1993; [32]Krahe, Scheinberger-Olwig, Waizenhofer, & Kolpin, 1999; [33]Wonderlich, Crosby, & Mitchell, et al. 2000; [34]Perkins & Luster, 1999; [35]Noll, Trickett, & Putnam, 2000; [36]Trickett, Noll, Horn, & Putnam, 2001; [37]Hunter, 1991; [38]Buist & Janson, 2001; [39]Zuravin & Fonatanella, 1999; [40]Whiffen, Thompson, & Aube, 2000; [41]Kamsner, & McCabe, 2000; [42]Bifulco, Brown, & Adler, 1991; [43]Abdulrehman & De Luca, 2001; [44]Mullen, Martin, Anderson, Romans, & Herbison, 1996; [45]Noll, Trickett, & Putnam, 2003, in press; [46]Messman-Moore & Long, 2000; [47]Widom & Shepard, 1996; [48]Widom & Kuhns, 1996; [49]Herrenkohl et al, 1998; [50]Smith, 1996; [51]Gutierrez, Thakkar, & Kuczen, 2000; [52]Nash, Hulsey, Sexton, Harralson, & Lambert, 1993; [53]Nereo, Farber, & Hinton, 2002; [54]Bremner, Randall, & Scott, et al, 1995; [55]Perez & Widom, 1994; [56]Noll, Horowitz, Norris, Bonanno, Trickett, & Putnam, 2002; [57]Trickett, Ghisletta, Horn, Noll, & Putnam, 1998; [58]Trickett, Noll, & Putnam, 1999; [59]Trickett, Noll, Reiffman, & Putnam, 2001.

of extant research is that, for the most part, research that has included male participants has not examined sex differences, because the number of males was so small. It is impossible to know how the results are affected by the small number of males in the sample. (Two of the adult studies reviewed have samples with both males and females—in both of these cases the samples were large and sex differences were examined. For this review only the findings for females are included.)

SEQUELAE OF SEXUAL ABUSE

Tables 1 and 2 summarize research findings and are organized developmentally. Table 1 covers early childhood (roughly from birth to age 6) and mid-to-late childhood (the elementary school years, roughly from 6 to 11 or 12 years of age). Table 2 covers adolescence (the secondary school years) and adulthood. The tables draw from cross-sectional, retrospective, and longitudinal studies. It is important to note that occasionally samples overlap the age grouping listed here, for example, ages from 4 to 11, or 6 to 17. If, in these cases, age differences were not examined, but a significant group effect was found for the sample as a whole, it was entered in the column and table that best represents the age and stage of the sample.

The findings in the tables are organized into three general domains: (a) physical and motor status or development which includes chronic effects of the sexual abuse, such as illness, physiological or other biological effects, and somatic complaints (such as headaches or stomach aches), but excludes immediate, acute injuries associated with the abuse (e.g., bruises, anal tears, etc.); (b) social and emotional development which includes findings concerned with personality and social relationships as well as behavior problems, psychopathology, and social deviancy; and (c) cognitive and academic development and attainment. Entries in the table indicate that significant group differences have been found between the abused group and the comparison group (e.g., in Table 1, the entry "enuresis" in column one means that sexually abused children were found to have a significantly higher frequency of this problem than were children in a nonabused comparison group.) Occasionally, to emphasize an inconsistency in findings, an entry in a table will indicate what was "not found." So for example, in Table 1, somatic problems are listed (as found) in early childhood but as "not found" in middle childhood.

Early Childhood

Although it is clear from Figure 1 that sexual abuse of young children is not uncommon, little research on abuse in early childhood exists. Only two studies met the criteria for inclusion in this review. Neither included infants in their samples. One had toddlers and preschoolers, the other included children four and older. As can be seen, the major effects seem to be somatic problems (enuresis, stomach aches, and headaches); inappropriate sexual behavior (e.g., masturbating excessively and/or in public); internalizing problems (especially anxiety and withdrawal); and developmental delays (Friedrich, Beilke, & Urquiza, 1987; White, Halpin, Strom, & Santilli, 1988).

Mid-to-Late Childhood

Considerably more research involves school-age children. Some new findings emerge for this age group and some findings are consistent with the research on younger children. Inconsistencies exist as well. In the physical/motor domain, while enuresis still exists as a problem (Trickett & Putnam, 1991), one study found no greater somatic complaints at this age (Friedrich et al., 1987). Another, however, (Trickett, Noll, Reifman, & Putnam, 2001) found more physical problems such as stomach aches and headaches as reported by mothers among sexually abused girls as compared with nonabused girls. The genital abnormalities referred to in Table 1 are lasting physical anomalies resulting from injury (Kolko, Moser, & Weldy, 1990). At this age evidence also suggests some psychobiological effects similar to those that have been associated with high levels of stress, e.g., disregulated cortisol, elevated catecholamines, and suggestions of immune problems (DeBellis, Chrousos, et al., 1994; DeBellis, Lefter, Trickett, & Putnam, 1994; DeBellis, Burke, Trickett, & Putnam, 1996).

In the social/emotional realm, inappropriate sexual behaviors and internalizing problems are still found, as was true for younger children (e.g., Friedrich et al., 1987; Kolko et al., 1990; Deblinger, McLeer, Atkins, Ralphe, & Foa, 1989; McBride-Chang, Trickett, Horn, & Putnam, 1992). Findings about anxiety are inconsistent, however—some research shows anxiety levels to be elevated, as was true for the younger children (Nash, Hulsey, Sexton, Harralson, & Lambert, 1993; Mannarino, Cohen, Smith, & Moore-Motily, 1991), but some does not (Grayston, de Luca, & Boyes, 1992; Trickett & Putnam, 1991). In addition, different problems seem to emerge in middle childhood; externalizing problems (e.g., aggression and conduct problems), elevated dissociation, and difficulties with peer relationships are all more common among sexually abused girls than among nonabused controls (Friedrich et al., 1987; Trickett, Noll Horn, & Putnam, 2001;Trickett, McBride-Chang, & Putnam, 1994; Putnam, Helmers, & Trickett, 1993; Helmers, Everett, & Trickett, 1991).

Despite some inconsistent findings in the cognitive/academic domain, most research suggests that abused girls show poorer school performance than their nonabused peers. Poor school performance may not, however, be reflected in grades, but rather in teacher ratings and, in some cases, achievement test scores (Trickett, McBride-Chang, & Putnam, 1994; Tong, Oates, & McDowell, 1987). Lower scores on crystallized ability at this age have been found (Trickett, Noll, Horn, & Putnam, 2001). In addition, one study found increased diagnosis of Attention Deficit Hyperactivity Disorder (ADHD) in sexually abused females (Trickett & Putnam, 1991). This may be particularly significant because this study had an all female sample and the diagnosis of ADHD is usually quite rare for females.

Adolescence

The findings for adolescents are for the most part similar to those for school-aged children. That is, studies with adolescent female samples have found cortisol disregulation and other psychobiological problems (DeBellis Chronsos et al., 1994), both internalizing and externalizing problems (Einbender & Friedrich, 1989), heightened dissociation (Trickett et al., 2001), and cognitive and school performance problems (Einbender & Friedrich, 1989; Tong et al., 1987, Trickett et al., 2001). The difference, in most cases, relates to how certain types of behavior are manifested. Thus adolescent sexually abused girls as compared with younger sexually abused girls are more likely to be actively delinquent (Kendall-Tackett, Williams, & Finkelhor, 1993); engage in earlier and sometimes more high-risk sexual activity (Noll et al., 2003; Wyatt, 1998); are more likely to have eating disturbances (Krahe, Scheinberger-Olwig, Waizenhofer, & Kolpin, 1999); report more physical health problems (Sickel, Noll, Moore, Putnam, & Trickett, 2002); and carry out more suicidal and self-injurious behaviors (Kendall-Tackett et al., 1993; Wyatt, 1988; Noll et al., 2003).

To date only limited research has examined the relationship of sexual abuse to the timing of puberty and it is inconsistent in its findings. Sexually abused girls have been found to have accelerated pubic hair growth and increased body mass, but not earlier menarche or earlier breast development than comparison group females (Trickett, Ghisletta, Horn, Noll, & Putnam, 1998; Trickett, Noll, & Putnam, 1999).

Adulthood

It is important to remember that almost all the studies with adult samples reflect retrospective designs and self-reported abuse. What is most notable is that almost all of these studies focused on the social/emotional domain, emphasizing psychopathology. Only a few adult studies have considered the physical/motor domain, or the cognitive/academic domain. One study found somatization to be elevated in a sample of women abused as children (Greenwald, Leitenberg, Cado, & Tarran, 1990). Another (Sickel et al., 2002) found more long-term health problems and more doctor visits and hospitalizations as compared with a nonabused group of adolescent and young adult women. Two studies indicate low hippocampal density in samples of women with a history of physical and sexual abuse (Bremner, Randall, Vermettan, et al., 1995; Bremner, Randall, Scott, et al., 1995). One of these studies reported poor short-term memory among the abused women (Bremner, Randall, Scott, et al., 1995). In contrast, another study (Trickett, Noll, Horn, & Putnam, 2001) found no differences in short- or long-term memory but did find lower scores on measures of fluid and crystallized abilities in sexually abused adolescents and young women.

Within the social/emotional domain, the adult studies indicate elevated alcohol and/or drug abuse, and externalizing problems (e.g., diagnoses of antisocial personality; Peters, 1988; Stein, Golding, Siegel, Burnam, & Sorenson, 1988) among women who report sexual abuse. Many reports document problems with depression and anxiety (Stein et al., 1988; Mullen, Romans-Clarkson, Walton, & Herbison, 1988; Sedney & Brooks, 1984; Fromuth, 1986; Murphy, Kilpatrick, Amick-McMullen, Veronen, Paduhovich, Best, Villeponteaux, & Saunders, 1988). Marital and other interpersonal relationship problems are common (Finkelhor, Hotaling, Lewis, & Smith, 1989; Mullen, Martin, Anderson, Romans, & Herbison, 1996), but findings regarding sexual adjustment or dysfunction are inconsistent (Briere & Runtz, 1990; Finkelhor et al., 1989; Fromuth & Burkhart, 1989; Greenwald et al., 1990; Harter, Alexander, & Neimeyer, 1988). Studies show greater revictimization rates (i.e., likelihood of being raped or battered; Fromuth, 1986; Noll, Horowitz, Bonanno, Trickett, & Putnam, 2003; Russell, 1986) and problems with child rearing (Burkett, 1991; Cole, Woolger, Power, & Smith, 1992).

To summarize, in the physical/motor domain, physical problems of one sort or another are common in sexually abused females both in early childhood and in adulthood. In childhood, enuresis and somatic complaints such as headaches and stomach aches are common. In adulthood, similar somatic complaints have been found. Research with school-age children is scant and findings are inconsistent. For adolescents, long-term physical health problems and more doctor visits and hospitalizations are reported.

Evidence of psychobiological disturbance in sexual abuse victims is also beginning to emerge. To date, cortisol disregulation has been examined directly in school-aged children and adolescents only. A few new studies suggest the possibility of hippocampal damage in adults who were abused both physically and sexually as children. Prolonged exposure to elevated levels of cortisol is hypothesized to be, at least in part, the cause of this damage. As will be discussed later in this chapter, these findings have potentially important implications for both physical and mental health and for cognitive development.

In the social/emotional domain, elevated risk of internalizing problems is found in female sexual abuse victims of all ages. These generally take the form of depression and/or anxiety. There also seems to be an enhanced risk of suicide and self-injurious behaviors from adolescence onward. Externalizing problems such as aggression, conduct problems, and delinquency are found from middle childhood onward. Sometimes the form of these problems changes as the girl transitions from one developmental stage to the next (e.g., delinquency emerges in adolescence). There is no evidence of these problems in early childhood but a few studies examined these issues. Levels of dissociation are higher for sexual abuse victims from middle childhood onward. This has not been examined among younger children.

Sexual behavior problems are apparent from early childhood through adolescence and young adulthood. For the younger child, these take the form of sexualized behavior such as excessive masturbation. For the older child and adolescents, they take the form of early onset of sexual activity, a preoccupation with sex and, sometimes, teen pregnancy. The adult studies are inconsistent about whether sexual problems persist into adulthood. One reason for this inconsistency may be that sexual abuse can lead to different trajectories including sexual preoccupation, sexual aversion, or, in extreme cases, sexual ambiguity (Noll, et al., 2003). Of all the problems associated with sexual abuse, this domain seems to be the most exclusively associated with sexual abuse per se, and not with other forms of abuse or violence (Trickett & McBride-Chang, 1995).

In the cognitive/academic domain, reasonably consistent evidence suggests that sexually abused girls and adolescent females have problems with poor school performance. The nature of these problems is not clear—little research has studied basic cognitive abilities or memory with this population, although the finding of higher rates of ADHD and of elevated dissociation among sexually abused participants suggests that these girls may have attentional problems. Only two studies investigated memory in adults abused as children, and these had conflicting findings. One additional study indicated lower crystallized and fluid abilities among sexually abused adolescent and young adult females. Both the longitudinal studies reviewed (the Widom, Putnam, and Trickett studies) show that there are important long term (i.e., 10 or 20 years) correlates of child sexual abuse. Equally important is the finding from these and other studies that in young adulthood, the development of women abused as children varies considerably. Some show resilience or adaptive development while others show maladaptation (Trickett et al., 2001; Kurtz, 2003; Trickett, Kurtz, & Pizzigatti, in press). Our knowledge of the important mediators of this variability is still quite sketchy, but information is beginning to emerge.

Intervening or Mediating Factors

What are the mediators or moderators of the impact of sexual abuse on development? Few studies have tried to answer this question and it is rare to see such models explicitly tested in the research. One study, however, demonstrated that for girls, being happier with males (either peers or adults) in childhood social networks mediated the effect of sexual abuse on birth control efficacy and sexual preoccupation in adolescence (Noll, Trickett, & Putnam, 2000). Other analyses with these data indicated that abuse status moderated the relationship between number of males in childhood social networks and later social competence. That is, for the comparison group there was a positive relationship but for the abuse group a negative relationship between number of males in the social network at a younger age and perceived social competence at a later age (Kurtz, 2003).

Are there gender, ethnic group, or social class relationships? As noted, most of the research to date is on females—we know very little conclusively about male victims of sexual abuse or how the impact of sexual abuse might differ by gender. Most of what we know comes from a few adult studies (Stein et al., 1988; Fromuth, & Burkhart, 1989). These suggest that adult males abused as children are less likely to exhibit depression and anxiety than are females, but are equally or more likely to be diagnosed as antisocial personality and to have substance abuse problems. For men, the studies concerned with marital and sexual relationships tend to be inconsistent—some finding dissatisfaction and dysfunction and some not. None of the studies reviewed here investigated whether there is a connection between being sexually abused as a child and being a perpetrator of abuse as an adult. Clearly this and other gender related issues are important areas for further research.

Also, almost no research has focused on ethnic group or social class differences and developmental outcomes. One exception is the research of Wyatt (1988). In her study, sexually abused and nonabused African-American and white women were studied in terms of their adolescent sexual histories and other aspects of adjustment. For the most part, ethnic group differences were minimal. Emerging evidence, however, suggests that there are ethnic differences in the *nature* of sexual abuse experiences (Huston, Parra, Prihoda & Foulds, 1995; Mennen, 1994; 1995; Pierce & Pierce, 1984; Trickett, Horowitz, Reiffman, & Putnam, 1997). For example, in the study by Trickett, Putnam, and colleagues, African-American females in the sample were more likely to be abused at an older age and for a shorter duration than were Caucasian females. To the degree that differences in sexual abuse experiences predict different developmental outcomes (see below), understanding such ethnic differences may be critical. Again, this is an area that needs further research.

Some research has been conducted on the importance of varying characteristics of the abuse as mediators of impact—e.g., the severity of the abuse (often defined as penetration), the age at which the abuse began, its duration and/or frequency, the relationship of the victim to the perpetrator, and whether the sexual abuse was accompanied by violence. The findings of these studies have been quite inconsistent. For example, a number of studies have found an association between abuse perpetrated by a father or father-figure and severity of negative impact (Adams-Tucker, 1982; Briere & Runtz, 1987; McLeer, Deblinger, Atkins, Foa, & Ralphe, 1988; Sirles, Smith, & Kusama, 1989; Tsai, Feldman-Summers, Edger, 1979). On the other hand, some studies have not shown this association (Einbender & Friedrich, 1989; Kiser et al., 1988; Mennen, 1993). In terms of the impact of duration or frequency of abuse, a number of studies have indicated that abuse that takes place over a longer period of time (Bagley & Ramsey, 1986; Sirles et al., 1989; Tsai et al., 1979), or more frequently (Friedrich, Urquiza, & Bielke, 1986) is associated with more severe negative outcomes. As before, other studies do not show this association (Einbender & Finkelhor, 1989; Tufts, 1984). Other abuse characteristics have shown even more inconsistency.

The variables most consistently associated with more adverse impact are longer duration of the abuse, force or violence accompanying the abuse, and father or father-figure as perpetrator. It is important to realize that this research has, for the most part, considered one variable at a time and has been concerned with *severity* of impact rather than differences in impact (i.e., the emergence of different types of problems being associated with different types of abuse). There is reason to believe that these characteristics of abuse may covary in ways that are important to understand. For example, in one study, abuse perpetrated by a biological father was found to begin at an earlier age and last longer than abuse by a stepfather or other father-figure (Trickett et al., 1997).

To really understand the impact of these different characteristics of abuse, it is important to consider them simultaneously. Two studies, so far, have used a multivariate approach to investigate this area (Mennen & Meadow, 1995; Trickett et al., 1997, 2001). Mennen and Meadow (1995) conducted a study in which several characteristics of abuse were considered simultaneously as predictors of adverse developmental outcomes in a sample of 134 girls and adolescents. They found that severity of abuse as indicated by penetration predicted a more serious outcome on a variety of measures indicating depression, low self esteem, etc., than did less severe abuse. There was also an interaction between force and the perpetrator's identity (father or father-figure vs. nonfather-figure): Girls abused with force by a nonfather-figure had much higher levels of distress than those abused by a nonfather-figure without force. Force did not predict a more serious outcome in girls abused by father figures. There was not a "main effect" for identity of perpetrator and neither age at onset of abuse nor duration of abuse were predictive of symptom levels.

The study by Trickett, Putnam, and colleagues (Trickett et al., 1997) also indicates the importance of looking simultaneously at multiple factors involved in abuse. Of about 80 sexually abused girls and female adolescents, multiple regression analyses were used to investigate the relationship between early onset of abuse, abuse severity, duration, use of force, and identity of perpetrator. In these analyses, when the predictive power of each of these variables was considered while controlling for the others, abuse severity (essentially whether there was penetration) and abuse by a biological father were found to be the most important mediators of impact. Abuse severity predicted amount of depression and hallucinatory symptoms. Abuse by a biological father (but not other "father-figures", e.g., stepfathers) predicted aggression, delinquency, and other "acting out" externalizing behavior problems. When controlling for these variables, age at onset of abuse, duration, and use of force were not significant predictors of developmental outcomes.

Although there is more to be learned in this area, it seems that for female victims of sexual abuse, the nature of the abusive acts and the identity of the perpetrator, perhaps in conjunction with use of force, are especially important. In longitudinal analyses with this same sample, it has been demonstrated that biological-father abuse was associated with greater aggression and other antisocial behavior both in childhood and adolescence, and with sexual aversion and sexual ambivalence in adolescence and early adulthood (Noll et al., in press). Multiple perpetrator (nonbiological father) abuse was associated with more gastrointestinal problems, and biological father abuse was associated with greater healthcare utilization in late adolescence (Sickel et al., 2002). This study also demonstrated that the single perpetrator (nonbiological father) group showed the least behavioral problems and maladjustment in childhood (i.e., within 6 months after disclosure) and were often indistinguishable from the comparison group. However, by adolescence, the females in this group seemed to be functioning as poorly, or more poorly, than the biological father subgroup (Trickett et al., 2001). This phenomenon may be explained by the possibility that these girls received less mental health treatment (specifically targeting the abuse) or other services at the time of disclosure because their distress symptoms were not as observable (Horowitz, Putnam, Noll, & Trickett 1997).

CONCLUSIONS

It is important to remember that in many cases there is only one or, perhaps, two studies supporting many of the findings reported here. The need for further research is clear and one should be cautious about concluding that we understand the long term impact of child sexual abuse on female development. The most important findings that need to be confirmed and expanded by further research include the following: First, the suggestion that there are psychobiological effects of child sexual abuse is extremely important. The few studies, to date, in this area, implicate cortisol elevation and dysregulation. Similar dysregulation has been associated with low social competence in preschoolers (Hart, Gunnar, & Cicchetti, 1995), with diagnoses of PTSD and major depression in adults, and, perhaps as a result of associated hippocampal damage (McEwen & Sapolsky, 1995; Sapolsky, 2000), with short-term memory problems and level of dissociation among women (Bremner, Randall, Vermettan, et al., 1995; Bremner, Randall, Scott, et al., 1995; Bremmer, Narayan, Anderson, Staib, Miller, & Charney, 2000). An intriguing and disturbing possibility is that such hormonal dysregulation may be related to other findings of long-term impact of sexual abuse on physical health including gynecological problems in women (Loewenstein, 1990), immune function, (DeBellis et al., 1996) and somatization symptoms (Greenwald et al., 1990).

A second important finding supported by a number of studies is the association between sexual abuse and, not only depression and anxiety disorders, but also "acting out" and externalizing problems in females, especially in adolescence and adulthood. These problems include aggression, delinquency, conduct disorders, antisocial personality, alcohol and substance abuse, and sexual acting out. It now seems clear that female maladaptation resulting from sexual abuse takes many more forms including social deviancies of several types than was previously thought.

Third, evidence suggests that sexual abuse of females is associated with later sexual risk-taking behaviors and reproductive decisions. Risky sexual behavior can lead to relatively early sexual initiation that occurs prior to the acquisition of necessary emotional maturity, leaving victims open to subsequent sexual exploitation and potential revictimization. High-risk sexual behaviors are also associated with higher rates of sexually transmitted diseases (including HIV/AIDS) and unintended pregnancies. Teen motherhood has far-reaching consequences both for the developmental transition of the mother into adulthood and for the health and well-being of offspring.

Finally, it seems quite important to consider the impact of sexual abuse on educational and occupational attainment and satisfaction. Here, the empirical evidence for childhood and adolescence is strong: school performance and achievement and certain cognitive abilities are low among sexual abuse victims as compared with nonabused children of comparable SES. This would suggest that a major long-term impact of sexual abuse would be lower educational attainment and, as a result, lower occupational attainment in adulthood. It is striking how few studies of adults have examined outcome variables in this domain. As noted earlier, one study investigated short-term memory in adults (Bremner, Randall, Scott, et al., 1995) and found deficits. Another did not find memory deficits but did find deficits in both fluid and crystallized abilities (Trickett et al, 2001). Because occupational attainment and satisfaction are so central to well-being during adulthood, this area demands more research. The notion that sexual abuse may have long-term consequences for education and occupational attainment also has implications for the selection of adult samples. A university sample is problematic to study the long term effects of sexual abuse because of likely overselection of adults with less severe impact of abuse. Also, this notion should be taken into account in adult research when matching abuse and comparison groups on SES because one may be matching on one of the outcomes of the abuse.

Treatment Implications

The research reviewed here suggests that the focus of treatment for females sexually abused in childhood should vary across individuals, be tailored to the specific types of abuse suffered, and be designed to address the major tasks and challenges of distinct developmental stages. The immediate and acute effects of sexual abuse should be dealt with in childhood, but treatment should continue into and through adolescence, and be revisited when developmentally salient issues arise and chronic psychopathology begins to manifest. There are a number of good, empirically-based treatments for sexually abused children which focus primarily on PTSD or other acute distress symptoms (see, e.g., Deblinger & Heflin, 1996; Kolko, 1998). Practitioners treating children should also be attuned to inappropriate sexualized behaviors and acute developmental and cognitive delays. Treatment might especially focus on peer relationships and conflict, and on internalizing behaviors such as withdrawal or somatic complaints. Treatment in the adolescent period might focus on increasing dissociative tendencies, more severe problems in school and with peers, externalizing behaviors such as delinquency, sexual acting out, and self-harm, and a greater risk for eating disorders. Treatment of sexual abuse in adulthood might focus on more severe psychopathology such as chronic depression, anxiety, and pathological dissociation. Alcohol and substance use, sexual dysfunction, and revictimization may also begin to manifest. Interpersonal relationships may be especially impacted during this period and issues of domestic violence, reproductive decision-making, and the challenges of parenting may be especially salient.

Across developmental stages from childhood to adulthood, it should be recognized that there may be psychobiological disturbances resulting from the stress and trauma of sexual abuse. Treatment should take into account that there may be hormonal dysregulation and perhaps even structural changes in the brains of sexual abuse victims that may be associated with diverse symptoms including memory or cognitive deficits, dissociation, depression, somatization, and physical illness.

An important conclusion generated by research in this area is that no sexual abuse should be presumed to be "mild" even if severe acute distress is not apparent. Results reported here indicate that distinct patterns of psychological and psychobiological problems may arise for childhood sexual abuse survivors at different stages of their lives. Contributing to these variations in response are a host of abuse characteristics, including perpetrator identity, duration of abuse, age at onset, the presence of physical force, etc., and, probably, a number of mediating factors as yet not well understood. Research to date has sketched out the impact of sexual abuse on the development of children. There is much yet to be learned. Research needs to continue if our knowledge is to be increased and it is important that this research include certain characteristics (see also National Research Council, 1993). One especially important emphasis is a developmental framework. There is much yet to learn about how the experience of sexual abuse in childhood interferes with development at the time it is experienced, or how it may affect the resolution of later developmental processes or tasks as the individual goes through adolescence and then adulthood. As such, research needs to include a focus on long-term effects and thus be either longitudinal and long-term, or include follow up studies of individuals documented to have been sexually abused as children. Finally, a multivariate perspective is required and as a result research samples need large Ns—larger samples than much of the extant research so that the impact of different forms of abuse, experienced by males as well as females, at different ages, by members of different ethnic groups or social classes, be teased apart. Only then can the complexities of this phenomenon be understood and can its adverse consequences across the lifespan be remediated.

REFERENCES

Abdulrehman, R. Y., & De Luca, R. V. (2001). The implications of childhood sexual abuse on adult social behavior. *Journal of Family Violence, 16*, 193–203.

Adams-Tucker, C. (1982). Proximate effects of sexual abuse in children: A report on 28 children. *American Journal of Psychiatry, 139*, 1252–1256.

Bagley, C., & Ramsey, R. (1986). Sexual abuse in childhood: Psychosocial outcomes and implications for social work practice. *Journal of Social Work and Human Sexuality, 4*, 33–47.

Beitchman, J. H., Zucker, K. J., Hood, J. E., daCosta, G. A., & Akman, D. (1991). A review of the short-term effects of child sexual abuse. *Child Abuse and Neglect, 15*, 537–556.

Beitchman, J. H., Zucker, K. J., Hood, J. E., daCosta, G. A., Akman, D., & Cassavia, E. (1992) A review of the long-term effects of child sexual abuse. *Child Abuse and Neglect, 16*, 101–118.

Bifulco, A., Brown, G. W., & Adler, Z. (1991). Early sexual abuse and clinical depression in adult life. *British Journal of Psychiatry, 159*, 115–122.

Bremner, J. D., Narayan, M. Anderson, E. R. Staib, L. H., Miller, H. L., & Charney, D. S. (2000). Hippocampal volume reduction in major depression. *American Journal of Psychiatry, 157*, 115–128.

Bremner, J. D., Randall, P., Scott, S., Capelli, S., Delaney, R., McCarthy, G., et al. (1995). *Deficits in short-term memory in adult survivors of childhood abuse.* Unpublished manuscript, Yale University, New Haven, CT.

Bremner, J. D., Randall, P., Vermetten, E., Staib, L., Bronen, R. A., Capelli, S., et al. (1995). *MRI-based measurement of hippocampal volume in postraumatic stress disorder related to childhood physical and sexual abuse.* Paper presented at the Annual Meeting of the American Psychiatric Association, August, New York.

Brewin, C. R., Andrews, B., & Gotlib, L. H. (1993). Psychopathology and early experience: A reappraisal of retrospective reports. *Psychological Bulletin, 113*, 82–98.

Briere, J., & Runtz, M. (1987). Post sexual abuse trauma: Data and implications for clinical practice. *Journal of Interpersonal Violence, 2*, 367–379.

Briere, J., & Runtz, M. (1990). Differential adult symptomatology associated with three types of child abuse histories. *Child Abuse and Neglect, 14,* 357–364.

Buist, A., & Janson, H. (2001). Childhood sexual abuse, parenting and postpartum depression—A 3-year follow-up study. *Child Abuse and Neglect, 25,* 909–921.

Burgdorf, K. (1980). *Recognition and reporting of child maltreatment: Summary findings from the National Study of the Incidence and Severity of Child Abuse and Neglect.* Washington, DC: National Center for Child Abuse and Neglect.

Burkett, L. P. (1991). Parenting behaviors of women who were sexually abused as children in their families of origin. *Family Process, 30,* 421–434.

Cole, P. M., Woolger, C., Power, T. G., & Smith, K. D. (1992). Parenting difficulties among adult survivors of father–daughter incest. *Child Abuse and Neglect, 16,* 239–249.

DeBellis, M. D., Burke, L. Trickett, T. K., & Putnam, F. W. (1996). Antinuclear antibodies and thyroid function in sexually abused girls. *Journal of Traumatic Stress, 9,* 369–378.

DeBellis, M. D., Chrousos, G. P., Dorn, L. D., Burke, L., Helmers, K., Kling, M. A., et al. (1994). Hypothalamic–pituitary–adrenal axis dysregulation in sexually abused girls. *Journal of Clinical Endocrinology and Metabolism, 78,* 249–255.

DeBellis, M. D., Lefter, L. Trickett, P. K., & Putnam, F. W. (1994). Urinary catecholamine excretion in sexually abused girls. *Journal of the American Academy of Child and Adolescent Psychiatry, 33,* 320–327.

Deblinger, E., & Heflin, A. H. (1996). *Treating sexually abused children and their nonoffending parents: A cognitive behavioral approach.* Thousand Oaks, CA: Sage.

Deblinger, E., McLeer, S. V., Atkins, M. S., Ralphe, D., & Foa, E. (1989). Post-traumatic stress in sexually abused, physically abused, and nonabused children. *Child Abuse and Neglect, 13,* 403–408.

Eckenrode, J., Laird, M., & Doris, J. (1993). The school performance of abused and neglected children. *Developmental Psychology, 29,* 53–62.

Einbender, A. J., & Friedrich, W. N. (1989). Psychological functioning and behavior of sexually abused girls. *Journal of Consulting and Clinical Psychology, 57,* 155–157.

Feldman-Summers, S., & Pope, K. S. (1994). The experience of "forgetting" childhood abuse: A national survey of psychologists. *Journal of Consulting and Clinical Psychology, 62,* 636–639.

Finkelhor, D., Hotaling, G. T., Lewis, I. A., & Smith, C. (1989). Sexual abuse and its relationship to later sexual satisfaction, marital status, religion, and attitudes. *Journal of Interpersonal Violence, 4,* 379–399.

Finkelhor, D., Hotaling, G., Lewis, I. A., & Smith, C. (1990) Sexual abuse in a national survey of adult men and women: Prevalence, characteristics, and risk factors. *Child Abuse and Neglect, 14,* 19–28.

Friedrich, W. N., Beilke, R. L., & Urquiza, A. J. (1987). Children from sexually abusive families: A behavioral comparison. *Journal of Interpersonal Violence, 2,* 391–402.

Friedrich, W., Urquiza, A., & Beilke, R. (1986). Behavior problems in young, sexually abused children. *Journal of Pediatric Psychology, 19,* 155–164.

Fromuth, M. E. (1986). The relationship of childhood sexual abuse with later psychological and sexual adjustment in a sample of college women. *Child Abuse and Neglect, 10,* 5–15.

Fromuth, M. E., & Burkhart, B. R. (1989). Long-term psychological correlates of childhood sexual abuse in two samples of college men. *Child Abuse and Neglect, 13,* 533–542.

Goldston, D., Turnquist, D. C., & Knutson, J. F. (1989). Presenting problems of sexually abused girls receiving psychiatric services. *Journal of Abnormal Psychology, 98,* 314–317.

Grayston, A. D., De Luca, R. V., & Boyes, D. A. (1992). Self-esteem, anxiety, and loneliness in preadolescent girls who have experienced sexual abuse. *Child Psychiatry and Human Development, 22,* 277–286.

Greenwald, E., Leitenberg, H., Cado, S., & Tarran, M. J. (1990). Childhood sexual abuse: Long-term effects on psychological and sexual functioning in a nonclinical and nonstudent sample of adult women. *Child Abuse and Neglect, 14,* 503–513.

Gutierrez, P. M., Thakkar, R. R., & Kuczen, C. (2000). Exploration of the relationship between physical and/or sexual abuse, attitudes about life and death, and suicidal ideation in young women. *Death Studies, 24,* 675–688.

Hart, J., Gunnar, M., & Cicchetti, D. (1995). Salivary cortisol in maltreated children: Evidence of relations between neuroendocrine activity and social competence. *Development and Psychopathology, 7,* 11–26.

Harter, S., Alexander, P. C., & Neimeyer, R. A. (1988). Long-term effects of incestuous child abuse in college women: Social adjustment, social cognition, and family characteristics. *Journal of Consulting and Clinical Psychology, 56,* 5–8.

Helmers, K., Everett, B. A., & Trickett, P. K. (1991). *Social support of sexually abused girls and their mothers.* Paper presented at the Biennial Meeting of the Society for Research in Development, March, Seattle, WA.

Herrenkohl, E. C., Herrenkohl, R. C., Egolf, B. P., & Russo, J. M. (1998). The relationship between early maltreatment and teenage parenthood. *Journal of Adolescence, 21,* 291–303.

Horowitz, L. A., Putnam, F. W., Noll, J. G., & Trickett, P. K. (1997). Factors affecting utilization of treatment services by sexually abused girls. *Child Abuse and Neglect, 21,* 35–48.

Hunter, J. A. (1991). A comparison of the psychosocial maladjustement of adult males and females sexually molested as children. *Journal of Interpersonal Violence, 6,* 205–217.

Huston, R. L., Parra, J. M., Prihoda, T. J., & Foulds, D. M. (1995). Characteristics of childhood sexual abuse in a predominantly Mexican-American population. *Child Abuse and Neglect, 19,* 165–176.

Jones, L. M., Finkelhor, D., & Kopiec, K. (2001). Why is sexual abuse declining? A survey of state child protection administrators. *Child Abuse and Neglect, 25,* 1139–1158.

Kamsner, S., & McCabe, M. P. (2000). The relationship between adult psychological adjustment and childhood sexual abuse, childhood physical abuse, and family-of-origin characteristics. *Journal of Interpersonal violence, 15,* 1243–1261.

Kendall-Tackett, K. A., Williams, L. M., & Finkelhor, D. (1993). Impact of sexual abuse on children: A review and synthesis of recent empirical studies. *Psychological Bulletin, 113,* 164–180.

Kiser, L. J., Ackerman, B. J., Brown, E., Edwards, N. B., McColgan, E., Pugh, R., et al. (1988). Post-traumatic stress disorder in young children: A reaction to purported sexual abuse. *Journal of the American Academy of Child and Adolescent Psychiatry, 27,* 645–649.

Kolko, D. J. (1998). Treatment and intervention for child victims of violence. In P. K. Trickett & C. J. Schellenbach (Eds.), *Violence against children in the family and community* (pp. 213–250). Washington, DC: American Psychological Association.

Kolko, D. J., Moser, J. T., & Weldy, S. R. (1990) Medical/health histories and physical evaluation of physically and sexually abused child psychiatric patients: A controlled study. *Journal of Family Violence, 5,* 249–267.

Krahe, B., Scheinberger-Olwig, R., Waizenhofer, E., & Kolpin, S. (1999). Childhood sexual abuse and revictimization in adolescence. *Child Abuse and Neglect, 23,* 383–394.

Kurtz, D. A. (2003). *Determining competent/resilient outcomes across multiple domains in sexually abused and nonabused females.* Unpublished doctoral dissertation, University of Southern California, Los Angeles, CA.

Lipovsky, J. A., Saunders, B. E., & Murphy, S. M. (1989). Depression, anxiety, and behavior problems among victims of father—Child sexual assault and nonabused siblings. *Journal of Interpersonal Violence, 4,* 452–68.

Loewenstein, R. J. (1990). Somatoform disorders in victims of incest and child abuse. In R. P. Kluft (Ed.), *Incest-related syndromes of adult psychopathology,* (pp. 75–112). Washington, DC: American Psychiatric Press.

Loftus, E. (1994). Memories of child sexual abuse. *Psychology of Women Quarterly, 18,* 67–84.

Mannarino, A. P., Cohen, J. A., Smith, J. A., & Moore-Motley, S. (1991). Six- and twelve-month follow-up of sexually abused girls. *Journal of Interpersonal Violence, 6,* 494–511.

McBride-Chang, C., Trickett, P. K., Horn, J. L., & Putnam, F. W. (1992). *The CBCL and behavior problems in sexually abused girls.* Paper presented at the Annual Meeting of the American Psychological Association, August, Washington, DC.

McEwen, B. S., & Sapolsky, R. M. (1995). Stress and cognitive function. *Current Opinion in Neurobiology, 5,* 205–216.

McGloin, J. M., & Widom, C. S. (2001). Resilience among abused and neglected children grown up. *Development and Psychopathology, 13,* 1021–1038.

McLeer, S. V., Deblinger, E., Atkins, M. S., Foa, E. B., & Ralphe, D. L. (1988). Post-traumatic stress disorder in sexually abused children. *Journal of the American Academy of Child and Adolescent Psychiatry, 27,* 650–654.

Mennen, F. E. (1993). Evaluation of risk factors in childhood sexual abuse. *Journal of the American Academy of Child and Adolescent Psychiatry, 32,* 934–939.

Mennen, F. E. (1994). Sexual abuse in Latina girls: Their functioning and a comparison with white and African American girls. *Hispanic Journal of Behavioral Sciences, 16,* 475–486.

Mennen, F. E., & Meadow, D. (1995). The relationship of abuse characteristics to symptoms in sexually abused girls. *Journal of Interpersonal Violence, 10,* 259–274.

Messman-Moore, T. L., & Long, P. J. (2000). Child sexual abuse and revictimization in the form of adult sexual abuse, adult physical abuse and adult psychological maltreatment. *Journal of Interpersonal Violence, 15,* 489–502.

Mullen, P., Martin, J., Anderson, J., Romans, S., & Herbison, G. (1996). The long-term impact of the physical, emotional, and sexual abuse of children: A community study. *Child Abuse and Neglect, 20,* 7–20.

Mullen, P. E., Romans-Clarkson, S. E., Walton, V. A., & Herbison, G. P. (1988). Impact of sexual and physical abuse on women's mental health. *Lancet, 1,* 841–845.

Murphy, S. M., Kilpatrick, D. G., Amick-McMullen, A., Veronen, L. J., Paduhovich, J., Best, C. L., et al. (1988). Current psychological functioning of child sexual abuse survivors. *Journal of Interpersonal Violence, 3,* 55–79.

Nash, M. R., Hulsey, T. L., Sexton, M. C., Harralson, T. L., & Lambert, W. (1993). Long-term sequelae of childhood sexual abuse: Perceived family environment, psychopathology, and dissociation. *Journal of Consulting and Clinical Psychology, 61,* 276–283.

National Center of Child Abuse and Neglect. (1988). *Study of national incidence and prevalence of child abuse and neglect,* 1988. Washington, DC: US Department of Health and Human Services.

National Center of Child Abuse and Neglect. (1996). *Third study of national incidence and prevalence of child abuse and neglect (preliminary findings).* Washington, DC: US Department of Health and Human Services.

National Research Council. (1993). *Understanding child abuse and neglect.* Washington, DC: National Academy Press.

Nereo, N. E., Farber, B. A., & Hinton, V. J. (2002). Willingness to self-disclose among late adolescent female survivors of childhood sexual abuse. *Journal of Youth and Adolescence, 31,* 303–310.

Noll, J. G., Horowitz, L. A., Bonanno, G. A., Trickett, P. K., & Putnam, F. W. (2003). Revictimization and self-harm in females who experienced childhood sexual abuse: Results from a prospective study. *Journal of Interpersonal Violence, 18,* 1452–1471.

Noll, J. G., Horowitz, L. A., Norris, J. A., Bonanno, G. A., Trickett, P. K., & Putnam, F. W. (2002). *The impact of childhood sexual abuse on revictimization and self-harm.* Poster presented at the 18th annual meeting of the International Society of Traumatic Stress Studies, November, Balitimore, MD.

Noll, J. G., Trickett, P. K., & Putnam, F. W. (2000). Social network constellation and sexuality of sexually abused and comparison group females in childhood and adolescence. *Child Maltreatment: Victimization and the Development of Romantic Relationships in Adolescence, 5,* 321–335.

Noll, J. G., Trickett, P. K., & Putnam, F. W. (2003). A prospective investigation of the impact of childhood sexual abuse on sexuality in adolescence and early adulthood. *Journal of Consulting and Clinical Psychologym, 71,* 575–585.

Perez, C., & Widom, C. (1994). Childhood victimization and long-term intellectual and academic outcomes. *Child Abuse and Neglect, 18,* 617–633.

Perkins, D. F., & Luster, T. (1999). The relationship between sexual abuse and purging: Findings from community-wide surveys of female adolescents. *Child Abuse and Neglect, The International Journal, 23,* 371–382.

Peters, S. D. (1988). Child sexual abuse and later psychological problems. In G. E. Wyatt & G. J. Powell (Eds.), *Lasting effects of child sexual abuse.* Newbury Park, CA: Sage.

Peters, S. D., Wyatt, G. E., & Finkelhor, D. (1986). Prevalence. In D. Finkelhor (Ed.), *A sourcebook on child sexual abuse.* Beverly Hills, CA: Sage.

Pierce, L. H., & Pierce, R. L. (1984). Race as a factor in the sexual abuse of children. *Social Work Research and Abstracts, 20,* 9–14.

Putnam, F. W., & Carlson, E. B. (1997). *Hypnosis, dissociation and trauma: Myths, metaphors and mechanisms.* In D. Bremer & C. Marmar (Eds.), Trauma, memory, & dissociation (pp. 27–55). Washington DC: American Psychiatric Press.

Putnam, F. W., Helmers, K., & Trickett, P. K. (1993). Development, reliability, and validation of a child dissociation scale. *Child Abuse and Neglect, 17,* 731–740.

Putnam, F. W., & Trickett, P. K. (1991). Cortisol abnormalities in sexually abused girls. Paper presented at the Annual Meeting of the American Psychological Society, May, Washington, DC.

Putnam, F. W., & Trickett, P. K. (1993). Child sexual abuse: A model of chronic trauma. *Psychiatry, 58,* 82–95.

Russell, D. E. H. (1986). *The secret trauma: Incest in the lives of girls and women.* New York: Basic Books.

Sapolsky, R. M. (2000). Glucocorticoids and hippocampal atrophy in neuropsychiatric disorders. *Archives of General Psychiatry, 57,* 925–935.

Sedney, M. A., & Brooks, B. (1984). Factors associated with a history of childhood sexual experience in a nonclinical female population. *Journal of the American Academy of Child Psychiatry, 23,* 215–218.

Sickel, A. E., Noll, J. G., Moore, P. J., Putnam, F. W., & Trickett, P. K. (2002). The long-term physical health and healthcare utilization of women who were sexually abused as children. *Journal of Health Psychology, 7*(5), 583–597.

Sirles, E. A., Smith, J. A., & Kusama, H. (1989). Psychiatric status of intrafamilial child sexual abuse victims. *Journal of the American Academy of Child and Adolescent Psychiatry, 28,* 225–229.

Smith, C. (1996). The link between childhood maltreatment and teenage pregnancy. *Social Work Research, 20,* 131–141.

Stein, J. A., Golding, J. M., Siegel, J. M., Burnam, M. A., & Sorenson, S. B. (1988). Long-term psychological sequelae of child sexual abuse: The Los Angeles Epidemiologic Catchment Area Study. In G. E. Wyatt & G. J. Powell (Eds.), *Lasting Effects of Child Sexual Abuse.* Newbury Park, CA: Sage.

Tong, L., Oates, K., & McDowell, M. (1987). Personality development following sexual abuse. *Child Abuse and Neglect, 11,* 371–383.

Trickett, P. K., Aber, J. L., Carlson, V., & Cicchetti, D. (1991). Relationship of socioeconomic status to the etiology and developmental sequelae of physical child abuse. *Developmental Psychology, 27,* 148–158.

Trickett, P. K., Ghisletta, P., Horn, J. L., Noll, J., & Putnam, F. W. (1998). *Latent growth curve models of pubertal development in sexually abused and nonabused girls.* Paper presented at the meeting of the International Society for the Study of Behavioral Development, July, Berne, Switzerland.

Trickett, P. K., Horowitz, L., Reiffman, A., & Putnam, F. W. (1997). Characteristics of sexual abuse trauma and the prediction of developmental outcomes. In D. Cicchetti & S. L. Toth (Eds.), *Rochester Symposium on Developmental Psychopathology. Vol. VIII: The Effects of Trauma on the Developmental Process* (pp. 289–314). Rochester, NY: University of Rochester Press.

Trickett, P. K., Kurtz, D. A., & Pizzigati, K. (2004). Resilient outcomes in abused and neglected children: Bases for strength-based interventions and policies. In K. Maton, C. Schellenbach, B. Leadbeater, & A. Solarz (Eds.), *Investing in children, youth, families, and communities: A strengths-based approach to research and policy* (pp. 73–95). Washington, DC: American Psychological Association.

Trickett, P. K., & McBride-Chang, C. (1995). The developmental impact of different forms of child abuse and neglect. *Developmental Review, 15,* 311–337.

Trickett, P. K., McBride-Chang, C., & Putnam, F. W. (1994). The classroom performance and behavior of sexually abused females. *Development and Psychopathology, 6,* 183–194.

Trickett, P. K., Noll, J. G., Horn, J. L. & Putnam, F. W. (April 2001). *The development of cognitive abilities in sexually abused females: Long-term effects.* Paper presented at the Society for Research in Child Development, Minneapolis, MN.

Trickett, P. K., Noll, J. G., & Putnam, F. W. (1999). *Age at menarche and acceleration of pubertal development in females who have been sexually abused.* Paper presented at the annual meeting of the Society for Research on Child Development, March, Albuquerque, NM.

Trickett, P. K., Noll, J. G., Reiffman, A., & Putnam, F. W. (2001). Variants of intrafamilial sexual abuse experience: Implications for long term development. *Journal of Development and Psychopathology, 13*(4), 1001–1019.

Trickett, P. K., & Putnam, F. W. (1991). *Patterns of symptoms in prepubertal and pubertal sexually abused girls.* Paper presented at the Annual Meeting of the American Psychological Association, August, San Francisco, CA.

Trickett, P. K. & Putnam, F. W. (1993). Impact of child sexual abuse on females: Toward a developmental, psychobiological integration. *Psychological Science, 4*, 81–87.

Trickett, P. K. & Putnam, F. W. (1998). Developmental consequences of child sexual abuse. In Trickett, P. K. Schellenbach, C. J. (Eds.), *Violence against children in the family and the community*, (pp. 39–56). Washington DC: American Psychological Association.

Tsai, M., Feldman-Summers, S., & Edger, M. (1979). Childhood molestation: Variables related to differential impacts on psychosocial functioning in adult women. *Journal of Abnormal Psychology, 88*, 407–417.

Tufts New England Medical Center, Division of Child Psychiatry. (1984). *Sexually exploited children: Service and research project* (Final report for the Office of Juvenine Justice and Delinquency Prevention). Washington, DC: US Department of Justice.

Whiffen, V. E., Thompson, J. M., & Aube, J. A. (2000). Mediators of the link between childhood sexual abuse and adult depressive symptoms. *Journal of Interpersonal Violence, 15*, 1110–1120.

White, S., Halpin, B. M., Strom, G. A., & Santilli, G. (1988). Behavioral comparisons of young sexually abused, neglected, and nonreferred children. *Journal of Clinical Child Psychology, 17*, 53–61.

Widom, Cathy S. (1989). The Cycle of Violence. *Science, 244*(4901), 160–166.

Widom, C. S., & Kuhns, J. B. (1996). Childhood victimization and subsequent risk for promiscuity, prostitution, and teenage pregnancy: A prospective study. *American Journal of Public Health, 86*, 1607–1612.

Widom, C. S., & Shepard, R. L. (1996). Accuracy of adult recollections of childhood victimization: Part 1. Childhood physical abuse. *Psychological Assessment, 8*, 412–421.

Williams, L. M. (1994). Recall of childhood trauma: A prospective study of women's memories of child sexual abuse. *Journal of Consulting and Clinical Psychology, 62*, 1167–1176.

Wonderlich, S. A., Crosby, R. D., Mitchell, J. E., Roberts, J. A., Haseltine, B., DeMuth, G., et al. (2000). Relationship of childhood sexual abuse and eating disturbance in children. *Journal of the American Academy of Child and Adolescent Psychiatry, 39*, 1277–1283.

Wyatt, G. E. (1988). The relationship between child sexual abuse and adolescent sexual functioning in Afro-American and white American women. *Annals of the New York Academy of Sciences*, 111–122.

Zuravin, S. J., & Fontanella, C. (1999). The relationship child sexual abuse and major depression among low-income women: A function of growing up experiences? *Child Maltreatment, 4*, 3–12.

13

Abuse and Violence in Adolescent Girls' Dating Relationships

DAVID A. WOLFE, KATREENA L. SCOTT, and CLAIRE V. CROOKS

Conceptualization of adolescent gender-based violence has been caught at the crossroads of the childhood peer aggression literature and the adult domestic violence literature. On the one hand, child peer aggression research recognizes female-perpetrated violence and "female types" of violence (Craig & Pepler, 1997; Olweus, 1991); on the other hand, the adult intimate relationship violence literature emphasizes a male-to-female, power- and control-based violence (Dobash & Dobash, 1992). In all likelihood, adolescent dating violence falls somewhere in the middle.

Despite the unique opportunities offered by the study of this "in between" period, there has historically been a lack of attention to research on adolescent dating relationships (Brown, Feiring, & Furman, 1999). Until recently, research in this area was curtailed by the notion that adolescent romantic relationships are somehow not authentic or not to be taken seriously. However, even with greater recognition of the developmental importance of adolescent dating, numerous logistical factors continue to impede research. For example, adolescent dating relationships are short-term (compared with adults') and their context and nature can change rapidly. As well, generational changes in adolescent subculture affect both the terminology of dating (e.g., "going out," "seeing someone," "hooking up") and the patterns of dating (e.g., in groups vs. dyads). Finally, public health concerns about teenage pregnancy and sexually transmitted infections have pushed the study of adolescent sexual behavior

DAVID A. WOLFE and CLAIRE V. CROOKS • University of WesternOntario,London,Ontario.
KATREENA L. SCOTT • University of Toronto, Toronto, Ontario.

to the forefront, eclipsing the context of romantic relationships in the process.

Although historically neglected, the amount and severity of all forms of violence both experienced and committed by adolescent girls is currently a topic of considerable research and clinical attention. Whereas there is wide acknowledgement that males are more involved in serious violence than females at all ages, violence committed by adolescent girls has been increasing rapidly over the past two decades (Snyder & Sickmund, 1999). Moreover, there is increased recognition that aggression in girls may take different forms than in boys (more indirect and relational-based), leading to higher estimates than previously obtained. We take a close look at gender differences throughout this chapter because, in conjunction with developmental considerations, they are a prominent focus of emerging research on aggression and violence among adolescent girls.

In addition, there is growing awareness of the need for developmentally informed theories and paradigms to adequately conceptualize aggression and violence in adolescent dating relationships. Theoretical approaches to understanding adolescent relationship violence have typically been downward applications derived from studies of adult relationships, despite crucial developmental differences between these age groups (Brown et al., 1999). Moreover, until the past decade, research on adolescent dating patterns and behaviors typically focused on college students or young adults, with little interest shown in the emergence of such behavior in early to mid-adolescence. When research has been conducted with younger adolescents it has tended to focus on boys, consistent with the bias in the general aggression literature that has historically overlooked girls (Odgers & Moretti, 2002; Pepler & Craig, 1999).

This chapter begins with a discussion of the significance of gender in defining abuse and violence with dating partners, followed by an overview of normative developmental transitions in adolescent romantic relationships that serve as contexts for relationship aggression. We then trace the changing nature of aggression across the stages of adolescent development, and describe developmental pathways to abusive or violent adolescent dating relationships. Finally, we discuss the implications for assessment and intervention that stem from these developmental paradigms.

CONCEPTUALIZING GIRLS' DATING AGGRESSION

Dating violence is distinguished from other, more general, forms of interpersonal violence in that such behaviors occur in the context of a romantic, or dating, relationship (though not always in the context of a "date"). Traditionally, this term has been used to describe a wide range of behaviors that function to control, dominate, or denigrate another person, causing some level of harm (Lewis & Fremouw, 2001). This definition provides a useful starting point for discussion; however, developmental and gender considerations need to be taken into account to clarify how dating violence is expressed by girls, in particular. As just one example, dating violence during early to mid-adolescence tends to be reciprocal or mutual. Therefore, unless noted, our discussion of dating violence refers to involvement of girls as both recipient and aggressor.

Abusive and violent behaviors fall along a broad continuum from relatively mild to more severe acts. The more common behaviors include insults, threats, and intimidation (i.e., mostly abusive but not violent), which are reported among a sizeable minority of youth (25–35%; Cascardi, Avery-Leaf, O'Leary, & Smith Slep, 1999; Malik, Sorenson, & Aneshensel, 1997). However, even the more severe forms of dating violence, such as physical and sexual assaults, are relatively prevalent: 10–20% of youth (boys as well as girls) report being hit, slapped, or forced to have sex by a dating partner (Centers for Disease Control and Prevention, 2000; Coker et al., 2000; Grunbaum et al., 2002; Silverman, Raj, Mucci, & Hathaway, 2001). When asked to report on specific behaviors (e.g., hitting, slapping, punching), 11% of high school students reported perpetrating physical abuse and 28% reported having been a recipient of such behavior on at least one occasion, with no significant reporting differences between girls and boys (Wolfe, Scott, Wekerle, & Pittman, 2001). Similarities in abuse perpetrated by adolescent boys and girls suggested by the above statistics are perhaps the most controversial issue in the conceptualization of dating violence, and as such warrants careful analysis. Gender differences in expression, form, intent, and consequences of aggression between adolescent dating partners, as well as the relational context in which it occurs, underscore the importance of a gender analysis in understanding this phenomenon.

Research on ethnic and cultural differences in the experiences of dating violence among adolescent girls have been limited to epidemiological studies, which have yielded variable patterns with respect to ethnicity. In a sample of 689 urban adolescents, for example, African American females were more likely to report rape or attempted rape compared with those of Puerto Rican ethnicity (Rickert, Wiemann, Vaughan, & White, 2003). Large-scale epidemiological studies are required, however, to identify overall trends as well as possible regional discrepancies in rates of dating violence among adolescent girls from a variety of ethnic and cultural backgrounds. Furthermore, the extent to which ethnicity or cultural differences play a role in the development, maintenance, and expression of dating violence remains unknown.

Gender-Specific Rates and Forms of Aggression

From a strictly prevalence viewpoint, there is little question that adolescent girls engage in aggressive behaviors toward dating partners at rates that are comparable to, or exceed, those for boys (Chase, Treboux, & O'Leary, 2002; Halpern, Oslak, Young, Martin, & Kupper, 2001). In a sample of over 2,000 high school students, for example, Cascardi et al. (1999) found that whereas victimization rates were similar (30.4 and 29.3%, for boys and girls, respectively), girls reported higher rates of perpetration of dating violence at this age (22.5 and 37.8%, for boys and girls, respectively). Similarity between boys and girls in rates of dating violence appears to extend into young adulthood. A recent meta-analysis of studies with young adults and college students found that young women were more likely to use physical aggression toward their dating partners, although males were more likely to injure their partners (Archer, 2000). Specifically, women were more likely than men to throw something, slap, kick, bite, or punch, and hit with an object whereas men were more likely than women to beat up, and to choke or strangle.

Whereas rates of physical abuse are similar, not surprisingly females are more likely than males to be victims of sexual coercion and abuse across all ages (O'Keefe, 1997; Swan & Snow, 2002). The 1999 National Youth Risk Behavior Survey (Centers for Disease Control and Prevention, 2000) found that 8.8% of students reported ever having been forced to have intercourse when they did not want to, with females reporting significantly more assaults than males (12.5 to 5.2%). Minority students were also more likely to have been forced to have sexual intercourse than nonminority students. Although females report greater sexual victimization and males endorse greater initiation of perpetration in most studies of this age group (Foshee, 1996), girls are more likely to instigate minor forms of sexual intrusiveness (e.g., kiss/touch) and boys are more likely to commit more severe acts such as attempted or forced intercourse (Poitras & Lavoie, 1995).

Finally, there may be gender differences in indirect and relational forms of aggression, a form of aggression that has only recently garnered research attention. Similar to relational aggression with peers (Crick, Bigbee, & Howes, 1996), such behavior in the context of dating relationships may include rumor-spreading and similar efforts directed at a partner's peer group, as well as verbal (e.g., sarcastic comments) and nonverbal (e.g., making faces, pointing) behaviors. Relational aggression is more common among younger teens (< Grade 10) than older ones, which likely reflects their relative immaturity in negotiating intimacy and handling relationship conflict (Wolfe, Scott, Reitzel-Jaffe, et al., 2001). Given their size disadvantage, girls may use indirect and verbal means in an attempt to gain advantage in a relationship (Berman, Straatman, Hunt, Izumi, & MacQuarrie, 2002).

One simple reason for reciprocal acts of violence, especially in less mature adolescent couples, is that the most common response to aggression is counteraggression (Watson, Cascardi, Avery-Leaf, & O'Leary, 2001). Although this partially explains why adolescents (and some adults) respond in kind to acts of aggression, it is important to examine more closely the developmental trends and situational events that are associated with mutual violence. From a developmental perspective, early patterns of abusive behavior during adolescence may be experimental and less rigidly established on the basis of gender role expectations and consequences than they are among adults. In addition, although men and women are similar in rates of relationship aggression, they may differ in more subtle ways in types of violence perpetrated and experienced, motivation for violence, and the impact of relationship aggression. Men and women may also differ in their ability to interrupt an emerging pattern of aggression in their relationships.

While this field develops, it is important to distinguish the severity and impact of such violence committed by boys versus girls. Despite similar reports of abusive and violent tactics with dating partners, girls receive more severe violence and suffer more severe physical and emotional reactions (Molidor & Tolman, 1998). At the same time, the dynamic that evolves between girls and boys in their early experiences at forming intimate relationships is different from the patterned forms of aggression seen among adult partners.

Motivation and Function of Dating Violence

Critical differences in intended function for acts of aggression toward dating partners clearly differ between boys and girls (Foshee, Linder, MacDougall, & Bangdiwala, 2001). Researchers have identified a number of different motivations cited by girls and boys for engaging in abusive or violent behavior toward their partners. By virtue of size and strength boys have more options available to escape a potentially dangerous or harmful situation; in contrast, adolescent girls are more likely to see self-defense as an acceptable reason for aggression (Cauffman, Feldman, Arnett-Jensen, & Jensen-Arnett, 2000). Beyond self-defense, abuse toward dating partners in mid- to late adolescence is often attributed to the dynamics of the relationship, the behavior of the partner, or one's attempt to gain control over one's partner. Not surprisingly, few teens recognize the "wrongness" of such behavior or take personal responsibility for their action, probably due in part to powerful messages from family, entertainment media, and peers, that imply coercive tactics are acceptable under certain circumstances (Wolfe, Wekerle, & Scott, 1997).

Motivation for relationship aggression is also tied to feelings of anger, jealousy, and emotional hurt. Male and female adolescents both report jealousy as a common motivator for relationship aggression (O'Keefe & Treister, 1998), which may be tied to its dual role as both an indication of caring as well as justification for aggression. Notably, girls are more likely to perpetrate relationship aggression as a means to demonstrate anger or to retaliate for emotional hurt, whereas boys use aggression in retaliation for being hit first and, according to their victims, as a means to gain control over their partners (Follingstad, Wright, Lloyd, & Sebastian, 1991; Gagne & Lavoie, 1993). Girls also report using abusive or violent tactics against their dating partners in an attempt to tease or engage (Jackson, Cram, & Seymour, 2000), as well as to fight back in response to partner aggression (Watson et al., 2001). Physical and emotional abuse by boys is also more likely to be attributed (by others) to behavior problems, or alcohol and drug consumption (Hammock & O'Hearn, 2002; Odgers & Moretti, 2002).

Consequences of Dating Violence

Childhood and adolescence are both critical and formative periods in which gender socialization is prominent, and profound lessons are imparted about gender inequality and sexism (Randall & Haskell, 2000). Even in adolescence, converging evidence suggests that the *impact* of experiencing relationship aggression differs significantly for boys and girls. Female victims of dating violence are more likely than males to experience fear, anxiety, hurt, and express a desire to leave the situation for self-protection. Male victims, in contrast, report being amused or angered by female aggression (Follingstad et al., 1991; Jackson et al., 2000). One study of high school youth found that girls reported their use of aggression as most typically expressive (i.e., feeling angry, frustrated), whereas boys reported their use of aggression as often playful (Scott, Wekerle, & Wolfe, 1997). In a similar vein, Cascardi et al. (1999) reported that in responding to their worst incident of violence, adolescent males typically reported that they laughed it off, while females reported responses of crying (40%), fighting back (36%), running away (11%), and obeying their partner (12%).

Related to impact is the possibility that boys and girls have different interpretations of violence in dating relationships. Currie (1998) found that young women were more likely to overlook a physically abusive experience whereas young men drew attention to their victimization, possibly to justify their own behavior. The possibility also remains that males may deny or minimize their violent behaviors and females may be too ready to assume blame, because of sex-role stereotypes that are part of Western culture (Sharpe & Taylor, 1999).

We next examine the developmental course of adolescent romantic relationships, and consider how this course provides the context for shifts from normative teasing to more malicious forms of physical and verbal aggression in the context of relationships for some teens.

DEVELOPMENTAL COURSE AND OUTCOMES

Normative Transitions in Adolescent Romantic Relationships

Developmental theorists describe the course of forming and maintaining adolescent romantic relationships as progressing through four phases. The first stage of dating involvement derives from teasing and cross-sex chasing in early elementary school, which by Grades 4 and 5, transforms into normative heterosexual interactions (Thorne & Luria, 1986). By early adolescence small groups of mixed-sex friends are common, which form the springboard for involvement in larger networks of mixed-sex peers. It is in these groups that romantic interest is first expressed with many group-based activities and little actual romantic interaction (Connolly, Pepler, Craig, & Taradash, 2000). As emphasized by Brown (1999), this early stage of dating is important for broadening the self-concept and increasing the confidence of youth in their capacity to relate to others romantically. Connolly and Goldberg (1999) add to this conceptualization the importance of youths' exploration of the concepts of physical attraction and passion.

In the second stage of dating, a "romantic flavor" is added to group-based interaction, and romantic relationships take on importance for peer status (Brown, 1999). Although there is likely considerable variation in time of entry to this stage, by age 14 or 15, about half of all adolescents report having had some single- or group-dating experience (Connolly & Johnson, 1996; Feiring, 1996). Dating at this stage is a short-term, rapidly shifting affair, as adolescents learn methods of interpersonal and sexual relatedness and experiment with romantic identities. For example, the average length of relationship among 15-year-olds in one study was approximately 4 months (Feiring, 1996).

Dating at this stage can be distinguished from later patterns of romantic involvement on a number of other dimensions as well. In particular, studies have found that young adolescents tend to describe their relationships in terms of companionship rather than characteristics of trust, support, intimacy, and stability that are emphasized in descriptions by young adults (Furman & Wehner, 1994; Paul & White, 1990; Shulman & Kipnis, 2001). At the same time, it is clear that early adolescent relationships are intense, consuming, and stressful (Seiffge-Krenke, 1998; Shulman & Kipnis, 2001). Because of the association of romance and status in this stage, adolescents are confronted with the pressure to engage in romantic relationships that receive peer approval. Romantic relationships may be used to gain status with peers, and a "poor" romantic choice may result in diminished peer acceptance. It is perhaps for this reason that among 12- to 17-year-olds, falling in love is one of the most frequently reported stressful experiences (Seiffge-Krenke, 1995). Younger adolescents in particular report high levels of negative affect such as shame and helplessness in association with falling in love.

After a period of experimentation in multiple casual relationships, youth generally progress to more serious, exclusive dating relationships that become increasingly important sources of support relative to parents and peers (Furman & Buhrmester, 1992). By 18 years of age most adolescents have had at least one steady relationship (Thornton, 1990), and dyadic relationships are the norm (Brown, 1999; Connolly & Goldberg, 1999). In addition, their romantic relationships have become more intense, committed, and satisfying.

At this point, many adolescents have begun to experiment with sexual intimacy. Results of the U.S. Youth Risk Behavior survey found that 34% of Grade 9 and 41% of Grade 10 students reported having had sexual intercourse, with 23 and 30%, respectively, indicating that they were currently sexually active (i.e. had engaged in sexual intercourse during the past 3 months; Grunbaum et al., 2002). Nieder and Seiffge-Krenke (2001) found that between the ages of 14 and 15, increases in the affection and intimacy of relationships are accompanied by a corresponding decrease in stress associated with romance. This reduction in stress may relate also to reduced peer interference, as youth at this age begin to resent the negative judgments or pressures of their peers (Zimmer-Gembeck, 2002).

Finally, youth progress to committed relationships that, to some extent, resemble marital relationships. Brown (1999) suggests that this progression to the bonding phase is marked by the addition of a pragmatic perspective. At this point adolescents work to balance in-depth romantic caring with practical considerations such as the possibility of lifelong commitment and similarity of adult goals and values. Connolly and Goldberg (1999) suggest a similar progression to committed romantic relationships, but focus on differences in expected duration and multiple roles (i.e., caring, attraction, intimacy) that these relationships entail.

In addition to the above issues, the trajectory for emerging romantic involvement across adolescence for gay/lesbian and bisexual youth is further complicated by the issue of sexual orientation identity and "coming out," which has received limited research attention. A four-stage model has been proposed as the "ideal" transition to an integrated same-sexual-orientation identity (Troiden, 1989). The stages involve a progression from sensitization (i.e., awareness of same-sex attraction), to confusion (marked by inner turmoil), to identity assumption (possibly following a same-sex sexual contact), to commitment. A recent attempt to delineate trajectories of significant events associated with sexual identity orientation (e.g., age of awareness, age of first disclosure, coming out) found five significant clusters of experience for these youth (Floyd & Stein, 2002). These clusters of youth differed from each other on dimensions of age of awareness, homosexual experience, age of first disclosure, disclosure to a parent, and gay/lesbian social immersion. The results suggested significant diversity in the experiences of gay/lesbian and bisexual youth with respect to these developmental experiences. For example, although the mean age for awareness (with respect to same-sex attraction) was 10.4 years ($SD = 3.4$), the responses ranged from 3 to 18 years. Clearly, it is difficult to chart age ranges for these significant events, given this variability of experience.

In sum, the developmental literature suggests that over the high school years there is a normative progression from multiple, casual, affiliative dating relationships to more committed and intimate partnerships. Continuity is normative, with high quality parent–child and peer relationships associated with more satisfying and adaptive adolescent romance. At the same time, there is a good deal of variation around this normative path, and there is almost certainly no single "best" path of romantic development (Furman & Wehner, 1997; Miller & Benson, 1999). The trajectories for gay/lesbian and bisexual youth have not received as much research attention, but recent attempts to describe the process of sexual identity formation suggests considerable variability for these youth. Although there may be many models of healthy adolescent dating, it is also clear that some paths lead toward maladaptive outcomes in intimate relationships. As with the characteristics of healthy relationships, examining the nature and scope of dating violence in adolescence must take into account the developmental context of intimate relationships. In the following section we review findings from three major developmental periods—early adolescence, midadolescence, and late adolescence—to clarify the ongoing progression of dating violence from early teasing and harassment to verbal, physical, and sexual assault.

Early Adolescence

In early adolescence, cross-sex relationships exist mostly in a group context. Thus, relationship aggression at this age also tends to be group based, and involves various forms of teasing and harassment. Teasing, a commonplace activity, typically involves making fun of the target individual, especially about some characteristic that deviates from the group norm, such as weight or appearance. However, teasing can escalate to the point of indignation, intimidation, and hostile discrimination. Although there are playful and beneficial aspects of teasing, teasing can be used by a more powerful (e.g., older, larger, more popular) individual to dominate a less assertive or less powerful one (Shapiro, Baumeister, & Kessler, 1991). Drawing on this parallel, some forms of teasing belong to the same class of behavior as coercive and openly hostile forms of abuse, and thus may warrant consideration as an entry-level behavior for those inclined to dominate others as they form their own intimate relationships.

Paradoxically, teasing also plays an important role in the development of cross-sex relationships and, as such, may signal the transition into romantic relationships. For example, as children approach puberty there is often a change from teasing about the presence of heterosexual interest to teasing about the absence of such interest (Shapiro et al., 1991). Teasing is also a viable strategy for the teaser to camouflage his or her intentions and express sentiments that could not otherwise be expressed. Because such teasing combines elements of sexual interest, aggression, and humor in an ambiguous manner, it permits the teaser to show romantic interest with little risk to self-esteem or social standing. The complex function of this behavior therefore represents one of the important developmental challenges accompanying the early formation of dating relationships.

Although adolescent banter is normative for showing romantic interest, teasing can also be used to camouflage aggressive and hurtful sentiments. Such harassment initially emerges in the context of same-sex relationships and can include malicious whispering, name-calling, and note-passing. Same-sex harassment can also include, or be based on, the romantic interests and choices of an individual. Like teasing, harassment can be predicted by an adolescent's interest, or lack of interest, in romance and often entails homophobic insults (McMaster, Connolly, Pepler, & Craig, 2002).

Between grades 6 and 8 cross-sex harassment becomes increasingly more common, with pubertal maturation and mixed-sex socialization both associated with increased cross-sex harassment (McMaster et al., 2002). Although same-sex harassment *sometimes* has a sexual component, cross-sex harassment *often* entails behaviors that might be construed as sexual advances. Examples of these behaviors include making sexual comments, jokes, or gestures, rating sexual parts of someone's body, pulling at someone's clothes in a sexual way (e.g., pulling up a shirt, pulling down pants), or brushing up against someone in a sexual way on purpose. Although younger teens have some concept of the various forms of harassment and why they are wrong, verbally, physically, and sexually abusive behaviors among peers or friends are usually discounted as "just joking" (Berman et al., 2002). This minimizing view continues throughout midadolescence, and becomes a familiar excuse for dating violence or a misperception of care and commitment from a partner, or both. At the same time these teasing behaviors are also ways of expressing interest, which is why it is difficult for teens and adults alike to differentiate the more harmful behaviors.

Notwithstanding teens' view of harassment as harmless, cross-sex harassment can and does have negative consequences. Young adolescent girls report that experiencing harassment leads to outcomes such as feeling afraid or embarrassed, being quiet in class, and achieving lower grades (American Association of University Women, 1993). Sexual and nonsexual forms of harassment take perhaps the greatest toll on girls in particular, who report reduced self-esteem, self-blame, a sense of needing to change to be accepted, embarrassment, and shame much more often than boys (Berman et al., 2002). Furthermore, sexual harassment of others is often a warning sign of a developmental pattern of interpersonal aggression and a precursor for hostile interactions with dating partners (McMaster, Craig, Connolly, & Pepler, 1997; Connolly, Pepler, Craig, & Taradash, 2000). In one of the few studies to track relationship aggression from childhood to adolescence, children who perpetrated the most same- and cross-sex harassment were substantially more likely to report perpetrating aggression in their dating relationships (Pepler, Craig, Connolly, & Henderson, 2002).

Midadolescence

In midadolescence youth make the transition from cross-sex group interactions to dyadic relationships. Relationship aggression follows this movement to the dyad, and dating violence as traditionally conceptualized emerges (Bethke & DeJoy, 1993). Dating relationships during this period contain aspects of both childhood friendships and adult intimacy, and function to meet conflicting strivings for autonomy and connection. Relationship aggression is similarly described with a mixture of characteristics, from child aggression to adult-like partner violence. Similar to early adolescence, reciprocal relationship aggression appears to be the norm, with girls perpetrating at least as much aggressive behavior toward their dating partners as boys, as previously described. However, motivation for and impact of relationship aggression at this stage may begin to resemble more closely that found in adult relationships.

The nature of youths' romantic involvement is important to consider in conceptualizing relationship aggression in midadolescence, because the early establishment of committed relationships may interfere with normal processes of adolescent social and emotional development. For example, premature stability in romantic relationships is thought to preclude healthy exploration and commitment to the process of identity formation, and affects the pursuit of other important goals, such as educational or career development (Samet & Kelly, 1987). Early dating initiation has been associated with a number of adolescent problem behaviors, such as teen pregnancy, decline in academic grades, smoking, drinking, and delinquency (Neeman, Hubbard, & Masten, 1995). Adolescents' limited skill and experience in negotiating self–other boundaries in intimate relationships may also explain why dating during this period is associated with high rates of abuse (Wolfe & Feiring, 2000).

Premature adolescent dating is not merely a correlate of other problematic behaviors, but part of a causal sequence that promotes precocious transition into adult sexual and social (i.e., drinking, smoking) activities, and corresponding neglect of adolescent developmental tasks (e.g., scholastic achievement). Using longitudinal data, Neeman et al. (1995) found that early romantic involvement predicted increased conduct problems and decreased academic achievement by midadolescence, even after controlling for continuity in problem behavior and romantic involvement (sex of participants was controlled in analyses but not examined as a potential moderator). Similarly, Davies and Windle (2000) found that developmental pathways characterized by high dating involvement (relative to their peers) over the high school period were associated with increased problem behaviors.

Late Adolescence

By late adolescence, relationships typically are relatively long-lasting, serious, and committed. At this point romantic relationships take on the function of support, care, and intimacy formerly accorded to parents and, to a lesser extent, friends and peers. For most youth these changes are positive, such as being related to decreased stress and increased feelings of intimacy and support. However, late adolescence is also when rates of violence against women peak, as reported in crime and police statistics. The National Crime Victimization Survey, for example, indicates an overall rate of 5.8 criminal intimate victimizations per 1,000 women over age 24, compared with rates of 15.6 per 1,000 for those aged 16 to 24 (Rennison, 2002).

Differences in motivation for abuse that emerge in midadolescence become more pronounced in late adolescence. Among college students, female victims are more likely to think their perpetrators' motivation for violence was domination, control, or retaliation to a female strike (Follingstad et al., 1991). In contrast, males who reported being victims of violence attributed their partners' aggression to a desire to demonstrate anger or retaliate against emotional hurt or mistreatment, a characterization with which female perpetrators agreed.

Despite differences in motivation, mutual violence remains the empirical norm in violent adolescent intimate relationships in late adolescence (Gray & Foshee, 1997). Youth involved in mutually violent relationships tend to report sustaining and initiating more total violence, more severe violence, and more injuries than those who reported victimization or perpetration alone. Gray and Foshee (1997) suggest that this occurs as a result of the coming together of two violent persons (i.e., assortative mating). Their supposition is that violent individuals select similar partners, and as a result violence escalates through gradually increased acceptance and mutual normalization of these actions. This finding underscores the need to study female dating violence within the context of male violence, and the reciprocal effects of aggressive male and female partners on each other.

In summary, teasing and harassment are likely entry-point behaviors for subsequent abusive and violent acts toward dating partners. Although these forms of relationship aggression typically begin with same-sex peers, by early adolescence harassment and other forms of abuse move into the realm of cross-sex relationships. By midadolescence relationship aggression becomes located more strongly in the dyad, with the importance of the peer group gradually decreasing. Initially, girls perpetrate abuse against their dating partners at a similar rate as boys do, but with very different consequences. Relationship aggression is relatively common during this period, with at least 10% of students reporting significant victimization experiences. As well, teens who prematurely engage in serious romantic involvement and who develop overly committed relationships during midadolescence are at increased risk for multiple negative outcomes, including partner abuse. By late adolescence, relationships become more adult-like and, for some, more stressful. Rates of relationship aggression peak in late adolescence and early adulthood as men and women come to depend more on romantic relationships for support and intimacy. Mutual, or reciprocal, abusive acts remain the norm, although the intention and types of acts vary for young men and women. The incidence of severe dating violence increases and peaks at this age, and other relationship choices, such as marriage or pregnancy, may be made with long-lasting negative repercussions.

Dating Violence Among Lesbian and Bisexual Adolescent Girls

Gay/lesbian and bisexual (GLB) youth are vulnerable to "typical" forms of dating violence (i.e., physical, sexual, and relational violence), in addition to being susceptible to the unique threat of being "outed" by a partner. To date, only one study has reported the prevalence of dating violence among GLB youth (Freedner, Freed, Yang, & Austin, 2002). A substantial proportion of the 333 youth who self-identified as gay/lesbian or bisexual (out of a sample of 521 youth, M age = 17 years) reported experiencing abuse. For girls, however, there were no significant differences in the amount of abuse experienced by sexual orientation, with approximately 37% of females in the total sample reporting at least one form of abuse. The nature of the perpetrator varied by sexual orientation, with 27% of bisexual youth and 19% of lesbians reporting perpetration by a male partner. In addition, there were some differences with respect to rates of specific types of violence experienced. Lesbians were more likely to report that a date or partner had made them scared (compared with heterosexual women), and bisexuals had a higher rate of being sexually abused by a date or partner. Among bisexual adolescent women reporting sexual abuse, 32% reported that the abusers were only female, 61% reported that the abusers were only male, and 7% reported abuse by both male and female partners. This study requires caution in that the data were collected from youth at a rally for

GLB youth rights. Nonetheless, this study represents an important preliminary step in beginning to describe the dating violence experience of these youth.

Clusters of Comorbidity

The issue of comorbidity with dating violence has been studied mainly using large-scale survey data. The cumulative results of these studies suggest that involvement with dating violence (as a perpetrator or victim) is essentially a nonspecific risk factor; that is, dating violence has been identified as a marker associated with a wide range of difficulties. For example, a study of 5,500 high school students in South Carolina found that severe dating violence (victim/perpetrator combined) was significantly related to physical fighting, drug use (illegal drugs, anabolic steroids, tobacco, or alcohol), and high-risk sexual behavior (Coker et al., 2000).

The common co-occurrence of dating violence, substance use, and high-risk sexual behavior may be indicative of an adolescent "risk triad" (Pittman & Wolfe, 2002). The notion of a triad that links these high-risk behaviors comes from separate, yet related, areas of study that together point to common developmental pathways and overlapping contributing causes. In studies by Pepler and colleagues, for example, alcohol use was significantly related to dating aggression for girls, and a trend existed for boys. Girls who reported dating aggression were 5 times more likely to use alcohol compared with girls who did not report dating aggression, whereas boys were 2.5 times as likely (Pepler, Craig, Connolly, & Henderson, 2002). Other researchers have found that teens who use alcohol and drugs are more likely to have sexual intercourse at an earlier age, have more partners, and have greater risk of sexually transmitted diseases (Pittman & Wolfe, 2002). While substance use may exert only a small effect size on violence in adolescence (U.S. Department of Health and Human Services [USDHHS], 2001), its known effects on lowering inhibitions and reducing judgment have been cited as one possible mechanism to explain this link (O'Keefe, 1997).

In Silverman and colleagues' investigations of common risk behaviors among youth, adolescent girls who had experienced physical dating violence also had difficulties with substance use and had high-risk sexual behavior, consistent with the risk triad model. However, there were also associations with unhealthy weight control (such as taking diet pills or laxatives) and suicidality (Silverman et al., 2001). The link between victimization and unhealthy eating practices was also evident in a survey of 2,700 adolescent girls (Thompson, Wonderlich, Crosby, & Mitchell, 2001). Experiences of dating violence and sexual victimization were significant predictors of both purging and diet pill consumption. These relationships provide the tentative basis for more exploration in this area; however, longitudinal data are required to follow the onset of these various behaviors and determine the direction of effects, and possible mechanisms.

DEVELOPMENTAL PATHWAYS TO TEEN DATING VIOLENCE

Adaptive progression of adolescents through phases of romantic involvement is predictable from their past relational experiences, primarily
those with peers and family members. In general, successful romance follows from peer competence, which follows from healthy and secure parent–
child relationships (Cicchetti & Rogosch, 2002; Scharf & Mayseless, 2001;
Shulman & Scharf, 2000; Seiffge-Krenke, Schulman, & Klessinger, 2001).
In one longitudinal study, for example, Zimmer-Gembeck, Siebenbruner,
and Collins (2001) found that progress toward commitment to a close and
satisfying romantic relationship between the ages of 12 and 16 was associated with psychosocial maturity in early and middle adolescence and
social adaptation in the friendship domain. Youths with poor individual
and social functioning, in contrast, tended to be overinvolved in dating.

Developmental psychopathology amalgamates many of the critical
mechanisms identified in related theories of normal and abnormal development, and this approach provides useful tenets for understanding teen
dating violence. A developmental psychopathology approach places dating violence in a broader context that includes teens' perceived emotional
climate of their families, their previous experiences with conflict and abuse,
their interpretations of violence and (past) maltreatment, and their available coping abilities and resources to countermand stress and seek supportive environments (Cicchetti & Tucker, 1994; Crittenden & Claussen,
2002). This viewpoint emphasizes the dynamic interplay of risk and
protective factors in contributing to the organization of the individual and
formation of the particular developmental trajectory. Rather than a single
prototype, different pathways are proposed that account for vulnerability
and diverse outcomes stemming from earlier experiences, such as child
maltreatment.

Specific mechanisms underlying pathways to dating violence stem primarily from social learning and attachment explanations for related problems, such as aggressive behavior, insecure relationship style, and the
impact of early childhood trauma on development. In particular, these theories connect early childhood events, such as parental conflict and maltreatment, to subsequent adolescent dating violence, and emphasize the
role of peers in developing and maintaining abusive behaviors. Potential
mechanisms offered by these theoretical perspectives are identified below,
including distal and proximal variables that have received empirical support.

Social Learning

Similar to aggressive youth in general, communication and problem-
solving skill deficits play an important role in describing violence in romantic relationships (Holtzworth-Munroe, 1992; Riggs & O'Leary, 1989).
Social learning theorists view abusive conflict-resolution techniques as
both learned and reinforced, often at the expense of more adaptive

(i.e., nonviolent) ways of resolving conflict. Thus, abusive conflict resolution tactics may be more common among individuals who have been exposed to violent conflict resolution methods in their families, as well as to media and other forms of community violence (Reitzel-Jaffe & Wolfe, 2001). Abusive husbands, for example, exhibit communication and problem-solving skills deficits, including a tendency to attribute hostile intent to their wives' actions (Holtzworth-Munroe & Hutchison, 1993), and difficulties in generating competent solutions to problems (Holtzworth-Munroe & Anglin, 1991).

Social learning and related social-cognitive models of coercive escalation may also account for the phenomenon of mutual aggression between adolescent dating partners. Coercive escalation refers to how one dating partner may use a milder form of abusive behavior (e.g., verbal insult), which then is matched or increased by the other partner in a chain of accelerating aggression or injury, or both. Aggression may also be met with humor or attempts at positive physical engagement (e.g., forced affection) and, hence, positively reinforced (Wekerle & Wolfe, 1999). In addition to modeling of abusive behavior by family members, social learning theory proposes mechanisms of self-efficacy, attitudes, and problem-solving skills as variables that would predict and maintain involvement in dating violence.

Attachment

An attachment theory perspective on teen dating violence is also relevant in terms of the intergenerational transmission of relational patterns (Crittenden & Claussen, 2002; Lyons-Ruth & Jacobvitz, 1999). Attachment theory proposes mechanisms of relational style (stemming from the early formation of secure vs. insecure caregiver relationship), as well as trauma-related symptoms (such as emotional dysregulation), as important in the initiation and maintenance of dating violence among adolescents (Wekerle & Avgoustis, in press). A main relational theme is the power imbalance where there is a helpless (victim) versus hostile/controlling (victimizer) dyadic dichotomy in relationship roles. Youths with more limited emotion regulation, such as those from abusive or maltreating families, would be expected to show a greater likelihood of regulation difficulties with fearful arousal. The greater the need of one partner to regulate such arousal, the more skewed the relational polarity becomes (Wekerle & Avgoustis, in press). Controlling behavior may emerge as aggression or as more subtle behaviors such as withdrawal, self-preoccupation, or imposing guilt on the other. Consistent with evidence of mutual violence among teen dating partners noted previously, an individual might alternate between victim and victimizer roles during the course of an argument or conflict.

How maltreatment contributes to insecure attachment models may lie in the expectation of a violent, not merely conflictual, dynamic. Early attachment and child maltreatment experiences inform the child that intimate relationships may involve stark power differentials, where power assertion and abuse are viable (even desirable) strategies to problem-solve and maintain relationships. In addition, such experiences pair experiences of anger and fear with close relationships, and establish views of others in terms of being threatening, abandoning, and not trustworthy (Wolfe et al., 1997). Attachment theory argues that both the victim and the victimizer sides of this dynamic would be learned and available (although perhaps not activated) in maltreated children's interactional repertoires.

In sum, adolescent dating violence may represent a bridge between negative childhood experiences (such as child maltreatment, exposure to marital violence, and insecure attachment) and the occurrence of similar relationship patterns of violence or victimization in adulthood. As they experiment with new roles and expectations, dating experiences are often indicative of past exposure to appropriate and inappropriate conflict resolution tactics, role models, and learning opportunities (Collins & Sroufe, 1999). Individuals exposed to healthy models are more likely to approach dating with greater self-confidence, problem-solving ability, and emotion regulation abilities, whereas those experiencing inconsistent, authoritarian, or neglectful caregiving, and who lack any suitable alternative role models or experiences, are most likely to enter the social dating arena with power-based expectations about the conduct of oneself and one's partner (Galliher, Rostosky, Welsh, & Kawaguchi, 1999).

From both social learning and attachment perspectives on relationship violence, childhood experiences that pair intimacy with either observed or experienced aggression may exert an influence on one's expectations and approach to romantic relationships. Several major risk factors emerge from the above theories. We begin with a discussion of child maltreatment and marital violence, since most theories posit these early experiences as playing a causal role in the formation of subsequent risk factors. Other prominent risk factors are then discussed, including relationship competence and self-efficacy, negative attitudes and beliefs, attachment style, reciprocal effects of past relationships, and trauma-related distress. Each of these risk factors is discussed below, followed by empirical findings.

Major Risk Factors

Child Maltreatment and Marital Violence

Youths with histories of maltreatment are especially at-risk for relationship-based difficulties (Bank & Burraston, 2001), and have more than a 3.5 times greater risk of involvement in adult domestic violence (Coid et al., 2001). Studies of the development of maltreated children, for example, have drawn connections between maltreatment and difficulties inferring emotions and intent of others, which in turn results in coercive interactions with peers (Rogosch, Cicchetti, & Aber, 1995) and dating partners (Wolfe, Wekerle, Reitzel-Jaffe, & Lefebvre, 1998). As well, some teens with maltreatment histories acquire a generalized tendency towards domineering and controlling behavior, which re-emerges in the context of intimate relationships (Follingstad, Bradley, Laughlin, & Burke, 1999). Because of these challenges, peer and social dating relationships among maltreated youth are more likely to be accompanied by poor interpersonal

adjustment (e.g., fear, mistrust, and hostility) and limited personal resources (e.g., poor problem-solving, lower self-efficacy, and distorted beliefs about relationships), which further tax their ability to form healthy,
non-violent relationships (Wolfe, Scott, Wekerle, & Pittman, 2001).

A connection between maltreatment and the emergence of dating violence was supported in a study of over 400 high school students, who
were divided into maltreated and nonmaltreated backgrounds on the basis of self-report (Wolfe et al., 1998). Compared with their nonmaltreated
counterparts ($n = 277$), maltreated youth ($n = 132$) reported more hostility and interpersonal sensitivity (e.g., self-depreciation, feelings of uneasi-
ness), lower problem-solving self-efficacy, and had higher self- and teacher
ratings on peer aggression. Past maltreatment was also significantly related
to boys' becoming perpetrators (as well as victims) of physical violence and
threats, and to girls being the recipient of such violence.

In addition to direct victimization (i.e., maltreatment), witnessing violence in one's family of origin has been connected to adult partner violence,
particularly for men (Hotaling & Sugarman, 1986). A study of young adults
(undergraduates) similarly found that those who witnessed their same-sex
parent perpetrate marital violence were at increased risk for being physically aggressive in their own dating relationships (Jankowski, Leitenberg,
Henning, & Coffey, 1999). There was no increased risk for dating violence
perpetration, however, when students witnessed only the opposite-sex parent perpetrate aggression. These same-sex modelling effects were not found
for dating violence victimization, although witnessing bidirectional marital
violence increased the risk for receiving aggression from a dating partner
(Jankowski et al., 1999).

Relationship Competence and Self-Efficacy

Some adolescents enter the dating arena ill-prepared to problem-solve
the complex issues that often emerge. Child maltreatment, in particular,
is related to the inhibition of healthy relationship skills development and
lower perceived competence and self-efficacy in social situations (Rogosch
& Cicchetti, 1994). As noted by Rogosch et al. (1995), maltreatment leads
to emotional and cognitive deficits associated with difficulty in accurately
inferring emotional reactions in others; these deficits, in turn, result in
problematic interpersonal interactions with both peers and dating partners. Not surprisingly, these relationship deficits appear to carry over into
adolescence. Adolescents with a history of maltreatment have a limited
ability to demonstrate basic relationship skills such as empathy and positive, nonthreatening communication (Birns, Cascardi, & Meyer, 1990). As
they form new partnerships in adolescence, this confluence of factors may
translate into an increased vigilance for signs of aggression, such as an
expectation to encounter hostility from others (Bugental, 1993), and the
belief that aggression is a viable and acceptable interpersonal conflict resolution strategy (Dodge, Pettit, & Bates, 1994).

Because self-efficacy is acquired through direct and indirect experiences, children who are abused or witness violence may form highly

situation-specific expectations regarding conflict resolution with intimate partners. Maltreated adolescents, especially girls, hold a low concept of their efficacy to resolve conflict in a nonviolent and nonthreatening manner, and are not confident that they can avoid being treated in a violent or threatening manner during a conflict (Wekerle et al., 2001). Whether direct or indirect exposure to parental aggression occurs, aggression is a viable, and perhaps preferred, behavioral option that may be learned. Murphy and Blumenthal (2000) found that female college students' interpersonal problems with dominance, intrusiveness, and vindictiveness fully mediated the association between childhood exposure to family violence and aggressive dating relationships (i.e., aggression by partner and aggression by self both indicated intimate aggression). These authors suggest that instead of acquiring a tendency to repeat specific forms of aggression (e.g., those specifically witnessed), the acquisition of a more generalized tendency toward domineering and controlling behavior may occur (i.e., a broad response set).

Attitudes and Beliefs

A social learning view of abuse specific to peer and romantic relationships highlights beliefs that aggression is normative, justifiable, and expected, and will increase the likelihood of desired outcomes (Dodge et al., 1994; Riggs & O'Leary, 1989). Accordingly, attitudes and beliefs justifying relationship violence under "certain conditions" have been linked to aggression in dating relationships among university (Reitzel-Jaffe & Wolfe, 2001) and high school students (Avery-Leaf, Cascardi, O'Leary, & Cano, 1997; Foshee et al., 2001), especially in accounting for male-to-female aggression. For example, Reitzel-Jaffe and Wolfe (2001) found that violence in men's family of origin predicted the development of negative beliefs about gender and interpersonal violence, which in turn predicted their own use of violence or coercion in relationships and their association with deviant peers. Another study found that attitudes accepting aggression as well as antisocial behavior toward partners and others accounted for more than 62% of the variance in dating violence among college-aged men, but only 32% of the variance in women's relationship aggression (Riggs & O'Leary, 1996). Among college-aged students, both males and females justify violence in self-defence, and females also justify violent tactics if humiliated by a dating partner (Foo & Margolin, 1995).

Although attitudes may initially be formed within the context of the family, by adolescence the shift toward the peer group creates an opportunity for social contagion of negative attitudes about male–female relationships. These powerful peer forces, including hostile talk about women among male peers (Capaldi, Dishion, Stoolmiller, & Yoerger, 2001) and sexual harassment with cross-gender peers (McMaster et al., 2002), reinforce beliefs and attitudes supporting aggression as a viable and acceptable interpersonal strategy with intimate partners. While boys are developing hostile attitudes about girls and women, girls may be learning to tolerate or accept such behavior (Berman et al., 2002).

Attachment Style

Past maltreatment is associated with rejection sensitivity among adolescent girls, which contributes to heightened expectations for commitment and a higher valuing of the relationship as an indicator of identity (Downey, Bonica, & Rincón, 1999). Girls and women also tend to report higher levels of emotional distress symptoms as a result of childhood maltreatment, and thus may be more vulnerable to distress mediated pathways to abuse (Kessler et al., 1999; Wolfe, Scott, Wekerle, & Pittman, 2001b).

Avgoustis and Wekerle (2001) examined the association between childhood maltreatment and violence in both dating relationships and peer relationships of youth, using adolescent attachment style as a moderator. Emotional neglect (e.g., not feeling loved) was a significant predictor above and beyond other forms of maltreatment (i.e., physical abuse, emotional abuse and physical neglect) of adolescent aggression. In predicting dating violence, emotional neglect was related to increased risk of being a victim in females, and of being a perpetrator in males (beyond the contribution of other forms of maltreatment). Attachment style moderated the relationship between emotional neglect and dating violence. High-risk girls (defined as those who perceive their relationship style as avoidant and who had high emotional neglect scores) were more likely to be victims of physical and emotional abuse from their dating partners. Similarly, high-risk boys were more likely to be physically and emotionally abusive toward their dating partner.

Relationship History and Experiences

Not surprisingly, adolescents' same-sex friendships, social networks, and perceptions of themselves have reciprocal effects on the nature and quality of their dating relationships (Davies & Windle, 2000). Ipso facto, lessons learned from peers and family members about the use of various abusive or violent tactics as a means to regulate and control interactions with others carries over to the dating context. Children who bully are much more likely to be violent in dating relationships than nonbullies (Connolly et al., 2000), as are those who grow up in maltreating homes (Wolfe et al., 1998). Other researchers have found that behavior observed in family problem-solving discussions among teenagers predicted relationship violence when the adolescents were in their early twenties (Andrews, Foster, Capaldi, & Hops, 2000). Similarly, Foshee et al. (2001) found that friend involvement in dating violence was correlated with dating violence by both males and females, and was a strong predictor of dating violence by females. Across time, girls were influenced by their friends' experiences of dating violence, as opposed to simply selecting similar friends after they have become involved in dating violence.

There are a number of possible social mechanisms through which relationships with parents and peers may facilitate healthy or unhealthy dating, that may act in concert with individual characteristics such as skills, attitudes, and attachment styles. Close friendship networks may increase contact with potential dating partners through group activities, provide a forum for discussion of dating, and a context for exchange of information (Connolly & Johnson, 1996; Paul & White, 1990). In addition, skills learned in friendships for resolution of conflict, regulation of affect, reciprocity and disclosure may be transferred to dating partners (Feiring, 1996; Lempers & Clark-Lempers, 1993). In contrast, a lack of close friendships and peer networks may preclude the development of dating, or conversely lead to a mismatch of romantic expectations. For example, youth who often have been exposed mostly to unhealthy relationships may be seeking support and intimacy at a time when most dating relationships are primarily affiliative (Gray & Steinberg, 1999).

Trauma-Related Distress

Trauma-related symptoms may be functionally related to relationship disturbances, including adolescent dating violence (Wolfe, 1999). For example, dissociation could contribute to asynchrony in and withdrawal from interacting, and hypervigilance could contribute to an agitated, highly reactive response to ambiguous or negative partner behavior. The former may relate to being a recipient of partner aggression, while the latter to being aggressive toward a partner. Girls and women tend to report higher levels of emotional distress symptoms as a result of childhood maltreatment, and thus may be more vulnerable to distress mediated pathways to abuse (Kessler et al., 1999; Wolfe, Scott, Wekerle, & Pittman, 2001). For maltreated girls, in particular, trauma symptoms may create a situation of vulnerability that may contribute to revictimization, interfering with accurate appraisal of threat and consequent appropriate escape/avoidance actions (Messman-Moore & Long, 2000).

Wekerle et al. (2001) supported a mediational model for females where posttraumatic stress symptoms accounted for the relationship between childhood maltreatment and dating violence in both high school and protective service samples. Emotional distress symptoms, which are especially elevated among girls with maltreatment backgrounds (Wolfe, Scott, Wekerle, & Pittman, 2001), may partially account for their involvement in abusive relationships. The critical mediational role of trauma-related symptoms is theoretically linked to potential structural and functional changes in brain development as a consequence of the maltreatment experiences (Glaser, 2000). Given that the dating context may involve strong feelings, physical proximity, and sexual involvement, there may be a resurgence of trauma-related symptoms owing to similar cues to the original abusive event(s) (Wekerle & Wolfe, 2003).

Role of Puberty

Navigating puberty is one of the major challenges faced by adolescents (Silbereisen & Kracke, 1997). The extent to which early or late onset of puberty may affect involvement in dating violence is worthy of consideration. Early onset of puberty in girls has been found to be associated with a number of risk behaviors including cigarette smoking and consumption of alcohol (Stattin & Magnusson, 1990). Furthermore, early-maturing girls tend to start dating earlier, and often choose older partners (Silbereisen & Kracke, 1997). Involvement with older partners has been identified as a mediator in the observed relationship between early physical maturation and earlier onset of sexual activity for girls (Stattin & Magnusson, 1990). Thus, early maturation poses a risk for many factors related to dating violence, but had not been investigated directly in this respect.

Integrating Models of Risk for Dating Violence

Although there has been steady progress in the identification of risk factors for adolescent dating violence, few comprehensive models integrate risk factors and elucidate common pathways to dating violence. We have been working on one such model that relates past child maltreatment and adolescent dating violence through the presence of trauma, attitudes that justify dating violence, and poor relationship competence (as measured by empathy and self-efficacy; Wolfe, Wekerle, Scott, Straatman, & Grasley, 2004). Longitudinal analyses involving a large sample of high school students (M age = 16.1; 55% female) found that girls' trauma symptoms (indicated by anger) and their attitudes justifying dating violence each predicted their dating violence perpetration 1 year later. Boys' trauma symptoms also predicted abuse of their dating partner 1 year later, when the model was adjusted to predict emotional abuse only. Hypotheses concerning the role of empathy and self-efficacy in predicting dating violence over time were not supported. This study also determined that a history of maltreatment increases one's risk for engaging in abusive behavior among both boys and girls, although it did not have a direct impact on dating violence across time after accounting for continuity in dating violence across time. This model represents a preliminary attempt to combine risk factors in a meaningful manner; however, further work is critically needed in this area.

ASSESSMENT AND TREATMENT

Given the importance of relationship development, efforts to accurately assess and effectively prevent or treat adolescent dating violence are warranted. The "initiation phase" of social dating in early to midadolescence, in particular, offers a prime opportunity to become aware of the ways in which violent and abusive behavior toward romantic partners may occur, often without purpose or intention. This premise holds true not only for individuals from violent and abusive family backgrounds where negative experiences were prominent, but it applies to other adolescents as well (Wolfe et al., 1997).

Assessment Issues

Adolescent dating violence is difficult to assess, in part because of privacy, and in part due to the range of intentions and consequences of potentially abusive acts, as previously discussed in this chapter. For example, teens often invoke a justification of "just joking" with respect to physical aggression. Thus, it is difficult to distinguish between playful wrestling that is experienced as such by all parties involved, and physically intrusive or intimidating acts that are being minimized by one or both dating partners. Despite these acknowledged difficulties, researchers have often relied on behaviorally based self-report measures to estimate incidence of dating violence, or proxy measures such as changes in attitudes and knowledge, to assess change over time. Behavioral indices, although more valid, are plagued by ethical, practical, and even definitional concerns (see, e.g., Yeater & O'Donohue, 1999; Wekerle & Wolfe, 1999). Unfortunately, there are often few reasonable alternatives for obtaining information about private relationships other than self-report or, in some limited circumstances, partner report.

With these limitations in mind, researchers have begun to describe some of the potential gender differences and biases commonly found in self-report. One source of difference may be in interpreting the actual language of items. For example, boys may interpret "hit" as involving a closed-fisted punch, whereas girls may see this more broadly (i.e., an open-handed slap). Similarly, boys tend to describe "force" as psychological pressure, whereas girls describe it as physical force (Muehlenhard & Cook, 1988; Watson et al., 2001). Moreover, there may be gender differences in the willingness and motivation to report or avoid reporting relationship aggression. Among adults, for example, women avoid reporting victimization to minimize personal hurt and relational problems and perhaps because they have a greater readiness to assume blame; men avoid disclosing perpetration to maintain control, deny problems and responsibility, and foster positive impression management (Wekerle & Wolfe, 1999). Such reporting biases have implications for interpreting similar, though not necessarily equivalent, rates of self-reported abuse perpetration and victimization among adolescents.

Conceptualization of dating and relationship violence must also distinguish between physical *acts* and physical *consequences* of violence (Lewis, Travea, & Fremouw, 2002). While the consequences of more subtle forms of abuse may differ from more serious physical and sexual assaults, subtle acts of abuse are important from a measurement perspective since they often proceed and cooccur with more serious physically and sexually violent acts in both adolescence (Capaldi & Crosby, 1997; O'Keefe, 1997) and adulthood (Babcock, Waltz, Jacobson, & Gottman, 1993). Thus, even though a punch may have a different consequence to the victim than a slap (for instance), these behaviors tend to cooccur and cluster into the same class of (aggressive) behavior. Following the lead of the field of sexual assault research, behaviorally specific, well-operationalized constructs will be critical for advancing the field and adding consistency to the definition of dating violence (Hanson, 2002). In addition, the measurement of teen dating violence needs to improve on ways to ensure that the context of conflict is adequately taken into account when asking respondents to describe their past actions. Merely counting discrete acts of violence can be misleading because the psychological significance and the context of abusive actions are key aspects in defining relationship violence.

A final difficulty in assessing adolescent dating violence is that few measures have been developed specifically for adolescent dating couples. The two most commonly used assessment instruments, the Conflict Tactics scales (CTS; Straus, 1979) and the Psychological Maltreatment of Women Inventory (PMWI; Tolman, 1989), were developed and normed almost exclusively in reference to adult and college-aged intimate relationships (e.g., Capaldi & Crosby, 1997; Foo & Margolin, 1995; O'Keefe & Treister, 1998; Pan, Neidig, & O'Leary, 1994; for exceptions see Avery-Leaf et al., 1997; Cascardi et al., 1999). From a developmental perspective, some items on these existing measures are simply inappropriate with adolescents (e.g., using children as a threat and control tactic; economic abuse). In addition, midadolescents' intimate partnerships vary greatly from those of adults in terms of duration, level of commitment, amount of prior experience, degree of sexual intimacy, the peer-like status of dating partners, and causes and resolutions of conflict (Furman & Wehner, 1997; Laursen & Collins, 1994). In response to these considerations, we developed the Conflict in Adolescent Dating Relationships Inventory (CADRI; Wolfe, Scott, Reitzel-Jaffe, et al., 2001) to fill this gap in adolescent-focused measures. The CADRI is completed by teens in reference to an actual conflict or disagreement with a current or recent dating partner over the past 2 months.

Intervention and Prevention Strategies

Because acts of violence and abuse in adolescent dating relationships are relatively commonplace and developmentally relevant, all teens can benefit from greater awareness of such issues. Therefore, intervention strategies are often based on a public health perspective of risk and protective factors, rather than individual psychopathology (Wolfe et al., 1997). A public health approach implies a focus on prevention and early intervention, with additional services available for targeted groups (e.g., high-risk youth), or to address the harmful consequences of victimization. Emerging prevention programs challenge inappropriate attitudes and behaviors and offer positive alternatives. They may also include resilience-promoting activities, such as skill building, recognition of early warning signs, awareness of forms of violence, and help-seeking strategies. Below are several considerations in addressing dating violence from a broad, prevention standpoint.

Gender Considerations

Program delivery must be sensitive to sex differences among adolescents, as described in this chapter. Programs on dating violence, for example, may create backlash among boys if they are perceived as an attack on males in general. In some cases, boys' attitudes *get worse* after they learn more about these issues (Hilton, Harris, Rice, Krans, & Lavigne, 1998). Backlash has also occurred because of attempts to impose adult-like explanations and solutions, rather than addressing dating violence from a teen perspective and motivation. Boys, in particular, are seldom willing to engage in discussion of relationship violence and personal responsibility that does not acknowledge, at some level, the reality of girls' aggression. Furthermore, girls may need to understand that relational and other forms of nonphysical aggression are inappropriate, regardless of their male partner's apparent lack of injury or indifference (Odgers & Moretti, 2002).

Girls may also benefit from discussion of the possible connections between previous (negative) relationships and their current patterns of attachment, and in some instances benefit from specific trauma counseling. Feminist approaches with adolescent girls include a mentoring model, which focuses on a positive relationship involving mutual sharing and supportive connection between girls and women. A common thread among these approaches is the importance of providing a safe, nonthreatening, nonjudgmental environment that allows adolescents to explore their own goals and choices in relationships. For boys, unique strategies for participation may include involvement of popular male peer and teacher role models, and more graduated approaches to introducing the underlying social issues and factors contributing to these problems (Jaffe, Wolfe, Crooks, Hughes, & Baker, 2004).

Program Delivery

Debate exists regarding the optimal locale for dating violence prevention efforts. On the one hand, community-based programming (often done in small co-ed groups) permits youth with common needs and strengths to become involved in their own communities, and to feel safe in participating in unfamiliar activities with minimal peer interference. On the other hand, school-based programs have the advantage of greater access to youth, space, time, and personnel. Even more fundamental is the elimination of any targeting or labeling of persons receiving the program by offering the program universally. School-based prevention concerning dating violence and sexual assault, however, must be equally sensitive to special needs (e.g., disclosures of past or current abuse in the classroom), and the importance of providing a safe place to discuss personal beliefs and attitudes. Other programmatic considerations include avoiding a "one size fits all" approach that ignores culturally relevant information and differences (Heppner, Neville, Smith, Kivlighan, & Gershuny, 1999), determining the best "dosage" of information and training (i.e., some programs are delivered in one session, whereas others are extended over 10–20 lesson plans), and the possible role of booster sessions that would expand the curriculum in accordance with developmental changes.

Primary prevention programs often involve activities aimed at increasing awareness and dispelling myths about relationship violence and sexual assault. Most often such activities include school auditorium presentations involving videotapes, plays, professional theatre groups, or a speech from a survivor; classroom discussions facilitated by teachers or service providers; or specific programs and curricula that encourage students to examine attitudes and behaviors that promote or tolerate violence. These curricula have primarily used didactic approaches to orient students to the different ways in which abuse and violence may be expressed, and examining their own attitudes and gender-role stereotypes (Avery-Leaf et al., 1997; Lavoie, Vezina, Piche, & Boivin, 1995).

One such program that has been evaluated is "Safe Dates" (Foshee, 1996, Foshee et al., 2000). Over 1,500 Grade 8 and 9 students participated in 10 classroom sessions and related activities, such as a poster contest. This project is one of the few studied that has included a follow-up to explore long-term prevention effects. Although some of the positive behavioral changes had disappeared at the 1-year follow-up, some of the critical changes in variables that mediate dating violence (e.g., dating violence norms, conflict-management skills, and awareness of community services for dating violence) were maintained.

In addition to school-based programs for adolescents, community-based programs with secondary prevention goals have been developed to target youth at risk of dating violence (on the basis of past family violence or maltreatment). The Youth Relationships Project (YRP; Wolfe et al., 2003) was developed to assist adults in empowering youth to end violence in relationships through education, skill development, and social competence. This program reflects an incremental strategy aimed at self-awareness and social change (i.e., examining oneself first, and moving on to one's peers, school environment, social institutions, and cultural influences), and is delivered through an 18-session program in community settings. The program targets not only abusive behaviors but also the social factors underlying discriminatory attitudes and assumptions, such as sexism, racism, and other forms of discrimination that make girls and minorities particularly susceptible to violence or oppression. Two-year follow-up results involving random assignment to the intervention or control condition support this approach in reducing physical and emotional abuse perpetration toward dating partners, for both girls and boys.

FUTURE DIRECTIONS

Throughout this chapter we have emphasized the importance of a developmentally sensitive conceptualization of adolescent dating violence. Adolescent dating violence is qualitatively different from both childhood peer aggression and adult intimate violence, although it has elements of both. Researchers in this area need to continue to investigate variables from both literatures, but integrate them into comprehensive models specific to adolescent relationship aggression. As these models emerge, they should inform practical applications related to assessment and treatment.

The need for comprehensive longitudinal models that combine risk factors and mechanisms that account for the emergence of dating violence has already been noted. Beyond a comprehensive dating violence model, however, there is a need to integrate theories from other domains of adolescent risk behavior (i.e., high-risk sexual behavior, substance use). The overlap between these areas is well documented in terms of comorbidity and common risk factors, but the reciprocal influences among these areas are not well delineated. The longitudinal study of partnerships and dating violence needs to take into account the stability of violence across different relationships, the trajectory when the first important teen partnership involves violence, the age differential of partners, the level of substance use in the partnership, the presence of sexual activity, and the overall quality of relationships. There are likely a number of trajectories along which adolescents navigate these various spheres, and a gender analysis of trajectories specific to boys and girls will be critical as these trajectories are explored.

Given the range of difficulties inherent in relying on self-report data, creative and innovative assessment strategies are required to complement existing data collection approaches. Behavioral measures provide one direction for efforts in this domain, as well as self-report diaries that permit ongoing recording of events. There is also a need to consider historical information to provide a developmental context for individual responses. For example, a comprehensive childhood history is an important component of assessment, as there is evidence that traumatic experiences in childhood have implications for differential response to subsequent violence because of neuropsychological vulnerabilities (DeBellis, 2001).

Finally, with respect to prevention and treatment, there is a need to move beyond a "one size fits all" approach to treatment, and begin to develop and evaluate a stepped series of interventions. The analogy of teaching children to read serves as a useful parallel. All children in school are automatically taught to read. As it becomes apparent that a percentage of these children will struggle with reading, they are given additional opportunities to hone their skills, often with the use of adult volunteers. The most intensive services are reserved for those that are clearly not meeting age-appropriate norms of competence.

Because universal approaches to preventing dating violence among adolescents are relatively new, there has not been the opportunity to explore the boundaries of effectiveness for these interventions. As yet we do not know who benefits from this approach and who may not, and we lack the necessary specificity to tailor universal interventions to adolescents' wide-ranging needs. As with any school subject, students do not learn and use the material in a uniform manner, and additional resources may be needed to assist those with greater needs. On the basis of current knowledge, we suspect that these needs may involve additional exposure to healthy role models and skill development (such as ample opportunity for "live rehearsal" of nonviolent problem-solving to overcome learned negative patterns), as well as efforts directed at supporting greater peer awareness and involvement in violence prevention. But it is not only a subset of teens who require additional efforts to overcome strong tendencies—violence prevention needs to borrow from other areas of health promotion and make a stronger effort to educate and involve parents, school personnel, and the community in promoting healthy, nonviolent relationships.

In summary, it may be that in adolescence an early version of violent coupling is emerging, one in which a history of maltreatment and peer aggression makes both male and female teens vulnerable to forming violent partnerships. Although boys and girls report equal rates of violent behaviors, these rates obscure numerous differences with respect to intention, consequences, severity, and impact. Further, incidents of hitting or punching may be the tip of the iceberg for a range of abusive behaviors, all of which need to be understood within a developmental context. The differential course for males and females as they navigate adolescence and begin to engage in dating relationships has only recently become a focus of study. As the next generation of research moves beyond attempting to quantify the problem of adolescent dating violence to a deeper understanding of the underlying dynamics and developmental trajectories, more developmentally sensitive assessment and treatment strategies will also emerge. In addition, as we move away from adult models of violence to new conceptualizations that capture the uniqueness of adolescence, the experience of adolescent girls as both victims and perpetrators of dating violence will be better understood.

ACKNOWLEDGEMENTS. This chapter was supported by a Senior Research Fellowship award from the Ontario Mental Health Foundation (DW), a grant from the National Institute of Alcohol Abuse and Alcoholism (DW), and a Postdoctoral Fellowship (KS) from the Social Sciences and Humanities Research Council.

REFERENCES

American Association of University Women. (1993). *Hostile hallways: The AAUW survey on sexual harassment in America's schools.* Washington, DC: American Association of University Women Educational Foundation.

Andrews, J., Foster, S. L., Capaldi, D., & Hops, H. (2000). Adolescent and family predictors of physical aggression, communication, and satisfaction in young adult couples: A prospective analysis. *Journal of Consulting and Clinical Psychology, 68,* 195–208.

Archer, J. (2000). Sex differences in aggression between heterosexual partners: A meta-analytic review. *Psychological Bulletin, 126,* 651–680.

Archer, J. (2002). Sex differences in physically aggressive acts between heterosexual partners: A meta-analytic review. *Aggression and Violent Behavior, 7,* 313–351.

Avery-Leaf, S., Cascardi, M., O'Leary, K. D., & Cano, A. (1997). Efficacy of a dating violence prevention program on attitudes justifying aggression. *Journal of Adolescent Health, 21,* 1, 11–17.

Avgoustis, E., & Wekerle, C. (April, 2001). *The importance of childhood emotional neglect in predicting adolescent interpersonal functioning.* Poster session presented at the biennial meeting of The Society for Research in Child Development, Minneapolis, MN.

Babcock, J. C., Waltz, J., Jacobson, N. S., & Gottman, J. M. (1993). Power and violence: The relation between communication patterns, power discrepancies and domestic violence. *Journal of Consulting and Clinical Psychology, 61,* 40–50.

Bank, L., & Burraston, B. (2001). Abusive home environments as predictors of poor adjustment during adolescence and early adulthood. *Journal of Community Psychology, 29,*
195–217.

Berman, H., Straatman, A. L., Hunt, K., Izumi, J., & MacQuarrie, B. (2002). Sexual harass-
ment: The unacknowledged face of violence in the lives of girls. In H. Berman & Y. Jiwani
(Eds.), *In the best interests of the girl child: Phase II Report.* London, Canada: Centre for
Research on Violence Against Women and Children. The University of Western Ontario.

Bethke, T., & DeJoy, D. (1993). An experimental study of factors influencing the acceptability
of dating violence. *Journal of Interpersonal Violence, 8*(1), 36–51.

Birns, B., Cascardi, M., and Meyer, S. (1990). Sexual socialization: Developmental influences
on wife abuse. *American Journal of Orthopsychiatry, 64,* 50–59.

Brown, B. (1999) . "You're going out with who?" Peer group influences on adolescent romantic
relationships. In W. Furman, B. Brown, & C. Feiring (Eds.), *The development of romantic
relationships in adolescence* (pp. 291–329). New York: Cambridge University Press.

Brown, B., Feiring, C., & Furman, W. (1999). Missing the love boat: Why researchers have
shied away from adolescent romance. In W. Furman, B. Brown, & C. Feiring (Eds.), *The
development of romantic relationships in adolescence* (pp. 1–16). New York: Cambridge
University Press.

Bugental, D. B. (1993). Communication in abusive relationships: Cognitive constructions of
interpersonal power. *American Behavioral Scientist, 36,* 288–308.

Capaldi, D. M., & Crosby, L. (1997). Observed and reported psychological and physical aggression in young, at-risk couples. *Social Development, 6,* 184–206.

Capaldi, D. M., Dishion, T. J., Stoolmiller, M., & Yoerger, K. (2001). Aggression toward female partners by at-risk young men: The contribution of male adolescent friendships.
Developmental Psychology, 37, 61–73.

Cascardi, M., Avery-Leaf, S., O'Leary, K. D., & Smith Slep, A. M. (1999). Factor structure
and convergent validity of the conflict tactics scale in high school students. *Psychological
Assessment, 11,* 546–555.

Cauffman, E., Feldman, S., Arnett-Jensen, L., & Jensen-Arnett, J. (2000). The
(un)acceptability of violence against peers and dates. *Journal of Adolescent Research,
15,* 652–673.

Centers for Disease Control and Prevention. (2000). Youth Risk Behavior Surveillance—United
States 1999. *Morbidity and Mortality Weekly Report, 49*(5), 1–96.

Chase, K. A., Treboux, D., & O'Leary, K. D. (2002). Characteristics of high-risk adolescents'
dating violence. *Journal of Interpersonal Violence, 17,* 33–49.

Cicchetti, D., & Rogosch, F. Q. (2002). A developmental psychopathology perspective on adolescence. *Journal of Consulting and Clinical Psychology, 70,* 6–20.

Cicchetti, D., & Tucker, D. (1994). Development and self-regulatory structures of the mind.
Development and Psychopathology, 6, 533–549.

Coid, J., Petruckevitch, A., Feder, G., Chung, W., Richardson, J., & Moorey, S. (2001). Relation
between childhood sexual and physical abuse and risk of revictimisation in women: A
cross-sectional survey. *The Lancet, 358,* 450–454.

Coker, A. L., McKeown, R. E., Sanderson, M., Davis, K. E., Valois, R. F., & Huebner, E. S.
(2000). Severe dating violence and quality of life among South Carolina high school students. *American Journal of Preventive Medicine, 19,* 220–227.

Collins, W. A., & Sroufe, L. A. (1999). Capacity for intimate relationships: A developmental
construction. In W. Furman, B. Brown, & B. Bradford (Eds.), *The development of romantic
relationships in adolescence. Cambridge studies in social and emotional development* (pp.
125–147). New York: Cambridge University Press.

Connolly, J., & Goldberg, A. (1999). Romantic relationships in adolescence: The role of friends
and peers in their emergence and development. In W. Furman, B. B. Brown, & C. Feiring
(Eds.), *The development of romantic relationships in adolescence* (pp. 266–291). New York:
Cambridge University Press.

Connolly, J. A., & Johnson, A. M. (1996). Adolescents' romantic relationships and the
structure and quality of their close interpersonal ties. *Personal Relationships, 3,* 185–
195.

Connolly, J., Pepler, D., Craig, W., & Taradash, A. (2000). Dating experiences of bullies in
early adolescence. *Child Maltreatment, 5,* 297–308.

Craig, W., & Pepler, D. 1997. Observations of bullying and victimization in the school yard. *Canadian Journal of School Psychology, 13,* 41-60

Crick, N., Bigbee, M., & Howes, C. (1996). Gender differences in children's normative beliefs about aggression: How do I hurt thee? Let me count the ways. *Child Development, 67,* 1003–1014.

Crittenden, P., & Claussen, A. (2002). Developmental psychopathology perspectives on substance abuse and relationship violence. In C. Wekerle & A.-M. Wall (Eds.), *The violence and addiction equation: Theoretical and clinical issues in substance abuse and relationship violence* (pp. 44–63). Philadelphia, PA: Brunner/Mazel.

Currie, D. H. (1998). Violent men or violent women? Whose definition counts? In R. Kennedy Bergen (Eds.), *Issues in intimate violence* (pp. 97–122). Thousand Oaks, CA: Sage.

Davies, P. T., & Windle, M. (2000). Middle adolescents' dating pathways and psychosocial adjustment. *Merrill-Palmer Quarterly, 46,* 90–118.

DeBellis, M. D. (2001). Developmental traumatology: The psychobiological development of maltreated children and its implications for research, treatment, and policy. *Development and Psychopathology, 13,* 539–564.

Dobash, R. E., & Dobash, R. P. (1992). *Women, violence and social change.* New York: Routledge.

Dodge, K. A., Pettit, G. S., & Bates, J. E. (1994). Effects of physical maltreatment on the development of peer relations. *Development and Psychopathology, 6,* 43–55.

Downey, G., Bonica, C., & Rincón, C. (1999). Rejection sensitivity and adolescent romantic relationships. In W. Furman, B. B. Brown, & C. Feiring (Eds.), *The development of romantic relationships in adolescence* (pp. 148–174). New York: Cambridge University Press.

Feiring, C. (1996). Concepts of romance in 15-year-old adolescents. *Journal of Research on Adolescence, 6*(2), 181–200.

Floyd, F. J., & Stein, T. S. (2002). Sexual orientation identity formation among gay, lesbian, and bisexual youths: Multiple patterns of milestone experiences. *Journal of Research on Adolescence, 12,* 167–191.

Follingstad, D. R., Bradley, R. G., Laughlin, J. E., & Burke, L. (1999). Risk factors and correlates of dating violence: The relevance of examining frequency and severity levels in a college sample. *Violence and Victims, 14,* 365–380.

Follingstad, D. R., Wright, S., Lloyd, S., & Sebastian, J. A. (1991). Sex differences in motivations and effects in dating violence. *Family Relations: Journal of Applied Family and Child Studies, 40,* 51–57.

Foo, L., & Margolin, G. (1995). A multivariate investigation of dating aggression. *Journal of Family Violence, 10,* 351–377.

Foshee, V. A. (1996). Gender differences in adolescent dating abuse prevalence, types and injuries. *Health Education Research, 11,* 275–286.

Foshee, V. A., Bauman, K. E., Greene, W. F., Koch, G. G., Linder, G. F., & MacDougall, J. E. (2000). The safe dates program: 1-year follow-up results. *American Journal of Public Health, 90,* 1619–1622.

Foshee, V. A., Linder, F., MacDougall, J. E., & Bangdiwala, S. (2001). Gender differences in the longitudinal predictors of adolescent dating violence. *Preventive Medicine: An International Journal Devoted to Practice and Theory, 32,* 128–141.

Freedner, N., Freed, L., Yang, W. & Austin, S. B. (2002). Dating violence among gay, lesbian and bisexual adolescents: Results from a community survey. *Journal of Adoelscent Health, 31,* 469–474.

Furman, W., & Buhrmester, D. (1992). Age and sex differences in perceptions of networks of personal relationships. *Child Development, 63,* 103–115.

Furman, W., & Wehner, E. A. (1994). Romantic views: Toward a theory of adolescent romantic relationships. In R. Montenayor, G. Adams, & G. Gullota (Eds.), *Advances in adolescent development. 6: Relationships during adolescence* (pp. 168–195). Thousand Oaks, CA: Sage.

Furman, W., & Wehner, E. A. (1997). Adolescent romantic relationships: A developmental perspective. In S. Shulman, & W. Collins, (Eds.), *New directions for child development, No. 78: Romantic relationships in adolescence: Developmental perspectives* (pp. 21–36). San Francisco: Josset-Bass.

Gagne, M. H., & Lavoie, F. (1993). Young people's views on the causes of violence in adolescents' romantic relationships. *Canada's Mental Health, 41,* 11–15.

Galliher, R. V., Rostosky, S. S., Welsh, D. P., & Kawaguchi, M. C. (1999). Power and psychological well-being in late adolescent romantic relationships. *Sex Roles, 40,* 689–710.

Glaser, D. (2000). Child abuse and neglect and the brain—A review. *Journal of Child Psychology and Psychiatry, 41,* 97–116.

Gray, H. M., & Foshee, V. (1997). Adolescent dating violence: Differences between one-sided and mutually violent profiles. *Journal of Interpersonal Violence, 12,* 126–141.

Gray, M. R., & Steinberg L. (1999). Adolescent romance and the parent-child relationship: A contextual perspective. In W. Furman, B. B. Brown, & C. Fering (Eds.), *The development of romantic relationships in adolescence* (pp. 235–262). New York: Cambridge University Press.

Grunbaum, J. A., Kann, L., Kinchen, S., Williams, B., Ross, J., Lowry, R., et al. (2002). *Youth Risk Behavior Surveillance,* United States, 2001. *Morbidity and Mortality Weekly Report, 51*(SS-4), 1–68.

Halpern, C. T., Oslak, S. G., Young, M. L., Martin, S. L., & Kupper, L. L. (2001). Partner violence among adolescents in opposite-sex romantic relationships: Findings From the National Longitudinal Study of Adolescent Health. *American Journal of Public Health, 91,* 1679–1685.

Hammock, G., & O'Hearn, R. (2002). Psychological aggression in dating relationships: Predictive models for males and females. *Violence and Victims, 17,* 525–540.

Hanson, R. F. (2002). Adolescent dating violence: Prevalence and psychological outcomes. *Child Abuse and Neglect, 26,* 449–453.

Heppner, M. J., Neville, H. A., Smith, K., Kivlighan, D. M., & Gershuny, B. S. (1999). Examining immediate and long-term efficacy of rape prevention programming with racially diverse college men. *Journal of Counseling Psychology, 46,* 16–26.

Hilton, N. Z., Harris, G. T., Rice, M. E., Krans, T. S., & Lavigne, S. E. (1998). Antiviolence education in high schools: Implementation and evaluation. *Journal of Interpersonal Violence, 13,* 726–742.

Holtzworth-Munroe, A. (1992). Social skills deficits in violent men: Interpreting the data using a social information processing model. *Clinical Psychology Review, 12,* 605–617.

Holtzworth-Munroe, A., & Anglin, K. (1991). The competency of responses given by maritally violent versus nonviolent men to problematic marital situations. *Violence and Victims, 6,* 257–269.

Holtzworth-Munroe, A., & Hutchison, G. (1993). Attributing negative intent to wife behavior: The attributions of maritally violent versus nonviolent men. *Journal of Abnormal Psychology, 102,* 206–211.

Hotaling, G. T., & Sugarman, D. B. (1986). Analysis of risk markers in husband to wife violence: The current state of knowledge. *Violence and Victims, 1,* 101–122.

Jackson, S. M., Cram, F., & Seymour, F. W. (2000). Violence and sexual coercion in high school students' dating relationships. *Journal of Family Violence, 15,* 23–36.

Jaffe, P., Wolfe, D. A., Crooks, C., Hughes, R., & Baker, L. (2004). The Fourth R: Developing healthy relationships in families and communities through school-based interventions. In P. Jaffe, L. Baker, & A. Cunningham (Eds.), *Innovative strategies to end domestic violence for victims, perpetrators, and their children* (pp. 200–218). New York: Guilford.

Jankowski, M.K., Leitenberg, H., Henning, K., & Coffey, P. (1999). Intergenerational transmission of dating aggression as a function of witnessing only same sex parents vs. opposite sex parents vs. both parents as perpetrators of domestic violence. *Journal of Family Violence, 14,* 267–279.

Kessler, R. C., Sonnega, A., Bromet, E., Hughes, M., & Nelson, C. B., & Breslau, N. (1999). Epidemiological risk factors for trauma and PTSD. In R. Yehuda (Ed.), *Risk factors for posttraumatic stress disorder* (pp. 23–59). Washington, DC: American Psychiatric Press.

Laursen, B., & Collins, W. A. (1994). Interpersonal conflict during adolescence. *Psychological Bulletin, 115,* 197–209.

Lavoie, F., Vezina, L., Piche, C., & Boivin, M. (1995). Evaluation of a prevention program for violence in teen dating relationships. *Journal of Interpersonal Violence, 10,* 516–524.

Lempers, J. D., & Clark-Lempers, D. S. (1993). A functional comparison of same-sex and opposite sex friendships during adolescence. *Journal of Adolescent Research, 8,* 1, 89–108.

Lewis, S. F., & Fremouw, W. (2001). Dating violence: A critical review of the literature. *Clinical Psychology, 21,* 105–127.

Lewis, S. F., Travea, L., & Fremouw, W. J. (2002). Characteristics of female perpetrators and victims of dating violence. *Violence and Victims, 17,* 593–606.

Lyons-Ruth, K., & Jacobvitz, D. (1999). Attachment disorganization: Unresolved loss, relational violence, and lapses in behavioral and attentional strategies. In J. Cassidy and P. R. Shaver (Eds.), *Handbook of attachment: Theory, research, and clinical applications* (pp. 520–554). New York: Guilford.

Malik, S., Sorenson, S., & Aneshensel, C. (1997). Community and dating violence among adolescents: Perpetration and victimization. *Journal of Adolescent Health, 21,* 291–302.

McMaster, L., Connolly, J., Craig, W., and Pepler, D. (1997, March). *Sexual harassment and dating violence among early adolescents.* Paper presented at the Biennial Meetings of the Society for Research in Child Development, Washington, DC.

McMaster, L. E., Connolly, J., Pepler, D., & Craig, W. M. (2002). Peer to peer sexual harassment in early adolescence: A developmental perspective. *Development and Psychopathology, 14,* 1, 91–105.

Messman-Moore, T. L., & Long, P. J. (2000). Child sexual abuse and revictimization in the form of adult sexual abuse, adult physical abuse, and adult psychological maltreatment. *Journal of Interpersonal Violence, 15,* 489–502.

Miller, B. C., & Benson, B. (1999). Romantic and sexual relationship development during adolescence. In W. Furman, & B. B. Brown, & C. Feiring (Eds.), *The development of romantic relationships in adolescence* (pp. 99–121). New York: Cambridge University Press.

Molidor, C., & Tolman, R.M. (1998). Gender and contextual factors in adolescent dating violence. *Violence Against Women, 4,* 180–194.

Muehlenhard, C. L., & Cook, S. W. (1988). Men's self-reports of unwanted sexual activity. *The Journal of Sex Research, 24,* 58–72.

Murphy, C. M., & Blumenthal, D.R. (2000). The mediating influence of interpersonal problems on the intergenerational transmission of relationship aggression. *Personal Relationships, 7,* 203–218.

Neeman, J., Hubbard, J., & Masten, A. S. (1995). The changing importance of romantic relationship involvement to competence from late childhood to late adolescence. *Development and Psychopathology, 7,* 4, 727–750.

Nieder, T., & Seiffge-Krenke, I. (2001). Coping with stress in different phases of romantic development. *Journal of Adolescence, 24,* 297–311.

O'Keefe, M. (1997). Predictors of dating violence among high school students. *Journal of Interpersonal Violence, 12,* 546–568.

O'Keefe, M. & Treister, L. (1998). Victims of dating violence among high school students: Are the predictors different for males and females? *Violence Against Women, 4,* 195–223.

Odgers, C. L., & Moretti, M. M. (2002). Aggressive and antisocial girls: Research update and challenges. *International Journal of Forensic Mental Health Services, 1,* 103–119.

Olweus, D., 1991. Bully/victim problems among school children: Some basic facts and effects of a school-based intervention program. In D. Pepler and K. Rubin (Eds.), *The development and treatment of childhood aggression* (pp. 411–438) Hillsdale, NJ: Erlbaum.

Pan, H. S., Neidig, P. H., & O'Leary, K. D. (1994). Male–female and aggressor–victim differences in the factor structure of the modified conflict tactics. *Journal of Interpersonal Violence, 9,* 366–382.

Paul, E. L., & White, K. M. (1990). The development of intimate relationships in late adolescence. *Adolescence, 24,* 375–400.

Pepler, D. J., & Craig, W. M. (1999). Understanding bullying and victimization from a dynamic systems perspective. In A. Slater and D. Muir (Eds.), *Developmental psychology: An advanced reader,* (pp. 441–451). Oxford, England: Blackwell.

Pepler, D. J., Craig, W. M., Connolly, J., & Henderson, K. (2002). Bullying, sexual harassment, dating violence, and substance use among adolescents. In C. Wekerle & A. Wall (Eds.),

The violence and addiction equation: Theoretical and clinical issues in substance abuse and relationship violence (pp. 153–168). New York: Brunner-Routledge.

Pittman, A. L., & Wolfe, D. A. (2002). Bridging the gap: Prevention of adolescent risk behaviors and development of healthy nonviolent dating relationships. In C. Wekerle & A. Wall (Eds.), *The violence and addiction equation: Theoretical and clinical issues in substance abuse and relationship violence* (pp. 304–323). New York: Brunner-Routledge.

Poitras, M., & Lavoie, F. (1995). A study of the prevalence of sexual coercion in adolescent heterosexual dating relationships in a Quebec sample. *Violence and Victims, 10,* 299–313.

Randall, M., & Haskell, L. (2000). *Gender analysis, sexual inequality, and violence: The lives of girls.* London, ON: Centre for Research on Violence Against Women and Children, The University of Western Ontario.

Reitzel-Jaffe, D., & Wolfe, D. A. (2001). Predictors of relationship abuse among young men. *Journal of Interpersonal Violence, 16,* 99–115.

Rennison, C. (2002). *Criminal victimization 2001: Changes 2000–01 with trends 1993–2001* (NCJ 194610): U.S. Bureau of Justice Statistics. Available from www.ojp.usdoj.gov/bjs/abstract/cv01.htm.

Rickert, V. I., Wiemann, C. M., Vaughan, R. D., & White, J. W. (2003). Date and acquaintance rape among urban female teens. *Journal of Adolescent Health, 32,* 155–156.

Riggs, D.S., & O'Leary, K. D. (1989). A theoretical model of courtship aggression. In M. A. Pirog-Good & J. E. Stets (Eds.), *Violence in dating relationships* (pp. 53–71). New York: Praeger.

Riggs, D. S., & O'Leary, K. D. (1996). Aggression between heterosexual dating partners: An examination of a causal model of courtship aggression. *Journal of Interpersonal Violence, 11,* 519–540.

Rogosch, F. A., & Cicchetti, D. (1994). Illustrating the interface of peer and family relations through the study of child maltreatment. *Social Development, 3,* 291–308.

Rogosch, F. A., Cicchetti, D., & Aber, J. L. (1995). The role of child maltreatment in early deviations in cognitive and affective processing abilities and later peer relationship problems, *Development and Psychopathology, 7,* 591–609.

Samet, N., & Kelly, E. W. (1987). The relationship of steady dating to self esteem and sex role identity among adolescents. *Adolescence, 22,* 231–245.

Scharf, M., & Mayseless, O. (2001). The capacity for romantic intimacy: Exploring the contribution of best friend and marital and parental relationships. *Journal of Adolescence 24*(3), 379–399.

Scott, K. L., Wekerle, C., & Wolfe, D. A. (1997). *Considered sex differences in youth self-reports of violence and their implications for the development of violent relationships.* Poster presented at the biennial meeting of the Society for Research in Child Development, April, Washington, DC.

Seiffge-Krenke, I. (1995). *Stress, Coping and Relationships in Adolescence.* Mahwah, NJ: Erlbaum.

Seiffge-Krenke, I. (1998). Social support and coping style as risk and protective factors. In I. SeiffgeKrenke (Ed.), *Adolescents' Health: A Developmental Perspective* (pp. 124–150). Mahwah, NJ: Erlbaum.

Seiffge-Krenke, I., Shulman, S. & Klessigner, N. (2001). Adolescent precursors of romantic relationships on young adulthood. *Journal of Social and Personal Relationships, 18,* 3.

Shapiro, J. P., Baumeister, R. F., & Kessler, J. W. (1991). A three-component model of children's teasing: Aggression, humor, and ambiguity. *Journal of Social and Clinical Psychology, 10,* 459–472.

Sharpe, D., & Taylor, J. K. (1999). An examination of variables from a social-developmental model to explain physical and psychological dating violence. *Canadian Journal of Behavioral Science, 31,* 165–175.

Shulman, S., & Kipnis, O. (2001). Adolescent romantic relationships: A look from the future. *Journal of Adolescence, 24*(3), 337–351.

Shulman, S., & Scharf, M. (2000). Adolescent romantic behaviors and perceptions: Age and gender related differences, and links with family and peer relationships. *Journal of Research on Adolescence, 10,* 99–118.

Silbereisen, R. K., & Kracke, B. (1997). Self-reported maturational timing and adaptation in adolescence. In J. Schulenberg, J. L. Maggs, & K. Hurrelmann (Eds.), *Health risks and developmental transitions during adolescence.* (pp. 85–109). New York: Cambridge University Press.

Silverman, J. G., Raj, A., Mucci, L. A., & Hathaway, J. E. (2001). Dating violence against adolescent girls and associated substance use, unhealthy weight control, sexual risk behavior, pregnancy, and suicidality. *Journal of the American Medical Association, 286,* 572–579.

Snyder, H. N., & Sickmund, M., (1999). *Juvenile offenders and victim: 1997 national report.* Washington, DC: Office of Juvenile Justice and Delinquency Prevention.

Straus, M. A. (1979). Measuring intrafamily conflict and violence: The Conflict Tactics (CT) scales. *Journal of Marriage and the Family, 41,* 75–88.

Stattin, H., & Magnusson, D. (1990). *Pubertal maturation in female development.* Hillsdale, NJ: Erlbaum.

Swan, S. C., & Snow, D. L. (2002). A typology of women's use of violence in intimate relationships. *Violence Against Women, 8,* 286–319.

Thompson, K. M., Wonderlich, S. A., Crosby, R. D., & Mitchell, J. E. (2001). Sexual violence and weight control techniques among adolescent girls. *International Journal of Eating Disorders, 29,* 166–176.

Thorne, B., & Luria, Z. (1986). Sexuality and gender in children's daily worlds. *Social Problems, 33,* 3, 176–190.

Thornton, A. (1990). The courtship process and adolescent sexuality. *Journal of Family Issues, 11,* 239–273.

Tolman, R. M. (1989). The development of a measure of psychological maltreatment of women by their male partners. *Violence and Victims, 4,* 173–189.

Troiden, R. R. (1989). The formation of homosexual identities. *Journal of Homosexuality, 17,* 43–73.

U. S. Department of Health and Human Services, National Center on Child Abuse and Neglect (2001). *Child maltreatment 1999: Reports from the states to the National Center on Child Abuse and Neglect.* Washington, DC: U.S. Government Printing Office. Available from http://www.axf.dhhs.goc/programs/cb/publications/cm99/high.htm.

Watson, J. M., Cascardi, M., Avery-Leaf, S., & O'Leary, K. D. (2001). High school students' responses to dating aggression. *Violence and Victims, 16,* 3, 339–348.

Wekerle & Avgoustis (2003). Child maltreatment, adolescent dating, and adolescent dating violence. In P. Florsheim (Ed.), *Adolescent romantic relations and sexual behavior: Theory, research and practical implications,* pp. 213–241. Hillsdale, NJ: Erlbaum.

Wekerle, C., & Wolfe, D. A. (2003). Child maltreatment. In E. J. Mash & R. A. Barkley (Eds.), *Child Psychopathology* (2nd ed.), (pp. 632–684). New York: Guilford.

Wekerle, C., Wolfe, D. A, Hawkins, D. L., Pittman, A.-L., Glickman, A., & Lovald, B. E. (2001). Childhood maltreatment, posttraumatic stress symptomatology, and adolescent dating violence: Considering the value of adolescent perceptions of abuse and a trauma mediational model. *Development and Psychopathology, 13,* 847–871.

Wekerle, C., & Wolfe, D. A. (1999). Dating violence in mid-adolescence: Theory, significance, and emerging prevention initiatives. *Clinical Psychology Review, 19,* 435–456.

Wolfe, D. A. (1999). *Child abuse: Implications for child development and psychopathology* (2nd ed.). Thousand Oaks, CA: Sage.

Wolfe, D. A., & Feiring, C. (2000). Dating violence through the lens of adolescent romantic relationships. *Child Maltreatment, 5,* 360–363.

Wolfe, D. A., Scott, K., Reitzel-Jaffe, D., Wekerle, C., Grasley, C., & Straatman, A. (2001). Development and validation of the conflict in adolescent dating relationships inventory. *Psychological Assessment, 13,* 277–293.

Wolfe, D. A., Scott, K., Wekerle, C., & Pittman, A. (2001). Child maltreatment: Risk of adjustment problems and dating violence in adolescence. *Journal of the American Academy of Child and Adolescent Psychiatry, 40,* 282–298.

Wolfe, D. A., Wekerle, C., Reitzel-Jaffe, D., & Lefebvre, L. (1998). Factors associated with abusive relationships among maltreated and non-maltreated youth. *Development and Psychopathology, 10,* 61–85.

Wolfe, D. A., Wekerle, C., & Scott, R. (1997). *Alternatives to violence: Empowering youth to develop healthy relationships.* Thousand Oaks, CA: Sage.

Wolfe, D. A., Wekerle, C., Scott, K., Straatman, A., & Grasley, C. (2004). Models of dating violence for adolescent girls and boys: Prediction over one year. *Journal of Abnormal Psychology, 113,* 406–415.

Wolfe, D. A., Wekerle, C., Scott, K., Straatman, A., Grasley, C., & Reitzel-Jaffe, D. (2003). Dating violence prevention with at-risk youth: A controlled outcome evaluation. *Journal of Consulting and Clinical Psychology, 71,* 279–291.

Yeater, E. A., & O'Donohue, W. (1999). Sexual assault prevention programs: Current issues, future directions, and the potential efficacy of interventions with women. *Clinical Psychology Review, 19,* 739–771.

Zimmer-Gembeck, M. J., Siebenbruner, J., & Collins, W. A. (2001). Diverse aspects of adolescent dating: Associations with psychosocial functioning from early to middle adolescence. *Journal of Adolescence, 24,* 313–336.

Zimmer-Gembeck, M. J. (2002). The development of romantic relationships and adaptations in the system of peer relationships. *Journal of Adolescent Health, 31*(6S), 216–225.

14

Girls' Adjustment to Divorce and Remarriage

CHRISTY M. BUCHANAN

Divorce and remarriage are common events in Western industrialized countries, particularly the United States. Approximately half of American children experience the divorce of their parents before they reach the age of 18 years (Furstenberg, 1990). The likelihood of experiencing parental divorce is higher among African American and Hispanic youth, and lower among Asian American youth, than it is among European American youth (Emery, 1999). Many divorced parents remarry, and subsequently divorce again. About 15% of children experience at least two family disruptions by the time they are young adults (Furstenberg, 1990).

Divorce and remarriage are unarguably stressful for children; in the short term, such changes inevitably disrupt children's customary routines and relationships. The good news is that the majority of children and families adapt such that—even though unhappy and even painful memories of the family changes remain (Emery, 1999; Emery & Coiro, 1997)—they live mentally healthy, productive, and satisfying lives. The bad news is that divorce, and perhaps also remarriage, raise the risk of maladaptive emotions and behaviors among children who experience these family changes.

In this chapter, I first highlight the primary ways in which females' experiences in situations of divorce and remarriage appear to be unique. I then review data on the association of both divorce and remarriage with risk of psychopathology. I focus primarily on longer-term adjustment (i.e., more than 2 years post-divorce). The immediate aftermath of divorce is typically stressful and chaotic for parents and children, but by about 2 years after the divorce many families have settled into new routines and adapted to the changes. For girls in particular, problems related to family disruption appear more likely to emerge in adolescence or young

CHRISTY M. BUCHANAN • Department of Psychology Wake Forest University, Winston-Salem, North Carolina, 27109-7778.

adulthood, even when the disruption occurred much earlier in childhood (e.g., Hetherington & Kelly, 2002). My focus in this chapter is, thus, on outcomes for children from disrupted families 2 or more years following the disruption.

Following discussion of outcomes associated with divorce and remarriage, explanations for the association between family structure and psychopathology are considered. Divorce is associated with a myriad of contextual and family characteristics (e.g., pre-divorce and post-divorce marital conflict, financial stressors, parental psychopathology, poor parent–child relationships) that are in themselves bad for children's development. Some of these characteristics are caused or worsened by divorce, some contributed to the divorce to begin with, and some are simply correlates of divorce. To the extent that divorce and other family transitions are associated with subsequent psychopathology among children, it is important to understand the relative role of divorce versus other factors in producing poor outcomes, as well as the various routes by which divorce might produce pathological outcomes. Furthermore, given that events such as divorce have a small average impact on psychological functioning, and that there is a great deal of variability in how children function in all family structures (e.g., Buchanan, Maccoby, & Dornbusch, 1996; O'Connor, Dunn, Jenkins, Pickering, & Rasbash, 2001), moderators of the impact of family change on adjustment are reviewed.

This review draws on literature that examines psychopathology directly as well as literature that measures adjustment more broadly. Understanding the continuum of normal development is informative for understanding psychopathology (Cummings, Davies, & Campbell, 2000; see Chapter 1). And research examining psychopathology per se and research examining a broader continuum of adjustment reach the same conclusions concerning the impact of family disruption, and concerning mechanisms and moderators of the impact of divorce. Therefore, an integrative review of literature on psychopathology as well as literature on broader aspects of adjustment seems justified.

DESCRIPTION OF THE PROBLEM FOR FEMALES

Throughout this chapter, unique risks of divorce and remarriage for females will be identified where appropriate. In this section, some of the major questions and issues relevant to female children of divorce are highlighted.

One might suspect that parents would be more willing to divorce, and that fathers would be less likely to stay involved with children following a divorce, when they have only female children. This might be true if parents emphasize the importance of a male parent's presence and involvement more for boys than for girls, or if fathers are more invested in their relationships with sons. In fact, however, although the samples of some studies do indicate a higher rate of divorce among parents of girls than parents of boys (e.g., Block, Block, & Gjerde, 1988; Kasen, Cohen, Brook, & Hartmark, 1996), other studies indicate equal rates of divorce for male and female children (e.g., Amato, 1991; Emery, Waldron, Kitzmann, & Aaron, 1999). Sex of child appears to be a less important influence on divorce rates than other factors such as parent race or education, or children's age (Emery, 1999). Research is also inconsistent concerning whether fathers are less likely to maintain contact with daughters than sons after divorce (e.g., Seltzer, 1991), although it is well established that girls are more likely than boys to live with mother, and less likely than boys to live in father's or joint custody (Buchanan et al., 1996; Emery, 1999; Maccoby & Mnookin, 1992).

With respect to the impact of divorce on adjustment, research overwhelmingly indicates more similarities than differences for males and females. More often than not, gender is *not* a significant moderator of the association between divorce and adjustment, and this is true even in large studies that have sufficient power to test the hypothesis (e.g., Chase-Lansdale, Cherlin, & Kiernan, 1995; Sun, 2001). In meta-analyses, effect sizes for divorce in all-male and all-female samples are more often statistically similar than statistically different (e.g., Amato & Keith, 1991a; 1991b). Sex differences have emerged somewhat more often in studies of the impact of remarriage than the impact of divorce, particularly those studies that provide relatively in-depth examinations of children's relationships with family members and children's adjustment. In particular, girls appear to exhibit more difficulty associated with a custodial mother's remarriage than do boys (e.g., Hetherington, 1991).

Despite the gender similarity that emerges from a broad look at the literature on divorce, sex differences sometimes occur for specific indices of adjustment. Consistent with reactions to stress in general, females seem more likely to react to divorce with internalizing problems and males more with externalizing problems (e.g., Doherty & Needle, 1991; McLeod, 1991). Yet, although internalizing problems might be a common reaction to stress for girls, divorce increases the risk of externalizing and antisocial behavior for them as well (Simons & Chao, 1996). Females may be more likely than males to suffer detrimental effects associated with divorce in the areas of educational attainment (Amato & Keith, 1991b) and quality of adult romantic relationships (Jacquet & Surra, 2001), although they appear less likely than males to exhibit poor social adjustment during childhood (Amato & Keith, 1991a) or to experience one-parent family status in adulthood (Amato & Keith, 199b) associated with divorce.

The timing of responses to family disruption may also be different for boys and girls. Studies examining post-divorce outcomes prior to adolescence often report that girls' adjustment is relatively good, and better than that of boys (Morrison & Cherlin, 1995; Shaw, Emery, & Tuer, 1993; Simons, Lin, Gordon, Conger, & Lorenz, 1999; Zaslow, 1988, 1989). In contrast, studies that examine post-divorce outcomes during adolescence and adulthood are more likely to report either equally negative associations between family disruption for boys and girls or, in some instances, more negative effects for girls (e.g., Chase-Lansdale et al., 1995; Fergusson, Horwood, & Lynskey, 1994). Thus, girls' risk of developing problems linked to divorce might increase over time, and might be worse when divorce occurs during adolescence.

Finally, although gender similarity in the overall impact of family disruption may be the norm, there are some instances in which family functioning changes uniquely for girls, so that the mechanisms by which family disruption affect children are different for girls than for boys. For example, although sexual abuse is relatively rare, girls more so than boys are at higher risk of sexual abuse by both fathers and stepfathers following divorce (Wilson, 2001). The route from family disruption to psychopathology via sexual abuse is thus more likely to be traveled by girls than boys.

DEVELOPMENTAL COURSE AND OUTCOMES

Divorce

Children whose parents divorce are at increased risk of negative emotional, behavioral, and academic or cognitive adjustment, including increased risk of psychopathology, compared to children whose parents do not divorce. This conclusion, put forth originally by relatively small and clinically oriented studies (e.g., Wallerstein & Blakeslee, 1989; Wallerstein & Kelly, 1980), has been confirmed with data that are prospective, longitudinal, and representative of large populations (e.g., Furstenberg & Kiernan, 2001; Kasen et al., 1996; Lee, Burkam, Zimiles, & Ladewski, 1994; Ross & Mirowsky, 1999; see also Emery, 1999, for a review). For example, Fergusson et al. (1994) found that the odds of several diagnosable conditions (e.g., conduct or oppositional defiant disorder, mood disorders, substance abuse and dependence) at the age of 15 years were up to four times higher among adolescents whose parents had separated during their childhood than they were among adolescents from intact families. Other studies demonstrate a link between childhood experience of divorce and increased risk of psychopathology for women and men (including depression, generalized anxiety disorders, and panic disorder) in adulthood (Chase-Lansdale et al., 1995; Cherlin, Chase-Lansdale, & McRae., 1998; Kendler, Neale, Kessler, & Heath, 1992).

The results of many studies are consistent in showing a small but significant increase in the probability of psychopathological problems among children and adults who have experienced their parents' divorce (see Amato & Keith, 1991a, 1991b, for meta-analyses). The negative impact of divorce appears reasonably consistent across ethnic and cultural groups (e.g., Amato, 1991; Amato & Keith, 1991a; Liu et al., 2000; Zhou, Bray, Kehle, & Xin, 2001), although it might be somewhat smaller among African Americans compared to European Americans (Amato & Keith, 1991b) and somewhat smaller among Americans compared to individuals from other cultures (Amato & Keith, 1991a).

The research on divorce thus points to an increased risk for psychopathology among children of divorce, but also to the resilience of these children. The increased odds of psychiatric problems reported by individual investigators are significant but modest (Fergusson et al., 1994; Chase-Lansdale et al., 1995), as are the effect sizes of divorce from meta-analyses

(Amato & Keith, 1991a, 1991b). The great majority of children, adolescents, and young adults whose parents divorce do not experience mental illness, and function in a normal range (Emery, 1999; Hetherington, 1993; Zill, Morrison, & Coiro, 1993). Nonetheless, even a small percentage of increase in mental illness in a large population translates into several thousand individuals experiencing mental illness as a result of divorce that might not otherwise have suffered such illness (Chase-Lansdale et al., 1995; Grych & Fincham, 1999). Furthermore, individuals seek psychological help even in the absence of psychiatric illness, and divorce raises the rate of seeking psychological help even more substantially than it raises the rate of psychiatric diagnosis (Zill et al., 1993).

Remarriage

Research linking remarriage with adjustment is more mixed in its findings than is the research on divorce. Remarriage, in comparison to single parenting, makes another adult available for parenting, presents the possibility of another positive adult relationship for the child, and improves the economic situation in most homes. Consistent with these potential benefits, stepfamily status is sometimes linked to better outcomes for children (Aseltine, 1996; Buchanan et al., 1996). In contrast, Kasen et al. (1996) found a higher incidence of psychiatric disorders among children from stepfamilies compared to children in intact families. Girls and boys had higher rates of attention deficit hyperactivity disorder (ADHD) in stepfamilies; girls exhibited higher rates of major depressive disorder and overanxious disorders in stepfamilies. In another study (O'Connor et al., 2001), children in "simple" stepfather families (i.e., all children biologically related to the mother) exhibited adjustment similar to that of children in intact homes, but children in "complex" stepfather families (i.e., some children not related to the mother) showed elevated emotional and behavioral problems compared to both intact and simple stepfather families. Adjustment in complex stepfather families was similar to that in single-parent families. These latter results in particular suggest that the link between stepfamily status and adjustment is complex. In any case, despite its potential benefits, stepfamily status is not always a protective factor.

Girls, more so than boys, seem to react negatively and are slow to adapt to a mothers' remarriage (Hetherington, 1991; Lee et al., 1994; Needle, Su, & Doherty, 1990). Girls' greater difficulties with remarriage may result from unique challenges related to the nature of their relationships with custodial mothers and stepfathers (these ideas will be discussed more fully in later sections). The impact of remarriage for girls and boys may also depend on when it occurs and how stable it is. For example, remarriages that occur relatively early in a child's life and that are stable over time are likely to be more beneficial to children than remarriages that come later or do not last (Chase-Lansdale et al., 1995; Zill et al., 1993).

In support of the importance of stability in new parental unions, cohabiting and otherwise unstable relationship histories are associated with more negative adjustment in children than is the existence of a remarried relationship (Ackerman, D'Eramo, Umylny, Schultz, & Izard, 2001; Buchanan et al., 1996; Isaacs & Leon, 1988). Remarried partners have demonstrated a clear commitment to the family, which may increase their authority and trustworthiness in the eyes of a child (Buchanan et al., 1996). Cohabitation itself might be less negative for girls than the instability of relationships in the home that typically accompanies cohabitation (Ackerman et al., 2000).

THEORIES AND ETIOLOGY

Current theories and evidence concerning the impact of divorce and remarriage on children emphasize a complex web of factors, including genetic and biological characteristics of parents and children, cognitive characteristics of children, and the environment—both within and outside the family—to which a child is exposed. Three categories of factors are useful in understanding the impact of family disruption. *Preexisting* factors (e.g., marital conflict or personality predispositions of the parent or child) differ between families that do and do not experience later disruption even prior to the disruption. These factors cooccur with family disruption but are not a result of the disruption per se. Nonetheless, preexisting factors may explain much of the negative impact of family disruption on children. *Mediating* factors (e.g., economic stress, poor-parenting, poor-quality parent–child relationships) are factors that change as a consequence of family disruption; changes in these factors consequently explain the link between disruption and poor adjustment. For example, family disruption might increase the probability of poor parenting, which in turn influences child adjustment negatively. *Moderating* factors (e.g., cognitive interpretations by the child, social support available to the child) alter the degree to which family disruption has an impact. For example, the impact of divorce is different for children who blame themselves for the divorce and those who do not. Preexisting, mediating, and moderating factors are not mutually exclusive; marital conflict, for example, may cooccur with divorce, change as a result of divorce, and moderate the impact of divorce on children.

To elucidate the impact of family disruptions on psychopathology in females, I review what is known about primary preexisting, mediating, and moderating factors. Because several factors are both preexisting and mediating, I discuss preexisting and mediating factors together, addressing the extent to which each factor appears to precede or mediate the impact of family disruption. Following this, I discuss moderating factors.

Preexisting and Mediating Factors

Pre-divorce Child Adjustment

Compared to children whose parents stay together, children whose parents subsequently divorce appear to have elevated rates of behavioral and emotional problems even prior to the divorce (e.g., Block et al., 1986;

Cherlin et al., 1991; Morrison & Coiro, 1999; Sun, 2001; for exceptions, see Morrison & Cherlin, 1995, Shaw et al., 1993). Why might this be? First, parental or family processes that exist prior to divorce in families that later divorce may already be detrimental to children's development (see later sections on marital conflict, parenting, and parent–child relationships). Alternatively, differences in children's adjustment prior to family disruption might reflect genetically influenced differences in personality or behavior that are shared between parents who divorce and the children of those parents (McGue & Lykken, 1992). Genetically influenced problematic traits in the parent or the child may raise the risk of future divorce and future psychopathology in the child.

Whereas studies of preadolescent children suggest that pre-divorce differences are similar for boys and girls, studies of adolescents prior to divorce suggest that predivorce differences may be larger for girls than for boys (Doherty & Needle, 1991). These findings are consistent with research showing that during adolescence, marital or family discord is more likely to predict problems for girls than for boys (Davies & Windle, 1997). Prior to adolescence, consistent sex differences in the impact of marital conflict have not been documented (Cummings & Davies, 1994; Reid & Crisafulli, 1990). Sex differences in response to the pre-divorce family context for adolescents might result in part from adolescent girls' heightened concerns with interpersonal relationships (Davies & Windle, 1991; Gore, Aseltine, & Colten, 1993; Leadbeater, Blatt, & Quinlan, 1995).

Controlling for pre-divorce emotional and behavioral problems in children substantially reduces or eliminates differences in childhood functioning related to divorce (e.g., Cherlin et al., 1991; Sun, 2001; but see Morrison & Coiro, 1999 for an exception). In contrast, controlling for pre-divorce emotional and behavioral problems appears less likely to eliminate differences in young adult functioning related to divorce (e.g., Chase-Lansdale et al., 1995; Cherlin et al., 1998) than it does differences in childhood functioning. Apparently, the sequelae of divorce tend to magnify the difference in functioning between groups over time, for both females and males, so that by adulthood, differences in adjustment are not completely explained by differences in pre-divorce functioning.

Parental Psychopathology

Adults who divorce have higher rates of psychopathology—including depression, antisocial problems, and schizophrenia—both prior to the divorce and subsequent to the divorce (e.g., Bruce, 1998; Emery et al., 1999; Hetherington & Kelly, 2002; Simons et al., 1996). Parental psychopathology is in some cases a reason for divorce; divorce can also precipitate problems in adjustment (Emery, 1999). Psychopathology among parents who divorce can lead to psychopathology in children of the divorce due to genetic relatedness or to impaired parenting associated with psychopathology (King, Segal, Naylor, & Evans, 1993; Landerman, George, & Blazer, 1991; O'Connor, Caspi, DeFries, & Plomin, 2000; Simons & Johnson, 1996). Accounting for parents' mental health both prior to and following divorce reduces the relation between family structure and children's behavioral and emotional problems (e.g., Carlson & Corcoran, 2001; Emery et al., 1999; O'Connor et al., 2001), indicating that parental psychopathology functions as both a preexisting factor and a mediating factor.

Marital and Family Conflict

Parents who later divorce experience more conflict and strain during their marriages than parents who do not divorce (Block, Block & Gjerde, 1988; Morrison & Coiro, 1999; Shaw et al., 1993; Sun, 2001). Marital conflict is a consistent predictor of problems, including psychopathology, in children (King, Radpour, Maylor, Segal, & Jouriles, 1995; Margolin, Oliver, & Medina, 2001). In general, conflict is a better predictor of maladjustment than is divorce per se (e.g., Borrine, Handal, Brown, & Searight, 1991; Dixon, Charles, & Craddock, 1998; Kozuch & Cooney, 1995; Morrison & Coiro, 1999; Vandewater & Lansford, 1998), and has been shown to account for the impact of divorce on children's adjustment (e.g., Dixon et al., 1998; Long & Forehand, 1987; Simons et al., 1999). In fact, conflict explains the increased rates of emotional and behavioral problems among children of divorce more effectively than other factors such as parental absence, economic disadvantage, parental well-being, and stressful life changes (Amato, 1993; Amato & Keith, 1991a).

Several theories attempt to explain the link between marital conflict and psychopathology (Margolin et al., 2001). One of these theories is *family systems theory*, in which it is proposed that children are negatively affected due to the impact of conflict on the constellation of relationships in the family. Research conducted from a family systems perspective has been helpful in illuminating the role of conflict in the adjustment of children from divorced families. From a family systems perspective, parents experiencing conflict with each other often attempt to bring the child into the conflict in some way in an attempt to diffuse that conflict for themselves; this process is called triangulation (Buchanan & Waizenhofer, 2001). Triangulation in divorced families is likely to take the form of pressure on the child to side with one of the parents (Buchanan & Waizenhofer, 2001). In response to real or felt pressure to side, children can respond in different ways: they might form an alliance with one parent; they might try to stay neutral in the conflict but experience torn loyalties; or they might disengage from both parents (Buchanan & Waizenhofer, 2001; Emery Joyce, & Fincham, 1987).

Alliances, loyalty conflicts, and disengagement from parents all represent dysfunctional patterns of family relationships that have been linked to adjustment problems in children. For example, alliances have been linked to lower anxiety in children, but also to heightened anger and inability to think in complex ways about relationships (Johnston & Campbell, 1988; Lampel, 1996). Loyalty conflicts predict increased depression or anxiety and increased deviance among adolescents, and mediate an association between child-perceived interparental conflict and adjustment (Buchanan et al., 1991, 1996; Healy, Stewart & Copeland, 1993). Consistent with other evidence that, during adolescence, girls more than boys are particularly sensitive to interpersonal problems, including marital conflict (Davies & Windle, 1997), adolescent girls are more likely to report feeling caught between parents than are adolescent boys (Buchanan et al., 1991, 1996).

In sum, although it can be handled in ways that it does not harm children (e.g., Cummings, Goeke-Morey, & Papp, 2001), research shows that conflict and hostility between parents is a critical factor in understanding the development of psychopathology among children of divorce. The impact of conflict may be direct (e.g., through modeling or its impact on emotions) or indirect (through its impact on triangulation in family relationships).

Parenting

The quality of parenting differs between families that divorce and those that do not divorce even prior to the divorce (Amato & Booth, 1996; Block et al., 1988; Shaw et al., 1993). In addition, divorce leads to decrements in effective parenting, especially in the short term but also in the longer term. For example, single parents are more likely than other parents to demonstrate inadequate control and monitoring of children and adolescents (Demo & Acock, 1996; Dornbusch et al., 1985; Hetherington, 1991; McLanahan & Sandefur, 1994) as well as punitive, coercive, and inconsistent discipline (Hetherington, 1991; Simons & Johnson, 1996), characteristics of parenting that have been linked with the development of psychopathology (Sroufe, Duggal, Weinfield, & Carlson, 2000).

Children of divorce or remarriage whose parents engage in more effective practices are better adjusted than children of divorce or remarriage whose parents do not parent as effectively (Buchanan et al., 1992, 1996; Deater-Deckard & Dunn, 1999; Wolchik, Wilcox, Tein, & Sandler, 2000), and quality of parenting—particularly that by custodial mothers—has been shown to mediate the association between family structure and adjustment (Conger & Chao, 1996; McLanahan & Sandefur, 1994; Simons & Chao, 1996; Simons et al., 1999).

Parent–Child Relationships

Unhealthy and insecure relationships with parents constitute a great risk factor for psychopathology (Cummings et al., 2000; Geiger & Crick, 2001; Kernberg, Weiner, & Bardenstein, 2000; Sroufe et al., 2000). To the extent that divorce disrupts attachments with parents or creates an environment unsuitable for the maintenance of secure and trustworthy relationships with parents, divorce clearly presents a threat to psychological well-being. Consistent with the idea that parental divorce interferes with the development of healthy relationships, adult children of divorce are more likely to mistrust others, and are more likely to have unhappy romantic relationships and marriages of their own, than adult children whose parents did not divorce (Amato, 1991; McLeod, 1991; Ross & Mirowsky, 1999); some evidence suggests that this is especially true for females (Jaquet & Surra, 2001). Furthermore, problems in close interpersonal relationships and young adult marital status help to explain the link between childhood experience of divorce and adult depression (Amato, 1991; Ross & Mirowsky, 1999), again perhaps especially for women (McLeod, 1991). Although problems in adult relationships may stem from some of the factors already discussed (e.g., parental psychopathology, marital conflict), they may also stem from inadequate parent–child relationships associated with divorce.

As with marital conflict and the quality of parenting, the quality of parent–child relationships differs between families even prior to divorce (Amato & Booth, 1996; Sun, 2001). Additionally, divorce changes the amount of time spent with each parent and sometimes the nature of parent–child interactions as well. Relationships with fathers are most likely to be affected, as time with fathers is most likely to change, and in some cases be very limited, after divorce (Furstenberg & Cherlin, 1991; Furstenberg & Harris, 1992; Seltzer, 1991). Children and adolescents from divorced homes see their fathers less, perceive them as less caring (Dunlop, Burns, & Bermingham, 2001), and have poorer quality relationships with them (Amato, 1999; Amato & Booth, 1996; Buchanan et al., 1996; Furstenberg & Harris, 1992; Zill et al., 1993) than do children and adolescents from intact homes. These differences exist for girls and boys, and even after controlling for pre-divorce differences in the quality of the relationship (Amato & Booth, 1996).

Among girls, at least during childhood, there are fewer differences by family structure in time spent with and the quality of relationships with mothers than there are in these aspects of relationships with fathers. Prior to adolescence, daughters and divorced single mothers tend to get along especially well, often having relationships that are "close, confiding, and harmonious" (Hetherington, 1993, p. 44). Problems in the mother-daughter relationship may emerge in adolescence or adulthood (Hetherington, 1991; Zill et al., 1993). Even though closeness, warmth, and time spent together between mothers and adolescent daughters does not differ by family structures (Amato & Booth, 1996; Dunlop et al., 2001; Hetherington, 1991, 1993), coercive behavior and conflict between mothers and children is higher in single-parent families than it is in other family types (Demo & Acock, 1996; Hetherington, 1991, 1993). Hetherington (1991, 1993) concludes that relationships between divorced mothers and their adolescent children are intense and ambivalent; this may be particularly true for girls. Furthermore, pubertal maturation that occurs early brings special trouble for divorced mothers and daughters. Early maturation in girls is associated with increased mother-daughter conflict for all families, but especially so when mothers are divorced (Hetherington, 1991).

Remarriage also appears to pose a special threat to the mother-daughter relationship. Remarried and cohabiting mothers spend less time doing things (e.g., sharing meals, engaging in activities together) with their children, both boys and girls, than do mothers in two-parent families (McLanahan & Sandefur, 1994). The experience of losing time with and attention from mothers as a result of their involvement in a new relationship may be particularly difficult for girls (Hetherington, 1991; Hetherington & Clingempeel, 1992; Kasen et al., 1996), who have typically maintained good, even overly close, relationships with their mothers after divorce (Hetherington, 1993; Kalter, Riemer, Brickman, & Chen, 1985). In fact, the quality of the relationship between a pre-adolescent girl and her mother declines with increases in the closeness of a new marital relationship (Hetherington, 1993), suggesting that this new relationships is in fact a threat of sorts to the mother-daughter relationship. This pattern is in stark contrast to that in other family structures, and that in established remarried families with boys, where closer marital relationships predict better outcomes for children.

Children's sense of security in relationships is likely related not only to the amount and quality of time with each parent, but also to the stability of relationships with adults in their lives. Thus, subsequent to divorce, when parents become involved in unstable and frequently changing relationships, the impact on children is likely to be negative. For example, Ackerman et al. (2000) found that an unstable history of relationships for the mother was a strong predictor of externalizing problems in 6- and 7-year-old children, and that controlling for instability in relationships markedly reduced the impact of family structure on externalizing. Other studies have documented that repeated family transitions are linked with especially poor outcomes for children (e.g., Brody & Neubaum, 1996; Hetherington & Kelly, 2002), although it is difficult to separate the impact of repeated transitions from parental dysfunction and psychopathology. It is possible, however, that the more transitions in relationships that a parent, and consequently a child, experiences the more likely that child will be to view relationships as insecure and untrustworthy. Children might also find it harder to know how to establish and maintain close relationships over time. Such problems in relationships appear to be one of the major mechanisms by which divorce affects mental health in adulthood (e.g., Ross & Mirowsky, 1999).

In sum, both divorce and remarriage are associated with increased problems in parent–child relationships. In the typical case, father-child relationships become more distant, and mother-child relationships become more conflicted, although for girls and mothers problems may not develop until the girl begins pubertal development or otherwise ages into adolescence. The quality of parent–child relationships is related to the quality of post-divorce adjustment (Buchanan et al., 1992, 1996; Demo & Acock, 1996; Dunlop et al., 2001), and although the quality of the relationship with the custodial parent appears especially important, children who maintain close relationships with both parents appear to be especially well off after divorce (Buchanan et al., 1996). Alternatively, in situations where conflict, psychopathology, or other factors result in the parent–child relationship becoming abusive (see Wilson, 2001, for evidence on the increased risk for daughters of abuse by single fathers), children are at heightened risk of psychopathological outcomes (Cicchetti, Toth, & Maughan, 2000; Flisher, Kramer, Hoven, & Greenwald, 1997). The quality of the parent–child relationship, particularly the mother-child relationship, mediates the association between divorce and adjustment (Demo & Acock, 1996; O'Connor et al., 2001; Vandewater & Lansford, 1998).

Life Stress and Economic Decline

Divorce is associated with increases in other life stresses (e.g., residential or school transitions, changes in parents' work status), including economic stresses (Furstenburg & Cherlin, 1991; Hetherington, 1993; Lee et al., 1994). Children of divorce suffer more economic hardship even as adults, in large part due to lower educational attainment (McLeod, 1991; Ross & Mirowsky, 1999). The impact of family disruption on educational attainment and income is especially strong for females (Amato & Keith, 1991b; McLanahan & Sandefur, 1994; McLeod, 1991; Powell & Parcel, 1997; but see Ross & Mirowsky for an exception). The link between parental divorce during childhood and later adult psychopathology is mediated, for both females and males, through lower educational attainment (Amato, 1991) and socio-economic problems (O'Connor et al., 2001; Ross & Mirowsky, 1999) precipitated by divorce.

Total life stress as experienced by the child is also a predictor of long-term adjustment following divorce (Amato, 1993; Buchanan et al., 1996; Hetherington, Cox, & Cox, 1985; Tschann, Johnston, Kline, & Wallerstein, 1990). Increases in negative events as well as decreases in positive events are associated with poorer adjustment (Sandler, Wolchik, Braver, & Fogas, 1991). Experiencing parental separation during childhood also increases the likelihood of developing problems such as depression and substance abuse in the face of other life stresses during adolescence and adulthood (e.g., Aseltine, 1996; Landerman et al., 1991). Sensitization to stress as a result of adversity in childhood appears to be a general phenomenon—not limited to divorce—and may result from the impact of early adversity on brain functioning or cognitive schemas concerning life events (Hammen, 2001). Perhaps the emergence of new or intensified problems among children of divorce during adulthood, often called the "sleeper effect" (Cherlin et al., 1998; Wallerstein & Blakeslee, 1989) results from a greater vulnerability to the normal stresses that emerge in adulthood among individuals who experienced family disruption in childhood.

Moderating Factors

The impact of any stressor such as divorce on children's mental health depends upon other factors such as the personal and social resources available to the child, the child's age at divorce, and the custody arrangement (e.g., Grych & Fincham, 1999; Margolin et al., 2001). In this section, evidence of the most important moderators of the relationship between divorce and negative outcomes is reviewed.

Mechanisms as Moderators

Several of the factors reviewed in the previous section can also function as moderators of the impact of divorce. For example, the impact of divorce is more likely to be detrimental if the marriage was low in conflict prior to the divorce (Amato, Loomis, & Booth, 1995; Booth & Amato, 2001); children whose parents had high-conflict marriages are often better off if their parents divorce than if they stay together. And the impact of divorce in high-conflict situations is worse if the divorce does not serve to reduce conflict between parents than if conflict is subsequently reduced. Similarly, the impact of divorce and stressors related to divorce is worse for children who do not have a warm relationship with at least one parent or who do not experience effective parenting practices (e.g., Dunlop et al., 2001; Wolchik et al., 2000).

Temperament and History of Adjustment

Children with temperaments marked by positive mood, adaptability, and the ability to regulate their emotions and behavior are less vulnerable to the negative effects of stress than children with more difficult temperamental attributes. The impact of family stressors such as divorce and remarriage, as well as the negative family processes (e.g., conflict) that accompany them, is no exception (Davies & Windle, 2001; Lengua, Sandler, West, Wolchik, & Curran, 1999). Children differ, for example, in their ability to maintain homeostasis and to regulate arousal in response to changes in the environment (El-Sheikh, Harger, & Whitson, 2001). Vagal tone provides a physiological indicator of this arousal regulation. In situations of marital conflict, children with low vagal tone are more likely to show internalizing and externalizing problems than are children with high vagal tone (El-Sheikh et al., 2001; Katz & Gottmann, 1995, 1997). Thus, children with a greater capacity to remain calm and regulate their own emotions are less likely to develop emotional and behavioral problems in response to family stresses. Consistent with these findings, family disruption and change is especially likely to increase the odds of psychiatric problems among adolescents who exhibit more immaturity and more affective problems in childhood, prior to the family disruption (Kasen et al.; 1996).

In contrast to these findings, Chase-Lansdale et al. (1995) found the impact of childhood divorce on young adults to be greater for those children who had fewer emotional problems in childhood. In their British sample, individuals who exhibited high levels of emotional problems in childhood, despite functioning at a lower absolute level during young adulthood than individuals who had low levels of emotional problems in childhood, were not as negatively affected by the divorce itself. Perhaps by adulthood, children who are least adaptable experience negative emotional responses to a variety of events and stressors in their lives, including but not predominantly divorce. In contrast, children who by temperament are more adaptable may show increased reactivity to new stressors predominantly because of the parental divorce (e.g., Landerman et al., 1991).

Thinking About the Divorce

Children interpret changes in family structure and the events surrounding such changes in different ways. Children who blame themselves for family troubles, particularly when self-blame lasts over time, adjust more poorly to divorce than children who do not blame themselves (Healy et al., 1993). Self-blame for marital conflict may be more common in (Kerig, 1998) and an especially important predictor of adjustment for girls (Cummings, Davies, & Simpson, 1994).

Although an internal locus of control is generally a protective factor, the findings regarding self-blame indicate that overestimating one's ability to influence divorce-related events may not be adaptive. However, an internal locus of control for positive events might be particularly adaptive; children who do not have an understanding of what causes positive events (i.e., who have an "unknown locus of control" for positive events) are more likely to show negative adjustment in the face of negative events in their lives than other children (Kim, Sandler, & Tein, 1997). In the authors' words, ". . . understanding why good things occur may enable children to reassure themselves that more positive conditions will occur in the future. In contrast, not knowing why good events occur may lead children to be pessimistic that their situation will improve." (Kim et al., 1997, p. 154).

Social Support

The positive impact of social support for individuals in stressful situations is well documented (e.g., Kahn & Antonucci, 1980; Werner & Smith, 1982, 1992), and applies to children who experience divorce and remarriage. Pennebaker's (1990) work with young adults showing the benefits of confiding in others under stressful situations, although not specifically about divorce, suggests that opportunities to confide about difficult family situations can promote better adjustment. Support from adults seems to buffer the stress of negative divorce-related events more effectively than does support from peers (Wolchick, Ruehlman, Braver, & Sandler, 1989), but intimate, supportive friendships can be helpful, at least for adolescent children (Buhrmester, 1990; Lustig, Wolchik, & Braver, 1992).

Girls in particular might also benefit from close, supportive sibling relationships. Sibling dyads that include girls are less troubled following divorce and remarriage than those that involve boys. Particularly in adolescence, female siblings are more likely to confide in one another and provide support for one another than other sibling dyads (Hetherington, 1991). Such support in female sibling dyads has the potential to aid girls in their adjustment to family stress.

Age at Divorce or Remarriage

Establishing the impact of age at divorce on children's longer-term reactions to divorce is a difficult endeavor, given the inherent confounds among a child's age at divorce, age at measurement, and time since divorce (Emery, 1999), as well as the possibility of parental separation(s) preceding divorce. It seems clear that children of all ages are affected in some way by divorce, although children may be affected more severely at some ages than others. For example, young children might have more difficulty interpreting divorce-related events, and early divorce might mean children are exposed for more of their childhood to negative sequelae of divorce such as economic difficulties and poor parent–child relationships. In fact, evidence exists that divorce is associated with worse long-term outcomes when it occurs at younger ages (Allison & Furstenberg, 1989; Fergusson et al., 1994; Zill et al., 1993). However, for females, short-term problems (i.e., in the first few years following divorce) are more likely to be detected when the divorce occurs during adolescence than when the divorce occurs prior to adolescence (e.g., Sun, 2001).

As already noted, early adolescence may be an especially vulnerable time for girls to experience a parent's remarriage (Hetherington, 1993; Hetherington & Clingempeel, 1992; Lee et al., 1994). Both girls and boys may resent the entrance of a new parental authority at a time in development when they desire more autonomy. Stepparents who enter a family when children are early adolescents have not had the opportunity to establish the trusting kind of relationship with the child that is helpful, even necessary, in eliciting the child's acceptance of that parent as an authority figure.

The entrance of a stepfather during early adolescence can create additional concerns for girls. I noted earlier that girls might especially resent the loss of time with and attention from their mothers. Perhaps more importantly, adolescent girls can be uncomfortable with or even threatened by the presence of a new man in the home at a time when their own sexuality is emerging. In fact, remarriages that occur when girls are 9 years or older show a reversal in the earlier-described pattern of association between marital closeness and girls' functioning. In these later remarriages, the closer the marital relationship is, the better the girls' relationships with her parents and the better her adjustment (Hetherington, 1993). Perhaps for adolescent girls, concerns about sexual boundaries are assuaged by closer mother-stepfather relationships, leading to relatively better outcomes when the new marital relationships are particularly strong. In fact, although most females are not sexually abused by their stepfathers, the risk of sexual abuse, including sexual abuse of the more severe kinds, is higher between stepfathers and adolescent girls than it is in other family dyads (Kendall-Tackett & Simon, 1992; Russell, 1984; Wilson, 2001). The experience of sexual abuse between stepfathers and stepdaughters has grave implications for the future mental health of girls (Nolen-Hoeksema & Girgus, 1994; Sroufe et al., 2000; Ussher & Dewberry, 1995). More generally, the discomfort over negotiating one's sexual development in the presence of an unrelated adult male may heighten the difficulty of this developmental task.

Custody Arrangement

There is tremendous variation in children's adjustment in every custody arrangement. One-size-fits-all prescriptions for the "best" custody arrangements, such as "children are better off with their same-sex parent" are overly simplistic (Buchanan et al., 1996); many girls fare well in the custody of their fathers and many boys fare well in the custody of their mothers. However, on average, joint custody is associated with positive outcomes for girls and boys (Bauserman, 2002; Buchanan et al., 1992, 1996), in part because more cooperative and well-adjusted families maintain joint custody over time, and in part because joint custody allows children to maintain close relationships with both parents.

In contrast, adolescents on average fare less well in the custody of their fathers than in mother—or joint custody, and this is particularly true for girls (Buchanan et al., 1991, 1996; Lee et al., 1994). The reasons for this difference have not been clearly elucidated, but it may reflect that mothers are more likely to have had psychological problems or relationship problems with their children when fathers get sole custody; that father custody arrangements are less stable and more likely to be associated with increased life stresses than other arrangements; that fathers get custody of more difficult children; or that fathers are less practiced and thus less effective in some aspects of parenting (Buchanan et al., 1992, 1996). All of these factors may be more likely for girls than for boys, as fathers are more likely to get custody of boys, compared to girls, for benign reasons (e.g., "boys need a male role model").

IMPLICATIONS FOR TREATMENT AND PREVENTION

Unquestionably, parental divorce and remarriage are stressful family transitions that raise the risk of negative outcomes, including psychopathology, in girls who experience them. However, it is just as clear that the events and relationships that occur in the family, both before and after divorce and remarriage, matter even more to the well-being of girls than does family structure (e.g., Borrine et al., 1991; Dixon et al., 1998; Lansford, Ceballo, Abbey & Stewart, 2001). On the one hand, even small increases in the odds of psychiatric illness as a result of divorce mean a substantial increase in the numbers of individuals that will need treatment for mental conditions as a result of family disruption. As such, efforts to reduce divorce rates are important. On the other hand, interventions targeted at changing family processes seem likely to reap more benefits than interventions targeted simply at family structure. As Fergusson et al. (1994) note, "... there may be considerable value in reducing the emphasis on parental separation as a cause of adolescent psychopathology and replacing this emphasis with a more general perspective involving social and contextual factors ..." (p. 1130). Interventions targeted at family processes among families at risk of divorce might have the dual benefit of reducing divorce rates and reducing the incidence of psychopathology in children who experience dysfunctional family relationships and poor parenting.

A serious look at the research on children's adjustment to divorce shows that attention must be paid to identifying stressed families prior to divorce. Families that subsequently divorce show higher marital conflict and poorer parenting and parent–child relationships prior to divorce, and both parents and children show elevated rates of emotional and behavioral problems prior to divorce. At least some, and perhaps a substantial amount, of the damage done to children's well-being that is attributed to divorce occurs prior to the divorce. This appears to be especially true for girls once they have reached adolescence, although the seeds of the problems that emerge in adolescence may have been planted earlier in childhood. Effort to help girls following parental divorce, while needed, will occur too late in some respects.

Interventions with families experiencing family transitions are also important. Interventions should not be limited to those families that seek it out or to children who display problems that require attention. Research showing the emergence of longer-term adjustment difficulties for young adults of divorce—even for individuals who did not exhibit severe negative reactions as children—suggests that all parents and children might benefit from help and support in the years following divorce. Girls should be helped to avoid self-blame as well as to find social support. Parents should be helped to recognize the difficulties they and their children are likely to face, such as ineffective parenting or pressuring daughters to take sides in post-marital conflict. Mothers can be alerted to the special issues of remarriage in young girls' development. Parents can be alerted to the importance of fathers' continued presence and affirmation in the lives of their daughters. Parents and other adults (e.g., school personnel) should perhaps be aware of the likelihood that girls' struggles with issues of family conflict and divorce might intensify during adolescence. Programs aimed at preventing, recognizing, and responding to instances of sexual abuse should be available to girls and their parents.

Interventions for divorcing parents such as mediation programs and parent education and support programs result in improved family processes such as lower conflict between parents and better parenting (Emery, 1994, 1999; Kelly, 1991; Wolchik et al., 1993). These programs have sometimes been shown to benefit children's adjustment as well (e.g., Forgatch & DeGarmo, 1999; Wolchik et al., 1993), although the short-term nature of most of these programs probably makes them less effective than they could be in affecting longer-term adjustment of families and children (Emery, 1999, Blaisure & Geasler, 1996). Extending these types of programs to more parents and over longer periods of time, and constructing them in ways that make social support readily available to parents and children over time as they face ongoing challenges of family disruption, is likely to help children avoid a future of psychopathology linked to family disruption.

FUTURE DIRECTIONS

Research on divorce and remarriage is plentiful; to a large extent it tells a consistent story. Family transitions raise the risk of psychopathology slightly but significantly. Family processes associated with family transitions explain a large part of the increased risk. Variability in children's adjustment after family transitions can be linked to predictable factors in the persons and environments of those experiencing transitions. Further research should continue to disentangle the many confounding factors in this area, such as marital conflict, parental psychopathology, parenting and parent–child relationships. All of these factors may be independently important, but it would be helpful to understand more clearly which factors are especially likely to play a causal role in the negative web of events and relationships that characterize many divorcing families.

Recent research extends our knowledge about the impact of divorce and remarriage into the young adult years, but continued efforts in this direction are needed. In particular, it would be helpful to investigate more closely the phenomenon whereby new or intensified problems related to parental divorce emerge during the adult years, a phenomenon that might be especially relevant to females. Research on vulnerability to life stresses is helpful in providing a theoretical framework for how such "sleeper effects" might arise, as is research on the negative ramifications of lowered educational attainment. However, this body of research is relatively new, and a closer look at those individuals who appear to have adjusted well to family transitions but then develop problems in adulthood (e.g., more intensive examination of their earlier functioning, and relationships and events in their preadult lives) might help to illuminate the developmental course of problematic reactions to divorce in the longer term.

Research examining the impact of family transitions in different ethnic groups is also relatively new. Thus, another important need is to understand the meaning of and events associated with changes in family structure for girls in different ethnic groups. The possibility that divorce has a less negative impact in Hispanic families (Amato, 1991) is intriguing, but needs replication and illumination. In what ways is the experience of divorce different for girls and boys in this ethnic group?

Finally, more research on the impact of different intervention and treatment programs for girls and their parents is sorely needed. We need to know the benefits but also the limits of the short-term interventions typically available to or even required of divorcing parents, as well as the extent to which programs should be lengthened in time and broadened in scope to maximize their impact (Salem, Schepard, & Schilissel, 1996). Increased efforts to identify and provide support and other resources to all children of families where divorce or remarriage occur—not just those who most obviously need help—might be important for reducing the incidence of longer-term problems.

REFERENCES

Ackerman, B. P., D'Eramo, K. S., Umylny, L., Schultz, D., & Izard, C. E. (2001). Family structure and the externalizing behavior of children from economically disadvantaged families. *Journal of Family Psychology, 15,* 288–300.

Allison, P. D., & Furstenberg, F. F. Jr. (1989). Marital dissolution affects children: Variations by age and sex. *Developmental Psychology, 25,* 540–549.

Amato, P. R. (1991). Parental absence during childhood and depression in later life. *The Sociological Quarterly, 32,* 543–556.

Amato, P. R. (1993). Children's adjustment to divorce: Theories, hypotheses, and empirical support. *Journal of Marriage and the Family, 55,* 23–38.

Amato, P. R. (1999). Children of divorced parents as young adults. In E. M. Hetherington (Ed.), *Coping with divorce, single parenting, and remarriage* (pp. 147–163). Mahwah, NJ: Erlbaum.

Amato, P. R., & Booth, A. (1996). A prospective study of divorce and parent-child relationships. *Journal of Marriage and the Family, 58,* 356–365.

Amato, P. R., & Keith, B. (1991a). Parental divorce and the well-being of children: A meta-analysis. *Psychological Bulletin, 100,* 26–46.

Amato, P. R., & Keith, B. (1991b). Parental divorce and adult well-being: A meta-analysis. *Journal of Marriage and the Family, 53,* 43–58.

Amato, P. R., Loomis, L. S., & Booth, A. (1995). Parental divorce, marital conflict, and offspring well-being during early adulthood. *Social Forces, 73,* 895–915.

Aseltine, R. H. (1996). Pathways linking parental divorce with adolescent depression. *Journal of Health and Social Behavior, 37,* 133–148.

Bauserman, R. (2002). Child adjustment in joint-custody versus sole-custody arrangements: A meta-analytic review. *Journal of Family Psychology, 16,* 91–102.

Blaisure, K. R., & Geasler, M. J. (1996). Results of a survey of court-connected parent education programs in U. S. counties. *Family and Conciliation Courts Review, 34,* 23–40.

Block, J. H., Block, J., & Gjerde, P. F. (1986). The personality of children prior to divorce: A prospective study. *Child Development, 57,* 827–840.

Block, J., Block, J. H., & Gjerde, P. F. (1988). Parental functioning and the home environment in families of divorce: Prospective and concurrent analyses. *Journal of the American Academy of Child and Adolescent Psychiatry, 27,* 207–213.

Booth, A., & Amato, P. R. (2001). Parental predivorce relations and offspring postdivorce well-being. *Journal of Marriage and the Family, 63,* 197–212.

Borrine, M. L., Handal, P. J., Brown, N. Y., & Searight, H. R. (1991). Family conflict and adolescent adjustment in intact, divorced, and blended families. *Journal of Consulting and Clinical Psychology, 59,* 753–755.

Brody, G. H., & Neubaum, E. (199). Family transitions as stressors in children and adolescents. In Pfeffer, C. R. (Ed.), *Severe stress and mental disturbance in children* (pp. 559–590). Washington, DC: American Psychiatric Press.

Bruce, M. L. (1998). Divorce and psychopathology. In B. Dohrenwend (Ed.), *Adversity, stress, and psychopathology* (pp. 219–232). New York: Oxford University Press.

Buchanan, C. M., Maccoby, E. E., & Dornbusch, S. (1991). Caught between parents: Adolescents' experience in divorced homes. *Child Development, 62,* 1008–1029.

Buchanan, C. M., Maccoby, E. E., & Dornbusch, S. (1992). Adolescents and their families after divorce: Three residential arrangements compared. *Journal of Research on Adolescence, 2,* 261–291.

Buchanan, C. M., Maccoby, E. E., & Dornbusch, S. M. (1996). *Adolescents after divorce.* Cambridge, MA: Harvard University Press.

Buchanan, C. M., & Waizenhofer, R. (2001). The impact of interparental conflict on adolescent children: Considerations of family systems and family structure. In A. Booth, A. C. Crouter, & M. Clements (Eds.), *Couples in conflict* (pp. 149–160). Mahwah, NJ: Erlbaum.

Buhrmester, D. (1990). Intimacy of friendship, interpersonal competence, and adjustment during preadolescence and adolescence. *Child Development, 61,* 1101–1111.

Carlson, M. J., & Corcoran, M. E. (2001). Family structure and children's behavioral and cognitive outcomes. *Journal of Marriage and the Family, 63,* 779–792.

Chase-Lansdale, P. L., Cherlin, A. J., & Kiernan, K. E. (1995). The long-term effects of parental divorce on the mental health of young adults: A developmental perspective. *Child Development, 66,* 1614–1634.

Cherlin, A. J., Chase-Lansdale, P., & McRae, C. (1998). Effects of parental divorce on mental health throughout the life course. *American Sociological Review, 63,* 239–249.

Cherlin, A. J., Furstenberg, F. F., Chase-Lansdale, P. L., Kiernan, K. E., Robins, P. K., Morrison, D. R., et al. (1991). Longitudinal studies of effects of divorce on children in Great Britain and the United States. *Science, 252,* 1386–1389.

Cicchetti, D., Toth, S. L., & Maughan, A. (2000). An ecological-transactional model of child maltreatment. In A. J. Sameroff, M. Lewis, & S. M. Miller (Eds.), *Handbook of developmental psychopathology* (2nd edition, pp. 689–722). New York: Kluwer Academic/Plenum.

Conger, R. D., & Chao, W. (1996). Adolescent depressed mood. In R. L. Simons (Ed.), *Understanding differences between divorced and intact families* (pp. 157–175). Thousand Oaks, Ca: Sage.

Cummings, E. M., & Davies, P. (1994). *Children and marital conflict: The impact of family dispute and resolution.* New York: Guilford.

Cummings, E. M., Davies, P. T., & Campbell, S. B. (2000). *Developmental psychopathology and family process: Theory, research and clinical implications.* New York: Guilford.

Cummings, E. M., Davies, P. T., & Simpson, K. S. (1994). Marital conflict, gender, and children's appraisals and coping efficacy as mediators of child adjustment. *Journal of Family Psychology, 8,* 141–149.

Cummings, E. M., Goeke-Morey, M. C., & Papp, L. M. (2001). Couple conflict, children, and families: It's not just you and me, babe. In A. Booth, A. C. Crouter, & M. Clements (Eds.), *Couples in conflict* (pp. 117–147). Mahwah, NJ: Erlbaum.

Davies, P. T., & Windle, M. (1997). Gender-specific pathways between maternal depressive symptoms, family discord, and adolescent adjustment. *Developmental Psychology, 33,* 657–668.

Davies, P. T., & Windle, M. (2001). Interparental discord and adolescent adjustment trajectories: The potentiating and protective role of intrapersonal attributes. *Child Development, 72,* 1163–1178.

Deater-Deckard, K., & Dunn, J. (1999). Multiple risks and adjustment in young children growing up in different family setting: A British community study of stepparent, single mother, and nondivorced families. In E. M. Hetherington (Ed.), *Coping with divorce, single parenting, and remarriage* (pp. 47–64). Mahwah, NJ: Erlbaum.

Demo, D. H., & Acock, A. C. (1996). Family structure, family process, and adolescent well-being. *Journal of Research on Adolescence, 6,* 457–488.

Dixon, C., Charles, M. A., & Craddock, A. A. (1998). The impact of experiences of parental divorce and parental conflict on young Australian adult men and women. *Journal of Family Studies, 4,* 21–34.

Doherty, W. J., & Needle, R. H. (1991). Psychological adjustment and substance use among adolescents before and after a parental divorce. *Child Development, 62,* 328–337.

Dornbusch, S. M., Carlsmith, J. M., Bushwall, S. J., Ritter, P. L., Liederman, H., Hastorf, A. H., & Gross, R. T. (1985). Single parents, extended households, and the control of adolescents. *Child Development, 56,* 326–341.

Dunlop, R., Burns, A., & Bermingham, S. (2001). Parent-child relations and adolescent self-image following divorce: A 10-year study. *Journal of Youth and Adolescence, 30,* 117–134.

El-Skeikh, M., Harger, J., & Whitson, S. M. (2001). Exposure to interparental conflict and children's adjustment and physical health: The moderating role of vagal tone. *Child Development, 72,* 1617–1636.

Emery, R. E. (1994). *Renegotiating family relationships: Divorce, child custody, and mediation.* New York: Guilford.

Emery, R. E. (1999). *Marriage, divorce, and children's adjustment* (2nd edition). Thousand Oaks, CA: Sage.

Emery, R. E., & Coiro, M. J. (1997). Some costs of coping: Stress and distress among children from divorced families. In D. Cicchetti & S. L. Toth (Eds.), *Rochester symposium on developmental psychopathology: The effects of trauma on developmental process* (Vol. 8, pp. 435–462). Rochester, NY: University of Rochester Press.

Emery, R. E., Joyce, S. A., & Fincham, F. D. (1987). The assessment of marital and child problems. In K. D. O'Leary (Ed.), *Assessment of marital discord* (pp. 223–262). Hillsdale, NJ. Lawrence Erlbaum Associates.

Emery, R., E., Waldron, M., Kitzmann, K. M., & Aaron, J. (1999). Delinquent behavior, future divorce or nonmarital childbearing, and externalizing behavior among offspring: A 14-year prospective study. *Journal of Family Psychology, 13*, 568–579.

Fergusson, D. M., Horwood, L. J., & Lynskey, M. T. (1994). Parental separation, adolescent psychopathology, and problem behaviors. *Journal of the American Academy of Child and Adolescent Psychiatry, 33*, 1122–1131.

Flisher, A. J., Kramer, R. A., Hoven, C. W., & Greenwald, S. (1997). Psychosocial characteristics of physically abused children and adolescents. *Journal of the American Academy of Child and Adolescent Psychiatry, 36*, 123–131.

Forgatch, M. S., & DeGarmo, D. S. (1999). Parenting through change: An effective prevention program for single mothers. *Journal of Consulting and Clinical Psychology, 67*, 711–724.

Furstenberg, F. F. Jr. (1990). Divorce and the American family. In W. R. Scott & J. Blake (Eds.), *Annual review of sociology* (Vol. 16, pp. 379–403). Palo Alto, CA: Annual Reviews.

Furstenberg, F. F., & Cherlin, A. J. (1991). *Divided families: What happens to children when parents part.* Cambridge, MA: Harvard University Press.

Furstenberg, F. F., Jr., & Harris, K. M. (1992). The disappearing American Father? Divorce and the waning significance of biological parenthood. In S. J. South & S. E. Tolnay (Eds.), *The Changing American Family* (pp. 197–223). Boulder, CO: Westview Press.

Furstenberg, F. F., & Kiernan, K. E. (2001). Delayed parental divorce: How much do children benefit? *Journal of Marriage and the Family, 63*, 446–457.

Geiger, T. C., & Crick, N. R. (2001). A developmental psychopathology perspective on vulnerability to personality disorders. In R. E. Ingram, & J. M. Price (Eds.), *Vulnerability to psychopathology: Risk across the lifespan* (pp. 57–102). New York: Guilford.

Gore, S., Aseltine, R. H., Jr., & Colten, M. E. (1993). Gender, social-relational involvement, and depression. *Journal of Research on Adolescence, 3*, 101–125.

Grych, J. H. & Fincham, F. D. (1999). Children of single parents and divorce. In W. K. Silverman & T. H. Ollendick (Ed.), *Developmental issues in the clinical treatment of children* (pp. 321–341). Boston, MA: Allyn and Bacon.

Hammen, C. (2001). Vulnerability to depression in adulthood. In R. E. Ingram, & J. M. Price (Eds.), *Vulnerability to psychopathology: Risk across the lifespan* (pp. 226–257). New York: Guilford.

Healy, J. M., Stewart, A. J., & Copeland, A. P. (1993). The role of self-blame in children's adjustment to parental separation. *Personality and Social Psychology Bulletin, 19*, 279–289.

Hetherington, E. M. (1991). Presidential address: Families, lies, and videotapes. *Journal of Research on Adolescence, 1*, 323–348.

Hetherington, E. M. (1993). An overview of the Virginia Longitudinal Study of Divorce and Remarriage with a focus on early adolescence. *Journal of Family Psychology, 7*, 39–56.

Hetherington, E. M., & Clingempeel, W. G. (1992). Coping with marital transition: A family systems perspective. *Monographs of the Society for Research in Child Development, 57* (2–3, Serial No. 227).

Hetherington, E. M., Cox, M., & Cox, R. (1985) Long-term effects of divorce and remarriage on the adjustment of children. *Journal of the American Academy of Child Psychiatry, 24*, 518–530.

Hetherington, E. M., & Kelly, J. (2002). *For better or for worse: Divorce reconsidered.* New York: W.W. Norton.

Isaacs, M. B., & Leon, G. H. (1988). Remarriage and its alternatives following divorce: Mother and child adjustment. *Journal of Marital and Family Therapy, 14*, 163–173.

Jacquet, S. E., & Surra, C. A. (2001). Parental divorce and premarital couples: Commitment and other relationship characteristics. *Journal of Marriage and the Family, 63*, 627–638.

Johnston, J. R., & Campbell, L. E. G. (1988). *Impasses of divorce: The dynamics and resolution of family conflict.* New York: Free Press.

Kahn, R. L., & Antonucci, T. C. (1980). Convoys over the life course: Attachment, roles, and social support. In P. B. Baltes & O. G. Brim, Jr. (Eds.), *Life-span development and behavior* (Vol. 3). New York: Academic Press.

Kalter, N., Riemer, B., Brickman, A., & Chen, J. W. (1985). Implications of parental divorce for female development. *Journal of the American Academy of Child Psychiatry, 24,* 538–544.

Kasen, S., Cohen, P., Brook, J. S., & Hartmark, C. (1996). A multiple risk interaction model: Effects of temperament and divorce on psychiatric disorder in children. *Journal of Abnormal Child Psychology, 24,* 538–544.

Katz, L. F., & Gottman, J. M. (1995). Vagal tone protects children from marital conflict. *Development and Psychopathology, 7,* 83–92.

Katz, L. F., & Gottman, J. M. (1997). Buffering children from marital conflict and dissolution. *Journal of Clinical Child Psychology, 26,* 157–171.

Kelly, J. B. (1991). Parent interaction after divorce: Comparison of mediated and adversarial divorce processes. *Behavioral Sciences and the Law, 9,* 387–398.

Kendall-Tackett, K. A., & Simon, A. F. (1992). A comparison of the abuse experiences of male and female adults molested as children. *Journal of Family Violence, 7,* 57–62.

Kendler, K. S., Neale, M. C., Kessler, R. C., Heath, A. C., & Eaves, J. L. (1992). Childhood parental loss and adult psychopathology in women: A twin study perspective. *Archives of General Psychiatry, 49,* 109–116.

Kerig, P. K. (1998). Moderators and mediators of the effects of interparental conflict on children's adjustment. *Journal of Abnormal Child Psychology, 26,* 199–212.

Kernberg, P. F., Wiener, A. S., & Bardenstein, K. K. (2000). Personality disorders in children and adolescents. NY: Basic Books.

Kim, L. S., Sandler, I. N., & Tein, J. (1997). Locus of control as a stress moderator and mediator in children of divorce. *Journal of Abnormal Child Psychology, 25,* 145–155.

King, C. A., Radpour, L., Naylor, M. W., Segal, H. G., & Jouriles, E. N. (1995). Parents' marital functioning and adolescent psychopathology. *Journal of Consulting and Clinical Psychology, 63,* 749–753.

King, C. A., Segal, H. G., Naylor, M., & Evans, T (1993). Family functioning and suicidal behavior in adolescent inpatients with mood disorders. *Journal of the American Academy of Child and Adolescent Psychiatry, 32,* 1198–1206.

Kozuch, P., & Cooney, T. M. (1995). Young adults' marital and family attitudes: The role of recent parental divorce, and family and parental conflict. *Journal of Divorce and Remarriage, 23,* 45–62.

Lampel, A. K. (1996). Children's alignment with parents in highly conflicted custody cases. *Family and Conciliation Courts Review, 34,* 229–239.

Landerman, R., George, L. K., & Blazer, D. G. (1991). Adult vulnerability for psychiatric disorders: Interactive effects of negative childhood experiences and recent stress. *The Journal of Nervous and Mental Disease, 179,* 656–663.

Lansford, J. E., Ceballo, R., Abbey, A., & Stewart, A. (2001). Does family structure matter? A comparison of adoptive, two-parent biological, single-mother, stepfather, and stepmother households. *Journal of Marriage and the Family, 63,* 840–851.

Leadbeater, B. J., Blatt, S. J., & Quinlan, D. M. (1995). Gender-linked vulnerabilities to depressive symptoms, stress, and problem behaviors in adolescents. *Journal of Research on Adolescence, 5,* 1–29.

Lee, V. E., Burkam, D. T., Zimiles, H., & Ladewski, B. (1994). Family structure and its effect on behavioral and emotional problems in young adolescents. *Journal of Research on Adolescence, 4,* 405–438.

Lengua, L. J., Sandler, I. N., West, S. G., Wolchik, S. A., & Curran, P. J. (1999). Emotionality and self-regulation, threat appraisal, and coping in children of divorce. *Development and Psychopathology, 11,* 15–37.

Liu, X., Guo, C., Okawa, M., Zhai, J., Li, Y., Uchiyama, M., et al. (2000). Behavioral and emotional problems in Chinese children of divorced parents. *Journal of the American Academy of Child and Adolescent Psychiatry, 39,* 896–903.

Long, N., & Forehand, R. (1987). The effects of parental divorce and parental conflict on children: An overview. *Developmental and Behavioral Pediatrics, 8,* 292–296.

Lustig, J. J., Wolchik, S. A., & Braver, S. L. (1992). Social support in chumships and adjustment in children of divorce. *American Journal of Community Psychology, 20,* 393–399.

Maccoby, E. M., & Mnookin, R. H. (1992). *Dividing the child: Social and legal dilemmas of custody.* Cambridge, MA: Harvard University Press.

Margolin, G., Oliver, P. H., & Medina, A. M. (2001). Conceptual issues in understanding the relation between interparnetal conflict and child adjustment. In Grych, J. H., & Fincham, F. D. (Eds.), *Interparental conflict and child development: Theory, research and application* (pp. 9–38). Cambridge, UK: Cambridge University Press.

McGue, M., & Lykken, D. T. (1992). Genetic influence on risk of divorce. *Psychological Science, 6,* 368–373.

McLanahan, S., & Sandefur, G. (1994). *Growing up with a single parent: What hurts, what helps.* Cambridge, MA: Harvard University Press.

McLeod, J. D. (1991). Childhood parental loss and adult depression. *Journal of Health and Social Behavior, 32,* 205–220.

Morrison, D. R., & Cherlin, A. J. (1995). The divorce process and young children's well-being: A prospective analysis. *Journal of Marriage and the Family, 57,* 800–812.

Morrison, D. R., & Coiro, M. J. (1999). Parental conflict and marital disruption: Do children benefit when high-conflict marriages are dissolved? *Journal of Marriage and the Family, 61,* 626–637.

Needle, R. H., Su, S. S., & Doherty, W. J. (1990). Divorce, remarriage, and adolescent substance use: A prospective longitudinal study. *Journal of Marriage and the Family, 52,* 157–169.

Nolen-Hoeksema, S., & Girgus, J. S. (1994). The emergence of gender differences in depression during adolescence. *Psychological Bulletin, 115,* 424–443.

O'Connor, T. G., Caspi, A., DeFries, J. C., & Plomin, R. (2000). Are associations between parental divorce and children's adjustment genetically mediated?: An adoption study. *Developmental Psychology, 36,* 429–437.

O'Connor, T. G., Dunn, J., Jenkins, J. M., Pickering, K., & Rasbash, J. (2001). Family settings and children's' adjustment: Differential adjustment within and across families. *British Journal of Psychiatry, 179,* 110–115.

Pennebaker, J. W. (1990). *Opening up: The healing power of confiding in others.* New York: Morrow.

Powell, M. A., & Parcel, T. L. (1997). Effects of family structure on the earnings attainment process: Differences by gender. *Journal of Marriage and the Family, 59,* 419–433.

Reid, W. J., & Crisafulli, A. (1990). Marital discord and child behavior problems: A meta-analysis. *Journal of Abnormal Child Psychology, 18,* 105–117.

Ross, C. E., & Mirowsky, J. (1999). Parental divorce, life-course disruption, and adult depression. *Journal of Marriage and the Family, 61,* 1034–1045.

Russell, D. E. (1984) The prevalence and seriousness of incestuous abuse: Stepfathers vs. biological fathers. *Child Abuse and Neglect, 8,* 15–22.

Salem, P., Schepard, A., & Schlissel, S. W. (1996). Parent education as a distinct field of practice: The agenda for the future. *Family and Conciliation Courts Review, 34,* 9–22.

Sandler, I., Wolchik, S., Braver, S., & Fogas, B. (1991). Stability and quality of life events and psychological symptomatology in children of divorce. *American Journal of Community Psychology, 19,* 501–520.

Seltzer, J. A. (1991). Relationships between fathers and children who live apart: The father's role after separation. *Journal of Marriage and the Family, 53,* 79–101.

Shaw, D. S., Emory, R. E., & Tuer, M. D. (1993). Parental Functioning and Children's adjustment in families of divorce: A prospective study. *Journal of Abnormal Child Psychology, 21,* 119–134.

Simons, R. L., & Chao, W. (1996). Conduct problems. In R. L. Simons (Ed.), *Understanding differences between divorced and intact families* (pp. 125–142). Thousand Oaks, CA: Sage.

Simons, R. L., & Johnson, C. (1996). Mother's parenting. In R. L. Simons (Ed.), *Understanding differences between divorced and intact families* (pp. 81–94). Thousand Oaks, CA: Sage.

Simons, R. L., Lin, K., Gordon, L. C., Conger, R. D., & Lorenz, F. O. (1999). Explaining the higher incidence of adjustment problems among children of divorce compared with those in two-parent families. *Journal of Marriage and the Family, 61,* 1020–1033.

Sroufe, L. A., Duggal, S., & Weinfield, N., & Carlson, E. (2000). Relationships, development, and psychopathology. In A. J. Sameroff, M. Lewis, & S. M. Miller (Eds.), *Handbook of developmental psychopathology* (2nd edition, pp. 75–91). New York: Kluwer Academic/Plenum.

Sun, Y. (2001). Family environment and adolescents' well-being before and after parents' marital disruption: A longitudinal analysis. *Journal of Marriage and the Family, 63,* 697–713.

Tschann, J. M., Johnson, J. R., Kline, M., & Wallerstein, J. S. (1990). Conflict, loss, change and parent-child relationships: Predicting children's adjustment during divorce. *Journal of Divorce, 13,* 1–22.

Ussher, J. M., & Dewberry, C. (1995). The nature and long-term effects of childhood sexual abuse: A survey of adult women survivors in Britain. *British Journal of Clinical Psychology, 34,* 177–192.

Vandewater, E. A., & Lansford, J. E. (1998). Influences of family structure and parental conflict on children's well-being. *Family Relations, 47,* 323–330.

Wallerstein, J. S., & Blakeslee, S. (1989). *Second chances: Men, women, and children a decade after divorce.* New York: Ticknor and Fields.

Wallerstein, J. S., & Kelly, J. B. (1980). *Surviving the breakup: How children and parents cope with divorce.* New York: Basic Books.

Werner, E. E., & Smith, R. S. (1982). *Vulnerable but invincible: A longitudinal study of resilient children and youth.* New York: McGraw-Hill.

Werner, E. E., & Smith, R. S. (1992). *Overcoming the odds: High-risk children from birth to adulthood.* Ithaca, NY: Cornell University Press.

Wilson, R. F. (2001). Children at risk: The sexual exploitation of female children after divorce. *Cornell Law Review, 86,* 251–327.

Wolchik, S. A., West, S. G., Westover, S., Sandler, I. N., Martin, A., Lustig, J., et al. (1993). The children of divorce parenting intervention: Outcome evaluation of an empirically based program. *American Journal of Community Psychology, 21,* 293–331.

Wolchik, S. A., Wilcox, K. L., Tein, J., & Sandler, I. N. (2000). Maternal acceptance and consistency of discipline as buffers of divorce stressors on children's psychological adjustment problems. *Journal of Abnormal Child Psychology, 28,* 87–102.

Wolchick, S. A., Ruehlman, L. S., Braver, S. L., & Sandler, I. N. (1989). Social support of children of divorce: Direct and stress-buffering effects. *American Journal of Community Psychology, 17,* 485–501.

Zaslow, M. J. (1988). Sex differences in children's response to parental divorce: 1. Research methodology and post-divorce family forms. *American Journal of Orthopsychiatry, 58,* 355–378.

Zaslow, M. J. (1989). Sex differences in children's response to parental divorce: 2. Samples, variables, ages, and sources. *American Journal of Orthopsychiatry, 59,* 118–141.

Zhou, Z., Bray, M. A., Kehle, T J., & Xin, T. (2001). Similarity of deleterious effects of divorce on Chinese and American children. *School Psychology International, 22,* 357–363.

Zill, N., Morrison, D. R., & Coiro, M. J. (1993). Long-term effects of parental divorce on parent-child relationships, adjustment, and achievement in young adulthood. *Journal of Family Psychology, 7,* 91–103.

15

Girls on their Own

Homelessness in Female Adolescents

**ANA MARI CAUCE, ANGELA STEWART,
LES B. WHITBECK, MATTHEW PARADISE,
and DAN R. HOYT**

When we first met 16-year-old Shana she was "spainging" (spare-changing) on the Ave. She agreed to participate in the study because she could make enough money to buy pizza and drinks for herself and her boyfriend. They met at a church-sponsored shelter and had been hanging together for almost a week. With a boyfriend, Shana felt protected and more willing to spend the night in a squat or even under the bridge if the weather was good. This was a welcome change from the shelter, which was always crowded and had lots of rules. She said that sometimes Mike could be difficult and demanding, but people were also less apt to mess with her when he was around. She liked that part.

Adolescence has long been considered a time of rapid biological, cognitive, and social changes and transitions. The body changes from that of a child to an adult and sexual reproduction becomes possible (Brooks-Gunn & Reiter, 1990). While these changes present challenges for most young people, within a supportive family context, adolescents can experiment with and try on adult roles within a relatively protected environment so that they emerge from this developmental period prepared to meet the tasks of young adulthood. Some adolescents, like Shana are not so lucky. They are afforded little protection from their social milieu and they enter, or are propelled into, independence prematurely. For these adolescents the normative challenges of this period are the least of their problems as they are faced with the prospect of making their own way

ANA MARI CAUCE and ANGELA STEWART • University of Washington, Seattle, WA 98195
LES B. WHITBECK and DAN R. HOYT • University of Nebraska-Lincoln 68588-0324
MATTHEW PARADISE • University of North Carolina-Greensboro 27402-6170

in an environment full of risk and where protection usually comes at a price.

In this chapter, we will examine the antecedents and consequences of youth homelessness, with special focus on homeless girls and young women. More specifically, we will examine their family backgrounds, their reasons for leaving home, and their experiences while on the streets. Finally, we will review several research studies that attempt to link their early history to their experiences on the street and mental health consequences. Throughout we will attempt to shed light on those risks and vulnerabilities that are unique to girls and young women, or that have special significance for them.

The best estimates of the national prevalence of youth homelessness range between one and two million, with numbers swelling during times of economic downturn and social turmoil (National Network of Runaway and Youth Service, Inc., 1985; Ringwalt, Greene, Robertson, & McPheeters, 1998). While there has been growing appreciation and concern among both policy makers and the general public that youth are living outside of a family context with increasing frequency, the research base on homeless and runaway youth is still in its infancy and they are considered the most understudied group within a broader homeless population that is itself understudied (Rotheram-Borus, Koopman, & Ehrhardt, 1991). The first few intensive, long-term examinations of these youths have only recently been completed or are nearing completion. In this chapter, we draw extensively from published data coming from three large studies of homeless youth, one a large-scale study conducted in various cities in the Midwest and two longitudinal studies in Seattle. Unpublished data from one of the latter studies was analyzed expressly for this project. Brief descriptions of these studies follow.

The Midwest Homeless and Runaway Adolescent Project (MHRAP; Whitbeck & Hoyt, 1999) consisted of interviews with 602 adolescents (241 boys, 361 girls), and 201 of their caretakers recruited by outreach workers primarily in five cities, St. Louis, Missouri; Kansas City and Wichita, Kansas; Lincoln, Nebraska; and Des Moines, Iowa. However, outreach interviewers in these cities also recruited youths from smaller cities like Cedar Rapids, Mason City, and Davenport, Iowa, and Scottsbluff, Nebraska. Youths ranged in age from 12 to 22 years, with a mean age of $16\frac{1}{2}$ years for boys, and 16 years for girls.

Three hundred and sixty-four adolescents (42% female) were interviewed for the Seattle Homeless Adolescent Research Project (SHARP). Youths were interviewed in conjunction with a case management evaluation study at a Seattle-based agency that provided a range of services to youth, including case management and shelter services. Most youths in the study were from Seattle, although youths were also recruited from Bremerton and Everett, smaller cities within a 100-mile radius. Youths ranged in age from 13 to 21 years, with an average age of just under $16\frac{1}{2}$ years.

The Seattle Homeless Adolescent Research and Education Study (SHARE) was a follow-up to the above study and included not only youths utilizing services at local agencies but also youths who were living on the street. These youths were contacted through street intercept interviews that took place in locations where street youths spend time. Three hundred and seventy-two youths (45% female) participated in this study. Youths ranged in age from 13 to 21 years, with a median age of 17 years. All data presented without specific citation comes from this study and most of the data from this study presented here were expressly analyzed for this study.

All three studies had recruitments rates over 90%. These high recruitment rates were, in part, made possible, because youths were offered payments, ranging from $25 to $60 for interviews. However, it was our impression that the opportunity to sit down with an interested and concerned listener in a protected place, often over coffee or a meal, served as the best enticement for participation. Youths almost uniformly enjoyed the opportunity to share their stories, even when these were painful.

In all three studies, the majority of homeless youth were White, although ethnic minority youth were overrepresented compared to the demographics of the community they were drawn from. Youth of mixed ethnicity were especially overrepresented in the Seattle samples, with close to a third of each Seattle sample reporting mixed ethnic background, most typically White and African or Native American. Although most of the data presented here are drawn from baseline interviews, it is worth noting that both the Seattle studies were short-term longitudinal, with youths interviewed every 3 or 4 months for between a year and a year and a half. In general, there was an attrition rate of 30 to 40% between the initial interview and first follow-up interview, growing to an attrition rate of almost half by the end of each study. Repeated contacts allowed our research team to get to know many of the participants quite well. In this chapter, we draw not only on the formal data from our interviews, but also on informal interaction with youths, which provided us with a richer understanding of their lives. Nonetheless, when observations are based on qualitative data or observations, that fact will be explicitly noted.

WHO ARE THESE HOMELESS GIRLS?

Characteristics of Homeless Youth

Most of the first studies of youth homelessness were conducted in major metropolitan areas on the coasts, most often in New York or Los Angeles, but homeless youth can be found within almost any community. This is highlighted by the work of Whitbeck, Hoyt, and colleagues (see Whitbeck & Hoyt, 1999) who have been studying homeless and runaway youth in both large and small towns in the Midwest. Indeed, while some homeless youth travel quite a distance from their homes, virtually every study of youth homelessness finds that most youth in their sample are from the surrounding area and that their ethnic backgrounds are similar to those of their community (Robertson, 1992), although some overrepresentation of ethnic minorities has been noted (Cauce, Paradise, Embry, Morgan, Lohr, Theopolis, Heger, & Wagner, 1998).

Our stereotypes of homeless youth are still shaped by the story of Huck Finn, and the image of an unruly young man hitchhiking his way across the country often comes to mind. Yet, in addition to youth who have left home of their own volition, homeless youth include those who have left home at the urging of their parents or guardians, typically called "throw-aways" or "push-outs," and "system kids" who enter the streets after being placed out of their parental homes into foster or institutional care. "Street kids" or "street youth" is used to refer to youths who have been homeless for extended periods of time and have become street-savvy, often support-ing themselves through theft, prostitution, and drug dealing (National Net-work, 1985). Most studies of homeless youth include youths from each of these groups and except for our exploration of how youth left home, we will not attempt to differentiate between them. Some distinctions between these groups surely exist, but the boundaries between them are quite fluid. Runaways may find they are not welcome at home when they attempt to return, and street kids may become system kids and then runaway from institutional care.

In a similar vein, unlike Huck Finn, a sizeable number of homeless adolescents are girls.[1] Studies using street intercepts, where youths are interviewed right off street corners, typically find more males than females in their samples (Cauce et al., 1998; Robertson, 1992) while studies con-ducted in shelters typically include more females than males (Whitbeck & Hoyt, 1999), suggesting that the gender distribution of street youth is at least roughly even.

WHERE DO HOMELESS GIRLS COME FROM?

The Family Life of Homeless Girls

Not surprisingly, youths rarely leave or are expelled from homes char-acterized by structure, warmth, and support. Homeless adolescents typi-cally leave homes marked by conflict, dysfunction, and instability. Empir-ical studies have consistently found that parents or caretakers of youth who become homeless engage in extremely high rates of substance abuse, many have had problems with the law, and family transitions are quite common (Cauce et al., 2000; Feitel, Margetson, Chamas, & Lipman, 1992; Whitbeck & Hoyt, 1999). One study found that fewer than half of all the homeless youth in their sample had lived with both their mother and father past the age of 6 years (Cauce et al., 1998). Somewhat more homeless girls than boys report coming from homes where there has been a remarriage or where a parent's boyfriend or girlfriend (usually the former) had moved in (Whitbeck & Hoyt, 1999).

Even more importantly, homeless girls characterize their relationships with their parents as marked by neglect, harsh parenting, or outright abuse. For example, in the Midwest study, more than three fourths of the

---

[1] The majority of homeless females in the studies that we review are between the ages of 16 and 18 years, with some as old as 21 years. In this sense, many are, in fact, young women. However, we have chosen to refer to them as homeless girls to clarify that we are not talking about adults and to emphasize their vulnerability.

girls report that their parents or caretakers have slapped them and pushed or grabbed them in anger. In addition, close to two thirds or more say that they were neglected, had something thrown at them in anger, or were hit with an object before they left home (Whitbeck & Hoyt, 1999). Rates for similar experiences among girls in the SHARE study were even higher (Tyler & Cauce, 2001). In all cases of neglect and harsh discipline, except for being hit with an object, girls report having experienced these more often than boys, suggesting that the home lives of girls who end up on the streets may have been harsher than that of boys in similar circumstances.

The risks that most homeless girls are exposed to during childhood become especially apparent when sexual abuse is examined (Ryan, Kilmer, Cauce, & Hoyt, 2001). Reported rates of sexual abuse vary somewhat from study to study and by method of data collection and range from 25 to 60% of homeless girls experiencing sexual abuse prior to leaving the home (Cauce et al., 1998; Rotheram-Borus & Koopman, 1991; Whitbeck & Hoyt, 1999).

Parents (78%) were most often the perpetrators of harsh discipline or physical abuse among this population. Fathers or stepfathers (42%) were somewhat more apt to be the abusers than mothers (36%). Girls rarely reported being the recipient of physical abuse at the hands of strangers or acquaintances (11%).

In contrast to findings for physical abuse, girls were somewhat more likely to report sexual abuse at the hands of nonfamily strangers or acquaintances (55%) than from family members. Sexual abuse within the family came most often from male siblings (25%), followed by biological fathers (10%) and step, adoptive, or foster parents (6%) (Tyler & Cauce, 2001). Clearly, girls who later become homeless experienced a high degree of violence and abuse within the family. Indeed, rates of sexual abuse among homeless youth have been estimated to be as much as five times higher than in the general population (Rotheram-Borus, Parra, Cantwell, Gwadz, & Murphey 1996).

Although we know little about the factors responsible for such high rates of family dysfunction, chaos, and abuse, there is some evidence suggesting that the family difficulties that affect homeless youth may be intergenerational and that the parents of homeless youth themselves may be caught in a cycle of dysfunction and abuse (Whitbeck & Hoyt, 1999). It does not appear that socioeconomic factors alone, such as poverty or economic disadvantage, account for the high degree of dysfunction in these families. In fact, when the family environments of homeless youth were compared with those of a closely matched comparison group of housed youth from the same or similar neighborhoods, the families of homeless youth were characterized by more dysfunction and instability, including intraparental violence and child maltreatment, and less warmth and support (McCaskill, Toro, & Wolfe, 1998; Wolfe, Toro, & McCaskill, 1999). Moreover, the socioeconomic status of the families of homeless youth, as indicated by their educational background, is surprisingly varied. More than a fourth of youth in the SHARP study reported that their parents had received some college or technical school education, with almost a fifth whose parent(s) were college graduates. An additional 7% had parent(s) who had received some education beyond college, whether graduate or professional school (Cauce et al., 2000).

Educational Backgrounds of Homeless Girls

Home is often not the only place where homeless girls have difficulties. Their school experiences are often ones of struggle and failure. In the Midwest Study, almost a fifth of the girls had been expelled from school at least once, almost a quarter reported that they had learning difficulties, and slightly more than a quarter were in special education at some point (Whitbeck & Hoyt, 1999). Reports of school difficulties were similar or somewhat higher among the SHARE sample. More than a quarter of these girls reported learning disabilities, with a similar number reporting that they had been enrolled in special education. Thirty percent had been expelled with almost twice as many reporting that they had been suspended from school.

Given their school problems before leaving home, it is not surprising that by the time they are on the streets, three quarters of the girls had dropped out at least once and only a handful were still enrolled in some sort of high school. However, it is worth noting that many have not given up on their education, with over 40% actively pursuing a GED. That so many girls are pursuing their high school equivalency, despite being homeless, is a good indication of both their persistence and strength, and to the fact that they have not yet given up on their future. Indeed, as we will see next, for many girls the decision to leave home is not simply an act of desperation and hopelessness, it is also an act of defiance, liberation, and hope for a better future.

Why Girls Leave Home

Studies that have tried to shed light on the process by which youths end up on the street have resulted in the typology of run aways, throwaways, system youths, that we described earlier. The Seattle SHARP study suggested that roughly a third of all youths have run away and another third have been kicked out or thrown out. Approximately a fifth of homeless youth were first separated from their home and parents when they were removed by the authorities. These youth ended up on the streets not because they left their "home," as we traditionally think of it, but rather because they ran away from, or aged out of, a foster family or foster home placement. The remaining 10% or so ended up on the streets for other reasons, or through circuitous routes. For example, a few youths ended up on the streets when a parent or parents ended up in a homeless shelter, and other youths described "couch surfing," moving out of their home to live with relatives, then friends, and eventually ending up on the streets. This same study also found that girls were more likely to report running away from home than boys, while boys were more apt to be kicked out of their home (MacLean, Paradise, & Cauce, 1999).

An examination of the girls in SHARE study found that most of the girls (63%) reported that it was their decision to leave home, a percentage slightly higher than that for boys (58%). On average, the girls in this study left home for the first time when they were 13 years old. In contrast, boys were more likely to be kicked out of their home (26%) than girls (16%). While we do not know for sure, girls' higher rate of leaving the home voluntarily may be a result of the more extreme conditions they faced there, including higher rates of sexual abuse. Boys' higher rate of leaving home involuntarily may be a result of more aggressive behaviors, which resulted in their being barred from home.

When asked to indicate as many reasons as they wanted for why they left home, family conflict and fighting was the reason most often mentioned by the girls in the SHARE study (60%), followed by not getting along with a family member (45%), parents too strict (25%), and violence at home (25%). Abuse in the home (physical, 22%; sexual, 7%), alcohol use at home (19%), and drug use at home (15%) were also mentioned quite often as reasons for leaving. It is worth noting that while girls reported that their parents' behavior played a major role in their homelessness, they also acknowledged that their own behavior often led to their exiting the home, with a fair number admitting that their own drug use (19%) or alcohol use (15%) was at least, in part, a deciding factor. In addition, more than half the girls (53%) reported that they left home because they wanted more freedom, but it is quite likely that this is not simply freedom from the normative parental restrictions imposed on teenagers, but freedom from the turmoil, conflict, and abuse that has been such a major part of their growing up.

Homeless young men and women left home for very similar reasons. However, for girls, serious family conflict may have played a more influential role in their decision to leave, as more girls than boys said that fighting and conflict within the family was a reason they left home. Youth homelessness, for both boys and girls, is typically a result of a long process of negative experiences within the family context and there is no single or simple explanation (Whitbeck & Hoyt, 1999). The results of an especially sophisticated event history analysis using the Midwest sample suggested that an unstable family environment characterized by abrupt changes in family structure, familial neglect, or sexual abuse is highly predictive of youths running away (Whitbeck, Hoyt, & Yoder, 1999).

FROM BAD TO WORSE: GIRLS ON THE STREET

Where Girls Stay

Once an adolescent girl is on her own, she must find a place to stay. Anecdotal reports from teens suggest that quite often, this takes them a significant part of the day, as friends they counted on staying with do not show up, shelters and even squats fill up, or the weather makes staying outdoors highly unattractive or next to impossible. Indeed, data from the

SHARP study suggested that, on average, youth changed their "residence" about every 45 days (Cauce et al., 2000).

When we asked girls in the SHARE study to list every place they had stayed in the last week, the most common response was a shelter or mission, with more than a third (38%) of the girls having spent at least one night at one of these. The next most common was at a friend's home, but specifically a friend's home without any parental supervision (31%), followed by actually staying on the street, often under a bridge (21%). Other responses given by more than 10% of the girls included a foster or group home (14%) and a squat, such as an abandoned home, building, or outdoor location (13%). Clearly a significant number of homeless girls are staying in extremely risky settings. While the risk of staying on the street or in an abandoned building is obvious, we even wonder about the relatively large number of girls staying at the home of a friend without a parent around. In at least some cases, we suspect that this may be a sexually exploitative situation. In more informal conversations with girls, it was not uncommon for them to tell us that they often accepted a place to stay from "friends" knowing that there was an expectation that they would have sex. Interestingly, these same girls were quite reluctant to label this exchanging shelter for sex, insisting that they did not *have* to have sex to stay there.

Survival Strategies and Street Risks

Finding a place to stay is not the only challenge confronting girls on their own; they also need to pay for meals and incidentals. The Midwest study provides a very detailed analysis of how homeless adolescents manage to get money and food (Whitbeck & Hoyt, 1999). This study found that, most often, youths got these necessities by using relatively conventional means. For example, this study found that almost half of the boys and girls in their study asked parents, relatives, or caretakers for money and slightly more than half got food from these same people. Even while on the streets, homeless youth typically remain in at least some contact with parents or relatives. In addition, almost a third of the youths had some sort of regular employment and about half did odd jobs when possible.

Nonetheless, given limited options for self-support using conventional means, homeless girls may use a range of deviant subsistence strategies, like panhandling or stealing to pay for food. Although strategies like panhandling, stealing, shop-lifting, and drug-dealing were more commonly used by boys than girls, the Midwest study found between 12% and 19% of girls engaged in each of these activities. In fact, numerous studies have found that the longer youths spend on their own, the more likely they are to engage in deviant subsistence strategies (Janus, McCormack, Burgess, & Hartman, 1987; Kufeldt, Durieux, Nimmo, & McDonald 1992; Whitbeck, Simons, Conger, Wickrama, Ackley, & Elder, 1997).

Time on the street is also apt to lead to youth becoming victimized. Studies of street youth have consistently found that they are extremely vulnerable to exploitation from both adults and peers (Cauce et al., 1998;

Greenblatt & Robertson, 1993; Whitbeck et al., 1997a, 1997b; Yates, MacKenzie, Pennbridge & Cohen, 1988). Half of the street youth in a Los Angeles sample reported fear of being sexually or physically assaulted (Kipke, Montgomery, Simon & Iverson, 1997) and a fifth of street youth interviewed in New York were actually robbed, physically assaulted, or sexually assaulted within their first 100 days on the street (Rotheram-Borus, Rosario, & Koopman, 1991). Our own work suggests that most young people who become homeless are victimized at least once. In general, young women are at increased risk for sexual victimization, while young men are more likely to be physically victimized (Whitbeck, Hoyt, Yoder, Cauce, & Paradise, 2001).

Although boys are more likely to be physically victimized, girls are also at risk for serious physical harm while on their own. In the SHARE study, approximately half of all homeless girls were in a serious fight or beaten up (51%) and about half were threatened with a weapon (52%). Some were subjected to life-threatening violence when they were assaulted and wounded by a weapon (21%) or were shot or shot at with a gun (16%).

Sexual victimization is a serious risk for homeless girls. More than a third of the girls were subjected to an attempted or actual rape (36%). Nearly half of all young women said they had unwanted and unpleasant experiences in which they were made to do something sexual against their will (49%) or were kissed or touched sexually on their breasts or buttocks when they did not want to be (49%). Some of the females were forced to watch someone do something sexual, such as masturbate (8%) and some were forced to expose themselves naked in front of a camera or in front of another person (7%).

Both these risks of physical and sexual assault increased exponentially with time spent on the streets. In the SHARP study, the probability of physical victimization increased by a multiplicative factor of 1.83 for each month of homelessness. The risk of sexual victimization for girls increased 3.75 times for each month on the street and prior sexual victimization increased the risk of subsequent sexual victimization by a factor of 3.97 (Hoyt & Ryan, 1997). Figure 1, provides a graphic portrait of how age, prior victimization, and time on the street increase the vulnerability of young girls to sexual assault. As this figure indicates, almost a third of the youngest girls are sexually assaulted within their first 2 months on the streets! This underscores the fact that while girls may be leaving abusive situations at home, the streets offer little relief.

Who gets victimized?

It appears to be quite clear that homeless youth, especially girls, face substantial risks for victimization on the street. Yet, some youth appear to experience more victimization than others. In a study combining the Midwest and SHARP samples, the predictors of physical and sexual victimization were examined separately. Results suggested that male gender, older age when leaving home, history of spending time on the streets, affiliation with deviant peers, and nonsexual deviant subsistence strategies

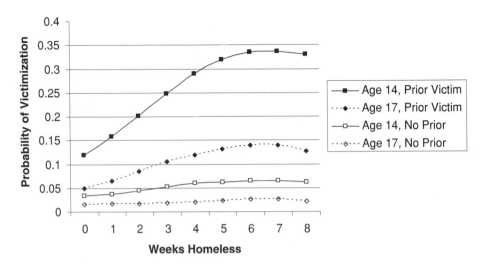

Figure 1. Probability of Sexual Victimization for Females Aged 14 and 17 years, Controlling for Prior Victimization, by Weeks Homeless[2]

predicted physical victimization. Female gender, history of family abuse, lower levels of social support from home, affiliation with deviant peers, and sexual deviant subsistence strategies predicted sexual victimization. In addition, the risk associated with sexual orientation and actual time on the streets (e.g., actually spending nights on the street, not just time on own) varied by gender. For boys, same-sex orientation put them at greater risk for sexual victimization, which was not the case for girls. Moreover, girls were at greater risk for sexual victimization when they spent time on the street, which was not the case for boys (Whitbeck, Hoyt, Yoder, Cauce & Paradise, 2001). Thus, while it is unclear to what degree youths have a "choice" in these matters, the peers they hang out with and subsistence strategies they use seem to, in part, increase their chances of being sexually victimized.

Circumstances in their past, such as prior abuse and victimization, may also increase youth's vulnerability. However, when attempts have been made to examine how past experiences, such as childhood sexual abuse, affect subsequent victimization, the effects appear to be indirect. More specifically, early sexual abuse magnified the risk of later sexual victimization by increasing the amount of time youths spent in risky environments, their involvement in deviant subsistence strategies and with deviant peers, and their participation in survival sex. So, ironically, it is the girls who were exposed to the most risk at home that are also at most risk on the streets. However, it is important to note that a history of early abuse and dysfunction does not affect later victimization directly. Rather, an abusive early history has its effect by placing youth on a trajectory of further risk that leads to further victimization (Tyler, Hoyt, Whitbeck, & Cauce, 2001).

[2]With prior weeks homeless set to the mean for the sample.

Additional Risks: Sexuality, Pregnancy, and Substance Use

Sexuality

While sexual victimization and assault is perhaps the most extreme risk that girls face on the street, there is a great deal of evidence that street youth are also at heightened risk for sexually transmitted diseases or unwanted pregnancies (D'Augelli & Bingham, 1993; Kral, Molnar, Booth, & Watters, 1997; Wagner, Carlin, Cauce, & Tenner, 2001). An examination of the sexual practices and behaviors of the girls in the SHARE study helps us to better understand the nature of such risks for young women on the streets.

Among homeless girls in the SHARE sample, most of were sexually active (83%) and initiated voluntary sexual activity[3] at early ages. We found that those who were sexually active typically became active quite young, just shy of their 14th birthday ($M = 13.9$, $SD = 1.96$ years). In terms of sexual orientation, most identified as heterosexual (61%), some as bisexual (25%), and a few as lesbian (4%).

During their first voluntary sexual activity, homeless girls had sexual partners who were, on average, 3 years older ($M = 16.8$, $SD = 3.05$ years), although there was a great deal of variability in partner age. While some girls had partners who were the same age or younger (29%), most had partners who were within 1 to 4 years older (54%). In contrast to some reports, these data suggest that the majority of first time voluntary sexual experiences did not involve exploitation by a much older partner. Nonetheless, exploitation by older partners may well have been the case for some girls. Among those who had sex for the first time at 16 years or younger, 6% had partners who were 21 years or older. Moreover, 18% of the girls had sex for the first time with a partner who was at least 5 years older, and 3% had sex for the first time with someone 10 or more years older.

The best indication of the risk for STD exposure and pregnancy, however, is the high frequency of sexual activity in which these young women are engaged. Among those who were sexually active, the average number of lifetime sexual partners was high ($M = 12.5$, $SD = 19.8$), as was the number of sexual partners during the last year ($M = 3.5$, $SD = 3.82$). However, it is also worth noting that the variability in the number of sexual partners was quite high. Among those who were sexually active, most had between 1 and 4 (28%) or between 5 and 10 (42%) lifetime sexual partners. Some had many more partners, including those who reported 11 to 50 (16%) and 100 or more (4%) lifetime partners. It is important to note that all but one of the girls who reported having 100 or more lifetime partners also reported that they had traded sex for money, food, shelter, or other necessities. In total, 13% of the girls actually reported trading for sex, although few considered their behavior prostitution.

---

[3]In this set of questions we explicitly asked girls not to include coerced sexual experiences or rape among their responses.

It is also worth noting that, in general, girls had romantic relation-ships with their sexual partners and thought of them as more than just sexual relationships. When asked how many of their sexual partners in the last year were steady boyfriends or girlfriends and how many were one-time only sexual encounters, the average number of steady relationship partners ($M = 2.23$, $SD = 2.44$) was greater than one-time only partners ($M = 1.47$, $SD = 4.84$).

Birth Control and STD Prevention

Not surprisingly, given their relatively high amount of sexual activity, many homeless girls reported that preventing pregnancy and reducing risk for exposure to sexually transmitted diseases (STDs) was an important concern. Moreover, three quarters (75%) of the young women said they sometimes or always used some form of protection. Of those who used protection some or all of the time, most reported that they did so explicitly to prevent STDs (62%) and HIV (62%). Pregnancy prevention (57%) was also reported as a major reason for using protection during sexual intercourse.

Still, while most used protection some of the time or all of the time, more than a fourth (27%) said they did not use any form of birth control at least half to all of the times they had sexual intercourse. Moreover, over half did not use any form of birth control or STD protection during at least one sexual encounter during their lifetime (63%). When asked specifically about condom use, the best form of protection against STDs, many young women reported inconsistent use. More than a third (35%) admitted they did not use a condom at least half to all of the times they had sex.

These young women were not entirely unaware of the risks to which they were exposing themselves. Indeed, about half (49%) of the young women said they worried about the possibility of getting AIDS. Nonethe-less, they may have underestimated their risk since very few considered themselves at high risk for AIDS (8%) and most considered their AIDS risk to be low (61%).

Even if young women are underestimating their HIV risk, in light of their concerns, why are they not using protection more consistently? Among those who had not used any form of birth control on at least one occasion, the most common reasons for not using protection were those related to their partner. Almost a third (30%) felt that knowing or trusting their partner obviated their need for protection. Quite a few (16%) also in-dicated that their partner objected to using protection. Some said they did not use protection because their partner did not like the feeling (16%) or their partner refused to use protection (11%). Still, although concerns for their partner led some to forego contraception use, extremely few (1%) said they did not use protection because they feared their partner would leave them if they used protection.

Quite a few young women also reported that using protection interfered with their own sexual enjoyment. Some did not use protection because they did not like they way it felt (24%), believed it ruined the mood (14%), or found protection too "messy" to use (4%). Others were more passive in their risk taking, saying they did not use protection because they did not want to think about it (14%) or simply thought they would not become pregnant or contract an STD (5%). In addition, some girls (11%) reported that they simply forgot to use protection.

One thing is certain; lack of knowledge or access to contraception is not the reason that so many girls expose themselves to sexual risk. In fact, fewer than 2% of all sexually active girls reported that they did not know how to use protection or how to get it. Still, consistent with previous research (Wagner et al., 2001), all too many girls seemed to believe that they did not really need to use protection if they were having sex with a steady boyfriend. This finding is especially troubling given the transitory nature of these so-called steady relationships. For example, in an informal encounter, one girl spoke to us, very excitedly and sincerely, about how she and her present boyfriend were planning to marry; they had met earlier that same day!

The lack of stability that is often a common experience of those living on the street, may have contributed to some girls' exaggerated sense of relationship stability and to their inconsistent use of protection, even with casual partners. In conversations we had with young homeless girls about HIV risk, several also noted that there were many worse things that could, or did, happen to them. Most appalling, one girl who had been on the streets for over a year noted that becoming HIV positive or pregnant was a route to better services. And, to some degree, she was right.

Pregnancy

In general, most homeless girls did not want to be pregnant at this time in their lives, although some said they wanted to become pregnant (9.4%) and some were actively trying to become pregnant (6%). Nonetheless, some girls reported that they were pregnant at the time of the interview (7%) and almost a third said that they had been pregnant at least once during their lifetime (32%). These pregnancies typically occurred during mid-adolescence ($M = 15.4$, $SD = 2.08$) and girls with a history of pregnancy, often reported that they were pregnant more than once ($M = 1.7$, $SD = 1.17$).

We do not know how many of these pregnancies were confirmed with a home- or doctor- administered pregnancy test. However, most of the pregnancies reported by homeless females ended in miscarriage (57%). Interviewer anecdotal reports indicated that some of these young women thought they were pregnant because they missed a menstrual period and once their period resumed, they believed they had miscarried. Given that a missed period may well be a function of inadequate nutrition, quite common among the homeless, these reports of pregnancies may be an overestimate. But even if inflated by 50%, the number of pregnancies among this young and unstable sample is worthy of concern.

It is more certain that among those with a history of pregnancy, some had an abortion (21%) and a few had a still-born baby (2%). Some young women remained pregnant and delivered their child (14%). Among these

live births (n = 8), most of the babies stayed with their mother right after
their birth (75%) while some went to live with an adoptive family (25%). Half
of the young women who gave birth to their child said they were currently
involved in providing care for their child at the time of interview. However,
only a quarter (n = 2) of these young mothers had daily contact with their
child.

Among the young women who reported that they were pregnant at least
once during their lifetime, 78% said they were not using birth control at
the time of conception. Forgetting to take or use protection was the most
common reason they did not use protection at the time when pregnancy occurred. Among those who were using protection, but still became pregnant
(21%), most were using condoms as their method of birth control.

Substance Use and Abuse

An additional factor that might put homeless girls at risk for sexual
exploitation and STDs is substance use and abuse. Some forms of substance use, such as intravenous drug use, put girls at risk for HIV directly.
But even simple alcohol or marijuana use can indirectly put girls at risk
by lowering their inhibitions or putting them in situations where sexual
assault is more likely. One study of nonhomeless youth in a community
sample found that after drinking alcohol, 16-to 24-year-olds were more apt
to have unprotected sex, to have sex that they regretted, or to be unable
to even remember if they had had sex the night before (Rondini, 2002).
Alcohol or drug use can lead to the misinterpretation of friendly cues as
sexual invitations (e.g., "beer goggles") and impaired coping resources, including a girl's lessened ability to ward off a come-on or out-and-out attack
(Rickert & Wiemann, 1998). On the flip side, research suggests that up to
45% of men who commit rape are under the influence of alcohol or drugs
(Bureau of Justice Statistics, 1994).

In light of these facts, substance abuse, which is considered a major
problem for many homeless youth, becomes doubly troubling. One recent
study of homeless youth in Southern California found that over 70% met
DSM-III criteria for substance abuse (Kipke et al., 1997), with a host of other
studies across the United States, Canada, and Australia also reporting elevated levels of alcohol and drug use (Fors & Rojek, 1991; Green, Ennett, &
Ringwalt, 1997; Kipke, Unger, Palmer, & Edgington, 1996; Maclean,
Paradise, & Cauce, 1999; Robertson, Koegel, & Ferguson, 1989). Most of
these studies do not find strong or consistent gender differences, but do
not report specifically on rates for homeless girls.

When we examined data from the SHARE project, focusing specifically on girls, we found that virtually all of them engaged in some sort of
substance use at some point. At least 90% have smoked cigarettes (96%),
drank alcohol (94%), or had marijuana (90%) at least once. Moreover, between a third and two thirds had tried cocaine or crack (47%), acid or LSD
(67%), mushrooms (44%), crank (45%), Heroin, opium, or morphine (38%),
speed or crystal methamphetamine (55%), or sniffed glue, nitrous oxide,
or other inhalants (38%). More than a fourth have also tried ecstasy (31%),

tranquilizers (31%) and other downers or quaaludes (27%). These rates are all extremely high, even if use is mostly experimental. Studies of youth in their senior year of high school, approximately the age of the typical youth in our study, find that between 7% and 12% of youth have ever tried "hard drugs," while about a third have tried marijuana (Johnston, O'Malley, & Bachman, 1992).

More disturbing, however, are the rates of more regular use. Almost half the girls (46%) report that they are drinking alcohol on at least a weekly basis, with almost a fourth (24%) drinking daily or almost daily. Moreover, it is quite clear when the girls drink, they often drink until they are drunk. When we asked about the amount they drank the most in the past month, more than a third (39%) reported having more that five drinks. In fact, almost a quarter (23%) had more than eight drinks in a single episode! This amount is consistent with the amount they reported they would drink if they could "have as much as you wanted." These high rates of substance use, and the especially high rate of binge drinking or drinking to get drunk, can put young women at considerable risk for victimization.

These data suggest that while there is a great deal of individual variability in substance use, very few girls abstained altogether and heavy use was not uncommon. As a rough basis for comparison, about 50% of 12th graders in a school-based sample had used any alcohol in the last month with 22% using any illicit drug (Johnston et al., 1992). Of added concern is the fact that for homeless girls, alcohol use is significantly related to depression. Our research with the SHARP sample found support for an affect-regulation model of substance use for girls, but not for boys. More specifically, there was some evidence that girls might be using alcohol or drugs as a way of coping with depression (MacLean et al., 1999). Given that alcohol is itself a depressant, this is not a very successful coping strategy and may serve to further heighten risk for precisely those girls who may already be at high risk.

In sum, being out of the home does not spell the end of risk for homeless girls. Once outside the house they face a level of risk, as high, if not higher, than the risk they left behind. Some of this risk comes from outright exploitation, such the high rate of physical and sexual assault that the girls experience. However, some of the risks to which these girls were exposed are at least somewhat under their own control. Although some degree of risk-taking is common in adolescence, what sets the risk-taking of these girls apart is that it happens in an environment that is already so risky. Experimentation with drugs and sex is risky enough within a suburban school or neighborhood, but the risk is exponentially higher for adolescents on the streets in neighborhoods that are typically marginal or outright dangerous.

Some girls justified their own risk-taking by noting that the risks they take do not significantly add to the unavoidable risks they face on a daily basis while living on the streets. In a life that is otherwise dull and dreary, romantic, sexual relationships or substance use may offer some relief and satisfaction. Even more ironically, as a few girls like Shana pointed out, the benefits associated with some risks, like voluntary sexual activity, might even protect them from other risks, like the risk of victimization. Boyfriends, even short-term ones, often help homeless girls find shelter and provide some protection from other boys or men.

Mental Health Problems

Given the dysfunctional families homeless girls come from, the abuse they experience both at home and after they leave, and the dangers they face on the street, it is not surprising that most studies of homeless youth find that they have very elevated rates of mental health problems including anxiety, depression, posttraumatic stress reactions, delinquent acting out, and aggressive behavior (see Farrow, Deisher, Brown, Kulig, & Kipke, 1992 for one review). Research studies that have used *DSM* diagnostic criteria have reported rates of conduct problems among homeless youth, including both girls and boys, ranging from 30% (Bukowski, Toro, & Wolfe, 1998) to 60% (Feitel et al., 1992) to 90% (Greenblatt & Robertson, 1993). Between 25% and 50% of homeless youth have been found to suffer from a major affective disorder (Bukowski et al., 1998; Feitel et al., 1992; Greenblatt & Robertson).

Using *DSM-III-R* criteria and focusing specifically on girls, the SHARP study similarly found high rates of mental health problems. Almost half (42%) of the girls reached diagnostic criteria for conduct disorder of oppositional defiant disorder, close to a third (29%) for attention deficit disorder, and close to or over a fourth for major despressive disorder (27%) and mania or hypomania (22%). A full 10% qualified for a diagnosis of schizophrenia.

These rates are extremely elevated when compared to findings from community samples of adolescents, albeit with boys and girls combined. For example, results from a large community sample of adolescents in the same region of the country found that overall rates of major depression in female adolescents was 3.7% (Lewinsohn, Hops, Roberts, Seeley, & Andrews, 1993). As another basis for comparison, a study of a normative sample of adolescents found that less than 10% of youth met diagnostic criteria for conduct disorder or major depression, fewer than 5% met criteria for attention deficit disorder, and less than 1% met criteria for schizophrenia (Kashani et al., 1987). Indeed, when we examined homeless youths' self-reported mental health symptoms, using the Achenbach Youth Self-Report scale, more than 40% of homeless youth in our sample met "clinical" or "borderline" criteria of internalizing disorders, with more than 50% meeting these same criteria for externalizing disorders. In normative samples, only 5% meet these clinical or borderline cut-off points.

Rates of posttraumatic stress disorder proved difficult to calculate. A full 17% of the girls qualified for a PTSD diagnosis. However, because the PTSD module of the DISC-R was not administered if the interview took more than 4 hours, which was the case for 7% of the sample, PTSD was not assessed among those most likely to have it. That is, typically those interviews that lasted the longest were those with complicated family histories and extensive reports of abuse. Thus, the prevalence of PTSD could have been as high as 24% for the girls.

In sum, compared to the boys, girls had lower rates of conduct disorder and higher rates of major depressive disorder and PTSD. It is also worth noting that more than half (54%) of the girls reported that they had attempted suicide in the past, a rate higher than that for the boys (40%) that was itself quite high. Looking across categories, about two thirds of the girls met criteria for at least one mental disorder, at rates that are alarmingly high.

FROM FAMILY DYSFUNCTION TO MENTAL DISORER: SUPPORT FOR A RISK AMPLIFICATION MODEL

Our examination of homeless and runaway girls does not make for a pretty picture. Their lives are clearly both troubled and troubling. We will not try to superimpose a silver lining where there is none. It is certainly the case that some, and perhaps many, girls handle the challenges of street life remarkably well given the hardships imposed by the instability and dangers of making it on their own are not readily surmountable. The extremely high rates or substance use and mental health problems are a testament to this fact.

However, it would be a mistake to totally blame street life for the problems these girls experience. What becomes most apparent in an examination of their lives is that for most of girls who end up on the streets, the instability, chaos, and risk began much earlier, often in the first few years of life. This is one of the reasons why Greenblatt and Robertson (1993) have called homelessness a "process" rather than an endpoint that can be traced to a specific event. Indeed, a fair number of the girls in our study had been living outside their homes well before adolescence as a result of a placement by child protective services. In this sense, it may be most apt to describe the lives of these girls as a trajectory of risk, beginning with a dysfunctional and chaotic home environment and ending with an unstable and often chaotic life on their own, moving in and out of shelters, living situations with friends, and in squats or on the street. The extremely high rates of victimization, including physical assault and rape, suggest that the degree of risk incurred by these girls and young women may actually be amplified once they begin living on their own.

Various versions of a risk amplification models for various forms of internalizing problems among homeless youth have been developed and tested by Whitbeck, Hoyt and colleagues (Whitbeck & Simons, 1990; Whitbeck & Hoyt, 1999; Whitbeck, Hoyt, & Yoder, 1999) using both the Midwest and SHARP samples. Drawing upon longitudinal data, they developed one risk amplification model that was specific to females and tested girls' depression and PTSD symptoms as the outcomes (Whitbeck & Hoyt, 1999). This model illustrates the route from parental problems, including alcohol use and criminality, to family abuse and time spent on the streets. Family abuse, in turn, is related to involvement with deviant peers, leading to girls' drug use, participation in deviant subsistence strategies, and dangerous sexual encounters. It is these involvements or activities that then lead to street victimization, which together with dangerous sexual encounters, directly affect internalizing problems.

Of particular interest is the fact that the effects of family problems are not directly related to internalizing problems; rather, they work through other factors. Affiliation with deviant peers plays an especially salient role once girls are on their own. These negative associations are strongly and directly related to risky sexual and subsistence behaviors on the street and to street victimization. Thus, each step these girls take magnifies the risk they were previously exposed to, eventually leading to the mental health problems we observe in them once they are on their own.

In sum, it was a constellation of risk factors, most notably, family abuse, time spent on their own, association with a deviant peer group, and engagement in deviant or sexual subsistence strategies, which placed girls at increased risk for both physical and sexual victimization and in turn, for increased likelihood of depressive and PTSD-like symptoms, and dysphoric affect. Thus, while family problems are the catalyst in the genesis of this risky developmental trajectory, it is time spent with a deviant peer group that propels girls further along the trajectory. Girls may be at particular risk for movement along this trajectory because they tend to be more oriented toward personal relationships.

Close and intimate friendships are considered especially important during adolescence (Savin-Williams & Berndt, 1990; Selman, 1980; Youniss & Smollar, 1985). And, it is worth noting that while deviant peers are a source of risk for these girls, their "street family," as they often refer to their street peers, is also an important source of support (see Paradise, Cauce, Ginzler, Wert, Wruck, & Brooker, 2001 for a description of relationships in the lives of homeless youth). In an ethnographic study of adolescents in a lower-income, inner-city public high school, Niobe Way (1996) found that friendships among adolescent girls were often marked by both closeness and a great deal of distrust. In our work with homeless girls, it was our sense that the distrust was focused predominantly on adults, and that similar-aged peers, especially other homeless youth, were too readily trusted. At least some of the victimization that youth experience on the streets is at the hand of other street youth. Nevertheless, for girls on their own, there are few alternatives but to turn to other youth for nurturance and protection, even if it does, at times, lead to harm.

DISRUPTING THE RISK TRAJECTORY: HELPING HOMELESS AND RUNAWAY GIRLS

Our observations suggest that their general distrust of relationships with adults can make homeless and runaway girls a difficult group to reach out to. They are often hesitant to come in for services and those who work with them typically report that, initially, they can be quite resistant to engaging in relationships with adults in helping relationships.

Still, there is good empirical evidence that providing girls with such services can make a positive difference in their lives. In conjunction with the SHARP study, adolescents were assigned to one of two case management conditions. In both conditions, they were provided a case manager whose job was to help them access appropriate services, from mental health counseling, to medical care, to shelter services. The intensive case management condition, compared to "regular" case management or treatement-as-usual, especially emphasized the development of a close, guardian-like relationship between the youth and case manager. In addition, compared to case managers who typically had a college degree or less, and whose training was primarily on the job, all intensive case managers had at least master's level training in psychology or social work (see Cauce et al., 1994 for a more detailed description of the case management conditions). One year after the start of the study, girls in both case management conditions showed statistically significant improvement over baseline on practically all measures of mental health and behavioral functioning. Girls who received intensive case management had the best outcomes (Cauce, Rodriguez, Paradise, Hoyt & Ryan, 2004). Indeed, statistical analyses revealed that the young women in the intensive case management condition not only evidenced psychological adjustment that was better, but those with a history of abuse were less apt to be revictimized on the streets (Ryan, Hoyt, Watanabe, & Cauce, 2001). This latter finding speaks especially well of the power of a supportive relationship with an adult. It may be difficult to establish a trusting and caring relationship with homeless youths, but when such relationships occur within the context of an appropriate intervention they may have the potential to break the cycle of victimization that is otherwise such a salient factor in the lives of these girls.

FUTURE DIRECTIONS OF RESEARCH AND TREATMENT

Adolescent girls who end up homeless or on the streets are far from typical. Thankfully, they represent only a small fraction of the population, although it is a growing fraction. However, despite the relative rarity of this condition or process, it tells us a great deal about the risks and special vulnerabilities of girls growing up in our society. The plight of homeless girls shines an especially bright light on the ways that sex and sexuality present a minefield for adolescent girls. For example, as we noted, having a boyfriend can be both a source of emotional support and physical protection, while at the same time exposing them to both emotional and physical risk at extremely close quarters.

The study of homeless girls can also shine the spotlight on our research methodologies and their strengths and weaknesses. One notable weakness in the research we present is that it is based, almost entirely, on self-report information. There is no good way to corroborate the information these girls and young women have provided us. Those who would wish to believe that the problems homeless youth face are almost entirely of their own making, or due to their deviance, can readily dismiss these youths reports of abusive or neglectful parenting. On the other hand, there are those who believe that youths underreport their experience of abuse and neglect and we have heard some youth workers say that *all* homeless youth have been sexually or physically abused.

The best counterargument to either of these claims is that the consistency of findings across study and study sites would argue for the reliability of the data obtained from youth. So too would the coherency of the portrait that such data paints. The relationships documented in these studies, such as that between abuse and depression or between alcohol use and unprotected sex, are similar to those found in normative studies of adolescents, where at least some multisource information is available. In this sense, we give most credence to findings that document relationships between variables and believe it is best to think of the more categorical information in terms of ranges. For example, we feel quite confident saying that between a third and two thirds of homeless girls have experienced physical or sexual abuse before leaving home and that youths who have experienced such abuse are most likely to be revictimized on the streets and to experience internalizing symptoms, including depression and PTSD.

Nonetheless, because of the biases inherent in self-report, it is especially important for future research to continue to look for ways in which information might be corroborated. For example, in SHARE we attempted to obtain some information from caretakers, but received data back from a very small portion of the sample. The Midwest study (Whitbeck & Hoyt, 1999) did a better job of obtaining reports from caretakers but most of that data are yet to be published. The best corroboration of the street experiences of these youth may come from friend or fellow street youth. Having youth report on each other is one promising strategy that has yet to be used.

Continuing emphasis on longitudinal investigations is also highly desirable. Examination of data over time can minimize self-report biases. A consistent bias for over- or underreporting is, in effect, canceled out over time-points. More importantly, we have just scratched the surface in our knowledge of the trajectories that these youth take. We do not even have good rough estimates of how many of them will end up as homeless adults, how many will end up in the penal system, and how many will go on to lead productive and stable lives.

What we do know is that providing girls access to services, may make a difference in that outcome. The proven capacity of homeless girls to engage in a positive relationship with a case manager, especially in the context of an intensive case management program, may be the silver lining in an otherwise dreary portrait. While involvement with a negative peer group is an important link in the cycle of victimization and dysfunction, girls end up homeless because adults have failed them. In most cases this failure has taken place at the hands of caretakers who have either been abusive, or have been unable to keep their daughters out of harm's way. Failure is also there at the societal level for not providing a safety net for girls that are not nurtured by their families. Thus, it is the responsibility of adults to reach out to these girls and develop services that are appropriate to the myriad of problems they experience. This will not be easy and it will not be inexpensive. Intensive case management is by its very nature, resource-intensive. But what is the alternative? The problem of youth homeless will not go away if it is simply ignored.

REFERENCES

Brooks-Gunn, J., & Reiter, E. (1990) The role of pubertal processes. In S. S. Feldman & G. R. Elliott (Eds.), *At the threshold: The developing adolescent* (pp. 16–53). Cambridge, MA: Harvard University Press.

Bulowski, P. A., Toro, P. A., & Wolfe, S. M. (1998). Homeless and matched housed adolescents: A comparative study of psychopathology. *Journal of Clinical Child Psychology, 27*, 306–319.

Bureau of Justice Statistics. (1994). *Violence against women.* washington, DC: U.S. Department of Justice.

Cauce, A. M., Morgan, C. J., Wagner, V., Moore, E., Wurzbacher, K., Weeden, K., et al. (1994). Effectiveness of case management for homeless adolescents: Results for the three month follow-up. *Journal of Emotional and Behavioral Development, 2*, 219–227.

Cauce, A. M., Paradise, M., Embry, L., Morgan, C., Lohr, Y., Theopolis, J., Heger, J. & Wagner, V. (1998). Homeless youth in Seattle: Youth characteristics, mental health needs, and intensive case management. In M. Epstein, K. Kutash, & A. Duchnowski (Eds.), *Outcomes for children and youth with behavioral and emotional disorders and their families: Programs and evaluation best practices* (pp. 611–632). Austin, TX: Pro-ed, Inc.

Cauce, A. M., Paradise, M., Ginzler, J. A., Embry, L., Morgan, C. J., Lohr, Y., & Theopolis, J. (2000). The characteristics and mental health of homeless adolescents. *Journal of Emotional and Behavioral Disorders, 8*, 230–239.

Cauce, A. M., Rodriguez, M. D., Paradise, M. A., Hoyt, D., & Ryan, K. (2004). Outcomes for intensive case management with homeless youth. Technical Manuscript. Seattle: University of Washington.

D'Augelli, A. R., & Bingham, C. R. (1993). Interventions to prevent HIV infections in young adolescents. In Richard M. Lerner (Ed.), *Early adolescence: Perspectives on research, policy, and intervention* (pp. 353–368). Hillsdale, NJ: Erlbaum.

Farrow, J. A., Deisher, R. W., Brown, R., Kulig, J. W., & Kipke, M. D. (1992). Health and health needs of homeless and runaway youth. *Journal of Adolescent Health, 13*, 717–726.

Feitel, B., Margetson, N., Chamas, J., & Lipman, C. (1992). Psychosocial background and behavioral and emotional disorders of homeless and runaway youth. *Hospital and Community Psychiatry, 43*, 155–159.

Fors, S. W., & Rojek, D. G. (1991). A comparison of drug involvement between runaways and school youth. *Journal of Drug Education, 21*, 13–25.

Green. J. M., Ennett, C. L., & Ringwalt, C. L. (1997). Substance use among runaway and homeless youth in three national samples. *American Journal of Public Health, 87*, 229–235.

Greenblatt, M., & Robertson, M. (1993). Life-styles, adaptive strategies, and sexual behaviors of homeless adolescents. *Hospital and Community Psychiatry, 44*(12), 1177–1180.

Janus, M., McCormack, A., Burgess, A., & Hartman, C. (1987). *Adolescent runaways: Causes and consequences.* Lexington, MA: Lexington Books.

Johnston, L. D., O'Malley, P. M., & Bachman, J. G. (1992). *Smoking, drinking, and illicit drug use among American secondary school students, college students, and young adults, 1975–1991.* Rockville, MD: National Institute on Drug Abuse.

Kashani, J. H., Beck, N. C., Hoeper, E. W., Fallahi, C., Corcoran, C. M., McAllister, J. A., Rosenberg, T. K., & Reid, J. C. (1987). Psychiatric disorders in a community sample of adolescents. *American Journal of Psychiatry, 144*(5), 584–589.

Kipke, M. D., Montgomery, S. B., Simon, T. R., & Iverson, E. G. (1997). "Substance abuse" disorders among runaway and homeless youth. *Substance Use and Misuse, 32*, 969–986.

Kipke. M. D., Unger, J. B., Palmer, R. F., & Edgington, R. (1996). Drug use, needle sharing, and HIV risk among injection drug-using street youth. *Substance Use and Misuse, 3*, 1167–1187

Kral, A. H., Molnar, B. E., Booth, R. E., Watters, J. K. (1997) Prevalence of sexual risk behavior and substance use among runaway and homeless adolescents in San Francisco, Denver, and New York City. *International Journal of STD and AIDS, 8*, 109–117.

Kufeldt, K., Durieux, M., Nimmo, M., & McDonald, M.(1992). Providing shelter for street youth: Are we reaching those in need? *Child Abuse and Neglect, 16*(2), 187–199.

Lewinsohn, P. M., Hops, H., Roberts, R. E., Seeley, J. R., & Andrews, J. A. (1993). Adolescent psychopathology: I. Prevalence and incidence of depression and other DSM-III-R disorders in high school students. *Journal of Abnormal Psychology, 102*, 133–144.

MacLean, M. G., Paradise, M., & Cauce, A. M. (1999). Substance use and psychological adjustment in homeless adolescents: A test of three models. *American Journal of Community Psychology, 27*, 405–427.

McCaskill, P., Toro, P. A., & Wolfe, S. M. (1998). Homeless matched housed adolescents: A comparative study of psychopathology. *Journal of Clinical Child Psychology, 27*(3), 306–319.

Mundy, P., Robertson, J., Greenblatt, M., & Roberston, M. (1989). Residential Instability in Adolescent Inpatients. *Journal of the American Academy of Child and Adolescent Psychiatry, 28*(2), 176–181.

National Network of Runaway and Youth Services (1985). *To whom do they belong? A profile of America's runaway and homeless youth and the programs that help them.* Washington, DC: Author.

Paradise, M., Cauce, A. M., Ginzler, J., Wert, S., Wruck, K., & Brooker, M. (2001). The role of relationships in developmental trajectories of homeless and runaway youth. In B. Sarason & S. Duck (Eds), *Person relationships: Implications for Clinical and Community Psychology* (pp. 159–179). New York: Wiley.

Richer, V. I., & Wiemann, C. M. (1998). Date rape among adolescents and young adults. *Journal of Pediatric Adolescent Gynecology, 11*, 167–175.

Ringwalt, C. L., Greene, J. M., Robertson, M., & McPheeters, M. (1998). The prevalence of homelessness among adolescents in the United States. *American Journal of Public Health, 88*(9), 1325–1329.

Robertson, M. J. (1992). Homeless youths: An overview of the recent literature. In J. Kryder-Coe, L. Salamon, & J. Monar (Eds.), *Homeless children and youth* (pp. 33–68). New Brunswick, NJ: Transaction.

Robertson, M. J., Koegel, P., & Ferguson, L. (1989). Alcohol use and abuse among homeless adolescents in Hollywood. *Contemporary Drug Problems, 16*, 415–452.

Rondini, A. (2002). Sex and alcohol: Some sobering thoughts. Retrieved September 20, 2004, from http://teenadvice.about.com/ library/weeky/aa121901a.htm.

Rotheram-Borus, M. & Koopman, C. (1991). Sexual risk behaviors, AIDS knowledge, and beliefs about AIDS among runaways. *American Journal of Public Health, 81*, 208–210.

Rotheram-Borus, M., Koopman, C., & Erhardt, A. (1991). Homeless youth and HIV infection. *American Psychologist, 46*, 1188–1197.

Rotheram-Borus, M., Parra, M., Cantwell, C., Gwadz, M., & Murphey, D. (1996). Runaway and homeless youth. In R. DiClemente, W. Hansen, & L. Ponton (Eds.), *Handbook of Adolescent Health Risk Behavior* (pp. 369–391). New York: Plenum.

Rotheram-Borus, M., Rosario, M., & Koopman, C. (1991). Minority youth at high risk: Gays males and runaways. In S. Gore & M. Colton (Eds.), *Adolescent stress: Courses and consequences* (pp. 181–200). Hawthorne, NY: Aldine de Gruyter.

Ryan, K., Kilmer, R. P., Cauce, A. M., & Hoyt, D. R. (2001). Psychological consequences of child maltreatment in homeless adolescents: Untangling the unique effects of maltreatment and family environment. *Child Abuse and Neglect, 24*, 333–352.

Savin-Williams, R. C. & Berndt, T. J. (1990). Friendship and peer relations. In S. Feldman & G. R. Elliot (Eds.), *At the threshold: The developing adolescent*. Cambridge, MA: Harvard University Press.

Selman, R. (1980). *The growth of interpersonal understanding: Developmental and clinical analyses*. New York: Academic Press.

Tyler, K. A., & Cauce, A. M. (2002). Perpetrators of early physical and sexual abuse among homeless and runaway adolescents. *Child Abuse & Neglect, 26*, 1261–1274.

Tyler, K. A., Hoyt, D., Whitbeck, L., & Cauce, A. M. (2001) The effects of a high-risk environment on sexual victimization of homeless and runaway youth. *Violence and Victims, 4*, 441–445.

Youniss, J., & Smollar, J. (1985). *Adolescent relations with mothers, fathers, and friends*. Chicago: University of Chicago Press.

Way, N. (1996). Between experiences of betrayal and desire: Close friendships among urban adolescents. In B. J. Leadbeater & N. Way (Eds.), *Urban girls: Resisting stereotypes, Creating identities*. New York: NYU Press.

Wagner, L. S., Carlin, L. Cauce, A. M., & Tenner, A. (2001). A snapshot of homeless youth in Seattle: Their characteristics, behaviors, and beliefs about HIV protective strategies. *Journal of Community Health, 26*, 219–232.

Whitbeck, L. B. & Hoyt, D. R. (1999). *Nowhere to grow. Homeless and runaway adolescents and their families*. Hawthorne, NY: Aldine de Gruyter.

Whitbeck, L. B., Hoyt, D. R., & Yoder, K. A. (1999). A risk-amplification model of victimization and depressive symptoms among runaway and homeless adolescents. *American Journal of Community Psychology, 27*, 273–296.

Whitbeck, L. B., Hoyt, D. R., Yoder, K. A., Cauce, A. M., & Paradise, M. (2001). Deviant behavior and victimization among homeless and runaway youth. *Journal of Interpersonal Violence, 16*, 1175–1204.

Whitbeck, L. B., & Simons, R. L. (1990). Life on the streets: The victimization of runaways and homeless adolescents. *Youth and Society, 22*(1), 108–125.

Whitbeck, L. B., Simons, R. L., Conger, R. D., Wickrama, K. A. S., Ackley, K. A., & Elder, G. H. (1997). The effects of parents' working conditions and family economic hardship on parenting behaviors and children's self-efficacy. *Social Psychology Quarterly, 60*, 291–303.

Wolfe S. M., Toro, P. A., & McCaskill, P. A. (1999). A comparison of homeless and matched housed adolescents on family environment variables. *Journal of Research on Adolescence, 9*(1), 53–66.

Yates, G. L., MacKenzie, R., Pennbridge, J., & Cohen, E. (1988) A risk profile comparison of runaway and non-runaway youth. *American Journal of Public Health, 78*, 820–821.

Yoder, K. A., Hoyt, D. R., & Whitbeck, L. B. (1998). Suicidal behavior among homeless and runaway adolescents. *Journal of Youth and Adolescence, 27*(6), 753–771.

VI

Health-Related Problems

16

Eating Disorders in Girls

LINDA SMOLAK

There is a scene in the Civil War epic *Gone With the Wind* in which Scarlett O'Hara is dressing to go to a barbeque at a neighboring plantation. Scarlett has her eye on one of the men who lives there and wants to appear particularly attractive. So, she orders her maid to tighten her corset so that her waist is abnormally small.

This fictional scene tells us at least two things. First, women have been concerned about attractiveness for a long time. The current emphasis on "image" is not born exclusively of late 20th century media (Brumberg, 1997), though today's media are not blameless in the widespread body dissatisfaction reported by girls and women. Women have long understood that *being looked at* is part of the feminine role. In fact, even young girls are aware that others are looking at—and judging—them.

Secondly, the scene from *Gone With the Wind* shows us that women have long been willing to do unnatural, and perhaps unhealthy, things in order to achieve a particular body type. Although many eating disorders specialists point to the emergence of Twiggy in the 1960s as the beginning of the trend toward unrealistic thinness, women in the 1950s routinely wore corsets and girdles to try to look slimmer. Brumberg (1997, pp. 102–103) describes a young woman who tried to restrict her caloric intake to 50 calories per day so as to lose weight before returning to school—in 1926.

Thus, today's eating problems are rooted in a long history of emphasizing attractiveness in general, and a preferred body shape in particular, in defining the success of a woman. Refusing to eat has long been a way for women to a gain a sense of personal control. Among medieval Catholic women, the discipline involved in self-starvation indicated spirituality and commitment to God that gave women status, and sometimes sainthood (Zerbe, 1993).

Both anorexia nervosa (AN) and bulimia nervosa (BN) have appeared in every edition of the *Diagnostic and Statistical Manual* since 1980

LINDA SMOLAK • Kenyon College, Gambier, Ohio, 43022-0000.

(*DSM-III*; American Psychiatric Association, 1980). AN, which is marked by self-starvation, had been recognized as a psychiatric disorder for over 100 years while BN, sometimes referred to as binge-purge syndrome, was not recognized as an eating disorder until it appeared in *DSM-III* (Herzog & Delinsky, 2001). Clinicians had noticed that many women seeking help for eating problems did not meet the criteria for AN but were clearly disturbed. Thus, BN was born of recent clinical experience and does not share AN's long history.

The current version of *DSM* (*DSM-IV*; American Psychiatric Association, 1994) has only one other official eating disorders category: eating disorders not otherwise specified (ED-NOS). This category includes anyone presenting with an eating problem who is currently clearly in clinical distress but does not meet the criteria for BN or AN. In addition, binge-eating disorder (BED) is a provisional *DSM-IV* category, requiring further research before it is included in *DSM*. BED involves frequent binge eating with no compensatory behavior.

Few *DSM-IV* (American Psychiatric Association, 1994) psychiatric disorders are as clearly gendered as AN and BN are. A review of epidemiological studies of AN suggests that AN occurs in 8.2 women for every one man affected (Pawluck & Gorey, 1998). The difference for BN may be larger. Even data examining less severe eating problems, such as weight and shape dissatisfaction or dieting, consistently show females to be more troubled than males. This difference is evident starting in elementary school and appears in all American ethnic groups (Smolak & Levine, 2001). Since ED-NOS is a vaguely defined category, gender differences are unknown. BED probably shows smaller gender differences than do BN and AN. Indeed, there may not be a gender difference in BED (Johnson & Torgrud, 1996).

At least among girls, poor body image has been prospectively related to the development of eating disorders (Attie & Brooks-Gunn, 1989; McKnight Investigators, 2003; Stice & Bearman, 2001). All people develop a body image. Indeed, body image is commonly conceptualized as part of self (e.g., Harter, 1986). That girls have more body image problems than boys do and that girls' body image problems sometimes lead to AN and BN, reflects developmental influences and trajectories. These developmental phenomena are the focus of this chapter. Such phenomena will help us to answer the questions raised by Striegel-Moore, Silberstein, and Rodin (1986) almost 20 years ago: (1) why are women so much more likely than men to be affected by eating disorders; and (2) why are some girls and women so severely affected?

DEFINING EATING DISORDERS

AN and BN are typically defined in terms of *DSM* criteria (American Psychiatric Association, 1994). Because AN and BN are relatively rare disorders, researchers often look at eating disorder symptoms rather than the full-blown clinical disorders. For example, elevated scores on the Eating Disorders Inventory (EDI; Garner, 1991) might serve as the dependent variable in a risk factor study. Such measures are, however, typically rooted in the *DSM-IV* criteria.

Anorexia Nervosa

Core symptoms

The hallmark characteristic of AN is an insistence on weighing substantially less than is expected for height and weight. *DSM-IV* suggests that "substantially less" means less than 85% of expected weight. A diagnosis of AN cannot be made without this symptom. Second, because there are a variety of reasons a person might be ≤85% of their expected weight, *DSM-IV* also requires that the person must show an intense fear or phobia of weight gain.

The third criterion is that the person must also be unrealistic in her experience of her body. She must overemphasize thinness as a component of self and must fail to recognize the risks associated with her current body weight. This symptom, in combination with the weight phobia, constitutes the cognitive component of AN.

Finally, amenorrhea is a criterion for postpubertal women. Body fat is involved in the production of estrogens and having so little body fat that menstruation ceases is considered indicative of pathology.

Related Symptoms

AN has a dramatic effect on physiological functioning. Indeed, AN's natural course may end in death. Estimates of the mortality rates differ widely, depending on length of follow-up and causes of death assumed to be attributable to AN. However, 5% to 10% is a realistic estimate of the number of girls and women receiving treatment for AN who will die from complications (Neumarker, 2000).

AN is associated with many physical problems (Hill & Pomeroy, 2001). These problems can assist in making the diagnosis of AN or in referring a girl for assessment. The girl may have dry, brittle hair and may even lose hair. Her skin, especially her palms, may be yellow and her nails may be brittle. She may develop a fine downy hair on her body (lanugo). Girls suffering from AN often feel cold and favor long-sleeved shirts and sweaters, even when others are wearing cooler clothing. Given their hypotension, they may even feel cold to the touch.

Perhaps the cardiac abnormalities are the most worrisome. Most AN victims suffer from bradycardia (abnormally slow heart rates) and hypotension, which can lead to fatal arrhythmias. Furthermore, if refeeding occurs too quickly, the weakened cardiovascular system may be strained to the point of failure (Hill & Pomeroy, 2001).

Even following weight gain, the AN victim may experience physiological problems. Bone density develops primarily during adolescence. If a girl is restricting calories and calcium intake at this time, bone growth may be permanently impaired (Hill & Pomeroy, 2001). Low levels of estrogen may exacerbate this problem. The losses may be severe enough to result in osteoporosis during young adulthood.

There are several behavioral indicators of AN that parents and teachers might watch for. These behaviors do not necessarily mean that a girl is anorexic, but they may be visible "warnings" of a problem. Girls suffering from AN do not want to eat. If parents or others pressure them to eat, they may resort to tricks to make it look as if they are eating. They might move food around on their plates or hide food in their napkins. These girls often have food-related rituals, such as cutting food into tiny pieces or smelling food before eating it. Girls suffering from AN often are interested in food, and may cook lavish meals or desserts for others without eating.

Some anorexic girls purge after they eat, particularly if they think they have eaten too much. These girls appear to have higher mortality rates than those who do not purge (Herzog & Delinsky, 2001). The purging may involve vomiting. If it does, signs may include frequent trips to the bathroom right after eating, the smell of vomit in a bathroom, the presence of emetics such as syrup of ipecac, and loss of tooth enamel on the back of the front teeth due to the acid in the vomit. Other girls will compensate for caloric intake by engaging in extreme exercise. Indeed, some girls may develop AN out of excessive exercise rather than dieting (Davis, Kennedy, Ravelski, & Dionne, 1994). Some girls may exercise for several hours a day, even if it involves staying up late or rising early. They may continue to exercise even when ill or injured and may protest vehemently if others try to prevent them from their workout. This may lead them to exercise in secret, for example, when everyone else in the house is asleep. Exercise may even interfere with other activities. When combined with trying to avoid food, this may mean that the girl gradually spends less time with her friends.

Bulimia Nervosa

Core symptoms

There are four diagnostic criteria for BN. The first is binge eating. A binge involves eating more in an identifiable time span than most people would eat. The binge eater knows she is eating more than others would find acceptable but feels unable to control her eating. She feels as if she is unable to stop.

The second criterion for the diagnosis of BN is "recurrent inappropriate compensatory behavior in order to prevent weight gain" (American Psychiatric Association, 1994, p. 549). BN can be categorized into a "purging" or "nonpurging" subtype. "Purging" refers to the compensatory behaviors of inducing vomiting or using enemas, laxatives, or diuretics. "Nonpurging" compensatory behaviors include fasting or excessive exercise. The compensatory behavior must follow the binge closely enough that the two can be considered a cycle. Third, *DSM-IV* stipulates that this cycle must have an average occurrence of twice a week over a 3-week period.

Fourth, the person must define themselves in terms of weight and shape. This ensures that the binge-compensatory behavior cycle is indeed related to weight concerns.

Finally, if a person shows symptoms of both AN and BN, she will be diagnosed with AN, binge-eating/purging type (American Psychiatric Association, 1994).

Related Symptoms

Like AN, BN is a potentially fatal disorder. One can choke to death on vomit. Vomiting and the techniques used to induce it may damage the esophagus or stomach, resulting in hemorrhaging. Cardiovascular complications, which may be fatal, also occur, partly because of electrolyte imbalances caused by vomiting. Ipecac, used to induce vomiting, may permanently damage the heart muscle (Hill & Pomeroy, 2001).

If vomiting is the compensatory method of choice, the signs noted earlier under AN will be present. Indeed, the pattern of dental erosion is often the first recognizable sign of BN. There may be cuts, scars, or calluses on the hand if the patient induces vomiting with her hand. Purging may also lead to enlarged parotid glands. While this is not a serious complication, it is easy to recognize, because it results in a squirrel-like appearance and because a doctor can feel the enlargement (Hill & Pomeroy, 2001).

People sometimes assume that girls and women who vomit after they eat must be thin. In fact, most people suffering from BN are within the normal weight range. Some are actually overweight. While vomiting and using laxatives will in fact harm the body, they are not effective ways to lose weight. Many of the ingested calories have been absorbed by the body before the purging occurs (Hill & Pomeroy, 2001).

People suffering from BN are very secretive. It is usually very difficult to "catch" someone binging or purging. However, there are signs that someone is binging. She may hide food, such as candy bars and cookies, in a drawer or closet. Food may disappear from the house. These will often be fairly large amounts of food; for example, an entire half-gallon of ice cream or a package of cookies. A bulimic might even shoplift food. However, many bulimics are sophisticated enough to not leave a "trail" of candy wrappers.

Eating Disorders—Not Otherwise Specified

Perhaps half of those seeking help for eating problems do not meet the full *DSM-IV* criteria for either AN or BN (Herzog & Delinsky, 2001). *DSM-IV* provides examples of possible constellations of behaviors considered ED-NOS but does not specific diagnostic criteria. People suffering from ED-NOS may experience body dissatisfaction and some of the cognitive symptoms of BN and AN to the same extent as people with those disorders. However, the psychological distress and social relations impairment tend to be less severe in ED-NOS than in BN and AN (Herzog & Delinsky, 2001).

Binge-Eating Disorder

Core symptoms. Binge-eating disorder (BED) is not officially a diagnostic category in *DSM-IV*. It is, instead, a set of "research criteria" that is in need of further research before inclusion in future *DSM* editions. Research is particularly needed regarding BED prior to adulthood, though there is now some evidence that BED might occur among adolescents (McKnight Investigators, 2003).

BED might be thought of as BN without the compensatory behaviors or investment in thinness. Research actually suggests that women suffering from BED are similar to those experiencing BN in terms of weight and shape concerns as well as comorbid psychiatric problems (Striegel-Moore et al., 2001). In addition to binge-eating, which is defined as it is in BN, someone must show concern about the binge-eating episodes (American Psychiatric Association, 1994). This may be indicated by feelings of disgust or embarrassment. Furthermore, the binges should occur or continue in the absence of hunger. The person must average two binges per week for 6 months to qualify for the disorder. As with BN, this frequency is not based on empirical data.

Related symptoms.   Given the lack of knowledge about BED, it is difficult to list associated behaviors. Binge-eating in BED may be secretive as it is in BN, though this is not actually documented empirically. Research with adults indicates that negative emotions, including anger and depression, often are associated with binges (Stice, 2001b). There is retrospective evidence that this association develops in childhood, perhaps in conjunction with sexual abuse (Thompson, 1994). Thus, children who are unable to express their emotions may turn to eating for comfort. This is an issue that urgently needs to be addressed in research.

In adulthood, BED is associated with an increased risk of obesity (Herzog & Delinsky, 2001; Striegel-Moore et al., 2001). This may also be true of children and adolescents, but the extant research does not permit us to draw a clear conclusion.

ISSUES IN DIAGNOSIS

The vast majority of research concerning eating disorders has been done with female participants. The diagnostic criteria for AN and BN, and to a lesser extent BED, have been developed based on clinicians' experiences with female clients. This focus is underscored by the inclusion of amenorrhea as a diagnostic criterion for AN. The problems with the diagnostic criteria then do not revolve a lack of sensitivity to the expression of these disorders in women. Rather, the problems include the arbitrariness of several of the criteria. This may be particularly pressing when diagnosing and treating young children. The frequency requirements, for example, may be too high to effectively identify children with problems.

The amenorrhea criterion may be problematic. Different girls and women require different levels of body fat before menstruation stops. There may well be other physical problems, including serious ones like cardiac arrhythmias, despite occasional menstruation. While poor nutrition may delay puberty (Netenmeyer & Williamson, 2001), it is difficult to establish delayed puberty prior to middle adolescence because of the substantial individual differences in development. This might lead to an underestimate of the number of prepubertal girls who suffer from AN.

It is also noteworthy that *DMS-IV* fails to consider several eating problems that occur among children (Lask, 2000). For example, children may refuse to eat or may refuse to eat certain foods. The latter may be temporary "food fads" but, particularly when these are long-lasting, health-endangering, or associated with trauma, depressive affect, or the refusal to also walk and talk, they may require psychological treatment.

Bryant-Waugh & Kaminski (1993) have suggested that *DSM-IV* criteria be modified for use with children. To be diagnosed with AN, children would have to lose or fail to maintain weight although no particular level of weight loss is required. The children also must show a determined effort to not eat and an associated fear of fat, extreme compensatory behaviors (e.g., vomiting, laxative use), body image distortion, or a preoccupation with caloric values or weight. These suggestions have not been widely implemented in diagnostic criteria or research.

COMMON COMORBIDITIES

Of the disorders that are comorbid with AN and BN, depression is the most frequently discussed. There is evidence that depression and eating problems, at subclinical levels, cooccur in girls starting before the age of 14 years (Graber & Brooks-Gunn, 2001). Depression and eating problems may be causally related. For example, Stice and Bearman (2001) reported that negative body image and disturbed eating predict the development of depression in adolescence.

EPIDEMIOLOGY

There have been several community-based studies examining the prevalence of eating disorders (see Garvin & Striegel-Moore, 2001 for a review). The most representative study, and the only one to include men, was the Epidemiological Catchment Area Study (ECA; Robins et al., 1984). However, this study only covers AN because data collection predated the official recognition of BN and BED as diagnoses (Garvin & Striegel-Moore, 2001). Other studies are poor in their coverage of pre-adolescents, adolescents, ethnic minority groups, males, ED-NOS, or BED (Garvin & Striegel-Moore, 2001). The limited data available indicate that peak ages of onset for AN are bimodally distributed at 14 and 18 years (American Psychiatric Association, 1994). BN most commonly onsets around the age of 18 years (Woodside & Garfinkel, 1992). Both AN and BN have been documented in prepubertal girls (Atkins & Silber, 1993; Stein, Chaloub, & Hodes, 1998). There is a clear need for much more epidemiological data before we can make definitive statements about the prevalence of eating disorders. Such data will be important for policy makers, researchers, and therapists.

Current estimates are that AN occurs in less than 1% of postpubertal American women (Garvin & Striegel-Moore, 2001). BN is considerably more common, with a lifetime prevalence rate of 3% (Garvin & Striegel-Moore, 2001). Among adolescents, the rates are probably lower with .5 to 1.0% suffering from AN, 1% meeting the criteria for BN, and perhaps 1% showing BED. Rates for prepubertal children are likely to be lower still (Thompson & Smolak, 2001).

These numbers do not fully capture the extent of eating problems. Many more girls and women suffer from subthreshold disorders, which are sometimes diagnosed as ED-NOS (Shisslak, Crago, & Estes, 1995). Among adolescents alone, the rate for the combination of subthreshold and full-syndrome eating disorders may be high as 10% (Agras, 2001).

Girls and adolescents may show individual symptoms of eating disorders without the full disorders. Some of these behaviors may be life threatening or at least may endanger the girls' health. Perhaps the best estimates we have of such behaviors come from a study by Alison Field and her colleagues (1999), which sampled over 16,000 9-to-14-year-old children. Even in this large cross-sectional sample, however, 93% of the respondents were White, so generalizability to ethnic minority girls is limited.

Among the girls, there were significant age-related increases in the percentage of girls who were not overweight but thought they were (4.2% at the age of 9 years, 19% of 14-year-olds), were trying to lose weight (20% vs. 44%), exercised daily to lose weight (5.9% vs. 12%), were always dieting (1.1% vs. 5%), purged at least monthly (0.9% vs. 2.9%), and binged at least monthly (0.4% vs. 3.6%). In general, the boys did not show comparable linear trends; rather, although 12-year-olds tended to demonstrate more eating problems than did 9-year-olds, 14-year-olds showed lower rates than the 12-year-olds.

Field et al.'s (1999) data exemplify two common findings. First, girls are more likely than boys to report disturbed eating attitudes and behaviors. This is true of everything from incorrectly thinking they are overweight to binge eating at least monthly. Second, girls' eating problems tend to increase with age, at least from middle childhood into middle adolescence. Boys do not show such clear-cut linearity. There are several possible interpretations of this. Perhaps as girls get older, the pressure to be thin becomes greater while the pressure on boys actually declines. This is consistent with findings suggesting that both boys and girls say that weight is a more important determinant of attractiveness for teenage girls than for boys (Jones, 2001). It may also be that puberty takes girls away from their thin ideal body shape while moving boys toward the greater size and muscularity valued as the male body ideal.

Ethnicity

There are several studies looking at ethnic group differences in at least some of the behavior and attitudinal problems associated with eating disorders (Douchinis, Hayden, & Wilfley, 2001). There are, however, relatively few studies of actual eating disorders among ethnic minority girls.

The first and clearest conclusion that can be drawn from this literature is that eating disorders and problematic eating attitudes and behaviors affect girls from all ethnic groups. No group is immune. Black girls do seem to have more flexible ideal body images and hence often report less body dissatisfaction, especially once BMI is controlled. This "protective" factor probably keeps down the rate of dieting and hence dieting-related disorders, such as AN, among Black girls. However, it does not completely eliminate them. Furthermore, it does not protect Black girls from binging behaviors and their disorders, BN and BED. Indeed, the McKnight Investigators (2003) reported no difference between Black and White adolescent girls in the rate of onset of partial or full-syndrome BN and BED.

More importantly, this more flexible body image is not a function of being a member of an American ethnic minority group. Studies have consistently found that Hispanic, Asian, and Native American girls show body dissatisfaction equal to or greater than that of White girls (Douchinis et al., 2001). For example, Field, Colditz, and Peterson (1997) found that 53.2% of Hispanic and 40.6% of White high school girls were dissatisfied with their bodies. In a very large sample, Croll, Neumark-Sztainer, Story, and Ireland (2002) found that American Indian high school girls vomited more than Hispanic girls who vomited more than White girls. Another large study (Story, French, Resnick, & Blum, 1995) found that Asian American girls were more likely than White or Hispanic girls, who were approximately equal to one another, to binge eat.

It is difficult to explain why ethnic groups within the United States show differences in rates of eating problems. The situation is made even more complex by differences *within* ethnic groups. Such differences may help us to partially understand the inconsistencies in the extant data. For example, the McKnight Investigators (2003) collected data from Hispanic, White, and Black girls in Arizona and California. They reported a significant site X Hispanic interaction for the development of BN and BED during the 3 years of the study. The Hispanic girls at the Arizona site were more likely to develop binge-eating disorders than were the Black or White girls. There was no ethnic group difference among the California girls. Further demographic analysis indicated that the Hispanic California girls were more likely to be from non-English speaking homes, and to identify as Latin American (as opposed to Mexican American) than were the Arizona girls.

DEVELOPMENTAL COURSE AND OUTCOMES

A developmental psychopathology approach to understanding eating disorders emphasizes the link between normal development and AN and BN. Eating disorders are seen as a pathway from normal development, a position underscored by the normative nature of body satisfaction and dieting among American girls and women (Smolak & Levine, 2001; Striegel-Moore et al., 1986). Developmental transitions are an example of a phenomenon where normal and abnormal development meet.

Transitions

Developmental psychologists have long been aware of the importance of transitions in creating or exacerbating coping problems. Transitions require the dismantling of personality, cognitive, and social structures and the re-configuration of these structures. Transitions are often triggered by biological or social changes. Puberty and high school graduation are examples of such triggers.

Figure 1 shows how the early adolescence transition might be involved in the development of eating problems (Smolak & Levine, 1996). There are several important points in this model. First, girls do not come to this transition as blank slates. They have existing personal and social structure characteristics that will interact with the demands of the transition. For example, Martin et al. (2000) found that negative emotionality during the preschool years was related to drive for thinness in early adolescence.

Second, the transition includes certain demands. For example, puberty brings with it an adult body, a body that is often inconsistent with cultural norms of beauty. Girls will routinely gain 40 pounds during puberty (Malina, 1975). The distribution of this weight will be different than it was in childhood or than it is for men. Women's normal bodies carry a higher percentage of fat than do men's bodies. The fat is not only located where girls would like it to be, that is, in their breasts but also in the hips, abdomen, and thighs—all of the places that popular culture suggests should be lean.

Third, it is possible that cumulative developmental demands and social pressures are particularly likely to trigger behavioral problems, including eating problems. Smolak, Levine, and Gralen (1993) reported that, compared to girls who experienced either early puberty or early dating or neither stressor, girls who went through puberty early and began dating early scored higher on a measure of disturbed eating later in adolescence.

Fourth, in addition to risk factors there are factors that may protect against the development of eating problems. Limited research suggests at least two possible protective factors. First, participation in non-elite high school sports appears to be correlated with a lower risk of body image disturbance (Smolak, Murnen, & Ruble, 2000). Second, elementary school girls who actively reject the objectified media image of women have more positive body esteem than girls who either accept or are neutral about the image (Smolak, Murnen, Mills, & Good, 2001).

Finally, the model as presented shows discrete categories of outcomes. This is probably an exaggeration of reality. Some girls and women who experience subthreshold disorders will eventually develop full-blown eating disorders, but others will not (Herzog & Delinsky, 2001). Secondly, even within eating disorders sufferers there is a certain fluidity of severity and diagnosis. A girl may, for example, meet the criteria for AN at some point in adolescence, appear to have improved, and then apparently develop BN later on (Herzog & Delinsky, 2001). Such movement across categories is not unusual.

Predispositions	Precipitators or Triggers	Developmental Tasks	Mediators	Outcomes
Personality	*Individual*			*Most adaptive*
GENDER*	Puberty, esp. wt. gain;	Adjust to adult	Cultural	In the absence of
Thinness schema	Heterosexual demands;	physique;	meaning of	predispositions, tasks
Need to fit in socially	School changes	Begin heterosexual	female body	may be interpreted
BMI	Non-normative stressors	relations	Simultaneity of	positively → healthy
Wt & Shape Concerns		Begin career search	task demands	outcome
Dieting	*Social Systems*	Assess relationships		*Moderate*
	▲ peer interaction & influence	with parents v. peers		With presence of thinness
Interacts with	Decreased parental support	Gender role intensifies		schema or wt concerns or
Systems	influence			moderate dieting, intensifi-
Family concerns with	Decreased support from teachers			cation of internalization of
wt & shape	Increased pressure from coaches			thin ideal and increased risk
Peer pressure	Increased exposure to media			of eating problems, esp. in
Hostile environment				cases of simultaneous stressors
for girls				*Least Adaptive*
				Presence of thinness schema, thin
				ideal internalization, substantial
				peer & family & media messages, previous
				history of dieting → high risk for eating
				disorders (clinical & subthreshold)

*Gender influences, perhaps even determines, the meaning of the transition. It is a pervasive influence throughout this transition and in the development of eating problems and disorders. Factors and tasks outlined here apply to girls only.

Adapted from: Smolak & Levine (1996, p. 214)

Figure 1. A developmental psychopathology model of adolescent eating problems

Other Developmental Systems

If we conceptualize eating disorders as developing along a path that bears direct relationships to normal developmental pathways, it is not surprising that we need to consider development in areas other than body image and weight control to understand the development of eating disorders.

Self-Development

Children and adolescents differ in terms of self-definition. Younger children do not tend to interpret personality and psychological characteristics of people as permanent traits that predict future behavior (Ewell, Smith, Karmel, & Hart, 1996). This may mean that the self-system of young children is relatively less integrated and consolidated, implying that young children may have some elements of a thinness schema but that it is fairly immature and still susceptible to prevention efforts (Smolak, 1999; Smolak & Levine, 1994).

There is also development from childhood through adolescence in terms of theory of self. Younger children explain their characteristics and behavior in terms of their own wishes and interests. By adolescence, explanations focus more on familial and peer influences (Ewell et al., 1996). This difference may make it easier to convince young children that they can resist social messages (e.g., advertisements) and affect their own body image (Smolak, 1999).

Gender Roles

Given the gendered nature of eating disorders, their symptoms, and the risk factors that contribute to their development, it should be clear that gender role development plays a role in the etiology of eating problems. However, developmental research linking gender role and eating problems is surprisingly limited.

First, masculinity, as measured by traditional sex role inventories, appears to have a small protective effect against eating problems while endorsement of femininity seems to be associated with a small but significant increase in risk for eating problems (Murnen & Smolak, 1998). Newer conceptualizations of gender roles, for example, superwoman, may also be related. Girls who adopt the superwoman ideology, trying to be everything to please others, seem to have more eating problems than other girls (e.g., Hart & Kenny, 1997; Steiner-Adair, 1986).

Second, girls appear to be more invested in relationships than boys are (Brown & Gilligan, 1992; Ewell et al., 1996; Taylor, Gilligan, & Sullivan, 1995). Girls may go to extremes in order to preserve friendships and social status. They may even being willing to sacrifice their sense of who they are (Brown & Gilligan, 1992; Taylor et al., 1995). All of this may lead them to try to please people more by adopting a particular appearance.

Gender is really a summary variable. It consists of a wide range of different experiences, opportunities, and stressors. For example, compared to American males, females are more likely to be sexually harassed, to be sexually abused, to be victims of relationship violence, and to be poor. Males, on the other hand, may suppress emotional expression, be victims of violence, and have less supportive friendships. Such gendered experiences may help to explain gender differences in psychopathology including, for example, the increased risk of eating disorders in females and of drug and alcohol abuse in males.

THEORIES OF THE DEVELOPMENT OF EATING DISORDERS

There are numerous theories and models of the development of eating problems (Huon & Strong, 1998; Johnson & Connors, 1987; Smolak & Levine, 1996, 2001). They all are multidimensional, acknowledging that a wide range of personal, social, and biological factors contribute to the onset and maintenance of eating disorders. One example, Smolak and Levine's model (Figure 1) examining developmental transitions, has already been presented.

Stice's (2001a) dual pathway model of the development of bulimia is also of substantial interest. This model postulates that bulimia nervosa might be rooted in dieting or in negative affect without dieting. Dieting, particularly if it is severe, may lead the body to react as if it is starving, resulting in an inability to stop eating once food is available. Further, women who are dieting feel a sense of control (Smolak & Murnen, 2001). Once the diet is "violated," for example, by eating a "forbidden food," eating may become disinhibited or unrestrained, resulting in a binge. Negative affect may lead to binge eating through a different mechanism. In effect, binge eating may be a method of coping with negative affect because food is comforting. Both dieting and negative affect are rooted in body dissatisfaction, which in turn is based on perceived pressure to be thin and thin-ideal internalization (Stice, 2001a). Stice's model reminds us that different pathways can lead to the same pathological outcome. Stice (2001a) has presented prospective, longitudinal data from adolescent girls supporting this model.

The remainder of this section focuses on two models, neopsychoanalytic theory and objectification theory, because they propose explanations for the gendered nature of eating problems.

Neopsychoanalytic Theory

The variants of neopsychoanalytic theory commonly cited by eating disorders specialists have their roots in Nancy Chodorow's (1978) work. The crucial point is that girls have an attachment to their mother that is unbroken from infancy. Boys, on the other hand, transfer their attachment to their fathers. The latter involves becoming independent of the mother. Girls do not have this opportunity and instead must negotiate a relationship with both parents. Hence, girls are raised in a way that emphasizes negotiation and relationships while boys' upbringing revolves around independence.

Carol Gilligan's (Brown & Gilligan, 1992; Gilligan, 1982) expansion of this theory suggests that, in childhood, girls are as assertive and self-assured as boys. She contends that it is not until the middle school years (ages 11 to 14 years) that girls feel the pressure to conform or risk losing important relationships. To girls, maintaining relationships is more important than establishing an independent sense of self. Gilligan (Brown & Gilligan, 1992; Gilligan, 1982; Taylor et al., 1995) has referred to this suppression of self as a loss of voice. This loss of voice may lead to a loss of a sense of control. Dieting may be a place to regain at least some control. Girls do not only become less assertive and less willing to express their wishes and interests as they move into adolescence. They actually lose touch with their own desires. So when they say "whatever you want to do is fine," they really no longer know what they want. There is, then, a loss of self as well as a loss of stated opinions. This may increase susceptibility to thin-ideal internalization as the girl searches for a self that is acceptable to others.

Research does suggest that, among college-age women, lower voice is associated with restrained eating, binge eating, and emotional eating (Smolak & Munsterteiger, 2002). More research is needed to ascertain the developmental trajectories of these relationships.

Objectification Theory

Fredrickson and Roberts' (1997) objectification theory is also relevant to the development of eating disorders in girls and young women. Fredrickson and Roberts have proposed that sex differences in body image result from differences in how men's and women's bodies are treated in American culture. Specifically, women's bodies are much more likely to be "looked at, evaluated, and always potentially objectified" (Fredrickson & Roberts, 1997, p. 175). This happens in face-to-face interactions, advertising, pornography, television, and film. Women do not tend to be the actors, in control of situations or even interactions. Instead, they are to be "looked at" and this "looking" is sexualized. Women's appearance is supposed to be pleasing to men rather than, for example, being functional. Thus, women learn that men's opinions about their appearance are important and, perhaps, even crucial to their well-being (see Fredrickson & Roberts, 1997).

Treating the female body as a sexual object begins early. Murnen and Smolak (2000) interviewed 3rd- through 5th-grade girls and found that about three fourths of them had experienced sexual harassment. Retrospective data (Bryant, 1993) also indicate that sexual harassment begins in elementary school. By middle school, sexual harassment becomes normative for girls and the threat of date rape is added to the already extant threat of child sexual abuse (Bryant, 1993; Silverman, Raj, Mucci, & Hathaway, 2001). Even schoolgirls understand that certain comments or looks from males are threatening. In one study (Bryant, 1993), middle and high school girls were five times more likely than boys to report being afraid at school. By middle school, girls modify their behaviors to reduce such threats, for example, by avoiding extracurricular events or not speaking in class.

Just as they learn that their bodies are an invitation to danger, girls also learn that being attractive may be a key to their success both professionally and socially. They realize or at least believe that the men and boys who watch and evaluate them can potentially make their lives happy or miserable. Therefore, girls gradually *internalize* that objectifying gaze and self-monitor their attractiveness, including whether they are thin enough. Fredrickson and Roberts (1997) claim this is what makes body dissatisfaction normative among adolescent girls and women.

Objectification theory is fairly new. However, predictions based on the theory in terms of objectification leading to body shame and eating problems (e.g., Fredrickson, Roberts, Noll, Quinn, & Twenge, 1998) have received some empirical support. Furthermore, consistent with objectification theory, both experimental and longitudinal data indicate that one of the best predictors of eating problems is internalization of the thin ideal (Thompson & Stice, 2001).

Objectification theory holds substantial promise for our understanding of eating problems and disorders. It is of particular interest because it focuses on cultural factors that create, or at least contribute to, the development of eating disorders. It thus suggests that prevention efforts focus on changing the environment in which girls develop, not just the girls themselves (Levine & Smolak, in press).

RISK AND PROTECTIVE FACTORS

Table 1 lists some of the documented risk and protective factors in the development of eating problems and disorders. Most of the listed factors have received experimental or prospective support. Such designs are important in identifying potential causal factors (Kraemer et al., 1997). However, not all variables can be subjected to such designs. Child sexual abuse and other forms of trauma are good examples. Therefore, variables that have been subjected to meta-analysis are also included.

Table 1. Risk factors for the development of eating problems

Individual	Familial	Peers	Other cultural
BMI	Parental comments re: own weight	Comments re: own weight	Use of media
Negative affect	Parental comments re: child's weight	Teasing	Elite, body shape-oriented sports
Female	Parental modeling of weight & shape concerns	Investment in thinness	Sexual abuse
Dieting			
Body dissatisfaction			
Femininity			
Thin-ideal internalization			

Biological Factors

Genetics

Some studies have shown fairly substantial rates of monozygotic twins' concordance for AN and BN (e.g., Bulik, Sullivan, Wade, & Kendler, 2000). Recent data suggest a genetic linkage signal for AN on chromosome 1 and for BN on chromosome 10p (Bulik et al., 2003; Devlin et al., 2002). However, the overall picture concerning genetic determinants of eating disorders remains murky (Fairburn, Crowne, & Harrison, 1999). Genetics are implicated in the development of obesity (Meyer & Stunkard, 1993). In addition, since high BMI is a risk factor for eating disorders (Stice, 2001b), genetics may also have an indirect effect on the development of eating disorders.

Biochemistry

It has been exceedingly difficult to investigate biochemical etiological factors. Given the low base rate of BN and especially AN and the high cost of biochemical tests, prospective studies are very expensive. Given this problem, researchers have tried a different approach. They have compared neurotransmitter and hormonal levels of recovered anorexic and bulimic patients to those of girls and women who have never suffered from the disorder. Using this technique, research has implicated serotonin and dopamine levels in the etiology of eating disorders (Kaye & Strober, 1999). The potential role of serotonin is supported by pharmacological studies showing some reduction in binge eating when clients are given selective serotonin reuptake inhibitors, such as fluoxetine, or tricyclics, such as amitriptyline (Mitchell, 2001). Furthermore, dieting is associated with serotonin reduction in women (Anderson, Parry-Billings, Newsholme, Fairburn, & Cowen, 1990).

There are, however, serious problems with these data. In terms of comparing recovered clients with control groups, it is difficult to ascertain when a client is recovered. Many girls continue at least some binge-eating, purging, or excessive exercise after treatment. Furthermore, there is no information as to how long it takes the body to return to normal functioning after a lengthy period of starvation (AN) or purging (BN). It is evident that AN and BN alter brain chemistry in ways that maintain the disorders (Kaye & Strober, 1999). Thus, the posttreatment differences may be attributable to, rather than a causal factor of, eating disorders.

Sociocultural Influences

Parents

There are data linking family functioning to the development of AN and BN (Steinberg & Phares, 2001). However, the data are difficult to interpret, perhaps because many studies are lacking a clinical control group. Those that do include a clinical control group often find that families of at least AN girls are not particularly different from those of other troubled girls.

However, parents may contribute to eating problems and disorders in other important ways. They may model body dissatisfaction by commenting on their own bodies or refusing to engage in certain activities, like swimming or having their picture taken, because they are afraid they look too fat. Clearly, women who suffer from AN or BN might model more extreme attitudes and behaviors to their daughters. Parents might also comment directly on their child's weight or shape, praising them for losing weight or warning them to not eat too much because of concerns about becoming fat.

Research shows that parental comments do affect children's body esteem, beginning in elementary school (e.g., Field et al., 2001; Smolak, Levine, & Schermer, 1999; Taylor et al., 1998). Furthermore, adolescents whose fathers were worried about the child's body shape were more likely to be constant dieters a year later (Field et al., 2001). Some researchers find that daughters are more affected by parental comments than sons are, although parents do not make such comments to their girls more than to their boys (Schwartz, Phares, Tantleff-Dunn, & Thompson, 1999; Smolak et al., 1999). Maternal modeling of body image and eating problems has been related to daughters' eating problems (e.g., Smolak et al., 1999) though not all studies find this (e.g., Attie & Brooks-Gunn, 1989).

Peers

Peer behavior also includes both peer modeling and comments about weight and shape. Some of the latter comments take the form of teasing; indeed, the single most frequent category of teasing is appearance-related. Teasing may also be considered part of the cultural objectification of girls and women, particularly when it takes the form of sexual harassment (Smolak & Murnen, 2001).

Peer comments and modeling are related to body image and eating behaviors among elementary school and adolescent girls (e.g., Levine, Smolak, & Hayden, 1994; Oliver & Thelen, 1996; Paxton, 1999; Taylor et al., 1998). Sexual harassment and girls' reactions to it are also related to body image and eating problems (Larkin, Rice, & Russell, 1999; Murnen & Smolak, 2000). Girls who link thinness and popularity have poorer body image (Oliver & Thelen, 1996; Taylor et al., 1998). Similar relationships for boys are either noteably smaller or do not exist at all.

Media

Girls start reading fashion magazines by late elementary school. Up to half of these girls read such magazines at least occasionally and about one fourth read them at least twice weekly (Field et al., 1999). Girls who compare themselves to magazine images have higher weight concerns and feel badly about the comparisons (Martin & Kennedy, 1993, 1994; Taylor et al.,

1998). Using magazines to obtain beauty and weight control information has been related to poor body image in girls (Field et al., 1999; Levine et al., 1994). Experimental evidence has linked exposure to media images of thin women to poor body esteem (Groesz, Levine, & Murnen, 2002). Prospective data suggest that girls who try to look like media models become very concerned with their own looks (Field et al., 2001).

Cumulative Effects of Peers, Parents, and Media

Girls are more likely to be influenced by messages from peers, parents, and media concerning body image than boys are. Admittedly, the data on boys are still sparse, so this conclusion must be considered tentative. Furthermore, there is some reason to believe that sociocultural images of the ideal male body are becoming more unrealistic (Pope, Olivardia, Gruber, & Borowiecki, 1999) indicating that pressures on boys might eventually equal those of girls.

There are several reasons why girls may be more susceptible to cultural pressures. First, as was already noted, girls may be more invested in social relationships than boys are. This may lead girls to make more social comparisons, whether they are to peers or media figures (Jones, 2001). Furthermore, girls may face consistent pressures across a wider range of socialization agents. For example, girls are more likely to discuss appearance with their friends (Jones, Vigfusdottir, & Lee, 2004) and may be more broadly exposed to media messages touting a particular body shape (Levine & Smolak, 1996). Thus, girls may be more likely to live within a "culture of thinness" (Levine et al., 1994), all of which may be internalized as suggested by Objectification Theory (Fredrickson & Roberts, 1997). Girls who perceive pressure to be thin from multiple sources are more likely to develop bulimic symptoms (McKnight Investigators, in press).

Sexual Abuse

Sexual abuse may be the single most controversial putative contributor to eating disorders. Some authors have argued that there is no specific relationship between eating disorders and child sexual abuse (CSA; e.g., Connors & Morse, 1993; Pope & Hudson, 1992). Others have argued that requiring that a risk factor be specific to eating disorders only is a somewhat unfair criterion to apply to CSA. Even body dissatisfaction is related to psychological problems other than eating disorders. Furthermore, accumulating evidence suggests that body image and eating problems are indeed related to CSA (Connors, 2001; Smolak & Murnen, 2002). Furthermore, methodological inadequacies, including definitional confusion, may be masking the extent of the relationship. For example, Smolak and Murnen (2002) reported in a meta-analysis that the magnitude of the relationship between CSA and eating problems depended on whether research participants were selected as CSA survivors or as eating problem sufferers.

ASSESSMENT CONSIDERATIONS

There are many available measures, ranging from parental reports to questionnaires to interview protocols, for assessing body dissatisfaction, eating problems, and eating disorders in female children and adolescents (for reviews, see Gardner, 2001 and Netenmeyer & Williamson, 2001).

There are two issues, however, that should be noted. First, many of the measures were developed and validated with college-age women. Whether these can be effectively used with children is an open question. It may be that more than wording changes are required. Changes in underlying ("molar") structures may require redefining concepts. For example, the Dutch Eating Behaviors Questionnaire (DEBQ; Van Strien, Fritjers, Bergers, & Defares, 1986) contains an emotional eating subscale. Some authors (Carper, Fisher, Orlet, & Birch, 2000) have revised the wording on the DEBQ emotional eating scale and have used it with children as young as 5 years of age. But the DEBQ's author has conducted interviews with children and now argues that the DEBQ cannot be effectively used with them (Braet & Van Strien, 1997).

Secondly, most of the measures have been validated only with White samples. Only additional research can ascertain whether these measures capture the range, intensity, and frequency of eating problems among ethnic minority groups.

TREATMENT AND PREVENTION

It is possible to treat eating disorders. But treatment is time consuming and expensive, especially if hospitalization is required to stabilize weight and eating. With insurance companies and HMOs demanding less-expensive treatment methods and hospitals closing inpatient programs because they are losing money, such hospitalization is becoming less common. This means we must rely on outpatient treatment, including self-help manuals, to treat body image and eating disorders.

Several forms of therapy have been found to be effective in treating eating disorders, particularly cognitive behavioral therapy and interpersonal therapy (e.g., Fairburn, 2002; Wonderlich, Mitchell, Peterson, & Crow, 2001). Success with drug treatments has been limited but there are some promising possibilities (Mitchell, 2001). Unfortunately, there are no controlled studies of the efficacy of any of these treatments with young children (Gore, VanderWal, & Thelen, 2001).

Even if there were effective treatments available, it is unlikely that they would reach everyone who needs them. Work on other public health problems has demonstrated that prevention is much more cost effective than is treatment (Levine & Piran, 2001). It is imperative, then, that we continue to work on prevention as the primary means for combating eating disorders.

A complete evaluation of prevention efforts and issues surrounding them is beyond the scope of this chapter (see Levine & Smolak, in press;

Piran, Levine, & Steiner-Adair, 1999; Vandereycken & Noordenbos, 1998 for reviews). Approaches that aim to change girls' developmental milieu seem particularly promising. Programs geared toward elementary school children may be able to stop the formation of thinness schema as well as cultures of thinness before they become entrenched.

FUTURE DIRECTIONS

While much progress has been made in the field of eating disorders, there are many exciting, and challenging, issues yet to be addressed.

More attention should be given to protective factors. This would provide greater latitude in the development of prevention programs, particularly those designed for high-risk girls. Some ideas concerning protective factors might come from a careful analysis of ethnic group differences. If a particular ethnic group has an unusually low rate of a disorder or symptom, their culture might be protecting for girls in ways that others do not.

In terms of treatments, we have to evaluate which treatments are effective with girls. Ethnicity also needs to be considered in evaluating treatment. Before this can be done, we need stronger epidemiological data. At this time, we do not really know who our audience is or ought to be.

The application of ecological models of eating disorders to the prevention of eating problems is also an exciting area for future research. Objectification theory and a growing body of research point to sociocultural factors as instrumental in the development of eating disorders. Indeed, when a girl's father points out that she would look better if she weighed a few pounds less while her mother refuses to even wear a bathing suit, her friends all talk about how fat they are (and she can see they are not), and her favorite television show is populated by thin women, it seems reasonable that she would become weight and shape conscious. This sort of unified, multipronged message to girls that it is important, perhaps even crucial, to be thin needs to be better understood so that it can be effectively interrupted in prevention and treatment programs.

We cannot wait until we completely understand the etiology of eating disorders before we begin to develop and implement prevention programs. Evaluations of such programs may, in fact, provide further tests of causal relationships. In any case, there are enough data to effectively guide the design of such programs. It is time to move ahead.

REFERENCES

Agras, W. S. (2001). The consequences and costs of the eating disorders. *Psychiatric Clinics of North America, 24*, 371–379.

American Psychiatric Association (1980). *Diagnostic and statistical manual of mental disorders* (3rd ed.). Washington DC: American Psychiatric Association.

American Psychiatric Association (1994). *Diagnostic and statistical manual of mental disorders* (4th ed.). Washington, DC: American Psychiatric Association.

Anderson, I., Parry-Billings, M., Newsholme, E., Fairburn, C., & Cowen, P. (1990). Dieting reduces plasma tryptophan and alters brain 5-HT in women. *Psychological Medicine, 20,* 785–791.

Atkins, D., & Silber, T. (1993). Clinical spectrum of anorexia nervosa in children. Journal of *Developmental and Behavioral Pediatrics, 14,* 211–216.

Attie, I., & Brooks-Gunn, J. (1989). Development of eating problems in adolescent girls: A longitudinal study. *Developmental Psychology, 25,* 70–79.

Braet, C., & Van Strien, T. (1997). Assessment of emotional, externally induced and restrained eating behaviour in nine to twelve-year-old obese and non-obese children. *Behavioural Research Therapy, 9,* 863–873.

Brown, L., & Gilligan, C. (1992). *Meeting at the crossroads.* Cambridge MA: Harvard University Press.

Brumberg, J. J. (1997). *The body project: An intimate history of American girls.* New York: Random House.

Bryant, A. (1993). Hostile hallways: The AAUW Survey on Sexual Harassment in America's schools. *Journal of School Health, 63,* 355–357.

Bryant-Waugh, R., & Kaminski, Z. (1993). Eating disorders in children: An overview. In B. Lask & R. Bryant-Waugh (Eds.), *Childhood onset anorexia nervosa and related eating disorders* (pp. 17–29). East Sussex, UK: Erlbaum.

Bulik, C., Devlin, B., Bacanu, S., Thornton, L., Klump, K., Fichter , M., et al. (2003). Significant linkage on chromosome 10p in families with bulimia nervosa. *American Journal of Human Genetics, 72,* 200–207.

Bulik, C., Sullivan, P., Wade, T., & Kendler, K. (2000). Twin studies of eating disorders: A review. *International Journal of Eating Disorders, 27,* 1–20.

Carper, J., Fisher, J., Orlet, J., & Birch, L. (2000). Young girls' emerging dietary restraint and disinhibition are related to parent control in child feeding. *Appetite, 35,* 121–129.

Chodorow, N. (1978). *The reproduction of mothering: Psychoanalysis and the reproduction of gender.* Berkeley: University of California Press.

Connors, M. (2001). Relationship of sexual abuse to body image and eating problems. In J. K. Thompson, & L. Smolak (Eds.), *Body image, eating disorders, and obesity in youth: Assessment, prevention, and treatment* (pp. 149–167). Washington, DC: American Psychological Association.

Connors, M., & Morse, W. (1993). Sexual abuse and eating disorders: A review. *International Journal of Eating Disorders, 13,* 1–11.

Croll, J., Neumark-Sztainer, D., Story, M., & Ireland, M. (2002). Prevalence and risk and protective factors related to disordered eating behaviors among adolescents: Relationship to gender and ethnicity. *Journal of Adolescent Health, 31,* 166–175.

Davis, C., Kennedy, S., Ravelski, E., & Dionne, M. (1994). The role of physical activity in the development and maintenance of eating disorders. *Psychological Medicine, 24,* 957–967.

Devlin, B., Bacnau, S., Klump, K., Bulik, C., Fichter, M., Halmi, K., et al. (2002). Linkage analysis of anorexia nervosa incorporating behavioral covariates. *Human Molecular Genetics, 11,* 689–696.

Douchinis, J., Hayden, H., & Wilfley, D. (2001). Obesity, body image, and eating disorders in ethnically diverse children and adolescents. In J. K. Thompson & L. Smolak (Eds.), *Body image, eating disorders, and obesity in youth: Assessment, prevention, and treatment* (pp. 67–98). Washington, DC: American Psychological Association.

Ewell, F., Smith, S., Karmel, M., & Hart, D. (1996). The sense of self and its development: A framework for understanding eating disorders. In L. Smolak, M. P. Levine, & R. Striegel-Moore (Eds.), *The developmental psychopathology of eating disorders: Implications for research, prevention, and treatment* (pp. 107–134). Mahwah, NJ: Erlbaum.

Fairburn, C. (2002). Interpersonal psychotherapy for eating disorders. In C. Fairburn & K. Brownell (Eds.), *Eating disorders and obesity: A comprehensive handbook* (2nd ed., pp. 320–324). New York: Guilford.

Fairburn, C., Cowne, P., & Harrison, P. (1999). Twin studies and the etiology of eating disorders. *International Journal of Eating Disorders, 26,* 349–358.

Field, A., Camargo, C., Taylor, C. Berkey, C., Frazier, L., Gillman, M., et al. (1999). Overweight, weight concerns, and bulimic behaviors among girls and boys. *Journal of the American Academy of Child and Adolescent Psychiatry, 38,* 754–760.

Field, A., Camargo, C., Taylor, C., Berkey, C., Robert, S., & Colditz, G. (2001). Peer, parent, and media influences on the development of weight concerns and frequent dieting among preadolescent girls and boys. *Pediatrics, 107,* 54–60.

Field, A., Colditz, G., & Peterson, K. (1997). Racial/ethnic and gender differences in concern with weight and bulimic behaviors among adolescents. *Obesity Research, 5,* 447–454.

Fredrickson, B., & Roberts, T. (1997). Objectification theory: Toward understanding women's lived experiences and mental health risks. *Psychology of Women Quarterly, 21,* 173–206.

Fredrickson, B., Roberts, T., Noll, S., Quinn, D., & Twenge, J. (1998). That swimsuit becomes you: Sex differences in self-objectification, restrained eating, and math performance. *Journal of Personality and Social Psychology, 75,* 269–284.

Gardner, R. (2001). Assessment of body image disturbance in children and adolescents. In J. K. Thompson & L. Smolak (Eds.), *Body image, eating disorders, and obesity in youth: Assessment, prevention, and treatment* (pp. 193–213). Washington, DC: American Psychological Association.

Garner, D. (1991). *Eating Disorder Inventory—2 manual.* Odessa, FL: Psychological Assessment Resources.

Garvin, V., & Striegel-Moore, R. (2001). Health services research for eating disorders in the United States: A status report and a call to action. In R. Striegel-Moore & L. Smolak (Eds.), *Eating disorders: Innovative directions in research and practice* (pp. 135–152). Washington DC: American Psychological Association.

Gilligan, C. (1982). *In a different voice.* Cambridge MA: Harvard University Press.

Gore, S., VanderWal, J., & Thelen, M. (2001). Treatment of eating disorders inchildren and adolescents. In J. K. Thompson & L. Smolak (Eds.), *Body image, eating disorders, and obesity in youth: Assessment, prevention, and treatment* (pp. 293–311). Washington, DC: American Psychological Association.

Graber, J., & Brooks-Gunn, J. (2001). Co-occurring eating and depressive problems: An 8-year study of adolescent girls. *International Journal of Eating Disorders, 30,* 37–47.

Groesz, L., Levine, M., & Murnen, S. (2002). The effect of experimental presentation of thin media images on body dissatisfaction: A meta-analytic review. *International Journal of Eating Disorders, 31,* 1–16.

Hart, K., & Kenny, M. (1997). Adherence to the superwoman ideal and eating disorder symptoms among college women. *Sex Roles, 36,* 461–478.

Harter, S. (1986). Processes underlying the construction, maintenance, and enhancement of the self-concept in children. In J. Suls & G. Greenwald (Eds.), *Psychological perspectives on the self* (Vol. 3), pp. (137–180). Hillsdale, NJ: Erlbaum.

Herzog, D., & Delinsky, S. (2001). Classification of eating disorders. In R. Striegel-Moore & L. Smolak (Eds.), *Eating disorders: Innovative directions in research and practice* (pp. 31–50). Washington, DC: American Psychological Association.

Hill, K., & Pomeroy, C. (2001). Assessment of physical status of children and adolescents with eating disorders and obesity. In J. K. Thompson & L. Smolak (Eds.), *Body image, eating disorders, and obesity in youth: Assessment, prevention, and treatment* (pp. 171–192). Washington, DC: American Psychological Association.

Huon, G., & Strong, K. (1998). The initiation and the maintenance of dieting: Structural models for large-scale longitudinal investigations. *International Journal of Eating Disorders, 23,* 361–370.

Johnson, C., & Connors, M. (1987). *The etiology and treatment of bulimia nervosa: A biopsychosocial perspective.* New York: Basic Books.

Johnson, W., & Torgrud, L. (1996). Assessment and treatment of binge eating disorder. In J. K. Thompson (Ed.), *Body image, eating disorders, and obesity: An integrative guide for assessment and treatment* (pp. 321–344). Washington DC: American Psychological Association.

Jones, D. C. (2001). Social comparison and body image: Attractiveness comparisons to models and peers among adolescent girls and boys. *Sex Roles, 45,* 645–664.

Jones, D. C., Vigfusdottir, T., Lee, Y. (2004). Body image and the appearance culture among adolescent girls and boys: An examination of friend conversations, peer criticisms, appearance magazines, and the internalization of appearance ideals. *Journal of Adolescent Research, 19*, 323–339.

Kaye, W., & Strober, M. (1999). Neurobiology of eating disorders. In D. Charney, E. Nestler, & W. Bunney (Eds.), *Neurobiological foundations of mental illness* (pp. 891–906). New York: Oxford University Press.

Kraemer, H., Kazdin, A., Offord, D., Kessler, R., Jensen, P., & Kupfer, D. (1997). Coming to terms with the terms of risk. *Archives of General Psychiatry, 54*, 337–343.

Larkin, J., Rice, C., & Russell, V. (1999). Sexual harassment and the prevention of eating disorders: Educating young women. In N. Piran, M. P. Levine, & C. Steiner-Adair (Eds.), *Preventing eating disorders: A handbook of interventions and special challenges* (pp. 194–207). Philadelphia: Brunner/Mazel.

Lask, B. (2000). Eating disturbances in childhood and adolescence. *Current Paediatircs, 10*, 254–258.

Levine, M. P., & Piran, N. (2001). The prevention of eating disorders: Toward a participatory ecology of knowledge, action, and advocacy. In R. Striegel-Moore & L. Smolak (Eds.), *Eating disorders: Innovative directions in research and practice* (pp. 233–254). Washington DC: American Psychological Association.

Levine, M. P., & Smolak, L. (1996). Media as a context for the development of disordered eating. In L. Smolak, M. P. Levine, & R. Striegel-Moore (Eds.), *The developmental psychopathology of eating disorders* (pp. 235–257). Mahwah NJ: Erlbaum.

Levine, M. P., & Smolak, L. (in press). *The prevention of eating problems and eating disorders: Theory, research, and practice.* Mahwah NJ: Erlbaum.

Levine, M. P., Smolak, L., & Hayden, H. (1994). The relation of sociocultural factors to eating attitudes and behaviors among middle school girls. *Journal of Early Adolescence, 14*, 471–490.

Malina, R. (1975). *Growth and development: The first twenty years in man.* Minneapolis: Burgess.

Martin, M., & Kennedy, P. (1993). Advertising and social comparison: Consequences for female preadolescents and adolescents. *Psychology and Marketing, 10*, 513–530.

Martin, M., & Kennedy, P. (1994). Social comparison and the beauty of advertising models: The role of motives for comparison. *Advances in Consumer Research, 21*, 365–371.

Martin, G., Wertheim, E., Prior, M., Smart, D., Sanson, A., & Oberklaid, F. (2000). A longitudinal study of the role of childhood temperament in the later development of eating concerns. *International Journal of Eating Disorders, 27*, 150–163.

McKnight Investigators (2003). Risk factors for the onset of eating disorders in adolescent girls: Results of the McKnight Longitudinal Risk Factor Study. *American Journal of Psychiatry, 160*, 248–254.

Meyer, J., & Stunkard, A. (1993). Genetics and human obesity. In A. Stunkard & T. Wadden (Eds.), *Obesity: Theory and therapy* (2nd ed., pp. 137–150). New York: Raven Press.

Mitchell, J. (2001). Psychopharmacology of eating disorders: Current knowledge and future directions. In R. Striegel-Moore & L. Smolak (Eds.), *Eating disorders: Innovative directions in research and practice* (pp. 197–212). Washington, DC: American Psychological Association.

Murnen, S., & Smolak, L. (1998). Femininity, masculinity, and disordered eating: A meta-analytic approach. *International Journal of Eating Disorders, 22*, 231–242.

Murnen, S., & Smolak, L. (2000). The experience of sexual harassment among grade-school students: Early socialization of female subordination? *Sex Roles, 43*, 1–17.

Netenmeyer, S., & Williamson, D. (2001). Assessment of eating disturbance in children and adolescents with eating disorders and obesity. In J. K. Thompson & L. Smolak (Eds.), *Body image, eating disorders, and obesity in youth: Assessment, prevention, and treatment* (pp. 215–233). Washington, DC: American Psychological Association.

Neumarker, K. (2000). Mortality and sudden death in anorexia nervosa. *International Journal of Eating Disorders, 21*, 205–212.

Oliver, K., & Thelen, M. (1996). Children's perceptions of peer influence on eating concerns. *Behavior Therapy, 27*, 25–39.

Paxton, S. (1999). Peer relations, body image, and disordered eating in adolescent girls: Implications for prevention. In N. Piran, M. P. Levine, & C. Steiner-Adair (Eds.), *Preventing eating disorders: A handbook of interventions and special challenges* (pp. 134–147). Philadelphia: Brunner/Mazel.

Pawluck, D., & Gorey, K. (1998). Secular trends in the incidence of anorexia nervosa: Integrative review of population-based studies. *International Journal of Eating Disorders, 23,* 347–352.

Piran, N., Levine, M. P., & Steiner-Adair, C. (Eds.). (1999). *Preventing eating disorders: A handbook of interventions and special challenges.* Philadelphia: Brunner/Mazel.

Pope, H., & Hudson, J. (1992). Is childhood sexual abuse a risk factor for bulimia nervosa? *American Journal of Psychiatry, 149,* 732–737.

Pope, H., Olivardia, R., Gruber, A., & Borowiecki, J. (1999). Evolving ideals of male body image as seen through action toys. *International Journal of Eating Disorders, 26,* 65–72.

Robins, L., Helzer, J., Weissman, M. Orvaschel, H., Gruenberg, E., Burke, J., et al. (1984). Lifetime prevalence of specific psychiatric disorders in three sites. *Archives of General Psychiatry, 41,* 949–958.

Schwartz, D., Phares, V., Tantleff-Dunn, S., & Thompson, J. (1999). Body image, psychological functioning, and parental feedback regarding physical appearance. *International Journal of Eating Disorders, 25,* 339–343.

Shisslak, C., Crago, M., & Estes, L. (1995). The spectrum of eating disturbances. *International Journal of Eating Disorders, 18,* 209–219.

Silverman, J., Raj, A., Mucci, L., & Hathaway, J. (2001). Dating violence against adolescent girls and associated substance use, unhealthy weight control, sexual risk behavior, pregnancy, and suicidality. *Journal of the American Medical Association, 28,* 572–579.

Smolak, L. (1999). Elementary school curricula for the primary prevention of eating problems. In N. Piran, M. P. Levine, & C. Steiner-Adair (Eds.), *Preventing eating disorders: A handbook of interventions and special challenges* (pp. 85–104). Philadelphia: Brunner/Mazel.

Smolak, L., & Levine, M. P. (1994). Toward an empirical basis for primary prevention of eating problems with elementary school children. *Eating Disorders: The Journal of Treatment and Prevention, 2,* 293–307.

Smolak, L., & Levine, M. P. (1996). Adolescent transitions and the development of eating problems. In L. Smolak, M. P. Levine, & R. Striegel-Moore (Eds.), *The developmental psychopathology of eating disorders: Implications for research, prevention, and treatment* (pp. 207–234). Mahwah, NJ: Erlbaum.

Smolak, L., & Levine, M. P. (2001). Body image in children. In J. K. Thompson & L. Smolak (Eds.), *Body image, eating disorders, and obesity in youth: Assessment, prevention, and treatment* (pp. 41–66). Washington, DC: American Psychological Association.

Smolak, L., Levine, M. P, & Gralen, S. (1993). The impact of puberty and dating on eating problems among middle school girls. *Journal of Youth and Adolescence, 22,* 355–368.

Smolak, L., Levine, M. P, & Schermer, F. (1999). Parental input and weight concerns among elementary school children. *International Journal of Eating Disorders, 25,* 263–271.

Smolak, L., & Munsterteiger, B. (2002). The relationship of gender and voice to depression and eating disorders. *Psychology of Women Quarterly, 26,* 234–241.

Smolak, L., & Murnen, S. (2001). Gender and eating problems. In R. Striegel-Moore & L. Smolak (Eds.), *Eating disorders: Innovative directions in research and practice* (pp. 91–110). Washington, DC: American Psychological Association.

Smolak, L., & Murnen, S. (2002). A meta-analytic examination of the relationship between sexual abuse and eating problems. *International Journal of Eating Disorders, 31,* 136–150.

Smolak, L., Murnen, S., Mills, J., & Good, L. (November, 2002). *Media objectification and body esteem in young children.* Presented at the conference of the Eating Disorders Research Society, Albuquerque, NM.

Smolak, L., Murnen, S., & Ruble, A. (2000). Female athletes and eating problems: A meta-analytic approach. *International Journal of Eating Disorders, 27,* 371–380.

Stein, S., Chalhoub, N., & Hodes, M. (1998). Very early-onset bulimia nervosa: Report of two cases. *International Journal of Eating Disorders, 24,* 323–327.

Steinberg, A., & Phares, V. (2001). Family functioning, body image, and eating disturbances. In J. K. Thompson & L. Smolak (Eds.), *Body image, eating disorders, and obesity in youth:*

Assessment, prevention, and treatment (pp. 127–147). Washington, DC: American Psychological Association.

Steiner-Adair, C. (1986). The body politic: Normal female adolescent development and the development of eating disorders. *Journal of the American Academy of Psychoanalysis, 14*, 95–114.

Stice, E. (2001a). A prospective test of the dual-pathway model of bulimic pathology: Mediating effects of dieting and negative affect. *Journal of Abnormal Psychology, 110*, 124–135.

Stice, E. (2001b). Risk factors for eating pathology: Recent advances and future directions. In R. Striegel-Moore & L. Smolak (Eds.), *Eating disorders: Innovative directions in research and practice* (pp. 51–73). Washington, DC: American Psychological Association.

Stice, E., & Bearman, S. (2001). Body image and eating disturbances prospectively predict increases in depressive symptoms in adolescent girls: A growth curve analysis. *Developmental Psychology, 37*, 597–607.

Story, M., French, S., Resnick, M., & Blum, R. (1995). Ethnic/racial and socioeconomic difference in dieting behaviors and body image perception in adolescents. *International Journal of Eating Disorders, 18*, 175–179.

Striegel-Moore, R., Cachelin, F., Dohm, F., Pike, K., Wilfley, & Fairburn, C. (2001). Comparison of binge eating disorder and bulimia nervosa in a community sample. *International Journal of Eating Disorders, 29*, 157–165.

Striegel-Moore, R., Silberstein, L., & Rodin, J. (1986). Toward an understanding of risk factors for bulimia. *American Psychologist, 41*, 246–263.

Taylor, J., Gilligan, C., & Sullivan, A. (1995). *Between voice and silence: Women and girls, race and relationship.* Cambridge MA: Harvard University Press.

Taylor, C. B., Sharpe, T., Shisslak, C., Bryson, S., Estes, L., Gray, N., et al. (1998). Factors associated with weight concerns in adolescent girls. *International Journal of Eating Disorders, 24*, 31–42.

Thompson, B. (1994). *A hunger so wide and so deep.* Minneapolis: University of Minnesota Press.

Thompson, J. K., & Smolak, L. (2001). Body image, eating disorders, and obesity in youth—The future is now. In J. K. Thompson & L. Smolak (Eds.), *Body image, eating disorders, and obesity in youth: Assessment, prevention, and treatment* (pp. 1–18). Washington DC: American Psychological Association.

Thompson, J. K., & Stice, E. (2001). Internalization of the thin-ideal: Mounting evidence for a new risk factor for body image disturbance and eating pathology. *Current Directions in Psychological Science, 10*, 181–183.

Van Strien, T., Frijters, J., Bergers, G., & Defares, P. (1986). The Dutch Eating Behavior Questionnaire (DEBQ) for assessment of restrained, emotional and external eating behavior. *International Journal of Eating Disorders, 5*, 295–315.

Vandereycken, W., & Noordenbos, G. (Eds.). (1998). *The prevention of eating disorders.* London: Athlone Press.

Wonderlich, S., Mitchell, J., Peterson, C., & Crow, S. (2001). Integrative cognitive therapy for bulimic behavior. In R. Striegel-Moore & L. Smolak (Eds.), *Eating disorders: Innovative directions for research and practice* (pp. 173–196). Washington DC: American Psychological Association.

Woodside, D., & Garfinkel, P. (1992). Age of onset in eating disorders. *International Journal of Eating Disorders, 12*, 31–36.

Zerbe, K. (1993). *The body betrayed: Women, eating disorders, and treatment.* Washington, DC: American Psychiatric Association.

17

Adjustment to Chronic Illness in Girls

KAREN BEARMAN MILLER and ANNETTE M. LA GRECA

A chronic illness is "one that lasts for a substantial period of time or has sequelae that are debilitating for a long period of time" (Perrin, 1985, p. 2). Epidemiological studies estimate that 10–20% of children and adolescents suffer from one or more chronic illnesses (Gortmaker & Sappenfield, 1984; Hobbs, Perrin, & Ireys, 1985). Recent medical advances in technology have drastically improved neonatal survival rates and reduced the risks of life-threatening complications of chronic illness (Elander & Midence, 1997). As a result of such advances, life expectancy among children and adolescents with more severe conditions is increasing. Thus, a current, prominent theme of child health research is enhancing the adaptation of children and their families to the stress associated with chronic disease conditions (Thompson & Gustafson, 1996).

Recent work has challenged the assumption that children and adolescents with chronic illnesses inevitably suffer from psychological and psychosocial difficulties. A meta-analysis (Lavigne & Faier-Routman, 1993) of the psychological adjustment of youth with chronic pediatric conditions revealed substantial variability in youngsters' adjustment. Specifically, many youth with chronic conditions had satisfactory family and peer relationships and did not exhibit adjustment problems, such as elevated levels of internalizing or externalizing behaviors. Nevertheless, youth with chronic diseases were two to four times more likely to have a psychiatric diagnosis during childhood and adolescence than youth without chronic illnesses (Kliewer, 1997). Such findings have stimulated researchers' interest in examining specific stressors and coping skills that influence how youth with

KAREN BEARMAN MILLER • St. Mary's Child Development Center, West Palm Beach, FL. ANNETTE M. LA GRECA • University of Miami, Coral Gables, Florida, 33124.

chronic disease adjust to their condition, as such information would ultimately enhance the effectiveness of health care services for youth with chronic illness (Midence, 1994).

Several variables have been consistently linked to adjustment to chronic illness, and these usually fall in one of the following categories: condition parameters (e.g., type, severity, functional status, duration), social–ecological parameters (e.g., socioeconomic status, family functioning, marital adjustment, parental support and adjustment), or child parameters (age, gender, coping strategies, and cognitive processes) (Thompson & Gustafson, 1996). One major criticism has been that many of these variables have been examined superficially. More specifically, variables have been related to child adjustment, but the specific *processes* by which the variables are related to adjustment have been largely neglected. Explanations for the underlying processes have been largely based on speculations drawn from developmental or social psychology literature rather than on empirical data with pediatric populations (e.g., La Greca, Bearman, & Moore, 2002). Furthermore, *moderating* variables that might help to explain the differential effects of illness on certain groups or populations have also been understudied (La Greca et al., 2002). Gender is one potential moderating variable, and may be especially important during childhood and adolescence when gender roles may shape the individual's development. Although several studies have examined mean differences in boys' and girls' adjustment to chronic disease conditions, for the most part, potential gender differences in the specific *processes* underlying boys' and girls' adjustment to chronic conditions have been neglected.

At present, the unique contribution of gender to children's psychological and psychosocial adjustment to chronic illnesses is unclear. Many illnesses are linked to gender, by genetics, physiology, or lifestyle factors (Revenson, 2001). Moreover, traditional gender-role stereotypes indicate that girls and boys are socialized to emphasize different aspects of behavior and emotions, suggesting that responses to chronic illness may vary by gender. However, investigations of gender differences in adjustment to chronic illness have yielded mixed results, and many studies have ignored gender issues altogether. For the purposes of this chapter, *gender differences* will include both gender-role issues as well as issues related to genetics and physiology, usually referred to as *sex differences*.

There may be several reasons why gender issues are ignored in child health research. First, sample sizes are often inadequate to examine gender differences. Second, gender is commonly "controlled" in analyses, although reasons for controlling gender are not reported in many studies. Finally, specific hypotheses regarding gender may not be formulated and, as a result, are not examined in the analyses. However, to advance our understanding of how gender may moderate the impact of chronic disease on adjustment, and to subsequently develop appropriate and effective interventions for girls (and boys), it is important to identify and examine gender-specific issues in pediatric populations. As a first step in this direction, researchers must delineate gender-specific factors that foster or hinder adaptation for youth with chronic illnesses.

With the foregoing issues in mind, the present chapter examines girls' adjustment to chronic illness in childhood and adolescence. It is organized into four primary sections. The first section reviews the prevalence of chronic illnesses in childhood. The second section discusses existing models of adaptation to chronic illness, with particular emphasis on issues that are pertinent for girls. The third main section reviews the most common chronic illnesses of childhood, examining available evidence on gender differences in adjustment. The fourth section explores adjustment issues specific to girls, noting the implications for child health research and intervention. Finally, at the end of the chapter, a brief summary highlights the main points and conclusions.

PREVALANCE OF CHRONIC ILLNESS IN CHILDHOOD

In a comprehensive review of epidemiologic studies of children's health and development, Gortmaker and Sappenfield (1984) concluded that 10 to 20% of children suffer from one or more chronic disorders. These figures may underestimate the problem, as more recent statistics from the Centers for Disease Control and Prevention report that asthma, the most common chronic illness in childhood, affects approximately 11% of youth under the age of 18 (Bloom & Tonthat, 2002). Moreover, chronic conditions regularly interfere with youngsters' daily activities and some may ultimately lead to childhood death. Table 1 illustrates prevalence rates for some of the more common chronic illnesses of childhood, as well as brief descriptions of their courses, treatments, and outcomes.

Over recent years, the prevalence of children with chronic illnesses has increased, and more and more children are living with the daily stress of managing an illness. Thompson and Gustafson (1996) suggest that several factors contribute to increased prevalence rates. First, advances in medical technology have improved early detection and treatment of chronic illnesses such that children are living with these illnesses longer than in previous decades. Not only are children and adolescents with chronic illnesses living longer, they also must adjust to more complex, demanding treatments. For example, life-saving treatments have produced long-term survivors of childhood cancer, but these treatments often require patient cooperation with aversive procedures (i.e., chemotherapy or bone marrow transplantation; Phipps & DeCuir-Whalley, 1990). Thus, medical advances increase the number of children who are affected by chronic illness and, subsequently, lead to new treatment challenges.

Second, Thompson and Gustafson (1996) suggest that the increase in the survival rates of premature infants has direct implications for the increasing rates of chronic illnesses in childhood. Premature infants are more likely to develop neurological, respiratory, and cognitive dysfunctions compared with healthy birth weight babies (see Thompson & Gustafson, 1996).

A third reason for increased prevalence rates of childhood chronic illnesses are the emergence of new conditions, such as pediatric HIV/AIDS

Table 1. Representative Chronic Illnesses of Childhood

Illness	Information/definition	Prevalence	Age of onset	Treatment	Complications/health risks
Arthritis (juvenile rheumatoid arthritis (JRA); Kewman, Warschausky, & Engel, 1995)	Type 1. "Systemic": Fever spikes with rash; half progress to polyarticular Type 2. "Polyarticular": Affects 5 or more joints for 6 weeks or more Type 3. "Pauciarticular": Affects fewer than 5 joints in first 6 weeks of onset	Overall: .22 per 1,000 Type 1. 10% of JRA cases; 50% females Type 2. 40% of JRA cases; females outnumber males 3:1 Type 3. 50% of JRA cases; males outnumber females 5:1	Type 1. Peaks at infancy – 3 yrs of age Type 2. Peaks at 1–3 yrs of age Type 3. Usually occurs before 10 yrs of age; peak at 1–2 yrs of age	Goals: Control inflammation, prevent joint deformities, maximize function, promote psychosocial adjustment Methods: Nonsteroidal drug treatment, physical therapy, occupational therapy, orthopedic surgery, psychological treatment	Muscle and joint pain, swelling and impaired limb function, eye problems, skeletal abnormalities, infections, hematological disorders
Asthma (Bloom & Tonthat, 2002; CDC/NCHS, 1998)	Episodes or attacks of small airways narrowing from inflammation and hyperresponsiveness to asthma "triggers" (e. g., allergens, weather changes, tobacco smoke) Severity levels: 1. Severe Persistent 2. Moderate Persistent 3. Mild Persistent 4. Mild Intermittent	Overall: 110 per 1,000 children and adolescents (0–17 yrs; (8. 1 million in United States) 41% female High risk: Racial/ethnic minorities who are poor and live in urban environments	Birth to adult 66% boys and 50% girls with asthma have first episode by age 3	Goals: Control acute exacerbations, maintain good breathing, dilate airways by relaxing smooth muscles Methods: Beta-adrenergic agonists and xanthines (control exacerbations), cromolyn sodium and inhaled corticosteroids (maintenance), bronchodilators (dilate airways], limited exposure to triggers	Course varies with patient, symptoms and severity vary with season of year Child death from asthma rare: 0.4 deaths per 100,000

Disease	Pathophysiology	Prevalence	Age	Treatment	Complications/Side effects
Cancer (Powers, Vannatta, Noll, Cool, & Stehbens, 1995; Thompson & Gustafson, 1996)	Most common: 1. Acute lymphoblastic leukemia (ALL): malignancy of bone marrow that produces blood cells, producing lymphoblasts which replace normal bone marrow with fewer red blood cells and more white blood cells 2. Brain tumors	Overall: Less than 1 in 600 children younger than 15 yrs 50% females 1. ALL: 30 to 40% of childhood cancer 2. Brain tumors: 20% of childhood cancer	Birth to adult	1. ALL: Phase 1: 4–6 weeks of intensive chemotherapy to destroy lymphoblasts (complete remission in 95%); phase 2: 2–3 yrs of maintenance chemotherapy; phase 3 (for children at risk for relapse): cranial irradiation and intrathecal chemotherapy; last resort: bone marrow transplantation 2. Brain tumors: Total or partial resection of tumor followed by radiation; chemotherapy can also be used prior to or in place or radiation	Side effects of chemotherapy (hair loss, nausea, vomiting, diarrhea, skin and mucosal inflammation, endocrine and growth retardation) Long term: Recurrent malignancy, growth retardation, neuropsychological deficits, cataracts, infertility Most common cause of disease-related death in childhood
Cystic fibrosis (Stark, Jelalian, & Miller, 1995)	Epithelia of the exocrine glands of several major organ systems (respiratory, digestive, pancreas, kidney, liver, reproductive) produce an abnormal mucus that is thick, viscous, and sticky	Overall: 1 in 2,000 live births (White); 1 in 17,000 births (Black) 50% female	Birth	Goals[a]: Improve pulmonary disease and malnutrition Methods[a]: Pulmonary: Chest physical therapy (45 min twice daily); aerosols to increase airflow, deliver antibiotics; hospitalization for intravenous antibiotics; oxygen; lung transplantation. Gastrointestinal: Diet and replacement enzyme preparations	Respiratory infection, pneumonia, graduate pulmonary function deterioration, malnutrition, sterility[a] In 1993, survival rate was 29. 4 yrs
Diabetes (type 1 diabetes; Johnson, 1995)	Destruction of insulin-producing islet cells within the pancreas	Overall: 1 in 600 children 50% female More prevalent in White children versus Black children	Birth to adult; peak onset in puberty	Goals: Keep blood glucose levels close to normal through exogenous administration of insulin Methods: Daily treatment of blood glucose monitoring, dietary constraints, injections of insulin, and balancing energy demands and insulin needs	Hyper or hypoglycemia; blindness, renal failure, nerve damage, heart disease

(Continued)

Table 1. (*Continued*)

Illness	Information/definition	Prevalence	Age of onset	Treatment	Complications/health risks
HIV/AIDS (Rotheram-Borus, Murphy, & Miller, 1996)	Human immunodeficiency virus (HIV): Body's immune system loses its effectiveness; opportunistic diseases may ultimately attack the body's organs, leading to sickness and possible death	Overall (CDC Web site): 40 million HIV adults in world; 17.6 million are women (48%): 2.7 million children under 15 yrs	Birth to adult	Goals: Slow progression to AIDS and preventing transmission to others Method: Antiretroviral drugs; psychological and psychosocial treatment	Early stage illnesses (in women): Vaginal candidiasis, pelvic inflammatory disease, cervical displasia Late stage diseases (in women): Neurological disease, pneumonia, tuberculosis, cervical cancer CDC Web site: In 2001, 3 million people died of AIDS (1.1 million women, 580,000 children under 15 yrs)
Sickle cell disease (Lemanek, Buckloh, Woods, & Butler, 1995)	Group of genetic disorders characterized by chronic hemolytic anemia and vasculopathy Sickle cell anemia is the most common form of SCD Clinical manifestations: Episodes of severe pain, infections, cerebrovascular accidents, anemic episodes, retarded growth, delayed sexual maturation	Overall: 3 of every 1,000 African American newborns Found in people of African, Mediterranean, Indian, and Middle Eastern heritage 50% female	6 months of age	Goals: Reduce morbidity and mortality; reduce pain Method: Screening programs for newborns (medical follow-up and parent education and genetic counseling); children (2 months—5 yrs of age) receive prophylactic penicillin twice daily	Physical effects: Varying degrees of pallor, scleral icterus, protuberant abdomen, frontal bossing and gnathopathy Complications: Central nervous system, ophthalmological, pulmonary, cardiac, hepatobiliary, genitourinary, musculoskeletal, immunological

and prenatal drug exposure (Thompson & Gustafson, 1996). The diagnoses of HIV and AIDS have reportedly been given to children only since 1982 (Thompson & Gustafson, 1996). However, current estimates reveal that 2.7 million children under the age of 15 have been diagnosed with HIV (Rotheram-Borus, Murphy, & Miller, 1996; see Table 1). With continued medical advances that improve the identification, course, or treatment of serious health conditions, rates of chronic disease in children and adolescents will inevitably continue to rise.

In summary, advances in medical technology, increasing numbers of infants surviving low birth weight, and new childhood diagnoses are most likely perpetuating the increase in prevalence rates of chronic illness in childhood. As a result, research examining risk and resilience factors in children with chronic illnesses is important because it could inform interventions to improve children's physical and emotional well-being, and to reduce health care costs associated with chronic disease.

MODELS OF ADAPTATION TO CHRONIC ILLNESS

Healthy and chronically ill children experience similar developmental tasks and challenges, yet youngsters' ability to master and deal with normative stressors may be complicated by the presence of a chronic disease (Midence, 1994). Various aspects of the illness, such as its physiological characteristics, hospitalizations, disruptions in daily activity, and changes in family relationships, in addition to the general stress of childhood, may lead to coping difficulties and, ultimately, to adjustment problems.

To better understand *how* disease-specific factors might influence youngsters' adjustment, several models of psychosocial adaptation to pediatric chronic illness have been developed. Each of the models has been influential in guiding research on children with chronic conditions and for developing interventions in pediatric settings. In these models, adjustment depends on the convergence of many interpersonal, intrapersonal, and environmental factors (Revenson, 2001), although none of the models specifically consider gender issues. This is particularly surprising, in light of developmental and clinical research that documents gender differences in several key factors that are consistently part of these psychosocial models. Because these models guide research and intervention efforts, it is important to consider how gender may contribute to the process of disease adjustment; that is the focus of the following section.

Pless and Pinkerton's Model of Adjustment

Pless and Pinkerton (1975) developed one of the first integrative models of adaptation to chronic illness, and it has influenced many of the later models that were developed. According to this model, an individual's interactions with his or her environment determine adaptation to illness. Specifically, the importance of feedback loops are stressed such that "current functioning influences the responses of others, which in turn, reciprocally influences future functioning" (Pless & Pinkerton, 1975, p. 30). In this way, adjustment is an ongoing process, and how one adjusts in childhood directly affects adjustment in adolescence and adulthood.

Two main components of Pless and Pinkerton's model are self-concept and coping style, which are influenced by biological and social processes. They are major determinants of how an individual reacts to stress, in that more positive self-esteem and more adaptive coping enable youth to process and deal with adverse circumstances in a more adaptive manner (Thompson & Gustafson, 1996).

Pless and Pinkerton's model does not consider gender issues, even though research strongly suggests that self-concept and coping style have substantially different determinants for boys and girls (Knox, Funk, Elliott, & Bush, 2000). For example, boys' and girls' self-concepts may be based on different self domains (Knox, Funk, Elliot, & Bush, 1998). Research has confirmed that, as children grow older, peer opinion and social feedback become pivotal in adolescents' self-worth (Chassin, Presson, Sherman, & McConnell, 1995). Specifically, for adolescent girls, self-concept is usually interpersonally oriented (Block & Robins, 1993), with higher levels of self-esteem associated with higher perceived interconnectedness (Josephs, Markus, & Tafarodi, 1992). Moreover, the feminine gender role traditionally emphasizes interpersonal relationships, expressiveness, and nurturing (e.g., Block, 1983). In contrast, adolescent boys' self-esteem is often characterized as self-oriented, with high self-esteem associated with believing that one has uniquely superior abilities (Block & Robins, 1993; Josephs et al., 1992). Thus, the role of interpersonal relationships seems more central to girls' formation of healthy self-concepts than to boys'.

In addition to self-concept, gender differences in coping have been studied extensively (e.g., Frydenberg & Lewis, 1993; Spirito, Stark, Gil, & Tyc, 1995). Girls are traditionally socialized to express emotion and seek social support (e.g., Frydenberg & Lewis, 1993; Spirito et al., 1995), so it is likely that they may be more inclined to use emotion-focused coping strategies than boys. For girls, it may be less threatening to their identity to discuss negative emotional experiences that may suggest that they are not coping well (Burke & Weir, 1978). Boys, on the other hand, are socialized to suppress emotion and to express themselves through more physical and sometimes aggressive ways. Indeed, literature suggests that boys are more likely to cope with stress with physical activity, aggression, attempts to control the situation, and distraction (Ryan-Wenger, 1996). Not surprisingly, then, the most salient finding in the current literature is that girls are more likely than boys to use social support and emotional expression to cope with general life stress (Williams & McGillicuddy-De-Lisi, 1999) as well as with disease-related stress (see Ryan-Wenger, 1996).

In summary, the two main determinants of adjustment to stress (self-concept and coping style) in Pless and Pinkerton's (1975) psychosocial model are very much interrelated for girls. Both factors rely heavily on girls' feelings about their interpersonal relationships. However, gender is not specifically considered in this psychosocial model.

Disability-Stress-Coping Model of Adjustment

Another conceptual model, which also considers the influences of self-concept and coping style on psychosocial adjustment, is Wallander and Varni's disability-stress-coping model (Wallander & Thompson, 1995; Wallander & Varni, 1992). This model incorporates condition-specific and general factors into a risk-and-resistance framework; stress is presumed to be the primary risk factor for developing psychosocial problems (Wallander & Thompson, 1995).

Specifically, this model purports that condition parameters (e.g., severity, chronicity) and general life stress are the key risk factors for child adjustment problems. Stress is believed to arise from children's physical conditions as well as from behavioral and environmental circumstances (Wallander & Thompson, 1995). Furthermore, stress may emanate from general life events, such as parents' divorce, which may not be related to illness. General life stress may be difficult for the children with chronic illness to tolerate, as they must also deal with disease-related stressors.

Moreover, Wallander and Varni's model proposes that certain resistance factors may moderate the relationship between stress and psychosocial adjustment, affecting how the stress is processed or perceived. Interpersonal factors (e.g., self-concept), social–ecological factors (e.g., social support), and stress-processing factors (e.g., coping style) may serve as such moderators. Various aspects of this model have been evaluated in pediatric populations (e.g., Bachanas et al., 2001; Hommeyer, Holmbeck, Wills, & Coers, 1999).

Although gender is not considered in the model, it is likely that girls are particularly vulnerable to difficulties during a specific developmental period. Consequently, gender and age may interact to influence youths' adjustment to chronic illness. Generally, girls report significantly more stressful life events than do boys (Coddington, 1972; Groer, Thomas, & Shoffner, 1992). Qualitatively, compared to boys, girls tend to report more worrying about self-concept issues, acceptance from peers, relationships with the opposite sex, and disagreements with parents; girls also report more feelings of isolation and loneliness (Burke & Weir, 1978; see Sharrer & Ryan-Wenger, 1995 for a review).

In fact, girls may experience a peak in their vulnerability to life stress in their early adolescent years. During these years, girls are exposed to two major transitions: physical changes associated with puberty and the transition from elementary school to junior high school (Simmons & Blyth, 1987). Boys usually undergo pubertal physical changes approximately 18 months later than girls, and thus they often experience these stressful transitions at different times, rather than concurrently (Eccles, Barber, Jozefowicz, Malenchuk, & Vida, 1999). In contrast, adolescent girls must simultaneously deal with physical and cognitive transformations as well as school transitions as they also experience peer group changes, increased social complexity, and higher educational demands and expectations (Frydenberg & Lewis, 1993).

Because chronic illness is a risk factor that increases girls' vulnerability to the stressors of daily life, the occurrence of numerous and simultaneous stressful life transitions may adversely affect girls' adjustment to their illness (Grey, Cameron, & Thurber, 1991). This observation is consistent with Wallander and Varni's (1992) model, which emphasizes an interactional relationship between general stress and condition-specific stress.

In summary, Wallander and Varni's model of psychosocial adaptation to chronic disease identifies life stress as a key risk factor for adjustment problems. Although developmental research has indicated that adolescent girls may simultaneously experience multiple significant life events, gender issues are not considered in their model. Also not considered in their psychosocial model are gender-related issues in self-esteem or coping.

Transactional Stress and Coping Model

Another integrative model of psychosocial adaptation, Thompson's transactional stress and coping model (Thompson, 1985), stems from ecological-systems theory and identifies chronic illness as a potential stressor to which the child and family systems must adapt. This model examines the influences of illness and demographic variables on youngsters' adjustment to illness, and also emphasizes the mediational nature of child and family processes in the illness–outcome relationship (Thompson & Gustafson, 1996; Wallander & Thompson, 1995). Thus, Thompson's transactional model purports that child adjustment affects and is affected by the stress experienced by family members (Thompson & Gustafson, 1996). Furthermore, certain adaptational processes account for the psychological adjustment of youngsters with chronic illness, including positive self-esteem and health locus of control (Thompson, 1985). This model has been evaluated in several pediatric populations, including youth with sickle cell disease (e.g., Thompson, Gustafson, Bonner, & Ware, 2002), cystic fibrosis (e.g., Thompson, Gustafson, Hamlett, & Spock, 1992), and diabetes (e.g., Murphy, Thompson, & Morris, 1997).

As with the conceptual models already discussed, Thompson's transactional model incorporates self-esteem and methods of coping in what the authors refer to as *child adaptational processes.* As with prior models, gender differences in self-esteem and coping are important, but have been neglected in the model. In addition, Thompson's model stresses the mediational nature of the interrelationship of child and maternal adjustment. This represents another area where gender issues are paramount.

Specifically, prior research suggests that mother–daughter relationships are distinctly different from mother–son relationships (see Debold, Brown, Weseen, & Brookins, 1999). Recent research in girls' psychological and social development illustrates that girls seek out meaningful connections with their mothers throughout development (Debold et al., 1999). As a result, positive, reciprocal mother–daughter relationships may serve as a protective factor in dealing with stress. However, mother–daughter relationships may also influence adjustment in negative ways. For example, parental verbalizations and pain-promoting behaviors (i.e., providing empathy, apologies, or mild criticism) may serve as signals for worry and, thus, precipitate and reinforce girls' distress more so than boys' (Chambers, Craig, & Bennett, 2002). In other words, the *quality* of the mother-child relationship may have more pronounced impact on girls' functioning (in both positive and negative ways) than on boys' functioning, suggesting that gender may moderate the association between "relationship quality" and "child adjustment."

In brief, Thompson's model of adjustment builds upon existing models that examine the roles of self-esteem and coping in youngsters' adjustment to chronic illness, emphasizing the mediational nature of child and family processes in the illness–outcome relationship. Although gender differences in parent–child relationships have been documented, Thompson's model does not take into account gender-specific aspects of these relationships.

Summary and Conclusions

In summary, the three key conceptual models highlighted in this section underscore the pivotal roles of interpersonal, intrapersonal, and environmental factors in children's and adolescents' adjustment to chronic illness. Specifically, the models suggest that self-esteem, methods of coping, life stress, and mother-child relationships are all important variables in understanding the linkages between chronic disease and youngsters' adaptation. Nonetheless, quantitative and qualitative gender differences in these variables, which are documented in developmental and clinical research, have yet to make an impact on how these psychosocial models are conceptualized and evaluated. Because it is possible that the processes or mechanisms by which girls and boys adjust to the stress of illness may differ, revisions to these psychosocial models are necessary.

Also striking is the absence of attention to peer relationship issues in the various conceptual models reviewed. Recent evidence underscores the role of close friendships and peer support in youngsters' adjustment to and management of chronic disease conditions (e.g., La Greca et al., 1995: La Greca, Bearman, & Moore, 2002). Greater attention to peer and friendship variables in understanding adjustment to chronic disease is desirable, particularly for girls. Girls' relationships often are more oriented toward intimacy, sharing, and support than are boys' (see La Greca & Prinstein, 1999), and it is possible that close friends play a greater role in girls' acceptance of and adjustment to their chronic disease than is the case for boys.

One final observation regarding the conceptual models reviewed is that none of them specify how the "predictors" of adjustment for chronically ill youth would be any *different* from those for "non-ill" youth. That is, the models essentially suggest how "stress" is related to "youngsters' adjustment"; yet many of the variables in the conceptual models (e.g., self-esteem, family support) also have been associated with better adjustment among non-ill youth. Thus, it is not clear how unique the models are to the area of chronic disease. For the most part, the disease-specific variables in the various models could be viewed as specific examples of "stressors" that could affect youngsters' functioning more generally.

Despite these caveats and observations, the psychosocial models reviewed have had, and continue to have, a tremendous influence on research and intervention in child health psychology. They are, therefore, important to consider and to further refine. In the next section of the chapter, gender issues in existing child health research are reviewed.

ADAPTATION TO SPECIFIC CHRONIC ILLNESSES

Gender Differences in Chronic Illnesses

Examining gender differences in physical and psychological adaptation to chronic disease is one way researchers can delineate factors that foster or hinder adaptation to chronic illness. In many ways, girls' and boys' health issues show different epidemiological patterns than those of other demographic groups (e.g., ethnic groups, developmental groups) (Dougherty, 1999). Moreover, girls and boys may have different mechanisms by which they adjust to the stress of chronic illness.

Table 2 illustrates a selective review of recent studies that have either analyzed gender differences in adjusting to chronic illness or have focused exclusively on girls with chronic illness. Although research in child health psychology has not consistently examined gender differences in adjustment, many studies listed in Table 2 have found significant gender differences. Their results highlight the need for research examining gender-specific aspects of disease adjustment. The following section discusses several common childhood illnesses (i.e., asthma, diabetes, sickle cell disease) and examines the existing research on gender differences in adjustment to these illnesses.

Asthma

In the most recent report by the National Institutes of Health (1997), *asthma* is defined as (a) a chronic inflammation disorder that causes airflow obstruction (narrowing/blocking), which is often reversible either spontaneously or with treatment, and (b) bronchial hyperresponsiveness to a variety of stimuli. In general, this obstruction, hyperreactivity of airways, and inflammation lead to the most common clinical feature of asthma, i.e. breathing difficulties, which are manifested as coughing, wheezing, or shortness of breath. Asthma is a relatively common chronic illness, occurring in approximately 11% of children less than 18 years old or, in 1997, an estimated 8.1 million children (Bloom & Tonthat, 2002; see Table 1).

As with other chronic illnesses, there has been wide variability in reports of children's adaptation to asthma. Some children adapt well to their illness, seeming to have few academic, social, emotional, and behavior

Table 2. Selected Studies of Gender Differences in Response to Chronic Illnesses of Childhood

Study	N	Adjustment variables	Disease-specific variables	Girls' adjustment/coping
Asthma				
Gabriels et al., 2000	23 children (10–14 yrs)	Verbalization of emotions	Detection of symptoms	Girls verbalized more emotions about their drawings and were better able to detect airflow changes in their small airways
Kitsantas & Zimmerman, 2000	172 girls (14–18 yrs) 22% with asthma	Self-efficacy, activity participation, physical fitness	Perceived lung efficacy	Compared to girls without asthma, girls with asthma were physically less fit, reported lower self-efficacy regarding their lung functioning during vigorous activities, and participated less often in those activities; perceived lung efficacy predicted girls' subsequent participation in physical activities
MacLean et al., 1992	48 boys 33 girls (6–14 yrs)	Perceptions of competence, internalizing and externalizing problems		Younger girls and older boys reported lower school competence than older girls and younger boys but no differences in other variables
Punnett & Thurber, 1993	125 children (10–13 yrs)	Self-perceptions of competence		Self-perceived athletic competence was less important for girls compared to boys; girls had positive self-perceptions about their behavioral conduct
Ryan-Wenger & Walsh, 1994	42 boys 36 girls (8–13 yrs)	Coping		No gender differences in coping
Cystic fibrosis				
Thompson et al., 1992	30 boys 15 girls (7–12 yrs)	Internalizing and externalizing problems; perception of self-worth		Girls reported more symptoms that met criteria for a DSM-III diagnosis than boys and more negative self-esteem than boys

(Continued)

Table 2. (*Continued*)

Study	N	Adjustment variables	Disease-specific variables	Girls' adjustment/coping
Type 1 diabetes				
Bearman & La Greca, 2002	45 boys 29 girls (11–18 yrs)	Social support from friends	Adherence	Girls reported more disease-specific support from peers than boys for emotions and for blood glucose testing; no gender differences in adherence
Frey, Guthrie, Loveland-Cherry, Park, & Foster, 1997	155 children (10–20 yrs)	Risky behaviors		Girls reported lower risk perception of risky behaviors; no gender differences in frequency of risky behaviors
Grey et al., 1997	89 children (8–14 yrs)	Coping	Metabolic control	Poorer metabolic control was associated with more use of avoidance and female gender
Hanson et al., 1990	Study 1: 139 adolescents (M = 14. 5 yrs) Study 2: 136 adolescents (104 with diabetes; 32 healthy; M = 13.4 yrs)	Self-esteem		Study 1: No gender differences Study 2: Girls had lower self-esteem than boys but did not differ from girls in normative data and healthy control sample
Johnson, Perwien, & Silverstein, 2000	62 boys 63 girls (10–17 yrs)		Response to physical symptoms	No gender differences in response to episodes of hypo- and hyperglycemia
Kovacs et al., 1990	44 boys 51 girls (8–14 yrs)	Anxiety, self-esteem, depressive symptoms	Reaction to disease implications and regimen	Over time (6-year longitudinal study), girls' anxiety increased, self-esteem remained stable, both boys and girls found disease implications and regimen more difficult (varied as a function of depression and anxiety), and girls were more upset by their illness
La Greca, Auslander, et al., 1995	45 boys 29 girls (11–18 yrs)	Social support from family and friends	Adherence	Girls reported more diabetes-specific support from friends and more general emotional support from friends; no gender differences in family support or in adherence

Study	Sample	Predictor	Outcome	Results
La Greca & Bearman, 2002	45 boys 29 girls (11–18 yrs)	Social support from family	Adherence	No gender differences in actual or perceived family support or in treatment adherence
La Greca, Schwartz & Satin, 1987	30 girls (15–35 yrs)	Binge eating	Metabolic control	85% reported binging, and they were in poorer metabolic control; higher number of binges associated with shorter disease duration and poorer control; those in fair or poor metabolic control coped by reducing or omitting insulin
La Greca, Swales et al., 1995	17 boys 25 girls (12–18 yrs)	Psychosocial functioning	Metabolic control	Girls were in worse metabolic control and reported more anxiety and depression; worse metabolic control explained by greater depression
Maharaj, Rodin, Connolly, & Olmstead, 2001	88 girls (11–19 yrs)	Eating problems, autonomy, and intimacy		Compared to girls with no eating problems, interactions of girls with eating problems' with their mothers constrained the expression of autonomy and intimacy
Rodin et al., 1991	103 girls (13–18 yrs)	Eating disorders	Disease compliance and metabolic control	13% of subjects reported having eating disorders and more than half of these girls reported omitting insulin to produce hyperglycemia and weight loss; those with eating disorders were less compliant and in poorer metabolic control
Rovet, Ehrlich, & Hoppe, 1987	26 boys 25 girls (6–14 yrs)	Adjustment		Girls reported less behavior problems than boys
Ryan & Morrow, 1986	125 with diabetes 82 controls (10–19 yrs)	Adjustment		Girls reported higher levels of anxiety and more negative perceptions of physical appearance than boys
Rydall et al., 1997	91 young women (baseline $M = 15$ yrs)	Prevalence of eating disorders	Metabolic control and disease complications	29% had disordered eating which persisted in 18% and improved in 9% 4–5 yrs later; 18% who were health at baseline had disordered eating at follow-up; disordered eating associated with poor metabolic control and risk of retinopathy
Seiffge-Krenke, 1998	89 adolescents (12–14 yrs) 106 health controls	Family environment		No gender differences in family climate
Vera, Nollet-Clemencon, Vila, Mouren-Simeoni, & Robert, 1997	40 girls (13–19 yrs) 35 healthy control girls	Social anxiety, depression, social functioning		In comparison to controls, girls with diabetes were not socially anxious and were not different in social functioning, but they did report more depression

(Continued)

Table 2. (*Continued*)

Study	N	Adjustment variables	Disease-specific variables	Girls' adjustment/coping
Recurrent pain				
Holden, Rawlins, & Gladstein, 1998	31 boys 26 girls ($M = 8.9$ yrs)	Perceived control and coping strategies		Girls who did not perceive control over their headache episodes more likely to report using active coping strategies; generally, girls more likely to use cognitive restructuring than boys
Sharrer & Ryan-Wenger, 1991	12 boys 13 girls (8–12 yrs)	Coping		Girls used less aggressive behavior and physical activity as coping mechanisms than boys; girls used more social support and emotional expression
Sickle cell disease				
Babarin et al., 1999	182 boys 145 girls (4–17 yrs)	Positive mood (maternal report)	Problem of disease	Disease was a greater day-to-day problem for girls and girls had higher maternal rating of positive mood
Conner-Warren, 1996	30 children (4–18 yrs)		Pain intensity	No differences in reported pain intensity according to gender
Gil et al., 1993	37 boys 33 girls (7–18 yrs)	Coping		No gender differences in coping
Hill & Zimmerman, 1995	32 children (2 months–22 yrs)	Caregiving (maternal report)	Illness perception	Mothers of daughters saw their children as less sick, were less likely to restrict their children's activities, and invested less effort in their caregiving
Hurtig, 1994	70 children (8–16 yrs)	Family relationships		According to parents' and children's reports, families of girls had more positive relations
Kell et al., 1998	42 boys 38 girls (12–18 yrs)	Family competence, psychological adjustment		Higher family competence was associated with fewer internalizing and externalizing behaviors, especially for younger adolescents and for girls
Sharpe et al., 1994	29 boys 25 girls (3–16 yrs)	Coping		Gender of the child was not related to mothers' or children's reported coping strategies
Chronic illnesses				
Eiser et al., 1992	134 boys 139 girls ($M = 9.4$ yrs)[a]	Adjustment: Peer relations, work	Disease restrictions	Overall, girls were better adjusted in terms of peer relationships and work; no gender differences in disease restrictions

Holden et al. 1997	72 diabetes 40 asthma (8–15 yrs)	Self-competence, family functioning, coping	Girls reported lower athletic competence and competence about physical appearance; mothers of girls reported higher family cohesion; no gender difference in maternal coping
Meijer et al. 2000	45 boys 53 girls (13–16 yrs)[b]	Peer interaction	Girls with chronic illnesses had lower level of social activities compared to healthy subjects; girls with cystic fibrosis displayed more assertive behavior than healthy girls
Olson et al. 1993	175 children (8–18 yrs) with chronic illness[c] 145 controls (8–18 yrs)	Coping skills	Gender did not significantly affect the predominant cognitive strategy (coping) used by chronic illness group or control group; no gender differences among illness subgroups
Perrin, Ayoub, & Willett, 1993	187 children (7–18 yrs)[d]	Behavior problems	Teachers perceived girls as having less behavior problems than boys, regardless of group
Schlundt et al., 1999	55 adolescents (12–18 yrs)[e]	Eating and weight related cognitions	Girls were significantly more concerned than boys about weight and restrictive dietary rules
Spirito et al. 1994	32 boys 22 girls (7–17 yrs) with chronic illnesses[f] (44 boys, 27 girls with acute illnesses)	Coping skills	No gender differences in coping
Spirito et al. 1995	93 boys 84 girls (7–18 yrs)[g]	Coping skills	Girls used less self-blame and cognitive restructuring than boys, and more emotional regulation and social support
Wallander et al. 1988	147 boys 123 girls (4–16 yrs)[h]	Behavioral and psychological problems	Girls had less externalizing problems than boys by maternal report; both boys and girls had more externalizing problems than a community sample

[a]Diabetes, asthma, cardiac disease, epilepsy, and leukemia.
[b]Cystic fibrosis, diabetes, juvenile chronic arthritis, osteogenesis imperfecta, eczema, and asthma.
[c]Asthma, juvenile rheumatoid arthritis, and diabetes.
[d]Grand mal seizures, petit mal seizures, cerebral palsy, visible conditions (spina bifida, rheumatoid arthritis, scoliosis, muscular dystrophy), and controls.
[e]Asthma, diabetes, renal failure, transplants, cystic fibrosis, rheumatological disorders, and hemophilia.
[f]Congenital orthopedic conditions, cancer, asthma, cystic fibrosis, diabetes, kidney disorders, ulcerative colitis, sickle cell anemia, hemophilia, and other disorders.
[g]Sickle cell disease, diabetes, cancer, migraine headache, congenital orthopedic problems, cystic fibrosis, ulcerative colitis, and other diagnoses.
[h]Diabetes, spina bifida, hemophilia, obesity, juvenile rheumatoid arthritis, and cerebral palsy.

problems. On the other hand, compared to children without asthma, children with asthma (especially those receiving inpatient treatment) present, in clinical settings, twice as often with behaviors considered to be indicative of poor adaptation to their illness (Furrow, Hambley, & Brazil, 1989; MacLean, Perrin, Gortmaker, & Pierre, 1992). Poor adaptation to asthma may be displayed in the form of internalizing behaviors (e.g., anxiety, depression), externalizing behavior problems (e.g., disruptive behaviors), deficient social interactions, academic difficulties, and inadequate illness management (Lemanek & Hood, 1999).

Gender differences in youngsters' adaptation to asthma suggest better adjustment for girls than for boys (see Table 2). Specifically, compared to boys with asthma, girls with asthma verbalize more emotions (Gabriels, Wamboldt, McCormick, Adams, & McTaggart, 2000), detect airway flow changes more effectively (Gabriels et al., 2000), and have more positive self-perceptions about their behavioral conduct (Punnett & Thurber, 1993). It is also noteworthy that some studies on children with asthma did not report gender differences (e.g., Ryan-Wenger & Walsh, 1994; see Table 2).

In contrast to these findings, Kitsantas and Zimmerman (2000) compared girls with asthma and without asthma and found that girls with asthma were less physically fit and that they reported less self-efficacy about their lung functioning during physical activities, which prevented them from participating in these activities. Thus, although girls with asthma may adjust better than boys with asthma, girls with asthma may still have more adaptation difficulties than healthy girls.

Diabetes

Type 1 diabetes is characterized by complete pancreatic failure and thus requires children to take daily exogenous insulin replacement (by injection) for survival (Johnson, 1995). In addition to insulin injections, children with diabetes must maintain a daily regimen that includes multiple blood glucose tests, eating restrictions, and regular sports activities. Type 1 diabetes is the third most frequent severe chronic condition of childhood (Sweeting, 1995), affecting approximately 150,000 children in the United States alone (Band & Weisz, 1990), with similar prevalence rates for girls and boys (see Table 1).

Perhaps because diabetes is a common and challenging disease to manage, it has been the focus of numerous investigations. Among the studies listed in Table 2, the largest number focused on youth with diabetes. These studies have examined a wide range of variables that reflect disease management, metabolic control, and psychosocial adjustment.

In terms of psychosocial functioning, studies of youth with diabetes have examined gender differences in variables such as social support, self-esteem, and internalizing and externalizing disorders. For the most part, these studies have yielded findings that parallel those for non-ill youth. For example, Bearman and La Greca (2003) found that girls reported more disease-specific emotional support than boys. Similarly, La Greca, Auslander, et al. (1995) reported that girls received more diabetes-specific and general support from their friends than did boys. In contrast, girls and boys do not appear to differ in their reports of family support (La Greca, Auslander, et al., 1995; La Greca & Bearman, 2002).

Other studies have examined gender differences in self-esteem among youngsters with diabetes, also obtaining findings that are similar to those for "healthy" populations. Specifically, girls with diabetes have reported lower self-esteem than boys with diabetes, but the girls' levels were similar to those in normative data and in reports from girls in a "healthy" control sample (e.g., Hanson et al., 1990).

In terms of internalizing and externalizing problems, studies have found that, compared to boys with diabetes, girls with diabetes become increasingly anxious over time (Kovacs et al., 1991). Other findings suggest that girls with diabetes are more upset about their illness (Kovacs et al., 1991), report more anxiety (La Greca, Swales, Klemp, Madigan, & Skyler, 1995; Ryan & Morrow, 1986) and depressive symptoms (La Greca, Swales, et al., 1995), and exhibit fewer externalizing problems (Rovet, Ehrlich, & Hoppe, 1987).

In general, such findings suggest that girls with diabetes may be vulnerable to internalizing problems compared to boys with diabetes, but friends seem to be an important source of general and disease-specific support for girls with diabetes. However, such findings are not surprising, in that they closely parallel those obtained in the developmental and clinical child literatures; typically, girls report more internalizing symptoms and fewer externalizing symptoms than do boys (e.g., Achenbach, Howell, Quay, & Conners, 1991), and girls describe their close friendships as more intimate and supportive than do boys (Belle, 1989; Berndt, 1982). Thus, it is not clear as to what extent the gender differences in psychosocial functioning observed among youth with diabetes are *specific* to youth with this chronic disease, or whether the findings simply mirror gender differences more broadly. Additional research that examines the *unique* implications of gender for the management of and adjustment to diabetes would be desirable.

On the other hand, studies that have examined gender differences in disease control and management have revealed that girls with diabetes have poorer metabolic control than boys with diabetes (e.g., Grey, Lipman, Cameron, & Thurber, 1997; La Greca, Swales, et al., 1995). It is not clear, however, what processes contribute to this gender difference in disease control. It is possible that certain behaviors that are common among adolescent girls may have an adverse impact on physical health when the adolescent has diabetes. For example, among girls with diabetes, disordered eating (i.e., binging, faulty weight loss strategies) has been associated with poor metabolic control (La Greca, Schwartz, & Satin, 1987; Rodin, Craven, Littlefield, Murray, & Daneman, 1991; Rydall, Rodin, Olmstead, Devenyi, & Daneman, 1997) and a high risk of disease complications (e.g., retinopathy) (Rydall et al., 1997). Thus, adolescent girls' typical concerns about weight, body shape, and diet (Striegel-Moore & Cachelin, 1999) could contribute to medical problems when the adolescent has diabetes. As another possibility, adolescent girls have been found to be less physically active than boys

(Cruickshanks, Orchard, & Becker, 1985); yet, physical exercise is important for regulating glucose levels and maintaining good metabolic control of diabetes (Davidson, 1986). Thus, common or normal developmental processes may place adolescent girls at greater risk than boys for problems with disease management and control. In general, additional research that examines the *unique* implications of gender for the management of and adjustment to diabetes would be desirable.

Sickle Cell Disease

Sickle cell disease (SCD) is a hematologic disease characterized by chronic anemia and frequent episodes of vascular occlusion, which is caused by sickling of abnormally shaped red blood cells (Sharpe, Brown, Thompson, & Eckman, 1994). Physical symptoms of the disease include skin ulcers; pneumococcal infections; dehydration; strokes; retinopathy; osteomyelitis (bone inflammation); necrosis of the hips, shoulders, and legs; and retarded growth (Sharpe et al., 1994).

SCD is distinct from many chronic illnesses in that children with SCD must cope with daily chronic pain and visible, severe physical symptoms. Pain is the most frequent symptom of SCD and is an important index of severity; the pain is caused by occlusions in circulatory pathways (Conner-Warren, 1996). Medically oriented pain management techniques include taking Tylenol with codeine, fluids, and ibuprofen (Conner-Warren, 1996; Elliot & Olson, 1983). Nevertheless, the pain of SCD is often variable in nature and contributes to significant limitations in physical activity and social behavior, as well as to low self-esteem and social competence (Charache, Lubin, & Reid, 1989; Gil et al., 1993; Robinson, 1999).

Because of the challenge of managing pain episodes, a significant portion of the psychosocial research on SCD has examined children's coping and adjustment to pain. In addition, unlike many other areas of child health psychology, minority youth have been the focus of most of these investigations. There is an especially high prevalence of SCD in African American youth, with approximately 3 in every 1,000 African American children affected (Lemanek, Buckloh, Woods, & Butler, 1995; see Table 1). Specifically, studies have found that African American parents of children with SCD frequently identify religiosity, a personal relationship with God, and social connectedness to a community of worship as key resources in coping with the stress of the illness and in contributing to the health psychological development of their children (Babarin, 1999).

In terms of gender issues, few studies have found gender differences in coping or adjustment to SCD (see Table 2.) For example, no consistent gender differences in coping strategies have been reported (e.g., Gil et al., 1993; Sharpe et al., 1994). Both girls and boys with SCD have similar rates of active and passive coping. In addition, Conner-Warren (1996) found no gender differences in reactions to painful episodes of SCD. On the other hand, Babarin, Whitten, Bond, and Conner-Warren (1999) reported that girls rated their disease as a greater day-to-day problem (greater disruption in their life) than did boys; however, the mothers of these girls also rated their daughters as having higher positive mood compared to the mothers of boys with SCD.

To some extent, the lack of gender differences in coping with pain from SCD are surprising, in that gender differences have been found in children's coping with headaches or recurrent abdominal pain. For example, Holden, Rawlins, and Gladstein (1998) found that girls with recurrent headache used more cognitive restructuring than did boys. Also, in a study of children's coping with recurrent abdominal pain, girls reported using more social support and emotional expression and less aggressive behavior and physical activity than did boys (Sharrer & Ryan-Wenger, 1991).

Although research in coping and reactions to SCD pain have yielded few gender differences, studies examining family characteristics of children with SCD have reported differences for girls and boys. Specifically, Hurtig (1994) found that, compared to the families of boys with SCD, the families of girls with SCD had more positive relations. Furthermore, Kell, Kliewer, Erikson, and Ohene-Frempong (1998) observed a link between higher family competence and fewer internalizing and externalizing behavior problems, particularly among girls. This research suggests that girls with SCD may be at an advantage compared to boys with SCD, because their family relationships may foster better adaptation. One explanation of this gender difference in family environment may be that mothers of girls with SCD may view their daughters as less sick as a result of gender-role stereotypes and, thus, are less likely to restrict their activities (Hill & Zimmerman, 1995). More research in gender differences in the family relationships of children with SCD would be useful and desirable.

Other Chronic Illnesses

Although many studies in child health psychology focus on children with one particular chronic illness, other studies aggregate children with different chronic conditions. An aggregated approach allows for themes or trends to be drawn across different diseases; this is particularly useful for studying psychosocial adjustment variables, but it is less conducive to studying disease-specific medical issues such as disease management or treatment adherence. Table 2 illustrates gender differences from studies with a general "chronic illness" category. These studies report gender differences across a variety of indicators of adjustment, including overall adjustment, coping strategies, self-competence, and peer interactions.

Wallander, Varni, Babani, Banis, and Wilcox (1988) reported that mothers of children with chronic illnesses report more externalizing symptoms in boys than in girls, results that are consistent with the literature on non-ill youth. However, when compared to a community sample, both boys' and girls' problem behavior ratings were higher than for control youth (Wallander et al., 1988). In a study by Eiser, Havermans, Pancer, and Eiser (1992), gender differences in several specific domains of adjustment were examined. Girls with chronic illnesses were found to have better adjustment in their peer relationships and work than did boys with chronic illnesses (Eiser et al., 1992). In both studies, gender differences were similar across the diseases that were represented.

Also, Investigators have found that girls with chronic illnesses perceived their athletic competence and physical appearance more negatively than did boys, results that are consistent with studies of non-ill youth. (Holden, Chmielewski, Nelson, Kager, & Foltz 1997). Girls with chronic disease are also more likely to be concerned with weight and restrictive dietary rules of their illness than are boys (Schlundt, Rowe, Pichert, & Plant, 1999).

One set of findings that is not consistent with studies of healthy adolescents pertains to the social functioning of youth with chronic illnesses. Specifically, Meijer, Sinnema, Bijstra, Mellenbergh, and Wolters (2000) found that girls with various chronic illnesses were involved in fewer social activities than were boys. Thus, it is possible that girl's concerns about the social impact of their disease might lead to greater disruption in their peer and social relationships. Further investigation of the social implications of girls' developing a chronic disease condition would be important and desirable.

Finally, studies of gender differences in children's coping strategies have yielded mixed results. Some have found no gender differences in the primary coping strategy used by children with chronic illnesses (e.g., Olson, Johansen, Powers, Pope, & Klein, 1993; Spirito, Stark, & Tyc, 1994). For example, Spirito et al. (1995) found that girls used more social support and emotional regulation and less cognitive restructuring and self-blame than did boys. However, another study of children with chronic illness revealed no gender differences in coping strategies (Spirito et al., 1994). Because gender differences in coping have yielded such discrepant findings, many researchers believe that it makes sense to examine coping in the context of a *specific* disease, rather than combing youth with various chronic illnesses. Coping skills, to a large extent, may depend on the specific demands imposed by a disease condition (e.g., pain management for SCD, allergen avoidance for asthma, multiplex daily tasks for diabetes).

Summary

From the above review of gender differences among youth with chronic disease conditions, it is clear that there is a general neglect of gender issues in this area of research. Nevertheless, a few general observations can be made.

First, in terms of girls' adjustment and psychosocial functioning (e.g., self-esteem, behavior problems), existing studies indicate that, compared to boys, girls with chronic illness report more internalizing problems, more problems with disordered eating, and lower levels of self-esteem and self-competence. However, these findings basically parallel those obtained with non-ill youth and do not appear to represent unique vulnerabilities for girls with chronic disease conditions. The one possible exception is that chronic disease conditions may have a greater social impact on girls than on boys; however, further investigation of this issue is necessary before firm conclusions can be drawn.

Second, in terms of disease management and control, there is some suggestion that "normative gender differences" may interact with the demands of a chronic disease in ways that have serious implications for girls' disease management and health. Perhaps the most obvious example is the linkage between adolescent girls' problematic eating and weight control behaviors (which are fairly common) and problems with metabolic control and treatment adherence for girls with diabetes.

Finally, studies of cultural and ethnic variables that may affect girls' disease management and adjustment to chronic conditions are seriously lacking. Very few studies have examined ethnic/cultural differences, particularly as they pertain to girls' adjustment and functioning; this is an important avenue for future investigation.

ADAPTATION TO CHRONIC ILLNESS: ISSUES SPECIFIC TO GIRLS

The above discussions of gender issues in models of adaptation to chronic illness and in adjustment to illness suggest that girls have unique characteristics that influence how they cope with and adjust to the stress of their illness. However, research on gender issues has been sparse and, in particular, the health needs of girls have received little attention. Most existing research has focused on mean gender differences, rather than on examining gender-specific *processes*. We believe it is important to explore the specific needs of girls with chronic illnesses in order to better understand "young women's health issues" and to develop interventions that are sensitive to and appropriate for girls with chronic illness. The section below describes some areas that warrant special consideration.

The Effects of Puberty

As girls move through childhood into adolescence, the biological and psychological stress of puberty may interact with and perhaps complicate chronic illness adjustment. Adolescence is characterized as a period of significant life changes (e.g., transitioning from grade school to junior high school to high school) and of considerable physical changes (e.g., weight gain; Marcotte, Fortin, Potvin, & Papillon, 2002; Simmons & Blyth, 1987). For adolescent girls, these changes often occur concurrently, predisposing adolescent girls to more life stress than adolescent boys, who often experience physical changes later than life changes (Eccles et al., 1999). Thus, adolescent girls' coping resources may be taxed from multiple stressors of adolescence, interfering with their abilities to cope with additional stressors, such as chronic illness. With this in mind, the assessment of stressful life events and physical development becomes particularly important for researchers and for clinicians who are working with adolescent girls, helping them cope with chronic illness.

Life Events

Research has consistently demonstrated that a convergence of stressful life events accounts for a significant rise in adolescents' rates of psychological adjustment problems—particularly, depressive symptoms (e.g., Brooks-Gunn & Warren, 1989; Peterson, Sirigiani, & Kennedy, 1991). An interactive model of adolescent depression proposed by Nolen-Hoeksema and Girgus (1994) provides an integrative context for examining gender differences in relation to individual predisposition, pubertal transitional challenge, and life stress. Indeed, the synchronicity of stressful events in puberty have accounted for higher rates of depression among adolescent girls compared to those among boys (Marcotte et al., 2002; Peterson et al., 1991).

The presence of a chronic illness in adolescence is usually construed as a major stressor (Holmes, Yu, & Frentz, 1999). The disease-related stress, coupled with the simultaneous occurrence of life changes in adolescence, may put adolescent girls with chronic illnesses at an increased risk of depression and other adjustment problems compared with girls without chronic illnesses. Unfortunately, the interrelationship of these particular stressors in adolescent girls has not been examined in child health research. However, research has indicated that children with chronic illnesses in other multiple stress conditions exhibit significantly more adjustment problems and poorer physical health than do children with chronic illness with no additional life stress. For example, Overstreet et al. (1995) found that children with diabetes who came from disruptive families experienced more behavioral problems and poorer metabolic control than did children with diabetes from intact families. Thus, for adolescent girls with chronic illness, it seems particularly important to examine the cooccurrence of puberty, life transitions, and perceived illness stress and how these factors contribute to their disease adjustment. Increased understanding of the interplay between these factors will most likely enhance the effectiveness of interventions developed for helping adolescent girls cope with chronic illnesses.

Eating Disorders

The physical changes of puberty alone account for adolescent girls' excessive focus on body image (Striegel-Moore, 1993). During puberty, hormonal changes lead to dramatic mood and bodily changes, including weight gain. Girls may be particularly vulnerable to adjustment problems associated with the physical changes of puberty. For adolescent girls, the value placed on thinness in Western society may bring about a preoccupation with weight and body shape (Striegel-Moore & Cachelin, 1999). Thus, adolescent girls are often caught in a struggle between the cultural ideal of female beauty and the physical reality of the female body (Striegel-Moore, 1993).

This normative developmental struggle is undoubtedly amplified for girls with chronic illnesses that involve strict dietary guidelines. Not surprisingly, eating problems have been found to be common and persistent in adolescent girls and young women with chronic illnesses. For example, Schlundt et al. (1999) found that, compared to boys with chronic illnesses, girls with chronic illnesses were significantly more concerned about weight and dietary restrictions.

Several researchers have focused on examining eating cognitions and behaviors in girls with type 1 diabetes (e.g., La Greca et al., 1987; Rodin et al., 1991; Rydall et al., 1997; see Table 2). During puberty, there is a peak onset of type 1 diabetes, and the onset is usually characterized by rapid weight gain (See La Greca et al., 1987). Not surprisingly, eating disorders are more prevalent among adolescent girls with diabetes compared to those among adolescent girls without diabetes (Jones, Lawson, Daneman, Olmstead, & Rodin, 2000). As many as 30% of girls with diabetes report having eating disorders or subclinical eating problems (e.g., insulin omission for weight loss, binge eating; Rydall et al., 1997; Stancin, Link, & Reuter, 1989). Eating problems in adolescent girls with diabetes may persist for several years and can lead to serious medical complications, such as retinopathy and chronic hyperglycemia (Rydall et al., 1997). Thus, it is important for health care professionals working with girls with diabetes (or other chronic conditions that may have an impact on body weight or diet) to evaluate their attitudes toward food and diet, and to take these into account when helping them cope with their disease. Furthermore, there is significant evidence that adolescent girls with other chronic illnesses that involve weight gain and dietary restraint may be at risk for eating problems. As a result, evaluating eating cognitions across other chronic illness groups is an important, additional concern for health care professionals.

Social Support

Social support represents a protective factor that can buffer the psychological and physical consequences of stress (Bearman & La Greca, 2003). For girls, social support is integral to developing a positive self-concept and coping with stress, both of which are major determinants of how individuals react to a chronic illness (Thompson & Gustafson, 1996). Because girls traditionally define themselves in relation to their interconnectedness to others (Block & Robins, 1993) and cope with stress by expressing emotion and seeking social support (Frydenberg & Lewis, 1993), it is important for health care professionals working with girls to evaluate the quality of their relationships with their friends and family and, when appropriate, involve their friends and family members in health care interventions. It seems particularly important to study *multiple* sources of social support, as these sources may relate differently to various social and psychological outcomes in youth with chronic illness (Varni, Katz, Colegrove, & Dolgin, 1994).

Friendships

Children's and adolescents' friendships and peer relations are important for cognitive, social, and moral development, as well as psychological and psychosocial health (see Brown, Way, & Duff, 1999). During adolescence, friendships become especially important as youth spend less time with their family members and more time with their friends. Moreover, gender differences in friendships become much more salient. For example, compared to adolescent boys, adolescent girls' friendships are more intimate, self-disclosing, and stable over time (see Brown et al., 1999). In addition, girls report more positive friendships with their same-sex peers than do boys (Bracken & Crain, 1994). In summary, friendships seem to be a particularly important outlet for the expression of support and the exchange of intimate feelings for girls, especially during adolescence.

For children and adolescents with chronic illness, support from close friends has been important for disease adjustment and treatment management. For example, Varni, Babani, Wallander, Roe, and Frasier (1989) found that perceptions of support from friends predicted adolescents' adaptation to diabetes. In other studies, higher perceived classmate support predicted, among other positive outcomes, lower levels of depression and anxiety symptoms in children with congenital and acquired limb deficiencies (Varni, Setoguchi, Rappaport, & Talbot, 1992) and in children with cancer (Varni et al., 1994). In addition to general support, La Greca, Auslander, Greca, Spetter, Fisher, & Santiago (1995) found that, compared to family members, friends provided more disease-specific emotional and companionship support for adolescents with diabetes. Overall, research suggests that friends are a critical source of support for adolescents with chronic illnesses.

Although few studies have examined gender differences in friends' support, several investigations have revealed that girls report more disease-specific support from close friends than boys (Bearman & La Greca, 2002; La Greca, Auslander, et al., 1995; see Table 2). These findings are consistent with developmental literature that suggests that girls' friendships are characterized by more intimacy and self-disclosure than are boys'. Future research in gender differences in friend support of youth with chronic illness is critical, so that health providers can understand the ways that friendships affect girls' (and boys') disease adaptation and adherence to medical regimens.

Family Relationships

As they grow older, children spend more time with friends and less time with family members. However, rather than moving away from parental relationships, girls appear to need meaningful connectedness with their mothers (Debold et al., 1999). Mothers are often considered by girls as significant, enduring sources of support (e.g., Furman & Buhrmester, 1992). Rather than distancing themselves from their mothers, adolescent girls are instead searching for new ways to relate to them (Debold et al., 1999). Girls' relationships with their mothers can provide an arena for the development of self-identity and resilience (Debold et al., 1999).

Although pediatric research has demonstrated the importance of family support in adjustment to pediatric chronic illness, gender differences have not been directly examined. Varni et al. (1994) found that girls reported more social support from family members than boys, but other studies have not found gender differences (e.g., La Greca & Bearman, 2002; La Greca, et al., 1995; see Table 2). As research on girls' social and emotional development suggests, mothers may be a particularly important source of support for girls with chronic illnesses throughout development. As a result, health care professionals working with girls with chronic illness should evaluate their relationships with their family members, particularly their mothers. In addition, it may be important to involve family members and other key sources of support in efforts to promote girls' coping with chronic illness (e.g., Anderson, Wolf, Burkhart, Cornell, & Bacon, 1989; Satin, La Greca, Zigo & Skyler, 1989).

SUMMARY AND CONCLUSIONS

Although youth with chronic illness may be at increased risk for psychosocial adjustment problems relative to non-ill youth, many youngsters adapt well, exhibit few internalizing or externalizing problems, and have successful interpersonal relationships. As a result, it is important for child health researchers to examine specific factors that may influence the *processes* by which youngsters adapt to chronic illness, and the factors that *moderate* youngsters' adaptation.

As reviewed in this chapter, several models of psychosocial adaptation to chronic illness have been influential in guiding research and intervention efforts in child health psychology. However, these models have not considered the role of gender as a main effect or moderating variable that may influence the process of adaptation. This is surprising, in that substantial research has documented gender differences in key aspects of these psychosocial models, such as self-esteem, coping, life stress, and mother-child relationships. By neglecting gender in these psychosocial models, important gender-related differences in youngsters' disease adaptation may be seriously overlooked by researchers and health care professionals. One implication of this chapter review is the importance of integrating gender issues into future adaptations and extensions of these psychosocial models, so that gender issues do not continue to be neglected in future research.

The sparse existing research examining gender differences in youngsters' adaptation to chronic illness has revealed some major themes. Specifically, compared to boys with chronic illness, girls with chronic illness may have higher levels of internalizing problems and more negative self-esteem and self-competence. Girls also have a tendency to place a greater emphasis on social support as a coping mechanism and report more support from their friends than do boys. Although these gender differences are similar to gender differences among youth who are *not* affected by chronic disease conditions, the findings suggest that the processes by which girls and boys with chronic illness adapt to (general and disease-related) stress may be different, and require further study.

On the other hand, there was also some suggestion that the interplay between adjustment and disease control may differ for girls and boys with chronic conditions. For example, girls with diabetes appear to have more problems with disease control than boys, although the specific processes contributing to these gender differences are not well understood. Additional research is needed that examines the *unique* issues or vulnerabilities of girls, in conjunction with the demands of disease management or a particular disease regimen. Furthermore, much of the existing research on chronic disease conditions focuses on adolescents, with little attention to younger children, or to older adolescents as they make the transition to adulthood. A developmental perspective is necessary to better understand girls' adaptation to chronic conditions. Longitudinal studies are especially needed so that the interplay between gender, disease management, and adaptation processes may be understood from a developmental perspective.

The last main section of the chapter highlighted several areas that may be useful in guiding researchers and clinicians in their future efforts to attend to gender-related issues. For example, as discussed earlier, puberty onset may have a more dramatic effect on girls' psychosocial adjustment than on boys. Specifically, in early adolescence, along with the onset of puberty and its associated physical changes come a number of stressful life transitions (e.g., changing schools, concerns about appearance) that can add to adolescent girls' accumulated life stress, especially in the already-stressful context of managing a chronic disease. As a result, researchers as well as health care providers would do well to evaluate the number and magnitude of daily life stressors that girls encounter, and to monitor and consider the extent of physiological changes that girls are experiencing.

Furthermore, researchers and health care providers should recognize that certain *aspects of chronic conditions* might complicate girls' adjustment. In this regard, it will be important for researchers and health care professionals to evaluate girls' eating- and weight-related concerns, and to develop treatment regimens that do not inadvertently contribute to psychosocial stress and adjustment difficulties.

Finally, another important theme discussed in the chapter, which also suggests directions for future research and intervention, is the differential role of social support from close friends and from key family members (e.g., mothers) in girls' adjustment to chronic disease. Future child health research should examine these interpersonal variables among girls with chronic disease. Increased understanding of the interplay between these factors and disease adaptation will most likely enhance the effectiveness of interventions developed for facilitating adolescent girls' coping with chronic disease conditions.

REFERENCES

Achenbach, T. M., Howell, C. T., Quay, H. C., & Conners, C. K. (1991). National survey of problems and competencies among four- to sixteen-year-olds. *Monographs of the Society for Research in Child Development, 56* (3, Serial No. 225).

Anderson, B. J., Wolf, F. M., Burkhart, M. T., Cornell, R. G., & Bacon, G. E. (1989). Effects of peer-group intervention on metabolic control of adolescents with IDDM: Randomized outpatient study. *Diabetes Care, 3,* 179–183.

Bachanas, P. J., Kullgren, K. A., Suzman Schwartz, K., Lanier, B., McDaniel, J. S., Smith, J. & Nesheim, S. (2001). Predictors of psychological adjustment in school-age children infected with HIV. *Journal of Pediatric Psychology, 26*, 343–352.

Babarin, O. A. (1999). Do parental coping, involvement, religiosity, and racial identity mediate children's psychological adjustment to sickle cell disease? *Journal of Black Psychology, 25*, 391–426.

Babarin, O. A., Whitten, C. F., Bond, S., & Conner-Warren, R. (1999). The social and cultural context of coping with sickle cell disease: II. The role of financial hardship in adjustment to sickle cell disease. *Journal of Black Psychology, 25*, 294–315.

Band, E. B., & Weisz, J. R. (1990). Developmental differences in primary and secondary control coping and adjustment to juvenile diabetes. *Journal of Clinical Child Psychology, 19*, 150–158.

Bearman, K. J., & La Greca, A. M. (2002). Assessing friend support of adolescents' diabetes care: The Diabetes Social Support Questionnaire—Friends Version. *Journal of Pediatric Psychology, 27*, 417–428.

Bearman, K. J., & La Greca, A. M. (2003). Social support. In T. H. Ollendick & C. S. Schroeder (Eds.), *The encyclopedia of clinical child pediatric and psychology* (pp. 628–629). New York: Kluwer Academic/Plenum.

Belle, D. (1989). Gender differences in children's social networks and supports. In D. Belle (Ed.), *Children's social networks and social supports* (pp. 173–188). New York: Wiley.

Berndt, T. J. (1982). The features and effects of friendships in early adolescence. *Child Development, 53*, 1447–1460.

Block, J. (1983). Differential premises arising from differential socialization of the sexes: Some conjectures. *Child Development, 54*, 1335–1354.

Block, J., & Robins, R. W. (1993). A longitudinal study of consistency and change in self-esteem from early adolescence to early adulthood. *Child Development, 64*, 909–923.

Bloom, B., & Tonthat, L. (2002). Summary health statistics for U. S. children: National Health Interview Survey, 1997. *Vital Health Statistics, 10*.

Bracken, B. A., & Crain, R. M. (1994). Children's and adolescents' interpersonal relations: Do age, race, and gender define normalcy? *Journal of Psychoeducational Assessment, 12*, 14–32.

Brooks-Gunn, J., & Warren, M. (1989). Biological and social contributions to negative affect in young adolescent girls. *Child Development, 60*, 40–55.

Brown, L. K., Way, N., & Duff, J. L. (1999). The others and I: Adolescent girls' friendships and peer relations. In N. G. Johnson, M. C. Roberts, & J. Worell (Eds.), *Beyond appearance: A new look at adolescent girls* (pp. 205–226). Washington, DC: American Psychological Association.

Burke, R. J., & Weir, T. (1978). Sex differences in adolescent life stress, social support, and well being. *Journal of Psychology, 98*, 277–288.

Centers for Disease Control National Center for Health Statistics. (1998). *New asthma estimates: Tracking prevalence, health care, and mortality.* Retrieved May 17, 2002, from www.cdc.gov/nchs/products/pubs/pubd/hestats/asthma/asthmahtm.

Chambers, C. T., Craig, K. D., & Bennett, S. M. (2002). The impact of maternal behavior on children's pain experiences: An experimental analysis. *Journal of Pediatric Psychology, 27*, 293–301.

Charache, S., Lubin, B., & Reid, C. D. (1989). *Management of therapy of sickle cell disease* (NIH Publication No. 89–2117). Washington, DC: National Institutes of Health.

Chassin, L., Presson, C. C., Sherman, S. J., & McConnell, A. R. (1995). Adolescent health issues. In M. C. Roberts (Ed.), *Handbook of pediatric psychology* (2nd Ed., pp. 723–740). New York: Guilford.

Coddington, R. D. (1972). The significance of life events as etiologic factors in the disease of children. II. A study of a normal population. *Journal of Psychosomatic Research, 16*, 205–213.

Conner-Warren, R. L. (1996). Pain intensity and home pain management of children with sickle cell disease. *Issues in Comprehensive Pediatric Nursing, 19*, 183–195.

Cruikshanks, K. J., Orchard, T. J., & Becker, D. J. (1998). The cardiovascular risk profile of adolescents with insulin-dependent diabetes mellitus. *Diabetes Care, 8*, 118–124.

Debold, E., Brown, L. M., Weseen, S., & Brookins, G. K. (1999). Cultivating hardiness zones for adolescent girls: A reconceptualization of resilience in relationships with caring adults. In N. G. Johnson, M. C. Roberts, & J. Worell (Eds.), *Beyond appearance: A new look at adolescent girls* (pp. 181–204). Washington, DC: American Psychological Association.

Dougherty, D. M. (1999). Health care for adolescent girls. In N. G. Johnson, M. C. Roberts, & J. Worell (Eds.), *Beyond appearance: A new look at adolescent girls* (pp. 301–326). Washington, DC: American Psychological Association.

Eccles, J., Barber, B., Jozefowicz, D., Malenchuk, O., & Vida, M. (1999). Self-evaluations of competence, task values, and self-esteem. In N. G. Johnson, M. C. Roberts, & J. Worell (Eds.), *Beyond appearance: A new look at adolescent girls* (pp. 53–84). Washington, DC: American Psychological Association.

Eiser, C., Havermans, T., Pancer, M., & Eiser, R. J. (1992). Adjustment to chronic disease in relation to age and gender: Mothers' and fathers' reports of their children's behavior. *Journal of Pediatric Psychology, 17,* 261–275.

Elander, J., & Midence, K. (1997). Children with chronic illnesses. *The Psychologist, 10,* 211–215.

Elliot, C. H., & Olson, R. A. (1983). The management of children's distress in response to painful medical treatments for burn injuries. *Behavioral Research, 21,* 675–683.

Frey, M. A., Guthrie, B., Loveland-Cherry, C., Park, P. S., & Foster, C. M. (1997). Risky behavior and risk in adolescents with IDDM. *Journal of Adolescent Health, 20,* 38–45.

Frydenberg, E., & Lewis, R. (1993). Boys play sports and girls turn to others: Age, gender, and ethnicity as determinants of coping. *Journal of Adolescence, 16,* 253–266.

Furman, W., & Buhrmester, D. (1992). Age and sex differences in perceptions of networks of personal relationships. *Child Development, 63,* 103–115.

Furrow, D., Hambley, J., & Brazil, K. (1989). Behavior problems in children requiring inpatient rehabilitation treatment for asthma. *Journal of Asthma, 26,* 123–132.

Gabriels, R. L., Wamboldt, M. Z., McCormick, D. R., Adams, T. L., & McTaggart, S. R. (2000). Children's illness drawings and asthma symptom awareness. *Journal of Asthma, 37,* 565–574.

Gil, K., Thompson, R., Keith, B., Tota-Faucette, M., Noll, S., & Kinney, T. R. (1993). Sickle cell disease pain in children and adolescents: Change in pain frequency and coping strategies over time. *Journal of Pediatric Psychology, 18,* 621–637.

Gortmaker, S., & Sappenfield, W. (1984). Chronic childhood disorders: Prevalence and impact. *Pediatric Clinics of North America, 31,* 3–18.

Grey, M., Cameron, M. E., & Thurber, F. W. (1991). Coping and adaptation in children with diabetes. *Nursing Research, 40,* 144–149.

Grey, M., Lipman, T., Cameron, M. E., & Thurber, F. W. (1997). Coping behaviors at diagnosis and in adjustment one year later in children with diabetes. *Nursing Research, 46,* 312–317.

Groer, M. W., Thomas, S. P., & Shoffner, D. (1992). Adolescent stress and coping: A longitudinal study. *Research in Nursing and Health, 15,* 209–217.

Hanson, C. L., Rodrigue, J. R., Henggeler, M. A., Harris, M. A., Klesges, R. C., et al. (1990). The perceived self-competence of adolescents with insulin-dependent diabetes mellitus: Deficit or strength. *Journal of Pediatric Psychology, 15,* 605–618.

Hill, S. A., & Zimmerman, M. K. (1995). Valiant girls and vulnerable boys: The impact of gender and race on mothers' caregiving for chronically ill children. *Journal of Marriage and the Family, 57,* 43–53.

Hobbs, N., Perrin, J. M., & Ireys, H. T. (1985). *Chronically ill children and their families.* San Francisco: Jossey-Bass.

Holden, E. W., Chmielewski, D., Nelson, C. C., Kager, V. A., & Foltz, L. (1997). Controlling for general and disease-specific effects in child and family adjustment to chronic childhood illness. *Journal of Pediatric Psychology, 22,* 15–27.

Holden, E. W., Rawlins, C., & Gladstein, J. (1998). Children's coping with recurrent headache. *Journal of Clinical Psychology in Medical Settings, 5,* 147–158.

Holmes, C. S., Yu, Z., & Frentz, J. (1999). Chronic and discrete stress as predictors of children's adjustment. *Journal of Consulting and Clinical Psychology, 67,* 411–419.

Hommeyer, J. S., Holmbeck, G. N., Wills, K. E., & Coers, S. (1999). Condition severity and psychological functioning in pre-adolescents with spina bifida: Disentangling proximal functional status and distal adjustment outcomes. *Journal of Pediatric Psychology, 24,* 499–509.

Hurtig, A. L. (1994). Relationships in families of children and adolescents with sickle cell disease. *Journal of Health and Social Policy, 5,* 161–183.

Johnson, S. B. (1995). Insulin-dependent diabetes mellitus in childhood. In M. C. Roberts (Ed.), *Handbook of pediatric psychology* (2nd Ed., pp. 263–285). New York: Guilford.

Johnson, S. B., Perwien, A. R., & Silverstein, J. H. (2000). Response to hypo- and hyper-glycemia in adolescents with type 1 diabetes. *Journal of Pediatric Psychology, 3,* 171–178.

Jones, J. M., Lawson, M. L., Daneman, D., Olmstead, M. P., & Rodin, G. (2000). Eating disorders in adolescent females with and without type 1 diabetes: Cross sectional study. *British Medical Journal, 10,* 1563–1566.

Josephs, R., Markus, H., & Tafarodi, R. (1992). Gender and self-esteem. *Journal of Personality and Social Psychology, 63,* 391–402.

Kell, R. S., Kliewer, W., Erickson, M. T., & Ohene-Frempong, K. (1998). Psychological adjustment of adolescents with sickle cell disease: Relations with demographic, medical, and family competence variables. *Journal of Pediatric Psychology, 23,* 301–312.

Kewman, D. G., Warschausky, S. A., & Engel, L. (1995). Juvenile rheumatoid arthritis and neuromuscular conditions: Scoliosis, spinal cord injuries, and muscular dystrophy. In M. C. Roberts (Ed.), *Handbook of pediatric psychology* (2nd Ed., pp. 384–402). New York: Guilford.

Kitsantas, A., & Zimmerman, B. J. (2000). Self-efficacy, activity participation, and physical fitness of asthmatic and nonasthmatic adolescent girls. *Journal of Asthma, 37,* 163–174.

Kliewer, W. (1997). Children's coping with chronic illness. In S. A. Wolchik & I. N. Sandler (Eds.), *Handbook of children's coping: Linking theory and intervention* (pp. 275–300). New York: Plenum.

Knox, M., Funk, J., Elliott, R., & Bush, E. G. (1998). Adolescents' possible selves and their relationship to global self-esteem. *Sex Roles, 39,* 61–80.

Knox, M., Funk, J., Elliott, R., & Bush, E. G. (2000). Gender differences in adolescents' possible selves. *Youth and Society, 31,* 287–309.

Kovacs, M., Iyengar, S., Goldston, D., Stewart, J, Obrosky, D. S., & Marsh, J. (1990). Psychological functioning of children with insulin-dependent diabetes mellitus: A longitudinal study. *Journal of Pediatric Psychology, 15,* 619–632.

La Greca, A. M., Auslander, W. F., Greco, P., Spetter, D., Fisher, E. B., & Santiago, J. V. (1995). I get by with a little help from my family and friends: Adolescents' support for diabetes care. *Journal of Pediatric Psychology, 20,* 449–476.

La Greca, A. M., & Bearman, K. J. (2002). The Diabetes Social Support Questionnaire—Family Version: Evaluating adolescents' diabetes-specific support from family members. *Journal of Pediatric Psychology, 27,* 665–676.

La Greca, A. M., Bearman, K. J., & Moore, H. (2002). Peer relations of youth with pediatric conditions and health risks: Promoting social support and healthy lifestyles. *Journal of Developmental and Behavioral Pediatrics, 23,* 1–10.

La Greca, A. M., & Prinstein, M. J. (1999). Peer group. In W. K. Silverman & T. H. Ollendick (Eds.), *Developmental issues in the clinical treatment of children* (pp. 171–198). Needham Heights, MA: Allyn & Bacon.

La Greca, A. M., Schwartz, L. T., & Satin, W. (1987). Eating patterns in young women with IDDM: Another look. *Diabetes Care, 10,* 659–660.

La Greca, A. M., Swales, T., Klemp, S., Madigan, S., & Skyler, J. (1995). Adolescents with diabetes: Gender differences in psychosocial functioning and glycemic control. *Children's Health Care, 24,* 61–78.

Lavigne, J. V., & Faier-Routman, J. (1993). Correlates of psychological adjustment to pediatric physical disorders: A meta-analytic review and comparison with existing models. *Journal of Developmental and Behavioral Pediatrics, 14,* 117–123.

Lemanek, K. L., Buckloh, L. M., Woods, G., & Butler, R. (1995). Diseases of the circulatory system: Sickle cell disease and hemophilia. In M. C. Roberts (Ed.), *Handbook of pediatric psychology* (2nd Ed., pp. 286–309). New York: Guilford.

Lemanek, K. L., & Hood, C. (1999). Asthma. In R. T. Brown (Ed.), *Cognitive aspects of chronic illness in children* (pp. 78–104). New York: Guilford.

MacLean, W. E., Perrin, J. M., Gortmaker, S., & Pierre, C. B. (1992). Psychological adjustment of children with asthma: Effects of illness severity and recent stressful life events. *Journal of Pediatric Psychology, 17,* 159–171.

Maharaj, S., Rodin, G., Connolly, J., & Olmstead, M. (2001). Eating problems and the observed quality of mother-daughter interactions among girls with Type 1 diabetes. *Journal of Consulting and Clinical Psychology, 69,* 950–958.

Marcotte, D., Fortin, L., Potvin, P., & Papillon, M. (2002). Gender differences in depressive symptoms during adolescence: Role of gender-types characteristics, self-esteem, body image, stressful life events, and pubertal status. *Journal of Emotional and Behavioral Disorders, 10,* 29–42.

Meijer, S. A., Sinnema, G., Bijstra, J. O., Mellenbergh, G. J., & Wolters, W. (2000). Peer interaction in adolescents with a chronic illness. *Personality and Individual Differences, 29,* 799–813.

Midence, K. (1994). The effects of chronic illness on children and their families: An overview. *Genetic, Social, and General Psychology Monographs, 120,* 311–326.

Murphy, L. M., Thompson, R. J., & Morris, M. A. (1997). Adherence behavior among adolescents with type 1 insulin dependent diabetes mellitus: The role of cognitive appraisal processes. *Journal of Pediatric Psychology, 22,* 811–825.

National Institutes of Health. (1997). *Guidelines for the diagnosis and management of asthma* (Publication No. 4857). Bethesda, MD: US Government Printing Office.

Nolen-Hoeksema, S., & Girgus, J. S. (1994). The emergence of gender differences in depression during adolescence. *Psychological Bulletin, 115,* 424–443.

Olson, A. L., Johansen, S. G., Powers, L. E., Pope, J. B., & Klein, R. B. (1993). Cognitive coping strategies of children with chronic illness. *Developmental and Behavioral Pediatrics, 4,* 217–223.

Overstreet, S., Goins, J., Chen, R. S., Holmes, C. S., Greer, T., Dunlap, W. P., & Frentz, J. (1995). Family environment and the interrelation of family structure, child behavior, and metabolic control for children with diabetes. *Journal of Pediatric Psychology, 20,* 435–447.

Perrin, J. M. (1985). Introduction. In N. Hobbs & J. M. Perrin (Eds.), *Issues in the care of children with chronic illness: A sourcebook on problems, services, and policies* (pp. 1–10). San Francisco: Jossey-Bass.

Perrin, E. C., Ayoub, C. C., & Willett, J. B. (1993). In the eyes of the beholder: Family and maternal influences on perceptions of adjustment of children with a chronic illness. *Journal of Developmental and Behavioral Pediatrics, 14,* 94–105.

Peterson, A. C., Sirigiani, P. A., & Kennedy, R. E. (1991). Adolescent depression: Why more adolescent girls? *Journal of Youth and Adolescence, 20,* 247–271.

Phipps, S., & DeCuir-Whalley, S. (1990). Adherence issues in pediatric bone marrow transplantation. *Journal of Pediatric Psychology, 15,* 459–475.

Pless, I. B., & Pinkerton, P. (1975). *Chronic childhood disorders: Promoting patterns of adjustment.* Chicago: Year-Book Medical Publishers.

Powers, S. W., Vannatta, K., Noll, R. B., Cool, V. A., & Stehbens, J. A. (1995). Leukemia and other childhood cancers. In M. C. Roberts (Ed.), *Handbook of pediatric psychology* (2nd Ed., pp. 310–326). New York: Guilford.

Punnett, A. F., & Thurber, S. (1993). Evaluation of the asthma camp experience for children. *Journal of Asthma, 30,* 195–198.

Revenson, T. A. (2001). Chronic illness adjustment. In J. Worell (Ed.), *Encyclopedia of women and gender* (Vol. 1, pp. 245–255). New York: Academic Press.

Robinson, M. R. (1999). There is no shame in pain: Coping and functional ability in adolescents with sickle cell disease. *Journal of Black Psychology, 25,* 336–355.

Rodin, G., Craven, J., Littlefield, C., Murray, M., & Daneman, D. (1991). Eating disorders and intentional insulin undertreatment in adolescent females with diabetes. *Psychosomatics: Journal of Consultation Liaison Psychiatry, 32,* 171–176.

Rotheram-Borus, M. J., Murphy, D. A., & Miller, S. (1996). Intervening with adolescent girls living with HIV. In A. O'Leary & L. S. Jemmott (Eds.), *Women and AIDS: Coping and care* (pp. 87–108). New York: Plenum.

Rovet, J. F., Ehrlich, R. M., & Hoppe, M. (1987). Behavior problems in children with diabetes as a function of sex and age of onset of disease. *Journal of Child Psychology and Psychiatry and Allied Disciplines, 28,* 477–491.

Ryan, C. M., & Morrow, L. A. (1986). Self-esteem in diabetic adolescents: Relationship between age at onset and gender. *Journal of Consulting and Clinical Psychology, 54,* 730–731.

Ryan-Wenger, N. A. (1996). Children, coping, and the stress of illness: A synthesis of the research. *Journal of the Society of Pediatric Nurses, 1,* 126–138.

Ryan-Wenger, N., & Walsh, M. (1994). Children's perspectives on coping with asthma. *Pediatric Nursing, 20,* 224–228.

Rydall, A. C., Rodin, G. M., Olmstead, M. P., Devenyi, R. G., & Daneman, D. (1997). Disordered eating behaviors and microvascular complications in young women with insulin-dependent diabetes mellitus. *New England Journal of Medicine, 336,* 1849–1854.

Satin, W., La Greca, A. M., Zigo, M., & Skyler, J. S. (1989). Diabetes in adolescence: The effects of a multifamily group intervention on parent simulation of diabetes. *Journal of Pediatric Psychology, 14,* 259–275.

Schlundt, D. G., Rowe, S., Pichert, J. W., & Plant, D. D. (1999). What are the eating cognitions of children whose chronic disease do and do not require attention to diet? *Patient Education and Counseling, 36,* 279–286.

Seiffge-Krenke, I. (1998). The highly structured climate in families of adolescents with diabetes: Functional or dysfunctional for metabolic control? *Journal of Pediatric Psychology, 23,* 313–322.

Sharpe, J. N., Brown, R. T., Thompson, N. J., & Eckman, J. (1994). Predictors of coping with pain in mothers and their children with sickle cell syndrome. *Journal of the American Academy of Child and Adolescent Psychiatry, 33,* 1246–1255.

Sharrer, V., & Ryan-Wenger, N. (1991). Measurements of stress and coping among school-aged children with and without recurrent abdominal pain. *Journal of School Health, 61,* 86–91.

Sharrer, V. W., & Ryan-Wenger, N. M. (1995). A longitudinal study of age and gender differences of stressors and coping strategies in school-aged children. *Journal of Pediatric Health Care, 9,* 123–130.

Simmons, R. G., & Blyth, D. A. (1987). *Moving into adolescence: The impact of school pubertal change and school context.* Hawthorn, NY: Aldine de Gruyter.

Spirito, A., Stark, L. J., Gil, K. M., & Tyc, V. L. (1995). Coping with everyday and disease-related stressors by chronically ill children and adolescents. *Journal of the American Academy of Child and Adolescent Psychiatry, 34,* 283–290.

Spirito, A., Stark, L. J., & Tyc, V. L. (1994). Stressors and coping strategies described during hospitalization by chronically ill children. *Journal of Clinical Child Psychology, 23,* 314–322.

Stancin, T., Link, D. L., & Reuter, J. M. (1989). Binge eating and purging in young women with IDDM. *Diabetes Care, 12,* 601–603.

Stark, L. J., Jelalian, E., & Miller, D. L. (1995). Cystic fibrosis. In M. C. Roberts (Ed.), *Handbook of pediatric psychology* (2nd Ed., pp. 241–262). New York: Guilford.

Striegel-Moore, R. H. (1993). Etiology of binge eating: A developmental perspective. In C. G. Fairburn & G. T. Wilson (Eds.), Binge Eating: Nature, assessment, and treatment (pp. 144–172). New York: Guilford.

Striegel-Moore, R. H., & Cachelin, F. M. (1999). Body image concerns and disordered eating in adolescent girls: Risk and protective factors. In N. G. Johnson, M. C. Roberts, & J. Worell (Eds.), *Beyond appearance: A new look at adolescent girls* (pp. 85–108). Washington, DC: American Psychological Association.

Sweeting, H. (1995). Reversals of fortune? Sex differences in health in childhood and adolescence. *Social Science and Medicine, 40,* 77–90.

Thompson, R. J. (1985). Coping with the stress of chronic childhood illness. In A. N. O'Quinn (Ed.), *Management of chronic disorders of childhood* (pp. 11–41). Boston: G. K. Hall.

Thompson, R. J., & Gustafson, K. E. (1996). *Adaptation to chronic childhood illness.* Washington, DC: American Psychological Association.

Thompson, R. J., Gustafson, K. E., Bonner, M. J., & Ware, R. E. (2002). Neurocognitive development of young children with sickle cell disease through three years of age. *Journal of Pediatric Psychology, 27,* 235–244.

Thompson, R. J., Gustafson, K. E., Hamlett, K. W., & Spock, A. (1992). Psychological adjustment of children with cystic fibrosis: The role of child cognitive processes and maternal adjustment. *Journal of Pediatric Psychology, 17,* 741–755.

Varni, J. W., Babani, L., Wallander, J. L., Roe, T. F., & Frasier, S. D. (1989). Social support and self-esteem effects on psychological adjustment in children and adolescents with insulin-dependent diabetes mellitus. *Child and Family Behavior Therapy, 11,* 1–17.

Varni, J. W., Katz, E. R., Colegrove, R., & Dolgin, M. (1994). Perceived social support and adjustment of children with newly diagnosed cancer. *Journal of Developmental and Behavioral Pediatrics, 15,* 20–26.

Varni, J. W., Setoguchi, Y., Rappaport, L. R., & Talbot, D. (1992). Psychological adjustment and perceived support in children with congenital/acquired limb deficiencies. *Journal of Behavioral Medicine, 15,* 31–44.

Vera, L., Nollet-Clemencon, C., Vila, G., Mouren-Simeoni, M. C., & Robert, J. J. (1997). Social anxiety in insulin-dependent diabetic girls. *European Psychiatry, 12,* 58–63.

Wallander, J. L., & Thompson, R. J. (1995). Psychosocial adjustment of children with chronic physical conditions. In M. C. Roberts (Ed.), *Handbook of pediatric psychology* (2nd Ed., pp. 124–141). New York: Guilford.

Wallander, J. L., & Varni, J. W. (1992). Adjustment in children with chronic physical disorders: Programmatic research on a disability-stress-coping model. In A. M. La Greca, L. J. Siegel, J. L. Wallander, & C. E. Walker (Eds.), *Stress and coping in child health* (pp. 279–297). New York: Guilford.

Wallander, J. L., Varni, J. W., Babani, L., Banis, H. T., & Wilcox, K. T. (1988). Children with chronic physical disorders: Maternal reports of their psychological adjustment. *Journal of Pediatric Psychology, 13,* 197–212.

Williams, K., & McGillicuddy-De-Lisi, A. (1999). Coping strategies in adolescents. *Journal of Applied Developmental Psychology, 20,* 537–549.

Index